# THE CONTENT AND CONTEXT OF HATE SPEECH

The contributors to this volume consider whether it is possible to establish carefully tailored policies for "hate speech" that are cognizant of the varying traditions, histories, and values of different countries. Throughout, there is a strong comparative emphasis, with examples, and authors, drawn from around the world. A recurrent question is whether or when different cultural and historical settings can justify different substantive rules without making cultural relativism an easy excuse for content-based restrictions that would gravely endanger freedom of expression.

Essays address the following questions, among others: Is "hate speech" in fact so dangerous and harmful, particularly to vulnerable minorities or communities, as to justify restricting freedom of speech? What harms and benefits accrue from laws that criminalize "hate speech" in particular contexts? Are there circumstances in which everyone would agree that "hate speech" should be criminally punished? Is incitement that leads to imminent danger a more reliable concept for defining restrictions than "hate speech"? Does the decision whether to restrict "hate speech" necessarily entail choosing between liberty and equality? What lessons can be learned from international law?

Michael Herz is the Arthur Kaplan Professor of Law at the Benjamin N. Cardozo School of Law of Yeshiva University, where he also serves as Co-Director of the Floersheimer Center for Constitutional Democracy. Previously, he clerked for Justice Byron White of the U.S. Supreme Court and for Chief Judge Levin H. Campbell of the U.S. Court of Appeals for the First Circuit. His publications include *Administrative Law and Regulatory Policy: Problems, Text, and Cases* (7th edition 2011, with Breyer, Stewart, Sunstein, and Vermeule), *A Guide to Judicial and Political Review of Federal Agencies* (2005, coedited with John F. Duffy), and articles on a variety of public law topics.

Peter Molnar is Senior Research Fellow and a founding researcher at the Center for Media and Communication Studies at Central European University, where he teaches courses on freedom of speech and access to information. Since 1994, he has taught at several other universities in Hungary including ELTE. He was a leading participant in Hungary's transition to democracy at the end of the 1980s. He has served as a Member of Parliament (1990–1998), as a principal drafter of the 1996 media law and related laws, and as a member of the National Radio-Television Board's Complaint Commission (2001–2010), and he has been an activist and legislative advisor. In 2006, he drafted the Budapest Declaration for the Freedom of the Internet, which was signed by many media scholars. In 2007, the staged version of his novel, *Searchers*, won awards for best alternative and best independent play in Hungary. He has been a visiting professor at several American universities, including the Graduate School of Journalism of the University of California at Berkeley and the Cardozo and Columbia Law Schools, and he has been a German Marshall Fellow, twice a Fulbright Fellow, and a Shorenstein Fellow at Harvard University. His publications include "A Failure in Limiting Restrictions on Freedom of Speech: The Case of the Audiovisual Media Services Directive," in *Freedom of the Media* (Beata Klimkiewicz ed. 2010) and "Towards Better Law and Policy Against 'Hate Speech' – The 'Clear and Present Danger' Test in Hungary," in *Extreme Speech and Democracy* (Ivan Hare and James Weinstein eds. 2009).

# The Content and Context of Hate Speech

## RETHINKING REGULATION AND RESPONSES

Edited by

**MICHAEL HERZ**

Benjamin N. Cardozo School of Law, Yeshiva University

**PETER MOLNAR**

Center for Media and Communication Studies, Central
European University

CAMBRIDGE
UNIVERSITY PRESS

CAMBRIDGE UNIVERSITY PRESS
Cambridge, New York, Melbourne, Madrid, Cape Town,
Singapore, São Paulo, Delhi, Mexico City

Cambridge University Press
32 Avenue of the Americas, New York, NY 10013-2473, USA

www.cambridge.org
Information on this title: www.cambridge.org/9780521138369

First published 2012

Printed in the United States of America

*A catalog record for this publication is available from the British Library.*

*Library of Congress Cataloging in Publication data*

The content and context of hate speech : rethinking regulation and responses /
[edited by] Michael Herz, Peter Molnar.
    p. cm.
Includes bibliographical references and index.
ISBN 978-0-521-19109-8 (hardback) – ISBN 978-0-521-13836-9 (paperback)
1. Hate speech.   2. Freedom of speech.   I. Herz, Michael E.   II. Molnar, Peter.   III. Title.
K5210.C66   2011
345′.0256–dc22        2011018357

ISBN 978-0-521-19109-8 Hardback
ISBN 978-0-521-13836-9 Paperback

# Contents

# Contributors

**Floyd Abrams** is a partner at the New York City law firm Cahill Gordon & Reindel LLP, where he specializes in free speech litigation.

**Kwame Anthony Appiah** is Laurance S. Rockefeller University Professor of Philosophy and the University Center for Human Values at Princeton University. In 2010 he was elected to a second term as president of the PEN American Center.

The late **C. Edwin Baker** was the Nicholas F. Gallicchio Professor of Law and Communication at the University of Pennsylvania Law School.

**Eduardo Bertoni** is Director of the Center for Studies on Freedom of Expression and Access to Information at the Palermo University School of Law in Buenos Aires. From 2002 to 2005 he served as Special Rapporteur for Freedom of Expression of the Inter-American Commission on Human Rights.

**Irwin Cotler** is a member of the Canadian Parliament and Professor of Law at McGill University. From 2003 to 2006, he was Minister of Justice and Attorney General of Canada.

**Ronald Dworkin** is Professor of Philosophy and Frank Henry Sommer Professor of Law at New York University.

**Katharine Gelber** is Associate Professor in Public Policy at the University of Queensland and the past president of the Australian Political Studies Association.

**Jamal Greene** is Associate Professor of Law at Columbia Law School.

**Miklos Haraszti** is an Adjunct Professor at Columbia University's School of International and Public Affairs. From 2004 to 2010 he served as Representative on Freedom of the Media for the Organization for Security and Co-operation in Europe.

**Alon Harel** holds the Phillip P. Mizock & Estelle Mizock Chair in Administrative and Criminal Law at the Hebrew University of Jerusalem.

**Stephen Holmes** is the Walter E. Meyer Professor of Law at New York University School of Law.

**Arthur Jacobson** is the Max Freund Professor of Litigation and Advocacy at the Benjamin N. Cardozo School of Law in New York City.

**Adam Liptak** is a columnist and the Supreme Court reporter for the *New York Times*. He was previously Senior Counsel in the *Times*'s legal department.

**Kenan Malik** is a writer, lecturer, filmmaker, and broadcaster living in London.

**Tarlach McGonagle** is Senior Researcher at the Institute for Information Law at the University of Amsterdam.

**Toby Mendel** is the founding Executive Director of the Centre for Law and Democracy in Canada. He was previously Senior Director for Law at ARTICLE 19.

**Yared Legesse Mengistu**, a former judge of the Federal High Court of Ethiopia, is Assistant Professor in the Graduate Program of the Law Faculty of Addis Ababa University.

**Peter Molnar** is a writer, activist, and former member of the Hungarian Parliament (1990–1998). He is Senior Research Fellow at the Center for Media and Communication Studies (CMCS) at Central European University in Budapest.

**Bhikhu Parekh** is a member of the British House of Lords and a former Professor of Political Philosophy at the University of Westminster and the University of Hull.

**Robert Post** is Dean and Sol and Lillian Goldman Professor of Law at Yale Law School.

**Monroe E. Price** is Director of the Center for Global Communication Studies at the Annenberg School for Communication at the University of Pennsylvania, Chair of CMCS, and the Joseph and Sadie Danciger Professor of Law and former dean at the Benjamin N. Cardozo School of Law in New York City.

**Andrei Richter** is Director of the Moscow Media Law and Policy Institute and Professor at the School of Journalism at Lomonosov Moscow State University.

**Julio Rivera Jr.** is Professor of Constitutional Law and Human Rights at Palermo University and at the San Andrés School of Law in Buenos Aires.

**Michel Rosenfeld** is the Justice Sydney L. Robins Professor of Human Rights and Director of the Program on Global and Comparative Constitutional Theory at the Benjamin N. Cardozo School of Law in New York City.

**Frederick Schauer** is the David and Mary Harrison Distinguished Professor of Law at the University of Virginia School of Law.

**Bernhard Schlink** is Professor of Law at Humboldt University of Berlin, a novelist, and a former judge.

**Theodore Shaw** is Professor of Professional Practice in Law at Columbia Law School. His many years at the NAACP Legal Defense and Educational Fund, Inc., included service as director-counsel and president from 2004 to 2008.

**Nadine Strossen** is Professor of Law at New York Law School. From 1991 through 2008, she was president of the American Civil Liberties Union.

**Julie C. Suk** is Professor of Law at the Benjamin N. Cardozo School of Law in New York City.

**Jeremy Waldron** is University Professor at New York University School of Law and Chichele Professor of Social and Political Theory at All Souls College at Oxford University.

# Foreword: Hate Speech and the Coming Death of the International Standard before It Was Born (Complaints of a Watchdog)

*Miklos Haraszti*

This collection of cutting-edge writing on hate speech is also a documentation of our day's passionate debate on democracies' free speech governance, a debate that not only reflects the change underway but also drives it forward. It is two changes in one, in fact. While concern over hate speech has grown from separate national anxieties into a global issue, the trend as to the preferred way of handling hate speech has gravitated toward restricting it by regulation rather than isolating it by more reasoned speech.

Both these approaches are defended in superbly crafted arguments in the present volume. The prize the authors want you to keep your eyes on are two very different "minimums." Proponents of keeping governments to a "minimal regulation" standard are powerfully rebutted by advocates of "extensive regulation" who believe, in Michel Rosenfeld's words, that "the state can no longer justify commitment to neutrality" and that it has a duty to "strive for maintenance of a minimum of mutual respect" and "secure a minimum of civility in the public arena."[1]

This is enjoyable intellectual fencing, but it should not blind us to the surprising hazards that the dispute represents for the global advocacy arena, quite apart from the question of which approach is best suited to handle hate speech.

The "minimal regulation" approach could be formulated this way: "Actual instigations to actual hate crimes must be criminalized, but otherwise offensive speech should be handled by encouraging further dialogue – in the press, through media ethics bodies, or in civil courts." It is most fully developed and firmly entrenched in the United States, but it is also embraced by most international watchdog institutions as their own. It was certainly my guiding principle in my years as the media freedom representative of the Organization for Security and Co-operation in Europe.

---

[1] Michel Rosenfeld, "Hate Speech in Constitutional Jurisprudence: A Comparative Analysis," Chapter 13 herein.

Yet it seems that the "minimalist" approach is losing out under a growing, punitive trend that is introducing new speech bans into national criminal codes. Most of them target "bad speech" specific to the country or to the worries of its ruling parties, the two being practically indistinguishable. In the wake of this legislative wave, "regulationist" thinking is on the rise in academia and also within all consensus-driven intergovernmental fora.

Treating society's exposure to hate discourses by local anesthesia may be promoted with very different motives, both progressive and oppressive. In any case, however, it should be clear that pursuing this approach means abandoning the prominent role that the "minimalist" approach had played in globally establishing the standard of free speech – or indeed, free speech as a standard. That would be a profound transformation, going well beyond just swapping the "suspicious" stamp on governmental intrusion for "dedicated to the common good," praise previously reserved for governmental self-restraint.

What is most at risk from this double-edged change may be the very existence of an international human rights standard for handling hate speech. Such a binding standard was virtually prescribed by that majestic free speech guarantee of the year 1948, Article 19 of the Universal Declaration of Human Rights (UDHR).[2] Now it seems it may disappear altogether before having been properly developed at all. The very notion of an international standard for limits on free expression becomes unnecessary – more than that: inappropriate – if the fragmentation into separate content-oriented, historically based, culturally defined, politics-shaped, country-specific approaches to speech restrictions becomes acceptable.

The painful reality is that we do not have a universally applicable agreement that could guide legitimate speech limitations. Article 19 of the UDHR gave an unreserved promise of a universal right to free speech; after twenty years of consensus labor, it has been balanced out by, among other concessions to state regulation, Article 20 of the International Covenant on Civil and Political Rights (ICCPR), which expressly prescribes legal restrictions on hateful incitement.[3]

As a matter of principle, and of logic, it has always been inescapable that any universal standard reconciling Article 19 with Article 20 would have to tend toward the minimal intrusion principle. If a universal standard allowed individual governments to define punishable hate speech or incitement as they pleased, it would be either not universal or not a free speech standard.

---

[2]  Article 19 provides:

> Everyone has the right to freedom of opinion and expression; this right includes freedom to hold opinions without interference and to seek, receive and impart information and ideas through any media and regardless of frontiers.

[3]  Article 20(2) specifically states:

> Any advocacy of national, racial or religious hatred that constitutes incitement to discrimination, hostility or violence shall be prohibited by law.

Toby Mendel provides the blueprint of a reconciled standard.[4] But the world has so far lacked a global institution equipped with autonomous authority, similar to that of the U.S. Supreme Court, and steered solely by the Declaration and the Covenant the way the Supreme Court is guided by the Constitution alone. Over time, such a body would surely come up with reconciled principles, just as the U.S. Supreme Court has in the last 100 years. In its absence, the consensus method characteristic of most international fora will in all probability be sufficient only to uphold – separately – the principles of both Article 19 and Article 20. Such a bifurcation can be seen in the case law of the European and the Inter-American Courts of Human Rights, which have simultaneously both blocked and enabled speech bans.

Nevertheless, looking back at my own intergovernmental work and that of the NGOs, *no* international advocacy would have been possible without a shared working assumption that the minimalist standard applies. My successor as media freedom representative also, I am sure, applies this test to speech bans. So do the Commissioner for Human Rights at the Council of Europe and the Special Rapporteurs for Freedom of Expression at the UN Human Rights Council, at the Organization of American States, and at the African Commission on Human and Peoples' Rights.[5] It would also be difficult to find a global NGO that thinks otherwise.

This is not because they all shut their eyes to the outpouring of hate speech, or are dogmatic about restricting governments. Rather, the reason is that these particular offices are not what might be called "consensus-stricken." Their mandate is to *independently* reconcile the right to free speech with the fight against hate speech (and the fight against misuse of hate speech prohibitions). So far, they have been quite free to define the tools used to fulfill their mandate.

I do not deny that diplomatic bargaining between local and global "values" can be fruitful; it may even open prison doors in some cases. But consistently rejecting manufactured, parochial constraints yields better results, even in practical terms. The international community may pay too high a price for too few concessions if it legitimizes local taboos and abandons insistence on every person's right to beliefs that are unpopular, even ugly, as long as they do not infringe on other people's rights. One may believe in gradual progress, but that will only come about if it remains clear for all players what is bargaining and what is the standard.

So there we stand, without an official universal standard, while another sobering bit of reality is the proliferation of new local hate speech laws that strive to protect citizens from their own rows.

In the West, pursuit of a benign utopia of an offense-free society takes its toll on freedom of expression. And when the model of ad hoc speech limitations is copied in new democracies, and even more so in new autocracies, it often becomes the

---

4  Toby Mendel, "Does International Law Provide for Consistent Rules on Hate Speech?," Chapter 22 herein.
5  *See* Annual Joint Declarations of the UN, OAS, OSCE, and ACHPR mechanisms on freedom of expression, *available at* http://www.article19.org/publications/law/igo-materials.html.

*old* "utopia" of an offense-free state, a specter of the dictatorial past believed to have been buried.

Of course, there are understandable motives pressing for this shift. One is the unquestionable abundance of poisonous hate speech, the sheer amount of which is compounded by increasingly easy access to it. The deepest cause for regulatory nervousness is probably that territorial jurisdiction over media content has evaporated. Thanks to the Internet and other global platforms, "organized" hate speech can now be delivered right at home, anonymously, without being restrained by distance, rules, or culture. (I wonder how the proponents of "extensive regulation" actually imagine curbing hate speech online. Can they avoid the only known "solution" to controlling the Internet – already realized by China or Iran – which is the carving up of the global network into nationally controlled intranets?)

Another explanation for the new regulatory zeal would focus on global crises: the Rushdie fatwa; the cartoon clashes; the post-9/11 security scare. Further, any cause or excuse that helps to avoid a rigorous, American-style enforcement of state neutrality is, unsurprisingly, welcomed by emerging new powers eager to keep their domestic public space as much under control as their economic might. Finally, not even Western Europe is still keen on the hard Voltaireian standard; it buzzes with well-meaning impromptu speech bans meant to help fight social battles.

I tend to agree with Bhikhu Parekh, whose eloquent *plaidoyer* for "regulationism" distinguishes between the West and the rest: today only the West can "afford to assign law a relatively limited role," whereas "making law a major instrument" is a necessity in the developing world.[6] Parekh bases this conclusion on nations' present political and cultural capabilities. But my agreement with his partition rests on a different criterion, namely the two regions' political and cultural relationship to *free* speech, not to bad speech or to the rule of law. I believe that the dispute over hate speech regulation is a real one only in countries where, as in most western nations, the level of freedom of expression would be left basically intact regardless of whether the debate favored a more "minimalist" or a more "regulationist" model. However, in countries where free speech itself is in trouble, and public speech gets overregulated quite apart from the hate speech conundrum, the "dispute" is hollow or even mere play-acting, its outcome preordained, because any step toward the "regulationist" model ends up by further – or again – curbing legitimate speech.

What I would add to the intra-western debate is exactly the notion of responsibility – solidarity if you wish – toward the possible global consequences.

The nascent standard was punctured early on in the noblest possible way, with a dozen or so European countries criminalizing Holocaust denial. Who could morally oppose these nations' efforts to honestly confront their own past? However, these morally appealing laws had features that served as a model for groups seeking to have their dignity guaranteed by a governmental ban on speech that offends them,

---

[6] Bhikhu Parekh, "Is There a Case for Banning Hate Speech?," Chapter 2 herein.

and also for governments seeking to assume the role of the judge over admissible speech. The Holocaust denial bans were content-based, instead of situation-based. From an ocean of nasty lies filling the public space every day, they picked out certain symbolically potent fallacies. They punished the hidden intent of the speaker. They abandoned what had been a primary value, peace of society – public order, rule of law, non-violence – in favor of the peace of soul of those who had experienced, and those who respected, the historical truth. Protection of a free public space gave way to protection of a hate-speech-free public space.

And so began the slide down the slippery slope. As usual, in the long run it was not the moral necessity of such activism that proved contagious; it was its arbitrariness.

Consider just a few examples of how the relativistic innovations have been mimicked and misused in other settings, in order simply to return to government oversight of the public space under the banner of a contemporary, noble cause.

"Defamation of religions," analyzed by Kwame Anthony Appiah,[7] is promoted internationally as a modern human right to dignity. But wherever it is invoked, it just reinvents the world's oldest hate speech provision, the prohibition of blasphemy.

Another popular hate speech provision punishes the questioning of a nation's official historical narrative. While Turkey has prosecuted writers for calling the massacre of Armenians in 1915 genocide, Switzerland in 2007 convicted a Turkish politician of incitement to hatred for calling the genocide claim an "international lie."[8] Attempts in Ukraine to criminalize denial of Holodomor, that is, the questioning of the genocidal character of the Soviet-induced famine of the 1930s, neatly pairs up with the push in Russia for criminalization of denial of the role played by the Soviet Union in World War II. One could list similar Baltic, Slovakian, Irish, and other "incitement of hatred of the historical truth"–type initiatives.

As Andrei Richter recounts, punishment of "extremism" is in fashion in the post-Soviet countries.[9] Legislators bundle the defamation of religions provisions with otherwise legitimate incitement laws, adding also the ban of "offensive criticism" of government. There is an echo here of the West's "promotion of terrorism" provisions, which is helpful in defusing possible criticism. But while western legislation was criticized domestically as being possibly conducive to illegitimate prosecution of political thought, the post-Soviet extremism packages are actually created for that purpose.

The original draft of Slovakia's infamous 2008 press law prohibited incitement to hatred on a *Guinness Book of World Records*–worthy *eighteen* different grounds, including hatred of a political conviction, punishable by the Ministry of Culture. I was successful in advocating the abandonment of this extreme proposal. Nonetheless,

7  Kwame Anthony Appiah, "What's Wrong with Defamation of Religion?," Chapter 9 herein.
8  *See* "Swiss Court Convicts Turkish Politician of Genocide Denial," *N.Y. Times*, March 9, 2007.
9  Andrei Richter, "One Step Beyond Hate Speech: Post-Soviet Regulation of 'Extremist' and 'Terrorist' Speech in the Media," Chapter 14 herein.

the enacted version of the extremism law included significantly enhanced state powers.[10]

My own country, Hungary, in its December 2010 media law, established a new method of punishing hate speech outside the criminal justice system. Just like Slovakia, Hungary has empowered an authority wholly controlled by the ruling party to punish all kinds of offending expression, notwithstanding the fact that these categories of speech had been held protected by the Constitutional Court in an earlier review of the Criminal Code.

This valuable collection not only contains current reports on the state of play in hate speech regulation. It also illustrates the state of the disintegration of the international standard and highlights the danger that disintegration poses for freedom of speech.

As new speech bans pour out of the national law pipelines, the international watchdog may wield only a rubber stamp. "Go in peace to prison, your country has a specific law banning just what you have uttered," could become a standard reply to complaints.

I am sure no proponents of the "extensive regulation school" wish to reach that point. In addition, my instinct is that the freefall of the international standard will do nothing to make the fight against hate speech more effective or successful.

But the impasse over the international standard is only one of the many lively issues touched upon by this thoughtful collection from Herz and Molnar. From it, all protagonists in the free speech saga will learn a lot about themselves, and will learn that the saga continues. Journalists who hate holding back their opinions; politicians who hate journalists for having opinions; extremists who love hating; scholars and students who love the issue of hate for being so illustrative of the dilemmas of regulating speech; and my lot, the free speech defenders – all will find splendid reading and a very usable book in their hands.

---

[10] Relevant materials, including my letters and press releases and a report on the draft law by Article 19, can be found on the OSCE Web site, osce.org/fom.

# Foreword: Hate Speech and Common Sense

*Adam Liptak*

Not long after the U.S. Supreme Court decided, by an 8–1 vote, that hateful speech from protestors at military funerals is protected by the First Amendment,[1] the father of the fallen Marine who had brought the case ventured an opinion of his own.

"My first thought," said Albert Snyder, "was that eight justices didn't have the common sense that God gave a goat."

There is, as Jeremy Waldron notes in his characteristically incisive contribution to this impressively varied and immensely valuable collection of chapters and interviews, a "weird artificiality" about how we think about hate speech.[2]

All Mr. Snyder had wanted to do was bury his son, Lance Cpl. Matthew A. Snyder, in peace and with dignity. What he endured instead was a protest from a small church that believes God is punishing the United States for its tolerance of homosexuality. Members of the church make this point by appearing at funerals and other public settings with signs bearing messages like "Thank God for Dead Soldiers" and "God Hates Fags."

"Since when did any of our military die so that a group of people could target their families and harass them?" Mr. Snyder asked me not long before the Supreme Court heard his case. He had won an $11 million jury verdict against the Westboro Baptist Church of Topeka, Kansas, saying the church had caused him emotional distress, but an appeals court reversed, invoking the First Amendment.

In March 2011, the Supreme Court agreed. Its decision confirmed a theme that runs through many of the chapters collected here: The United States' commitment to the protection of hate speech is distinctive, deep, and authentic – and also perhaps reflexive, formal, and unthinking.

Chief Justice John G. Roberts Jr.'s majority opinion in the case, *Snyder v. Phelps*, was not inattentive to the pain the protests had caused. "The record makes clear that

---

[1] *Snyder v. Phelps*, 131 S. Ct. 1207 (2011).
[2] Jeremy Waldron, "Hate Speech and Political Legitimacy," Chapter 16 herein.

the applicable legal term – 'emotional distress' – fails to capture fully the anguish Westboro's choice added to Mr. Snyder's already incalculable grief," the chief justice wrote.[3] But the court responded to that pain with what was, depending on your point of view, ringing rhetoric from the First Amendment canon or an unthinking and formulaic set of platitudes.

"Given that Westboro's speech was at a public place on a matter of public concern, that speech is entitled to 'special protection' under the First Amendment," Chief Justice Roberts wrote. "Such speech cannot be restricted simply because it is upsetting or arouses contempt."[4]

That form of analysis was anticipated by the fascinating interview that kicks off this volume, one in which Michael Herz and Peter Molnar have collected illuminating perspectives from the leading scholars and practitioners in this area.

In the United States, Robert Post told Professor Molnar in 2009, "Hate speech that is part of public discourse will receive the same protection that public discourse generally receives."[5]

A little later in the interview, Dean Post acknowledged, however, that even American courts reserve some doctrinal running room in this area. "Often hard cases within public discourse are handled by courts classifying speech as outside public discourse," he said.

Did the speech at issue in the *Snyder* case include contributions to public discourse? Chief Justice Roberts took a broad view:

> The placards read "God Hates the USA/Thank God for 9/11," "America is Doomed," "Don't Pray for the USA," "Thank God for IEDs," "Fag Troops," "Semper Fi Fags," "God Hates Fags," "Maryland Taliban," "Fags Doom Nations," "Not Blessed Just Cursed," "Thank God for Dead Soldiers," "Pope in Hell," "Priests Rape Boys," "You're Going to Hell," and "God Hates You." While these messages may fall short of refined social or political commentary, the issues they highlight – the political and moral conduct of the United States and its citizens, the fate of our nation, homosexuality in the military, and scandals involving the Catholic clergy – are matters of public import.[6]

But did the speech *solely* involve public discourse? This is the point on which the *Snyder* decision is most vulnerable, at least under conventional American legal reasoning.

Aspects of the church's messages, notably including an Internet screed that the Supreme Court refused to consider on technical grounds, did seem to target the Snyder family directly and without making an obvious contribution to public discourse even as generously defined by the court.

[3]  *Snyder*, 131 S. Ct. at 1217–18.
[4]  *Id.* at 1219.
[5]  "Interview with Robert Post," Chapter 1 herein.
[6]  *Snyder*, 131 S. Ct. at 1216–17.

Chief Justice Roberts dismissed the concern in the circumstances:

> We are not concerned in this case that Westboro's speech on public matters was in any way contrived to insulate speech on a private matter from liability. . . . There was no preexisting relationship or conflict between Westboro and Snyder that might suggest Westboro's speech on public matters was intended to mask an attack on Snyder over a private matter.[7]

The negative pregnant in the passage is an acknowledgment of Dean Post's point about the fluid definition of public discourse.

In the wake of the *Snyder* decision, which does seem to put the United States at one extreme in the international spectrum in its commitment to protecting hate speech, it is particularly interesting to hear the voices in this volume cautioning against making too much of the claim of American exceptionalism in this area.

It is a particular privilege to hear some final reflections on this point from the late C. Edwin Baker, who first of all reminds us of just how much hate speech in the United States is unprotected against regulation by nongovernmental actors in, for instance, workplaces and schools.[8]

"Interestingly," he goes on, "putting aside official legal doctrine, some political scientists have concluded that in practice as opposed to rhetoric the United States is not exceptional in the way typically suggested." He reminds us, too, of "the historically *inadequate* protection of speech freedom in the United States."

But in the area of hate speech, at least, the weight of the evidence seems to me to support the claim of exceptionalism. Consider, for instance, Michel Rosenfeld's reflections on the Canadian experience. Although the Canadian Supreme Court is attentive to the views of the U.S. Supreme Court, Professor Rosenfeld writes, it has expressly declined to follow them in protecting hate speech.[9]

I looked into the contrasting American and Canadian approaches to hate speech in 2008 in the context of proceedings before the British Columbia Human Rights Tribunal over whether a news magazine had violated Canadian law by publishing an article arguing, in biting tones, that the rise of Islam threatened western values.[10] In the process, I had occasion to interview some of the lawyers involved.

"Canadians do not have a cast-iron stomach for offensive speech," one of them, Jason Gratl, said. "We don't subscribe to a marketplace of ideas. Americans as a whole are more tough-minded and more prepared for verbal combat."

Mr. Gratl, you may be surprised to learn, was a lawyer with the British Columbia Civil Liberties Association.

---

[7] *Id.* at 1217.

[8] C. Edwin Baker, "Hate Speech," Chapter 3 herein.

[9] Michel Rosenfeld, "Hate Speech in Constitutional Jurisprudence: A Comparative Analysis," Chapter 13 herein.

[10] *See* Adam Liptak, "Freedom to Offend," N.Y. *Times*, June 12, 2008, at A1.

I suspect Professor Waldron would have some sympathy for Mr. Gratl's measured defense of offensive speech. That is because Professor Waldron, like the other contributors to this splendid volume, eschews the reflexive in favor of the reflective.

"There are a number of arguments in the literature that link the protection of free expression to the flourishing of self-government in a democracy," Professor Waldron writes. "Some say little more than that, though they say it sonorously and at great length."

That amusing accusation does not hold here, which is a tribute to the editors, although it might have some purchase in the *Snyder* case. Mr. Snyder would certainly think so.

# Acknowledgments

It is a pleasure to acknowledge the wonderful assistance and support that we have enjoyed during the long process of producing this volume.

Appropriately for a project about speech, this book began with a conversation. The conversation was between Monroe Price and Miklos Haraszti. Miklos had become the Representative for Freedom of Expression of the Organization for Security and Co-operation in Europe (OSCE), in which capacity he was confronted by wildly divergent approaches to "hate speech," such as that taken by the European Convention on Human Rights on the one hand and the First Amendment to the U.S. Constitution on the other. Monroe, who sees all problems as opportunities, suggested we take on a comparative examination of "hate speech" regulation. Monroe continued to offer support and helpful ideas throughout the project. The result was two conferences, one hosted by the Cardozo School of Law in New York City and the other by the Center for Media and Communication Studies (CMCS) at Central European University in Budapest. The bulk of this book consists of papers from those conferences. We are grateful to Monroe and Miklos and are pleased both are represented within these pages.

We received institutional support for the conferences, as well as a colloquium and conference at Cardozo in spring 2010, from several sources. The Floersheimer Center for Constitutional Democracy at the Cardozo School of Law was indispensable. It is a source of deep regret that Stephen Floersheimer did not live to see this volume in print, but we are deeply indebted to him and the Center for making it possible. The Center for Media and Communication Studies (CMCS) at Central European University was essential to the book's existence. In addition, the Open Society Justice Initiative and the Organization for Security and Cooperation in Europe provided generous support for the Budapest conference.

All of the authors have our heartfelt thanks, but among them Robert Post stands out. Despite overwhelming professional obligations, Robert has shown unflagging enthusiasm for and support of this project and, among other contributions, was generous enough to give the keynote speech at both the original Budapest conference and the May 2010 conference at Cardozo.

Sandra Coliver of the Open Society Justice Initiative (the editor of an enormously valuable book, *Striking a Balance*, about the subject of this volume) was a constant source of generous guidance, advice, and hospitality throughout this project.

Thanks also to David Rudenstine, who was hugely helpful both as Cardozo dean and as conference and workshop participant.

Several of the chapters herein were further honed through presentation at a spring 2009 colloquium co-sponsored (with CMCS) by the Center for Law and Culture at the Columbia Law School convened by Peter Molnar and Kendall Thomas. We are grateful for Columbia's support.

John Berger of Cambridge University Press is a model editor, combining patience and flexibility with high standards and a clear vision of what a book can and should be.

Two anonymous reviewers consulted by Cambridge University Press provided very helpful comments on several chapters.

Zelma Rios, Program Director of the Floersheimer Center, went above and beyond, as she so often does, in reading and providing invaluable comments on the entire manuscript.

Between the four of them, Cardozo students Jocqueline Cheever, Todd Grabowsky, Brooke Menschel, and Marissa Rothstein proofread and cite-checked the entire manuscript. They did a superb job.

Finally, we would like to thank the many friends, not identified here, who helped in ways large and small and, most of all, our families for inspiration and support.

Michael Herz
New York City

Peter Molnar
Budapest & New York City

# Introduction

## Michael Herz and Peter Molnar

As we write this introduction, in early 2011, our home countries, Hungary and the United States, are both preoccupied (convulsed would be too strong a term) with concerns over appropriate limits on public discourse. On January 8, 2011, several people were killed and Congresswoman Gabrielle Giffords severely wounded by a gunman who opened fire on a crowd in Tucson, Arizona. That state has been riven by debates over immigration policy, gun control, abortion, and other divisive issues that have been at least sharp and often hostile and abusive. The shooting produced a great deal of soul-searching and hand-wringing over whether the corrosive terms and rhetoric of the political debate had produced such violence. There were many calls to tone down the rhetoric. At a memorial service, President Obama urged: "[A]t a time when our discourse has become so sharply polarized, at a time when we are far too eager to lay the blame for all that ails the world at the feet of those who happen to think differently than we do, it's important for us to pause for a moment and make sure that we are talking with each other in a way that heals, not in a way that wounds."[1] Yet it is not at all clear that the rhetoric, abhorrent as it often is, in fact produced this particular act of violence, and the rhetoric itself grows out of deeply held beliefs and is very well received by those who view the world the same way, so fundamental change seems unlikely.[2]

---

[1] Barack Obama, Speech (Tucson, AZ, Jan. 12, 2011). Consciously or not, the President was echoing a seminal early scholarly contribution to the contemporary "hate speech" debate. *See* Mari J. Matsuda et al., *Words That Wound: Critical Race Theory, Assaultive Speech, and the First Amendment* (Westview Press 1993).

[2] One prominent conservative commentator decried the focus on violent political rhetoric in the wake of the Tucson shooting as a "hate speech inquisition." Michelle Malkin, "The Hate Speech Inquisition," *National Review Online* (Jan. 19, 2011), http://www.nationalreview.com/articles/257432/hate-speech-inquisition-michelle-malkin.

Meanwhile, in the last few years Hungary has seen significant increases in (public expressions of) anti-Semitism and anti-Roma prejudice.[3] For many, these trends became all the more worrisome with the 2010 election of a two-thirds majority right-wing government. Years before its election the governing party endorsed the use of a flag similar to the one used by the Nazi arrow cross party, which ruled Hungary at the end of World War II,[4] and an extreme right-wing opposition party is the third-strongest in Parliament. This troubling increase in visible racist sentiments coincides with the passage of highly restrictive media laws,[5] targeted in part at racist and other "hate" speech.[6] The members of the media board that will implement and enforce the new laws were all appointed by the governing supermajority, raising a threat that enforcement of these provisions will be arbitrary or skewed – for example, the limitations on racist expressions might be applied primarily, or disproportionately, *against* those who would attack racism. The constitutional treatment of "hate speech"[7] has been highly contested in Hungary,[8] and in classrooms, cafes, private homes, on the streets, and in the media Hungarians wrestle with how to handle this communication pollution in the current political-legal setting.

Our countries are not unusual. Hardly a day goes by without another report of a legal controversy somewhere in the world regarding the regulation of "hate speech." Communities beset by deep sectarian and racial divisions and conflicting worldviews – characteristics that seem, discouragingly, to define an ever greater number of human societies – are in a constant struggle to preserve and perhaps to balance values of free expression, equality, tolerance, diversity, and respect. The regulation of "hate speech" is arguably the most literal, concrete, and contested setting for this struggle.

Whether and how to restrict speech that denies (both in its substantive content and in its practical effects) equal dignity and liberty for all, speech that expresses and promotes hatred of particular groups, poses one of the most difficult challenges regarding free speech. Not surprisingly, responses to this challenge have not been uniform. In most of the world, "reasonable" regulation of "hate speech" is accepted

---

[3] *See, e.g.*, Erich Follath, "Europe's Capital of Anti-Semitism: Budapest Experiences a New Wave of Hate," *Der Spiegel* (Oct. 14, 2010), *available at* http://www.spiegel.de/international/europe/0,1518,722880,00.html.

[4] On the use of this flag, see Peter Molnar, "Towards Better Law and Policy Against 'Hate Speech' – The 'Clear and Present Danger' Test in Hungary," in *Extreme Speech and Democracy* (Ivan Hare & James Weinstein eds., Oxford University Press 2009).

[5] *See* http://www.cmcs.ceu.hu/node/297/; http://hungarianwatch.wordpress.com/.

[6] The new media regulation extended the previous content-based ban on "hate speech" on radio and television programs to printed and online media content. *See* http://hungarianwatch.wordpress.com/2011/02/02/in-rare-interview-with-israeli-daily-orban-says-hungarys-new-media-law-is-good-for-the-jews-and-anti-semitism-exists-but-is-not-a-concern/.

[7] In light of the slippery and contestable nature of the term "hate speech," one of us is resolved never to use it without quotation marks. *See* Peter Molnar, "Responding to 'Hate Speech' with Art, Education, and the Imminent Danger Test," Chapter 10 herein, at n. 2. The other of us defers.

[8] *See generally* Molnar, *supra* note 4.

as both important and supportive of democratic values. (What counts as "reasonable" varies widely, however.) In contrast, our countries have opted for a quite different approach, providing constitutional protection to abhorrent speech. American courts have been consistently hostile to regulation of "hate speech," applying the First Amendment with vigor and insisting that the solution to the harms such speech causes is found not in suppression but in more speech countering the hateful messages. And since the early 1990s, postcommunist Hungary has been largely in the "the-more-speech-the-better" camp, notwithstanding the experience of the Hungarian Holocaust.[9]

If one accepts that there exists a category of unprotected degrading or abusive speech that justifies a governmental response of some sort, the next challenge is definitional. The general understanding is that the problematic speech must be directed at a group, or an individual on the basis of membership in a group, as opposed to being merely personal. (Telling an ex-lover "I hate you" might be an expression of hate, but it is not "hate speech.") But which groups count? All classes that are protected under other legal regimes (not that that is a fixed, agreed-on list)? Only minorities? Only those groups or those minorities that have been historically discriminated against or even persecuted? (Here a central disagreement in the affirmative action debate – is the problem racial classifications as such, or are racial classifications that disadvantage historically oppressed groups different from those that disadvantage the historical oppressors? – resurfaces.) If so, will majorities accept a law that protects only minorities, or only those groups or those minorities who have been historically discriminated against or even persecuted? If not, is a facially neutral law prone to uneven or abusive enforcement *against* minorities? Finally, at what point does condemnation, insult, or disdain cross the line to become a message of persecution, inhumanity, degradation, or whatever other term one uses to identify what is substantively beyond the pale? A particular problem is posed by coded speech: insults and attacks and maybe even calls to violence that on their face seem benign enough but stand in for blatantly hateful expressions and are understood to do so. Here again the immigration debate provides examples; many observers find that supposedly dispassionate policy statements about the threat from illegal immigration (in the United States especially by Hispanics, for example) is a sort of de facto "hate speech."[10] Reaching such speech, but only such speech, may be an

---

9  Largely, but not entirely. One of the exceptions is that in 2010 Hungary criminalized holocaust denial, making it punishable by up to three years in prison.

10  *See, e.g.,* Anti-Defamation League, *Immigrants Targeted: Extremist Rhetoric Moves into the Mainstream* (2008). The report states:

> The demonization of immigrants has led to an increased sense of fear in communities around the country and created a toxic environment in which hateful rhetoric targeting immigrants has become routine.
>
> Unlike the Ku Klux Klan and neo-Nazis, who make no attempt to hide their racism and bigotry, these anti-immigrant groups and coalitions often use more subtle language to demonize immigrants and foreigners. They are frequently quoted in the media, have been called to testify

impossible challenge for any regulatory regime, especially because it is at least likely that the more a country needs content-based regulation of "hate speech," the less chance it has for an evenhanded application of such restrictions.

Another definitional concern involves incitement. Preventing incitement is a central goal of "hate speech" regulations, and it provides a justification that rests on a larger, societal harm beyond solicitude for the target of the "hate speech." But incitement to what? Incitement to violence, assuming sufficient immediacy, is constitutionally unprotected and legally prohibited everywhere, and is the focus of the American-Hungarian principle that holds general content-based restrictions on "hate speech" unconstitutional. But if it is the threat of *violence* that justifies regulation, then the concern is no longer with "hate speech" per se. What about incitement to discrimination? Incitement to hatred? The first promotes acts that are (likely) themselves prohibited; the second promotes an attitude or belief system which can be maintained without engaging in prohibited acts.

Even if one concludes that the category of problematic speech can be identified, there arises a whole set of questions regarding the nature and scope of the governmental response. Most obviously, the response might take the form of legal liability (criminal? civil? administrative?). Arguably, however, art, education, and other affirmative measures, although usually off the main stage of the debate, are more effective than regulation and can enable communities – the targeted groups and the broader community as well – to engage in counterspeech to rebut, defuse, and prevent "hate speech," instead of relying on the state to silence hateful speakers.

Finally, the answers to these sorts of questions are unlikely to be uniform across all countries, times, and settings. Context matters. It is at least questionable whether it would be either possible or desirable to establish a standard global regulatory policy toward "hate speech." International law can be helpful in pushing for narrower restrictions on freedom of speech and thus reducing the risk of regulatory abuses, but one premise of almost every contribution to this collection is that there is no single means by which "hate speech" can and should be addressed. In the words of this book's title, both "content *and* context" count.

These challenges are longstanding. The settings have changed, in particular with the move online. But the issues are recurrent. The Internet has increased mutual engagement and understanding in meaningful ways, but it has also produced more polarized, aggressive, unrestrained, and often anonymous attacks on those groups the speaker disagrees with or dislikes. *Plus ça change.* Thus, while the Internet may have made "hate speech" more easily accessible, it has not made the issues surrounding it qualitatively different.

> before Congress, and often hold meetings with lawmakers and other public figures. However, under the guise of warning people about the impact of illegal immigration, anti-immigrant advocates often invoke the same dehumanizing, racist stereotypes as hate groups.

*Id.* at 1.

The contributors to this volume address these issues from a range of perspectives, backgrounds, and starting points. Throughout, there is a strong comparative emphasis, with examples, and authors, drawn from around the world. Few of the authors are completely firm or absolutist in their positions, and none are deaf to competing claims.

The book consists of four parts. The chapters in Part I offer the broadest overviews. In the first of a set of interviews with Peter Molnar, Robert Post examines his concept of public discourse and the dangers of regulating it to fight "hate speech." Bhikhu Parekh and Ed Baker both are deeply convinced of their respective, and opposing, positions, but both carefully examine the counterarguments. Parekh offers a sweeping review of the reasons not to regulate "hate speech," finding that they are ultimately wanting. Baker also starts from first principles, puzzling out what kind of showing would justify the restriction of such speech and ultimately concluding that it has not been made. Kenan Malik, in another interview, also takes a strong speech-protective position, arguing in part that active social responses and vibrant dialogue can change prejudiced attitudes and their expression more effectively than can legal prohibitions. Jamal Greene explores the influence of public attitudes on the constitutional status of "hate speech," articulating the possibilities of a popular constitutionalism in which constitutional meaning is not solely the province of the courts. First Amendment lawyer Floyd Abrams defends the American approach, not necessarily for all places and all times, but certainly for America.

Part II turns to a set of more specific concerns. Frederick Schauer takes on John Stuart Mill, analyzing, in depth and detail, the (in)applicability in this setting of Mill's argument that suppression on the basis of falsity is always a mistake because what we think is false may prove to be true. Julie Suk's chapter offers an account of the criminalization of Holocaust denial in France, drawing our attention to the possibility that, contrary to the premises of American free speech jurisprudence, the direct regulation of public debate can be a mechanism to promote national solidarity and state legitimacy. Anthony Appiah dissects and rejects the arguments for legal prohibitions on or remedies for defamation of religion, an idea that has at times made real headway within the United Nations and elsewhere. Peter Molnar proposes that art and other forms of education (in the broadest sense possible) combined with a more workable concept of incitement to imminent danger, is the best response to expressions of hatred. Katharine Gelber takes on the question of counterspeech; she values such speech, but is skeptical that counterspeech, let alone effective counterspeech, will arise spontaneously, arguing instead that the state has a role in encouraging, nurturing, and facilitating private responses. Arthur Jacobson and Bernhard Schlink offer an illuminating corrective to the received wisdom about the American constitutional protection of "hate speech," describing three ways in which such speech is in fact meaningfully regulated in the United States. Michel Rosenfeld provides a comparative study of the constitutional treatment of "hate speech" in several western democracies. Andrei Richter reports on the use and abuse of laws against extremism and terrorism in the biggest postcommunist country, Russia, and other post-Soviet republics. Alon Harel, unusually for these debates, focuses not on the speech itself or its harmful effects, but rather on its meaning *to the speaker*, venturing the argument that "deeply rooted" "hate speech" merits protection that more casual, transient, or thoughtless speech does not.

One of the central conceptual, jurisprudential, and practical challenges posed by the question of regulating "hate speech" is the (perceived) clash between free speech values and equality values. It is common to see this as precisely the setting where those concerns intersect and conflict. For many, to prohibit "hate speech" is to privilege equality over liberty; to protect it is to privilege liberty over equality. The chapters in Part III address this concern. The chapters by Jeremy Waldron, Ronald Dworkin, and Stephen Holmes form a trio. Waldron is sympathetic to certain speech restrictions, finding liberty concerns often quite dilute and equality concerns compelling; in particular, he is dubious about Dworkin's (and to some extent Post's) claim that governmental action in a democracy is legitimate only if the process that preceded it was open to participation by all. Dworkin defends his position, and Holmes offers further comments on both Waldron's and Dworkin's arguments. Yared Mengistu is particularly sensitive to the liberty/equality conflict; drawing mostly on the experience of his native Ethiopia, he argues that equality concerns require controlling "hate speech" directed at oppressed minorities, but that speech in the other direction should be protected. This part concludes with interviews with two of the most celebrated civil liberties advocates in the United States. Nadine Strossen (former president of the American Civil Liberties Union [ACLU]) offers a full-throated and unapologetic defense of robust constitutional protection for "hate speech," denying that this position undermines or sets back the cause of equality. Theodore Shaw (former director-counsel and president of the NAACP Legal Defense and Educational Fund, Inc.) takes a less firm position, although he also is wary of regulating speech, in part because of a fear that such regulations would be used to silence rather than to protect vulnerable minorities – in other words, that in practice, restrictions of liberty will prove harmful to the goal of equality.

The last section of the book turns to questions of international law, which increasingly has taken on the issue of regulating "hate speech." Toby Mendel reviews the relevant international law, arguing that it provides a coherent and useful set of principles that can be applied domestically. Irwin Cotler's chapter concerns what may be the most gruesome and abhorrent form of "hate speech": incitement to genocide. Tarlach McGonagle focuses on the Council of Europe, providing a sweeping review of the many different legal instruments and fora in which the Council has grappled with this issue. Eduardo Bertoni and Julio Rivera Jr. report on the American Convention on Human Rights, an international agreement with its own particular approach. This part concludes with Monroe Price's study of the somewhat anarchic way in which states have sought to control content, including "hate speech," that is broadcast internationally via satellite.

These chapters are wide-ranging in subject matter. They share open-mindedness, seriousness of purpose, engagement with competing views, and respectful disagreement. By both substance and example, then, they offer some hope of progress on these intractable and profoundly important questions.

Elsewhere we gratefully acknowledge the many people and institutions that have provided such wonderful support for this volume.[11] Allow us here simply to thank the authors for their extraordinarily thoughtful, learned, and serious contributions.

---

[11] *See* "Acknowledgements," *supra.*

**PART I**

# Overviews

# 1

# Interview with Robert Post

**Peter Molnar:** When I first came to the United States, a friend told me that the supposedly strong protection of freedom of speech in this country is simply a myth. Would you agree?

**Robert Post:** I suppose it would depend upon what one means by "myth." In certain communicative contexts – like the Internet, newspapers, magazines, or movies – constitutional protections for speech are quite robust. But in many other settings there is far less, if any, constitutional protection. So can we conclude that the reputation of a strong First Amendment is merely a myth?

**PM:** More narrowly, then: It is often stated that in the United States "hate speech"[1] is constitutionally immune from regulation. Is this correct?

**RP:** In many settings speech that is demeaning or degrading to particular minorities or genders or sexual orientations is regulated in the U.S. with few, if any, constitutional impediments. In private settings, for example, where there is no state action, constitutional restrictions do not apply. In such private settings hate speech can be regulated without constitutional constraint. There are also many public settings in which hate speech can be and is suppressed regularly and effectively. These tend to be settings in which the regulation of hate speech does not compromise public discourse.

**PM:** For example?

**RP:** In courtrooms, for example. Attorneys and judges will be penalized for hateful expression. So will teachers and students in public elementary and high schools,

[1] Peter Molnar explains why he places "hate speech" in quotation marks in "Responding to 'Hate Speech' with Art, Education, and the Imminent Danger Test," Chapter 10 herein, at n. 2.

This interview was conducted in New York City on October 29, 2009. Dean Post subsequently revised and expanded his remarks. Eds.

and even, in some contexts, in public universities. Prisoners, guards, and administrators will be regulated for hate speech in prisons, as will government employees in bureaucracies. There are lots and lots of settings in which in the United States government regulates or prohibits hate speech and First Amendment issues are not thought to arise.

This is an area in which conceptual precision is essential. First Amendment protections attach to speech acts, not to speech per se. The identity of a speech act is in part determined by its context. The same vile words, epithets, and concepts can therefore in different contexts be constitutionally conceptualized as entirely different kinds of speech acts and in consequence receive entirely different degrees of constitutional protection.

Speech acts that comprise "public discourse" – speech acts that we recognize as appropriate ways to influence the formation of public opinion – receive what we ordinarily conceive as the full measure of First Amendment protection. Hate speech that is part of public discourse will receive the same protection that public discourse generally receives. Hate speech that is not part of public discourse will not receive this kind of protection. So, for example, hateful words addressed by one employee to another in the context of employment within the Social Security Administration will receive only the minimal forms of constitutional protection that we accord to speech expressed by employees in the context of government employment about matters of private concern.

Because First Amendment protections depend on how a speech act is classified, and because "hate speech" is not in the United States itself recognized as a distinct constitutional category of speech act, it is never clear what circumstances people have in mind when they speak of the regulation of hate speech in the United States. Typically the claim that hate speech is constitutionally immune from regulation imagines hateful communications within public discourse, like expression in newspapers. Such speech does indeed tend to be protected from regulation. But because speech uttered in the workplace is not typically classified as public discourse, hate speech expressed in such a context is routinely suppressed.

**PM:** So how do we distinguish between those parts of the public sphere that comprise public discourse as you define it and those that do not?

**RP:** The concept of the "public sphere" is a sociological one. It refers to a sociological formation created by the circulation of texts. It typically comes into being when persons seek access to common facts and common information, and typically for some common purpose. There is a large and complicated literature, and much disagreement, on what the public sphere entails.[2] When I use the term "public

---

[2]  *See, e.g.*, Jürgen Habermas, "The Public Sphere: An Encyclopedia Article," in *Media and Cultural Studies: Key Works* 102 (Meenakshi Gig Durham & Douglas M. Kellner eds., Wiley-Blackwell 2001); Nancy Fraser, "Rethinking the Public Sphere," 25/26 *Social Text* 56 (1990).

discourse," by contrast, I am using it stipulatively to refer to those forms of communication which in our society are viewed as necessary to the processes by which public opinion is formed. We believe that such processes must be left relatively unregulated and that persons participating in such processes must be regarded by the law as autonomous and self-determining.[3] We believe that the legitimacy of our democracy depends upon these principles. Public opinion is formed within the public sphere, but which forms of communication are included within public discourse and which are not is ultimately a normative constitutional question.[4]

The distinction between public discourse and the public sphere can be seen in courtroom speech. The speech of the attorneys in the courtroom in a political trial no doubt forms part of the *public sphere*. Yet attorney speech within a courtroom is routinely and extensively regulated. Attorneys are regarded as officers of the court, not as autonomous private citizens. Attorney speech is therefore pervasively controlled by rules of evidence, rules of procedure and decorum, and so on. No judge would allow attorney speech to degenerate into racist diatribes, because such diatribes would undermine the organizational objective of a court to achieve justice. Attorney speech in a political trial would be part of the "public sphere" but it would not for normative constitutional purposes be regarded as "public discourse."

A more complicated example is radio and television broadcasting. Such broadcasting is certainly constitutive of the public sphere, but in the United States countervailing considerations prevent broadcasting from being unequivocally categorized as public discourse. Broadcasting represents a hybrid case, which is in some ways free and unregulated, and in many ways highly regulated. The categorization of broadcasting is a question of deep confusion within American constitutional law.[5] We do not permit mere indecency to be suppressed in public discourse, but we do permit its censorship within broadcasting. The Internet, by contrast, cannot be regulated in this way.

**PM:** It seems that in the United States much of the regulation of "hate speech" in the public sphere (though not the public discourse) has been done not by the state but by other organizations. Examples would include university speech codes.[6]

**RP:** One needs to distinguish various dimensions of the public sphere. There are aspects of the public sphere, like the courtroom example, which involve what I

---

[3] Robert Post, "Meiklejohn's Mistake: Individual Autonomy and the Reform of Public Discourse," 64 *U. Colorado L. Rev.* 1109 (1993); Robert Post, "Democracy and Equality," 1 *Law, Culture and the Humanities* 142 (2005), *republished in* 603 *Annals Amer. Acad. Political Soc. Science* 24 (2006).

[4] I discuss some of the enormously complicated considerations that form part of this normative question in Robert Post, "The Constitutional Concept of Public Discourse: Outrageous Opinion, Democratic Deliberation, and *Hustler Magazine v. Falwell*," 103 *Harv. L. Rev.* 601 (1990).

[5] *See* Robert Post, "Subsidized Speech," 106 *Yale L.J.* 151 (1996).

[6] *See generally* Arthur Jacobson and Bernhard Schlink, "Hate Speech and Self-Restraint," Chapter 12 herein.

have elsewhere called managerial domains. A managerial domain is an institution created to accomplish a specific function, to achieve a particular goal. The goal of a courtroom is to produce justice. The function of a university is to dispense education and to produce knowledge. Once a bounded institution exists that is oriented toward a specific mission, the institution will regulate persons within its domain in ways necessary successfully to achieve its function. And this implies that the institution will also regulate the speech of persons within its domain as is necessary to be instrumentally effective.[7] The constitutional rationale of public discourse is precisely the opposite of that of a managerial domain. The objective of the latter is to achieve its purposes; the objective of public discourse is to determine what our purposes are. Within public discourse, goals must perennially be taken as provisional and revisable.

**PM:** Control of "hate speech" in these "managerial settings" does not exhaust the instances of actual regulation in the United States. For example, Jacobson and Schlink point to two others: regulation of employers, making them liable for harassing speech by their employees, and the self-regulation of the broadcast and cable industries.[8] How do these latter contexts fit within your conceptual schema?

**RP:** With regard to workplace regulation, writers such as Cynthia Estlund contend that workplace speech should be considered part of public discourse, that is to say it should be considered part of public-opinion formation.[9] The proposition is serious and debatable, but it is clear that it does not represent the current normative perspective of the contemporary American legal system. Title VII[10] places significant restrictions on workplace speech which creates a hostile environment,[11] and courts do not evidence any serious inclination to use the First Amendment to restrict these aspects of Title VII.[12]

The situation with regard to broadcasters is very different. Self-regulation by broadcasters is a response to the threat of regulation by the Federal Communications

---

[7] For the general theory of this point, see Robert Post, "Between Governance and Management: The History and Theory of the Public Forum," 34 UCLA L. *Rev.* 1713 (1987). For an elaboration of the point in the specific context of university speech codes, see Robert C. Post, "Racist Speech, Democracy, and the First Amendment," 32 *Wm. & Mary L. Rev.* 267, 317–25 (1991).

[8] Jacobson and Schlink, *supra* note 6.

[9] *See, e.g.,* Cynthia Estlund, "Harmonizing Work and Citizenship: A Due Process Solution to a First Amendment Problem," 2006 *S. Ct. Rev.* 115 (criticizing the Supreme Court for underprotecting public employees' free speech rights and undervaluing the public interest in hearing what they have to say); Cynthia L. Estlund, "The Workplace in a Racially Diverse Society: Preliminary Thoughts on the Role of Labor and Employment Law," 1 *U. Pa. J. Labor & Empl. L.* 49, 73 (1998) (describing "the workplace as a uniquely valuable setting for speech and as an important satellite forum for public discourse").

[10] Title VII of the Civil Rights Act of 1964, codified at 42 U.S.C. § 2000e.

[11] *See* Jacobson and Schlink, *supra* note 6.

[12] Arguments that Title VII does violate the First Amendment have been made, generally by scholars with very different politics than Estlund's. *See, e.g.,* Kingsley Browne, "Zero Tolerance for the First Amendment: Title VII's Regulation of Employee Speech," 27 *Ohio N.U.L. Rev.* 563 (2001). For cites to the literature, see *id.* at 576 n. 77.

Commission (FCC). American constitutional law currently accepts a number of distinct rationales for regulating the content of broadcasting, most especially for prohibiting the broadcast of indecent speech during certain hours of the day when children are likely to be in the audience. One traditional justification concerned spectrum scarcity;[13] in these days of the Internet and of a virtually infinite number of cable channels, that rationale has become less and less convincing. The justification that presently retains pride of place is the one offered in the *Pacifica* case,[14] in which the Court reasoned, roughly, that because broadcasting is a powerful method of socializing the young, it is necessary to regulate broadcasting to ensure that its intrusion into the home does not disrupt the transmission of essential community values from parents to children. Any such disruption would undermine the very decency and civility that public discourse in a democracy requires to fulfill its function of democratic legitimation.[15]

**PM:** So you read *Pacifica* to permit limits not only on indecency but also on some sorts of "hate speech"? If so, is it a special limitation on broadcast "hate speech," an exception from what you call "the paradox of public discourse," that there seems to be no way for the state under the prevailing interpretation of the First Amendment to uphold civility rules in public discourse, although a minimum of civility rules might seem to be necessary for public discourse to function properly?

**RP:** This is currently a matter of constitutional speculation, but my guess is that if the FCC imposed on broadcast television the kind of regulations that Jeremy Waldron is talking about – limitations designed to provide members of vulnerable groups the "assurance" necessary to go about their lives in a secure and dignified manner[16] – and these limitations were defined in a suitably precise and limited way, those regulations would be upheld by the courts. But that's merely a prediction. Such a conclusion would be consistent with the rationale of *Pacifica*. Of course, a court that disagreed with *Pacifica* might reach a different conclusion about the extent to which enforcement of community norms might be necessary to sustain the function of public discourse.

The Internet, in contrast to broadcasting, is understood to be a medium of communication in which adults can control the participation of children by filters and other devices, so that adult communication on the Internet cannot be regulated to make it appropriate for the socialization of children.[17] The Internet is therefore for constitutional purposes analogous to media such as newspapers and movies. *Pacifica*'s justification for content regulation, which sounds in the socialization of children, drops out of the picture.

[13] *See, e.g.,* Red Lion Broadcasting Co. v. FCC, 395 U.S. 367, 388–91 (1969).
[14] FCC v. Pacifica Foundation, 438 U.S. 726 (1978).
[15] Robert Post, "Community and the First Amendment," 29 *Az. St. L.J.* 473 (1997).
[16] *See* Jeremy Waldron, "Hate Speech and Political Legitimacy," Chapter 16 herein.
[17] Reno v. American Civil Liberties Union, 521 U.S. 844 (1997).

**PM:** In your previous work, notably your book *Constitutional Domains*,[18] you have distinguished the model of democratic self-government, in which "autonomous wills" are coordinated and reconciled, from the form of social organization that you label "community." Public discourse may operate very differently, and be subject to very different regulation, in these two settings. Could you explain the tension between democracy and community and how they can be reconciled?

**RP:** The scope and nature of public discourse depends upon the scope and nature of what is "public." In my work, I contrast the social formation of the "public" with the social formation of what I call "community."

I define "community" as a social structure that inculcates common norms into the identities of its members.[19] Only feral children grow up outside communities. Normal human beings, as George Herbert Mead explained, are raised in a community that socializes them into its norms. All normal human beings "internalize" these norms, so that they become part of the structure of their personality.[20] Normal human beings know how to treat other human beings within their culture, how to distinguish friends from enemies, how to evince respect and contempt, and so on. The same norms that are powerfully built into the structure of individual personalities are also powerfully built into the collective identity of the community, so that there is a continuous symmetry between collective and individual identity. I use the term "community" to refer to this deep and inevitable form of social solidarity in which ongoing processes of socialization ensure that social norms reciprocally define individual and collective identity. Building on Mead's work, I think of community as a primal and indispensable form of social organization. It creates identities; it creates values; it creates structures of attitudes and motivations; it creates social solidarity and unity that allows for group identification, and so on.

The social formation of the "public" is not at all like this. The public is a space that encompasses many communities. This idea was developed in America through sociologists, particularly at the University of Chicago in the early years of the twentieth century, who were studying major urban metropolitan areas in which there were many distinct communities.[21] Take the complex and diverse city of Chicago. It encompassed neighborhoods in which persons congregated from distinct communities, from Italy, Poland, Slovakia, neighborhoods in which there lived primarily Jews, or African Americans, or White Anglo-Saxon Protestants (WASPs), and so on. Each of these distinct communities possessed a unique identity, a particular form of social solidarity based on particular customs, traditions, histories, and norms. Yet these various neighborhoods somehow had to come together to govern the common

---

[18]  Robert C. Post, *Constitutional Domains: Democracy, Community, Management* (Harvard University Press 1995).

[19]  *Id.* at 300.

[20]  Robert Post, "Between Democracy and Community: The Legal Constitution of Social Form," in *Nomos XXXV: Democratic Community* 163 (John W. Chapman & Ian Shapiro eds., NYU Press 1993).

[21]  *See* Post, *supra* note 3.

metropolitan area of Chicago, which was a vast space that embraced many diverse communities. The common space of what I call the "public" is that into which persons enter as they leave their insular neighborhoods and communities and seek to work together with those who have been socialized into distinct norms. Because we are a multicultural nation, we have been forced in the United States to forge a healthy public space in which persons from diverse neighborhoods can meet each other, on terms of equality and mutual respect, *outside* of their respective communities. Of course the public space would be neither safe nor equal if persons entering it would automatically be subject to the norms of an alien community.

As the need for a safe and neutral public space became increasingly apparent in the third decade of the twentieth century, which is to say as WASP dominance of the public sphere that had heretofore been accepted as natural began to weaken, we developed in the United States a First Amendment doctrine designed to ensure that the state would remain neutral with respect to the enforcement of community norms within public discourse, which is to say within those forms of speech necessary for the common project of democratic self-governance. The First Amendment sought to ensure that public discourse was safe and welcoming to all individuals; it refrained from suppressing speech that might be inconsistent with the norms of any particular community. The First Amendment ensured not merely a marketplace of ideas, but also a marketplace of communities.

The key case in this development was *Cantwell v. Connecticut*,[22] which interpreted the First Amendment to hold that in public discourse we meet each other as equal persons who are immune from the condemnation that might be imposed by the norms of an alien community. Even if communicating according to the norms of a speaker's own community profoundly insults and demeans another, because the community norms of an addressee regard such communication as offensive and degrading, the First Amendment will nevertheless typically prohibit the law from enforcing the community norms of an addressee.

Our unique separation of church and state is a good example of the way in which we have interpreted our Constitution to ensure a public space that remains permanently outside the domain of any single community. The Establishment Clause does not prohibit the establishment of religion because we are an irreligious nation. To the contrary, we are the most religious of all modern developed nations. We instead prohibited the establishment of religion because religion was so important to Americans in the eighteenth century and because they understood that they were so religiously diverse. Each sect was afraid that it would come under the control of another, alien sect. They therefore agreed that *no sect* would be able to seize control of the common resources of the federal government. The Establishment Clause guaranteed that the federal government would remain neutral ground, and hence

---

[22] 310 U.S. 296 (1940) (setting aside breach of the peace convictions of Jehovah's Witnesses proselytizing on the sidewalk).

that religious practices could safely remain voluntary and privatized with respect to federal control.

Norms of civility, by which we distinguish speech that is hateful from all other forms of speech, are like the tenets of a religion. Different communities have different norms of civility, and hence they classify different forms of speech as hateful. In the 1940s, when the notion of public discourse was being constructed by our Supreme Court, multiple communities were seen as vying for control of the public space. The upstanding decent people on the right side of the tracks wanted to prohibit one form of one discourse, whereas the working classes wanted to ban a different kind of discourse, and the churches wanted to suppress yet a third form of discourse. Which form of civility would the law impose to control public discourse? The Court's answer was that no form of civility could be imposed.

Precisely because in the United States community was fragmented, precisely because there was deep, sincere, and divisive disagreement about the forms of speech that should be prohibited as hateful, the Court adopted a rule that was analogous to the Establishment Clause. It said that *no* community could seize the power of the state to impose its own norms on public discourse. That is the true meaning of such reiterated but fundamentally odd Supreme Court maxims as "one man's vulgarity is another's lyric,"[23] or "one man's amusement teaches another's doctrine."[24] The Court is not really advocating a kind of hopeless relativism. In many contexts the law distinguishes vulgarities from lyrics, amusements from doctrines. These distinctions, however, turn on community norms, and what such maxims really mean is the First Amendment will not permit such norms to be enforced within public discourse.

Underlying this marketplace of communities is one additional and important qualification. Karl Polanyi once argued that any marketplace must be "embedded" in a larger community.[25] That principle also applies to the marketplace of communities. If one is going to tolerate different forms of speech, that toleration itself must reflect an image of the public good; it must reflect a particular normative image of the good state that is democratically responsive to the public opinion of its citizens. Absent such an image, public discourse cannot perform its allotted function of underwriting democratic legitimacy. So without an image of a state like, say, Hungary, an image of a social order that is larger and more encompassing than any single particular community within Hungary, there is no reason for particular Hungarians to leave their own particular communities to participate with strangers to make a public opinion that will direct the larger Hungarian state. There is no reason to tolerate alien communities at all. One can see here that the whole idea of democratic self-governance is itself a community norm that must be sustained through typical forms of community socialization, including specifically democratic

---

[23] Cohen v. California, 403 U.S. 15, 25 (1971).
[24] Winters v. New York, 333 U.S. 507, 510 (1948).
[25] *See generally* Karl Polanyi, *The Great Transformation* (Farrar & Rinehart 1944).

education. And this, in turn, means that if the toleration of incivility fundamentally threatens the community norms that sustain democracy itself, then the logic I have been explicating no longer applies.

In the United States, therefore, courts always face a dilemma. With respect to any particular government regulation enforcing a civility rule within public discourse, it can be argued either that enforcement of the civility rule is necessary to sustain the community life of the nation, so that striking down the regulation would ultimately undermine democratic self-governance, or that, to the contrary, the enforcement of the civility rule violates the tolerance required by democratic self-determination, so that allowing the regulation needlessly displaces and therefore damages democratic self-governance. One sees this dilemma endlessly reiterated within American jurisprudence.

**PM:** Do you think this model can work only in the United States?

**RP:** Habermas argues that it can work in Europe. Habermas's idea of "constitutional patriotism" is quite relevant to what I have been saying.[26] Habermas believes that one can have loyalty to an entity that is defined by inclusiveness and difference. He initially based his notion of constitutional patriotism on the United States, which at one point he considered an appropriate model for Europe.

**PM:** Your model seems to have both a normative and a descriptive/cultural element. The normative element requires that the state respect the authorship of everyone in the public discourse; the cultural/descriptive element holds that everyone accepts that others might have different views about civility rules in the public discourse but that in the background there is something common that holds people together in some shared enterprise.

**RP:** That's right; there is some *unit* that defines public discourse. If we protect public discourse so that we might engage in "self-government," we must first ask who the "self" is that seeks to govern. If we answer "the people," then we must join with Rousseau, who properly observes that we must first "examine into that by which a people became a people; for, on this . . . rests the true foundation of society."[27] However we define "the people" who have thrown themselves together into the common enterprise of self-government through the perpetual formation of public opinion, the success of democratic self-government requires that the unit we define must

---

[26] *See* Jürgen Habermas, "Struggles for Recognition in the Democratic Constitutional State," in Jürgen Habermas, *The Inclusion of the Other: Studies in Political Theory* 225–6, 203–36 (Ciarin Cronin & Pablo DeGrieff eds., Ciarin Cronin trans., MIT Press 1998). Frank Michelman describes "constitutional patriotism" as naming "a motivational disposition . . . of attachment to one's country, specifically in view of a certain spirit sustained by the country's people and their leaders in debating and deciding disagreements of essential constitutional import." Frank Michelman, "Morality, Identity and 'Constitutional Patriotism'," 76 *Denv. U.L. Rev.* 1009, 1022 (1999).

[27] Jean-Jacques Rousseau, *A Treatise on the Social Compact, Or, the Principles of Political Law* 18 (J. Murray 1791).

necessarily share a common commitment to, at a minimum, the community norm of self-determination as the proper form of social solidarity. The implication is that democracy is always founded on some larger notion of an encompassing community that creates the public and that requires common collective authorship.[28] Without this normative premise, I think it will be very hard to construct a coherent concept of freedom of speech. Somehow the preconditions for loyalty and tolerance must be constructed on the basis of antecedent forms of social solidarity, on some form of community.

**PM:** Do you mean that this normative premise provides a precondition for Hungary or Central European and Eastern European countries generally if they want to construct a coherent concept of freedom of speech, and that countries in which the cultural elements that you described are missing are not, or cannot be, legitimate democracies?

**RP:** I don't know. I don't know enough about what it is like to live in a democracy like Russia or Hungary. Do citizens there experience authorship? Or do they feel oppressed no matter what party is in power? In my country, George W. Bush was in power for eight years and he did many things I abhorred. Nevertheless, I did not and could not refuse to accept an identification with my government. My loyalty transcends the particular actions of a particular party, however much I disagree with the actions it may be taking. My relationship to my government is based upon a larger time horizon than the Bush presidency. Does that larger time horizon exist in Russia or Hungary? If it does, then you have the resources to construct a real democracy.

**PM:** How might a country go about developing the two cultural elements of loyalty and tolerance if they are meager or underdeveloped?

**RP:** I think that an important resource is collective memory. There has to be a continuous story of national development and ideals. In this country, our tradition of freedom of speech is itself an essential collective memory that inspires loyalty and tolerance. And I suspect the same would be true for many European countries. If they don't have such a story, if they don't have the resources for collective memory – and this is István Rév's point about Hungary[29] – it will be very difficult to create the normative resources for public discourse and the marketplace of communities. Without some larger community value, nothing will constrain the exercise of raw power, which frequently does not experience the need to be either tolerant or loyal.

Another way of saying this is that in the United States we believe that even the positive enactments of the state are ultimately accountable to the most deeply held norms of the community that underwrites the state. This is the area of our

---

[28] *See* Robert Post, "Democracy, Popular Sovereignty, and Judicial Review," 86 *Cal. L. Rev.* 429 (1998).
[29] István Rév, *Retroactive Justice: Pre-History of Post-Communism* (Stanford University Press 2005).

doctrine we call substantive due process, which constrains state action on the basis of fundamental traditions and values.

**PM:** At the gay pride parade in Budapest in 2009 (a topic to which I will return), the government protected the marchers very professionally. That shows both an ability and a certain political commitment to do so, indicating that the cultural element of tolerance is developing in Hungary.

**RP:** The example would be powerful if the government were acting to demonstrate toleration for speech with which it radically disagreed. Holmes put this most dramatically when he said that the true test of guarantees of freedom of speech turns on "freedom for the thought that we hate."[30] But note that such tolerance cannot be only for progressive causes. There must be tolerance for speech hated by the left as well as speech hated by the right.

**PM:** Yes, obviously.

**RP:** Not obviously.

**PM:** For many people not obviously.

**RP:** There are many who would construct asymmetries between the toleration of the left and the right. In fact we heard this position articulated in our symposium.[31]

**PM:** I wonder how complete this model of unregulated discourse between competing communities is. Suppose community A has civility rules under which members are not only free to engage in anti-gay speech, for example, but even required to do so, whereas community B, in this example, a gay community, has a norm of respecting the freedom of speech even of community A, which is engaging in "hate speech" aimed directly at community B. Then it is not really a fair fight. Can the state intervene in such circumstances?

**RP:** Once again, it is important to avoid a picture in which the state either acts in an aggressive and intolerant way or is paralyzed and cannot act at all. In the United States, as I mentioned, the regulation of speech is quite fragmented and discontinuous. The government can intervene in some contexts, but not in others. In the workplace, rules against anti-gay speech are permissible. So communities are not in this sense equal in the workplace; we permit the suppression of some forms of uncivil speech. But public discourse is a limited and specialized form of communication in which communities must politically be regarded as equal. The reason why we impose such odd rules on public discourse is that it is the precise location in which the "self" in "self-government" is created. It is the location in

---

[30] United States v. Schwimmer, 279 U.S. 644, 655 (1929) (Holmes, J., dissenting).
[31] Post is referring here to an international workshop on "hate speech," organized by Jeremy Waldron, that took place at NYU Law School on October 23–24, 2009. Eds.

which we collectively decide what is and what is not fundamental. And if that question is already decided and imposed upon public discourse, then we lose the capacity collectively to think through the problem. That is why the state cannot intervene to tip the scales within public discourse.

Notice also, however, that even though we prevent the state from regulating public discourse in the name of a community norm, we nevertheless freely allow the state to participate within public discourse as a speaker. The state is a frequent, powerful, and loud participant in public discourse. We respect a president who stands up and asserts we should treat each other with civility and respect and that we should raise the tone of public conversation.[32]

**PM:** I have heard you elsewhere mention the example of the U.S. government expressing support for civil rights by issuing a commemorative stamp in honor of Martin Luther King. That's also forceful speech.

**RP:** Precisely so.

**PM:** But in the public discourse, under the prevailing First Amendment model, special protection of certain groups is not possible.

**RP:** For speech purposes. The state can adopt affirmative action programs; it can regulate conduct in many ways. But as a general matter the First Amendment prevents the state from restricting what people do and do not *say* in public discourse, although this generalization has exceptions. There are limits that the Court has found it necessary to impose. The way I conceptualize those limits is that the social form of community is logically and sociologically prior to that of democracy. So if incivilities occurring in public discourse threaten to undermine the very idea of a democratic community, if they threaten to undermine the norms of civility that allow public discourse to serve its function, the Court will permit regulation. But what is permissible will be a very thin form of regulation at the margins, and we will characterize unprotected speech with labels like fighting words,[33] or "true threats,"[34] or incitement to imminent violence.[35] These are marginal cases, but they do definitely exist, and they teach us an important lesson. They stand for the proposition that the Court will allow the maximum possible degree of freedom that is

---

[32]  For two strikingly direct governmental condemnations of what most would characterize as hate speech, see the statements approved by the houses of the U.S. Congress in 1994 condemning a November 1993 speech by Khalid Muhammad of the Nation of Islam at Kean College in New Jersey. H.R. Res. 343, 103d Cong., 2d Sess. (1994) (condemning the speech as "outrageous hatemongering of the most vicious and vile kind"); 140 *Cong. Rec.* S687 (February 2, 1994) (adopting by a vote of 97–0 an amendment expressing the sense of the Senate that the speech "was false, anti-Semitic, racist, divisive, repugnant and a disservice to all Americans and is therefore condemned").

[33]  *See* Chaplinsky v. New Hampshire, 315 U.S. 568 (1942).

[34]  *See* Virginia v. Black, 538 U.S. 343 (2003); R.A.V. v. City of St. Paul, 505 U.S. 377, 388 (1992); Watts v. United States, 394 U.S. 705 (1969).

[35]  *See* Brandenburg v. Ohio, 395 U.S. 444 (1969).

compatible with the survival of the democratic community.[36] So not even in public discourse is there anything like "absolute protection." Not even close.

**PM:** The examples you give all turn on the context of the speech.

**RP:** Most fundamentally, they turn on the legal characterization of the speech act at issue. Courts typically ask whether a particular speech act constitutes an effort to participate in public opinion formation, or whether it instead is really a threat, or a fight, or an incitement to immediate illegal action. These characterizations are intuitive and pre-theoretical, and, as you say, they are very influenced by context. Many of the most basic First Amendment judgments turn on such pre-theoretical acts of classification.

Here's an example. As I have mentioned, there is an essential difference between state regulation of speech within a managerial domain and within public discourse. But if a soldier in a military barracks is writing his Senator complaining about his commanding officer, should the speech act be classified as within the managerial domain of the military, in which case it can be punished because inconsistent with the discipline required for the effective functioning of the military, or should it be classified as the public discourse of a citizen petitioning his government? This is a normative question, and it is the kind of pre-theoretical determination that is constantly made and continuously underlies First Amendment doctrine. If speech is within the managerial domain of the military, it can be regulated as hate speech. Hate speech between soldiers can be and is suppressed insofar as it is inconsistent with the mission of the military. When such speech is within public discourse, by contrast, it is relatively immune from state regulation. Often hard cases within public discourse are handled by courts classifying speech as outside public discourse.

**PM:** Do you mean to imply that democracies must allow people to engage in "hate speech" so long as "hate speech" is expressed within the public discourse, otherwise they undermine their legitimacy regardless their cultural context?

**RP:** I was surprised at a recent conference[37] to hear several speakers say that each country should regulate hate speech in its own way. This is not the usual way in which I have heard this question discussed, which tends to be in a universalist register. It is argued that hate speech either does or does not come within a universal right to freedom of speech, and hence it is either suppressible in every state or in no state. This cosmopolitan approach is consonant with a highly internationalist doctrine of human rights that extend universally around the globe. The thought that hate speech may be constitutionally protected in one country but not in another seems inconsistent with a global vision of rights.

---

[36] On the concept of "democratic community," see Post, *supra* note 20.
[37] Post is referring to a conference based on the contributions to this book which took place at the Cardozo School of Law on May 13, 2010. Eds.

My own view, I should hasten to say, is highly contextualist. I believe that "A" can be a right in country "B" but not country "C" if the history, customs, traditions, and political circumstances of the two countries are relevantly different. Until this conference, I have always considered myself as something of an outlier for taking this view.

I rest my own contextualism on the conclusion that it does not make much sense to speak of a right of freedom of speech *simpliciter*. To speak of a simple right to speech, one would have to be able to distinguish speech from action. But no such distinction exists, because all words are also deeds. "Speech" and "action" are not distinct natural categories that exist in the world. Instead we determine the reasons why we wish to protect speech, and we then classify as speech those transactions that serve these reasons. The fundamental question for us is therefore what purposes we wish to serve by protecting speech. This is the way, for example, Fred Schauer talked about freedom of speech in his 1982 book,[38] which set the modern agenda for thinking about First Amendment jurisprudence.

For a variety of reasons I will not go into now, I do not think that the search for truth is particularly helpful in defining which speech acts are protected.[39] Nor do I think, even though the late great Ed Baker would have disagreed,[40] that the value of autonomy is particularly helpful as a guide to protecting speech, because it is too vague and broad-gauged. What seems to me most useful in describing the actual shape of constitutional protections throughout the world, not just in the United States, is the thought that we protect freedom of speech because we believe that certain kinds of communications must be free if democracy is so succeed as a form of governance.

Roughly speaking, the thought is that democracy rests on the value of self-governance. It must mediate between individual and collective autonomy. We do this through the medium of public opinion. Public discourse is the technical legal term used to describe the speech acts necessary for public opinion to mediate between individual and collective autonomy. In a culturally heterogeneous society, free participation in public discourse is a necessary but not sufficient condition for my faith that my government can be responsive to my beliefs. We reinforce this faith with a wide range of institutions, ranging from elections to juries, designed to tether the state to public opinion. This suggests that the right to freedom of speech is logically and sociologically dependent on an anterior right to democratic participation

---

[38]  Frederick Schauer, *Free Speech: A Philosophical Enquiry* (Cambridge University Press 1982).

[39]  For a general discussion, see Robert Post, "Reconciling Theory and Doctrine in First Amendment Jurisprudence," 88 *Cal. L. Rev.* 2353 (2000).

[40]  In his chapter in the current volume, Baker rests his skepticism regarding regulation of hate speech on two propositions that are central to much of his writing about freedom of speech: that the legitimacy of the state depends on its respect for people's equality and autonomy, and that, as a purely formal matter, the state only respects people's autonomy if it allows them to express their own values in their own speech. C. Edwin Baker, "Hate Speech," Chapter 3 herein.

or self-rule. This turn suggests that international human rights instruments have it conceptually backward.

If there is a right to participate in the formation of public opinion, that right exists to make the state more democratically legitimate. This creates something of a paradox. The content of this right is exquisitely contextual, because which forms of speech will and will not make the state more democratically legitimate is in part an historical question. Yet the right is also formal, because it extends equally to all who are subject to democratic rule.

It could be that participation in opinion formation in certain ways, in certain countries, in certain national contexts, destabilizes democracy rather than legitimizes it. Legitimacy is a contingent historical condition. The right of participation is a formal universal right. The two therefore fit uneasily together. The formal right exists so long as it serves the contextual value. That is why, at root, one might adopt a contextualist position about the regulation of hate speech. In some contexts, hate speech might so delegitimize democracy as to justify excluding hate speech from the formal definition of freedom of speech; in other contexts, excluding hate speech from the right of freedom of expression would constitute a paradigmatic example of censorship. It all depends.

As a formal matter, we can say that suppressing hate speech in public discourse contradicts the formal right of participation. It prevents persons from participating in a process of public-opinion formation in ways that would make the law responsive to them. With respect to such persons, the state has *pro tanto* ceased to be legitimated, because it has excluded them from the process of public-opinion formation. There is thus always a steep cost to prohibiting the participation in public discourse of those who wish to engage in hate speech. The default rule should therefore be that hate speech should not be excluded from public discourse. But there is another side to the question. It could be that the costs of hate speech to the overall democratic legitimation of the nation are so high that the default rule should be overturned. This is a matter of particular historical contingencies and circumstances.

**PM:** Your discussion of public discourse offers one test of legitimacy: the results of the democratic process are legitimate only if all communities have participated in the discourse that produces the relevant consensus or decision. That in turn disables the state from proscribing certain messages, including "hate speech." Julie Suk provides a different account with regard to France, arguing that after World War II, the very legitimacy of the republic required outlawing racist speech and Holocaust denial.[41]

**RP:** I can't speak to the particular historical claims that Julie makes. I know that Patrick Weil has offered an analogous account. In the abstract, of course, we can

---

[41] Julie C. Suk, "Denying Experience: Holocaust Denial and the Free-Speech Theory of the State," Chapter 8 herein.

say that to the extent that a state firmly commits to a particular identity, so much so that it prohibits persons from thinking or communicating about any other identity, then it *pro tanto* ceases to be a democratic state because it refuses to be responsive to what its citizens are actually thinking and so withdraws from the project of self-governance. Julie has contrasted the French state's refusal to be neutral with the impotence of the American state, which she regards as effectively paralyzed by a misconceived commitment to neutrality that is mandated by the First Amendment. For the reasons I've already discussed, I think this contrast is overdrawn. The First Amendment prohibits content discrimination in the civil and criminal regulation of public discourse. But as a general matter, the American state is far from neutral. The American state takes substantive positions all the time. It affirms civil rights, equality, toleration, and so forth. Consider our regulation of workplace actions and speech. Consider our stamps and monuments. Consider the ongoing expression of American government officials about issues of race and toleration. Consider the rules and regulations that the American state imposes on the army, on government institutions, on contractors, and so on. No one should confuse the American state with a neutral state. What is true is that the American state will not regulate public discourse through civil or criminal sanctions in ways that are based on content. So the contrast between us and the French is actually much smaller than I think Julie implies.

**PM:** So to ensure legitimacy and self-government, the government cannot intervene in the public discourse – through civil or criminal sanctions in ways that are based on content – other than in exceptional situations.

**RP:** It can and does intervene in public discourse in the sense that the government itself *speaks* in public discourse. But you are correct that a concern with democratic legitimation prevents it from using civil and criminal sanctions to regulate public discourse except in very unusual situations.

**PM:** All right. And what about the claim that another way for the state to achieve legitimacy is by excluding certain messages from the public discourse?

**RP:** Jeremy Waldron makes an analogous point. For him, democratic legitimacy does not require including in public discourse attacks on accepted "fundamentals" as to which there is no longer a meaningful, ongoing debate. Jeremy's position presupposes that we agree about the fundamentals; that they are not controversial. In his model, something like in the old picture of Patrick Devlin,[42] the legitimacy of the state depends upon enforcing what we already all agree upon.[43] Such a position would have much to recommend it if in fact there was universal agreement about what was "fundamental." But, as in Devlin's case, those who advocate for

[42] Patrick Devlin, *The Enforcement of Morals* 10 (Oxford University Press 1965).
[43] *See* Waldron, *supra* note 16.

the enforcement of fundamentals are most apparently attempting to discredit and exclude those who precisely disagree with their view of fundamental values. In the context of hate speech, we are by hypothesis addressing a situation in which many persons deny "fundamental" principles and wish to speak in ways that are inconsistent with them. This suggests to me that in fact we do not all agree on such fundamentals at all. Waldron of course concedes that there is not unanimity on these principles, stating only that "these matters are more or less settled."[44] But this is a significant concession, and it seems to imply that ultimately his claim is that such principles *should be* fundamental and beyond dispute. That amounts to the proposition that persons should be prevented from communicating because in our view they have nothing of value to say.

**PM:** Let me turn to a specific example involving "hate speech." In Budapest in 2008, extreme right-wing Internet sites encouraged "counter-demonstrators" to block the gay pride parade, by force if necessary. At the parade itself, "counter-demonstrators" were throwing rocks, acid-filled eggs, and bottles when they could get close enough, and many of them were shouting homophobic and anti-Semitic epithets. Let's assume that at the parade some people did not call for stopping the parade, by force if necessary, or for physically hurting participants of the parade, but they did express their homophobic and racist ideas. Would, or should, such speech be protected under *Brandenburg*?[45]

**RP:** It would be helpful closely to parse the case that you put. First, there are marchers who wish to express their point of view, which concerns pride in gay culture. Presumably their message is that gay culture should be accepted in Hungary. The parade is in this sense the public expression of an idea. A central principle of freedom of speech is that the state cannot suppress expression of an idea in public discourse merely because it disagrees with that idea. This principle follows from the thought that public discourse is the medium within which democratic will is formed, so that if the state were to control which ideas could be expressed in that medium, it would no longer be responsive to a democratic will. The right to express this controversial idea in the parade should therefore be protected.

Second, a parade is not simply words. It is not abstract text. It is a material manifestation that can cause physical effects, like trash, traffic jams, noise, and so on. Most communicative acts have physical dimensions of this kind. Loudspeakers cause sound, movie houses cause congestion and fire hazards, newspapers cause litter, DVDs consume chemicals, and so on. How the necessary physical dimensions of communication can be regulated without compromising freedom of speech is a continuous and complex problem. In the context of parades, this problem includes

---

44 *Id.*
45 Brandenburg v. Ohio, 395 U.S. 444, 447 (1969) (holding that speech advocating violence or lawlessness is constitutionally protected "except where such advocacy is directed to inciting or producing imminent lawless action and is likely to incite or produce such action").

how parades can be reconciled with traffic control, pedestrian safety, commercial and other usages of street space, and so on. On the constitutional side of the question is the importance of persons being able to deploy the medium of parades in ways normatively regarded as integral to the formation of public opinion.

Third, the message I convey in my parade or speech may provoke others to violent acts. The question posed here is whether the costs caused by speech – the negative reactions and effects – should be internalized by the speakers. Because participation in public discourse is so precious, we typically do not permit hecklers' vetoes.[46] The state protects the right to speak, even if private citizens who detest the speech seek to suppress it. Nevertheless, this presumption, like all default positions, has limits. At some point the state is justified in suppressing speakers if their speech will cause extreme and unavoidable harm to themselves or to others. Where this point is reached is a judgment call. If the state is too quick to suppress the speaker, we may be suspicious that the supposedly paternalist intervention is merely an excuse for siding with those who oppose the speaker. And yet the state is also derelict if it ignores the safety of the speaker altogether.

In the situation you propose, the counterdemonstrators have as much right as the initial paraders to voice sentiments, even unpopular sentiments that disagree with the marchers. They have every right to oppose gay rights. They have every right to show up and shout homophobic slogans. Just like gay persons have every right to burst forth from the closet and demand acceptance, so those who oppose gay rights have every right forcefully to assert that they do accept gays. There is a real public controversy between these two groups.

It follows that the state cannot suppress the anti-parade demonstrators on the ground that the state disagrees with their message, just as the state cannot stop the parade on the ground that the state disagrees with *its* message. The state must be neutral as between these messages. An antipathy to hate speech would not seem particularly helpful to me in guiding the state in how to proceed. What the state does need to do is to ensure that both sides of this demonstration can peacefully express their opinions. In doing so the state has the obligation of preserving the peace and of constraining those who would violate the peace. How in the end this must be done is a highly contextual question of judgment. But antipathy would seem to me to have little to do with it.

**PM:** Even if the "counter-demonstrators" would deny equal citizenship?

**RP:** The question of what does and does not constitute equal citizenship is itself a question of political opinion. Those who argue against naturalizing undocumented immigrants are taking a position about equal citizenship, yet it is also a position

---

[46] That is, we do not empower a hostile audience to silence a speaker through their very hostility and the harm or violence it threatens to produce. *See* Harry Kalven, Jr., *The Negro and the First Amendment* 140 (Ohio State University Press 1965).

in an ongoing political controversy. The question of which sexual practices should be regulated and which should be constitutionally immune from regulation is similarly a question about the political constitution of the state. For this reason, the counterdemonstrators should be entitled to express their message of disapproval.

If we assume, as might perhaps be inferred from your statement of the case, that the goal of the counterdemonstrators was not to express a message but to intimidate and harm participants in the gay parade, then we no longer have a symmetrical question of two parties each wishing to influence the formation of public opinion by conveying a message. Instead we have a question of one party wishing to communicate and a second party wishing through violence to prevent this communication. Nothing in the theory of freedom of speech would prevent the suppression of the latter. We would conceptualize the counterdemonstrators as attempting to commit a crime. The state is justified in preventing that crime. That the crime is expressive would no more implicate freedom of speech than would the attempt of the perpetuators of 9/11 to communicate a message immunize their crime under the First Amendment.

In short, it is one thing to have a counterdemonstration that seeks to convey a message, however hateful, and it is quite a different thing to use force and violence to prevent someone from speaking. There is no question at all that the state may and should prohibit the second.

**PM:** Sure, but what about "counter-demonstrators" who are engaged only in speech, but are expressing their views in a setting, in a context, when doing so directly and potentially decisively contributes to creation of the imminent danger of violence? Some people might not engage in violence except if they were encouraged to do so, either by Web sites urging that the parade should not be allowed to happen by any means necessary or by others on the spot, who might or might not be engaged in *express* incitement to violence.

**RP:** One question you may be now asking is when advocacy of illegal action can be regulated as illegal action. This is not a question that is unique to hate speech. It occurs in innumerable contexts. In the United States, we have for several generations subsumed this question under the so-called *Brandenburg* test that you mentioned earlier, which holds that the state cannot "forbid or proscribe advocacy of the use of force or of law violation except where such advocacy is directed to inciting or producing imminent lawless action and is likely to incite or produce such action."[47]

The reason we require such a strict connection between advocacy of illegal action and illegal action is that we have learned through bitter experience that it is quite easy for a state to postulate some causal connection between speech and subsequent illegal conduct, however attenuated, and to use this connection as a pretext for suppressing speech which it wishes to silence because it disagrees with its content. During World War I, the United States Supreme Court, per Justice Holmes, allowed

---

[47] *Brandenburg*, 395 U.S. at 447.

speech to be suppressed if it merely had the "tendency" to cause future illegal conduct, and on this ground the state savagely suppressed the expression of all kinds of antiwar sentiments.[48] From the perspective of the United States, therefore, the question is whether the counterdemonstrators in your example would pass or fail the *Brandenburg* test.

Your example raises real difficulties in the theory of freedom of speech. There are many ambiguities that course through the case law. The *Brandenburg* test requires judgments that are necessarily discrete and contextual, and so subject to abuse. And while courts without a doubt read the relationship between speech and violence with an eye to how acceptable they find the speech,[49] this suggests that judicial judgments are made by fallible human beings. As a general matter, however, I cannot see how these difficulties are connected to the question of hate speech. I do not see why we would not apply in the context of hate speech the same rules for connecting speech to illegal conduct that we would apply in any other context.

**PM:** A possible reason for special rules for connecting speech to illegal conduct in the context of "hate speech" may be that such speech can create imminent danger of violence even if the speaker claims that he/she did not intend to incite those actions; he/she only wanted to express his/her opinions. How would you conceptualize the connection between speech and the imminent danger of the sort we are talking about that speech can create or directly and decisively contribute to?

**RP:** Analogous difficulties are created in all situations in which the *Brandenburg* test applies. It used to be said that the speech of even insignificant communists was like a spark that carried the potential of igniting the flame of revolution. I fail to see why hate speech presents a situation that is uniquely complicated.

**PM:** This discussion supports the view that, as you said earlier, responses to "hate speech" should be contextual. Given that perspective, do you think it would be possible to develop international standards for the regulation of "hate speech"?

**RP:** I myself tend to be skeptical toward efforts to implement universal standards. Universal standards tend to be articulated at such a high level of abstraction, and to be filled with so many exceptions and qualifications, as to lose the capacity to guide and control state action. In my view, the impulse to regulate hate speech, and the degree of immunity it will claim from regulation, will depend upon such particular and historical circumstances as the need of specific countries to ensure freedom of speech to underwrite democratic legitimation. The greater the need of a nation for mechanisms of democratic legitimation, the more freedom of speech it will allow.

---

[48] *See, e.g.*, Debs v. United States, 249 U.S. 211 (1919).
[49] *Compare* NAACP v. Claiborne Hardware Co., 458 U.S. 886 (1982), *with* R.A.V. v. City of St. Paul, 505 U.S. 377 (1992), *and* Virginia v. Black, 538 U.S. 343 (2003).

We should also recognize that the significance of rules of civility will vary from country to country. The fundamental diversity in the nature and meaning of civility rules has been demonstrated by my colleague Jim Whitman.[50] The need to allow freedom of speech will always be balanced against the need to enforce civility rules, and these balances will work themselves out differently in different countries. The balance will necessarily be path-dependent and particular.

**PM:** Could there be a universal definition of "hate speech"?

**RP:** We can always construct a definition. The question is whether the definition will do any work. In law, we have to define hate speech carefully to designate the forms of the speech that will receive distinctive legal treatment. This is no easy task. Roughly speaking, we can define hate speech in terms of the harms it will cause – physical contingent harms like violence or discrimination; or we can define hate speech in terms of its intrinsic properties – the kinds of words it uses; or we can define hate speech in terms of its connection to principles of dignity; or we can define hate speech in terms of the ideas it conveys. Each of these definitions has advantages and disadvantages. Each intersects with first amendment theory in a different way. In the end, any definition that we adopt must be justified on the ground that it will achieve the results we wish to achieve.

**PM:** There can be many definitions then. If so, are all of them arbitrary?

**RP:** Any definition of "hate speech" will be constructed to serve a particular purpose. We must evaluate the status of "hate speech" so defined in order to determine whether it achieves what we wish to accomplish and whether the harms of the definition will outweigh its advantages.

**PM:** Toby Mendel argues that Articles 19 and 20 of the International Covenant on Civil and Political Rights could be the basis of a consistent standard, though courts are not clearly interpreting these provisions.[51]

**RP:** I am skeptical that these Articles in fact articulate a useful standard. If we look only at Article 19, for example, what is "the freedom of expression"? Is it the right of a student to talk in class regardless of the instruction of her teacher? Is it the right of a lawyer to talk in court regardless of the instructions of a judge? Article 19 contains such general language as to be practically useless. In order to determine the actual parameters of "freedom of expression," we will have to define the values served by freedom of speech, and these values will invariably become context specific.

---

[50] James Q. Whitman, "Enforcing Civility and Respect: Three Societies," 109 *Yale L.J.* 1279, 1383–90 (2000).
[51] Toby Mendel, "Does International Law Provide For Consistent Rules on Hate Speech?," Chapter 22 herein.

To take another example, Article 19 requires freedom of speech "regardless of frontiers."[52] What does that mean? If freedom of speech is, as I suggest, logically and sociologically connected to democratic self-determination, how can its regulation be separated from the units of self-determination? Almost all international statements I have seen suffer from immediate and obvious deficits of this kind. They join together goods that are in tension and assume that all is well. They are very nice in the abstract, but in the concrete world of law they do not seem to me to provide much analytic clarity, precision, or guidance.

Article 20 suffers from analogous ambiguities. To know how to interpret Article 20, one would need a persuasive theory of meaning of words like "hatred" and "incitement" and "hostility." As we interpret these words differently, so Article 20 will come to be more or less in tension with other principles of freedom of speech.

**PM:** You emphasized that education specifically should contribute to sustaining the deeper structures of democracy. What sort of educational policies would you suggest?

**RP:** Amy Gutmann has a good discussion of this question in her book *Democratic Education*.[53] Democratic education is necessary in order to sustain our commitment to and understanding of the value of democratic self-government. It is necessary in order to inculcate the practical virtues that democratic citizens must exercise if democracy is to succeed. These virtues include sustaining the balance between toleration and self-authorship; maintaining faith in the long-run dependence of state policy upon evolving public opinion despite short-run defeats; balancing national imperatives against local needs and values; affirming the priority of civilian authority as against the temptations of military force; prizing peaceful transitions of power; protecting freedom of speech; and so on. There are innumerable necessary democratic virtues that we take for granted. All are premised on the belief that a stable democratic polity is of fundamental value and must be preserved. This belief doesn't come from God, from human rights instruments, from natural law, or from nature. It comes from community commitments that instilled through socialization and education.

Public education in a democracy takes many forms. There is primary socialization, which occurs in the family and in elementary institutions of education. There is the continuous education of the state, which occurs through public education, public monuments, art, prizes, stamps, and street names. There is the peer-to-peer education that occurs through forms of civic engagement. And so on.

---

[52]  Section 2 of Article 19 provides: "Everyone shall have the right to freedom of expression; this right shall include freedom to seek, receive and impart information and ideas of all kinds, regardless of frontiers, either orally, in writing or in print, in the form of art, or through any other media of his choice." International Covenant on Civil and Political Rights, art. 19(2), December 16, 1966, 999 U.N.T.S. 171.

[53]  Amy Gutmann, *Democratic Education* (Princeton University Press rev. ed. 1999).

**PM:** Would it be acceptable if the U.S. government gave awards for the best achievement in the last year in the struggle against prejudice and the promotion of diversity?

**RP:** Of course. Restraints on what the government chooses to praise are chiefly political. We give prizes for cultural achievement at the Kennedy Center; we give prizes for essays on a many different topics; we award research grants; we endow lectures, and so on. Courts do not typically review such activities.[54]

**PM:** Law, too, can be educative. Some defend the prohibition of "hate speech" on the ground that it has considerable educational value, instructing the public about certain important virtues.

**RP:** It is entirely true that law is educational.[55] But law is not *only* educational. The law also regulates and controls behavior. Thus the criminal law not only expresses society's extreme condemnation and abhorrence of certain conduct, it also uses the state's monopoly on legitimate violence to prevent that conduct. It does this through stigmatization as well as punishment. If law were merely expressive, then it would make sense to regard hate speech regulation as a form of public education. On this view, hate speech regulation would do no more than express our society's abhorrence of intolerance and bigotry. It would teach health lessons in social respect and solidarity. Hate speech regulation would be no different than a president's exhortation to mutual respect.

But because law is much more than merely expressive and educational, because it is also punitive and regulatory, the view you describe does not rest on an adequate account of hate speech regulation, which also penalizes participation in public discourse by those who hold certain views condemned by the state. This not only sends a message of intolerance – that those who believe certain ideas are not welcome within processes of public opinion formation – but it also undercuts democratic legitimation with respect to such persons. It stands as an open invitation to exclude from public-opinion formation those who hold views that a majority believes should be beyond the pale. These are very dangerous and costly moves in a democracy. The expressive message of hate speech regulation is thus very complicated. It can breed intolerance as easily as tolerance; it can promote resentment and social instability as easily as it can promote solidarity and respect. The actual effects of hate speech regulation will be highly contextual, depending upon national traditions, histories, and so forth.

**PM:** One last question about education, connecting the need for education and the need for the cultural preconditions for legitimacy through public discourse. To

---

54 Post, *supra* note 5; National Endowment for the Arts v. Finley, 524 U.S. 569 (1998).
55 Robert Post, "The Social Foundations of Privacy: Community and Self in the Common Law Tort," 77 *Cal. L. Rev.* 957 (1989).

what extent can countries like Hungary create these preconditions by developing history books that can support a common sense of history?

**RP:** One cannot create collective memory merely by writing excellent history. But certainly excellent history is a helpful aid in the creation of a stable narrative of collective memory. I tend to think that stable historical narratives both depend upon a healthy respect for facts and upon a compelling and perhaps non-historical sense of the meaning of facts. If the political victors in Hungary can change the facts and the significance of those facts every few decades, the nation cannot establish a coherent narrative about its fundamental values. Respect for facts thus cabins the efforts of the state unscrupulously to manipulate history.

**PM:** Since Hungary became democratic in 1989, it should be able to develop a common sense of history, including an at least largely shared interpretation and conceptualization of our history in the last century.

**RP:** That would be wonderful.

**PM:** Suppose *two* countries are involved; for example, consider the Israel/Palestine conflict.

**RP:** Israel and Palestine have two different historical narratives. Dialogue between Israel and Palestine is complicated by the difficulty of persons talking to each other out of two entirely distinct historical frameworks that create incompatible visions of justice and of the future. There is no easy or simple solution to that problem.

**PM:** Slovakian and Hungarian historians and history teachers have also been working for years on common history books in which they try to harmonize their distinct national narratives.

**RP:** That's very hopeful.

**PM:** A standard argument for leaving "hate speech" unregulated is that the most effective response is more speech. But it raises the question whether the state should go further than engaging in counterspeech; should it encourage and facilitate private counterspeech? Katharine Gelber argues that the state and the political community of a country should enable members of the targeted minority – say, Roma in Hungary – to answer forcefully.[56] What do you think about this argument?

**RP:** It depends on exactly what this argument means. Should the president of Hungary speak out against anti-Roma hate speech? Of course. Should the Hungarian parliament speak out against such hate speech? Of course. Should the Hungarian prime minister? Of course. I can't think of any argument against the state participating in the formation of public opinion in this way. It is a separate question

---

[56] Katharine Gelber, "Reconceptualizing Counterspeech," Chapter 11 herein.

what it might mean for the state to "facilitate" the speech of the Roma themselves. Much would depend upon the exact steps taken. So, for example, to permit Roma to use public fora but to prevent their opponents from using the same fora would be quite problematic. Yet for the state to offer remedial assistance to groups otherwise excluded from public discussion would present an entirely different question.

**PM:** What do you make of Charles Lawrence's suggestion that when racist, or homophobic, or religiously bigoted speech occurs at a university, then the whole university must react? That proposition can be analogized to the idea that the whole state has to do something.

**RP:** There is a sense in which I regard Lawrence's observation as correct, and a sense in which I regard it as very misguided. It seems right to me that a university is a community and it must defend itself as a community. Racist attacks within a university are the concern of the entire community, and those who speak for the community have an obligation to defend it by articulating the values proper to the community. But if universities were to be held "responsible" for the speech of their members, there could be no academic freedom.[57] If a university were to be held accountable for the ideas and expressions of its members, it could not cede to its faculty or students the freedom to think independently, and this independence is required by the very idea of a university. So in most cases a university should not be held accountable for the racist speech of its faculty or students (as distinct from its administrators), but at the same time a university must assume the responsibility for ensuring the conditions of mutual respect and safety necessary for the functioning of a university. By analogy, no state that imagines itself as democratically responsive to public opinion can assume responsibility for what is said within public discourse. Nevertheless, any democratic state must ensure that public discourse remains sufficiently civil as to perform its function of democratic legitimation.

**PM:** What about the argument that restricting alleged defamation of religions is necessary in order to protect religious sensibilities? Under your model of public discourse, how could we deal with the challenge posed by religious sensitivities?

**RP:** Religious sensitivity is fast becoming an increasingly salient problem in Europe. In my view, however, there should be no structural difference between our analysis of speech that is defamatory of groups (racist speech) and speech that is defamatory of religions (blasphemy). There are some very early and very poor opinions by the European Court of Human Rights[58] that seem to imply that speech offensive to religious sensibilities can be suppressed as blasphemy, but these opinions would seem to cede control of public opinion formation to religious groups, and in a civil society

---

57  *For the Common Good: Principles of American Academic Freedom* (Matthew W. Finkin & Robert C. Post eds., Yale University Press 2009).
58  *See* Robert Post, "Religion and Freedom of Speech: Portraits of Muhammad," 14 *Constellations* 72 (2007).

that is not defensible. It makes little practical sense because religious sensibilities can be, and indeed frequently are, logically incompatible with each other. What offends Catholics does not offend Muslims, and vice versa. Sometimes what is offensive to one religion is affirmatively necessary to another. Oliver Cromwell famously issued a directive regarding the religious liberty of the Catholics in Ireland: "As to freedom of conscience, I meddle with no man's conscience; but if you mean by that, liberty to celebrate the Mass, I would have you understand that in no place where the power of the Parliament of England prevails shall that be permitted."[59] For these reasons, any test that would seek to determine the acceptability of public speech by reference to subjective religious sensibilities would instantly entangle itself in absurdities and self-contradictions of the worst kind. The test for the acceptability of public speech must in the end turn on a neutral secular standard.

**PM:** The United Nations General Assembly and Human Rights Council still approved resolutions aimed at "combating defamation of religions."[60]

**RP:** I confess I don't understand the meaning of such a resolution. If I say that Jesus Christ is the only true God, the statement could simultaneously affirm my deepest faith and defame Islam. An international standard of defaming religion would instantly lead to heated internal contradictions.

**PM:** Hopefully our global community will not restrict freedom of speech in such an absurd way.[61] Thank you so much for the interview.

**RP:** Thank you, Peter.

---

[59] McDaniel v. Paty, 435 U.S. 618, 631 n. 2 (1978) (Brennan, J., concurring) (quoting Oliver Cromwell).

[60] *See, e.g.*, UN General Assembly, Office of Public Information, Press Release GA/SHC/3966, *Third Committee Approves Resolution Aimed at "Combating Defamation of Religions"* (November 12, 2009), *available at* http://www.un.org/News/Press/docs/2009/gashc3966.doc.htm. The Resolution passed by a vote of 81 to 55, with 43 abstentions. *Id.* The United States voted against the Resolution "because it would not agree that prohibiting speech was the way to promote tolerance." *Id.* Support for this resolution has weakened over the years. It was approved again in March 2010, but by the narrowest margin to date. U.N. Human Rights Council, Res. 13/16, Rep. of the Human Rights Council, U.N. Doc. A/65/53 (Mar. 25, 2010). The vote was 20 to 17, with 8 abstentions.

[61] In 2011, the Human Rights Council adopted a resolution condemning violence, discrimination, and incitement to religious hatred without reference to "defamation of religions." U.N. Human Rights Council, Res. 16/18, Rep. of the Human Rights Council, A/HRC/16/2, chap. I (Mar. 24, 2011). *See also* Robert Evans, "Islamic Bloc Drops U.N. Drive on Defaming Religion," Newsmax.com, Mar. 24, 2011, *available at* http://www.newsmax.com/Newsfront/article/2011/03/24/id/390671.

## 2

# Is There a Case for Banning Hate Speech?

## *Bhikhu Parekh*

During the past few decades, there has been an almost universal trend toward banning so-called hate speech directed at individuals or groups on the basis of their race, ethnicity, nationality, or religion. The prohibited forms of expression vary from country to country, but the basic thrust is the same. Britain bans abusive, insulting, and threatening speech; Denmark and Canada prohibit speech that is insulting and degrading; and India and Israel ban speech that incites racial and religious hatred or is likely to stir up hostility between groups. In the Netherlands, it is a criminal offense to express publicly views insulting to groups of persons. Australia prohibits speech that offends, insults, humiliates, or intimidates individuals or groups, and some of its states have laws banning racial vilification. Germany goes further, banning speech that violates the dignity of an individual, implies that he or she is an inferior being, or maliciously degrades or defames a group.

Many of these countries claim to be guided by or find support in the International Covenant on Civil and Political Rights, particularly Article 20, which requires a ban on "any advocacy of national, racial or religious hatred that constitutes incitement to discrimination."[1] Some of them are also signatories to the International Convention on the Elimination of All Forms of Racial Discrimination, Article 4 of which requires parties to "condemn all propaganda or organisations based on theories of racial superiority and incitement to racial discrimination and acts of violence" and to eradicate "all dissemination of ideas based on racial superiority or hatred, incitement to racial discrimination, as well as all acts of violence or incitement to such acts against any race or group of persons of another colour or ethnic origin, and also the provision of any assistance to racist activities, including the financing

---

[1] International Covenant on Civil and Political Rights, art. 20, G.A. Res. 2200 (XXI), U.N. GAOR 21st Sess., Supp. No. 16, U.N. Doc. A/6316 (Dec. 16, 1966).

An earlier version of this chapter was published under the title "Hate Speech," 12 *Public Policy Review* 213 (2006).

thereof."[2] Although the United States restricts some speech on the grounds that it threatens national security, constitutes obscenity or child pornography, presents a danger of an imminent breach of peace, or is patently offensive and directed at a captive audience or used in a workplace, it is, with the recent exception of Hungary, the only country to resist the trend to ban hate speech.[3] Even here, however, such a broad interpretation of the First Amendment of its Constitution is of relatively recent origin, going back no further than the 1960s, and several writers have argued that the country needs to reconsider its position.[4]

## I. DEFINING HATE SPEECH

In the course of enforcing their laws, different countries have punished or sought to punish different instances of speech, of which the following are a small sample:

1. Shouting "Niggers go home," making monkey noises, and chanting racist slogans at soccer matches.[5]
2. "Islam out of Britain. Protect the British people."[6]
3. "Arabs out of France."[7]

---

[2] International Convention on the Elimination of All Forms of Racial Discrimination, art. 4, G.A. Res. 2106 (XX), U.N. GAOR 20th Sess., Supp. No. 14, U.N. Doc. A/6014 (Dec. 21, 1965).

[3] Some argue that although the origins of this trend can be traced to the late 1910s, it emerged in its current forms in the Supreme Court's judgment in Brandenburg v. Ohio, 395 U.S. 444 (1969), which held that speech may be curtailed only when there is "incitement to imminent lawless action." *See* Rodney Smolla, *Free Speech in an Open Society* (Vintage 1992). The United States made an extensive reservation when ratifying the International Convention on the Elimination of All Forms of Racial Discrimination.

[4] For a sympathetic exploration of the differences between European and American approaches to free speech, see Aernout Nieuwenhuis, "Freedom of Speech: U.S.A. vs Germany and Europe," 18 *Netherlands Quarterly Human Rights* 195 (2000). For a comparative overview by an American law professor critical of the American position, see Michel Rosenfeld, "Hate Speech in Constitutional Jurisprudence: A Comparative Analysis," Chapter 13 herein. *See also* Stephen H. Shiffrin, *Dissent, Injustice and the Meaning of America*, ch. 9 (Princeton University Press 1999).

[5] *See* Michael Walker, "The Mask of Sufferance Removed," *Irish Times*, Oct. 23, 2000.

[6] Englishman Mark Norwood was prosecuted, convicted, and fined for displaying in his apartment window a poster with this slogan and a picture of the World Trade Center. The European Court of Human Rights rejected his complaint that this was a breach of his right to freedom of expression. Norwood v. United Kingdom, App. No. 23131/03, decision of Nov. 16, 2004, Eur. Ct. HR (Second Section). The case is summarized in Conference on Security and Cooperation in Europe, *Countering Terrorism, Protecting Human Rights* 228 (Organization for Security and Cooperation in Europe 2007).

[7] For one typical example of this sentiment, consider a recent post in the comments to an online article. Under the subject line "Arabs out of France," the writer states: "The arabs wanted France out of their countries. France left and then the arabas infest France with crime and reactionalry ideas and no contributions to science or art.; Throw them into the Mediterannean and let them swim back to Morocco and Algeria." (All spelling errors are in the original.) Comment to Michael T. Klare, "A Planet on the Brink: Economic Crash Will Fuel Social Unrest," *AlterNet*, Feb. 24, 2009, *available at* http://www.alternet .org/rights/128716/ a_planet_on_the_brink:_economic_crash_will_fuel_social_unrest/?comments= view&cID=1146119&pID=1145646#c1146119.

4. "Serve your country, burn down a mosque."[8]
5. Blacks are inherently inferior, lecherous, predisposed to criminal activities, and should not be allowed to move into respectable areas.
6. Jews are conspiratorial, devious, treacherous, sadistic, child killers, and subversive; want to take over the country; and should be carefully watched.
7. Distribution by a political party of leaflets addressed to "white fellow citizens" saying that, if it came to power, it would remove all Surinamese, Turks, and other "undesired aliens" from the Netherlands.[9]
8. A poster of a woman in a *burka* with text that reads: "Who knows what they have under their sinister and ugly looking clothes: stolen goods, guns, bombs even?"[10]
9. Salman Rushdie's *Satanic Verses* was banned in several countries for causing distress and grave offense to Muslims and stirring up hostility to them.[11]
10. Holocaust denial is an offense in Germany, France, Austria, the United Kingdom, and several other countries.[12] The offense generally includes denying the existence, extent, or enormity of the Holocaust.[13] In some countries, "trivializing" it is also an offense.[14]
11. The Council of Europe has adopted a Framework Decision requiring member states to criminalize "publicly condoning, denying or grossly trivialising crimes of genocide, crimes against humanity and war crimes as defined in Articles 6, 7 and 8 of the Statute of the International Criminal Court, directed against a group of persons or a member of such a group defined by reference to race, colour, religion, descent or national or ethnic origin when the conduct is carried out in a manner likely to incite to violence or hatred against such a

---

[8] A card with this text was received by a member of the House of Lords in 2005 and referred to the police for prosecution. *See* Lords Daily Hansard, vol. 674, col. 220 (Oct. 11, 2005).

[9] *See* Glimmerveen and Hagenbeek v. Netherlands, Oct. 11, 1979, Application No. 8406/78 (Eur. Comm'n on H.R.).

[10] This poster, headed "The Burka Bombers," was described by Lord Falconer of Thoroton during debate on the racial and religious hatred bill in the House of Lords. *See* Lords Daily Hansard, vol. 674, col. 168 (Oct. 11, 2005).

[11] *See generally* Daniel Pipes, *The Rushdie Affair: The Novel, the Ayatollah, and the West* (Transaction Publishers 1990).

[12] Raffi Berg, "The Fight Against Holocaust Denial," *BBC News*, Apr. 14, 2005, *available at* http://news.bbc.co.uk/2/hi/europe/4436275.stm.

[13] *See generally* Kevin Boyle, "Hate Speech – The United States versus the Rest of the World," 53 *Maine L. Rev.* 488, 497–99 (2001). The European Court of Human Rights has rejected free speech challenges to these laws. *See, e.g.*, Lehideux and Isorni v. France, 55/1997/839/1045, 1998-VII Eur. Ct. HR 92 (1998).

[14] The German Constitutional Court argued that the remarks of a Holocaust denier (David Irving) robbed the German Jews of their "individual and collective identity and dignity" and created a "social and political environment in which they cannot feel an integral part of the German society." Holocaust Denial Case, Entscheidungen des Bundesverfassungsgerichts [Federal Constitutional Court] 1994, 90 *BVerfGE* 241 (Germ.).

group or a member of such a group."[15] This has provoked considerable public protest by European intellectuals.[16]

These and related forms of prohibited speech are not all of the same kind. Some of them express or advocate views but do not call for action. Some are abusive or insulting but not threatening. Some express dislike of a group but not hatred, and some of those that do are so subtle as not to be obviously abusive or insulting. Some take a demeaning or denigrating view of a group but wish it no harm and even take a patronisingly indulgent attitude to it. Because forms of speech can be offensive and morally unacceptable without amounting to hate speech properly so called, they should not all be lumped together and treated in an identical manner. Hate speech is a distinct kind of speech, and much conceptual confusion is created – and the net of prohibited speech unduly widened – by subsuming all forms of uncivil and hurtful speech under it. We may therefore rightly proscribe hate speech without also proscribing insulting, abusive, denigrating, and similarly objectionable speech. This does not mean that we may not choose to ban the latter as well, but rather that the reasons for doing so are not necessarily the same as those that apply to hate speech. Even the term "hate speech" is unsatisfactory because it stresses hatred, an extremely strong emotion. However, given that it is widely used and there is no obvious alternative, I shall continue to use it in this chapter and give it a reasonably precise meaning.

Hate speech expresses, encourages, stirs up, or incites *hatred* against a group of individuals distinguished by a particular feature or set of features such as race, ethnicity, gender, religion, nationality, and sexual orientation. Hatred is not the same as lack of respect or even positive disrespect, dislike, disapproval, or a demeaning view of others. It implies hostility, ill will, severe contempt, rejection, a wish to harm or destroy the target group, a silent or vocal and a passive or active declaration of war against it. Hate speech has three essential features. First, it is directed against a specified or easily identifiable individual or, more commonly, a group of individuals based on an arbitrary and normatively irrelevant feature. To say that one hates all human beings or all living beings is not hate speech. It is nondiscriminatory in the sense of not being targeted against a particular section of humankind and includes even the speaker; is too abstract to mean much, if anything, in practice; and implies no concrete course of action. To say that one hates murderers and wants them all locked up or executed is not a case of hate speech either. It advocates a policy and does not incite to action, and it is based not on a normatively irrelevant ascriptive identity, but on what the individuals involved have done.

[15] Council of the European Union, Council Framework Decision on combating certain forms and expressions of racism and xenophobia by means of criminal law, art. 1.1(c), 2008/913/JHA (Nov. 28, 2008).

[16] *See* Timothy Garton Ash, "The freedom of historical debate is under attack by the memory police," *The Guardian*, Oct. 16, 2008, at 27.

Second, hate speech stigmatizes the target group by implicitly or explicitly ascribing to it qualities widely regarded as highly undesirable. Stigmatization is a matter of degree. The negative qualities might be considered remediable and contingent, in which case the speaker is implying that the target group is required to rid itself of them to be accepted. Or they might be considered an inherent part of the group's identity, in which case it is permanently condemned.

Third, because of its negative qualities, the target group is viewed as an undesirable presence and a legitimate object of hostility. It cannot be trusted to be a loyal member of society and presents a threat to its stability and well-being. Because society would be better off without it, it may legitimately exterminate or expel the target group. And if that should prove impossible, it may rightly discriminate against and tolerate it as an unavoidable evil confined to a shadowy existence on the margins of society. Thus, hate speech encourages and purports to justify discrimination.[17]

Although hate speech breathes the spirit of exclusion and violence, it does not necessarily or by definition result in violence or public disorder. The speaker or his/her audience might consider it prudent not to act on it. Also, the targeted group might either exercise self-restraint or be too timid or intimidated to fight back. It is therefore a mistake, commonly made, to define hate speech as only that which is likely to lead to public disorder and to proscribe it because or only when it is likely to do so. What matters is its content – what it says about an individual or a group – and its long-term effect on the group and the wider society, rather than its immediate consequences in terms of public disorder.

Hate speech is often expressed in offensive, angry, abusive, and insulting language, and its impact generally depends on that, but it is not necessary that it should be so expressed. Hate speech can also be subtle, moderate, nonemotive, even bland; its message conveyed through ambiguous jokes, innuendoes, and images. Although its mode of expression provides a useful clue to its nature, it is not the only one. Every form of speech occurs within a particular historical and cultural context, and its content, import, insinuations, and moral and emotional significance are inseparable from, and can only be determined in the light of, that context. An utterance that appears innocent on the face of it might not in fact be so, or one that is harmless in one context might be a case of hate speech in another. Holocaust denial, for example, is not by itself a case of hate speech. Although untrue, it is an opinion like any other and should be tolerated in a free society in the same way that we put up with believers in witchcraft and a flat earth. However, it could also be a coded way of saying that Jews cannot be trusted; would resort to any tricks, including invention of imaginary horrors, to serve their interests; represent a subversive presence and that no shared life is possible with them; and that they therefore represent a hostile

---

[17] It is striking that both Article 20 of the International Covenant on Civil and Political Rights and Article 4 of the International Convention on the Elimination of All Forms of Racial Discrimination make "incitement to discrimination" central to hate speech. *See supra* nn. 1 & 2 and accompanying text.

and subversive group deserving of discriminatory treatment and worse. It then has all three features of hate speech.

If we examine the cases of prohibited speech listed earlier in terms of these three criteria, we see that some of them constitute hate speech and others do not. Examples (1) to (7) are all cases of hate speech. Examples (2) and (3) do not explicitly stigmatize British Muslims and French Arabs, but they do so implicitly. The two groups are presented as an undesirable presence because of the kind of people they are believed to be, that is, because of their customs, practices, alleged lack of loyalty to the host society, inability to integrate, and so on, and hence the French and British societies are seen as better off without them. Although (1) through (7) differ in the degree of active ill will they express, making some weak and others strong forms of hate speech, they all meet its basic test. Item (8) is a comment on the person's dress, but also an ill-disguised reference to Muslim women as not to be trusted. It arouses suspicion and mistrust but not necessarily hatred of them. *The Satanic Verses*, item (9), neither ascribes undesirable qualities to Muslims nor impugns their ability to share a common life. It mocks Prophet Mohammed and casts doubt on the authenticity of some of the Qur'anic verses but does not advocate hostility to Muslims, and is not a case of hate speech.[18] As observed earlier, (10) could be a case of hate speech depending on its context and import. As for (11), its first part is loosely worded and too wide. It does not distinguish clearly between expressing a view and incitement to action, and it covers a large number of historical events. However, it is only intended to provide a framework for future legislation, and much depends on how the member states translate it into law.

## II. WHY HATE SPEECH IS UNACCEPTABLE

The importance of free speech is too obvious to need elaboration. Speech occurs at many levels, including interpersonal relations, public life, and intellectual inquiries. At each level it plays a vital but different role, and its defense is based on somewhat different grounds. While making a general case for free speech, we also need to take full account of these differences and may rightly allow a greater degree of it in one area than in others.

First, free speech is the indispensable basis of free thought and critical self-consciousness. When it is denied or severely curtailed, the human capacity to think, and all that is distinctive to human beings, is undermined. At the most basic level, thought is inseparable from speech. Speech is objectified thought, and thought is articulated in speech and represents a form of speaking to oneself. When individuals externalize and express their thoughts and give them a worldly reality, they systematize and impose a measure of order on them, become clearer about their content,

---

[18] As the European Commission of Human Rights concluded. *See* Choudhury v. United Kingdom, in 12 *Human Rights L.J.* 172, 172 (1991).

create a vitally necessary space or distance between themselves and their thoughts and feelings, and are able to reflect on them critically.

Second, free speech is the basis of a meaningful human life. It is through the medium of speech that individuals disclose themselves, appear before others, are recognized and affirmed by them, and acquire a sense of who they are. They communicate their thoughts and feelings, build bonds, construct shared memories, and create and sustain a rich and varied individual and collective life. When speech is drastically curtailed and subjected to all manner of constraints, human relations remain shallow and fragile; are marred by ignorance, misunderstanding, dishonesty, and falsehoods; and lack the capacity for transparency and permanence.

Third, free speech is just as vital in political life. It enables citizens to submit their beliefs and opinions to critical scrutiny, assists the formation of an informed public opinion and collective will, provides the only effective check on the government, creates a vibrant civil society, and in general ensures an easy and constant flow of ideas among citizens and between them and the government.

Finally, free speech is just as crucial to intellectual inquiries. It enables us to challenge inherited dogmas, critically examine different bodies of ideas, rise above our biases, pursue truth, expand the range of intellectual and moral sympathy, secure a firmer grasp of the grounds of our beliefs and practices, and develop vital human capacities.

Given that free speech is so central to human life, we rightly place a high value on it and protect and nurture it by making it a constitutionally protected right. It is not a natural right, one we possess "by nature," but a moral right we believe we ought to enjoy for the ontological, epistemological, moral, and other reasons mentioned earlier. Like all rights, it presupposes a moral community whose members share a broad consensus on fundamental human interests and are willing to accept the corresponding restraints and obligations. Because such a community alone makes rights possible, all rights including free speech have certain limits built into them. They must not undermine the moral community and must be balanced against other rights and values.

Although free speech is an important value, it is not the only one.[19] Human dignity, equality, freedom to live without harassment and intimidation, social harmony, mutual respect, and protection of one's good name and honor are also central to the good life and deserve to be safeguarded. Because these values conflict, either inherently or in particular contexts, they need to be balanced. Although we may rightly privilege some of them over others either in general or in particular contexts, none can be so absolutized as always to trump others. Even social harmony and national security, which are vital to the very existence of society, do not override

---

[19] For a valuable discussion, see Stanley Fish, *There's No Such Thing as Free Speech... and It's a Good Thing Too* (Oxford University Press 1994), especially chapters 8 and 9. *See also* Bhikhu Parekh, *Rethinking Multiculturalism*, ch. 10 (Palgrave Macmillan 2000).

the demands of human dignity and free speech, which is why we rightly refuse to sacrifice the latter even when faced with terrorist attacks. We want security and peace but not at all cost, and we do not wish to live in a society that can only be maintained by locking up everyone who arouses our suspicion or by subjecting convicted criminals, including terrorists, to inhuman and degrading punishment or torture. Every value makes claims that limit those of others, and every right is limited in its content and scope by other rights. This is as true of the right to free speech as of others, which is why it is subject to limits in all societies. The important question is whether prohibition of the expression and promotion of hatred as defined earlier should be one of these.

Hate speech is objectionable for both intrinsic and instrumental reasons, for what it is or manifests and for what it does. It lowers the tone of public debate, coarsens the community's moral sensibility, and weakens the culture of mutual respect that lies at the heart of a good society. It views members of the target group as an enemy within, refuses to accept them as legitimate and equal members of society, lowers their social standing, and in these and other ways subverts the very basis of a shared life. It creates barriers of mistrust and hostility between individuals and groups, plants fears, obstructs normal relations between them, and in general exercises a corrosive influence on the conduct of collective life. Hate speech also violates the dignity of the members of the target group by stigmatizing them, denying their capacity to live as responsible members of society, and ignoring their individuality and differences by reducing them to uniform specimens of the relevant racial, ethnic, or religious group.

Because hate speech intimidates and displays contempt and ridicule for the target group, group members find it difficult not only to participate in the collective life, but also to lead autonomous and fulfilling personal lives. They lead ghettoized and isolated lives with a knock-on effect on their children's education and career choices. In Britain and many other European countries, blacks and Asians, for example, long avoided football matches because of the all-too-familiar racist chants. Some of them also resisted the temptation or the invitation to stand for elections because of the fear of racist insults. Targets of hate speech understandably feel nervous in public spaces lest they should be humiliated. They are afraid to speak their minds and behave normally, and they worry constantly about how the negative stereotypes that others hold of them will lead them to interpret their words and actions. As a result, they are likely to feel alienated from the wider society, to lead shadowy lives, and to feel trapped in a cramped mode of being. When hate speech is allowed uninhibited expression, its targets rightly conclude that the state either shares the implied sentiments or does not consider their dignity, self-respect, and well-being important enough to warrant action. In either case, the state forfeits its legitimacy in their eyes and weakens its claim to represent them and demand their loyalty.[20]

---

[20] The Canadian Supreme Court spells this out well in *Regina v. Keegstra* [1990] 3 S.C.R. 697. Hate speech, it argues, creates discord in the community, harms the target group, infringes equality, and

Hate speech is also unacceptable because of its likely long-term consequences. It encourages a climate in which, over time, some groups come to be demonized and their discriminatory treatment becomes accepted as normal. Vicious and widespread hatred of a group does not spring up overnight. It builds up slowly through isolated utterances and actions, each perhaps trivial individually, but all cumulatively capable of coarsening the community's sensibility, poisoning the minds of the young, weakening the norms of civility and decency, and creating a situation in which it becomes common practice to ridicule, mock, malign, and show hostility to the target group and, over time, to others. The violence implicit in hate speech then comes to the fore, initially in isolated incidents but gradually gathering a momentum of its own. If anything can be *said about* a group of persons with impunity, anything can also be *done to* it. This is because if a group can be treated with contempt, its interests and feelings are viewed as of no consequence. It is stripped of dignity, dehumanized, treated as belonging to an inferior species, and a moral climate is created in which harm done to it is seen as right and proper and does not arouse a sense of outrage. It is not surprising that, with some exceptions, Europeans, who witnessed the rise of Fascism and Nazism and watched the ease with which these movements created a racist climate that swept millions, should be some of the strongest advocates of the need for a timely ban on hate speech.

Even when a society does not travel all the way in this direction, the impact of hate speech can be considerable. It legitimizes and generates pressure for discrimination against the target group and provides moral support and encouragement to those inclined to discriminate. The target group is unable to relax and lead a life without fear and harassment. Some of its members either internalize their negative image and develop self-abasement and low self-esteem or compensate for it by becoming aggressive and self-righteous. They tend to avoid activities, occupations, and careers where they fear hatred, cannot be sure of equal treatment and basic respect, and have to watch out for signs of suppressed resentment and hostility. Although the moral and psychic injury that all this can cause, and the restricted life chances to which it leads, are not easy to identify and measure, they can be profound and real. We lose sight of these subtle and deeply damaging long-term consequences of hate speech if we concentrate only on, and judge it in terms of, the likely immediate threat to public disorder.

The argument that speech may be restricted only when there is "imminent danger" of violence also fails to probe further the idea of imminent danger. No action occurs in a historical vacuum, and every action produces consequences not inherently but against a particular background. If a group came into existence urging people to "kill all elderly parents" or to "kill all beautiful women," its intended audience as well as its target group would think it was mad or joking and dismiss its utterances without a moment's thought. But if it expressed similar sentiments about blacks, Jews, or

has only slight social value. *See also* Robert C. Post, "Racist Speech, Democracy and the First Amendment," 32 *Wm. & Mary L. Rev.* 267 (1991).

gays, the latter would feel intimidated and insecure, and the group's statements could provoke those so inclined, or their long-suffering victims, to resort to violence because of the deeply rooted prejudices against these groups built up over time. Imminent danger occurs against, and is imminent because of, the prevailing social climate, and consistency demands that we concentrate our efforts not only on fighting the immediate source of danger, but also on changing the climate.

## III. THE ROLE OF LAW

Because hate speech is unacceptable for these and related reasons, it has no place in a decent society and deserves to be discouraged. The difficult and much-debated question is whether it should be not merely discouraged by moral and social pressure but prohibited by law. Although law must be our last resort, its intervention cannot be ruled out for several important reasons. Most obviously, assuming meaningful levels of enforcement and compliance, direct prohibition would reduce or eliminate speech that causes very real harm to the targets of such speech.

Second, a legal prohibition is valuable for the message it sends. Such a law reassures all members of society – not only the currently targeted group, but also other members of society, for every one of them can under certain circumstances be a target – that the state values them all equally and is committed to maintaining a civil public discourse and protecting their fundamental interests. So far as the currently targeted group is concerned, the law legitimizes the state in its eyes, earns its trust, and acquires the right to its loyalty. It also lays down norms of civility and sends out clear messages concerning what is or is not an acceptable way of talking about and treating other members of society. Being a collective and public statement of the community's moral identity and guiding values, the law affirms and enforces these values, has a symbolic and educational significance, and helps shape the collective ethos.

Third, proscription of hate speech plays an important role in preventing political mobilization of hostility against particular groups. This is especially true if the limits are enacted before hate-based organizations have built up powerful networks and support and before their rhetoric has coarsened public sensibility. As I argued earlier, a climate of intimidation and violence against identified groups develops over time. Once it takes deep roots and poisons the relations between different groups, law lacks a supportive public opinion and is either not enacted or not enforced or takes a drastic form and risks provoking widespread resistance. In the developing societies, and even in such mature democracies as Britain, France, Germany, and the Netherlands, it is common for politicians and political parties to outbid each other by pandering to base political instincts and provoking hatred of whatever group appears to arouse popular dislike. Banning hate speech discourages them from doing so and inflaming the all-too-easily aroused passions in pursuit of short-term gains. Although other factors played a part as well, it is worth noting that British elections, their media coverage, and political discourse in general have been healthier and more moderate as a result of the law proscribing incitement to racial hatred.[21] Similar things have happened in India, Germany, Austria, the Netherlands, South Africa, and elsewhere, in all of which crude expressions of racial and religious hatred have declined in recent years. This is not to say, of course, that these sentiments have disappeared or even substantially declined in these countries, but rather that public life is conducted in a more civil language, and that politicians appealing to such sentiments are generally treated with disdain by the general public and disowned by their leaders.

While agreeing that hate speech is morally and politically unacceptable, many writers oppose a legal ban on it, notwithstanding the foregoing benefits. Their reasons are varied, but the following six are the most common. On analysis, none is ultimately convincing.

First, free speech is a highly important value, indeed the lifeblood of democracy, and should only be restricted when the rights of other individuals, public order, and compelling public interest are at stake. The harm caused by hate speech is generally relatively minor in its intensity and extent, and even when it is serious, its tolerance is a small price to pay in the larger interest of a free and vibrant democracy.

Although the argument has some merit, for a comprehensive and undiscriminating ban on all forms of hate speech is often counterproductive and fraught with difficulties, the argument in its unqualified form is deeply flawed. Rather than talk of liberty in the abstract, we need to ask what sort of liberty or liberty to do what is restricted by a ban on hate speech. As Sir Frank Soskice put it during debate on the race relations bill in the British House of Commons, "What is the loss of liberty they fear? Is it other than the loss of liberty by the use of outrageous language to stir up actual hatred against most completely harmless people . . . for something they cannot possibly help?"[22] We rightly ban obscenity, libel, defamation, public display of pornography, and so forth, partly because of the harm they cause and partly because we believe that our public life should be guided by certain norms. It is not clear why these norms should not exclude utterances that intimidate, bring into contempt, provoke hatred of, and damage the dignity and life chances of sections of society. Social harmony, public faith in the legitimacy of the political system, equality of treatment, and the right to live one's life without harassment and intimidation are also important values. It is difficult to see on what grounds free speech can be made a "preferred right" and allowed always to trump them. Free speech is the lifeblood of democracy when it advances reasoned arguments, subjects ideas and opinions to critical public scrutiny, exposes falsehoods, aims to arrive at a rational view of the matter, and so on. Hate speech does none of these. In fact it weakens democracy

---

[21]  The Public Order Act of 1986 outlawed "incitement to racial hatred"; the prohibition was extended to incitement to religious hatred by the Racial and Religious Hatred Act 2006.

[22]  Commons Daily Hansard, vol. 711, col. 938 (May 3, 1965).

by arousing passions and irrational fears, making sweeping and indiscriminate generalizations about groups, creating a sense of insecurity among target groups, and
discouraging their political participation. Like free speech, mutual respect, spirit of
tolerance, equal dignity, and unconstrained and enthusiastic participation in the
conduct of public life are also the lifeblood of democracy.

Second, it is argued that evil ideas are best defeated not by banning them but by
subjecting them to a critical scrutiny and confronting them with better ideas. The
answer to hate speech is not less but more speech.[23] This argument makes a valid
point but exaggerates it. It is true that respect for fellow human beings requires us to
engage critically with their misguided but sincerely held beliefs, and that it is more
effective in the long run to refute the basis of these beliefs than to suppress their
public expressions. There are, however, limits to this approach.

The marketplace of ideas, on whose competitive scrutiny and fairness this argument relies, is not neutral and does not provide level playing fields. It has its biases
and operates against the background of prevailing prejudices. When racist, anti-
Semitic, and xenophobic beliefs are an integral part of a society's culture, they
appear self-evident, commonsensical, and obvious, and therefore enjoy a built-in
advantage over their opposites. Indeed the latter rarely get heard, and if they do, they
tend to be dismissed out of hand. Furthermore, a fair competition between ideas
requires that they all enjoy equal access to the marketplace, including the popular
media and other agencies through which they are communicated and critically
engage with each other. This is rarely the case.

Even assuming that the market is or can be made neutral and equally accessible to
all bodies of ideas, it is naive to imagine that false ideas will always lose in their battle
with true ones.[24] Ideas do not operate in a social vacuum. They are bound up with
interests, the prevailing structure of power, and so on, and the victory often goes to
those bodies of ideas that enjoy the patronage of powerful groups or prey on people's
fears and anxieties. Even as far as material products are concerned, competition does
not ensure that quality triumphs over cheap and poorly made products. There is no

---

[23] *See, e.g.,* Collin v. Smith, 447 F. Supp. 676, 702 (N.D. Ill.) ("The ability of American society to
tolerate the advocacy even of the hateful doctrines espoused by the plaintiffs without abandoning its
commitment to freedom of speech and assembly is perhaps the best protection we have against the
establishment of any Nazi-type regime in this country."), *aff'd,* 578 F.2d 1197 (7th Cir.), *cert. denied,*
439 U.S. 916 (1978); American Civil Liberties Union, "Hate Speech on Campus" (Dec. 31, 1994),
*available at* http://www.aclu.org/studentsrights/expression/12808pub19941231.html ("[W]here racist,
sexist and homophobic speech is concerned, the ACLU believes that more speech – not less – is the
best revenge."). *See generally* Whitney v. California, 274 U.S. 357, 376 (1927) (Brandeis, J., dissenting)
(ascribing to the framers the view that "the fitting remedy for evil counsels is good ones").

[24] John Milton famously observed: "Let [Truth] and Falsehood grapple; who ever knew Truth put to the
worse in a free and open encounter?" John Milton, *Areopagitica: A Speech for the Liberty of Unlicensed
Printing* (1644). One hesitates to label Milton naive; nonetheless, the intervening centuries have done
little to provide empirical support for this confident assertion. Frederick Schauer's chapter in this
volume usefully discusses the shortcomings of the belief that "truth will out." *See* Frederick Schauer,
"Social Epistemology, Holocaust Denial, and the Post-Millian Calculus," Chapter 7 herein.

reason to expect a different outcome at the level of ideas. This is not to deny the importance of the marketplace of ideas, but rather to argue that, like the market in general, it needs to be subjected to certain regulatory controls. This is what the ban on hate speech does. By allowing ideas to be freely expressed provided that they do not violate norms of mutual respect and civility, it ensures their fair competition, counters the weight of prevailing prejudices, and encourages the participation of those likely to be intimidated or alienated by hate speech.

Third, it is argued that a ban on hate speech inhibits and has a chilling effect on public discussion and debate, and that once we go down this road, we open the floodgates to all kinds of restrictions. The argument makes an important point. As the experiences of societies with a ban on hate speech show, people do sometimes feel inhibited and hold themselves back from making robust criticisms of and even expressing their views on the beliefs and practices of different groups. This happens because the ban on it is worded vaguely and applied inconsistently or in a biased manner. Given that the ban on hate speech is necessary for reasons mentioned earlier, the answer lies in rectifying these flaws and not in leaving hate speech unregulated.

The argument we are considering presupposes that an uninhibited freedom of expression is necessarily a good thing. There is no obvious virtue in allowing everyone to say anything that comes into his or her head and requiring those affected to put up with it. Speech can have social consequences that need to be balanced against its benefits; it cannot be absolutized or allowed to override any and all other values. Furthermore, this argument relies on the misleading metaphor of the slippery slope and the implied fear that once we go down a particular road, we would not know where to stop.[25] If this were true, we would not be able to make any exception to a principle or a value lest it should open the floodgates to others. We make such exceptions all the time; indeed human life, which is not a slope at all, let alone a slippery one, would be impossible unless we did so. When we distinguish between different situations on clearly stated grounds, we do not helplessly slide from one to the other. We ban defamation of individuals without jeopardizing fair critical comment, and we ban obscenity without discouraging acceptable forms of erotic expression. It is all a question of knowing the limits one may not cross. A ban on hate speech is no different.

Fourth, some critics of the ban on hate speech argue that it gives the state the right to judge the content of speech and to decide what sort of speech is good or bad and should or should not be allowed. In their view, this violates its moral neutrality, may skew political debate, and constricts individual liberty.[26] Although this argument

---

[25] Frederick Schauer, "Slippery Slopes," 99 *Harv. L. Rev.* 361 (1985).

[26] The principle that content-based restrictions are more suspect than content-neutral ones is entrenched in American First Amendment doctrine. For a description and defense, see Geoffrey R. Stone, "Content-Neutral Restrictions," 54 *U. Chi. L. Rev.* 46 (1987); Geoffrey R. Stone, "Content Regulation and the First Amendment," 25 *Wm. & Mary L. Rev.* 189 (1983).

rests on a justified fear of the state, it is flawed. It is not true that the state does not judge or has no right to judge the content of speech. Every state enjoys and exercises the right to limit speech in the interest of other equally important values, and it cannot do so without passing some judgment on its content. This is as true in the United States as it is elsewhere. First of all, the First Amendment places no requirements of neutrality when the government *itself* is the speaker.[27] Second, even in its regulatory capacity, the government need not always be neutral. When an American state bans public display of hardcore but not softcore pornography, commercial advertisements that tell blatant lies, release of military secrets, and libel of private individuals, it clearly judges the content of speech. To restrict speech is to restrict what may or may not be said, that is, its content and likely effect. While watching a film in a crowded cinema hall, the law stops me from shouting "fire" but not "rubbish" or "how moving."

Beyond a certain point, the moral neutrality of the state is itself problematic. A liberal state should not enforce a particular view of the good life on its citizens and should allow a free flow of ideas, but some values are so central to its moral identity that it cannot remain neutral with respect to them. A state committed to human dignity, gender and race equality, or the spirit of free inquiry cannot be neutral between forms of speech or behavior that uphold or undermine these values. This is why it teaches these values and not others in its schools, discourages and keeps a close watch on faith schools, supports or grants charity status to some organizations and activities but not others, and so on. As long as the ideas subversive of its central values remain confined to a tiny and eccentric minority or a matter of academic debate, and largely harmless, it should rightly leave them alone. But if they were to gain momentum and threaten its fundamental values, it should not remain an uninterested bystander. Ideally it should act earlier, but if that was not possible or effective, legal prohibition becomes necessary.

Fifth, it is sometimes argued that human beings are responsible and autonomous individuals, or at least that an assumption that they are such is the basis of a democratic society, and that they can and should be trusted to see through hate speech.[28] A ban on hate speech smacks of paternalism or moral authoritarianism, which should

---

[27] *See, e.g.*, Pleasant Grove City v. Summum, 555 U.S. 460, 467 (2009) ("The Free Speech Clause restricts government regulation of private speech; it does not regulate government speech."). Justice Scalia, with his usual directness, has asserted that "[i]t is the very business of government to favor and disfavor points of view." National Endowment for the Arts v. Finley, 524 U.S. 569, 598 (1998). Robert Post explores this point in Chapter 1 herein.

[28] Ronald Dworkin, "The Coming Battles Over Free Speech," *N.Y. Rev. Books*, June 11, 1992, at 55. Dworkin explains that this constitutive, as opposed to instrumental, justification for freedom of speech has two dimensions:

> First, morally responsible people insist on making up their own minds about what is good or bad in life or in politics, or what is true and false in matters of justice or faith. Government insults its citizens, and denies their moral responsibility, when it decrees that they cannot be trusted to hear opinions that might persuade them to dangerous or offensive convictions. . . .

have no place in a society of free and equal citizens. This objection highlights an important point, but it takes an idealized view of personal autonomy and ignores the conditions of its development. Human beings, even in a democracy, are not as autonomous and self-critical as it assumes; otherwise we would not be able to explain the centuries-long hold of racist ideas and religious bigotry, or the ease with which millions even in "mature" societies fell for and continue to fall for populist demagogues and their murderous political programs. Autonomy in the sense of a critical evaluation of ideas and forming one's convictions after a rigorous assessment of evidence and arguments is a matter of degree. Some develop it to a greater degree than others, and more so in some areas than in others, depending on their social background, education, and opportunity for self-development. We should not make the mistake of homogenizing our fellow citizens or taking an abstract and uniform view of autonomy.

Autonomy, further, is exercised under certain conditions. It requires, among other things, that one has equal access to different bodies of ideas so that one can judge and arbitrate between them. As we observed earlier, this is not the case. Some ideas are hegemonic and become part of a society's shared understanding whereas others lead a marginal existence, making it extremely difficult even for otherwise autonomous individuals to see through and resist the power of the former. In almost all societies, including the western ones, racism, sexism, nationalism, and xenophobia represent powerful currents of thought reflected in and regularly reinforced by the media. Not surprisingly, even the most self-critical liberals sometimes find it difficult to resist their appeal. It is because of these limits of individual autonomy that the law needs to lay down norms of decency. It does not ban ugly ideas per se, which are left free to circulate privately, but only when they take the form of publicly expressing and promoting hatred of, and poisoning relations between, individuals and groups.

Sixth, there is a body of interrelated practical objections to bans on hate speech. Law, it is argued, cannot by itself change people's attitudes and eliminate hatred. This is true, but it does not entail the required conclusion. Because law throws the society's collective moral and legal weight behind a particular set of norms of good behavior, it does have some influence on attitudes; its role is limited but nonetheless important. Besides, our concern is not so much to change attitudes in the first instance as to deny some of them public expression, and law is best equipped to achieve that. As Aristotle observed, ethics is a matter of social ethos, and the latter is shaped by habits developed through acting in certain ways. On the conventional

[Second,] moral responsibility has another, more active, aspect as well: a responsibility not only to form convictions of one's own, but to express these to others, out of respect and concern for them, and out of a compelling desire that truth be known, justice served, and the good secured. Government frustrates and denies that aspect of moral personality when it disqualifies some people from exercising these responsibilities on the ground that their convictions make them unworthy participants.

*Id.* at 56–7.

liberal view, our beliefs are the ultimate determinants of our behavior and are, or should be, a result of rational reflection. As Aristotle argued, the relationship between belief and conduct is reciprocal and complex. Our beliefs shape our conduct, but they are also in turn influenced by it. By acquiring the habit of acting in certain ways, we build up an appropriate character and develop certain attitudes and ways of thinking. Law is primarily concerned with conduct, but it also shapes citizens' character, attitudes, and beliefs.

It is sometimes argued that banning hate speech drives extremist groups underground and leaves us no means of knowing who they are and how much support they enjoy. It also alienates them from the wider society, even makes them more determined, and helps them recruit those attracted by the allure of forbidden fruit.

This is an important argument and its force should not be underestimated. However, it has its limits. A ban on hate speech might drive extremist groups underground, but it also persuades their moderate and law-abiding members to dissociate themselves from these groups. When extremist groups go underground, they are denied the oxygen of publicity and the aura of public respectability. This makes their operations more difficult and denies them the opportunity to link up with other similar groups and recruit their members.

While the ban might alienate extremist groups, it has the compensating advantage of securing the enthusiastic commitment and support of their target groups. Besides, beyond a certain point, alienation need not be a source of worry. Some religious groups are alienated from the secular orientation of the liberal state, just as the communists and polyamorously inclined persons bitterly resent its commitment (respectively) to market economy and monogamy. We accept such forms of alienation as inherent in collective life and do not seek to redress them by abandoning the liberal state. The ban might harden the determination of some, but it is also likely to weaken that of those who seek respectability and do not want to be associated with ideas and groups considered so disreputable as to be banned, or who are deterred by the cost involved in supporting them. There is the lure of the prohibited, but there is also the attraction of the respectable.

It is sometimes argued that a ban on hate speech can easily become an end in itself and an excuse to avoid well-conceived antidiscrimination policies. Although this can happen, as arguably it has in France,[29] there is no obvious reason why it should. As the cases of Britain, Netherlands, Germany, and Australia show, the ban on hate speech has gone hand in hand with a wider campaign to address the causes of racism, sexism, or homophobia by pressing for a well-worked-out strategy to tackle discrimination and disadvantage. This is not accidental and has a complex internal logic. Once people realize that ban on hate speech has made only a marginal

---

[29] For a helpful discussion of the (underenforced) prohibition on Holocaust denial in France, a country that is not "a model of success as far as racial equality is concerned," see Julie Suk, "Denying Experience: Holocaust Denial and the Free-Speech Theory of the State," Chapter 8 herein.

difference in their lives, they look for the deeper causes and see the need for an antidiscrimination struggle in other areas of life. The ban on hate speech alerts the target groups to other goals to aim at and gives it the confidence to fight for them by actively participating in public life.

Some critics of the ban argue that law is a blunt instrument and cannot define hate speech precisely enough to avoid two important dangers. First, it is unlikely to stand up in a court of law and not only brings the law into disrepute, but also disappoints those whom it claims to help. Second, it could be misused by the government to suppress legitimate dissent and struggle for human rights and even to whip up fears of national disintegration and social disharmony for which minorities are blamed. Such abuses have occurred in Sri Lanka, apartheid South Africa, the erstwhile Soviet Union, and even in such democracies as India and Israel.

This is a powerful argument whose force advocates of the ban do not always fully appreciate. However, it is not as fatal as is sometimes made out. It does not challenge the ban in principle, but rather its practicability. Law is a blunt instrument because it is necessarily articulated in terms of general categories, which cannot be sharply defined and distinguished, and because it cannot deal with the nuances and complexities of unique situations. This is true of all laws and is not unique to one banning hate speech. Because we cannot live without laws, we cope with their bluntness in three important ways. First, we make them precise by defining the relevant concepts as sharply and unambiguously as humanly possible. The precision is never absolute and incontrovertible but adequate and reasonably workable. This is why hate speech must be defined with great care and distinguished from such vague expressions as offensive, hurtful, and distressing remarks, as I suggested earlier. Secondly, we entrust the enforcement of the criminal law to public authorities and expect them to initiate prosecutions with due regard to their likely results and the public interest. Thirdly, we rely on judges to apply the law and adapt it to the complex circumstances of each case with sensitivity and good judgment. The resulting case law elucidates the law's key concepts, explores the full range of its meaning and implications, and builds up an appropriate tradition of discourse on it. The First Amendment jurisprudence in the United States shows how the Supreme Court has wrestled with the concept of speech, at times rendered conflicting judgments, and over time built up a broad but not unquestioned consensus on what constitutes speech.[30] We should expect the same in relation to hate speech.

I might take the British experience to indicate how the ban on hate speech has worked in practice. Between 1987, when the Public Order Act 1986 Act came into effect, and 2004, there were sixty-five prosecutions for incitement to racial hatred. On three occasions, the Attorney-General had declined to give his consent to prosecution on grounds of public interest. Of the sixty-five prosecutions, forty-four resulted in

---

[30] *See generally* Eugene Volokh, "Speech as Conduct: Generally Applicable Laws, Illegal Courses of Conduct, 'Situation-Altering Utterances,' and the Uncharted Zones," 90 *Cornell L. Rev.* 1277 (2005).

convictions, twenty-six of these resulted in immediate sentences of imprisonment of between three months and two years, five in suspended prison sentences, and the rest in conditional discharge, fine, or community service. Five prosecutions resulted in acquittal, six were dropped by the prosecution for various reasons, and ten had other outcomes such as that the defendants were judged medically unfit or had absconded or died. These statistics show that the ban, if carefully drafted, can stand up in a court of law, has teeth, and can act as a check on hate speech.

The danger that the ban can be misused is real, but that does not undermine the case for it. It is interesting that the African National Congress, which had suffered much from such an abuse under the apartheid regime, continued with the ban on hate speech in a suitably revised form on establishing a democratic South Africa. Many laws, including those relating to public order and national security, are open to abuse, but that does not mean that we should dispense with them. Furthermore, repressive governments can easily invoke all kinds of familiar reasons to justify suppression of dissenting movements and minority protests. No doubt a ban on hate speech provides them with one legitimizing reason, but it is not the only one and its absence would not make any difference to their actions.

Determined governments are able to misuse the ban because it is formulated in vague terms and applied in a biased manner, and it is this that needs to be addressed. Given that the general point of the ban is to protect vulnerable groups against intimidation and violence, we could demand a more stringent judicial scrutiny when it is used for opposite purposes. An independent judiciary, a representative legislature, a popularly accountable government, a free press, and so on are our best protection against misuse of laws, including the ban on hate speech. Once these institutions are established, a ban has a good chance of success. If they are not, the ban is open to abuse as indeed are all other laws. We cannot, therefore, discuss it in the abstract or in isolation from the wider political institutions and culture.


## IV. CONCLUDING REFLECTIONS

I have argued that hate speech strikes at the root of the shared communal life and represents a gross misuse of the right to free speech. It breathes the spirit of aggression and violence, lowers the tone of public discourse, expresses and promotes hostility to a group of persons, subjects them to harassment and intimidation, inhibits their participation in communal life, and damages their sense of dignity and equal life chances. Although law has its obvious limits, it has an important role in discouraging hate speech. It affirms the community's commitment to equality and civility, sets standards of good behavior, reassures vulnerable groups, and prevents the normal intergroup conflicts and prejudices of a multiethnic society from getting out of control. Law is most effective and the risk of its abuse is considerably reduced when it is part of a wider antidiscrimination and conciliation strategy, is accompanied by a campaign of public education, and is carefully drafted and directed against clearly defined forms of hate speech.

The role of law varies with society. Western societies have several mechanisms to cope with hate speech and its consequences, such as an open and competitive economy, a vibrant civil society, a reasonably cohesive and integrated society, a varied media representing a wide spectrum of views, and a plural and self-limiting public culture. They can, therefore, afford to assign law a relatively limited role. As their recent actions show, even they had to increase that role to cope with the rabid rhetoric and militant activities of right-wing organizations, joined now by their jihadist Islamist cousins spouting hatred of what the West most values.

So far as the developing countries are concerned, the situation could not be more different. Most of them are composed of ethnic, religious, and racial groups with little experience of working together and a long legacy of mistrust, ignorance, misunderstanding, and hostility. Rumors, jokes, inflammatory or ill-conceived remarks by politicians seeking short-term gains, and even reasoned criticisms made in the course of an uninhibited exercise of free speech can arouse deep-seated fears, trigger unrest, and undo years of good work in nation building. Extralegal mechanisms on which the developed societies rely are not yet strong enough to cope with the consequences of hate speech, making law a major instrument of collective action, at least until such time as the society acquires reasonable cohesion and stability and throws up informal mechanisms of control.

Context plays an important part in our assessment of the value of a law. Banning Holocaust denial has a particular meaning in Germany. It is part of reparative justice, a public statement of the country's acknowledgment of and apology for its past, a way of fighting neo-Nazi trends in German society, and so on. The ban is justified not only because Holocaust denial is a form of hate speech, but on other moral and historical grounds as well. This is also the case, albeit to a lesser extent, in some other European countries that have a history of rabid anti-Semitism. The ban has no meaning in India where there is no history of hostility to Jews and where anti-Semitism is not a problem. Although all forms of hate speech properly so called deserve to be discouraged, how strict a view we should take of different forms of it, how far we should resort to law, and whether the law should rely on civil remedies alone or should also involve criminal penalties are best decided in the light of the history and the prevailing circumstances of the society in question.

Free speech flourishes and is indeed only possible under certain conditions, such as some degree of political stability, social stability, intercommunal harmony, and a culture of civility. In their absence, the nervous society lacks both the confidence to live with dissent and vigorous debate and the ability to cope with their consequences. The ease with which western societies, including the United States, have in recent years introduced an extensive system of surveillance – some have even made praising or "glorifying" terrorism a criminal offense, and imposed or encouraged severe formal and informal restrictions on free speech, shows how much their commitment to it is primarily a result of their social and political stability rather than their greater love of liberty.[31] Political stability and social harmony are not external to free speech but make it possible and lie at its very basis. When hate speech is banned to create and maintain these conditions, we restrict free speech not only in the interest of other values, but also its own. Indeed, while restricting it at one level, we consolidate and deepen it at another.

---

[31] A polite but firm request from the White House was enough to "persuade" CBS, NBC, ABC, FOX, and CNN not to broadcast unedited videotapes by Osama Bin Laden in 2001. Bill Carter and Felicity Barringer, "Networks Agree to U.S. Request to Edit Future bin Laden Tapes," *N.Y. Times*, Oct. 11, 2001, at A1. Network officials stated that Secretary of State Condoleezza Rice had not tried to "coerce" them, but had been, in the words of one executive, "very gentle, very diplomatic, very deft." *Id*. The official reason – that the tapes might be sending out secret messages – was widely known to be spurious, as the Al-Jazeera Web site, easily accessible in the United States, continued to show them uncensored.

# 3

# Hate Speech

## C. Edwin Baker

Given the evils of hate, any argument for protecting hate speech is, at best, an uphill effort and, at worst, simply misguided. Many people either accept, or at least wonder whether they should accept, an argument that goes something like this:

> Anyone sensitive to the horror of genocide knows that hate pervades the atmosphere at such times. Few goals can rank higher than preventing genocide and the murderous racial conflicts presented to the world during the twentieth century. Lesser instances of race-based violence also should be prevented. It is difficult to find any value in the freedom to engage in racist hate speech. Important but ultimately less significant values such as free speech cannot, for any sensitive person, lead to any pause in outlawing the speech that contributes to these horrors. Exceptions to any free speech principle should be made for hate speech. Whether or not the ban will be effective in even a few cases to prevent genocide or racial violence, the mere possibility that it will more than justifies the ban.

As an advocate of almost absolute protection of free speech,[1] I should explain the grounds for my valuation of free speech and rejection of the just mentioned claim. That explanation, it turns out, is too ambitious for this essay. Nevertheless, Section II of this chapter describes but does not defend a theory of why racist or hate speech

---

[1] The misguided nature of a common argument against the absolutist position in respect to free speech and in favor of finding hate speech as an appropriate exception to the "free speech principle" should be mentioned. The argument assumes both that there are in fact and that there should be many exceptions to the free-speech principle. Most of what these claimants assert as exceptions is considered such by absolutists, making their point irrelevant. No absolutist – not Justices Black or Douglas, nor Thomas

Versions of this chapter were presented at conferences on hate speech at the Cardozo Law School in New York City (November 2005) and the Central European University in Budapest (April 2006). I received helpful comments from many people but particularly Peter Molnar and Monroe Price. This chapter revises and extends "Autonomy and Hate Speech," in *Extreme Speech and Democracy* 139 (Ivan Hare & James Weinstein eds., Oxford University Press 2009).

[Editors' Note: Ed Baker died, unexpectedly and much too soon, before final revisions to this chapter were complete. We have made a few grammatical corrections and slight changes in the footnotes but otherwise left his text intact.]

should be protected – a theory that I believe provides the best, albeit often unrecognized, explanation of existing American case law but one that is surely a controversial, probably minority, view even in the United States. There are, of course, arguments that emphasize different evils about hate speech, evils presumably less dramatic but more common than those just mentioned, about the harms caused by hate speech. Although these will mostly not be discussed here, my expectation is that the arguments for and against prohibitions discussed here will, with variable force, also apply to those arguments – and I will occasionally note how a focus on these rationales could weaken or strengthen arguments against regulation.

Most readers will realize, as do I, that the abstract theoretical grounds offered here will not and should not satisfy my imagined proponent of regulation. Thus, Section III describes the empirical evidence that would cause me to abandon the theory described in Section II, at least in the context of some category of racist or hate speech, but then gives reasons to doubt that this evidence will be forthcoming. In the end, this essay could be seen as a call for more knowledge – I stand ready to be shown that relevant evidence overrides my doubts about the wisdom and efficacy of suppression.

Given the inevitable uncertainties about empirical evidence, Section III does not answer the last sentence of the imagined argument for regulation set forth earlier about the mere *possibility* of making a contribution toward prevention. Thus, Section IV offers a different answer: it considers reasons to expect, as a practical matter, that hate speech regulation is more likely to contribute to genocidal events and lesser forms of racial violence than to reduce them. Historical horrors help justify – or so I suggest – greater, not lesser, protection for speech. My hypothesis is that a concern with racism and racial violence empirically supports a gamble on strong speech protection. Section V is a brief conclusion.

I

Before beginning, however, I offer the following preface. Constantly, references to "American exceptionalism" are made in discussions of free speech. Usually the

---

Emerson, nor any other major absolutist scholar – ever suggests that all of (or only) something describable as verbal speech should be exempt from legal regulation. Rather, all have a theory of what a proper free speech principle covers and then argue that (at least) government abridgments or violations of that principle are impermissible. This approach is evident in the argumentative structure of judicial opinions – illustrated by many of the most famous First Amendment decisions of the U.S. Supreme Court – that consider whether the speech at issue is covered by the idea of free speech. If it is not, the absolutist favors upholding the regulation; if it is, the absolutist would strike down any regulation that abridges the freedom without even considering (sometimes without noting) as possible justifications the important state reasons for regulating. *See* C. Edwin Baker, "Harm, Liberty, and Free Speech," 70 *S. Cal. L. Rev.* 979 (1997). Thus, the absolutist would entertain – and what I explain later in the chapter is why I would reject – the argument that hate speech is not covered by the rationale for free speech. Nevertheless, to the extent that she maintains her absolutist position, she would not accept arguments about interests that purported to justify an exception.

suggestion is that the United States is extremely protective of free speech, disregarding most contrary values, whereas Europeans and others, although generally protective of core speech freedoms, allow restrictions that are "prescribed by law and are necessary in a democratic society."[2] Although if the view I present were accepted, no laws invalid under the First Amendment in the United States could meet this "necessity" standard, Europeans interpret it with a "margin of appreciation" that allows restraints. Under this standard, they recognize other important values in determining the extent of protection of speech – basically an approach Americans call "balancing." Nevertheless, this suggestion of difference is, at best, overblown. First, in many contexts, many Europeans favor – including some justices on the European Court of Justice – something close to what has been portrayed as the strongly speech-protective American position. For example, a 2004 decision of the Hungarian Constitutional Court followed its earlier 1992 decision in repeatedly invoking the American "clear and present danger" test in finding unconstitutional a law that punished speech provoking racial hate.[3] In contrast to these European defenders of strong speech protection, many, if not most, American First Amendment scholars and jurists favor a "balancing" that is quite like what is portrayed as the European approach.[4]

There is also a historical point. Though some Americans – I am one – favor the strongly speech-protective approach identified with American exceptionalism, that approach has been in the United States a "fighting faith" that often has not (yet) prevailed. Admittedly, the last half of the twentieth century saw generally increasing protection of speech in America. Still, especially early in the twentieth century and before, American courts regularly approved limits, jailing or fining people for their speech activities. All sorts of expression have been prohibited and punished – speech favoring socialism, communism, anarchism,[5] and an even more mainstream political editorial;[6] racist speech[7] or sexually explicit

---

[2] *See, e.g.*, European Convention on Human Rights §10(2). The Canadian Charter of Rights and Freedoms protects freedom of expression "subject only to such reasonable limits prescribed by law as can be demonstrably justified in a free and democratic society." Canadian Charter of Rights & Freedoms, § 1.

[3] Hungarian Constitutional Court, Decision 18/2004 (v.25) AB, *available at* http://www.mkab.hu/admin/data/file/675_18_2004.pdf; *see* Peter Molnar, "Towards Improved Law and Policy on 'Hate Speech' – The 'Clear and Present Danger' Test in Hungary," in *Extreme Speech and Democracy* 237 (Ivan Hare & James Weinstein eds., Oxford University Press 2009).

[4] Virtually all First Amendment opinions of Chief Justice Burger or Justice Powell adopt a form of balancing. This approach, which received one of its best defenses in Steven H. Shiffrin, *The First Amendment, Democracy, and Romance* (Harvard University Press 1990), would probably require reversal of many of the great modern First Amendment decisions in which no hint of balancing occurs. *See* Baker, *supra* note 1.

[5] *See* Zachariah Chafee, Jr., *Free Speech in the United States* 36–107 (Harvard University Press 1964) (describing cases).

[6] An editorial cartoon criticizing political corruption was the basis for a fine, with the court refusing to hear the publisher's offer to prove its truth. Patterson v. Colorado, 205 U.S. 454 (1907).

[7] Beauharnais v. Illinois, 343 U.S. 250 (1952).

speech;[8] publication and sale of great novels,[9] feminist materials important for sex education;[10] labor picketing[11] and public assemblies.[12] To this day, the First Amendment, which applies only to governmental, not private, activity, offers people no protection from being fired by private employers for their speech or political associations.

Interestingly, putting aside official legal doctrine, some political scientists have concluded that in practice, as opposed to rhetoric, the United States is not exceptional in the way typically suggested. The impression of one commentator is that, as "compared to nine European democracies, the U.S. has imposed the most severe legal and social 'obstacles to political dissent.'"[13] Later this chapter will raise general doubts about causal claims. Still, I cannot help wondering if the extraordinarily sad state not only of American foreign policy but also of domestic policies, which have left the United States with greater income inequality than any other industrialized democratic country, reflects in part the historically *inadequate* protection of speech freedom in the United States. How would our politics have gone if we had not suppressed labor activists from early in our history, the liberal internationalists during or after World War I, or wiped progressive thinkers out of the universities and cultural industries during the McCarthy period, a cleansing that took decades to repair? Much of Zachariah Chafee's classic book on free speech can be read as supporting his speculative comment that greater respect for free speech at the time of World War I might have led to a better treaty after the war, to support in the United States for the League of Nations, and to "sav[ing] English children from German bombs in 1941."[14] In any event, even though many of the most prominent advocates of rather

---

[8] Roth v. United States, 354 U.S. 476 (1957).

[9] Courts upheld, for example, bans on Theodore Dreiser, *American Tragedy* in 1930, Lillian Smith, *Strange Fruit* in 1945, Edmund Wilson, *Memories of Hecate County* in 1947, Erskine Caldwell, *God's Little Acre* in 1950. *See* Thomas I. Emerson, *The System of Freedom of Expression* 468–70 (Random House 1970). Beyond the judicial approval of censorship of specific books was, of course, the effect of this potential on what was written and deleted. This censorship of great – as well as not so great – literature in the United States is well and exhaustively described in Edward deGrazia, *Girls Lean Back Everywhere: The Law of Obscenity and the Assault on Genius* (Random House 1992).

[10] Most famous is Margaret Sanger's prosecution under the Comstock law for trying to circulate birth control information. Margaret A. Blanchard, "The American Urge to Censor: Freedom of Expression Versus the Desire to Sanitize," 33 *Wm. & Mary L. Rev.* 741, 766–78 (1992).

[11] Giboney v. Empire Storage Co, 336 U.S. 490 (1949); Hughes v. Superior Court, 339 U.S. 460 (1950); International Brotherhood of Teamsters v. Vogt, 354 U.S. 284 (1957).

[12] A conviction for public speaking in a public place was famously affirmed by Justice Holmes in the now discredited decision of Commonwealth v. Davis, 162 Mass. 510 (1895), *aff'd*, 167 U.S. 43 (1897), and later echoed in decisions such as Cox v. Louisiana, 379 U.S. 559 (1965) (upholding ordinance that prohibited picketing near a courthouse, although reversing conviction because of selective application of statute against defendants) and Adderley v. Florida, 385 U.S. 39 (1966) (upholding conviction for peacefully demonstrating outside a county jail).

[13] Robert J. Goldstein, *Political Repression in Modern America: From 1870 to the Present*, xiv (Schenkman Publishing 1978) (quoting Robert Dahl, *Political Oppositions in Western Democracies* xvi, 390–2 [Yale University Press 1968]).

[14] Chafee, *supra* note 5, at xiii, 561–2.

absolutist speech freedom may be American scholars and jurists, identifying that position with an American and contrasted with a European reality is exaggerated. Still, relatively absolutist protection is the view that my comments endorse.

Finally, I might note that the argument of the three parts of this chapter respond to only some, albeit I believe the most common and most powerful, arguments supporting legal prohibitions on hate speech, and some of the considerations developed here apply somewhat more broadly. Other arguments for prohibitions are mostly outside the chapter's scope. Still, I will briefly comment on one somewhat startling argument made by Jeremy Waldron.[15] He claims that he can "test" the liberal belief that a free society (of which he says a Rawlsian well-ordered society is a subcategory) would not have laws against hate speech. He performs the test by asking "what does a *well-ordered society* look like?" Noting that a society that "permits [racial hate] publications may *look* quite different from a society" in which these are not legally permitted, he concludes that a well-ordered society would look like the second. From this, he appears to offer a non sequitur: laws prohibiting racist publications would be appropriate in a free society. He also takes the Rawlsian claim that in a well-ordered society, "everyone accepts, and knows that everyone else accepts, the very same principles of justice," and that people "assure each other of . . . their joint allegiance" to these principles, an assurance that "dignity requires," as a central premise for his conclusion that such prohibitions are proper. To achieve this required assurance of each by the other, Waldron argues, laws can make a contribution – they can provide "public guarantees." Put only somewhat differently, in a Rawlsian well-ordered society, "citizens have and can rely on public assurance of one another's commitments to justice," which includes the dignity that is Waldron's concern.[16] He claims that "a well-ordered society is supposed to provide [these assurances]" and that this assurance is provided in part by the government, presumably this being a justification for laws prohibiting at least some hate speech.[17]

Consider three points about this argument. First, most importantly, it seems that Waldron's proposal *eliminates all possibility* of achieving his goal *of a well-ordered society*. A person's general behavior and speech *cannot* be taken to give the necessary

---

[15] Jeremy Waldron, "Dignity and Defamation: The Visibility of Hate," 123 *Harv. L. Rev.* 1596 (2010).

[16] Dignity is subject to quite diverse understandings. For Waldron – following views particularly common in Europe – among other things, a person's dignity involves the legal right to control other people's thoughts and attitudes or at least some of their expressions of their thoughts, attitudes, and beliefs. Rather than viewing dignity as dependent on control of (ownership of) other people's minds and expression, other views find this conception directly contradicts human dignity. The idea of dignity implicit in this chapter encompasses a person's status as an agent who has a right and, to some extent, an ability to have and express attitudes and beliefs. Even though much is left to be said, the first conception seems more natural and necessary for an inegalitarian status-based society, and the second for an action-based society in which people live self-authored lives or, at least, lives for which they claim ultimate responsibility. Illustrative of this difference is the original development of the law of defamation as a means to protect political and social elites from damage to their reputational status by false, or even worse, true reports of their foibles.

[17] Waldron, *supra* note 15, at 1617–35.

assurance of – indeed to give *any* assurance of – one's recognition of another's dignity or equality if one is not free to assert the contrary. If, as Waldron, echoing Rawls, suggests, a well-ordered society depends on people *knowing* what other people believe, it cannot be such a society unless people are free to say what they believe. True, a just order may rely on laws against murder to provide public assurance that murder is not tolerated, but this is because law *can* properly deal with individual behavior – but cannot determine, and certainly cannot guarantee knowledge of, what people think. Any chance of knowing what another person thinks depends on her freedom to express her commitments or other attitudes.

Second, creating a society that *looks* well-ordered does not show that it *is* a free society (a category that includes well-ordered as an idealized subcategory). To really be a free well-ordered society, the society must not only look well-ordered but must meet the prerequisites of being free and well-ordered – requirements that include, first, freedom and more specifically, the capacity of people to assure each other of their mutual commitments. A "well-ordered" Potemkin village is probably the best example of Waldron's "political aesthetics" but it guarantees nothing about what the society *is* like other than, if coercive laws were necessary to create the appearance, that the society is not free.

Third, there is a question of how a society becomes well ordered. Waldron is surely right that "societies do not become well-ordered by magic" and even right that the state and the law have an important "expressive role" – the law should not communicate people's lack of equality or dignity, which was a major evil of segregation and other laws that violate the Fourteenth Amendment's equal protection clause.[18] As the U.S. Supreme Court said in rejecting compulsory flag salutes by children in school, "the end" – there "national unity," here each person's respect for and assurance of each other person's respect for people's dignity and equal status as citizens – as something that "officials may foster by persuasion and example[,] is not in question."[19] What is in question is whether Waldron is persuasive that "the disciplinary role of the law" – presumably including prohibitions on hate speech – may be "necessary," as he says it is "natural to think" – or, as the Court asks, "whether . . . compulsion . . . is a permissible means. . . ."[20] In saying that the government cannot coerce speech, the Court opined that it was not "choos[ing] weak government over strong government," but rather "adher[ing] as a means of strength to individual freedom of mind in preference to officially disciplined uniformity for which history indicates a disappointing and disastrous end."[21] In asking whether the "slow and easily neglected route to aroused loyalties," which corresponds to means

---

[18]  Charles R. Lawrence III, "If He Hollers Let Him Go: Regulating Racist Speech on Campus," 1990 *Duke L.J.* 431 (1990); C. Edwin Baker, "Outcome Equality or Equality of Respect: The Substantive Content of Equal Protection," 131 *U. Pa. L. Rev.* 933 (1983).

[19]  West Virginia State Board of Education v. Barnette, 319 U.S. 624, 640 (1943).

[20]  *Id.*

[21]  *Id.* at 637.

that Waldron characterizes as "spectacularly dumb" if relied on in neglect of coercive laws, "may be short-cut by substituting [compulsion]," the Court answered "no."[22] According to the Court, "to believe that patriotism will not flourish if patriotic ceremonies are voluntary and spontaneous instead of a compulsory routine is to make an unflattering estimate of the appeal of our institutions to free minds."[23] The same can reasonably be said about the appeal of attitudes necessary to sustain a realistically just or well-ordered society or the people for whom having these attitudes is important.

## II

My premises are: (1) that the legitimacy of the legal order depends on it respecting people's equality and autonomy; and (2) that as a purely formal matter, the legal order only respects people's autonomy if it allows people in their speech to express their own values – no matter what these values are and irrespective of how this expressive content harms or leads to harms of other people or makes government processes or achieving governmental aims difficult. Pursuit of substantive aims, such as helping people experience fulfillment and dignity, must occur within a legal structure that as a formal matter respects people's equality and autonomy.

The conception of autonomy that the state must respect is, as noted, in a sense *formal*, not *substantive*.[24] A legal order must generally ascribe autonomy to people, usually withdrawing this attribution only to certain behavior within and purportedly controlled by institutional structures frameworks steered by mechanisms other than communication and a person's choices or on basis of individualized assessments of lack of competence. The state cannot coherently *ask* a person to obey its laws unless it treats the person as capable of making choices for herself, for example, the choice to obey the law.[25] As so conceived, respect for a person's autonomy is in general an on/off value. A government regulation either is or is not consistent with the required respect. A person is not treated as formally autonomous if the law denies her the right to use her own expression to embody her views. As used here, formal autonomy applies to individual activity or choice, not claims to control others or achieve particular results. (I have gone further and argued that an individual also must have a general right over the value-expressive uses of oneself – one's own body – but that raises interpretive difficulties not necessary to examine here.) Moreover, meeting the requirement of respecting her choice autonomy, granting this expressive right,

---

[22] *Id.* at 631.

[23] *Id.* at 641.

[24] C. Edwin Baker, "Autonomy and Informational Privacy or Gossip: The Central Meaning of the First Amendment," 21 *Soc. Phil. & Pol'y* 215 (2004).

[25] Seeing the law this way represents the most important transformative element of H.L.A. Hart's transformation of positivism. See H.L.A. Hart, *The Concept of Law* (2d ed., Clarendon Press 1994) (1961); C. Edwin Baker, *Hart's Transformation of Positivism* (2008) (unpublished manuscript).

creates no actual or even potential conflict with respect for others' formal autonomy, that is, no conflict with recognizing their equivalent choice or expressive rights with respect to their body or speech. Law's respect for formal autonomy of one person never denies respect for the formal autonomy (or, for that matter, the formal equality) of another. This lack of conflict is possible precisely because formal autonomy does not involve claims to achieving or even capacity to achieve any particular results, claims that would create potential for conflicts between different claimants.

In contrast to respect for a person's formal autonomy as an absolute requirement of legal legitimacy, a central aim of a democratic state should be to promote people's *substantive autonomy*. Substantive autonomy involves a person's actual capacity and opportunities to lead the best, most meaningful, self-directed life possible. Laws that advance one person's substantive autonomy – by allocating resources to her or providing her information, for example – often reduce the substantive autonomy of another person. In making policy choices, a state is properly influenced by potentially conflicting substantively egalitarian aims, welfare-maximizing considerations, and various inevitably non-neutral collective self-definitional or majoritarian values. These policy or legal *choices*, as compared to others the state might make, inevitably favor some people's substantive autonomy over that of others.

Democratic legitimacy, I believe, and certainly the civil libertarian commitment, requires that, in advancing people's substantive autonomy as well as in advancing substantive egalitarian aims and other proper policy goals, the legal order neither have the purpose to nor use general means that disrespect people's formal autonomy (or their formal equality). On this view, respect for free speech is a proper constraint on the choice of collective or legal means to advance legitimate policy goals. Typically racist hate speech embodies the speaker's at least momentary view of the world and, to that extent, expresses her values. Of course, her speech does not respect others' equality or dignity. It is not, however, the speaker but the state's legitimacy that is at stake in evaluating the content of the legal order. Law's purposeful restrictions on such racist or hate speech violate the speaker's formal autonomy, whereas her hate speech does not interfere with or contradict anyone else's formal autonomy even if such speech does cause injuries that sometimes include undermining others' substantive autonomy. For this reason, prohibitions on racist or hate speech should generally be impermissible – even if arguably permissible in special, usually institutionally bound, limited contexts where the speaker has no claimed right to act autonomously – such as when, as an employee, one has given up one's autonomy to meet role demands inconsistent with expressions of racism.

Admittedly, other influential theories of free speech could lead to different conclusions – or different explanations for similar conclusions. Pragmatic balancers are likely to treat the notion of formal autonomy as incoherent or lacking moral appeal and instead seek to advance people's substantive autonomy, possibly in a roughly egalitarian manner, or to advance other substantive goals. Undoubtedly, the mere expression of racist hate speech can cause real injuries and has the potential to stimulate further harms. As will be noted later in the chapter, however, those disparaged by hate speech might well be better off without legal restrictions on the speech. Without offering any sympathy for the racists, the pragmatic balancer could plausibly come out on either side in this debate about legal restrictions on hate speech.[26]

Equally interesting is a more foundational approach to free speech. Some view free speech guarantees as a necessary implication of democracy – with the scope of protection limited by its rationale.[27] To many thoughtful observers, this democratic basis for the protected legal status of speech suggests justifiable restrictions on at least some racist hate speech. The assertion is that racist speech contradicts the democratic premise – an equality in being self-governing – that justifies protection of speech. For example, hate speech that portrays a particular group as unfit to participate in the governing process or that advocates crimes against members of a particular group rejects basic premises of democracy. The critique observes that the hate speech does not take a position *within* democratic discourse but rather aims at thwarting democracy and democracy's discourses by means of actual or expressive exclusion. For this reason, it is argued, hate speech can be prohibited.

In the past, a number of jurists have accepted roughly that view – arguing that antidemocratic speech is permissibly prohibited. Judge Learned Hand treated counseling or advocacy of law violation as inconsistent with the democratic methods of change and, therefore, properly made illegal.[28] Justice Felix Frankfurter explained that communists' speech ranked low on any scale of values.[29] Presumably the low ranking occurred because the communists recommended change by nondemocratic means; for that reason, their speech was not "political" within Frankfurter's understanding of democratic practice. Robert Bork likewise denied that advocacy of law violation – for example, advocacy of revolution or even peaceful civil disobedience – could be "political speech," which is the only category that he would protect.[30] At mid-century, Carl Auerbach argued that the basic postulate behind the First Amendment allows Congress to "exclude from the struggle," to restrict the speech of "those groups which, if victorious, would crush democracy and impose totalitarianism."[31] Such arguments could apply equally to racist hate speech, at least to the extent the speech rejects the premise of democratic inclusion.

---

[26] Steven H. Shiffrin, *Dissent, Injustice, and the Meanings of America* 49–87 (Princeton University Press 1999).

[27] Alexander Meiklejohn, *Political Freedom: The Constitutional Powers of the People* (Harper 1960).

[28] *See* Masses Publishing Co. v. Patten, 244 F. 535 (S.D.N.Y. 1917).

[29] *See* Dennis v. United States 341 U.S. 494 (1951) (Frankfurter, J., concurring).

[30] Robert Bork, "Neutral Principles and Some First Amendment Problems," 47 *Indiana L.J.* 1, 20, 29–31 (1971). At about the time of publication, in a lecture given at Yale Law School, Bork argued, as I remember it, for an even more restrictive understanding of the scope of political speech.

[31] Carl A. Auerbach, "The Communist Control Act of 1954: A Proposed Legal-Political Theory of Free Speech," 23 *U. Chi. L. Rev.* 173, 189 (1956).

Others argue, however, that this conclusion does not follow, at least does not follow for "our" (meaning the American) particular version of democracy.[32] They claim that all speech, no matter how disrespectful of others, that is part of public discourse merits protection, possibly absolute protection. Emphatic about locating the basis of free speech in "our" conception of democracy, which is premised on people's autonomously arriving at their own political views – that is, arriving at their views without legal restriction on the public discourse leading to those views. A person must be able to explore (advocate or hear) even views inconsistent with democracy to formulate her own commitments – although this strong protection of speech applies only to speech that is part of public discourse, which arguably covers only speech evocative of possible public issues and which is part of a possible public sphere or public discourse.

This view has undeniable strengths both interpretatively and normatively and may very well reach the same conclusion about most regulation of hate speech as does my emphasis on formal autonomy. Still, unlike a theory grounded on respect for individual autonomy, this democratic approach does not cover protection of speech not properly characterized as part of public discourse. (Interestingly, albeit for different reasons, both the autonomy and the democratic discourse approaches either completely or largely deny protection to "commercial speech."[33]) My theoretical objection to this view relates to its initial premise – that we should protect speech fundamentally because the protection is essential to democracy or, more precisely, to the conception of democracy that we accept. My question is *why* are we so concerned with democracy? Why does democracy provide a foundational premise? The strategy of my question is the expectation that any sound normative answer to this inquiry, outlined in the last paragraph of this section, will both explain the proper contours of democracy and show that an explanation of the *nature and significance* of democracy's contribution to the legitimacy of the legal order requires and reflects acceptance of value premises that go beyond the structure of the political order to matters such as protection of even nonpolitical self-expression.

One response could attempt to avoid the normative question and merely say – perhaps for the United States but maybe not those European countries that restrict hate speech – that we are not only in fact deeply committed to democracy, but also that *our* conception of democracy requires virtually complete citizen autonomy within public discourse. This essentially sociological response, however, leaves two problems. First, it does not answer the skeptic, the person who wonders why we

---

[32] Robert C. Post, *Constitutional Domains* 119–78 (Harvard University Press 1995); Robert C. Post, "Hate Speech," in *Extreme Speech and Democracy, supra* note 3, at 123; James Weinstein, "Hate Speech, Viewpoint Neutrality, and the American Concept of Democracy," in *Boundaries of Free Expression & Order in American Democracy* 146–69 (Thomas R. Hensley ed., Kent State University Press 2001); James Weinstein, "Extreme Speech, Public Order, and Democracy: Lessons from *The Masses,*" in *Extreme Speech and Democracy, supra* note 3, at 23.

[33] *See, e.g.,* C. Edwin Baker, "Commercial Speech," 84 *Indiana L.J.* 981 (2009).

should be committed to democracy or, if we should be, why to *our* particular conception of democracy, especially given, as Meiklejohn commented, "the sheer stupidity of the policies of this nation."[34] Second, even more fundamentally, to the extent that we do in fact adopt laws punishing hate speech – even if invalidated by courts – it seems that *our* conception of democracy is at least contested. It even seems that, in the view of the majority, our conception of democracy is more like the one that Justice Frankfurter and Judge Hand describe than the one Professors Post and Weinstein propose. They may be right but they need a normative, not merely sociological, rationale for their position.

Instead of the contextual sociological claim, I have argued that the best answer to this normative question of what it is about democracy that justifies our allegiance is that democracy is the *only* political order that embodies a normative principle of *equal* respect for people's right to be engaged in *self-determination* when self-determination occurs at the group level, leads to legal allocation of resources, and involves coercion – that is, is the only form of government that respects people as free and equal in the process of choosing laws. But if legitimacy (or the justification of legal obligation) requires respect for people's right of self-determination, there is no reason why this required respect applies only when people act to decide about the collective but not when they act to decide about themselves. If this is right, the fundamental status of each person's equality and autonomy provides *both* the normative basis for democracy and a set of normative principles that democratic laws must not violate. These values both require democracy and require limits on democracy. The logic of this rationale for democracy does not so much place free speech at the center of democracy as locates democracy as an offshoot of respect for individual autonomy (and equality) that encompasses free speech. Respect for ascribed autonomy is both definitive of, and restricts the scope of, both foundational free speech and democracy. Thus, I reject an emphasis on democratic foundations for free speech in favor of this more basic premise of respect for individual autonomy to which the law must conform even as it pursues practices that favor people's substantive autonomy. On this basis, the legal order must respect the autonomy even of the individual who would deny such respect to others in the community – the law must respect the freedom of the racist to express her views.

III

Abstract theory is fine. But a convincing case that a different approach to free speech might prevent occurrences such as the Holocaust, more recent genocides like that in Rwanda, or other virulent, murderous racist practices would lead me – and I suppose any person of goodwill – to revise abstract commitments that counsel against legal

---

[34] Alexander Meiklejohn, "The First Amendment Is an Absolute," 1961 *Sup. Ct. Rev.* 245, 263.

prohibitions of racist speech. So the natural question is: What evidence or argument would such a convincing case require?

First, historical evidence should be available. But then the question becomes: What specific historical evidence should be tellingly relevant to us today? Germany's experience with Nazism is often noted in explaining their current prohibitions on hate speech, but it is less than clear that this history shows that these prohibitions are now needed. Historical accounts will likely find racist hate speech prominent in periods leading up to the genocide. But that finding is clearly not enough. It would not show whether this speech was causal or merely symptomatic, reflecting attitudes, prejudices, and underlying forces that would have led to violence without being crystallized in anything that would be covered by any plausible legal category of hate speech. The hate speech might have even been usefully symptomatic in exposing a serious problem with which society needed to deal. And the history would not show whether, even if causal of violence in that historical context, it would be so under different historical conditions – for example, the conditions that exist in modern democracies.

Still, even in the absence of good empirical evidence, a causal claim about racist hate speech – at least as a contributing cause within a longer chain of causation – seems intuitively very plausible. Genocide or virulent racial discrimination presumably reflects attitudes. It is difficult to understand how such attitudes could first arise and then persist if not in some way embodied in people's communications, their expression. Of course, such expression is unlikely to arise out of nothing. Material conditions and social orientations that are not themselves equivalent to the expression of racism are also likely to be a central part of the causal chain. If so, the question becomes where in this causal chain, where in its fight against virulent racism, a legal order should target its intervention(s). Pragmatically, the question is where political interventions would actually be needed, effective, and politically feasible. The reality may be that the second and third (effective and politically feasible) and the first (needed) come apart in respect to hate speech regulation but not in respect to other possible responses. As to effectiveness, as noted earlier, the problem is that the causally significant racist speech may take a broader, ideological, more general attitude creating form than the narrower, more specific category that any plausible restriction of hate speech would cover. As to politically feasible, it may be that effective passage *and adequate enforcement* of hate speech restrictions would only occur when they are not needed. (Many countries that have experienced the worst racist violence have, in fact, had such prohibitions without successfully preventing racist or genocidal results.[35])

---

[35] I was told at the conferences where this chapter was presented that both Rwanda and Germany are examples.

The seriousness of the evil surely justifies multiple interventions if their multi-plicity increases the likelihood of favorable outcomes. Still, pragmatically to justify hate speech regulation seems to require that the following be shown:

1. Hate speech occurs in cases of genocide or virulent racial discrimination – a demonstration that usually – maybe always – can be made.
2. As a causal matter, hate speech – or, more specifically, the hate speech that would be outlawed by hate speech regulation – contributes to these evils. The more general version of this claim is probably right, although the more specific claim about the specific hate speech that would be barred is considerably more speculative. As noted, most proposed legal restrictions on hate speech target a relatively narrow category (even if to those caught up it, often members of racial minorities, an unduly broad category) that might be characterized as emotional epithets, while leaving calmer (or coded) expositions of racism untouched although the later may be the more causally significant. Evidence or careful argument on the point is seldom offered and, I suspect, any offering would seldom be fully convincing.

Even if these two points are right, a sound argument for legal prohibitions also requires persuasive grounds to believe the following additional claims:

3. Legal prohibitions of hate speech are actually an effective place (even if not the exclusive place) to intervene in the causal chain: I have seen little empirical evidence supporting this claim. Later in the chapter, I will suggest doubts that this argumentative burden can be met.
4. Enactment of the hate speech prohibitions creates greater benefits than costs. The latter may include costs, which some people might characterize as ben-efits, related to the extent or nature of democracy and to human freedom. Moreover, the benefits should be calculated in terms of the excess of benefits over those that could be achieved by more modest (and politically feasible) measures justified in terms of their having greater benefits than costs – a point very roughly embodied in standard First Amendment doctrine by the require-ment that restrictions on speech be not only adequate but also "necessary" to serve a compelling state interest.
5. These legal bars on hate speech would not reduce the efficaciousness or likelihood of other (legal or social) interventions that would be more effective in preventing virulent racist acts; or, at least, that any negative effects would not be greater than any benefits the bars on hate speech provide.

An assessment of these five essentially empirical matters is crucial. I will put aside the fourth, assume the first two *arguendo*, and focus on the third and fifth.

The third point requires two doubtful claims. It must assume that political forces will be able to secure adoption and adoption of the needed prohibitions on hate speech *in those situations* where the prohibitions are needed and that the prohibitions would be causally effective as a means to prevent virulent racism or genocide. Clearly, many places in the modern world have adopted such prohibitions. The possibility is real, however, that the prohibitions will be adopted and enforced *only* in places where not needed. Nevertheless, maybe the proper purpose of international conventions requiring their adoption is precisely to add to the political pressure to adopt such restrictions, thereby increasing the likelihood of their adoption where needed.

Even more problematic, to be an effective place to intervene, adopted prohibitions must be efficacious in reducing the likelihood of serious racist evils. Most obviously, this result probably requires sufficient enforcement of the prohibitions against the relevant targets. Nevertheless, maybe the argumentative burden can be met here too. Still, even mere adoption may help create a cultural climate where racist speech – and even more importantly, virulent racist practices – are unacceptable. As to sufficient enforcement, the question is made more difficult because it is not clear at what stage enforcement would be meaningful in preventing the polity from devolving in an unacceptably racist direction or whether enforcement could be effective at reversing cultural directions. Active enforcement (against appropriate targets) is likely only if racist groups have not become too established. By the time Nazis were gaining power, or during the year immediately preceding the genocide in Rwanda, effective enforcement was unlikely. At the relevant time, enforcement would likely either be blocked, create a backlash against the enforcers and sympathy for the "suppressed" racists, or – as will be discussed later – enforced primarily against "unpatriotic" or "racist" speech of those most needing protection – Jews or Tutsis, for example, or against African Americans in the United States or Algerians in France.

Thus, the hope of those favoring hate speech prohibitions must be that enforcement will be meaningful and effective at a quite early stage. Pessimism about this speculative hope seems justified. First are generic doubts about the likelihood of effective legal enforcement. More important, however, is the likelihood that at this most relevant stage, the speech that meaningfully contributes to developing or sustaining racism will be subtle, quotidian, and, to many people, seemingly inoffensive or at least not "seriously" offensive speech. This speech is likely to fly under the legal radar screen and, in any event, meaningful enforcement of prohibitions against this speech is even less likely. Thus, even given a belief that racist speech contributes significantly to virulent racism and genocidal practice, my hypothesis is that at earlier stages, legal prohibitions will not cover or be effectively enforced against the most relevant speech, and at later stages enforcement will not occur, will be counterproductive in creating martyrs for a racist cause, or will focus on the wrong targets.

Even if there is reason to doubt the effectiveness of legal prohibitions in preventing the reign of racist practices, the horrific evil feared (as well as the noxious quality of speech properly covered by a prohibition) recommend that error should be on the side of caution. Here is where the fifth point about possible negative effects of restrictions on hate speech, preliminarily suggested by some previous comments, is crucial. Caution – it is awful speech, and any possibility of reducing the evils it may contribute to justifies restriction – is often given as a reason to prohibit hate speech. This reason, however, depends crucially on rejecting two further real empirical possibilities: (1) that the prohibitions themselves will contribute to the racist nature of society, and (2) that adoption of hate speech prohibitions will make other, more effective interventions against the development of a racist, genocidal culture or polity less likely or less effective. Of course, the opposite empirical results are possible. Advocacy of and then adoption of hate speech prohibitions and pressure for their enforcement could invigorate an antiracist politics that makes other, maybe even more significant interventions, more likely. And, if the first possibilities turn out to be true, adoption of hate speech prohibitions would contribute to the evil outcomes that a country must try to prevent. That is, official legal suppression of "evil" speech could generate the very evil that motivates suppression.

Given these alternative empirical possibilities, the debate is not between idealistic but uncaring "liberal" defenders of free speech and fierce opponents of the worst forms of racism. Rather the pragmatic debate is about different empirical predictions concerning the most effective strategy for opposing racism. Empirical evidence suggesting which scenario – or when – is most likely should be welcome. Perhaps the evidence exists, although I do not know of it at a level where confidence in a particular conclusion is warranted. Thus, Section III describes considerations supporting the judgment that speech prohibition will actually exacerbate racist practice. Finally, if the issue remains in doubt, I will consider which direction merits our gamble.

Before engaging in that discussion, however, I will note an invocation of the exacerbation hypothesis in a judicial opinion favoring free speech. In the late 1940s and early 1950s, the United States prosecuted leaders of the Communist Party for what could be benignly characterized as advocating (teaching), or conspiracy to teach, the necessity and propriety of violent means to achieve a proletarian dictatorship (although without any relevant evidence, some Justices gave the speech at issue a more malignant characterization). When their convictions were affirmed by the Supreme Court in *Dennis v. United States*, Justice Douglas in dissent powerfully asserted:

> Communism in the world scene is no bogeyman; but Communism as a political faction or party in this country plainly is. Communism has been so thoroughly exposed in this country that it has been crippled as a political force. *Free speech* has destroyed it as an effective political party.[36]

Essentially Douglas's account claims "exceptionalism" for the American response to communism. The claim is implicitly twofold: that the American response was to

---

[36] Dennis v. United States, 341 U.S. 494, 588 (1951) (emphasis added).

rely on free speech and that this response was more effective than other responses tried elsewhere in the world. Unfortunately, specifics of Douglas's historical account and causal claim are either doubtful or much too simplistic. Nevertheless, Douglas illustrates the logic of a view that favoring free speech provides a central aspect of the best response to a major evil to which objectionable speech is said to contribute. Crucially, nothing in Douglas's argument for allowing the expression of evil views counsels neutrality toward or even toleration of those objectionable revolutionary views. The same lack of toleration even more obviously applies to the expression of racial hatred. Nothing about legally allowing the speech – either in the *Dennis* case or in the hate speech context – suggests that the views expressed do not present a serious threat to the existence of an acceptable world. Rather, the *pragmatic* claim is that to allow people the option to express their dreadful views is less dangerous than to attempt to outlaw this expression.

## IV

Finally, consider reasons that hate speech prohibitions are likely to backfire. My hypothesis has two reciprocal prongs. First, as an empirical matter, my suspicion is that the prohibitions will not be effective at reducing the chances of horrendous results. Reasons for that suspicion have been discussed earlier. Second, also as an empirical matter, my suspicion is that prohibitions on hate speech will actually exacerbate problems, will increase the likelihood of horrendous results. I consider six interrelated points that suggest this hypothesis.

First, enacting and defending prohibitions on hate speech may divert energy from and dampen the sense of necessity of the more vital activity of responding expressively to and critiquing racist views. Prohibitions, to the extent that they take overt expression of racism out of public discourse, create a danger about which John Stuart Mill warned. Without people having the experience of responding to and opposing expressions of misguided views, truth is in danger of becoming sterile dogma, ineffective for good because people will have lost the ability to justify and explain the truth when challenged.[37] This point – the need for any noxious doctrine that exists within a community to be publicly expressed and then persuasively rejected – was probably the underlying lesson offered by Justice Douglas's account in *Dennis* of the discursive defeat of communism in the United States.

Here is a place to repeat the point that, even if human rights, including the right of everyone to express their views no matter how horrifying, require rejecting legal prohibitions of hate speech, this *legal* toleration does not imply state neutrality or complacence toward the evil views. *State* neutrality or *social* toleration is the opposite of what society needs. In any free discussion – or in wide-open debate where speech may be "vehement, caustic, and sometimes unpleasantly sharp" in

---

[37] John Stuart Mill, *On Liberty*, chapter 2 (1859).

its attacks[38] – conversational partners (or political opponents) should be committed to each being able to express her view. But the response of the other can be: "no, your view is entirely unacceptable, it is wrong for the following reasons, and I will do everything within my (legal) power to prevent it from being realized." Despite conservative objections, people *should seek political correctness*, like all forms of correctness. Of course, ideal responses to the people whom a person believes is offering evil counsels is a subject too extensive to take up here, but I should note that I am hardly recommending retributivist responses or denial of rights. Still, to the extent they are able, people should reject, not socially or discursively tolerate, evil counsels and evil endeavors. Specifically, people should condemn the racist expression and react accordingly to the people who purvey it.

As an empirical hypothesis, I suggest that more active (and thus more effective) opposition to racist views is likely to come from the social practice of not tolerating racist expression than from laws making it illegal. People in positions of power or authority do and should lose their influence, and often even their position of authority, for public or exposed private racist expression. Society should be and apparently is prepared to maintain strong social norms rejecting racist viewpoints. I fear, however, that laws prohibiting racist expression would weaken, maybe even replace, such social practices. Legal prosecutions focus on the wrong issues – legal requirements, legal line drawing, the propriety of prosecution of this rather than other cases. In any minimally decent society that legally *permits* hate speech, such expression of hate reflexively creates, for those who object to racism, a platform to explain and justify their objections. This expressive activity may provide the greatest safeguard against racist cultures and polities. In contrast, legal repression creates a platform for racists to claim victimhood and to appeal to the many who value liberty to oppose the suppression of their freedom, shearing off the energy of a significant group from the chorus that condemns the racist views.

Second is a closely related point. By causing racism to (largely) go underground, speech prohibitions are likely to obscure the extent of the problem and the location or the human or social carriers of the problem, thereby reducing both the perceived necessity and the likely effectiveness of opposition to racism. My experience has been that among those people who are likely targets of hate speech but who still favor free speech, the reason most often given for favoring speech is the advantage of "knowing the enemy." Knowledge of the existence, views, and, importantly, the identity of those with racist attitudes increases the capacity of those potentially subject to racist harms to protect themselves and to make meaningful rhetorical, strategic, political, and legal responses.

Third, speech prohibitions can increase (or create) racist individuals' or groups' sense of oppression and thereby increase their rage and belief that they must act. Of course, the empirical issue could go either way. Prohibitions that push the more

---

[38] New York Times v. Sullivan, 376 U.S. 254, 270 (1964).

virulent expressions of hate underground may reduce its salience, whereas allowing it may increase the sense among its purveyors and their audience of the justification, maybe the necessity and entitlement, of their acting even criminally against its targets. Thus, whether prohibitions on racist speech do more to prevent than to fan the development of racist attitudes is an empirical issue. I can only speculate here. Still I suggest that causes are deeper and prohibitions may do little. If this suggestion is right, the primary immediate effect of the speech prohibition may be simply to suppress (or to attempt to suppress) people's expression of their racist views whereas the primary dynamic and longer-term consequence of suppression is to outrage and alienate those suppressed. Those suppressed may reasonably and rationally experience the majority (that is, those who back the law) and the legal order as specifically denying their basic rights, their right to express their truthfully held views in the public sphere (or in whatever contexts the specific law applies) while everyone else has this freedom. For this reason, they may conclude, they can no longer accord allegiance to (or view as legitimate) this legal order. That is, the prohibition is likely to increase the virulence of their views and their self-understanding of being treated unjustly by a legal order that they see as unequally coddling those whom they despise. Under these conditions, those whose speech the prohibitions make illegal are likely to feel more increasingly justified in using any means – including violent or illegal means – to pursue their values. Essentially, this is the point of Thomas Emerson's fourth, often neglected reason to protect free speech.[39] Speech freedom, he argues, helps create a balance between stability and change, which reduces the likelihood that pent-up anger, when almost inevitably it *eventually* expresses itself, will be expressed with irrational violence. The prediction is that even if speech prohibitions decrease the short-term level of expression of the forbidden views, they will increase the likelihood that those views will periodically be expressed by violent outbreaks rather than a social contestation in which any group numerous and strong enough to pass and enforce speech-repressive laws would surely prevail.

Fourth, prohibiting the *expression* of any values – even the most offensive views such as expression that denies democratic values or calls for violent or illegal actions – in the context of discourses where verbal responses are possible – is likely to reduce the democratic cultural self-understanding that conflicts are to be dealt as a political rather than violent struggle. This self-understanding, as suggested earlier, helps decrease the likelihood (without eliminating the danger) that racism will be expressed in overt violence. This is basically Ralf Dahrendorf's vision that the idea of democracy is not to embody the naive goal to eliminate conflict but rather to move society's inevitable real conflicts from the plane of violence to the plane of politics.[40]

---

[39]  Emerson, *supra* note 9, at 7; Thomas I. Emerson, *Toward a General Theory of the First Amendment* 11–15 (Random House 1967).
[40]  Ralf Dahrendorf, *Class and Class Conflict in Industrial Society* (Stanford University Press 1959).

Fifth, a political program of enacting and enforcing hate speech prohibitions runs the danger of diverting political energy from arguably more meaningful political responses to the underlying causes of racism. Three obvious and arguably more valuable places to put these energies can be noted – improving the material conditions of those who are the typical targets of hate, affirmative and public expressive rejection of hate (the more speech solution), and changes the conditions that fester hate among some portions of society. As to this last, often purveyors of racism have themselves experienced forms of social or material discrimination (or deprivation) – and sometimes they even list their depressed material condition as evidence justifying disparaging racist views. Changing their material conditions is crucial to a long-term nonrepressive response to hate. Even though full consideration of the causes of racism is far beyond the scope of this chapter (and my understanding), social and material conditions, including those that generate feelings of economic and social marginalization, are likely contexts in which racial resentment flourishes. Changing these conditions, combined with creating contexts that can defuse racist attitudes, could make a significant difference in the likelihood of outbreaks of racial violence as well as in the ubiquity of racial hate. The prospects of successful suppression of hate speech may not be good, and may even exacerbate the problem, but the possibility of reducing (albeit probably not eliminating) underlying causes may be real. Political energy should be devoted to this task.

Anticensorship feminists made a similar point in debates about regulation of pornography. Although their substantive views about pornography varied greatly, the anticensorship feminists were united both in the view that the existing social order operated to oppress women in many spheres and that a strategy of trying to suppress pornography was a misdirection of their political energy.[41] Similarly, the more meaningful political responses to racism include fighting racism within public discourse, referred to in the first point earlier, but also efforts to change social conditions that generate the alienation of groups among which racism flourishes. Equally important are policy endeavors aimed at integrating into the culture and economy typical targets of racist oppression. Creation and effective enforcement of laws prohibiting discrimination in employment and education, as well as affirmative recruitment or subsidy of typical targets of racism, could help change the material conditions that create racial oppression. The goal should be to change the material conditions that reflect, breed, and sustain racial hatred.

As an example of wrongly directed energies, I once observed corporate leaders showing their liberality by favoring suppression of hate speech (which, in any event, is not conducive to a good business climate). They thereby seemed to be (as I expect they are) caring people who, as individuals, oppose racism. These same

---

[41] Carlin Meyer, "Sex, Sin, and Women's Liberation: Against Porn Suppression," 72 *Texas L. Rev.* 1097 (1994); Nadine Strossen, "A Feminist Critique of 'the' Feminist Critique of Pornography," 79 *Virginia L. Rev.* 1099 (1993).

leaders, however, often oppose legal civil rights provisions that would force their firms to take responsibility for a lack of minorities in their workforce or discrimination against minorities on the job. It is hard to avoid the cynical view that this politics favors the superficial, and, for these businesses, the inexpensive remedy over real material responses to underlying social conditions that contribute to racism and racial subordination.[42]

Finally, a prohibition on even a narrowly formulated category of hate speech embodies a principle that will be hard to circumscribe. There are two problems here. First, these laws are likely to be abused by those in power, who will often be able to characterize the speech or politics of their opponents as amounting to hate speech or its equivalent. Consider possible characterizations: that labor agitators ferment class hatred and, potentially, class violence; lesbians ferment hatred of and violence against men; black nationalists make racist attacks on whites; Algerians insult the French. Today I suspect that mainstream majorities, with prosecutors ready to do their part, see the main purveyors of hate to be the many radical Muslims who, if not terrorists themselves, seem to be nurturing the hate that leads to terrorism. Majoritarian prejudices have an almost inescapable capacity to seem, to these majorities, as simply a description of reality and their expression not dangerous. Thus, it is much more likely that "vile" radical mullahs will be prosecuted than that those who hold this view of Muslims will be. Nadine Strossen has argued that the typical use of laws prohibiting hate speech or related offenses against honor, even if adopted to protect minority groups, are most often used to defend dominant groups and punish minority group members or suppress their speech.[43] Minorities in Ethiopia have been punished under hate speech laws for their criticisms of Ethiopia's dominant ethnic group.[44] In Rwanda today, the dominant regime appears to find criminal expressions of genocidal ideology everywhere, even among its moderate democratic adversaries and former and would-be supporters.[45] That is, hate speech prohibitions have been continually used to punish activists among oppressed groups for the criticism of dominant groups.

The second problem involves the slippery slope both in application of these categories and use of the justification. Any principle that allows restrictions on speech that preaches hate will be hard to contain. Suppression of other "harmful" speech to

---

[42] See a similar suggestion in James Weinstein, *Hate Speech, Pornography, and the Radical Attack on Free Speech Doctrine* 155–6 (Westview Press 1999).

[43] Nadine Strossen, "Hate Speech and Pornography: Do We Have to Choose Between Freedom of Speech and Equality?" 46 *Case W. Res. L. Rev.* 449, 465–70 (1996).

[44] Yared Legesse Mengistu, "Shielding Marginalized Groups from Verbal Assaults Without Abusing Hate Speech Laws," Chapter 19 herein. Similar reports of the use of hate speech laws to suppress democratic opposition to the regime in power were offered by speakers at a panel, of which I was the moderator, entitled "Freedom of Speech and the Legislation of Memory," at *Healing the Wounds: Speech, Identity, and Reconciliation in Rwanda*, Cardozo School of Law (Mar. 30, 2009) (panel of Jacqueline Bakamurera, Susan Benesch, Peter Molnar, and Lars Waldorf).

[45] This point was made manifest both by speakers and in informal conversation at the March 2009 Cardozo panel, *supra* note 44.

deal with other nasty problems will seem similar. Virtually all laws aiming to restrict speech can use as a justification that the law responds to real harms. However, most laws restricting speech see application only or primarily against marginal individuals and groups – the outsiders or dissenters who should be the primary beneficiaries of speech protection.[46] A real danger to free speech is that prohibitions on hate speech, justified because of the serious harm the expression can cause, are likely to justify other restrictions on the basis of arguments about other purported harms with the net effect of further subordinating the disempowered.

Even without any certainty that the prohibitions will have meaningfully beneficial effects, caution might at first seem to justify prohibitions of hate speech. If, however, the six points listed here are right, that is precisely the wrong conclusion. Instead, if these points are right, caution would accept the necessity of some real harm out of a realistic fear that prohibitions would overall be counterproductive and lead to even worse results. Those six reasons were: (1) allowing and then combating hate speech discursively is the only real way to keep alive the understanding of the evil of racial hatred; (2) forcing hate speech underground obscures the extent and location of the problem to which society must respond; (3) suppression of hate speech is likely to increase racists' sense of oppression and their willingness to express their views violently; (4) suppression is likely to reduce the societal self-understanding that democracy means not eliminating conflict through suppression – what Justice Jackson described as the unanimity of the graveyard[47] – but rather moving conflict from the plane of violence to the plane of politics; (5) legal prohibition and enforcement of laws against hate speech are likely to divert political energies away from more effective and meaningful responses, especially those directed at changing material conditions in which racism festers, material conditions of both the purveyors and targets of hate; and (6) the principle justifying prohibitions and the specific laws prohibiting hate speech are likely to be abused, creating a slippery slope to results contrary to the needs of victims of racial hatred (including jailing the subjects of racial hatred for their verbal responses) and to the needs of other marginalized groups.

Thus, my fear is the precedent of punishing racial hate speech, even punishing loosely defined genocidal speech, may itself contribute to tragedy. For example, as I understand the facts, the International Tribunal's conviction of Rwandan radio broadcasters for genocide based on their speech, speech which was integrated into the actual practice of murder much like that of the leader of a pack of gunmen who directs subordinates as to whom to shoot, was proper and would have been proper under the relevant U.S. free-speech doctrine relating to intentional creation of a clear and present danger of crime.[48] The First Amendment does not protect a person in using speech in an attempt to commit a crime.[49] The speaker who gives

---

[46] Shiffrin, *supra* note 26, at 121–30.
[47] *Barnette*, 319 U.S. at 641.
[48] *Brandenburg v. Ohio*, 395 U.S. 444 (1969).
[49] Hans A. Linde, "'Clear and Present Danger' Reexamined: Dissonance in the *Brandenburg* Concerto," 22 *Stan. L. Rev.* 1163 (1970).

orders to her associated gunmen is properly treated as having participated in any murder they commit. However, conviction for genocide of the Rwandan newspaper publisher, Hassan Ngeze, who periodically published racist diatribes against the Hutus' traditional oppressors and purported to speak in defense of his historically subordinated group, under circumstances where they were under armed attack by those oppressors,[50] and who published his views substantially before the occurrence of the genocidal murders, sets a troubling precedent.[51]

As I see it, if cycles of oppression and societal violence are to be broken, a society desperately needs to create a culture of open expression where all views, especially the most extreme views, are openly expressed and debated. In contrast, legal prohibitions on racist speech – to the extent that they would (often did) exist where "needed" but given how much and against whom these laws most likely would be (or were) enforced – would not have, or perhaps rather might not have, prevented the occurrence of the genocide in Rwanda or elsewhere. But the mere existence of the International Tribunal's precedent of jailing this publisher is likely to be used – I have been told informally, has been used – by those in power in African countries at a similar stage in the development of civil society and of democracy to suppress expression of opposition groups. The precedent might even be used (or, more accurately, "abused") to justify punishment of "disrespectful" or "inaccurate" speech about those in power. The impact of this precedent on a nation, through its impact on press freedom, can be hugely significant. Any consequent lack of free press will contribute greatly to the likelihood of corruption in existing governments and to making any replacements of ruling elites much more likely to come only through violence. If my fears are right, the International Tribunal could have hardly given Africa a worse present.

My main pragmatic point, I suppose, is to doubt the validity of the hypothesis that a legal prohibition of (necessarily only some) racist speech, speech that admittedly occurs in contexts that produce genocidal results, would contribute to preventing such events. More specifically, the empirical suppositions justifying this opposition to hate speech regulation are:

1.   Speech prohibitions will be ineffective. Contexts in which genocide practices occur are ones in which enforcement of hate speech prohibitions will not occur, and the development of such contexts will not be effectively prevented by earlier attempts to legally suppress hate speech. Too many bigoted practices and expressions will fly below the radar screen of any speech prohibitions.

---

[50]   The complicated and frequently deadly political background of the Rwanda genocide is often ignored in popular accounts, but some of the groundwork was laid by the 1959 revolution, the transfer of power from the traditional minority Tutsi elite to a Hutu elite, the subsequent racialized contestations, and then, most importantly, the invasion by the basically Tutsi Rwanda Patriotic Front (RPF) continuing from 1990. See Mahmood Mamdani, *When Victims Become Killers* (Princeton University Press 2001).

[51]   See Prosecutor v. Nahimana, Yagwiza, and Ngeze, No. ICTR-99–52-T (Dec. 3, 2003); C. Edwin Baker, "Genocide, Press Freedom, and the Case of Hassan Ngeze," U. Penn. Law School, Public Law Working Paper No. 46 (2003), *available at* http://ssrn.com/abstract=480762.

2. Regulation of hate speech may affirmatively contribute to the rise of racist genocidal cultures or polities.
3. A key, albeit hardly the only, element in the most effective strategy of preventing the rise of such a culture or polity is to provide for more robust protection of speech.

V

As a concluding comment, I want to indicate awareness of the fact that hate speech causes many real harms, many real injuries. Although I reject such a conclusion, these injuries could plausibly justify suppression of hate speech even if suppression were not a wise way to respond the most dramatic evils of racism. For two reasons, this chapter does not address arguments for suppression of hate speech based on these other injuries. First, much of the commentary explaining America's purported exceptionalism, its (purportedly) greater protection of speech, especially of hate speech, involves Europe's twentieth-century close-up experience with fascism and the Holocaust. I wanted therefore in this chapter to rebut the suggestion that some countries have reasons to restrict hate speech different from the reasons operable in the United States. Thus, I needed to argue that this historical experience does not justify, whether or not it explains, a purportedly different European evaluation of free speech. In this regard, I might note that the single most defining element of the American experience, continually reflected in countless aspects of American law, especially in our policy failures, is the legacy of African-American slavery and the American Civil War. Europe hardly has a monopoly on hate, on hate speech, or on racism.

Second, even though the arguments that racist speech causes real harms is surely right, that point is hardly unique to racist speech. Real harm is caused by most speech that judges or legislatures consider as possible bases for legal liability or punishment.[52] Here is not the place to discuss the point, but one or both of the reasons given here to protect speech – either normative views that protection is necessary to justify the legitimacy of the legal order or pragmatic arguments about bad consequences of accepting the propriety of regulation – justify a speech-protective stance despite the harm speech can and does cause. This is especially true given the inevitable errors of identifying what speech causes greater harm than benefits and given the inevitable chilling effect of speech regulation on valuable speech.

Justice Holmes argued that our theory of free speech "is an experiment, as all life is an experiment." It is a "wager . . . based on imperfect knowledge."[53] Given lack of

---

[52] *See* Baker, *supra* note 1, at 979–82, 986–8.
[53] Abrams v. United States, 250 U.S. 616, 624 (1919) (Holmes, J., dissenting). Holmes observed the impotence of what he characterized as the "silly leaflet[s] by an unknown man" involved in the case. *Id.* at 628. But he was hardly basing protection of speech on its being impotent, as Waldron suggests (*see* Waldron, *supra* note 15, at 1617), when he said that "we should be eternally vigilant against attempts

adequate evidence for any certainty about the guess whether suppression or freedom provides the best security, I think wisdom requires that choice favor liberty. Liberty is the choice if people are fundamentally good and worthy of respect – suppression is the choice if the opposite holds factually. We are worthy of intellectual and legal concern only if the former is true. For this reason, recognizing that the guess may turn out to be wrong, I would rather have hazarded the guess that justifies a concern with the circumstances and future of humanity. Only then would being right in the guess matter. Moreover, I suspect, given that the answer is not writ in stone, that such a guess can be part of a self-fulfilling prophesy. If so, it is clear which prophesy should be favored.

to check the expression of opinions that we loathe and believe to be fraught with death," 250 U.S. at 630, or when, in a later case, he argued that "[i]f in the long run the beliefs expressed in proletarian dictatorship are destined to be accepted by the dominant forces of the community, the only meaning of free speech is that they should be given their chance and have their way," Gitlow v. New York, 268 U.S. 652, 673 (1925) (Holmes, J., dissenting).

# 4

# Interview with Kenan Malik

**Peter Molnar:** Would you characterize some speech as "hate speech," and do you think that it is possible to provide a reliable legal definition of "hate speech"?

**Keenan Malik:** I am not sure that "hate speech" is a particularly useful concept. Much is said and written, of course, that is designed to promote hatred. But it makes little sense to lump it all together in a single category, especially when hatred is such a contested concept.

In a sense, hate speech restriction has become a means not of addressing specific issues about intimidation or incitement, but of enforcing general social regulation. This is why if you look at hate speech laws across the world, there is no consistency about what constitutes hate speech. Britain bans abusive, insulting, and threatening speech. Denmark and Canada ban speech that is insulting and degrading. India and Israel ban speech that hurts religious feelings and incites racial and religious hatred. In Holland, it is a criminal offense deliberately to insult a particular group. Australia prohibits speech that offends, insults, humiliates, or intimidates individuals or groups. Germany bans speech that violates the dignity of, or maliciously degrades or defames, a group. And so on.[1] In each case, the law defines hate speech in a different way.

One response might be to say: Let us define hate speech much more tightly. I think, however, that the problem runs much deeper. Hate speech restriction is a means not of tackling bigotry but of rebranding certain, often obnoxious, ideas or arguments as *immoral*. It is a way of making certain ideas illegitimate without bothering politically to challenge them. And that is dangerous.

**PM:** Setting aside legal restriction, would you differentiate between claims (that target certain groups) that should be challenged in political debate and claims

---

[1] *See generally Striking a Balance: Hate Speech, Freedom of Expression and Non-discrimination* (Sandra Coliver ed., Article 19 and University of Essex 1992).

This interview was conducted as an email exchange in January and February 2011. Eds.

(that also target certain groups) that should be simply rejected as so immoral that they don't deserve an answer other than the strongest rejection and moral condemnation?

**KM:** There are certainly claims that are so outrageous that one would not wish to waste one's time refuting them. If someone were to suggest that all Muslims should be tortured because they are potential terrorists, or that rape is acceptable, then clearly no rational argument will ever change their mind, or that of anyone who accepts such claims.

Much of what we call hate speech consists, however, of claims that may be contemptible but yet are accepted by many as morally defensible. Hence I am wary of the argument that some sentiments are so immoral they can simply be condemned without being contested. First, such blanket condemnations are often a cover for the inability or unwillingness politically to challenge obnoxious sentiments. Second, in challenging obnoxious sentiments, we are not simply challenging those who spout such views; we are also challenging the potential audience for such views. Dismissing obnoxious or hateful views as not worthy of response may not be the best way of engaging with such an audience. Whether or not an obnoxious claim requires a reply depends, therefore, not simply on the nature of the claim itself, but also on the potential audience for that claim.

**PM:** What do you think about proposals for restricting defamation of religion?

**KM:** It is as idiotic to imagine that one could defame religion as it is to imagine that one could defame politics or literature. Or that the Bible or the Qur'an should not be criticized or ridiculed in the same way as one might criticize or ridicule *The Communist Manifesto* or *On the Origin of Species* or Dante's *Inferno*.

A religion is, in part, a set of beliefs – about the world, its origins, and humanity's place in it – and a set of values that supposedly derive from those beliefs. Those beliefs and values should be treated no differently than any other sets of beliefs, and values that derive from them. I can be hateful of conservatism or communism. It should be open to me to be equally hateful of Islam and Christianity.

Proponents of religious defamation laws suggest that religion is not just a set of beliefs but an identity, and an exceptionally deeply felt one at that. It is true that religions often form deep-seated identities. But then, so do many other beliefs. Communists were often wedded to their ideas even unto death. Many racists have an almost visceral attachment to their beliefs. Should I indulge them because their views are so deeply held? And while I do not see my humanism as an Identity with a capitol "I," I would challenge any Christian or Muslim to demonstrate that my beliefs are less deeply held than theirs.

Freedom of worship – including the freedom of believers to believe as they wish and to preach as they wish – should be protected. Beyond that, religion should have no privileges. Freedom of worship is, in a sense, another form of freedom of expression – the freedom to believe as one likes about the divine and to assemble and enact rituals with respect to those beliefs. You cannot protect freedom of worship, in other words, without protecting freedom of expression. Take, for instance, Geert Wilders' attempt to outlaw the Qur'an in Holland because it "promotes hatred."[2] Or the investigation by the British police a few years ago of Iqbal Sacranie, former head of the Muslim Council of Britain, for derogatory comments he made about homosexuality.[3] Both are examples of the way that defense of freedom of religion is inextricably linked with defense of freedom of speech. Or, to put it another way, in both cases, had the authorities been allowed to restrict freedom of expression, it would have had a devastating impact on freedom of worship.

That is why the attempt to restrict defamation of religion is, ironically, an attack not just on freedom of speech but on freedom of worship too – and not least because one religion necessarily defames another. Islam denies the divinity of Christ; Christianity refuses to accept the Qur'an as the word of God. Each Holy Book blasphemes against the others.

One of the ironies of the current Muslim campaign for a law against religious defamation is that had such a law existed in the seventh century, Islam itself would never have been born. The creation of the faith was shocking and offensive to the adherents of the pagan religion out of which it grew, and equally so to the two other monotheistic religions of the age, Judaism and Christianity. Had seventh-century versions of today's religious censors had their way, the twenty-first-century versions may still have been fulminating against offensive speech, but it certainly would not have been Islam that was being offended.

At the heart of the debate about defamation of religion are actually not questions of faith or hatred, but of political power. Demanding that certain things cannot be said, whether in the name of respecting faith or of not offending cultures, is a means of defending the power of those who claim legitimacy in the name of that faith or that culture. It is a means of suppressing dissent, not from outside, but from within. What is often called offense *to* a community or a faith is actually a debate *within* that community or faith. In accepting that certain things cannot be said because they are offensive or hateful, those who wish to restrict free speech are simply siding with one side in such debates – and usually the more conservative, reactionary side.

**PM:** Do you support content-based bans of "hate speech" through the criminal law, or do you instead agree with the American and Hungarian approach, which permits prohibition only of speech that creates imminent danger?

**KM:** I believe that *no* speech should be banned solely because of its content; I would distinguish "content-based" regulation from "effects-based" regulation and permit the prohibition only of speech that creates imminent danger. I oppose content-based

---

2  *See* Ian Traynor, "'I don't hate Muslims. I hate Islam,' says Holland's rising political star," *The Observer*, Feb. 17, 2008, at 40.
3  Nigel Morris, "Hate crime inquiry into 'anti-gay' Sacranie," *The Independent (London)*, Jan. 12, 2006, at 5.

bans both as a matter of principle and with a mind to the practical impact of such bans. Such laws are wrong in principle because free speech for everyone except bigots is not free speech at all. It is meaningless to defend the right of free expression for people with whose views we agree. The right to free speech only has political bite when we are forced to defend the rights of people with whose views we profoundly disagree.[4]

And in practice, you cannot reduce or eliminate bigotry simply by banning it. You simply let the sentiments fester underground. As Milton once put it, to keep out "evil doctrine" by licensing is "like the exploit of that gallant man who thought to pound up the crows by shutting his Park-gate."[5]

Take Britain. In 1965, Britain prohibited incitement to racial hatred as part of its Race Relations Act.[6] The following decade was probably the most racist in British history. It was the decade of "Paki-bashing," when racist thugs would seek out Asians to beat up. It was a decade of firebombings, stabbings, and murders. In the early 1980s, I was organizing street patrols in East London to protect Asian families from racist attacks.

Nor were thugs the only problem. Racism was woven into the fabric of public institutions. The police, immigration officials – all were openly racist. In the twenty years between 1969 and 1989, no fewer than thirty-seven blacks and Asians were killed in police custody – almost one every six months. The same number again died in prisons or in hospital custody.[7] When in 1982 cadets at the national police academy were asked to write essays about immigrants, one wrote, "Wogs, nignogs and Pakis come into Britain take up our homes, our jobs and our resources and contribute relatively less to our once glorious country. They are, by nature, unintelligent. And can't at all be educated sufficiently to live in a civilised society of the Western world." Another wrote that "all blacks are pains and should be ejected from society."[8] So much for incitement laws helping create a more tolerant society.

Today, Britain is a very different place. Racism has not disappeared, nor have racist attacks, but the open, vicious, visceral bigotry that disfigured the Britain when I was growing up has largely ebbed away. It has done so not because of laws banning racial hatred but because of broader social changes and because minorities themselves stood up to the bigotry and fought back.

---

4  The classic statement of this proposition in Anglo-American jurisprudence is from Justice Holmes: "[I]f there is any principle of the Constitution that more imperatively calls for attachment than any other it is the principle of free thought – not free thought for those who agree with us but freedom for the thought that we hate." United States v. Schwimmer, 279 U.S. 644, 654–55 (1929) (Holmes, J., dissenting). *See also* Anthony Lewis, *Freedom for the Thought That We Hate* (Basic Books 2008).

5  John Milton, *Areopagitica: A Speech for the Liberty of Unlicensed Printing to the Parliament of England* (1644).

6  Race Relations Act, 1965, c. 73, § 6 (Eng.).

7  Figures adapted from Institute of Race Relations, *Deadly Silence: Black Deaths in Custody* (Institute of Race Relations 1991).

8  *See Policing London*, No. 4 (Greater London Council Nov. 1982).

Of course, as the British experience shows, hatred exists not just in speech but also has physical consequences. Is it not important, critics of my view ask, to limit the fomenting of hatred to protect the lives of those who may be attacked? In asking this very question, they are revealing the distinction between speech and action. Saying something is not the same as doing it. But, in these post-ideological, postmodern times, it has become very unfashionable to insist on such a distinction.

In blurring the distinction between speech and action, what is really being blurred is the idea of human agency and of moral responsibility. Because lurking underneath the argument is the idea that people respond like automata to words or images. But people are not like robots. They think and reason and act on their thoughts and reasoning. Words certainly have an impact on the real world, but that impact is mediated through human agency.

Racists are, of course, influenced by racist talk. It is they, however, who bear responsibility for translating racist talk into racist action. Ironically, for all the talk of using free speech responsibly, the real consequence of the demand for censorship is to moderate the responsibility of individuals for their actions.

Having said that, there are clearly circumstances in which there is a direct connection between speech and action, where someone's words have directly led to someone else taking action. Such incitement should be illegal, but it has to be tightly defined. There has to be both a direct link between speech and action and intent on the part of the speaker for that particular act of violence to be carried out.

Incitement to violence in the context of hate speech should be as tightly defined as in ordinary criminal cases. In ordinary criminal cases, incitement is, rightly, difficult legally to prove. The threshold for liability should not be lowered just because hate speech is involved.

**PM:** How tightly should we define the connection between incitement and the imminent danger of action? What about racist slogans in a soccer stadium, and imminent danger of violence on the crowded streets after the end of the game?

**KM:** Racist slogans, like any racist speech, should be a moral issue, not a legal one. If supporters are clearly set to attack others, or are directly inciting others to do so, then, of course, it becomes a matter for the law.

**PM:** What about this example: At the 2009 gay pride parade in Budapest, peaceful marchers were attacked. Some onlookers merely shouted homophobic statements; others, no doubt encouraged by the taunting, threw eggs and rocks at the marchers. If the hecklers later stated that they had not intended to incite violence, should they be subject to punishment or liability?

**KM:** Such questions cannot be answered in the abstract; it depends on the context. I would need to know more factual details than you have provided. If the two groups you mention were independent of each other and happened to turn up at the gay march at the same time, and if the perpetrators of violence would have attacked the marchers anyway, then I don't see that the non-violent homophobes have a legal case to answer. The non-violent homophobes are no more responsible for the violence of the violent homophobes in those circumstances than peaceful anti-globalization protestors are responsible for the actions of fellow-protestors who trash Starbucks or set cars alight.

If, on the other hand, there was a relationship between the two groups, or if the one was clearly egging on the other, and if without such encouragement the violent protestors would not have been violent, then, yes, there may well be a case to answer.

**PM:** What if the two groups of anti-globalization protestors are not independent from each other, if they belong to the same group, just some/most of them are peacefully shouting slogans, while others are acting violently? Would you draw a line between slogans – uttered without violence – that are hateful and slogans that might be angry but do not incite hatred?

**KM:** People should have the legal right to shout slogans, even hateful ones, and even though we might morally despise them for doing so. The law should deal with people acting violently, or those that directly incite others to violence. To "incite hatred," as you put it, should not, of itself, be a criminal offense; the distinction is again between a particular *attitude* and a particular *action*.

**PM:** In that case, suppose the action is not violence but discrimination. That is, should it be only the imminent danger of violence that can justify restriction to speech, or does the imminent danger of discrimination suffice?

**KM:** I support laws against discrimination in the public sphere. But I absolutely oppose laws against the advocacy of discrimination. Equality is a political concept, and one to which I subscribe. But many people don't. It is clearly a highly contested concept. Should there be continued Muslim immigration into Europe? Should indigenous workers get priority in social housing? Should gays be allowed to adopt? These are all questions being keenly debated at the moment. I have strong views on all these issues, based on my belief in equality. But it would be absurd to suggest that only people who hold my kind of views should be able to advocate them. I find arguments against Muslim immigration, against equal access to housing, against gay adoptions unpalatable. But I accept that these are legitimate political arguments. A society that outlawed such arguments would, in my mind, be as reactionary as one that banned Muslim immigration or denied gays rights.

**PM:** But what about advocacy of discrimination that creates imminent danger of discrimination? For example, when members of a minority group would like to enter a restaurant or a bar and someone vehemently tells the security guard at the door that those people should not be allowed in.

**KM:** An individual who advocates such discrimination may be morally despicable but should not be held to have committed a legal offense. The security guard, however, and the establishment that so discriminates should be answerable to the law.

**PM:** Do you think that we can find a universal approach to criminal law restriction to incitement to hatred? Or should the regulation depend on the cultural context, and if so, in what way regulation could be different?

**KM:** I believe that free speech is a universal good and that all human societies best flourish with the greatest extension of free speech. It is often said, for example, even by free-speech advocates, that there is a case for Germany banning Holocaust denial. I don't accept that. Even in Germany – especially in Germany – what is needed is an open and robust debate on this issue.

**PM:** Would you suggest the same for Rwanda?

**KM:** Yes I would. What Rwanda requires is not the suppression of the deep-seated animosities but the ability of people openly to debate their differences. It's worth adding, given the argument for state regulation of hate speech, that in Rwanda it was the state that promoted the hatred that led to such devastating consequences.[9]

**PM:** What would imminent danger caused by incitement to hatred mean in such an environment? In other words: Do you think that the legal concept of this imminence of danger can be contextual?

**KM:** The meaning of "imminent danger" clearly depends upon circumstances. What constitutes imminent danger in, say, London or New York, where there exists a relatively stable, relatively liberal society, and a fairly robust framework of law and order, may be different from what constitutes imminent danger in Kigali or even in Moscow. And the meaning of imminent danger for a Jew in Berlin in 1936 was clearly different from that for a Jew – or a Muslim – in Berlin in 2011. At the same time, in those times and in those societies in which particular groups are being made targets of intense hostility, this debate becomes almost irrelevant. In a climate of extreme hatred, as in Rwanda in 1994, or in Germany in the 1930s, it may be easier to incite people into harming others. But in such a climate, the niceties of what legally constitutes "imminent harm" would, and should, be the least of our worries. What would matter would be to confront such hatred and prejudice head on, both politically and physically.

What I am wary of is that in accepting the commonsense view that what constitutes danger is dependent on circumstances, we should not make the concept so elastic as

---

9 *See* Report on the Situation of Human Rights in Rwanda submitted by Mr. René Degni-Ségui, Special Rapporteur of the Commission on Human Rights, under paragraph 20 of Commission Resolution E/CN. 4/S-3/1 of 25 May 1994, U.N. ESCOR, Comm'n on Hum. Rts., 51st Sess., Prov. Agenda Item 12, P 25, U.N. Doc. E/CN. 4/1995/71 (1995), P 9(a), 26(a), 26(b). *See also* United State Institute for Peace, *Rwanda: Accountability for War Crimes and Genocide* (1995), *available at* http://www.usip.org/publications/rwanda-accountability-war-crimes-and-genocide.

to render it meaningless. Whether in London, New York, Berlin, or Kigali, speech should only be curtailed if such speech directly incites an act that causes or could cause physical harm to others and if individuals are in imminent danger of such harm because of those words. What is contextual is that in different circumstances, different kinds of speech could potentially place individuals in the way of such harm.

**PM:** Do you think that violent acts committed by hateful motivation deserve stricter punishments?

**KM:** I accept that intentions are not just morally but also legally relevant, and that different intentions can result in the imposition of different sentences. But when we make a distinction between, say, murder and manslaughter, we are making a distinction based on the kind or degree of harm the perpetrator intended. When it is suggested, however, that a racist murderer should receive a greater punishment than a non-racist murderer, a different kind of distinction is being drawn. The distinction here is not between the degrees of harm intended – in both cases the killer intended to kill – but between the thoughts that were in the minds of the respective killers. The distinction is between someone who might be thinking, "I am going to kill you because I hate you because you looked at me the wrong way" and someone who might be thinking, "I am going to kill you because I hate you because you are black."

What is being criminalized here is simply a thought. And I am opposed to the category of thought crimes. Racist thoughts are morally offensive. But they should not be made a criminal offense.

Proponents argue that raising the punishment for hate crimes will (1) protect those who are abused or attacked simply because they belong to a particular group, and (2) send a message about the kind of society we wish to promote.[10] But that is not fundamentally different from the argument for the criminalization of hate speech. And I am opposed to it for the same reason that I am opposed to the criminalization of hate speech.

**PM:** But does it not make a substantial difference that one might be able to avoid being attacked by not looking at her/his potential attackers the wrong way, while one cannot change her/his skin color?

**KM:** To the victim, such a distinction is, of course, of little comfort. There is also an implication here that some victims cannot help being victims, while others could, by having behaved differently, have avoided their misfortune. While this is not the same as suggesting that some victims ask to be victims, it is moving in that direction, and we should be careful about how far down this road we go.

The real issue remains the same: Should murderers with racist intent be punished to a greater degree than those with other kinds of malicious intent? I accept that

---

[10] *See generally* Frederick M. Lawrence, "The Punishment of Hate: Toward a Normative Theory of Bias-Motivated Crimes," 93 *Mich. L. Rev.* 320 (1994).

racism is a pernicious social evil that needs specifically to be combated. But I reject the idea that we can, and should, combat racism by outlawing racist thoughts. If you accept, as I do, that thoughts in themselves – even racist thoughts – should not be legally prohibited, then you have to accept that a racist thought that leads to murder should not be seen as legally different from a nonracist thought that leads to murder.

**PM:** How, in your view, could we improve the social (non-legal) responses to "hate speech"?

**KM:** The whole point of free speech is to create the conditions for robust debate, to be able to challenge obnoxious views. To argue for free speech but not to utilize it to challenge obnoxious, odious, and hateful views seems to me immoral. It is morally incumbent on those who argue for free speech to stand up to racism and bigotry.

At the same time, however, we should be clear that what often legitimizes bigotry are the arguments not of the bigots but of mainstream politicians and intellectuals who denounce bigotry and yet accept bigoted claims. Throughout Europe, mainstream politicians have denounced the rise of the far right. And throughout Europe, mainstream politicians have adapted to far-right arguments, clamping down on immigration, pursuing anti-Muslim measures, and so on. They have sometimes even adopted the language. In his first speech at the Labour Party conference after gaining the top office, former British Prime Minister Gordon Brown talked of ensuring "British jobs for British workers,"[11] a slogan first popularized by the neofascist National Front.[12] The National Front had twinned it with a second slogan: "Three million blacks. Three million unemployed. Kick the blacks out."

Gordon Brown was, of course, not guilty of hate speech. But his use of that phrase probably did far more to promote xenophobic sentiment than any amount of "hate speech" by far-right bigots. Challenging bigotry requires us to challenge the mainstream ideas that give it sustenance, and to campaign against those discriminatory social practices and laws that help make the arguments of the racists, the sexists, and the homophobes more acceptable.

**PM:** Do you think that banning "hate speech" undermines, or at least weakens, the legitimacy of a democracy?

**KM:** Free speech and democracy are intimately linked. Without free speech there is no democracy. That is why any restriction on speech must be kept to the absolute minimum.

There are two ways in which banning hate speech undermines democracy. First, democracy can only work if every citizen believes that their voice counts. That

[11] Gordon Brown, Speech to the Labour Conference (Sept. 24, 2007) (transcript *available at* http://news.bbc.co.uk/2/hi/uk_news/politics/7010664.stm).

[12] John Rentoul, "'British jobs' blows up in the PM's face; Gordon Brown's disastrous mistake in using the language of the BNP on immigration is a gift to the Tories," *The Independent on Sunday*, Nov. 4, 2007, at 40.

however outlandish, outrageous, or obnoxious one's belief may be, they nevertheless have the right to express it and to try to win support for it. When people feel they no longer possess that right, then democracy itself suffers, as does the legitimacy of those in power.

Not just the banning of hate speech but the very categorization of an argument or a sentiment as "hate speech" can be problematic for the democratic process. I am in no doubt that some speech is designed to promote hatred. And I accept that certain arguments – like the direct incitement of violence – should indeed be unlawful. But the category "hate speech" has come to function quite differently from prohibitions on incitement to violence. It has become a means of rebranding obnoxious political arguments as immoral and so beyond the boundaries of accepted reasonable debate. It makes certain sentiments illegitimate, thereby disenfranchising those who hold such views.

And this brings me to the second point as to why the banning of hate speech undermines democracy. Branding an opinion as "hate speech" does not simply disenfranchise those holding such a view; it also absolves the rest of us of the responsibility of politically challenging it. Where once we might have challenged obnoxious or hateful sentiments politically, today we are more likely simply to seek to outlaw them.

In 2007, James Watson, the codiscoverer of the structure of DNA, claimed of Africans that their "intelligence is not the same as ours" and that blacks are genetically intellectually inferior.[13] He was rightly condemned for his arguments. But most of those who condemned him did not bother challenging the arguments, empirically or politically. They simply insisted that it is morally unacceptable to imagine that blacks are intellectually inferior. Britain's Equality and Human Rights Commission studied the remarks to see if it could bring any legal action. London's Science Museum, at which Watson was to have delivered a lecture, canceled his appearance, claiming that the Nobel Laureate had "gone beyond the point of acceptable debate."[14] New York's Cold Spring Harbor Laboratory, of which Watson was director, not only disowned Watson's remarks but forced him eventually to resign.[15]

I fundamentally disagree with Watson. Indeed I have written more than one book challenging such ideas,[16] and have many times publicly debated their supporters. But I also think that it was as legitimate for Watson to have expressed his opinion as it is for me to express mine, even if I believe his assertion was factually wrong, morally

[13] Cahal Milmo, "Celebrated scientist attacked for race comments," *The Independent (London)*, Oct. 17, 2007, at 2.

[14] Cahal Milmo, "Science Museum cancels talk by Watson after 'racist' comments," *The Independent (London)*, Oct. 18, 2007, at 6.

[15] Cornelia Dean, "James Watson Quits Post after Remarks on Races," *N.Y. Times*, Oct. 26, 2007, at A18.

[16] See, e.g., Kenan Malik, *Strange Fruit: Why Both Sides are Wrong in the Race Debate* (Oneworld Publications 2008); Kenan Malik, *The Meaning of Race: Race, History and Culture in Western Society* (Macmillan Press/NYU Press 1996).

suspect, and politically offensive.[17] Simply to dismiss Watson's claim as beyond the bounds of reasonable debate is to refuse to confront the actual arguments, to decline to engage with an idea that clearly has considerable purchase, and therefore to do disservice to democracy.

**PM:** Thank you so much for the interview.

**KM:** My pleasure.

---

[17] Nadine Strossen makes a similar point with regard to the contretemps regarding Harvard President Larry Summers raising the question whether the underrepresentation of women in the sciences might have a biological basis. *See* "Interview with Nadine Strossen," Chapter 20 herein.

# 5

# Hate Speech and the Demos

## Jamal Greene

It is sometimes said that the statist and aristocratic traditions of Europe render its political institutions less democratic than those of the United States. Richard Posner writes of "the less democratic cast of European politics, as a result of which elite opinion is more likely to override public opinion than it is in the United States."[1] If that is true, then there are obvious ways in which it figures into debates over the wisdom of hate-speech regulation. The standard European argument in favor of such regulation may easily be characterized as antidemocratic: Restrictions on hate speech protect unpopular minority groups from democracy run amok. The Nazi example states the paradigm case, even if the paradigm no longer describes the usual targets of such regulation.[2] By contrast, the American argument against hate-speech regulation is typically framed in democratic terms: Informed deliberation requires that all sides have an opportunity to be heard, with the most able policies emerging through a form of intellectual competition.[3] Or, more interestingly, full participation in a democratic community requires that self-expression not be limited to what others have deemed orthodox.[4]

There is another way, however, in which the relatively democratic character of American politics influences – or rather, should influence – the debate over

---

[1] Richard A. Posner, "The Supreme Court, 2004 Term – Foreword: A Political Court," 119 *Harv. L. Rev.* 31, 86 (2005); *see* Robert Post, "Hate Speech," in *Extreme Speech and Democracy* 123, 137 (Ivan Hare & James Weinstein eds., Oxford University Press 2009) (arguing that "democratic legitimation is a less pressing issue in Europe").

[2] *See* Michel Rosenfeld, "Hate Speech in Constitutional Jurisprudence: A Comparative Analysis," Chapter 13 herein ("Whereas in Nazi Germany hate speech was perpetrated by the government as part of its official ideology and policy, in contemporary democracies it is by and large opponents of the government and, in a wide majority of cases, members of marginalized groups with no realistic hopes of achieving political power who engage in hate speech.").

[3] *See* Abrams v. United States, 250 U.S. 616, 630 (1919) (Holmes, J., dissenting).

[4] *See* West Virginia State Board of Education v. Barnette, 319 U.S. 624, 642 (1943); C. Edwin Baker, "Autonomy and Hate Speech," in *Extreme Speech and Democracy, supra* note 1, at 139, 142–6.

regulation of offensive speech. Scholars of U.S. constitutional law have increasingly recognized that constitutional argument must not simply appeal to democratic norms but must also attend to democratic conditions. Constitutional law is not fashioned through Socratic argument among scholars and judges, nor does it follow merely from the currents of elite opinion, but it results rather from a dialogue between political institutions – including the Supreme Court – and social and political movements, against a background of often exogenous cultural conditions. Thus, we should understand *Brown v. Board of Education* not as an epiphany inspired by the force of Earl Warren's charisma or Felix Frankfurter's intellect but as a piece of a movement strategy led by the National Association for the Advancement of Colored People (NAACP) and enabled, in part, by antipathy toward fascism and Stalin's Soviet Union.[5] Changes in U.S. sex-equality law in the 1970s can be tied directly to the sexual revolution of the 1960s and the political forces behind the Equal Rights Amendment.[6] The difficulty of formal constitutional amendment through Article V requires that judges and other constitutional actors retain a degree of receptivity to popular preferences expressed through movement politics and occasioned by social change. As Robert Post and Reva Siegel write, "if the Court's interpretation of the Constitution seems wholly unresponsive, the American people will in time come to regard it as illegitimate and oppressive."[7]

The lessons of what Post and Siegel have called "democratic constitutionalism" have seldom been applied to the debate over regulation of hate speech. A ban on hate speech is a decision of constitutional dimension, and yet arguments for or against it typically rely wholly on the force of their reasoning, with little or no attention given to what more will be required for those arguments to be accepted and to acquire constitutional status. In the free-speech area no less than in other realms of constitutional law, a brilliant argument is neither sufficient nor even necessary to effect constitutional change in the United States.[8] Such arguments must engage the American people in the right way, and at the right time. This chapter, then, explores some of the positive conditions relevant to reform of hate-speech regulation. Although I glean some insight through comparison with Europe, I focus primarily on the United States, where empirical data are most complete and where the idea of democratic constitutionalism has been most fully developed.

The affluents of constitutional change in the United States include, on the one hand, political and social movements, and on the other, cultural changes that may be exogenous to those movements. Sections I and II of this chapter consider each

---

5  Brown v. Board of Education, 347 U.S. 483 (1954); *see* Mary Dudziak, *Cold War Civil Rights: Race and the Image of American Democracy* (Princeton University Press 2000).

6  *See* Reva B. Siegel, "Constitutional Culture, Social Movement Conflict and Constitutional Change: The Case of the de facto ERA," 94 *Calif. L. Rev.* 1323 (2006).

7  Robert C. Post and Reva B. Siegel, "Democratic Constitutionalism," in *The Constitution in 2020*, at 25, 28 (Jack M. Balkin & Reva B. Siegel eds., Oxford University Press 2009).

8  *See* Daniel A. Farber, "The Case Against Brilliance," 70 *Minn. L. Rev.* 917 (1986).

dimension in turn. Section I discusses the role that movement politics has played in developing and retaining a strong speech-protective norm in the United States. As Samuel Walker and others have persuasively argued, hate-speech regulation has been generally unsuccessful in the United States over the last half century in large measure because of opposition within the civil rights community.[9] Those who have organized in favor of antidiscrimination laws of other sorts have viewed speech codes as either counterproductive or outright contrary to their aims. Europe has not, by and large, seen comparable opposition to hate-speech regulation by its putative beneficiaries.

Section II addresses the cultural conditions that must attend any successful movement for reform of hate-speech laws. I begin by discussing public opinion on regulation of offensive speech. The reader will not be surprised to learn that Americans today appear to support hate-speech regulation far less than Europeans. The reader may be surprised to learn, however, that Americans support such regulation far less today than they did a decade ago. Indeed, survey data suggest that, with respect to the desirability of legal restrictions on racially offensive speech, the views of the American people of 1997 approximate those of Europeans of 2002. The relative receptivity of Americans just ten years ago to regulation of offensive speech suggests that a set of mutable conditions influences public opinion in this area. I offer and evaluate three possible considerations that might account for these changes: trust of government; sensitivity to international opinion; and opportunity for exit from prevailing community norms.

Section III discusses strategies for altering the current U.S. consensus on regulation of hate speech. Federalism's preference for piecemeal legislation may frustrate any reform movement but may at the same time allow for the trial and error needed for well-targeted intervention. Reforms might aim either at actively altering the background conditions I have identified or merely tailoring energy to opportunity. Whether or not public attitudes permit a norm in favor of hate-speech regulation to calcify may ultimately be beyond the control of reformers, but greater attention to public attitudes can at least tell them whether the iron is hot.

I

The cleavage between the restrictive European and the permissive American legal postures toward hate speech has generated extensive discussion, including in this volume. In brief, although laws and prosecutorial practices vary from state to state, virtually every European country has enacted content-based restrictions on racially insulting or inciting speech that would be patently unconstitutional in the United

---

9  Samuel Walker, *Hate Speech: The History of an American Controversy* (University of Nebraska Press 1994).

States.[10] As interpreted by the Supreme Court, the U.S. Constitution forbids states or the federal government from adopting laws required by Article 4 of the International Convention on the Elimination of All forms of Racial Discrimination (ICERD) and by Article 20(2) of the International Covenant on Civil and Political Rights (ICCPR), and the Senate has accordingly attached reservations to the United States' ratifications of those treaties.[11] Both the federal government and many state and local governments provide enhanced criminal penalties for violent crimes motivated by racial or religious animus,[12] but over the last half century, the Supreme Court has repeatedly ruled against content-based restrictions on offensive speech, and few jurisdictions have sought to test those decisions.[13]

Although it is tempting to ascribe the American position on hate speech to a kind of libertarian cultural DNA, it was not inevitable that differences with the rest of the western world would develop in this area. Consider the state of the United States in 1952. Proposed legislation outlawing group libel had been cropping up at all levels of American government; a bill introduced in Congress in 1943 by New York Congressman Walter Lynch that would have prohibited the mailing of writings expressing racial or religious hatred received three days of hearings before the Committee on Post Offices and Post Roads.[14] *New York ex rel. Bryant v. Zimmerman*, in which the Supreme Court upheld a New York requirement that the Ku Klux Klan provide membership lists, was good law, as was *Chaplinsky v. New Hampshire*, which exempted "fighting words" from First Amendment protection.[15] The Court had just decided *Dennis v. United States*, in which it upheld a conviction for conspiracy to advocate overthrow of the government; *Feiner v. New York*, in which it allowed the state to prosecute Irving Feiner for arousing public anger from a soapbox; and *Beauharnais v. Illinois*, upholding the conviction of a white supremacist who had violated the state's group libel law.[16]

---

[10] *See* Frederick Schauer, "The Exceptional First Amendment," in *American Exceptionalism and Human Rights* 29, 34–8 (Michael Ignatieff ed., Princeton University Press 2005).

[11] Article 4 of the ICERD requires States Parties to criminalize "all dissemination of ideas based on racial superiority or hatred," and to prohibit any organizations or propaganda "which promote and incite racial discrimination." Article 20(2) of the ICCPR requires prohibition of "[a]ny advocacy of national, racial or religious hatred that constitutes incitement to discrimination, hostility or violence."

[12] *See* 18 U.S.C. § 245; Wisconsin v. Mitchell, 508 U.S. 476 (1993).

[13] *See, e.g.,* R.A.V. v. City of St. Paul, 505 U.S. 377 (1992); Texas v. Johnson, 491 U.S. 397 (1989); Cohen v. California, 403 U.S. 15 (1971); Brandenburg v. Ohio, 395 U.S. 444 (1969); *see also* Collin v. Smith (*The Skokie case*), 578 F.2d 1197 (7th Cir. 1977), *cert. denied*, 439 U.S. 916 (1978). *Cf.* Virginia v. Black, 538 U.S. 343 (2003).

[14] *See* Joseph Tanenhaus, "Group Libel," 35 *Cornell L.Q.* 261, 294 (1950); Joseph Tanenhaus, "Group Libel and Free Speech," 13 *Phylon* 219 (1952).

[15] New York *ex rel.* Bryant v. Zimmerman, 278 U.S. 63 (1928); Chaplinsky v. New Hampshire, 315 U.S. 568 (1942).

[16] Dennis v. United States, 341 U.S. 494 (1951); Feiner v. New York, 340 U.S. 315 (1951); Beauharnais v. Illinois, 343 U.S. 250 (1952). Notably, three years before the Court's decision in *Beauharnais*, the Truman Administration helped draft and endorsed the German Basic Law, which expressly grounds

It was also in 1952 that the Supreme Court first set *Brown v. Board of Education* for argument.[17] That case, and the movement that agitated for it, bears crucially on the doctrine that would follow. The anti–hate speech laws that swept across Europe in the 1960s, 1970s, and 1980s were born of the same human rights impulse that facilitated the American civil rights movement. And it is easy to see how a Court primed to open the nation's racially segregated schools to black students would have sympathies for the law it allowed Illinois to apply to Joseph Beauharnais, who had distributed a leaflet calling for the mayor of Chicago to "halt the further encroachment, harassment and invasion of white people, their property, neighborhoods and persons, by the Negro."[18]

But civil rights groups were at best ambivalent toward legislation aimed at curbing offensive speech, and the NAACP actively opposed the Lynch bill.[19] An example will show why. In 1966, the Congress of Racial Equality (CORE) led a march into the all-white Chicago suburb of Cicero, Illinois, to demand open housing. Cicero, which sits 13 miles due south of Skokie, had been the site of a notorious riot in 1951 in which thousands of angry white residents had burned and looted an apartment building to prevent a black family from moving in. A year before the CORE demonstration, a black teenager looking for a summer job in Cicero had been beaten to death by a white gang.[20] The CORE marchers were met by several hundred hecklers who hurled bottles, rocks, eggs, and small explosives and had to be restrained by National Guard troops and local police.[21]

Civil rights activism required protection against a heckler's veto.[22] It required subversive organizing. It required fighting words. Indeed, during the Jim Crow era, otherwise pacific words – "No!" comes readily to mind – could, when uttered by members of particular communities, lead immediately and predictably to violence. Feiner had been made to get off his soapbox because he had given "the impression that he was endeavoring to arouse the Negro people against the whites, urging that they rise up in arms and fight for equal rights."[23] The sanction given in *Bryant* for states to require membership lists of subversive organizations had been used against the NAACP and leftist groups in the South in the 1950s, until the Supreme Court

---

limitations on its guarantee of freedom of expression in the competing "right to personal honor." Art. 5(2). The Basic Law also outlaws associations "that are directed against the constitutional order or the concept of international understanding." Art. 9(2).

[17] Brown v. Board of Education, 344 U.S. 1 (1952).

[18] *Beauharnais*, 343 U.S. at 252.

[19] Walker, *supra* note 9, at 85.

[20] *See* Paul L. Street, *Racial Oppression in the Global Metropolis: A Living Black Chicago History* 103–4 (Rowman & Littlefield 2007).

[21] *See* Donald Janson, "Guards Bayonet Hecklers in Cicero's Rights March," N.Y. *Times*, Sept. 5, 1966, at 1.

[22] I refer here to restrictions on speech imposed because of the anticipated (or actual) incivility of offended listeners.

[23] *Feiner*, 340 U.S. at 317.

declared such practices unconstitutional in *NAACP v. Alabama ex rel. Patterson*.[24] When the Court gave First Amendment protection to libelous statements in 1964, it was in the service of protecting the ability of civil rights groups to mobilize public opinion in their favor.[25]

It is not just that any speech regulation aimed at maintaining civility in public life may disproportionately affect out-groups.[26] Hate-speech restrictions in particular have a history of missing their originally intended marks. New Jersey's 1935 race-hate statute, born of violent confrontations between Nazi sympathizers and their antagonists, was used only against a group of Jehovah's Witnesses before the New Jersey Supreme Court declared the law unconstitutional in 1941.[27] In Great Britain, the Public Order Act 1936, enacted in response to the fascist threat, was used against Bertrand Russell and other antinuclear protesters in 1961. High-profile prosecutions under Britain's Race Relations Act 1965 included that of Black Power leader Michael Abdul Malik, who received a one-year prison sentence for alleged incitement of hatred against whites, and four members of the Universal Coloured People's Association, three of whom were convicted and fined a total of £270 for the same.[28] Laws aimed at protecting civil society from groups seeking to disrupt the social and political order may be a form of "militant democracy," but they may not gain the unqualified support of those who wish to dismantle a majoritarian regime marked by apartheid or other indicia of fundamental injustice. "In the absence of real political power," writes Walker, "words – extreme, emotionally loaded words – are one of the few devices available to the powerless for capturing attention, dramatizing an issue, and motivating people for change."[29]

All of which is to say that the pronounced American trend away from hate-speech restrictions when much of the world was heading the opposite way was not for lack of an argument but for lack of an arguer. The ACLU fervently opposed such laws. Civil rights groups were disapproving or, at best, conflicted. Racists – no small constituency – were understandably self-interested. Other Americans were ambivalent or did not much care. That is no formula for a constitutional moment. Jack Balkin has written that "[e]ach generation makes the Constitution their Constitution by calling upon its text and its principles and arguing about what they mean in their own time."[30] Mobilized groups in the United States in the 1950s and 1960s decided

---

[24]  357 U.S. 449 (1958).

[25]  New York Times v. Sullivan, 376 U.S. 254 (1964).

[26]  *See* Kent Greenawalt, *Speech, Crime, and the Uses of Language* 298 (Oxford University Press 1992).

[27]  Walker, *supra* note 9, at 55–6; *see* State v. Klapprott, 22 A.2d 877 (N.J. 1941).

[28]  *See* Richard P. Longaker, "The Race Relations Act of 1965: An Evaluation of the Incitement Provision," 11 *Race & Class* 125, 129 (1969); R. v. Malik, 52 Crim. App. 140 (1968) (Eng.); "Sentences Today on Four Coloured Men," *The Times* (London), Nov. 29, 1967, at 3; "Race Speeches: £270 Fines," *The Times* (London), Nov. 30, 1967, at 20.

[29]  Walker, *supra* note 9, at 111–12.

[30]  Jack M. Balkin, "Abortion and Original Meaning," 24 *Const. Commentary* 291, 302 (2007).

that cases like *West Virginia State Board of Education v. Barnette*,[31] *Terminiello v. Chicago*,[32] *NAACP v. Alabama ex rel. Patterson*,[33] and *Cohen v. California*[34] better expressed the meaning of the free-speech guarantee in their time and for their purposes than cases like *Bryant*,[35] *Chaplinsky*,[36] *Feiner*,[37] and *Beauharnais*.[38]

No serious domestic movement to challenge the American position on hate speech emerged until the 1980s, during controversies over campus speech codes. In part because of affirmative-action programs, once marginalized minorities were reaching critical mass on college campuses. A series of racist incidents across a surprisingly wide range of schools prompted many universities to adopt restrictions on certain racially offensive or intimidating speech and conduct. Minority groups and white sympathizers, many born well after the peak of the civil rights movement, viewed such restrictions in the same self-evident terms that many Europeans do today, and organized to promote them.[39]

The courts saw matters differently. Federal district courts invalidated the codes at the University of Michigan and the University of Wisconsin.[40] The Supreme Court struck down state and federal laws outlawing the burning of the American flag and a city ordinance criminalizing the display of symbols likely to arouse racial or religious hatred.[41] The doctrinal carapace against content-based regulation of offensive speech was too thick for speech-code activists to penetrate. Some measure of organization was present, but it was not sufficient to animate the population or move the courts. The activists failed to make their issue, and their pain, the nation's. Understanding why the movement failed is critical to assessing the prospects for bridging the present hate-speech divide between the United States and the rest of the western world. The episode illustrates, not for the first time, that while an argument and an arguer are necessary to produce constitutional change, they are not sufficient. Constitutional argument also needs the right audience.

---

[31] 319 U.S. 624 (1943) (holding that the First Amendment forbids compelling students to salute the American flag).

[32] 337 U.S. 1 (1949) (striking down a Chicago ordinance criminalizing speech that "stirs the public to anger, invites dispute [or] brings about a condition of unrest").

[33] 357 U.S. 449 (1957) (holding that a state law requiring the Alabama NAACP affiliate to submit membership lists violated the group members' associational rights).

[34] 403 U.S. 15 (1971) (invalidating the conviction of a man arrested for wearing a jacket with the words "Fuck the Draft" in a Los Angeles courthouse).

[35] 278 U.S. 63 (1928).

[36] 315 U.S. 568 (1942).

[37] 340 U.S. 315 (1951).

[38] 343 U.S. 250 (1952).

[39] *See* Walker, *supra* note 9, at 129–30. On campus speech codes generally, see Arthur Jacobson and Bernhard Schlink, "Hate Speech and Self-Restraint," Chapter 12 herein.

[40] Doe v. University of Michigan, 721 F. Supp. 852 (E.D. Mich. 1989); UWM Post v. Board of Regents of the University of Wisconsin, 774 F. Supp. 1163 (E.D. Wisc. 1991).

[41] Texas v. Johnson, 491 U.S. 397 (1989); United States v. Eichman, 496 U.S. 310 (1990); R.A.V. v. City of St. Paul, 505 U.S. 377 (1992).

## II

Those who promoted campus speech codes in the 1980s might have had a significant audience in the 1940s, and perhaps in the 1950s, but did not have enough of one in their own time. At least two possible lessons emanate from their experience. It might be that the American people are inalterably libertarian on speech issues, our collective consciousness permanently fixed by the Warren Court rulings and their progeny. But it is more plausible, and more true to our constitutional heritage, to conclude that the American people are inalterably dynamic, viewing arguments in the different lights of changing circumstance. In light of that condition, it would be useful to know what it takes to move public attitudes on hate-speech regulation, whether or not one supports reforming the American posture in this area. The literature on hate speech contains surprisingly little, however, even on what those attitudes might be.

The space of this chapter is too short for a comprehensive treatment, but it is possible to report some data and to critically evaluate some hypotheses. In brief, and as discussed in Subsection A, the American public today is far less enthusiastic about hate-speech regulation than its European counterpart, and, significantly, has become increasingly opposed to such regulation over the last decade. Subsection B proposes and assesses three possible explanations: a relative lack of trust in government; a frosty disposition toward international and transnational norms; and increasing opportunities for "exit" from community life.

## A

Two U.S. studies are most relevant for our purposes. Each year since 1997 (with the exception of 1998), the First Amendment Center (FAC) has commissioned a survey in which it asked American adults whether they strongly agree, mildly agree, mildly disagree, or strongly disagree with the following proposition: "People should be allowed to say things in public that might be offensive to racial groups." FAC has asked the same question with respect to religious groups each year since 2000 (with the exception of 2004). I report the FAC results in Table 5.1.

I supplement the FAC results with original data from a July 2009 Massachusetts Institute of Technology (MIT) survey of Americans' constitutional perceptions and political values.[42] The MIT survey asked 1,677 American adults the same two hate-speech questions as the FAC survey.[43] The results of the MIT survey are reported in Table 5.2. These results are of interest both as a snapshot and longitudinally. First, Americans are divided on whether people should be allowed to say things in public

---

[42] The MIT survey was commissioned by Stephen Ansolabehere with the collaboration of Nathaniel Persily and me.

[43] The MIT survey was an Internet-based survey and did not include a "don't know" option. The FAC survey comprised in-person interviews.

TABLE 5.1. *First Amendment Center survey, 1997–2008*

People should be allowed to say things in public that might be offensive to racial groups.

|  | 1997 | 1999 | 2000 | 2001 | 2002 | 2003 | 2004 | 2005 | 2006 | 2007 | 2008 |
|---|---|---|---|---|---|---|---|---|---|---|---|
| Strongly agree | 8% | 8% | 15% | 16% | 14% | 18% | 17% | 21% | 22% | 21% | 24% |
| Mildly agree | 15% | 13% | 17% | 18% | 20% | 20% | 18% | 22% | 20% | 21% | 19% |
| Mildly disagree | 14% | 16% | 15% | 15% | 16% | 14% | 14% | 14% | 13% | 12% | 12% |
| Strongly disagree | 61% | 62% | 52% | 49% | 48% | 47% | 49% | 39% | 42% | 44% | 42% |
| DK/Ref. | 2% | 1% | 1% | 2% | 1% | 1% | 1% | 3% | 2% | 2% | 2% |

People should be allowed to say things in public that might be offensive to religious groups.

|  | 2000 | 2001 | 2002 | 2003 | 2005 | 2006 | 2007 | 2008 |
|---|---|---|---|---|---|---|---|---|
| Strongly agree | 22% | 25% | 29% | 26% | 23% | 31% | 32% | 32% |
| Mildly agree | 24% | 22% | 28% | 23% | 25% | 24% | 28% | 23% |
| Mildly disagree | 15% | 16% | 14% | 14% | 15% | 16% | 12% | 12% |
| Strongly disagree | 38% | 35% | 28% | 36% | 35% | 27% | 26% | 30% |
| DK/Ref. | 1% | 3% | 2% | 1% | 4% | 2% | 2% | 2% |

*Source:* The First Amendment Center, 1997–2008, State of the First Amendment 1997–2008 [computer files] (Storrs, CT, Center for Survey Research and Analysis, University of Connecticut [producer and distributor]).

that might be racially or religiously offensive. Forty-eight percent of MIT survey respondents said that people should be permitted to make racially offensive comments, and 56 percent said the same of religiously offensive comments. Affirmative responses in the MIT survey are slightly higher in each category than in the most recent FAC survey, in which 43 percent said yes as to racially offensive speech and 55 percent said yes as to religiously offensive speech. There are also marginal differences in intensity of viewpoint. Only 20 percent of MIT respondents, compared

TABLE 5.2. *MIT survey, 2009*

|  | People should be allowed to say things in public that might be offensive to racial groups | People should be allowed to say things in public that might be offensive to religious groups |
|---|---|---|
| Strongly agree | 20% | 26% |
| Mildly agree | 28% | 30% |
| Mildly disagree | 23% | 21% |
| Strongly disagree | 29% | 24% |

*Source:* Massachusetts Institute of Technology, 2009, *Attitudes & Perceptions About the Constitution* (Menlo Park, CA: Knowledge Networks).

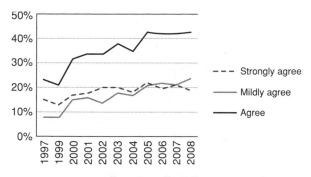

CHART 5.1. Allow Racially Offensive Speech

to 24 percent of FAC respondents, "strongly" agreed that racially offensive speech should be permitted, and 26 percent of MIT respondents said the same of religiously offensive speech, compared to 32 percent in the FAC survey. There is sense in the observed distinction between race and religion. Certain strongly held religious views may be impossible to disaggregate from disparagement of the religious views of others. As Ivan Hare writes, "[R]eligions inevitably make competing and often incompatible claims about the nature of the true god, the origins of the universe, the path to enlightenment, and how to live a good life and so on."[44] Religious offense is therefore, categorically, a more problematic candidate for hate-speech regulation than racial offense.[45]

The most striking survey result is the trend over time, particularly on race. As Chart 5.1 illustrates, the proportion of Americans who believe that racially offensive speech should be permitted nearly doubled from 1997 to 2008; the proportion holding that view "strongly" nearly tripled. The proportion of Americans who strongly disagree that racially offensive speech should be permitted – that is, those espousing a more stereotypically European view – decreased by nearly a third. The MIT survey, although reflecting a different distribution in intensity of viewpoint, is consistent with the overall picture: Americans are far more permissive of hate speech today than they were in the mid-to-late 1990s.

The upward trend in acceptance slices clean through demographics. As one might expect, tolerance of hate speech is more prevalent among whites than blacks and Hispanics, and among the college educated. Minorities are usually the intended beneficiaries of hate-speech restrictions, and educated people are more likely to be familiar with the First Amendment. But the sharp upward slope in tolerance for offensive speech persists across racial groups and regardless of education level.

[44] Ivan Hare, "Blasphemy and Incitement to Religious Hatred," in *Extreme Speech and Democracy*, *supra* note 1, at 289, 308.

[45] Witness, for example, the controversy in the United Kingdom over the Racial and Religious Hatred Act 2006, which some feared would outlaw certain passages in the Bible and the Koran. *See* "The Tongue Twisters," *The Economist*, Oct. 13, 2007.

People with postgraduate degrees were nearly twice as likely to agree that racially offensive speech should be permitted in 2006 than they were in 1999. Those with only high-school educations were slightly more than twice as likely.[46] Black Americans are roughly two-thirds as likely as whites to take a permissive attitude toward racially offensive speech, but both groups are just about two and a half times as likely to hold that view today compared to a decade ago.

These results should alarm advocates for reform of the American position. Without an explanation for so dramatic a trend and a strategy for reversing it, the best arguments for reform will fall on deaf ears. At the same time, it may hearten reformers to know that Justice Jackson was only partly right: Rejecting government prescription of political orthodoxy is surely a star in the American constitutional constellation, but it is by no means fixed.[47] I have already discussed the crossroads of 1952. There is little evidence that Americans before that period were unusually tolerant of offensive speech. In the 1930s, numerous state and local governments banned either pro-Nazi or pro-Communist propaganda and made life generally difficult for fascist groups.[48] In 1946, at the height of the proliferation of group libel bills, six in ten Americans told Gallup that it should be illegal to join the Ku Klux Klan,[49] even as a former Klansman – Hugo Black – sat on the Supreme Court. As of 1952, the United States might easily have taken a different direction on hate-speech restrictions.

Was 1999 also a crossroads? Was 2009 a crossroads, with some Americans beginning to moderate their absolutism? If so, then why? The next subsection takes up that question, but first it is useful to consider whether American opinion is in fact an outlier compared to Europe. We lack comprehensive comparative data on European attitudes toward hate-speech regulation during the period for which U.S. data are available. The best available data may be from the European Social Survey (ESS), which in 2002 asked respondents in twenty-one European countries and Israel to rate on a scale of 0 to 10 whether a law against promoting racial hatred was a good or a bad thing for a country. More than three in ten respondents (31 percent) gave a response of "10," indicating that such a law was "extremely good" for a country. Nearly six

---

[46] I do not have sufficient data to compile these numbers for 2007 and 2008, but it may be useful to report that the educational distribution in the 2009 MIT survey differs in important ways from the most recently available FAC survey. Namely, less educated people seem relatively less inclined to favor speech restrictions in the 2009 survey. Approximately half of all high school graduates in the MIT survey agreed that offensive speech should be allowed, compared to one-third in the 2006 FAC survey. Conversely, slightly more than half of MIT survey respondents with postgraduate degrees agreed that offensive speech should be permitted, compared to more than 60 percent in the 2006 FAC survey.

[47] Cf. *Barnette*, 319 U.S. at 642 (Jackson, J.) ("If there is any fixed star in our constitutional constellation, it is that no official, high or petty, can prescribe what shall be orthodox in politics, nationalism, religion, or other matters of opinion, or force citizens to confess by word or act their faith therein.").

[48] Walker, *supra* note 9, at 40; *see* Joel H. Spring, *Images in American Life: A History of Ideological Management in Schools, Movies, Radio, and Television* 52, 92–3 (SUNY Press 1992).

[49] Roper Center for Public Opinion Research, Gallup Poll (Aug. 16–21, 1946).

in ten (59 percent) gave a response of "8" or higher, and nearly three-quarters (73 percent) answered "6" or higher.[50]

Drawing reliable comparisons between the ESS data and the FAC and MIT surveys is perilous given the differences in question wording, which cannot be regarded as trivial. The best we can say, perhaps, is that nearly three out of four Europeans in 2002 would at least mildly disagree that racially offensive speech should be permitted. That figure meaningfully exceeds the number of Americans holding similar views in 2002, vastly exceeds the number holding such views in 2009, and approximates the number holding such views in the late 1990s.

We can draw a more direct comparison from the 2004 International Social Survey Programme (ISSP), which asked respondents in thirty-nine countries around the world various questions related to citizenship, one of which was "Should people prejudiced against any racial group be allowed to hold public meetings?" Respondents were asked whether such groups should definitely, probably, probably not, or definitely not be permitted to hold such meetings.[51] Of the countries surveyed, which included much of Europe, no country had a greater proportion of respondents answer "definitely" or "probably" than the United States (39 percent). As Chart 5.2 shows, within Europe, only Norway (37 percent) was comparably tolerant of meetings of racist groups. Notably, only 9 percent of respondents in Hungary answered this question in the affirmative, even though Hungary may be Europe's most speech-protective country.[52] In a large majority of countries surveyed, the proportion of respondents who answered "definitely" or "probably" was less than half the proportion in the United States.

## B

Explaining the differences between Europe and the United States on hate speech has engaged some of the brightest minds in the world of international and comparative public law.[53] Far less attention has been paid to the differences within the United States over time. Yet understanding these internal differences is vitally important for those who wish to moderate the American posture. Dramatic evolution in American public attitudes, even over relatively brief periods, suggests that events short of catastrophic genocide may indeed be capable of changing the minds of the American people. We lack sufficient data to draw firm conclusions as to what those events might be, but some possibilities recommend themselves. I propose three considerations that

---

[50] European Social Survey Round 1 Data (2002/2003), Data file edition 6.1. Norwegian Social Science Data Services, Norway (Data Archive and distributor of ESS data).

[51] International Social Survey Programme 2004: Citizenship (ISSP 2004). For ease of comparison over time, the ISSP separately samples East German and West German respondents.

[52] *See* Peter Molnar, "Towards Improved Law and Policy on 'Hate Speech' – The 'Clear and Present Danger' Test in Hungary," in *Extreme Speech and Democracy, supra* note 1, at 237.

[53] *See, e.g.,* Rosenfeld, *supra* note 2. *See also* Post, *supra* note 1; Schauer, *supra* note 10.

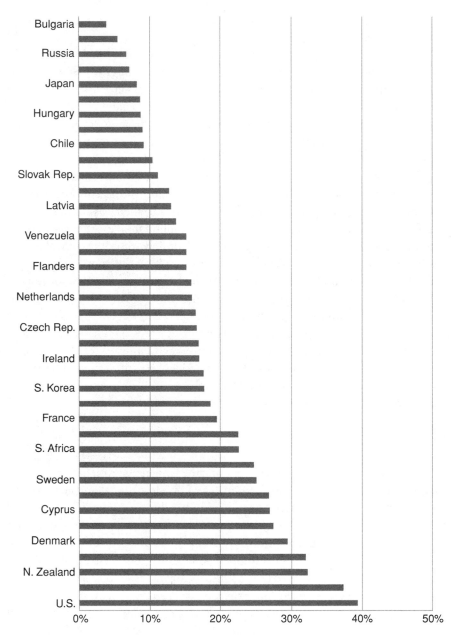

CHART 5.2. Racist Meetings Should Definitely or Probably Be Permitted

may affect whether the American people of a particular time are relatively receptive to laws restricting hate speech: trust in government; sensitivity to international norms; and opportunities for exit.

## 1. Trust in Government

The Rasmussen polling organization asked in a 2008 survey of American adults whether it would be "a good idea for the United States to ban hate speech." Twenty-eight percent of respondents answered yes, 53 percent said no, and 19 percent were unsure.[54] Those numbers are loosely consistent with the numbers reported in the FAC and MIT surveys.[55] The same Rasmussen survey followed up, however, with the following question: "Which is better – allowing free speech without government interference or letting government decide what types of hate speech should be banned?" Only 11 percent of respondents said that it is better to let government decide; 74 percent said it was preferable to allow unfettered free speech. Even for many of those who were not bothered by restrictions on hate speech, the specter of government deciding which speech would be permitted and which would not was unacceptable.

One need only sit in on a grade-school social studies class to glean that mistrust of government is part of the national operating instructions for the United States. Suspicion of top-down political authority is evident in the bill of particulars detailed in the Declaration of Independence and in the system of checks and balances embedded in the Constitution and celebrated by *The Federalist*. "If angels were to govern men," Madison says in Federalist No. 51, "neither external nor internal controls on government would be necessary."[56]

Significantly, however, Americans today trust government far less than they used to. Various polls over the last half century have measured trust in government by asking Americans the following question: "How much of the time do you think you can trust the government in Washington to do what is right? Just about always, most of the time, or only some of the time?"[57] The number of Americans saying they can trust the federal government all or most of the time stood at 73 percent in 1958; it was 17 percent in October 2008. Of course, October 2008 was just before

---

[54] Toplines – Free Speech, June 12, 2008, Rasmussen Reports (2008).

[55] It is not entirely clear how "yes" or "no" in the Rasmussen survey best correspond to the scale of agreement reported in the FAC and MIT surveys. It should also be noted that Rasmussen primed respondents by noting that "[m]any European countries and Canada do not have full freedom of speech, but instead have laws to prevent hate speech." There is reason to believe that this kind of priming is likely to depress the number of respondents in favor of such laws. See *infra* Section II.B.2.

[56] *The Federalist* No. 51, at 322 (James Madison) (Clinton Rossiter ed., New American Library 1961).

[57] The data from 1958 to 1996 come from the American National Election Studies. *See Deconstructing Distrust: How Americans View Government* 87 (Pew Center for People & the Press 1998). Subsequent data comes from surveys conducted by the Pew Center for People & the Press (1998), ABC News/*Washington Post* (2000), and CBS News/*New York Times* (2002–2008).

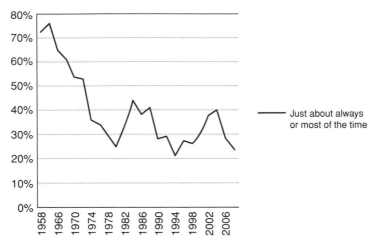

CHART 5.3. Trust Government to Do Right Thing

an unpopular President, George W. Bush, was replaced by Barack Obama. But as Chart 5.3 demonstrates, the downward secular trend in Americans' trust in their government extends beyond any one administration. The last time a majority of Americans said they trusted government all or most of the time was in 1972, just before the Watergate scandal ended Richard Nixon's presidency.

A people who believe that government usually cannot be trusted will not lightly task that same government with prosecuting citizens for offensive speech.[58] Both *Brandenburg v. Ohio*, which states the modern American standard for criminalizing incitement,[59] and *Cohen v. California*, which allowed clothing bearing a profane message to be worn in a courthouse,[60] were handed down amid a precipitous decline in Americans' faith in their government. Indeed, Henry Louis Gates Jr. has argued that the campus speech-code movement resulted in part from the newfound trust of minority groups for authority figures on campus. "The contemporary aim is not to resist power," wrote Gates, "but to enlist power."[61] If some minorities have been feeling increasingly close to power within collegiate gates, other Americans have

---

[58] *See* Frederick Schauer, *Free Speech: A Philosophical Inquiry* 86 (Cambridge University Press 1982) ("Freedom of speech is based in large part on a distrust of the ability of government to make the necessary distinctions, a distrust of governmental determinations of truth and falsity, an appreciation of the fallibility of political leaders, and a somewhat deeper distrust of governmental power in a more general sense.").

[59] 395 U.S. 444, 447 (1969) ("[T]he constitutional guarantees of free speech and free press do not permit a State to forbid or proscribe advocacy of the use of force or of law violation except where such advocacy is directed to inciting or producing imminent lawless action and is likely to incite or produce such action.").

[60] 403 U.S. 15 (1971).

[61] Henry Louis Gates Jr., "Let Them Talk: Why Civil Liberties Pose No Threat to Civil Rights," *New Republic*, Sep. 20 & 27, 1993, at 44.

been feeling increasingly alienated from political institutions more generally. And those who distrust government appear less likely to favor hate-speech restrictions. The MIT survey asked respondents to indicate which of the following statements they agreed with: "The less government, the better," or "There are more things that government should be doing." Even controlling for whether people generally identify as liberal or conservative, opponents of hate-speech restrictions are somewhat more likely to oppose big government.[62]

It is not clear whether Europeans, for their part, in fact trust the state any more than Americans do. A 1998 survey commissioned by Pew found that only 45 percent of respondents in the United Kingdom, France, Germany, Italy, and Spain said "no" when asked whether they "basically trust the state," compared to 56 percent of Americans. But the most recent ESS, in 2006, found that in rating trust of their parliaments on a scale of 0–10 – from "no trust at all" to "complete trust" – 54 percent of Europeans registered 4 or lower.[63] And in the 2002 ESS survey, neither trust in parliament nor trust of politicians was significantly correlated with whether respondents believe a hate-speech law is desirable. The 2004 ISSP asked a similar question to the one that has been most frequently asked in the United States: whether and to what extent respondents agree that "[m]ost of the time we can trust people in government to do what is right." The United States is no particular outlier on this question, nor are responses to the trust question significantly correlated with responses to the racist public meeting question.[64]

All told, we lack both the data and a sufficiently persuasive story to establish trust in government as any more than a partial explanation for the recent surge in American tolerance for hate speech. It is true that in the years since 2002, Americans' distrust in government has correlated quite nicely – on the order of 0.8 – with permissive attitudes toward racial hate speech. But from 1997 to 2001, the correlation was insignificant, indeed marginally negative. Results from the FAC survey indicate that American tolerance for certain other kinds of speech regulation – for example, restrictions on religious hate speech and flag burning – have correlated significantly with Americans' trust in government over the last decade. But attitudes toward restrictions on offensive song lyrics are largely unchanged over the same period.[65] It may be that, at least in the United States, trust in government is a precondition for an anti–hate speech constitutional norm, but is not sufficient without more.

---

[62] *See* MIT Survey, *supra* note 42.
[63] The Pew results and the ESS results are not necessarily inconsistent. Each of the four Western European countries surveyed in the Pew study that were included in the 2006 ESS – Italy did not participate – had a proportion of "5 or lower" responses on the ESS scale of relative trust in parliament that was below the Europe-wide average.
[64] *See* ISSP 2004, *supra* note 51.
[65] *See* FAC Survey, *supra* Table 5.1.

## 2. Sensitivity to International Norms

Shame is an essential weapon in the arsenal of the international human rights advocate.[66] Louis Henkin writes of enforcement of human rights norms: "Intergovernmental as well as governmental policies and actions combine with those of NGOs and the public media, and in many countries also public opinion, to mobilize and maximize public shame. The effectiveness of such inducements to comply is subtle but demonstrable."[67] The notion that shame can provoke nations to act against their own interest may come across as naively anthropomorphic, and the internal dynamics of the process are indeed more complicated than the invocation of raw human emotion suggests.[68] It is difficult to dispute, however, that a people's basic sensitivity to world opinion is nearly indispensable in encouraging them to internalize international norms.

It is a familiar complaint within the international human rights community that, as Frederick Schauer has written, "American courts, American lawyers, and the American constitutional culture have been stubbornly anti-international, far too often treating foreign influence as a one-way process, in which Americans influenced others but were little influenced in return."[69] Jed Rubenfeld suggests quite plausibly that while the Second World War's principal lesson for Europe was that nationalism is dangerous, the take-home across the Atlantic was that Americans are exceptional.[70] Within American domestic politics, the fact that the United States stands alone on some question of international law has long been an argument both for and against compliance. This at-best ambivalent posture poses particular challenges for those who wish to elevate hate-speech restrictions to the status of customary international law.

Domestic enthusiasm for American exceptionalism appears to have become particularly pronounced since September 11, 2001.[71] A foreign-planned attack on domestic soil is bound to provoke nationalism, but international criticism of the U.S. intervention in Iraq seemed to exacerbate the usual jingoism that accompanies military retaliation. The reaction by some to occasional citation of foreign or transnational law in U.S. court decisions provides a microcosmic window into the new nationalism. Three months after the U.S.-led invasion of Iraq, the Supreme Court decided *Lawrence v. Texas*, in which it invalidated the state's prohibition on

---

[66] *See* Robert F. Drinan, *The Mobilization of Shame: A World View of Human Rights* (Yale University Press 2002).

[67] Louis Henkin, "Human Rights: Ideology and Aspiration, Reality and Prospect," in *Realizing Human Rights: Moving from Inspiration to Impact* 3, 24 (Samantha Power & Graham Allison eds., Palgrave Macmillan 2000).

[68] *See, e.g.,* Harold Hongju Koh, "Why Do Nations Obey International Law?," 106 *Yale L.J.* 2599 (1997).

[69] Schauer, *supra* note 10, at 51.

[70] Jed Rubenfeld, "Unilateralism and Constitutionalism," 79 *N.Y.U. L. Rev.* 1971 (2004).

[71] *See* Harold Hongju Koh, "American Exceptionalism," 55 *Stan. L. Rev.* 1479, 1496 (2003).

same-sex sodomy.[72] In the course of his majority opinion, Justice Kennedy cited four decisions of the European Court of Human Rights, most prominently *Dudgeon v. United Kingdom,* and referred to a brief filed by former U.N. High Commissioner for Human Rights Mary Robinson, which discussed the laws of other nations.[73] Within one year of the *Lawrence* decision, several interest groups had called for the impeachment of any federal judge who cites foreign law while interpreting the U.S. Constitution.[74] Both the House and the Senate introduced measures that would forbid any federal court from relying on any law or precedent of any foreign adjudicator in interpreting the Constitution.[75] Steven Calabresi, a cofounder of the Federalist Society, is characteristically direct. "Those of us concerned about citation of foreign law . . . believe in something called American exceptionalism, which holds that the United States is a beacon of liberty, democracy and equality of opportunity to the rest of the world," he writes. "The country that saved Europe from tyranny and destruction in the 20th century and that is now saving it again from the threat of terrorist extremism and Russian tyranny needs no lessons from the socialist constitutional courts of Europe on what liberty consists of."[76]

For all this chest-thumping, it is not clear that Americans identify much less with the international community than Europeans or others. Over a four-year period from 2005 to 2008, the World Values Survey asked respondents in forty-five countries whether and to what extent they "see [themselves] as a world citizen."[77] As Chart 5.4 indicates, only ten countries registered less agreement with that statement than the United States (69 percent), but eight of those ten were European countries: Bulgaria (46 percent), Georgia (48 percent), Germany (53 percent), Romania (54 percent), Ukraine (60 percent), Italy (62 percent), Moldova (65 percent), and Finland (65 percent). Including Turkey, nine European countries registered greater agreement with the sentiment of world citizenship than did the United States: Poland (74 percent), Cyprus (74 percent), Slovenia (74 percent), Switzerland (78 percent), Serbia (78 percent), Spain (79 percent), Sweden (84 percent), Turkey (85 percent), and Andorra (87 percent). If there is a leitmotif here, it is hardly obvious.

One's regard for international opinion may be unrelated to one's tolerance for hate speech. Or it may be that between-group differences between the United States and Europe record separate phenomena than within-group differences between the United States of 1997 and the United States of 2009. It may be that, as with

---

72 Lawrence v. Texas, 539 U.S. 558 (2003).
73 *See id.* at 576 (citing Dudgeon v. United Kingdom, 45 Eur. Ct. H.R. 52 (1981); P.G. & J.H. v. United Kingdom, App. No. 00044787/98, 56 (Eur. Ct. H.R., Sept. 25, 2001); Modinos v. Cyprus, 259 Eur. Ct. H.R. (1993); Norris v. Ireland, 142 Eur. Ct. H.R. (1988); Brief of Mary Robinson et al. as Amici Curiae at 11–12).
74 *See* Dana Milbank, "And the Verdict on Justice Kennedy Is: Guilty," *Wash. Post,* Apr. 9, 2005, at A3.
75 Constitution Restoration Act of 2004, S. 2323, H.R. 3799, 108th Cong. 2d Sess. (2004).
76 Steven G. Calabresi, Letter to the Editor, *N.Y. Times,* Sept. 18, 2008, at A18.
77 World Values Survey 2005–2008.

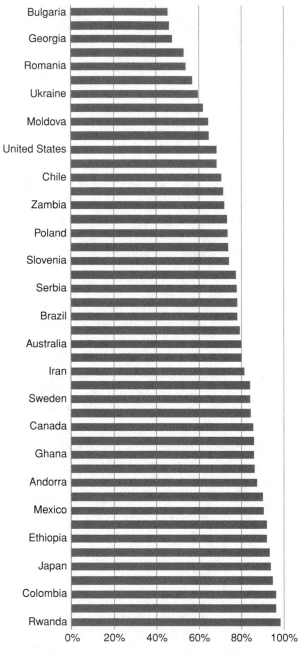

CHART 5.4. Consider Self a World Citizen

government distrust, rising scorn for international opinion is a hurdle to Americans' tolerating hate-speech regulation but does not, without much more, explain American attitudes. Additional data would help answer these important questions.

### 3. Opportunities for Exit

In his classic treatment of competition between firms or organizations, the economist Albert Hirschman counterposed two possible consumer or member responses to a decline in product or organizational quality. A person may stop buying the firm's products or leave the organization, that is, choose the "exit" option, or the person may complain to management, that is, choose the "voice" option.[78] Hirschman and others have usefully extrapolated his observations to the realms of political and social decision making. Referring to the country's origins as a settler nation, Hirschman writes that "[t]he United States owes its very existence and growth to millions of decisions favoring exit over voice."[79] The frontier, which then became the suburb and the exurb, has been a powerful symbol more available in the expansive United States than in the traditionally denser populations of Europe. Hirschman writes:

> Even after the closing of the frontier, the very vastness of the country combined with easy transportation make it far more possible for Americans than for most other people to think about solving their problems through "physical flight" than either through resignation or through ameliorating and fighting *in situ* the particular conditions into which one has been "thrown."[80]

Hirschman suggests that Americans are more apt than Europeans to vote with their feet rather than to engage in a contest of words or ideas.

This contestable macro account of social behavior and of American psychology, if true, should be of great interest to the discourse on hate-speech regulation. If material conditions or social expectations require that voice is preferred to exit, then a people may well be inclined to call on the state to moderate the terms of discourse. If we must stand and fight, let us at least be civilized about it. Whether or not the macro account is true, however, Hirschman's theoretical insight still offers lessons at the micro level. There is plenty of reason to believe that a permissive norm toward hate speech is likely to flourish where various forms of exit are readily available. As I have suggested, the American suburb was the twentieth-century embodiment of exit.[81] And to the extent we seek an account that tells us what happened to hate-speech regulation circa 1952, it is tempting to ascribe a role to the rapid, subsidized

---

[78] Albert O. Hirschman, *Exit, Voice, and Loyalty: Responses to Decline in Firms, Organizations, and States* 4 (Harvard University Press 1970).

[79] *Id.* at 106.

[80] *Id.* at 107.

[81] Although this might be changing. *See* Nicole Stelle Garnett, "Suburbs as Exit, Suburbs as Entrance," 106 *Mich. L. Rev.* 277 (2007).

suburbanization of the United States. The pushback in the form of college speech codes then provides a compelling counterpoint, wherein the gates of university campuses become a powerful metaphor for the absence of exit, the classroom a stylized arena for voice.

This story may also be helpful in explaining the more recent surge in Americans' tolerance for offensive speech. Although U.S. growth in metropolitan areas in recent years has exceeded that outside of such areas since 2000, the growth rate of outlying counties within metropolitan areas grew 67 percent faster than central counties from 2000 to 2007.[82] Moreover, a greater proportion of U.S. population growth from 2000 to 2004 resulted from domestic migration (as opposed to immigration or natural growth) than in the 1990s.[83]

Geography is not the only space across which individuals seeking to escape unwanted intimacy either isolate themselves or form communities of interest. As Robert Putnam has famously detailed, traditional forms of civic engagement have vanished from the American social landscape in recent decades.[84] Others have replaced them – Facebook, Twitter, and MySpace, to name three – but the communities these exponentially multiplying forms of social networking create are voluntary associations devoted to predetermined common interests. They are designed, almost willfully, to defeat the need for the face-to-face interactions characteristic of voice-based communities. Rather, like suburbs, they permit socialization and exit to coexist.[85]

The viral proliferation of such communities over the past several years is self-evident. For those still in need of convincing, consider that as of December 2008, 35 percent of American adults had a profile on a social networking site, and one in five used such sites on any given day. In February 2005, less than four years earlier, those numbers were, respectively, 8 percent and one in fifty.[86] It is also self-evident, I think, that, as P. M. Forni writes, "online communication has unleashed a new magnitude of rudeness."[87] Online discourse promises not only anonymity but minimal barriers to community entry and exit, with predictable results. First, individuals may feel more liberated to engage in offensive speech and therefore become acculturated to, even solicitous of, uncivil discourse. Second, and relatedly, our default conception of the public sphere might gradually shift from the physical to the cyber world.

---

[82] U.S. Census Bureau, *Population Change in Central and Outlying Counties of Metropolitan Statistical Areas: 2000 to 2007* (2009).

[83] U.S. Census Bureau, *Domestic Net Migration in the United States: 2000–2004* (2006).

[84] Robert D. Putnam, *Bowling Alone: The Collapse and Revival of American Community* (Simon & Schuster 2000).

[85] *See The Internet in Public Life* 90–1 (Verna V. Gehring ed., Rowman & Littlefield 2004); *cf.* Laura E. Buffardi and W. Keith Campbell, "Narcissism and Social Networking Web Sites," 34 *Personality & Social Psychol. Bull.* 1303 (2008).

[86] *See* Pew Internet & American Life Project, *Adults and Social Network Websites* 3–4 (2009).

[87] Pier M. Forni, *The Civility Solution: What To Do When People Are Rude* 149 (St. Martin's Griffin 2008).

Asked whether racially offensive speech should be permitted "in public," we might understand the metes and bounds of that "location" – and therefore its rules of discourse – far differently than our children do.

If this explanation is valid and adequate, we might expect a like dynamic elsewhere in the world. Online communication is not unique to the United States, nor should we imagine it to be uniquely effective at altering *American* norms of civility. It may be that similar forces are at play in Europe and elsewhere; we lack the data to assess changes over time in world attitudes toward hate-speech restrictions. It may also be, however, that the Supreme Court's First Amendment decisions over the last decades, and the social and political movements that inspired them, helped create the space within which a norm of hate-speech tolerance can flourish.[88] This story again suggests the possibility that one or the other – the effects of online discourse or the Court's handiwork – is necessary but not sufficient to produce the American attitude on hate-speech regulation.

## III

That attitude is influenced by an additional consideration that will be crucial to any efforts at reform. Lawmaking in the United States is not, of course, the exclusive province of the national government. Rather, the great majority of laws, ordinances, and regulations occur at the state and local levels. Any constitutional change requires a mixture of movement energy and cultural change, but federalism is the straw that stirs the drink. And in most cases it stirs ever so slowly. Whereas the Supreme Court may invalidate a law with the requisite five signatures, making the free-speech norm less permissive of offensive speech would require state-by-state action slow enough to delay premature Supreme Court review but massive enough to push national public opinion.

---

[88] Political scientists have long questioned the notion, popularized by Eugene Rostow and Alexander Bickel, that the Supreme Court is an effective educative body. *See* Eugene V. Rostow, "The Democratic Character of Judicial Review," 66 *Harv. L. Rev.* 193, 208 (1952) (calling the Justices "teachers in a vital national seminar"); Alexander M. Bickel, *The Least Dangerous Branch: The Supreme Court at the Bar of Politics* 26 (Yale University Press 1962) (calling the courts "a great and highly effective educational institution"). The principal objection is that the public is generally ignorant of a large majority of the Court's business. *See, e.g.,* Walter F. Murphy and Joseph Tanenhaus, "Public Opinion and the United States Supreme Court: Mapping of Some Prerequisites for Court Legitimation of Regime Changes," 2 *Law & Soc'y Rev.* 357 (1968); Stephen M. Griffin, "What Is Constitutional Theory? The Newer Theory and the Decline of the Learned Tradition," 62 *S. Calif. L. Rev.* 493, 522 (1989) ("In the absence of adequate public knowledge about its activities, the Court cannot be said to educate or to have the power to legitimize government policies."). *But see* James L. Gibson and Gregory A. Caldeira, "Knowing the Supreme Court? A Reconsideration of Public Ignorance of the High Court," 71 *Journal of Politics* 429 (2009). Even accepting low levels of public knowledge of the Court's ordinary workload, it is difficult to dispute the Court's role in reinforcing, if not creating, thick constitutional norms. *See* Robert Post and Reva Siegel, "Popular Constitutionalism, Departmentalism, and Judicial Supremacy," 92 *Calif. L. Rev.* 1027, 1038 (2004).

Thus, when a wave of anti-Nazi laws was sweeping across Europe in the 1930s, the only race-hate law the United States could muster during the period at the state level was New Jersey's law of 1935. Massachusetts and Indiana passed group libel laws in the 1940s, but the rest of the states were silent.[89] Congress was constitutionally forbidden from enacting a general race-hate law without a commerce hook, and the bills that were proposed were blocked by veto gates. The presence of multiple fora for lawmaking tends to disperse the energies of a popular movement. It also enables time for reflection and evaluation of the effectiveness of measures in sister jurisdictions. The feebleness of the National Socialist Party of America march in Chicago's Marquette Park – where the neo-Nazi group relocated from Skokie in 1978 – was a national object lesson in the efficacy of the American position. Hate speech can be remarkably self-refuting.

This chapter's aim, then, has not been to suggest an easy time for reformers. Rather, it has been to suggest, in Barry Friedman's delightful phrase, the importance of being positive.[90] American public opinion on hate-speech regulation appears to have trended dramatically in one direction over the last several years. That trend may be reversible through directed action. If my hypotheses as to causes are correct, then it will be useful to promote the effectiveness of government regulation and international institutions more generally. Perhaps, as Putnam argues, civics education, a renewed focus on public service, and innovations in urban planning can alter Americans' conception of community and encourage us to internalize a sense of mutual obligation.[91]

This will all sound Pollyanna-ish to some, but public opinion offers lessons even for cynics. I have several times referred to the conditions that foster a norm for or against hate-speech regulation as potentially exogenous. It may be that those conditions resist directed action, or else are too complex to alter proactively. Even so, it is useful for reformers to have the tools to recognize the moment to strike. If Americans have a low opinion of government and international institutions, and are becoming increasingly insular and self-regarding in our social relations, it is anything but an obvious opportunity to import new, heretofore unconstitutional restrictions on offensive speech. More modest proposals – changes in the definition of hate crime or workplace harassment, for example – are better uses of reformers' energies.[92] In this regard, federalism may act as both sickness and cure. The opportunity for localized experimentation means that constitutional norms may be chipped at rather than detonated.

---

[89] Walker, *supra* note 9, at 82–3.

[90] Barry Friedman, "The Importance of Being Positive: The Nature and Function of Judicial Review," 72 *U. Cincinnati L. Rev.* 1257 (2004).

[91] Putnam, *supra* note 84, at 404–8.

[92] *See, e.g.*, H.R. 1913, 111th Cong., 1st Sess. (proposing to add sexual orientation-motivated violence to the federal hate crimes law).

My hypotheses as to causes are defeasible. But they must be evaluated both theoretically and empirically and, if necessary, supplemented or replaced. The posture I wish to discourage is the one that views the differences between the United States and much of the democratized world on hate-speech regulation as engrained, inalterably, within our cultural DNA. It may be true that Americans have certain instincts that predispose us to oppose content-based restrictions on speech. We are typically suspicious of government, fond of our own perceived exceptionalism, and able and willing to migrate, both physically and psychosocially. But to speak of genetic predisposition as destiny is a too-common fallacy. "[E]ven when a trait has been built and set, environmental intervention may still modify inherited defects," writes Stephen Jay Gould. "Millions of Americans see normally through lenses that correct innate deficiencies of vision."[93] Adjusting the American – or, if one prefers, the European – attitude toward hate speech calls for neither philosophizing nor despair, but rather careful surgery.

[93] Stephen Jay Gould, *The Mismeasure of Man* 186 (W.W. Norton 1996).

# 6

## On American Hate Speech Law

### Floyd Abrams

### I. INTRODUCTION – FIRST PRINCIPLES

So often has the constitutional protection afforded to "hate speech" by the First Amendment to the U.S. Constitution been contrasted with more restrictive laws in other democratic societies, that it may be useful to offer a bit of context to the American approach. Consider two U.S. Supreme Court decisions from 2010 in what may seem to be unrelated areas.

The first is *United States v. Stevens*,[1] which held unconstitutional under the First Amendment a federal statute that criminalized the commercial creation, sale, or possession of "a depiction of animal cruelty."[2] Seeking to persuade the Court to affirm the constitutionality of the statute, the United States proposed a novel legal test, one never before adopted by American courts. As the Court summarized the government's position, it urged "that a claim of categorical exclusion [from the First Amendment] should be considered under a simple balancing test."[3] The test was "[w]hether a given category of speech enjoys First Amendment protection depends upon a categorical balancing of the value of the speech against its societal costs."[4]

That proposal – one that, if adopted, might be promising indeed for proponents of what Professor Greene characterizes as "reform" of the American treatment of hate speech[5] and what others might view as the suppression of speech – was soundly rejected by the Court in the following language:

As a free-floating test for First Amendment coverage, that sentence is startling and dangerous. The First Amendment's guarantee of free speech does not extend only

[1]   130 S. Ct. 1577 (2010).
[2]   18 U.S.C. § 48(a) (2006).
[3]   *Stevens*, 130 S. Ct. at 1585.
[4]   *Id.* (quoting Brief for Petitioner at 10, 2009 WL 1615365, at *8).
[5]   *See* Jamal Greene, "Hate Speech and the Demos," Chapter 5 herein.

to categories of speech that survive an ad hoc balancing of relative social costs and benefits. The First Amendment itself reflects a judgment by the American people that the benefits of its restrictions on the Government outweigh the costs. Our Constitution forecloses any attempt to revise that judgment simply on the basis that some speech is not worth it.[6]

So the Supreme Court is of no mind simply to "balance" the harm said to be inflicted by hate speech against any supposed benefits of continuing to protect it.

Similarly, in the highly controversial *Citizens United v. Federal Election Commission*[7] decision, which struck down congressional limits on the right of corporations and unions to spend their funds on advertisements or other speech about who to vote for late in political campaigns, the Court's analysis was anything but blurry. Political speech, the Court emphasized, receives the highest protection under the First Amendment, protection that will allow the speech to "prevail against laws that would suppress it, whether by design or inadvertence."[8] Limitations on political speech based on its content cannot be constitutionally sanctioned unless narrowly tailored to a compelling governmental interest,[9] if ever.[10] The only question, then, was whether the fact that corporations were the putative speakers changed that calculus, and (citing twenty-five prior decisions of the Court, which had found speech by corporations to be protected by the First Amendment[11]) the Court concluded that it did not. It therefore held the statute at issue unconstitutional. Here too, what the Court did *not* do was simply "balance" what might be viewed as the advantages of stricter campaign finance reform against whatever harm to First Amendment interests the statute occasioned.

I do not propose to discuss these cases here, although the much (and I think wrongly) criticized *Citizens United* in particular is certainly fertile ground.[12] But any consideration of the American approach to hate speech must begin by acknowledging that American constitutional rulings protecting (or not permitting punishment of) hate speech are not outliers but well within the nation's constitutional mainstream. The United States does not protect such speech because it is hate speech,

6   *Stevens*, 130 S. Ct. at 1585.
7   130 S. Ct. 876 (2010).
8   *Id.* at 898.
9   *Id.*
10  In his opinion for the Court, Justice Kennedy observed that "it might be maintained that political speech simply cannot be banned or restricted as a categorical matter," *id.*, a position he had urged in Simon & Schuster v. Members of N.Y. State Crime Victims Board, 502 U.S. 105, 124 (1991) (Kennedy, J., concurring) (arguing against use of the compelling-interest standard to assess content-based restrictions of speech). Such a blanket prohibition was unnecessary to reject the restrictions challenged in *Citizens United* and the opinion does not address whether to adopt the more protective standard.
11  *Citizens United*, 130 S. Ct. at 899–900.
12  *See* Floyd Abrams, "*Citizens United* and Its Critics," 120 *Yale L.J. Online* 77 (2010), http://yalelawjournal.org/2010/9/29/abrams.html.

but because as a general matter, the First Amendment "reflects a judgment by the American people that the benefits of its restrictions on the Government outweigh the costs."[13] Indeed, to allow hate speech to be sanctioned or banned would be at odds with both principles identified in the *Citizens United* case – it would be a restriction based on content and it would relate to speech on political or social topics that routinely receives the highest level of First Amendment protection.

## II. HATE SPEECH LIMITATIONS IN HISTORICAL CONTEXT

That the American position rests on well-settled principles does not begin to answer the question of whether a wholesale shift in approach would be a salutary step for the United States. Nor does it begin to establish that such an approach is appropriate in other countries.

For example, Professor Suk offers an arresting analysis of French law, drafted, as was that of postwar Germany, "to face their collective responsibility for the Holocaust."[14] So viewed, the adoption by nations of laws banning hate speech makes a good deal of sense. Who could object, on either moral or pragmatic grounds, to the same German nation that engaged, within living memory, in murderous barbarism and genocide as a matter of considered state policy making it a crime to deny the reality of the Holocaust? As Michel Rosenfeld has observed, "[v]iewed from the particular perspective of a rejection of the Nazi experience and an attempt to prevent its resurgence, the suppression of hate speech seems both obvious and commendable."[15]

The experience in another democratic nation, India, is also of particular interest. With more than 600,000 lives having been lost in the communal violence that occurred during the period after the partition of the subcontinent into India and Pakistan, the Indian Constitution and a variety of criminal statutes sought to limit such violence in the future by limiting the speech thought to cause or contribute to it. Although it may be an overstatement to conclude that the real issue in drafting the Indian Constitution "was identifying acceptable ways to limit the basic freedoms of speech, assembly, association and movement," it is certainly no exaggeration to conclude that "[t]he horrible communal violence that occurred in India during the time of the debates undoubtedly had a profound impact upon the nature and shape of the constitutional provisions."[16] As a result, Section 153A of the Indian penal code, entitled "Promoting enmity between different groups on grounds of religion,

---

[13] *Stevens*, 130 S. Ct. at 1585.
[14] Julie Suk, "Denying Experience: Holocaust Denial and the Free-Speech Theory of the State," Chapter 8 herein.
[15] Michel Rosenfeld, "Hate Speech in Constitutional Jurisprudence: A Comparative Analysis," Chapter 13 herein.
[16] C. Raj Kumar, "Human Rights Implications of National Security Laws in India: Combating Terrorism While Preserving Civil Liberties," 33 *Denv. J. Int'l L. & Pol'y* 195, 200 (2005).

race, place of birth, language, etc., and doing acts prejudicial to the maintenance of harmony," criminalizes speech that is so characterized.[17]

Throughout India's history, the communal violence that such provisions were adopted to prevent has recurred during electoral campaigns after critical, sometimes damning, comments were directed at religious groups. As summarized by Samuel Issacharoff:

> Indian history does not lack for examples of election agitation leading to scores of deaths. The question is what steps may be taken to permit genuine, even if distasteful, political expression while maintaining public order in the face of likely violent outbursts.... India's response is to narrow the definition of permissible political speech....
>
> In the stable framework of the United States, it may well be that reactions to suppress political participation have been overwrought and largely unnecessary.... The decision of India, a country forged in fratricidal religious conflict, seeking to suppress election day incitements likely to engender communal violence is not a move so readily discounted.[18]

As Professor Issacharoff suggests, it is difficult, perhaps impossible, to extrapolate from the experience of the United States to the so-different experiences of all others. What the history of nations as diverse as Germany, France, and India does suggest, at the very least, is that democratic nations may properly reach different decisions based on their quite painfully different on-the-ground historical realities.

## III. HATE SPEECH ABSOLUTES

Some decisions to ban what is characterized as hate speech should, however, be rejected everywhere. Consider the repeated resolutions introduced and adopted by the Human Rights Council and the General Assembly of the United Nations urging nations to ban speech viewed as "defamatory" of religion, "inciting to hatred" of religion, or the like.[19] Initially introduced in 1999 by Pakistan before the Commission

---

[17] The relevant provision – quite striking to American eyes – provides for a fine and up to three years in prison for whoever

> by words, either spoken or written, or by signs or by visible representations or otherwise, promotes or attempts to promote, on grounds of religion, race, place of birth, residence, language, caste or community or any other ground whatsoever, disharmony or feelings of enmity, hatred or ill-will between different religious, racial, language or regional groups or castes or communities....

The Indian Penal Code, No. 45 of 1860, § 153A(1)(a). *See also id.* at § 153B(1)(c) (making it a crime to "make[] or publish[] an assertion, counsel, plea or appeal concerning the obligation of any class of persons, by reason of their being members of any religious, racial, language or regional group or caste or community, [if] such assertion, counsel, plea or appeal causes or is likely to cause disharmony or feelings of enmity or hatred or ill-will between such members and other persons").

[18] Samuel Issacharoff, "Fragile Democracies," 120 *Harv. L. Rev.* 1405, 1424, 1452–3 (2007).

[19] As of this writing, the most recent version of these resolutions, entitled "Combating Defamation of Religions," was approved, albeit barely, by the UN's Human Rights Council in March 2010. Human

on Human Rights on behalf of the Organization of the Islamic Conference ("OIC"), at a time when it related, by its terms, only to defamation of Islam, such resolutions have increasingly been pressed by Islamic states as a sort of response to, among other supposed verbal misconduct, the Danish cartoons that inflamed many in the Islamic world.[20]

Although these resolutions, by focusing on "defamation" of religion, have significant vagueness problems – just how critical must one be to be characterized as engaging in defamation? – we can get an idea of how such an approach would work in practice, given that many nations already have such laws. In a 2008 letter to the United Nations Office of the High Commissioner for Human Rights criticizing these resolutions, the United States set out a telling list of examples of how antidefamation provisions have been used to punish minority religious communities or dissident members of a majority faith:

- In January 2008, a provincial court sentenced a student to death for distributing "blasphemous" material regarding the role of women in Islamic societies. The student was arrested in October 2007 for downloading the material from the Internet and passing it to students at the university he attended.
- In December 2007, a court reportedly sentenced two foreigners to six months in prison for allegedly marketing a book deemed offensive to Aicha, one of Prophet Mohammed's wives.
- In November 2007, a court sentenced a British teacher to fifteen days in jail for "insulting religion," after she named a class teddy bear Mohammed. A seven-year-old student named Mohammed had reportedly requested that the bear be named after him. The teacher was pardoned and deported the following month.
- In February 2007, a court sentenced an Internet blogger to three years in prison for his comments that critiqued the practice of Islam. He remains in prison.
- In January 2007, a court gave two writers a three-year suspended sentence and fined them $8,000 for "defaming Islam" in a magazine article. Publication of the magazine was also suspended for two months.
- In January 2007, authorities arrested a Christian on charges of blasphemy for allegedly making derogatory remarks about the Qur'an. She was held until May and released on bail.[21]

Rights Council Res. 13/L.1, Rep. of the Human Rights Council, 13th Sess., Mar. 1–26, 2010, U.N. Doc. A/HRC/13/L.1 (Mar. 11, 2010). The vote was 20 to 17, with 8 abstentions, a closer vote than that by which previous versions had passed. For a general description and the suggestion that international enthusiasm for prohibiting defamation of religions is waning, see Lorenz Langer, "The Rise (and Fall?) of Defamation of Religions," 35 *Yale J. Int'l L.* 257 (2010).

[20] *See generally* Jytte Klausen, *The Cartoons That Shook the World* (Yale University Press 2009).

[21] United States Government Response to the United Nations Office of the High Commissioner for Human Rights concerning Combating Defamation of Religions (2008), *available at* http://geneva .usmission.gov/2009/08/12/usg-response-tab1/. The document does not identify the particular countries in which these events occurred.

There is an additional deeply troubling aspect to the imposition of sanctions for so-called religious defamation. As the European Centre for Law and Justice ("ECLJ") pointed out in a study of the issue, it appears "that laws based on the concept of 'defamation of religion' actually help to create a climate of violence. Violators of these laws, as applied in most Muslim countries, are subject to the death penalty, which frequently encourages people to take matters into their own hands."[22] The ECLJ study cites an example from Pakistan, in which a twenty-two-year-old Hindu "was beaten to death by co-workers at a factory for allegedly committing the crime of blasphemy, which is a crime punishable by death in the country. The three workers who carried out the beating were arrested, charged not with murder but with 'failure to inform the police that blasphemy was underway.'"[23] The ECLJ study quotes a human rights activist based in Islamabad who observed that: "Not a single murderer who killed anyone for blasphemy has been punished for murder. In fact, such murderers get hero's treatment in police stations. And those police officials who openly honour such murderers have never been tried for their illegal and reprehensible action."[24]

To say this is not to suggest that hearing someone defame one's own religion is not disturbing or that one does not wish sometimes – "often" might be a better word – that offensive criticism had not been voiced at all. Consider the following offering: Jews are "an ignorant and barbarous people, who have long united the most sordid avarice with the most detestable superstition and the most invincible hatred for every people by whom they are tolerated and enriched. Still, we ought not to burn them."[25] Who authored that passage, including its last line? Voltaire, no less, writing in 1756 – the same enduring proponent of tolerance and brotherhood that we so often honor for just that advocacy.

Another historical example comes to mind. The year was 1517, the writer was Martin Luther, and the writing was the first great act in moving the world into the Reformation. Luther's courage in posting his ninety-five Theses on the Castle Church in Wittenberg has long been recognized as a signal moment in world history. But it should not be forgotten just how ferocious what Luther had to say about the Roman Catholic Church really was. He condemned the Church for selling indulgences; he characterized as "madness" the notion that papal pardons could absolve someone for sins committed; he criticized the Pope for not paying for the restoration of St. Peter's Cathedral out of "his own money rather than with

---

[22] European Centre for Law and Justice, "Combating Defamation of Religions," Submission to the UN Office of the High Commissioner of Human Rights, at 8 (June 2008), *available at* http://www.eclj.org/PDF/080626_ECLJ_submission_to_OHCHR_on_Combating_Defamation_of_Religions_June2008.pdf.

[23] *Id.*

[24] *Id.*

[25] François-Marie Arouet (Voltaire), *Jews* (1756), reprinted in *The Jew in the Modern World: A Documentary History* 304, 305 (Paul Mendes-Flohr & Jehuda Reinharz eds., Oxford University Press, 2d ed. 1995).

the money of poor believers."[26] At least as viewed from Rome, Luther had accused the Church, maligned the Church, *defamed* the Church. That conduct ultimately led to his excommunication and, in time, the creation of a Protestant Church in Germany and a Reformation throughout Europe.

It may seem a touch too hypothetical to consider the impact of the OIC resolution on Martin Luther's sixteenth-century offerings. But the potential impact today of that effort is anything but hypothetical. For there is no ambiguity about what it seeks to do. Its purpose is nothing less than to stifle criticism of Islam. In fact, earlier versions of the resolution limited its scope to defamation of Islam and no other religion. It would suppress such speech by subjecting writers, publishers, artists, and all others to sanctions if they came too close to the all-but-unknowable line that separates "defamation" of Islam from . . . what? Consider the examples set forth earlier in the U.S. submission to the UN Office of the High Commissioner for Human Rights. Would it – could it – constitute defamation of religion to criticize regimes that punish as blasphemers those who criticize Islam for its treatment of women? Or to criticize Islam itself for the same thing? Is it, could it be viewed as, religious defamation to mock those involved in sentencing a British teacher to jail time for naming a class teddy bear Mohammed? The answer is all too clear.

We know, after all, that a prime impetus for the current efforts to adopt this resolution is the anger of many in the Islamic community as a result of publication of the Danish cartoons. And that, in a sense, is all we really need to know about the resolution. For even putting aside the distortions of what those cartoons actually portrayed by too many people who knew better, the cartoons were a form of political commentary of just the sort that any democratic state should respect. By their nature, political cartoons are, as the U.S. Supreme Court unanimously observed in *Hustler Magazine v. Falwell*[27] in 1988, often not at all "even-handed, but slashing and one-sided."[28] Yet, as the Court rightly observed, "our political discourse would have been considerably poorer without them."[29] There is, quite simply, no reading of either Article 19 of the Universal Declaration of Human Rights[30] or the First Amendment that would not protect the Danish cartoons. And there is no reading of Article 19 or

---

[26]  Martin Luther, "Disputation on the Power and Efficacy of Indulgences ('The Ninety-Five Theses')," reprinted in *Martin Luther's Basic Theological Writings* 40–6 (Timothy F. Lull ed., Augsburg Fortress, 2d ed. 2005). As their actual title indicates, the 95 *Theses* were an extended attack on indulgences; the quotes in the text are from theses 75 and 86.

[27]  485 U.S. 46 (1988).

[28]  *Id.* at 54.

[29]  *Id.* at 55.

[30]  Universal Declaration of Human Rights, G.A. Res. 217 (III) A, art. 19, U.N. Doc A/RES/217 (Dec. 10, 1948) ("Everyone has the right to freedom of opinion and expression; this right includes freedom to hold opinions without interference and to seek, receive and impart information and ideas through any media and regardless of frontiers."). Article 19 reappears, with almost identical wording, as article 19 of the International Covenant on Civil and Political Rights, which provides that, subject to certain restrictions, "[e]veryone shall have the right to freedom of expression; this right shall include freedom to seek, receive and impart information and ideas of all kinds, regardless of frontiers, either orally,

the First Amendment that could possibly be deemed consistent with the adoption of the OIC resolution.

## IV. "IN AMERICA THERE IS NO HERESY, NO BLASPHEMY"

How different is the American approach? In some respects, it is all but unique. The International Covenant on Civil and Political Rights, drafted in 1966 and thereafter ratified by most nations in the world, provides in Article 20 that "[a]ny advocacy of national, racial or religious hatred that constitutes incitement to discrimination, hostility or violence shall be prohibited by law."[31] Although the United States does recognize that even in the face of an extremely broadly written First Amendment, incitement to violent acts can in certain narrow circumstances be penalized, the notion of "incitement to discrimination" could be interpreted far more broadly than our Constitution permits. As a result, when the United States ratified the convention in 1992, it was with an express reservation that "[a]rticle 20 does not authorize or require legislation or other action by the United States that would restrict the right of free speech and association protected by the Constitution . . . of the United States."[32]

The classic American case on the subject, *Cantwell v. Connecticut*,[33] began on a street corner in New Haven in 1938, ten years before the Universal Declaration was adopted.

On April 26, 1938, Newton Cantwell and his two sons, all of whom were Jehovah's Witnesses, arrived on a street in New Haven in a neighborhood in which 90 percent of the residents were Roman Catholic. The Cantwells were equipped with a record player and a bag containing books and pamphlets of their preachings. They went door to door and with the answerer's permission played one of their records. The Cantwells stopped two passersby, both Catholics, and asked for and received their permission to play a record. What they heard, entitled "Enemies," was an angry, sometimes venomous, attack on organized religion in general and the Roman Catholic Church in particular. Among the materials contained on the record, and played for and to its listeners, were passages such as this:

> The most seductive and subtle instrument employed to deceive man is religion, because religion has the appearance of doing good, whereas it brings upon the people great evil. There are many different religions, all of which are deceptive, are the instruments of the enemy Satan, and all work to the injury of men. This book submits the conclusive proof that for more than fifteen hundred years a great

---

in writing or in print, in the form of art, or through any other media of his choice." International Covenant on Civil and Political Rights art. 19, ¶ 2, Mar. 23, 1976, 999 U.N.T.S. 171.

[31] International Covenant on Civil and Political Rights art. 20, ¶ 2, Mar. 23, 1976, 999 U.N.T.S. 171.

[32] 138 Cong. Rec. S4781–01, at I(1) (daily ed., April 2, 1992) (U.S. reservations, declarations, and understandings, International Covenant on Civil and Political Rights).

[33] 310 U.S. 296 (1940).

religious system, operating out of Rome, has by means of fraud and deception brought untold sorrow and suffering upon the people. It operates the greatest racket ever employed amongst men and robs the people of their money and destroys their peace of mind and freedom of action. That religious system is vigorously pushing its political schemes amongst all the nations of earth, with the avowed purpose of seizing control of the nations and ruling the people by cruel dictators. Some of the nations have fallen under that wicked power, and all nations are now greatly endangered. Because of the increasing power of the enemy the liberties of the people are rapidly passing away and all nations are rushing into infidelity and into ultimate destruction.

Upon hearing such assertions and others that referred to the Church as a "harlot" that brought fascism and Nazism into being, one of the two listeners told the Cantwells that they had better leave the area before something happened to them. They did so, but were later convicted of, among other things, inciting breach of the peace. The U.S. Supreme Court ultimately reversed the convictions, concluding that "the fundamental law declares the interest of the United States that the free exercise of religion be not prohibited and that freedom to communicate information and opinion be not abridged."[34] While a state has a right to preserve peace and order within her borders, the Court said, it "may not unduly suppress free communication of views, religious or other, under the guise of conserving desirable conditions."[35]

Here, the Court said, the Cantwells were on a public street, where they had every right to be and to impart their views peacefully to others. They had sought and received the permission of those they had met to play their record. They had not impeded traffic.

The essential characteristic of political and religious liberty, the Court concluded, was that people could express their views "unmolested and unobstructed."[36] In a country such as the United States in which people from so many nations and creeds coexisted, the Court said, the shield that protects the right to exercise and disseminate different religions was especially necessary. "In the realm of religious faith," the Court explained, as well as

> that of political belief, sharp differences arise. In both fields the tenets of one man may seem the rankest error to his neighbor. To persuade others to his own point of view, the pleader, as we know, at times, resorts to exaggeration, to vilification of men who have been, or are, prominent in church or state, and even to false statement. But the people of this nation have ordained in the light of history, that, in spite of the probability of excesses and abuses, these liberties are, in the long view, essential to enlightened opinion and right conduct on the part of the citizens of a democracy.[37]

[34] *Id.* at 307.
[35] *Id.* at 308.
[36] *Id.* at 310 ("The essential characteristic of these liberties is, that under their shield many types of life, character, opinion and belief can develop unmolested and unobstructed.").
[37] *Id.*

How far does protection of speech go in the United States? What does the First Amendment protect? Certainly speech such as that of the Cantwells that harshly criticized one religion in the service of trying to persuade listeners to join another. Certainly the Danish cartoons themselves. Certainly books such as Salmon Rushdie's *The Satanic Verses*, which offended many Muslims. Certainly movies such as Mel Gibson's "The Passion of the Christ," which offended many Jews, and "The Last Temptation of Christ," which offended many Christians. And certainly works of art such as Chris Ofili's "The Holy Virgin Mary," a painting which contained elephant dung (considered regenerative in Nigerian tribal culture) on the depiction of the Virgin Mary and which so inflamed New York's then-mayor Rudolph Giuliani for supposedly being sacrilegious that he, quite literally, sought to close down the Brooklyn Museum.[38] Are any of those – all of them? – the stuff of "defamation of religion"?

One way to articulate the American approach is nicely encapsulated in Professor Suk's correct observation that "[t]o the American legal mind, the punishment of Holocaust denial would not even constitute a hard case: such a prohibition would be a paradigmatic violation of the First Amendment's free speech guarantee."[39] The harder question is whether the United States *should* change that view (if the First Amendment allowed it).

The answer to that question ought not, I suggest, to be based on the sort of ad hoc balancing rejected in the *Stevens* case, in which one seeks to compare the general advantages of living in a society free enough to permit that grossest calumnies to be uttered with the potential harm caused by such speech. The Court in *Stevens* had it right, and not only as a historical matter, when it observed that the First Amendment presupposes generally that "the benefits of its restrictions on the Government outweigh the costs."[40]

I refer now not to the data provided by Professor Greene demonstrating the increasing loss of confidence in government reflected in polling data in the United States.[41] I refer instead to the lesson of history that banning or punishing "bad" speech leads inexorably to the empowering of governments to ban speech that others may think of as good, that censorship of speech leads to more censorship.

For myself, I start by thinking of the woman with whom then-Prime Minister Gordon Brown had the misfortune to meet less than a week before the 2010 British election. She spoke disparagingly of immigrants; he later spoke (he thought privately) disparagingly of her. As it happens, her speech was moderately phrased but her views nonetheless were clear enough to lead Brown to characterize her as a "bigot." But suppose she had been clearer still, denouncing immigrants in a manner deemed

---

[38] *See* Floyd Abrams, *Speaking Freely: Trials of the First Amendment* 188–230 (Viking 2005).
[39] Suk, *supra* note 14.
[40] *Stevens*, 130 S. Ct. at 1580.
[41] *See* Greene, *supra* note 5.

sufficiently "hateful" to fall within a hate-speech statute. Punishing her would put at issue the very legitimacy of the society that did so.[42]

To many people who live in democratic nations elsewhere than the United States, the American approach may sound rather romantic, unreal, unworldly. A world that has witnessed genocidal conduct in post-Holocaust areas ranging from Cambodia to Rwanda and now Darfur should take care not to deceive itself that the dangers of murderous conduct abetted by speech advocating it are ones of the past alone.

Some scholarly works have attributed thousands of deaths to the publication of a single book, *The Protocols of the Elders of Zion*.[43] So it is difficult to offer a "no, never" response to the notion of agreeing to the adoption in the United States of the rules so often applied in other democratic nations. And, as I have observed previously, I cannot condemn or even criticize states such as Germany and India, which have acted in light of their own historically demonstrated needs. But I do believe that any such action in the United States would impair democratic legitimacy, that the country would become bogged down in seemingly endless and surely overheated debate about which speech to ban, and that, as Professor Greene has observed, in practice "[h]ate speech restrictions in particular have a history of missing their originally intended marks."[44]

In the end, however, neither definitional difficulties nor those of rational implementation are the basis for my personal opposition to hate speech limitations in the United States. This is an issue of principle and Professor Harry Kalven had it right when he observed that in *"America there is no heresy, no blasphemy."*[45]

Justice Harlan put it this way:

> The constitutional right of free expression is powerful medicine in a society as diverse and populous as ours. . . .
>
> To many, the immediate consequence of this freedom may often appear to be only verbal tumult, discord, and even offensive utterance. These are, however, within established limits, in truth necessary side effects of the broader enduring values which the process of open debate permits us to achieve. That the air may at times seem filled with verbal cacophony is, in this sense not a sign of weakness but of strength.[46]

A system based on such values may not be fit for all nations. So far, however, it has served the United States well.

---

[42] This point about legitimacy is elaborated by Ronald Dworkin and Robert Post, and debated by Jeremy Waldron, in their contributions to the present volume. *See* Chapters 17, 1, and 16 herein.

[43] *See generally* Norman Cohn, *Warrant for Genocide: The Myth of the Jewish World Conspiracy and the Protocols of the Elders of Zion* (Penguin Books 1970).

[44] Greene, *supra* note 5.

[45] Harry Kalven, Jr., *A Worthy Tradition: Freedom of Speech in America* (Jamie Kalven ed., Harper & Row 1988).

[46] Cohen v. California, 403 U.S. 15, 24–5 (1971).

# PART II

# Refinements and Distinctions

# 7

# Social Epistemology, Holocaust Denial, and the Post-Millian Calculus

## Frederick Schauer

## I

It is no longer news that there are countries in which it is unlawful to deny the existence of the Nazi Holocaust.[1] Nor is it surprising that among these countries are Austria, Germany, and Israel, given the obvious historical reasons for their treatment of Holocaust denial with special sensitivity. But Holocaust denial is also a crime in Belgium, Canada, France, Spain, and Switzerland, among other countries, and a similar prohibition is now being proposed in Argentina. Moreover, existing

[1] The literature is extensive. In English, see, for example, *Extreme Speech and Democracy* 509–79 (Ivan Hare & James Weinstein eds., Oxford University Press 2009); Robert A. Kahn, *Holocaust Denial and the Law: A Comparative Study* (Palgrave Macmillan 2004); Lawrence Douglas, "Policing the Past: Holocaust Denial and the Law," in *Censorship and Silencing: Practices of Cultural Regulation* 67–88 (Robert C. Post ed., Getty Institute 1998); Stanley Fish, "Holocaust Denial and Academic Freedom," 35 *Valparaiso U. L. Rev.* 499 (2001); Credence Fogo-Schensul, "More Than a River in Egypt: Holocaust Denial, the Internet, and International Freedom of Expression Norms," 33 *Gonzaga L. Rev.* 241, 241–76 (1998); Emanuela Fronza, "The Punishment of Negationism: The Difficult Dialogue Between Law and Memory," 30 *Vt. L. Rev.* 609 (2006); Robert A. Kahn, "Cross-Burning, Holocaust Denial, and the Development of Hate Speech Law in the United States and Germany," 83 *U. Det. Mercy L. Rev.* 163 (2006) ; John Knechtle, "Holocaust Denial and the Concept of Dignity in the European Union," 36 *Florida St. U. L. Rev.* 41 (2008); Kenneth Lasson, "Holocaust Denial and the First Amendment: The Quest for Truth in a Free Society," 6 *Geo. Mason L. Rev.* 35 (1997); Lawrence McNamara, "History, Memory and Judgment: Holocaust Denial, the History Wars and Law's Problems with the Past," 26 *Sydney L. Rev.* 353 (2004); Eric Stein, "History against Free Speech: The New German Law against the 'Auschwitz' – and Other – 'Lies'," 85 *Mich. L. Rev.* 277 (1986); Peter R. Teachout, "Making 'Holocaust Denial' a Crime: Reflections on European Anti-Negationist Laws from the Perspective of U.S. Constitutional Experience," 30 *Vt. L. Rev.* 655 (2006); Richard H. Weisberg, "Fish Takes the Bait: Holocaust Denial and Post-Modern Theory," 14 *Law & Literature* 131 (2002).
Earlier versions of this chapter were delivered at the Columbia Law School, at the Conference on Unchallengeable Orthodoxies held at Arizona State University, and in a session of Vincent Blasi's course at the University of Virginia on the ideas of the First Amendment. I am grateful to Blasi and his students for the opportunity to try out my ideas and subject them to valuable critique, and for the comments of Michael Herz, Peter Molnar, and Kendall Thomas.

or proposed laws also deal with denial of genocide in, for example, Armenia and Rwanda,[2] and thus it is safe to say that the question of legal prohibitions on Holocaust denial is one of worldwide and not just regional or local interest.

Although the criminalization of Holocaust denial is thus hardly unique, it is also the case that in other countries, most obviously, but not only,[3] the United States, the very idea of punishing the expression of an idea on account of the idea's falsity goes to the heart of principle of freedom of speech. It is not simply that Holocaust denial is legally permitted and constitutionally protected in the United States. It is that the legal and constitutional permissibility of Holocaust denial is understood as a core and not merely a fringe application of the very idea of freedom of speech under the First Amendment.

The legal, constitutional, and political[4] protection of Holocaust denial in the name of freedom of expression owes its principal intellectual debt to John Stuart Mill. In *On Liberty*,[5] and especially in its second chapter, Mill provided us with what is still the canonical argument against enforced orthodoxy in opinion and expression.[6] As is well-known, Mill's argument for allowing even the most widely and firmly accepted truths to be criticized and contradicted is a three-pronged one. The second of those prongs is directed at the way in which the belief in accepted truths that are in fact true will be stronger if those beliefs must respond to challenges,[7] and the third focuses on the fact that the truths of even true accepted truths will typically be partial, such that we increase our knowledge when we allow even that which is largely true to be modified by seeing the truths in even that which is largely false.

Yet although these aspects of Mill's argument are important and enduring, it is the first prong of the argument in *On Liberty* that constitutes the core of Mill's claim, and that is of greatest relevance in considering the possibility of legal prohibitions on Holocaust denial, for now we are into the realm of prohibiting the expression

---

[2] *See* Pablo Salvador-Coderch and Antoni Rubí-Puig, "Genocide Denial and Freedom of Speech," 4 InDret (2008), *available at* www.indret.com/code/getPdf.php?id=1186&pdf=591_en.pdf.

[3] On Hungary, which did not prohibit Holocaust denial until 2010 despite its own close connection with the history of the Holocaust, see Peter Molnar, "Towards Better Law and Policy Against Hate Speech – The 'Clear and Present Danger' Test in Hungary," in *Extreme Speech and Democracy, supra* note 1, at 237.

[4] By "political" protection I mean only the unwillingness to prohibit Holocaust denial, usually for freedom-of-expression reasons, even in countries in which such a prohibition would be constitutionally permissible.

[5] John Stuart Mill, *On Liberty* (David Spitz ed., W.W. Norton 1975) (1859).

[6] The origins of the Millian position are somewhat earlier, and even as far back as 1644 John Milton in the *Areopagitica* asked, rhetorically, "who ever knew Truth put to the wors[e], in a free and open encounter?" John Milton, *Areopagitica: A Speech for the Liberty of Unlicensed Printing* 45 (H. B. Coterill ed., Macmillan & Co. 1957) (1644). On Milton as the precursor of the basic Millian position, see Vincent Blasi, *The Ideas of the First Amendment* 366 (West Publishing 2006).

[7] As Mill put it, even if the received opinion is true, allowing the expression of the false opinion will create "the clearer perception and livelier impression of truth, produced by its collision with error." Mill, *supra* note 5, at 18.

of that which seems plainly false. This is Mill's argument from fallibility, and it is the component of *On Liberty* that has been most influential in shaping the western culture of freedom of expression. Even that which we believe most confidently to be true, Mill argues, might be false, and so too with that which we are convinced is false, for that might in reality be true. To hold otherwise is not only to assume our own infallibility, but is also to risk losing the actual truths that are now mistakenly rejected. Only by permitting the expression of that which we most fervently and confidently believe to be false, he argues, do we retain the possibility of learning new truths and of rejecting as false that which we now mistakenly take to be true.

Millian fallibilism[8] and the related broader arguments from truth[9] – the "marketplace of ideas"[10] as a reliable, even if not perfect, method for separating true from false ideas – have waned somewhat as dominant themes in the law and literature of freedom of expression generally, but they are hardly dead.[11] Every time a civil liberties organization argues that the best remedy for false speech is more speech, for example, it relies on Mill's basic idea. So too when academics and others make claims for a special privilege of academic freedom, insisting that the goals of searching for truth and increasing the stock of human knowledge are central to the mission of the academy. Most relevantly here, however, is the way in which people are urged to "tolerate" that which they believe to be plainly false, with Holocaust denial being one of the persistent examples. My goal in this chapter, therefore, is to examine closely the Millian position – in some circles we might even think of it as the Millian orthodoxy – in the hope that understanding its assumptions and implications will assist us in determining where, if anywhere, its prescriptions ought to hold sway.

---

[8]  On Mill as fallibilist, see John Skorupski, *John Stuart Mill* 376–84 (Taylor & Francis 1989). Fallibilist ideas figure even more prominently in the work of Karl Popper. *See, e.g.*, Karl Popper, *The Logic of Scientific Discovery* (Routledge & Kegan Paul 1959); Karl Popper, *Conjectures and Refutations: The Growth of Scientific Knowledge* (Routledge & Kegan Paul 1963). Popper's defense of freedom of speech and inquiry in Karl Popper, *The Open Society and Its Enemies* (Routledge & Kegan Paul, 5th ed. 1966), is largely consistent with Mill. *See also* Jagdish N. Hattiangadi, "To Save Fallibilism," 92 *Mind* 407, 407–9 (1983).

[9]  *See* Frederick Schauer, *Free Speech: A Philosophical Enquiry* chapter 2 (Cambridge University Press 1982).

[10]  "[T]he best test of truth is the power of [a proposition] to get itself accepted in the competition of the market." Abrams v. United States, 250 U.S. 616, 630 (1919) (Holmes, J., dissenting). For the view that Holmes's reference to the "competition of the market" is less concerned with truth-finding than is commonly supposed, see Vincent Blasi, "Holmes and the Marketplace of Ideas," 2004 *Sup. Ct. Rev.* 1.

[11]  *See, e.g.*, Eric Barendt, *Freedom of Speech* 7–13 (Oxford University Press 1985); L. Wayne Sumner, *The Hateful and the Obscene: Studies in the Limits of Free Expression* 18–35 (University of Toronto Press 2004); Vincent Blasi, "Reading Holmes Through the Lens of Schauer: The *Abrams* Dissent," 72 *Notre Dame L. Rev.* 1343 (1997); Matthew Lynch, "Closing the Orwellian Loophole: The Present Constitutionality of Big Brother and the Potential for a First Amendment Cure," 5 *First Amend. L. Rev.* 234, 301–2 (2007).

II

An important preliminary qualification is in order: I address here only Mill's claim that it is wrong to suppress the expression of an idea on the grounds of its alleged falsity because it is always possible that the view we suppress as false may in fact be true. In so limiting the inquiry, I bracket the important question of whether nonepistemic goals might occasionally or even more often prevail over the goal of locating new truths, identifying errors, and in general advancing the store of human knowledge. Restrictions on Holocaust denial are again a key example, as are less formal inhibitions on discussing (or researching) the possibility that there may be race-based differences in human intelligence. I will return presently to the epistemic side of such restrictions and inhibitions, but it is important to bear in mind that many such restrictions are often motivated not by epistemic goals, but by a desire to reduce offense, create a comfortable environment for living or learning, or lessen the degree of religious or racial tension, discrimination, and violence. Even if the suppressed view were true, it might be argued, losing that truth is a price well worth paying to achieve various other goals that are important even if the suppressed view is in fact sound. Even if there actually were racially correlated differences in human intelligence, for example, allowing the discussion of those differences would likely impair the educational and social experiences of those statistically likely to be less intelligent, and might also increase the probability of discrimination or violence against them. Because maximizing the educational and social experiences of even the less intelligent is important, and preventing discrimination and violence against them (or retaliatory violence by them) even more so, there could be a social value in suppression of a view that would be largely or entirely independent of the truth or falsity of the view. So too with Holocaust denial. Even if the Holocaust had not taken place, or even if the claims of its magnitude are grossly exaggerated, it may nevertheless be the case that accepting the fact and the size of the Holocaust is important in lessening the manifestations of anti-Semitism, and thus there might be arguments for restricting Holocaust denial that were largely unrelated to the question of whether the Holocaust actually happened or whether it is merely a socially useful myth.

It is a serious omission of Mill's that he rarely, if ever, considers the possibility of suppression for reasons other than the alleged falsity of the suppressed view.[12] Implicitly, therefore, he treats the increase in knowledge as a value having a lexical priority over all other values.[13] By neglecting the possibility that various nonepistemic benefits might be worth the cost of some epistemic loss, Mill finds himself in the

---

[12] The most noteworthy exception is Mill's famous example of saying to an angry mob in front of the home of the corn dealer that corn dealers are starvers of the poor. But short of the threat of immediate violence, Mill does not discuss the nonepistemic goals that might justify restrictions on expression.

[13] L. Wayne Sumner argues that Mill's absolutism is best understood from a rule-utilitarian perspective, and thus Mill's act-absolutism might be a function of having already negatively evaluated the likelihood

position, odd for a professed utilitarian, of presupposing that the intrinsic good of knowledge is of greater value than any other human good, and is so much greater that no amount of nonepistemic benefit is worth the cost of even the smallest sacrifice of increased knowledge.

Mill is properly faulted on these lines, and the failure to consider that in many settings the argument for suppression is often social and psychological rather than epistemic is a flaw in much modern debate about these topics. Nevertheless, the weighing of epistemic against nonepistemic goals is not my primary concern here. Rather, I propose to evaluate the epistemic arguments on their own terms, and consider the implications and presuppositions of the argument, taken alone, that suppression is bad because, by denying us the possibility to replace false beliefs with true ones, and by denying us the possibility of replacing ignorance with knowledge, suppression of the nonreceived opinion is epistemically disadvantageous.

### III

It will be useful to explicate in greater detail the structure of the Millian claim that "[w]e can never be sure that the opinion we are endeavoring to stifle is a false opinion."[14] Thus, "the opinion which it is attempted to suppress by authority may possibly be true."[15] For Mill, to eliminate the possibility that the opinion rejected on account of its falsity may in actuality be true is to assume one's infallibility. And Mill believes that it is irrational to so assume one's infallibility, for that is to confuse one's own (psychological, or subjective) certainty with an (ontological) absolute certainty. We may think we are sure, but without access to reality in any way other than through our own minds, we must, he argues, be careful not to be overconfident of our own abilities to determine the truth.[16]

It is worth noting that Mill's argument is entirely epistemic and not at all ontological. He is no extreme (or even mild, for that matter) social constructionist, and plainly believes in the existence of a mind-independent reality. For Mill, the truth of a proposition, whether factual or moral, is not a matter of social consensus or individual perception. But although Mill evidences no doubts about the concept of objective truth, he is highly skeptical of the ability of fallible human beings to locate it with certainty, and even more skeptical of the ability of fallible human beings to assess accurately the reliability of their own opinions. Indeed, one might even describe Mill's position as less epistemic than psychological, in the sense that he

---

that some expression-outweighing consideration would prevail in a particular case. *See* Sumner, *supra* note 11.

[14] Mill, *supra* note 5, at 18.

[15] *Id.*

[16] Note also Holmes's warnings that "certitude is not the test of certainty," Oliver Wendell Holmes, "Natural Law," 32 *Harv. L. Rev.* 40, 40 (1918), and that time has "upset many fighting faiths," *Abrams*, 250 U.S. at 630 (Holmes, J., dissenting).

appears to believe that real human beings can rationally have more confidence in the truth of some propositions than in others. Where our rationality fails us, however, is in our ability to match our confidence in the truth of a proposition with the likelihood that the proposition is true. And because we are likely to be overconfident in assessing the reliability of our own opinions,[17] we are accordingly unlikely to be able to gauge with any reliability the size of the possibility that what we now believe to be false might in reality be true.

Because of this psychological proclivity toward overconfidence, Mill argues, and because our confidence increases to the extent that others share our opinions, the problems of epistemic or psychological overconfidence are even greater with respect to widely held beliefs than for individual opinions. Thus, "ages are no more infallible than individuals; every age having held many opinions which subsequent ages have deemed not only false but absurd; and it is as certain that many opinions, now general, will be rejected by future ages, as it is that many, once general, are rejected by the present."[18]

Mill is too perceptive to ignore the way in which some degree of confidence in the correctness of our judgments is a prerequisite for acting on those judgments. "We may, and must, assume our opinion to be true for the guidance of our own conduct," he acknowledges, but he refuses to draw from this seeming concession the conclusion that there is no difference between taking action on the basis of our presumed certainty and suppressing opposing opinions on the basis of that same certainty. "There is the greatest difference between presuming an opinion to be true, because, with every opportunity for contesting it, it has not been refuted, and assuming its truth for the purpose of not permitting its refutation. Complete liberty of contradicting and disproving our opinion, is the very condition which justifies us in assuming its truth for the purposes of action; and on no other terms can a being with human faculties have any rational assurance of being right."[19]

Yet for Mill, the virtue of allowing the expression of opinions opposed to our best current assessment of truth is not only a matter of justifying the truth of our opinions for purposes of action. It is also the way in which knowledge advances: "Wrong opinions and practices gradually yield to fact and argument: but facts and

---

[17] A century and a half later, cognitive and social psychologists would show that the tendency to be overconfident in one's judgments is as great, if not greater, for experts as for novices, a finding that lends much support to Mill's conclusions. *See* Markus Glaser, Thomas Langer, and Martin Weber, "Overconfidence of Professionals and Lay People: Individual Differences Within and Between Tasks?" (2010), *available at* http://papers.ssrn.com/abstract=712583; Leilani Greening and Carla C. Chandler, "Why It Can't Happen to Me: The Base Rate Matters, but Overestimating Skill Leads to Underestimating Risk," 27 *J. Applied Soc. Psychol.* 760, 760–74 (1997). Mill does observe that "[a]bsolute princes, or others who are accustomed to unlimited deference, usually feel this complete confidence in their own opinions on nearly all subjects," Mill, *supra* note 5, at 19, and can thus be credited with anticipating in a less systematic matter what has now been observed more scientifically.

[18] Mill, *supra* note 5, at 23.

[19] *Id.* at 20.

arguments, to produce any effect on the mind, must be brought before it."[20] And it is for this reason that Mill rejects as a "pleasant falsehood" the "dictum that truth always triumphs over persecution."[21] Rather, "[h]istory teems with instances of truth put down by persecution."[22] But if the persecution, whether official or social, persists, then we will have eliminated the possibility of exchanging error for truth, and thus advancing the state of human knowledge.

We can now recapitulate the core of the Millian argument: We increase our knowledge by leaving our current opinions constantly open to revision, and in this way we justify acting on our current imperfect knowledge. Allowing the expression of that which we believe most fervently to be false thus gives us both the opportunity to increase our knowledge and the confidence that what we now believe imperfectly to be true is at least more likely true than any of the now-known alternatives.

IV

Mill's argument has been profoundly influential in identifying the negative consequences of suppression, especially the consequence of losing the possibility of gaining new knowledge. It is quite remarkable, however, especially for a utilitarian committed to evaluating both the benefits *and* costs of any proposed action, that Mill seemingly ignores any of the consequences, even the epistemic ones, of non-suppression. He is eloquent and persuasive on the question of what we might lose if we refuse to allow the expression of that which we believe most fervently to be false, but strangely silent on the question of what we might lose if we allow that expression. In other words, we find nothing in Mill that addresses the potential benefits of orthodoxy, or the potential benefits of using the enforcement apparatuses of the state and of nonstate social norm enforcement to enforce belief (by way of a prohibition on expression of the contrary view) in a prevailing opinion.

To put a somewhat sharper edge on this question, we should consider the possibility – the probability, most likely – that many of the things we believe to be true really are true. Perhaps we cannot, as Mill warns us, be totally, absolutely, completely sure that what we think is true is actually true, but it is important not to confuse possibly or conceivably untrue with probably untrue. And once we see this, we then must consider, as Mill and his followers seem not to have, the consequences of allowing the expression of that which not only seems false, but in fact is false, and the consequences of encouraging challenges to that which not only seems true, but in fact is true. What, then, would be the (epistemic) consequences of allowing or encouraging challenges to the view that the Holocaust actually happened in roughly the way most people now understand it if in fact the way that most people

[20]  *Id.* at 33.
[21]  *Id.* at 28.
[22]  *Id.*

now understand the Holocaust is more or less accurate? In other words, what are the epistemic consequences of allowing Holocaust denial if Holocaust denial is false?

The principal potential consequence of allowing the expression of that which is false is that the expression of the falsity may increase the number of people who believe in the proposition despite its falsity, or who have greater confidence in the truth of a false proposition than they did prior to its frequent or prevalent expression.[23] Mill is surely right in observing the way in which confidence in an opinion increases insofar as others hold the same opinion, but if this is so, then confidence in a false opinion – and a willingness to act on a false opinion – will increase in just the same way when its expression proliferates.

Mill seems to exclude the possibility of proliferation of error by expression because of his reliance on the belief that "wrong opinions and practices gradually yield to fact and argument,"[24] but is this true? We might say that every propositional speech act contains a variety of attributes. These would include, for example, the identity and attributes of the speaker, the identity and attributes of the hearer, the prior beliefs of the hearer, the form of expression chosen by the speaker, the hearer's opinion of the speaker, society's opinion of the speaker, and many others, one of which – but only one of which – is the truth of the proposition being articulated. We can then reformulate the question by asking how powerful the truth of a proposition is in determining which propositions will be accepted and which rejected, as compared to all of the other attributes of a propositional speech act in producing the phenomenon of acceptance or rejection. Not surprisingly for a rationalist like Mill, he implicitly

---

[23] There is an important but rarely discussed (a noteworthy exception is Alvin I. Goldman, *Knowledge in a Social World* [Cambridge University Press 1999]) question of social epistemology here – the question of just what it is for a group or a society to know something. In a society of a thousand people, say, is there more knowledge when a hundred people know something that is true than when just ten know it? And so too in reverse. Is there less knowledge when a hundred people have a false belief than when merely ten do? Is a society in which a hundred people have a false belief a less *epistemically* desirable one than a society in which only ten have a false belief, or is the degree of prevalence of false belief epistemically inconsequential so long as one member of the society has a true belief about the same subject? And thus suppose if we have one society of one hundred people, twenty have a true belief in $x$, ten have a false belief in not-$x$, and seventy have no beliefs at all about $x$. And then suppose that in another society (or in the same society at some later time), forty people have a true belief in $x$, fifty people have a false belief in not-$x$, and ten have no beliefs at all about $x$. We can then ask two interrelated questions: first, does the second society have more knowledge about $x$ because more people have true beliefs in $x$, or does the second society have less knowledge about $x$ because more people have false beliefs about $x$; and, second, apart from the question of how we *define* collective knowledge, which between the first or second societies is epistemically better off? And even if we could sort out what it was for a population to know something, is a society that believes $n$ true propositions and $p$ false ones more or less epistemically well off than one that believes $n+1$ true propositions but also $p+1$ false ones? Much of the free-speech tradition, and especially that part of the tradition influenced by Mill, appears to have assumed that any society with more beliefs in the truth, or with beliefs in more truths, is better than a society with less, but has done so without considering the trade-offs between true and false beliefs and the possibility that a process for producing more true beliefs might produce more false beliefs as well.

[24] Mill, *supra* note 5, at 28.

believes that the truth of a true proposition will be the dominant (exclusive?) factor in producing its acceptance. There are, however, alternative hypotheses, especially the hypothesis that the acceptance of a proposition is less dependent on its truth than Mill believed, and more dependent on, for example, the style (words chosen, visuals, emphasis, rhetoric, and much else) in which the proposition is expressed, the prior beliefs of the listeners (who are more likely to believe false propositions when they accord with their previously held false beliefs), the charisma, expertise, and authority of the speaker, the frequency with which the proposition is expressed, and the extent to which the proposition satisfies various pragmatic, psychological, or emotional needs of the listener.[25] Ultimately this is an empirical question, one subject to genuine examination using modern experimental and other methods in the social sciences.[26] Mill provides a few selected historical anecdotes but no systematic evidence or examination,[27] and the insights of modern social science and the experience of modern marketing should give us pause before we too quickly assume that the truth of a proposition is the most significant factor in determining whether that proposition will be accepted by a given person or audience.[28]

## V

We must thus consider the possibility that the suppression of challenges to orthodoxies such as the orthodoxy that the Holocaust is historical fact at times serve to decrease

---

[25] Since the 1976 publication of Richard Dawkins, *The Selfish Gene* (Oxford University Press 1976), there has developed a substantial literature on the cultural evolution of the ideas, symbols, and the like that Dawkins calls "memes." Dawkins and his followers are Millian insofar as they believe that a process of evolution and natural selection leads desirable or useful or valuable memes to survive while memes that are less so will wither, but the value of a meme to Dawkins and his successors is not strictly a function of its propositional truth, even if a meme is one that is capable of being true or false.

[26] And from a less empirical perspective, the modern analytic and formal insights about the economics of information may assist us in understanding the ways in which markets for ideas and information are like and unlike markets for goods and services.

[27] The larger point here is that the causal relationship between communications and research environment, as the independent variable, and the acceptance of true propositions and the rejection of false ones, as the dependent variable, is an empirical and not a philosophical question, although its development and discussion has been left largely to the philosophers and the lawyers. But Alvin Goldman recognizes this and draws on the psychological research showing that factual opinions are far less open to evidence-based revision than Mill supposes. Alvin I. Goldman, "Epistemic Paternalism: Communication Control in Law and Society," 88 *J. Phil.* 113, 113 31 (1991).

[28] Consider, for example, the case of Henry Fonda's character in the classic 1957 film *Twelve Angry Men*. As is well known, the Fonda character eventually persuaded eleven of his fellow jurors to exchange their false belief in the defendant's guilt for the true belief that the defendant might not be guilty. But he had at his disposal not only the truth of the proposition that he was urging, but also his good looks, his charm, his rhetorical ability, his persistence, his passion, and his white suit. If we were to hold constant his looks, his charm, his rhetorical ability, his persistence, his passion, and his sartorial accoutrements, but change the proposition he urged from a true one to a false one, would the outcome have been different? Possibly, but there is also the possibility that all of these attributes other than truth could or would have persuaded eleven people to exchange their true belief for a false one.

the likelihood that false ideas will spread (and be acted on) despite their falsity. And although when and where this might happen, as well as for which propositions or types of propositions it is most likely, are irreducibly empirical issues, recognizing this possibility enables us to understand what we might call the post-Millian calculus. That is, when we allow the expression of that which we believe to be false, we, as Mill properly insisted, increase the probability of increasing our knowledge with respect to any given proposition, and we likely produce an aggregate increase in knowledge across a population and over time. But we also may increase the number of people who hold false beliefs, which is itself an epistemic negative, and possibly also increase the frequency with which those false beliefs may produce action with unfortunate consequences. The post-Millian calculus, which Mill directed us to but did not himself embrace, suggests that an institution or practice of suppression, for some category of utterances within some domain of speakers and listeners (or writers and readers), can be justified only when (but not always when) it is predicted that the consequential losses from the spread of false opinions that might be accepted and acted on despite their falsity will be greater than the consequential gains that will come from the discovery of previously unknown truths and the increase in knowledge that is the corollary of that discovery.

It is of course true that we cannot make these determinations with anything close to certainty. We cannot know what we do not know, and thus any predictions of what we might learn from discouraging orthodoxy will be highly speculative, and so too, obviously, will be the future value of learning what we do not now know. And so too on the other side of the calculus. Our predictions about the likelihood that people will be persuaded of this or that false belief are only guesses, as are our estimates of the harms, if any, that will ensue when people hold false beliefs.

Therefore, decision to encourage or discourage some enforced or unchallengeable orthodoxy, as well as the decision to encourage or discourage all orthodoxies, or orthodoxies of some type, will be a decision made under extreme uncertainty. But decisions under uncertainty are a pervasive feature of the human predicament. And we are thus familiar with thinking of them as decisions involving the comparison of the likelihood and consequences of different types of errors. In this context, therefore, the question is whether the expected harm – the likelihood of error times its severity – of stifling those beliefs that are in fact true is greater than the expected harm of allowing the circulation of those beliefs that are in fact false.

Once we understand the orthodoxy problem as a problem in decision theory involving assessing the expected harm of two different types of errors – statisticians label them the Type I and Type II errors, and others think in terms of false negatives and false positives – we can understand Mill's perspective, or, to put a sharper point on it, perceive Mill's error. In pointing out eloquently and persuasively the harms that may come from suppressing that which is in fact true, and in glossing over the harms that may come from allowing that which is in fact false, Mill appears to have adopted one or both of two background assumptions. One is that he may have believed that the conceivably permanent harms coming from lost truths are so great as to outweigh all other harms, and certainly the harms coming from the possibly only temporary spread of false beliefs. If the loss (or even the delay) of a truth is so great a harm as to be lexically prior to all other harms,[29] then the error of losing a truth is so great that there is no need to consider the error of allowing the spread of a falsehood. To the extent that Mill believed that the value of knowledge so dominated all other values, therefore, it is not surprising that for him the error of suppressing that which is in fact true was so great that there was no need to consider the error ensuing from not suppressing that which is in fact false. In this respect, Mill may be seen as adopting a version of what, in the context of regulation of environmental hazards, nuclear material, and genetically modified foods, for example, goes by the name of the *precautionary principle*.[30] If we are unsure of the consequences of some phenomenon or material or process, the principle holds, we should err on the side of restriction for fear of an unknown disaster. Better to be safe than sorry, as the venerable expression would put it. And thus Mill might be understood as applying a precautionary principle to public epistemology, believing that we should guard at almost all costs against the possibility that we will lose a truth we do not now know, whose currently unknown value may turn out to be vast, and which, if lost now, may never be recovered.[31]

Alternatively, Mill appears also to have believed that the harms flowing from failing to suppress that which is in fact false would not be large, this being largely the consequence of his faith in the ability of people to identify truth when it is shown to them. For Mill the rationalist, echoing Milton in the *Areopagitica* two centuries earlier in believing that truth would always win in an open fight with falsity, the harms that would come from allowing the propagation of error would be temporary and small, for human reason could, if only given the opportunity, identify error and keep it from doing much harm. Without the benefit of official suppression or social intolerance, falsities would rarely ripen into orthodoxies.

---

[29]  For discussion, see Frederick Schauer, "Reflections on the Value of Truth," 41 *Case W. Res. L. Rev.* 699, 699–724 (1991).

[30]  *See, e.g.*, Cass R. Sunstein, *The Laws of Fear: Beyond the Precautionary Principle* (Cambridge University Press, 2005); Arie Trouwborst, *The Evolution and Status of the Precautionary Principle in International Law* (Kluwer Law International 2002); David A. Dana, "A Behavioral Economic Defense of the Precautionary Principle," 97 *Nw. U.L. Rev.* 1315 (2003); Jonathan Remy Nash, "Standing and the Precautionary Principle," 108 *Colum. L. Rev.* 494 (2008); Gary E. Marchant and Kenneth L. Mossman, "Please Be Careful: The Spread of Europe's Precautionary Principle Could Wreak Havoc on Economies, Public Health, and Plain Old Common Sense," *Legal Times*, Aug. 15, 2005.

[31]  Of course the precautionary principle could be reversed in this context, because those urging restriction might be seen as wishing to take all possible precautions against speech-caused harms, arguably different in kind as well as degree with respect to Holocaust denial and genocide denial, that we cannot now comprehend. *See generally* Frederick Schauer, "Is it Better to Be Safe than Sorry?: Free Speech and the Precautionary Principle," 36 *Pepp. L. Rev.* 301 (2009).

VI

Mill's belief in the preeminent value of truth seems narrow, but it is his confidence in the power of human rationality to distinguish truth from falsity and thus to minimize the negative effects of the latter that seems to many a contemporary reader almost quaint. Demonstrable falsehoods thrive despite their demonstrated falsity – consider astrology, *The Protocols of the Elders of Zion*, the view that AIDS was intentionally introduced into the population by the American government, the beliefs that President Obama was born in Kenya and that President Bush knew in advance about the 9/11 attacks, and the vast sums earned by those who promote, for example, diet slippers and diet earrings as sure-fire cures for obesity.[32] Moreover, the persistence of so many so-called urban legends[33] is a valuable caution against assuming too quickly that truth is a highly effective remedy against false belief.

The normative narrowness and empirical doubtfulness of the Millian account[34] explains part of why Millian epistemic arguments for freedom of expression have taken a back seat in recent years, typically replaced by arguments premised on the values of democratic deliberation, individual self-expression, personal autonomy, personal identity, human dignity, self-governance, challenges to authority, and many others. But once we understand the assumptions of the Millian perspective, we can understand why such arguments still have a special importance in the context of discussions about the value of open inquiry and unrestricted communication in academic settings.[35] It may be that for an entire polity the discovery of truth is only one value among many, but we live in a world of differentiated institutions serving different social roles and thus having different missions. Perhaps the institution of academic inquiry and research – an institution that ought not to be confused with the universe and functions of schools, colleges, and universities[36] – is one that has been implicitly entrusted with the task of increasing knowledge. Insofar as that is true, we might conclude that Mill's presupposed transcendent value of truth, even

[32] *See* Federal Trade Commission, Deception in Weight Loss Advertising: A Workshop (Nov. 19, 2002), *available at* http://www.ftc.gov/bcp/workshops/weightloss/transcripts/transcript-full.pdf.

[33] *See* Chip Heath and Dan Heath, *Made to Stick: Why Some Ideas Survive and Others Die* (Random House 2007).

[34] *See* Alvin I. Goldman and James C. Cox, "Speech, Truth, and the Free Market for Ideas," 2 *Legal Theory* 1 (1996); Stanley Ingber, "The Marketplace of Ideas: A Legitimizing Myth," 1984 *Duke L.J.* 1 (1984). *Cf.* William P. Marshall, "In Defense of the Search for Truth as a First Amendment Justification," 30 *Ga. L. Rev.* 1 (1995).

[35] *See, e.g.,* Paul Horwitz, "*Grutter*'s First Amendment," 46 *B.C. L. Rev.* 461 (2005); Paul Horwitz, "Universities as First Amendment Institutions: Some Easy Answers and Hard Questions," 54 *UCLA L. Rev.* 1497 (2007); John A. Scanlan, "Aliens in the Marketplace of Ideas: The Government, the Academy, and the McCarrant-Walter Act," 66 *Texas L. Rev.* 1481 (1988); Frederick Schauer, "Towards an Institutional First Amendment," 89 *Minn. L. Rev.* 1256 (2005); James Weinstein, "Institutional Review Boards and the Constitution," 101 *Nw. U.L. Rev.* 493 (2007).

[36] The qualification is based on the fact that much important research is done in think tanks and research centers with no formal teaching function and often with no university affiliation. Conversely, many junior colleges, community colleges, and even universities have little or no research mission.

if not necessarily sound for society at large, might nevertheless be so within the confines of academic research and inquiry. Even if Mill is properly criticized for not recognizing the full panoply of nonepistemic considerations that might inform the question of when to encourage and when to discourage orthodoxies, it may still be that in academic settings these nonepistemic considerations are properly relegated to a decidedly secondary status.

Furthermore, on the other side of the calculation of consequences, it may also be that the risks of accepted falsity are much less in research domains. Mill may have been wildly optimistic in believing human beings generally to be reliably capable of distinguishing truth from falsity, but it may be much closer to the mark to imagine such capacities within the rarified precincts of academic inquiry. And if this is true,[37] then the dangers of unsuppressed falsity will be diminished dramatically, because here, even if more rarely elsewhere, falsity may be identified for what it is far more frequently and far more quickly. Even if truth does not have huge explanatory power in determining which ideas the public (or their political and cultural leaders) will accept and which they will reject, it may have substantially more explanatory power in predicting or determining which ideas will be accepted and which rejected in academic inquiry.

These suppositions about academic domains are also empirical to the core, and abstract academic speculation is no substitute for serious empirical research about the role of truth in actual academic inquiry. But if the hypothesis that truth does (empirically) matter more in academic inquiry than it does for the world at large, and if it is also true that as a matter of normative institutional design truth *should* matter more in academic inquiry than it in fact does (or should) for the world at large, then Mill may have provided us with the foundations for a freedom of academic inquiry and research even if his arguments for freedom of expression have long since been relegated to a subsidiary position.

## VII

We return to Holocaust denial. The topic of Holocaust denial is itself important, and the pervasiveness of Holocaust denial in contemporary anti-Semitic discourse invites consideration of just why it is that Holocaust denial, which obviously is of far more recent vintage than anti-Semitism itself, figures so prominently in contemporary anti-Semitism.

Even apart from the role that Holocaust denial plays in modern anti-Semitism, however, the question of Holocaust denial provides a prime example of a central

---

[37] Which, as an empirical matter, it may not be. Whether academics, even in their research and inquiry functions, are less prone than nonacademics to groupthink, susceptibility to status rather than argument, and many other impediments to rational inquiry, is an investigatable empirical question, the answer to which involves examining more than the self-serving pronouncements of academics themselves.

theme in the history of free-speech thought – the belief that restricting the expression of a view because of its falsity is fundamentally inconsistent with the idea of free speech itself. Indeed, the tension between restricting Holocaust denial and one of the central themes of the free speech tradition is implicitly (and sometimes explicitly) acknowledged in the view that restrictions on Holocaust denial are different from other restrictions on falsity precisely because of the persistence of anti-Semitism and because anti-Semitism has historically taken a particular form.

But is Holocaust denial in fact a special case? The arguments for restricting Holocaust denial typically rely on the extent to which the belief that the Holocaust never occurred persists in the face of overwhelming and widely accessible evidence to the contrary. The persistence of such apparently counterfactual belief is undeniable, but is it as unique to Holocaust denial as is often assumed. Perhaps instead, Holocaust denial is simply a dramatic example of the widespread resistance of popular (and sometimes academic) opinion to argument and factual demonstration?[38] If this latter supposition is true, then the case of Holocaust denial may tell us much about epistemic arguments for free speech in general, and not just about the supposedly special case of Holocaust denial.

Moreover, what Holocaust denial tells us about the epistemic arguments for free speech may have some application to other rationales often understood to undergird the principle of free speech. Arguments from democratic decision making, from individual self-realization (or self-governance or self-expression), and from autonomy, among others, remain somewhat connected to a rationalist view of human thought that Holocaust denial may well call into question. If the resistance of Holocaust denial to argument and evidence tells us something about human thought in general, then it may tell us something about free speech in general as well.

Acknowledging the lessons for freedom of expression generally that can be drawn from controversies about Holocaust denial is not to deny the extent to which Holocaust denial is a component of the category of hate speech as well as, arguably, a component of the category of freedom of expression. Although hate speech is treated in contemporary debates as a distinct category, all of the arguments for restricting a particular variety of hate speech are connected with arguments for restricting (or not restricting) some larger category not necessarily limited to race, ethnicity, religion, gender, sexual orientation, and so on. Controversies about racial insults, for example, are also controversies about insults, and are thus about the extent to which, if at all, a racial insult is different from the nonracial insults that also generate free-speech controversies.[39] So too with race-based or religion-based or ethnicity-based offensive speech, where the dispute is about whether such offensiveness is different from or similar to the kinds of offensiveness that, at least in the United States, has long been

---

[38]  *See* Frederick Schauer, "Facts and the First Amendment," 57 *UCLA L. Rev.* 897 (2010).

[39]  Chaplinsky v. New Hampshire, 315 U.S. 568 (1942) ("You are a God damned racketeer . . . and Fascist"); Rosenfeld v. New Jersey, 408 U.S. 901 (1972) ("mother-fucker"); Gooding v. Wilson, 405 U.S. 518 (1972) ("son of a bitch").

constitutionally protected.[40] And issues regarding the extent to which incitement to racial hatred should be prohibited take place in the shadow of determinations about whether and when incitements to illegality should be prohibited.[41]

Once we recognize that virtually all of the harms typically alleged by those urging hate speech controls have potential counterparts apart from the domains of hate speech, we can see that much the same applies to the form of hate speech that consists of Holocaust denial or genocide denial. Here the larger category is the category of public falsity, and we can no more understand why we should (or should not) tolerate the particular type of public falsity that is Holocaust denial without first understanding the issues involved in deciding to tolerate public falsity in general than we can understand racial insults without understanding insults, racially offensive speech with understanding offense, and incitement to racial hatred without understanding incitement.

This is not to say that the harms involved in Holocaust denial are necessarily similar to or even, magnitude aside, commensurable with the harms involved in other forms of public falsity, and so too with insult, offense, and incitement. But we cannot understand the arguments that a certain form of hate speech is an exception to otherwise prevailing free speech principles unless we understand both those principles and the relationship between the harms of a certain kind of hate speech and the harms that any nontrivial free speech principle routinely tolerates.[42] To suppose that hate speech is some sort of entirely unique category is a blunder, and we will understand the arguments for restriction and protection only if we comprehend the full range of issues involved in the domain to which a certain type of hate speech is alleged to be an exception. Holocaust denial is a type of hate, but it is also a type of falsity, and we can deal with the issue of hate-based falsity only when we understand not only the harms of hate, but also the harms of falsity and the arguments for tolerating them in the name of freedom of speech. These arguments have been around since Milton and Mill, among others, but they may rest on faulty empirical premises and an unduly crude decision theory. Recognizing this is far from sufficient to justify regulation of Holocaust denial, but it may be sufficient to recognize that the slogans we have inherited from Milton, Mill, Holmes, and others may raise more questions than they answer.

---

[40]  Cohen v. California, 403 U.S. 15 (1971) ("Fuck the draft").

[41]  Brandenburg v. Ohio, 395 U.S. 444 (1969).

[42]  *See generally* Schauer, *supra* note 9; Frederick Schauer, "The Phenomenology of Speech and Harm," 103 *Ethics* 635 (1993).

# 8

# Denying Experience

## *Holocaust Denial and the Free-Speech Theory of the State*

### *Julie C. Suk*

American constitutional law is exceptionally protective of racist speech. Racist speech is criminally punishable in many western democracies,[1] even though these countries' laws also protect the freedom of expression. Furthermore, many European countries punish Holocaust denial,[2] based on the understanding that it is a form of racist, anti-Semitic propaganda. In the United States, however, racist speech is protected by the First Amendment's free-speech guarantee. To the American legal mind, the punishment of Holocaust denial would not even constitute a hard case: such a prohibition would be a paradigmatic violation of the First Amendment's free-speech guarantee.[3]

---

[1] For an extensive account of the prohibitions of hate speech and their application in Canada and various European countries, see Michel Rosenfeld, "Hate Speech in Constitutional Jurisprudence: A Comparative Analysis," Chapter 13 herein.

[2] Holocaust denial is criminally punishable in France, Germany, Austria, Belgium, Spain, Portugal, Poland, Italy, and Switzerland. Until recently, Hungary had not prohibited Holocaust denial, an approach consistent with the Constitutional Court's generally protective stance toward speech. *See* Peter Molnar, "Towards Improved Law and Policy on 'Hate Speech' – The 'Clear and Present Danger' Test in Hungary," in *Extreme Speech and Democracy* 237 (Ivan Hare and James Weinstein eds., Oxford University Press 2009). In 2010, however, Hungary too made Holocaust denial a criminal offense.

[3] As Frederick Schauer puts it:

> It is not only that Holocaust denial is legally permitted and constitutionally protected in the United States. It is that the legal and constitutional permissibility of Holocaust denial is understood as a core and not merely a fringe application of the very idea of freedom of speech under the First Amendment.

Frederick Schauer, "Social Epistemology, Holocaust Denial, and the Post-Millian Calculus," Chapter 7 herein.

Thanks to Youngjae Lee, Peter Molnar, Robert Post, and an anonymous reviewer for Cambridge University Press for helpful comments on earlier drafts, and to Henry Rousso for fascinating discussions of the topics discussed in this chapter. The author is grateful to the participants in the hate speech conferences at Cardozo Law School in November 2005 and Central European University in March 2006 for their reactions and criticisms. Translations, unless otherwise indicated, are my own.

A close engagement with the foreign practice of prohibiting Holocaust denial can shed light on the normative and descriptive propositions underlying our protection of racist speech. In contrasting American racist-speech doctrine with the French experience of prohibiting and punishing Holocaust denial, this chapter compares the two legal cultures' different understandings of the processes by which a democratic state legitimates its authority to govern a society in which racial minorities are now equal citizens. These divergent accounts of democratic legitimacy have implications for the manner in which the legal system pursues racial equality.

American First Amendment cases addressing racist speech rest not on an individual right to express hatred, but rather on a particular theory of the state.[4] The Supreme Court has held that even though the First Amendment does not protect "fighting words," it nonetheless prohibits the state from singling out *racist* fighting words for punishment.[5] The primary concern in racist-speech doctrine is not the speaker's autonomy, or even the contribution of racist speech to the marketplace of ideas. Rather, it is that the state would be undermining its own democratic legitimacy were it to discriminate against certain viewpoints. According to this theory, the state cannot maintain its democratic legitimacy if it "cuts off any citizen from the possibility of participating in collective self-determination."[6] It cannot cut off racists and Holocaust deniers from the opportunity to influence democratic will formation.

In France, by criminalizing Holocaust denial, the state makes clear that racism has no place in collective self-determination. This exclusion enhances, rather than undermines, the state's legitimacy, because the state cannot govern legitimately unless it makes a strong, clear break with a past racist regime. The law against Holocaust denial participates in this legitimating rupture. To explore this process of legitimation, I examine the historical dynamics that led to the reestablishment of the French republic following World War II and the defeat of the Vichy regime. Laws prohibiting racist speech and Holocaust denial do not play the same role in every society, but in France, the law participates in the society's self-conscious construction of its own past. The history and genealogy of the current laws prohibiting racist speech and Holocaust denial show how significant these laws are to the legitimacy of the current republic.

---

[4] The Supreme Court has been generally hostile to content-based regulation of speech. Geoffrey Stone has identified four underlying concerns for this hostility: equality, communicative impact, distortion of the public debate, and motivation. *See* Geoffrey Stone, "Content Regulation and the First Amendment," 25 *Wm. & Mary L. Rev.* 189, 201–33 (1983). On close examination, all four of these underlying concerns are premised on the assumption that the state should be neutral, antipaternalistic, facilitating of impartial and unbiased public debate, and tolerant of ideas of which it disapproves. *See id.* at 203, 212–14, 225–6, 229.

[5] *See* R.A.V. v. City of St. Paul, 505 U.S. 377, 391–2 (1992).

[6] Robert C. Post, "Community and the First Amendment," 29 *Ariz. St. L.J.* 473, 481 (1997). A similar argument is made by Ronald Dworkin. *See* Ronald Dworkin, "Foreword," in *Extreme Speech and Democracy, supra* note 2, at v–ix.

Comparative engagement with the French experience can lead to sharper articulations of the explanations for America's distinctive commitment to protecting racist speech. Why does the American state's legitimacy depend on the opportunity of all communities, including racist ones, to participate in collective self-determination? How does our current legal order understand the significance of the state's past participation in perpetuating racism? And what are the consequences of our approach for the ways in which our law pursues racial equality?

## I. THE FREE-SPEECH THEORY OF THE STATE

I shall begin by articulating the theory of state legitimacy that underlies our racist-speech doctrine. In *R.A.V. v. City of St. Paul*, the Supreme Court struck down on First Amendment grounds a criminal ordinance prohibiting "the display of a symbol which one knows or has reason to know arouses anger, alarm, or resentment in others on the basis of race, color, creed, religion, or gender."[7] The case grew out of the prosecution of several teenagers who burned a cross inside a fenced yard belonging to a black family.

The Court's reasoning is ultimately that the state cannot limit the speech of those expressing racial hatred while permitting other hateful messages:

> Displays containing some words – odious racial epithets, for example – would be prohibited to proponents of all views. But "fighting words" that do not themselves invoke race, color, creed, religion, or gender – aspersions upon a person's mother, for example – would seemingly be usable *ad libitum* in the placards of those arguing *in favor* of racial, color, etc., tolerance and equality, but could not be used by those speakers' opponents. One could hold up a sign saying, for example, that all "anti-Catholic bigots" are misbegotten; but not that all "papists" are, for that would insult and provoke violence "on the basis of religion." *St. Paul has no such authority to license one side of a debate to fight freestyle, while requiring the other to follow Marquis of Queensberry rules.*[8]

Even when messages are expressed through forms of expression not otherwise protected under free-speech doctrine, the state must refrain from expressing special hostility to racist fighting words. The First Amendment prevents the state from proscribing some fighting words and not others, based on content: "The government may not regulate use based on hostility – or favoritism – towards the underlying message expressed."[9]

According to this theory, what is wrong with the St. Paul ordinance is not that it bans too much speech, but that it bans too little. Under this analysis, a blanket ban on all fighting words would be constitutionally permissible, because nobody

---

[7]  *See R.A.V.*, 505 U.S. at 381.
[8]  *Id.* at 391–2 (emphasis added).
[9]  *Id.* at 386.

has a First Amendment right to express fighting words, but a narrower ban on racist fighting words is unconstitutional because it reflects state favoritism toward antiracist or antisexist points of view. What renders the law illegitimate is the state's hostility to a particular viewpoint, not the burdens on the individual autonomy interests in speaking. In public discourse, the state compromises its legitimacy by taking sides against racists, because it implies that democratic deliberation is not open to all. This message can undermine the state's legitimacy in a pluralistic society, in which the state is supposed to be open to all of its citizens.

This vision of the state is perpetuated in the more recent case of *Virginia v. Black*.[10] There the Court upheld the criminal punishment of cross burning with intent to intimidate, but it did so precisely because the statute in question prohibited *all* cross burnings with such intent, without singling out racist cross burnings in particular. Unlike the St. Paul ordinance at issue in R.A.V., the Virginia statute made no reference to race, religion, gender, or other demographic characteristics:

> It does not matter whether an individual burns a cross with intent to intimidate because of the victim's race, gender, or religion, or because of the victim's "political affiliation, union membership, or homosexuality." Moreover, as a factual matter it is not true that cross burners direct their intimidating conduct solely to racial or religious minorities.[11]

As R.A.V. made clear, if the Virginia statute had only banned cross burnings intended to express racial hatred, it would have been unconstitutional.

Recent American hate speech jurisprudence justifies the protection of racist speech based on its understanding of the bounds of legitimate state authority. As the R.A.V. Court put it, "In fact the only interest distinctively served by the content limitation is that of displaying the city council's special hostility towards the particular biases thus singled out. That is precisely what the First Amendment forbids."[12] A state undermines its own legitimacy by favoring antiracist viewpoints over racist ones through the regulation of speech. Antiracist viewpoints are characterized as "majority preferences," and "the point of the First Amendment is that majority preferences must be expressed in some fashion other than silencing speech on the basis of its content."[13] Curiously, our constitutional law has not taken this rhetoric to its logical conclusion by prohibiting the state from enacting employment discrimination laws that may express the state's hostility to racism. But the R.A.V. Court is articulating a sentiment that has powerful resonance in our legal and political culture: The state's disapproval of racism can alienate people who remain equal participants in the democratic polity, and in so doing, compromises the state's legitimate authority

---

[10] Virginia v. Black, 538 U.S. 343 (2003).
[11] *Id.* at 362.
[12] R.A.V., 505 U.S. at 396.
[13] *Id.* at 392.

to govern us all.[14] That idea is the focus of this chapter, namely a theory of state legitimacy that extends beyond free-speech doctrine and affects other state pursuits of racial equality.

Robert Post has interpreted American First Amendment doctrine through the concept of democratic legitimacy: "[T]he American First Amendment tends to regard speech necessary for the maintenance of democratic legitimacy, which I shall call 'public discourse,' as a unique domain in which the state is constitutionally prohibited from enforcing community norms."[15] In the United States, "public discourse is an arena of competition of many distinct communities, each trying to capture the law to impose its own particular norms."[16] In this "marketplace of communities," the state's legitimacy depends on its refraining from the punishment of a community's attempts to shape collective self-determination through public discourse.

## II. CRIMINAL PUNISHMENT OF RACIST SPEECH AND HOLOCAUST DENIAL IN FRANCE

The significance of this particular vision of democratic legitimacy can be illuminated by close engagement with an alternative model. In France, the state's legitimacy is not undermined by its prohibition of racist speech and Holocaust denial. In fact, I shall argue that, as a result of the complex historical trajectory of the Holocaust denial laws, the state's legitimacy appears to *depend* on its punishment of Holocaust denial rather than its protection of such speech.

Criminal law is not merely a mode of regulation or a means of deterring undesirable behaviors. Criminal law can uniquely enshrine a community's constitution of itself as a moral entity. It imposes responsibilities on the members of a particular community, responsibilities that must be discharged as a condition of their remaining members of the community. As Joel Feinberg explained, criminal law has the capacity not only to condemn, but to authoritatively disavow certain acts.[17]

France's criminal punishment of Holocaust denial takes on a largely expressive rather than regulatory function. The very purpose of French laws prohibiting racist speech and Holocaust denial is to take a strong expressive stance of hostility toward the viewpoints expressed. Any equivalent statute would be a paradigmatic violation of the American free-speech theory of the state. Furthermore, the French state's punishment of Holocaust denial functions more in this expressive capacity than as

---

[14] As I note in Section IV, antidiscrimination law has always been understood to include claims of "reverse" discrimination, that is, claims by whites challenging affirmative action or other initiatives to promote the equality of racial minorities by addressing the presence of effects of past racism. Thus, antidiscrimination law does not clearly express a message condemning racism, and this may be an important element in maintaining its legitimacy in our legal culture.

[15] See Robert Post, "Hate Speech," in *Extreme Speech and Democracy, supra* note 2, at 123, 133.

[16] *Id. See also* "Interview with Robert Post," Chapter 1 herein.

[17] Joel Feinberg, "The Expressive Function of Punishment," in *Doing and Deserving: Essays in the Theory of Responsibility* 95, 101–2 (Princeton University Press 1970).

a means of minimizing the availability of racist speech or Holocaust denial to the public's eyes and ears.

In France, as in Germany and other European nations, criminal law has played a critical role in enabling the state and the society to face their collective responsibility for the Holocaust. The criminal process can be described as a "realm of memory,"[18] through which the nation collectively remembers the historical circumstances that engendered its current constitutional commitments. In France, a generation after World War II, there were several highly publicized criminal trials of Vichy and Nazi officials for their crimes against humanity during the Holocaust, the most famous ones being the trials of Klaus Barbie and Paul Touvier.[19] The memory of Vichy has been a central theme, if not an obsession, in French public discourse since the 1970s,[20] when new historical research[21] and films[22] established and exposed the shared responsibility of the French state for the Holocaust.

The social function of criminal punishment in France in general is somewhat different from that in the United States. French law tends to criminalize acts that are only subject to civil liability in the United States.[23] There are several gradations of crimes: "contravention," "délit," and "crime." Holocaust denial is a *délit*. Criminal punishments in France are mild compared to those in the United States, and for *délits*, imprisonment is rarely imposed; the punishment is usually a fine.[24] But the difference between a criminal fine and a civil remedy is that criminal punishment enables the state to express condemnation unambiguously.

The criminal provisions punishing racist speech are found in the 1972 law "relative to the fight against racism." The 1972 statute amended an existing statute on the "freedom of the press," which had been in force since 1881.[25] The 1972 amendment added the following provision to the "freedom of the press" statute:

---

[18] Here I borrow Pierre Nora's terminology; in French, "les lieux de mémoire." *See Realms of Memory: The Construction of the French Past* (Pierre Nora & Lawrence D. Kritzman eds., Arthur Goldhammer trans., Columbia University Press 1998) (vol. 3, "Symbols"); *see also Rethinking France: Les Lieux de Mémoire* (Pierre Nora ed., David P. Jordan trans., University of Chicago Press 2010) (vol. 4, "Histories and Memories").

[19] For an account of these trials, see Henry Rousso, *The Haunting Past* (Ralph Stoolcraft trans., University of Pennsylvania Press 2002); Eric Conan and Henry Rousso, *Vichy: An Ever-Present Past* (Nathan Bracher trans., Dartmouth College – University Press of New England 1998).

[20] *See* Henry Rousso, *The Vichy Syndrome: History and Memory in France since 1944* (Arthur Goldhammer trans., Harvard University Press 1994) (1991).

[21] *See, e.g.,* Robert Paxton, *Vichy France: Old Guard and New Order 1940–1944* (Columbia University Press 2001) (1972).

[22] *See, e.g., The Sorrow and the Pity* (Marcel Ophüls 1970).

[23] To name just a few examples, employment discrimination, sexual harassment, and defamation are all prohibited by the Penal Code. *See* Code pénal [C. pén.] art. 225–2, 222–33, 226–8 (Fr.).

[24] *See* James Q. Whitman, *Harsh Justice: Criminal Punishment and the Widening Divide Between American and Europe* 83 (Oxford University Press 2003).

[25] *See* Loi du 29 juillet 1881 sur la liberté de la presse [Law of July 29, 1881 on the Freedom of the Press], J.O.R.F., July 30, 1881.

Whoever, by means described in article 23, will have provoked to discrimination, hatred, or violence with regard to a person or a group of persons by reason of their origin or their membership or non-membership to an ethnicity, a nation, a race, or religion, shall be punished by imprisonment of one month to one year or a fine of 2,000 Francs to 300,000 francs or only one of these punishments.[26]

Article 23 of the Freedom of the Press statute refers to writings, prints, drawings, engravings, paintings, emblems, or images, any other support of writing, speech, or images sold and distributed, put up for sale or exposed in public places, whether by signs exposed to the public or any audiovisual communication.[27] Thus, it appears that the 1972 law banned most forms of public expression with racist content because all such materials could provoke discrimination, hatred, or violence on the basis of race.

In addition to its speech provisions, the 1972 statute made it a criminal offense to discriminate on the basis of race in certain contexts.[28] The law criminalized the refusal to provide a good or service, interference with the normal exercise of economic activity, refusal to hire, firing or sanctioning, the denial of offers of employment or employment training, and refusal of access to internships on the basis of race.[29] Unlike the United States, which only imposes civil liability for these types of discrimination, France imposes criminal punishment as well as civil liability for intentional racial discrimination.[30] Although the statute authorizes up to three years' imprisonment for racial discrimination, prison sentences in discrimination cases have always been suspended when they are imposed.[31] The usual punishment for racial discrimination is a criminal fine, often in an amount equivalent or lower than the damages awards often awarded in American civil employment discrimination suits.[32]

Holocaust denial was explicitly banned in 1990, in a law explicitly aimed at "repressing all racist, anti-Semitic, or xenophobic acts."[33] Known as the "loi Gayssot," the statute criminalized Holocaust denial by prohibiting the public contestation of "the existence of 'crimes against humanity.'" It defined "crimes against humanity"

---

[26] Loi 72–546 du 1 juillet 1972 relative à la lutte contre le racisme [Law 72–546 of July 1, 1972 on the fight against racism], J.O.R.F., July 2, 1972, at 6803. Note that, under the current version of the statute, the maximum fine is €45,000 and one year of imprisonment.

[27] Loi du 29 juillet 1881 sur la liberté de la presse, *supra* note 25, art. 23.

[28] Loi no. 72–546, *supra* note 26, tit. II, art. 6–8.

[29] *Id. See also* C. pén. art. 225–1; 225–2 (Fr.).

[30] For a discussion of the procedural and institutional explanations for France's continued use of criminal law to enforce employment discrimination law, see Julie C. Suk, "Procedural Path Dependence: Discrimination and the Civil-Criminal Divide," 85 *Wash. U.L. Rev.* 1315 (2008).

[31] For a discussion of convictions under the racial discrimination provisions of the 1972 statute, see *id.* at 1340–5.

[32] *See id.* at 1365.

[33] Loi 90–615 du 13 juillet 1990 tendant à réprimer tout acte raciste, anti-Semite, ou xenophobe, art. 9 [Law 90–615 of July 13, 1990 on repressing all racist, anti-Semitic, or xenophobic acts, art. 9], J.O.R.F., July 14, 1990, at 8333.

according to article 6 of the statute of the international military tribunal annexed to the treaty of London of August 8, 1945.[34] The statute also reaffirmed the principle prohibiting any discrimination based on membership or nonmembership to an ethnicity, nation, race, or religion.[35] In addition, the statute empowered antiracist associations and organizations devoted to defending the honor of the Resistance to initiate and participate in proceedings prosecuting the denial of crimes against humanity.[36]

In practice, investigations and prosecutions under the laws prohibiting racist speech and Holocaust denial are few and far between. Most of them are initiated by antiracist groups against academics and politicians who are already well known for their racist or revisionist views. Many of the defendants are repeat offenders. As is the case with criminal racial discrimination offenders, Holocaust deniers rarely serve prison sentences. When imposed, prison sentences are usually suspended. The usual punishment is a criminal fine. In many cases, the fine, too, is suspended. Despite convictions and criminal fines for incitement to racial hatred and Holocaust denial, convicted Holocaust deniers continue to publicly avow their views. All of the Holocaust denial literature for which these offenders are punished is available for perusal in French libraries. These realities support the conclusion that the main function of criminalizing Holocaust denial is to strongly express the state's moral outrage rather than to silence an unpopular viewpoint.

There have been several well-publicized prosecutions of Holocaust deniers in the last two decades. The first highly publicized conviction under the 1990 Gayssot law occurred in 1991, when Robert Faurisson, a well-known Holocaust denier, was convicted for stating in a magazine interview that the "the myth of the gas chambers is a dishonest fabrication," and that he had "excellent reasons not to believe that there was a policy of exterminating the Jews, or in the magic of gas chambers."[37] Faurisson's prosecution was initiated by eleven associations of French resistance fighters and deportees to German concentration camps. He was sentenced to a 100,000 FF fine. The editor of the magazine was sentenced to a 30,000 FF fine and ordered to pay 20,000 FF to each of the eleven associations that had participated in the proceedings. Another important provision of the criminal judgment was that the judgment had to be published in advertisements in four daily publications, costing 15,000 FF for each publication. Faurisson's criminal fine was suspended, meaning that he would only have to pay it if he committed the same offense within five years

---

[34] Loi du 29 juillet 1881 sur la liberté de la presse, *supra* note 25, art. 24; Law No. 90–615, *supra* note 33, art. 9.

[35] Loi no. 72–546, *supra* note 33, art. 1.

[36] Loi 90–615, *supra* note 33, art. 13. Note that art. 2–1 of the *Code de la procédure pénale* authorizes antiracist organizations to participate as civil parties in prosecutions of racial discrimination in violation of the *Code pénal* art. 225–2, which codified the antidiscrimination provision of the 1972 statute.

[37] "Pour 'contestation de crimes contre l'humanité' M. Robert Faurisson est condamné à 100 000 francs d'amende avec sursis," *Le Monde* (Fr.), Apr. 20, 1991.

of the sentence.[38] Faurisson then unsuccessfully challenged his conviction and the 1990 Gayssot law, on freedom-of-expression grounds, before the United Nations Committee on the International Covenant on Civil and Political Rights.[39]

Nonetheless, Faurisson persisted in publicizing his views that there were no gas chambers to execute the Jews. He was convicted five times between 1992 and 1998 for Holocaust denial.[40] In 2005, he broadcast this view on an Iranian satellite television channel, stating: "There never existed a single gas chamber for execution by the Germans, not one. As a consequence, the gas chamber that millions of tourists visit at Auschwitz, that's a lie, a falsification, a trick for tourists." For these statements, he was convicted again under the Gayssot law, fined €7,500, and sentenced to a suspended prison sentence of three months.[41] The prosecution was initiated by MRAP (Mouvement contre le racisme et pour l'amitié entre les peoples) (Movement against racism and for friendship between peoples) and LICRA (Ligue contre le racisme et l'antisémitisme) (League against racism and anti-Semitism), two of the antiracist organizations that had participated in the first case in 1991.

Throughout the last two decades, these associations have initiated several more prosecutions of well-known Holocaust deniers. In 1998, Roger Garaudy, a philosopher and author, was prosecuted for expressing doubt about the existence of the gas chambers in his 1995 book, *Les mythes fondateurs de la politique israélienne (The founding myths of Israeli politics)*.[42] In several passages, he referred to the "myths" of six million exterminated Jews, of justice at Nuremberg, and of the Holocaust.[43] Garaudy was convicted and fined 120,000 FF. Damages were also awarded, largely as a symbolic measure, to MRAP and LICRA, which had participated in the litigation.[44]

The following year, LICRA and other organizations initiated the prosecution of Jean Plantin for publishing the journal *Akribeia*, devoted to questioning the extermination of Jews in gas chambers in Nazi concentration camps. Plantin received a criminal fine of 10,000 FF and a suspended six-month prison sentence.[45] Plantin became the first Holocaust denier whose suspended sentence was converted into an

---

[38]  *Id.*

[39]  Faurisson v. France, UNHRC Comm. No. 50/1993, U.N. Doc. CCPR/C/58/D/550/1993, decided Nov. 8, 1996.

[40]  "Le négationniste Robert Faurisson a été condamné à trois mois de prison avec sursis," *Le Monde* (Fr.), Oct. 3, 2006.

[41]  *Id.*

[42]  Roger Garaudy, *Les mythes fondateurs de la politique israélienne [The Founding Myths of Israeli Politics]* (1995). Note that Garaudy's book is available for perusal in several French libraries. For instance, at the Bibliothèque Nationale de France, it is available under the call number Tolbiac – Rez-de-jardin – magasin 1999–19003s; at the Sciences-Po library, it is available under the call number 8°182.236.

[43]  "Roger Garaudy 'doute' toujours de l'existence des chambres à gaz," *Le Monde* (Fr.), Jan. 11, 1998.

[44]  "Le philosophe Roger Garaudy est condamné pour contestation de crimes contre l'humanité," *Le Monde* (Fr.), Mar. 3, 1998.

[45]  "Un éditeur Lyonnais comdamné pour 'publicité' en faveur d'oeuvres révisionnistes," *Le Monde* (Fr.), May 29, 1999.

actual sentence, when the Lyon Court of Appeal revoked the suspension after Plantin violated the terms of the suspension by publishing writings denying the Holocaust on an Internet site.[46] However, the Cour de Cassation nullified the Court of Appeal's decision, reinstating the suspended sentence.[47]

Since then, a handful of Holocaust deniers have served actual prison sentences. In 2004, Vincent Reynouard was convicted under the 1990 statute for distributing a pamphlet and videocassette questioning the massacre of Jews in Oradour-sur-Glane in 1944.[48] Reynouard, who had been convicted previously in 1991 for distributing materials to high school students questioning the existence of the gas chambers, was sentenced to twenty-four months in prison, only eighteen of which were suspended. More recently, Georges Theil, a Front National politician who had served in the elected position of regional adviser in the Rhônes-Alpes region, was sentenced to six months in prison, unsuspended, for saying on local television that the existence of gas chambers was a physical and chemical impossibility.[49]

But these recent prison sentences do not necessarily signal a trend toward sending Holocaust deniers to jail. More recent convictions involved suspended prison sentences. Bruno Gollnisch, the second-in-command of the Front National, was convicted in January 2007 under the Holocaust denial statute for having stated in a press conference that there should be a debate about how the Jews died in Nazi camps. Gollnisch was fined €5,000 and then ordered to pay €55,000 in damages to the organizations that initiated his prosecution. He was given a suspended three-month prison sentence. Faurisson's October 2006 conviction also led to a suspended three-month sentence.

These examples illustrate the significance of the symbolic function of France's criminalization of Holocaust denial. The laws against racist speech do not censor racist or Holocaust denial literature. They do not prohibit anyone from perusing these materials. Indeed, all of the offending works, including Garaudy's book and Plantin's periodical, are freely available to readers in the Bibliothèque Nationale de France and other libraries. While the criminal prosecutions have resulted in fines, payment of damages to antiracist, resistance, and deportees' organizations, and publication of the judgment in newspaper advertisements, the judgments have not removed the voices of Holocaust deniers from public discourse. These prosecutions draw public attention to Holocaust denial rather than shielding the public from these viewpoints. Thus, the most important function of these laws in actual operation is not censorship or suppression, but the state's strong expression of disapproval of the content of the message.

---

[46] *See* "Le négationniste Jean Plantin condamné à de la prison ferme," *Le Monde* (Fr.), Jan. 24, 2003.

[47] Cour de cassation [Cass.] [Supreme Court for Judicial Matters], Chambre criminelle [crim.] Apr. 27, 2004, 03–85288.

[48] "Oradour-sur-Glane: le révisionniste Reynouard condamné à six mois de prison ferme," *Le Monde* (Fr.), June 9, 2004.

[49] "Un ancien élu frontiste condamné à six mois de prison," *Le Monde* (Fr.), Jan. 5, 2006.

It is tempting to interpret this reality as an argument against the criminalization of Holocaust denial. Alan Dershowitz, for instance, has argued that criminalizing Holocaust denial is counterproductive and ineffective, as it helps spread rather than suppress the prohibited message.[50] Such arguments assume that the sole purpose of criminalizing Holocaust denial is to deter, suppress, and drive out such views from French society. This view fails to capture something far more significant that is going on: Each time the state prosecutes Holocaust denial, it reminds the French people that the Holocaust occurred, and this memory is essential to the legitimacy of its current political authority. Examining the legal history of prohibiting racist speech in France reveals the ways in which the current legal order is understood, by way of remembering the past, as a commitment to avoiding the past regime's failures.

## III. A LEGAL HISTORY OF PROHIBITING RACIST SPEECH

In France, the state's ability to express hostility to anti-Semitism affirms, rather than undermines, the legitimacy of the current republic. This is largely due to the political and legal history of banning racist speech in France. The statute providing for the punishment of racism in its various manifestations was embedded in the legal processes by which the state dismantled the anti-Semitic Vichy regime and reestablished the republican constitutional order following World War II.

Unlike the U.S. constitution, the French constitution explicitly links the values it protects to the historical events that precipitated their proclamation. The constitution now in force was adopted in 1958. Although the 1958 constitution's main purpose was to restructure then existing political and legal institutions, it explicitly integrated two older texts: the 1789 Declaration of the Rights of Man, the founding document of the French Revolution, and the Preamble to the 1946 constitution, which enabled France to emerge from World War II as a constitutional republic.

The Holocaust is directly referenced, albeit in broad and general language, in the 1946 preamble, the first article of which reads:

> Following the victory won by free people over regimes that attempted to enslave and degrade the human person, the French people proclaim again that every human being, without distinction of race, religion, or belief, possesses inalienable and sacred rights. It solemnly reaffirms the rights and liberties of man and citizen consecrated by the Declaration of Rights of Man of 1789 and the fundamental principles recognized by the laws of the Republic.[51]

The language of the Preamble self-consciously characterizes the antiracist vision of human rights as something that is being proclaimed *again*. The constitutional order

---

[50] *See* Jamie Glazov, "Symposium: Criminalizing Holocaust Denial," *Front Page Magazine*, July 27, 2007, *available at* http://97.74.65.51/readArticle.aspx?ARTID=27525.

[51] 1946 Const. Preamble (Fr.).

that emerged after World War II was a "reaffirmation," a new regime that had to establish both a break with the Vichy regime that preceded it and continuity with the republic that preceded Vichy. The text framed the French people's commitment to human rights, particularly human rights regardless of race, religion, and faith, as importantly connected to a rejection by the French people of the Nazi regime that had just been defeated to make way for this constitutional moment. Establishing a break with the Nazi acts in recent memory was thus important to legitimizing the new constitutional order that emerged when the French people reconstituted the republican state.

Not only did the constitutional text of 1946 express condemnation of recent Nazi atrocities; the regime change itself, which transformed Nazi-dominated Vichy France into the liberated French Republic, included the restoration of a 1939 law prohibiting racist and anti-Semitic speech. The 1939 decree, known as the Marchandeau law, amended the 1881 Freedom of the Press law to prohibit "defamation and insults against a group of persons belonging by their origin to a particular race or religion, which have for their purpose to incite hatred against citizens or residents."[52] The report to the President justifying this decree noted that the law was part of a "vigorous effort at national defense," as hateful speech had the effect of dividing citizens and weakening the morale of the nation.[53] The purpose of the law, it appears, was not only to protect the victims of these insults, but, more importantly, to promote solidarity between French citizens of different races and religions.

The 1939 law was a reaction to the proliferation of anti-Semitic propaganda in the French press throughout the 1930s. Céline published his infamous *Bagatelles pour un massacre* in 1936; shortly before that, Marcel Jouhandeau had published *Le péril juif*. Céline's second anti-Semitic pamphlet, *L'Ecole des cadavres*, appeared in 1938. These pamphlets depicted Jews as a threat to French civilization. In the popular anti-Semitic literature of the period, the hatred of Jews was largely based on resentment of Jews' perceived economic success and intellectual stature. During the period leading up to the Vichy government's ascension to power, racism against Jews was largely manifested through the press. Unlike race discrimination in the American context, racism was not manifested in legal segregation leading to severe economic inequality. Racism was evident primarily in the expression of anti-Semitic ideas in writing, which contributed significantly to the success of the anti-Semitic politicians who established the Vichy regime. Political opposition to Léon Blum, the socialist prime minister, was often framed in anti-Semitic terms. The popular

---

[52] Décret modifiant les articles 32, 33, et 60 de la loi du 29 juillet 1881 sur la liberté de la presse, 21 avril 1939, [decree modifying articles 32, 33 and 60 of the law of July 29, 1881 on the Freedom of the Press, April 21, 1939], J.O.R.F., Apr. 25, 1939, at 5295.

[53] Rapport au président de la république française, 21 avril 1939, [Report to the President of the French Republic on Apr. 21, 1939], J.O.R.F., Apr. 25, 1939, at 5295.

press depicted Jews as conspiring to take over France, repeating the themes of the popular 1886 book by Edouard Drumont, *La France juive*.[54]

The 1939 Marchandeau Law sought, unsuccessfully, to stop racism from destroying the French republic. The framers of the Marchandeau law explained why they thought the suppression of racist speech did not alter or conflict with the fundamental commitment to free speech:

> [The law] has no purpose other than to unite liberty [of the press] with others that are inseparable from the republican device itself. To this end, no reason related to race or religion can destroy the equality of citizens; no legacy born of hereditary circumstances could attack, in the way one sees another, the sentiment of fraternity which unifies all the members of the French family.[55]

The purpose of the law was not only to protect individuals subject to racist speech, but to reconceptualize the victim of racist speech as the republic itself, which could not survive if its citizens regarded each other through the lens of racism instead of the lens of fraternity. The goal was national solidarity. Racist speech harms "the sentiment of fraternity" that is necessary for the proper functioning of the republic, just as free speech is necessary for the proper functioning of the republic. Thus, because protection of the "republican device"[56] is the ultimate goal of freedom of speech, the framers of the Marchandeau law saw the punishment of racist speech as fully compatible with the values underlying freedom of speech.

Nonetheless, the anti-Semitic Vichy regime ascended to power on June 16, 1940. A few months later, the new government passed laws abridging the rights of Jews, thus destroying the republican commitment to equality. One of the first acts of the Vichy regime was to abrogate the Marchandeau law itself[57] and pardon everyone who had been convicted under it.[58] At the time, the popular view was that the Marchandeau law had established a special legal privilege for Jews[59] that was no longer compatible with the "new French state."[60] Thus, Vichy's abrogation of the Marchandeau law is now seen as the first legal step that the Vichy regime took in its persecution of Jews. Laws that explicitly stripped Jews of rights and privileges began to appear

---

54 Edouard Drumont, *La France Juive* (1886). For an excellent and detailed account of anti-Semitic propaganda in the 1930s, and its role in the political evolution that led to Vichy's success, see Gérard Noiriel, *Immigration, antisémitisme et racisme en France (XIXe-XXe siècle)* 433–81 (Fayard 2007).

55 Rapport au président de la république française, *supra* note 53.

56 *Id.*

57 Loi portant abrogation du décret-loi du 21 avril 1939, modifiant les articles 32, 33, et 60 de la loi du 29 juillet 1881 sur la liberté de la presse, [Law repealing the decree law of April 21, 1939 modifying articles 32, 33, and 60 of the law of July 29, 1881 on the Freedom of the Press], J.O.R.F, Aug. 30, 1940, at 4844.

58 *See* Loi portant abrogation, *supra* note 57, art. 2.

59 *See* Ralph Schor, *L'Antisémitisme en France dans l'entre-deux-guerres: Prelude à Vichy* 142–43 (Editions Complexe 2005).

60 *See* Michael Marrus and Robert Paxton, *Vichy France and the Jews* 3 (Basic Books 1981).

in October and November of that year.[61] An early example was the abrogation of another important law dating back to 1870, known as the Cremieux decree, which had granted French citizenship to Jews in Algeria.[62] Many more laws followed, one at a time, denying Jews the opportunity to work in government, excluding them from various professions, one at a time, limiting their property rights, requiring their identification, and, ultimately, authorizing their deportation and extermination.[63]

When France was liberated from German occupation, the new regime issued an ordinance on August 9, 1944 that effectively declared all the legal acts of the Vichy regime to be null and void.[64] The French constitutional order of 1946 could only be established after Vichy's anti-Semitic laws had been dismantled. The 1944 ordinance declared: "The form of the Government of France is and remains a Republic. In law, it never ceased to exist."[65]

The ordinance nullified all the "constitutional, legislative, and regulatory acts" of the government after June 16, 1940. It explicitly nullified all acts "that established or applied a discrimination founded on Jewish characteristics."[66] For many other laws, however, the project of reestablishing the Republic was complicated. For one thing, the Resistance had also passed laws and decrees after June 1940 on behalf of "France libre" (Free France) or "France combattante" (France at War), and the ordinance of August 9, 1944 did not intend to nullify these acts. Furthermore, the new regime wanted to restore some but not all aspects of the Third Republic that had fallen to Vichy. Thus, tables annexed to the ordinance specified the particular Vichy acts that were nullified, as well as the scope of the nullification. Laws on Tableau I were nullified with the effect of reverting back to the state of affairs prior to the adoption of the Vichy law in question.[67] Laws on Tableau II were nullified prospectively, and thus without undoing the effects of the law prior to passage of the August 9, 1944 ordinance.[68] Vichy's abrogation of the racist speech law was on Tableau I.

The current French statute criminalizing racist speech cannot be understood in isolation from the history by which the postwar French state established its break

[61] *See* Loi portant statut des juifs, 3 octobre 1940, [Act of Oct. 3, 1940 on the status of Jews], J.O.R.F., Oct. 18, 1940, at 5323; Loi portant réorganization des corps municipaux, 16 novembre 1940, [Law regarding the reorganization of municiple bodies, Nov. 16, 1940], J.O.R.F., Dec. 12, 1940, at 6074.

[62] Loi portant abrogation du décret du Gouvernement de la defense nationale du 24 octobre 1870 fixant le statut des juifs indigènes des département de l'Algérie, 7 octobre 1940, [Law repealing the decree of the Government of National Defense of Oct. 24, 1870 setting up the statute of the native Jews of the departments of Algeria, Oct. 7, 1940], J.O.R.F, Oct. 8, 1940, at 5234.

[63] *See generally* Richard Weisberg, *Vichy Law and the Holocaust in France* (Routledge 1996).

[64] Paxton, *supra* note 21, at 330.

[65] Ordonnance du 9 août 1944 relative au rétablissement de la légalité républicaine sur le territoire continental, [Order relating to the restoration of republican legality on the continental territory, Aug. 9, 1944], J.O.R.F, Aug. 10, 1944, at 688.

[66] *Id.* art. 3.

[67] *See id.* art. 4 & Tableau I, at 688–9.

[68] *See id.* art. 4 & Tableau II, at 688–9.

with Vichy, as well as its continuity with the republic that preceded Vichy.[69] Tracing the genealogy of the 1939 law reveals its embeddedness in the project of reclaiming antiracism as a republican value that had existed before and after Vichy.

More importantly, the 1939 Marchandeau law continues to occupy a central place in contemporary French legal discourse around racism and discrimination. The law was explicitly remembered as a critical element of the reconstitution of a legitimate republic when France adopted its modern antiracism laws in 1972. Legislators invoked the 1939 law and designated it as the legal template on which modern antiracism law, including the prohibition of discrimination, would be built. When the 1972 law prohibiting incitement to racial hatred was being debated, legislators discussed the memory of the Holocaust and framed the 1939 Marchandeau law as the foundation for the legislation they were proposing. Indeed, one member of the National Assembly reminded his colleagues of the Marchandeau decree's legal history: its abrogation by the Vichy regime and return into force when republican legality was reestablished.[70]

By invoking this history, the legislators in 1972 implicitly tied the antiracism law to the constitutional order established after the Vichy regime was dismantled. When the 1990 law strengthening antidiscrimination law and prohibiting Holocaust denial was passed, legislators invoked the Marchandeau law again as the origin of "antiracist legislation."[71] Indeed, the memory of French anti-Semitism has influenced the contemporary legal understanding of racial equality in France today.[72]

The legitimacy of the postwar constitutional order depended on the state's vehement rejection, not only of anti-Semitism as an idea, but of anti-Semitism as a social movement. Anti-Semitism is characterized as harmful not only to Jews, but to national solidarity. This idea motivated the adoption of the 1939 law punishing racist speech, and it endured in the legislative debates leading to the adoption of the 1990 law explicitly banning Holocaust denial.[73] The 1990 "Gayssot" law presented itself as an extension of the 1972 law punishing incitement to racial hatred. The 1990 law

---

[69] Indeed, when De Gaulle was asked formally to proclaim the Republic on August 25, 1944, he replied: "The Republic has never ceased to exist. Free France, fighting France, the French Committee for National Liberation has always encompassed it. Vichy was always and remains null and void. Myself, I am the president of the government of the Republic. Why would I have to proclaim it?" *See* Henry Rousso, *Le syndrome de Vichy De 1944 à Nos Jours* 31 (1987).

[70] *See* Assemblée Nationale, Débats Parlementaires, 7 juin 1972, [National Assembly, Parliamentary Debate of June 7, 1972], J.O.R.F., June 8, 1972, at 2282.

[71] *See* Assemblée Nationale, Débats Parlementaires, 2e séance du 2 mai 1990, [National Assembly, Parliamentary Debate meeting 2E of May 2, 1990], J.O.R.F., May 3, 1990, at 936 (remarks of Jacques Toubon).

[72] For a detailed discussion of the importance of the memory of Vichy for French antidiscrimination law, see Julie Chi-hye Suk, "Equal by Comparison: Unsettling Assumptions of Antidiscrimination Law," 55 *Am. J. Comp. L.* 295, 314–24 (2007).

[73] *See* Assemblée Nationale, Débats Parlementaires, 2e séance du 2 mai 1990, [National Assembly, Parliamentary Debate meeting 2E of May 2, 1990], J.O.R.F., May 3, 1990, at 919 (remarks of Jean-Claude Gayssot).

prohibited, *inter alia*, the denial of the "crimes against humanity" defined by article 6 of the international military tribunal statute attached to the Treaty of London. The statute prohibiting Holocaust denial wrote into law the growing acknowledgment that the denial of the Holocaust was a new, more subtle manifestation of anti-Semitism in French society.[74] Thus, the criminalization of Holocaust denial could easily be characterized as an extension of existing laws that already criminalized incitement to racial hatred and racial defamation.

At the same time, it was difficult to prosecute Holocaust denial under these existing laws, because the Holocaust deniers tend to use the legitimating posture of historical research to disguise their acts of racist propaganda.[75] Instead of making overt anti-Semitic statements of the sort that proliferated in the late 1930s, leading up to the passage of the Marchandeau law, today's anti-Semites invoke the objective academic discipline of history to assert that the Jews were not exterminated in gas chambers by Nazis. The subtle implication of such an assertion is that Jews fabricated the stories of their own persecution to mobilize the world's support for the creation of Israel.[76] The image of Jews as lying to seize power is a familiar one – the same image was perpetuated in anti-Semitic propaganda in the 1930s, culminating in Vichy France's persecution and deportation of French Jews.[77] As Michel Troper puts it, Holocaust denial "takes part in an anti-Semitic and anti-Democratic movement, which did not stop with the genocide itself, and which nourished it."[78] Troper, like many legislators who supported the 1990 Gayssot law, recognized that Holocaust denial is not merely the expression of a historical viewpoint, but a way of participating in the same social movement that destroyed the republic in the past.

France's antiracism laws punish the forms of racist propaganda that resemble those that facilitated the Vichy regime's ascent to power and the subsequent participation by the French state in the Holocaust. Today, the purpose is not necessarily to "regulate" such speech to avert a tangible danger of genocide, but to recognize the collective memory of racism's complex social manifestation and its potential to destroy the republic. This recognition is critical to the current republic's establishment of a clear break with the Vichy regime.

---

[74] As the Justice Minister noted during the legislative debates, Holocaust denial was "the principal contemporary vector of antisemitism." *See* Assemblée Nationale, Débats Parlementaires, 2e séance du 2 mai 1990, [National Assembly, Parliamentary Debate meeting 2E of May 2, 1990], J.O.R.F., May 3, 1990, at 905. This understanding was also articulated in Pierre Vidal-Naquet, *Les assassins de la mémoire* (Jeffrey Mehlman trans., Columbia University Press 1992) (1990).

[75] The Justice Minister noted that contemporary anti-Semites, aware of existing laws against racist speech, had begun to reframe their racist views as historical research. *See* Débats Parlementaires, *supra* note 74. *See also* Michel Troper, "La loi Gayssot et la constitution," 54 *Annales, Histoire, Sciences Sociales* 1239 (1999).

[76] Walter Laqueur gives a cogent account of how historical refutation of the so-called "Auschwitz lie" manifests anti-Semitism throughout Europe today. *See* Walter Laqueur, *The Changing Face of Anti-Semitism: From Ancient Times to Today* 125–50 (Oxford University Press 2006).

[77] *See* Schor, *supra* note 59, at 83–99.

[78] Troper, *supra* note 75, at 1255.

## IV. RETHINKING THE FREE-SPEECH THEORY OF THE STATE

The comparison with France highlights several unique elements of the American First Amendment justification for protecting racist speech. Why is it that in the United States, the state's exclusion of racist speech from public discourse would undermine its legitimacy instead of strengthening it? Robert Post notes that, "in effect, the First Amendment pressures the state to be neutral with respect to the many competing communities that seek to control the law by enforcing their own particular ways of distinguishing decency from indecency, critique from hatred."[79] America, unlike many other societies, recognizes the fact that it is made up of diverse communities, and thus our constitutional law is "concerned to protect public discourse as a sphere that remains equally open to all communities."[80] This includes communities whose values contradict fundamental constitutional principles such as racial equality.

However, the idea that the diversity of America's communities requires First Amendment protection of racist speech is of relatively recent vintage. In fact, in the 1952 case of *Beauharnais v. Illinois*,[81] the Supreme Court suggested that the diversity of America's communities justified state attempts to curb racist speech. In *Beauharnais*, the Supreme Court upheld the conviction of a man who had distributed leaflets accusing blacks of encroaching, harassing, invading, and mongrelizing the white race.[82] In so doing, the Court offered the following account of the state's legitimacy in prohibiting speech exposing any race to contempt:

> Illinois did not have to look beyond her own borders or await the tragic experience of the last three decades to conclude that willful purveyors of falsehood concerning racial and religious groups promote strife and tend powerfully to obstruct the manifold adjustments required for free, ordered life in a metropolitan, polyglot community. From the murder of the abolitionist Lovejoy in 1837 to the Cicero riots of 1951, Illinois has been the scene of exacerbated tension between races, often flaring into violence and destruction. In many of these outbreaks, utterances of the character here in question, so the Illinois legislature could conclude, played a significant part.[83]

In footnotes, the Court documented the various race riots that had occurred around the time that the law was passed, as well as academic accounts of these riots. It continued:

> [T]he State was struggling to assimilate vast numbers of new inhabitants, as yet concentrated in discrete racial or national or religious groups – foreign-born brought

---

[79] *See* Robert Post, "Hate Speech," *supra* note 15, at 133.
[80] *Id.*
[81] 343 U.S. 250 (1952).
[82] *Id.* at 252.
[83] *Id.* at 259.

to it by the crest of the great wave of immigration, and Negroes attracted by jobs in war plants and the allurements of northern claims.[84]

On this account the state had a legitimate interest in promoting solidarity against racism in a diverse society by punishing racist speech. The Court was unwilling to compel the state to ignore this history:

> In the face of this history and its frequent obligato of extreme racial and religious propaganda, we would deny experience to say that the Illinois legislature was without reason in seeking ways to curb false or malicious defamation of racial and religious groups. . . . [85]

Although *Beauharnais* has never been formally overruled, American First Amendment doctrine has clearly moved away from this approach. This shift is accompanied by the Court's increased reluctance to distinguish decent from indecent, dangerous from unpopular, hatred from critique. This determined neutrality regarding different substantive messages can appear extreme. For example, in *Brandenburg v. Ohio*, which invalidated the conviction of a Ku Klux Klan member advocating violence against blacks, Justice Douglas's concurrence analogized to punishing draft-card burning and the "infamous loyalty-security hearings" of the McCarthy era.[86] A central feature of American diversity is that there is constant disagreement between communities about where the line between hatred and critique falls.

In the United States, the Constitution ensures that these communities – "we the people" – will remain sovereign regardless of what their values and political commitments become. In France, by contrast, the Republic remains sovereign, and this means that some values and political outcomes are not up for grabs. When the Second Empire fell and the Third Republic was established, it was forbidden to introduce or debate proposals in Parliament that would propose a return to the monarchy.[87] Although the French constitution is much easier to amend than the U.S. constitution, it nevertheless declares that the republican form of government can never be subject to revision.[88] In the United States, what keeps the state legitimate is the constitution's guarantee of the sovereignty of the people, whereas in France, the state's legitimacy depends on its consistency with the republican values in the constitution.

The French experience draws attention to something that is entirely absent from the American legal culture: conscious attempts to forge a collective memory through law. In both the United States and France, the current constitutional orders emerged after the state participated in racist exclusions of persons whom they now embrace as

---

[84] *Id.*

[85] *Id.*

[86] Brandenburg v. Ohio, 395 U.S. 444, 457 (Douglas, J., concurring).

[87] *See* Patrick Weil, "The Politics of Memory: Bans and Commemorations," in *Extreme Speech and Democracy, supra* note 2, at 562, 570.

[88] 1958 Const. art. 89 (Fr.).

equal citizens. In France, the state recognizes the Vichy regime's anti-Semitism and its participation in the Holocaust in various ways. One mundane example is that, at a public preschool in the 15th arrondissement, a plaque prominently displayed above the main entrance invokes the memory of children who were deported from the school because they were Jewish, "with the active participation of the Vichy government." In addition, a law commemorates the state's participation in racist and anti-Semitic persecution. Passed two and a half years after the Loi Gayssot, a decree establishes July 16 as a national day of commemoration of the victims of racist and anti-Semitic persecution.[89] The date was chosen because it was the anniversary of the roundup of the Vélodrome d'hiver in 1942, when the French police arrested and eventually deported thousands of Jews, including children. Patrick Weil situates the criminal punishment of Holocaust denial "in the context of a series of actions that, at certain key moments, the Republic initiates. These actions are always triggered by the end of times of great division, with a goal of creating a new feeling of common citizenry, a new unity surrounding fundamental values, through two paired means: celebration and a radical ban."[90] Through the punishment of Holocaust denial and the commemoration of the deportations, the state is directing its citizens to remember past atrocities for which the nation is collectively responsible. The collective memory serves as a justification for excluding anti-Semitism as a possibility for future exercises of collective self-determination. The fight against racism thus becomes a collective national project, the success of which depends on citizens' solidarity.

The significance of this solidarity becomes salient when comparing French and American approaches to racial discrimination. French law treats the manifestations of racism as an injury to the entire polity and to the state rather than as individual injuries with individual victims. Thus, it criminalizes racial employment discrimination, whereas U.S. law only imposes civil liability. In France, criminal prosecution is the central method by which the law responds to race discrimination in employment, even though civil remedies are also available.[91] Although there are many explanations for this, an extremely important function of criminalization is the recognition that racist acts injure the entire polity, not only the racial minorities at which the racism is targeted. In the United States, law has commemorated slavery and segregation through nonbinding resolutions apologizing to African Americans.[92] An apology

---

[89] Décret 93–15 du 3 février 1993 instituant une journée nationale commemorative des persecutions racistes et anti-Sémites commises sous l'autorité de fait dite "gouvernement de l'Etat française" (1940–1944), [Decree 93–15 of Feb. 3, 1993 commemorating the state's participation in racist and anti-Semitic persecution], J.O.R.F, Feb. 4, 1993, at 1902.

[90] Weil, _supra_ note 87 at, 577.

[91] I discuss both the procedural and substantive significance of the criminalization of racial discrimination in Suk, _Procedural Path Dependence, supra_ note 30, at 1340–5, 1368.

[92] _See_ Bernie Becker, "Senate Approves Slavery Apology, with Reparations Disclaimer," The Caucus, The Politics and Government Blog of the _New York Times_, June 18, 2009, 4:33 PM, _available at_ http://thecaucus.blogs.nytimes.com/2009/06/18/senate-approves-slavery-apology-with-reparations-disclaimer/.

is probably better than no commemoration at all, but it is striking that American commemorations understand the state's past atrocities as injuries to particular groups rather than threats to the entire state's legitimacy.

What are the consequences of these differences? In the United States, antidiscrimination law is the primary means by which the law combats racism. It, too, is open to all communities. Thus, in the United States, antidiscrimination law is powerfully utilized by whites complaining about the jobs they did not get due to employer actions undertaken to promote employment opportunities for racial minorities. Indeed, such plaintiffs prevailed in the recent Supreme Court case of *Ricci v. DeStefano*.[93] In France, by contrast, the discourse of "reverse discrimination" is noticeably absent. Affirmative action is controversial, but for different reasons: It is discussed by reference to whether racial differentiation is compatible with the abstract republican principle of equality, but never on the grounds that it helps minority communities at the expense of whites. In short, racial equality is a collective goal to be achieved through national solidarity, not a political agenda in which some communities will win and others will lose.

I do not mean to propose a ban on racist speech in America to generate the solidarity necessary to achieve racial equality. Nor is it clear that the French have done a better job at achieving racial equality. But the comparison should lead Americans to reflect more deeply about the significance of solidarity's absence. The French experience of punishing Holocaust denial demonstrates a legal order in which the legitimacy of the state is not undermined by, and in fact depends on, its exclusion of anti-Semitic propaganda. This is because the new legal order is consciously repudiating past anti-Semitism, not only for the sake of French Jews or other minorities, but for the possibility of republican government itself. Under such conditions, the state's project of combating racism is conceived as a collective one rather than a way of favoring some communities at the expense of others. Furthermore, as *Beauharnais* demonstrates, our First Amendment tradition has not always been averse to punishing racist speech to promote solidarity between diverse communities. These comparative and historical perspectives should lead us to imagine alternative possibilities for the state's relationship to racism and its past, beyond the free-speech theory of the state.

---

[93] *See* Ricci v. DeStefano, 129 S. Ct. 2658 (2009). The Supreme Court held that the New Haven (Connecticut) Fire Department violated Title VII by declining to promote white firefighters on the basis of promotion tests on which black and Hispanic firefighters had performed poorly.

# 9

## What's Wrong with Defamation of Religion?

*Kwame Anthony Appiah*

In March 2010, in Geneva, the UN's Human Rights Council (HRC) voted by a narrow margin to accept a nonbinding Resolution on "Combating Defamation of Religions."[1] (Hereafter, "the Resolution.") Resolutions like this one have been offered regularly at the HRC and in the General Assembly, have the support of the Organization of the Islamic Conference (OIC) and the Arab League, and have passed regularly over the last decade in all of these various fora.[2] I think this widespread support is regrettable and I hope that this idea does not gain a serious foothold in international human rights law. In fact, the Resolution had less support in March 2010 than it had had in the past and, as this volume goes to press, it appears that the resolution's proponents have abandoned their efforts, at least for the foreseeable future.[3] I am glad that this is so, and in this chapter I want to explain why. To do this, I will have first to say something about the considerations that I think favor laws against defamation in general; my aim is to make the best case for legal sanctions against defamation of religion in particular before recommending against such legal sanctions.

---

[1] U.N. Human Rights Council, Res. 13/16, Rep. of the Human Rights Council, U.N. Doc. A/65/53 (Mar. 25, 2010) [hereinafter *HRC Resolution*]. The vote was 20 to 17, with 8 abstentions.

[2] For an overview, see International Freedom of Expression Exchange, "'Defamation of religions' resolution suffers major loss of political support," *available at* http://www.ifex.org/international/2010/03/30/cihrs_reaction/.

[3] Robert Evans, "Islamic Bloc Drops U.N. Drive on Defaming Religion," Newsmax.com, Mar.24, 2011, *available at* http://www.newsmax.com/Newsfront/article/2011/03/24/id/390671. In its place, the Human Rights Council adopted a resolution condemning violence, discrimination, and incitement to religious hatred without reference to "defamation of religions." U.N. Human Rights Council, Res. 16/18, Rep. of the Human Rights Council, A/HRC/16/2, chap. I (Mar. 24, 2011).

I am very grateful to the editors for their comments on an earlier draft and for helping clarify my claims. The obscurities that remain are, of course, my own responsibility.

## I. THE BACKGROUND

The Resolution weaves the concept of "defamation of religion" into a text that endorses many other more conventional moral and legal ideas. The text "strongly deplores" violence and incitement to violence, both physical and psychological, directed against people on the basis of religious belief,[4] for example, and urges governments to offer legal protections to their targets,[5] as well as to religious "places, sites, shrines and symbols" threatened with destruction.[6] What reasonable person could object to that? (Although one might quibble that states ought ordinarily to protect people and property from violence, whether or not it is motivated by hostility to their religion.)

However, the Resolution also endorses some more controversial notions, including the idea that states ought to prevent the "targeting of religious symbols" in the media; thus, apparently, proposing to extend the protections of human rights law from persons to symbols, and so – again, apparently – aiming to limit the freedom of individual men and women to criticize religious ideas, even where there is no showing that their criticism will lead to any harm – save perhaps offense – to any human being.[7]

The document makes no attempt to define (or even give examples of) defamation of religion, but the expression occurs most often in the phrase "defamation of religion and incitement to religious hatred in general," which might suggest that defamation of religion is a *species* of incitement to religious hatred.[8] Granted the tradition of understanding human rights as the rights of individual persons, this suggests that it is incitement to hatred of individual members of particular religious groups that the Resolution has in mind. Were this all that it had in mind, however, the Resolution would be otiose, given that Article 20 of the International Covenant on Civil and Political Rights already requires that "*[a]ny advocacy of national, racial or religious hatred that constitutes incitement to discrimination, hostility or violence shall be prohibited by law.*"[9]

So part of what motivates the Resolution, one is bound to conclude, is the thought that states ought to sanction speech and writing that is contemptuous of religious

---

[4] *HRC Resolution, supra* note 1, at ¶ 3.

[5] *Id.* at ¶ 14.

[6] *Id.* at ¶ 16.

[7] Other harms that might flow from criticism of religions include damage to life, limb, or property incited by that criticism, as I discuss later in the chapter.

[8] *HRC Resolution, supra* note 1, at Preamble, ¶11. Incitement to religious hatred, an established idea in international law, began to be introduced in these resolutions in 2009. *See* Human Rights First, "Focus Paper on Defamation of Religions" 3 (March 2010), *available at* http://www.humanrightsfirst. org/discrimination/pdf/3–2010-focus-paper-defamation-of-religions.pdf.

[9] International Covenant on Civil and Political Rights art. 20, ¶ 2, Mar. 23, 1976, 999 U.N.T.S. 171 (emphasis added).

symbols or ideas, not just because of any harm it threatens to people, but because it is wrong in itself to display contempt for any religion; and this interpretation of the Resolution's agenda is supported by the way that the preamble to the Resolution speaks of "recognizing the valuable contribution of all religions to modern civilization."[10] I take it, that is, that although rather loosely conceived, the idea of legal action against defamation of religion attracts people who see something especially wrong about speaking about religions – usually, other people's religions – in ways that display disrespect for them. Left unanswered is why criminal punishment is an appropriate or fruitful response. We certainly owe respect to what deserves respect, and that includes more than people. (The rule of law deserves respect, for example. And so, for that reason, do the people who are struggling around the world today to implement it.) But even though there are many people and things we ought to respect, it does not follow that displays of disrespect – even if directed at people and things we ought to respect – should be subject to criminal sanction.

In the context of global interreligious dialogue, indeed, it seems unlikely that the criminalization of speech offensive to some religious community will be helpful in building respect between religious communities. When some Christians or Jews say things that some Muslims regard as defamatory of Islam, locking those Jews or Christians up (or fining or flogging them) is unlikely to advance dialogue between the Abrahamic faiths. Nor is it likely to help create the sort of atmosphere of mutual respect that most people now hope for. *Mutatis mutandis*, the same is true when the insults are made by Muslims or Jews against Christianity, or Christians or Muslims against Judaism.

And there are, in any case, people and things that deserve not respect but contempt. Disrespect for Pol Pot or Radovan Karadžić, for example, strikes me as not just morally permissible but morally required. So, too, for racism. And we ought to be permitted, *ceteris paribus*, to express the sentiments that morality demands of us. At the very least then, if the expression of disrespect were to be penalized, it ought to be possible to claim a defense of justification. So if there were a reason why we should *never* display disrespect for a religious idea or symbol or tradition, there would have to be something special about religions.

It might be a presupposition, for example, of the proposal that every one of us ought to have respect for every religion (or every religious idea), whatever our own faith. Or, at the very least, that we should keep our disrespect for any religion to ourselves. But I doubt this is what the supporters of the Resolution have in mind. After all, one religious idea long current in the Christian world is that the Prophet Mohammed is probably in hell. Is that idea one that every Muslim ought to treat with respect? Or to avoid disagreeing with except, perhaps, in the very politest of terms? When you find yourself faced with questions like these, it is sometimes helpful to go back to basics.

---

[10]  *HRC Resolution, supra* note 1, at Preamble, ¶ 4.

## II. DISTINGUISHING BLASPHEMY

We should begin, however, by putting one issue out of the way. The list of the enthusiasts for bans on defamation of religion includes many who are clearly concerned simply to gain support in international law for laws against blasphemy. Those of us who are not offended by blasphemy need to do more, I think, to try to understand what motivates those who want the state to criminalize speech that dishonors God or other persons or objects or practices important to religious communities. I have always thought, myself (as someone who grew up as an evangelical Christian), that God was particularly well placed to protect His own honor and His own people without the help of the state. State laws – as opposed to religious proscriptions – against blasphemy have always struck me as aimed at protecting someone who should be perfectly capable of protecting Himself.

In multireligious societies, laws against blasphemy are problematic if they commit the state to the truth of particular religious claims, which will be denied by some citizens, even if they are accepted by a majority of others. It is hard even to define blasphemy without such religious claims. (As people in the United Kingdom discovered in the *Satanic Verses* case.[11]) And if you define blasphemy as speech that is regarded as dishonoring by any religious community at all, then you have moved into the sphere of defamation of religion and you are no longer really talking about blasphemy – which is an offense against God, not His people – at all.

It is easy to see why believers are often offended by assaults on the dignity of their God or of other important religious objects: After all, we are all upset by the disparagement of those whom we love and respect, and the offense is likely to be greatest when it is God, whom believers are supposed to love and respect the most, who is disparaged. So the thought that people are not being unreasonable when they react with violence to defamation of religion, and that we may place the burden of avoiding this violence on those who enrage them, is, in my view, not unnatural, even if, in the end, we decide it is a mistake. Even granted that thought, however, it surely matters not just *that* religious persons or ideas have been disparaged but where and how and why. In particular, we should want to ban the simple denial of a religious claim – announcing, say, that Christ was not divine, that Mohammed was not the last prophet, or that the Exodus did not occur – only if those who are offended by such a denial are reasonably *entitled* to respond with violence. To find such entitlement, I think, even once we understand the motivations for a concern

---

[11] Publication of Salmon Rushdie's *Satanic Verses* led not only to the *fatwa* sentencing Rushdie to death; in England, a blasphemy action was brought by a Muslim against Rushdie. The courts dismissed the claim on the ground that the English law of blasphemy only protects Christianity. R. v. Chief Metropolitan Stipendiary Magistrate ex parte Choudhury, 3 W.L.R. 986 (1990), *aff'd*, 1 Q.B. 429 (1991). The European Commission then concluded that the law's limited scope did not constitute discrimination on the basis of religion in violation of articles 9 and 14 of the European Convention. *See* Choudhury v. United Kingdom, App. No. 17439/90, 12 Hum. Rts. L.J. 172–73 (1991).

with blasphemy is either to suppose that religious people are incapable of reasonable self-restraint or to regard such self-restraint as something that should never be asked of them. The first of these premises insults most religious people; the second is hard to defend in a multireligious world because it undervalues freedom of expression in religious matters.[12]

A state, like Pakistan or Britain, that has an established religion, does take a view on the question who God is, what He is like, and what behavior toward Him is proper, and, while I am against establishment – I think it has bad effects on both church and state – I think it can be carried on without breaching the fundamental human rights of members of religious minorities.[13] I do not think the fact that Lutheranism is the established church in Norway in itself ensures that Catholics or Baptists there must think that the state tramples on their rights.[14] But blasphemy laws do fail to protect minority religions when they expose their adherents to criminal sanctions for asserting what they take to be religious truths, such as that the religious claims of the established religion are false. Given the fact that religions make incompatible claims, freedom of religious expression necessarily entails that you be permitted to utter words that imply the falsity of other faiths and the wickedness of other people's religiously motivated behavior. The old Muslim practice of toleration in el-Andalus did not require Christians and Jews to accept the claims of Islam, although it did require them to avoid dishonoring the Prophet in the public spaces of the community.[15] For evangelical religions, like Christianity and Islam, the free exercise of religion is going to require freedom to talk to others about your religion, and in a society where private life is religiously segregated, this will have to involve discussion in public. But there is a difference, in principle, between public dissent from the truth of religious claims and dishonoring religious symbols. Construed as a constraint on the latter, the laws of el-Andalus look less worrying than if we suppose they ruled out the former.

## III. BUILDING A CASE FOR ANTIDEFAMATION LAW

Three broad classes of considerations offer reasonable grounds for banning public speech (or published writing) that is insulting or defamatory. So, to be clear (which

---

[12] There is also a moral hazard problem here. Allowing ourselves to be worried by the threat of violence encourages violent responses (and threats of violence) from people who want to enforce codes of blasphemy on people who do not share their faith.

[13] Among the bad effects on the church are the sorts of abuse of state powers that go with Caesaropapism. Among the bad effects on the state is an exaggerated sense of the moral authority of the government over citizens' lives.

[14] Of course, some people no doubt think that every citizen has an individual human right to have their religion treated exactly like every other by the state. I myself think that states ought to be neutral among religious identities. But the point is that toleration of minority religions and equal treatment under the law in all matters other than the symbolic fact of establishment is consistent with establishment. I do not believe Norwegian Catholics reasonably regarded themselves as second-class citizens.

[15] _See_ Kwame Anthony Appiah, "How Muslims Made Europe," _N.Y. Rev. Books_, Nov. 6, 2008, at 59–62.

the Resolution was not), the issue I am addressing is legal restraint of expression backed by sanctions, not legal adjudication of claims to compensation for harms resulting from one person's expression about another. The first class has to do with public order; the second reflects a concern for the mental state or reputation of the person insulted; and the third has to do with questions of honor.

### A. *Public Order: Insults and Violence*

Obvious threats to public order flow from the use of language that is calculated to offend, for two rather different reasons. One sort of offensive speech consists of the sort of insult that might lead a normal person exposed to it to be so outraged that she would respond violently to her insulters. From this point of view, it is the consequences for public order – or rather disorder – that flow from such speech that matters, not the protection of the victim from verbal abuse. A rather different idea is that words can have the aim or effect of inflaming passions in ways that will lead to crimes against people or property, especially crimes against those defamed. Here, protection of the defamed from physical harm is at the center of concern, and the speech amounts to incitement to violence against them.

Whether we are worried about insult leading to violence initiated by its victims or against them, context and style of utterance are relevant, because an insult shouted angrily is more likely to produce a violent response, and riot and mayhem are more likely to be produced by speech addressed to a spirited crowd than murmured in a quiet classroom. Also, with both of these rationales, we can identify contexts where the expression of the view can be allowed without risk, and so it is not strictly speaking the content of the expression – even if the heart of it is an insult intended to be recognized as insulting – that is being regulated as its occurrence in circumstances where it is likely to have unfortunate consequences.

When we have to decide between regulating expression, on the one hand, and allowing it while controlling the violence it may elicit, on the other, it matters both what the costs of each will be and whether we think the violence of the responses is reasonable. Enraging someone because you know her weak spots may be a bad thing to do, but if she responds by hitting you, that may still be her problem. So the question of how people ought to respond to defamatory words – the question which responses are warranted or, at any rate, not unreasonable – is always in the offing. It is not the mere fact that affray results from insult that makes us willing to regulate it; the fact that affray is one not unreasonable response to insult also plays a part.[16]

So, too, does the fact that speech is sometimes easier to regulate than responses to insult. Riots, once underway, are notoriously difficult to restrain; crowds can go crazy under the impact of speech and writing, and when they do, they can do great

---

[16] Those of a pacific temperament may think that it is always wrong to be provoked to violence. My own view is that this is, at least, not obvious.

harm. Unleashing the madness of crowds is always something that the state has good reason to seek to avoid, so limiting speech on occasions where it will have these effects is an essential role of public authorities and they need the legal means to carry out the task. In doing this, however, it is never what is being said that triggers concern, but rather the effects of saying it. In the right context, insulting an alien religion could be an effective way of *controlling* a crowd's violent impulses. In such a context, defaming another religion might be exactly what pubic order requires.

It is not, then, the content of what is being said that should trigger the thought of restraining speech for reasons of public order. This is true even though there are better reasons to protect public speech about some topics than about others. In American free-expression jurisprudence, political speech rightly ranks high among the contents worth protecting – higher than commercial speech, for example.[17] So it may be that it is worth expending more resources to allow speech and prevent the risk of the violence it might elicit, when the speech, while inflammatory in its effects, is about topics of concern to our common life. Democratic political communities need to discuss what laws should regulate and how they should regulate them. Debates about these matters can, and perhaps sometimes should, raise high emotions. A concern for public order can raise the issue whether speech should be barred; but even if speech poses a threat to public order, it may be worth expending the resources to allow it. If freedom of speech is worth something, sometimes the public should pay the costs of allowing it.[18] The presence of a credible threat to public order is only the beginning of the analysis.

## B. *The Costs of Defamation for Its Victims*

A second sort of consideration favoring the criminal regulation of defamation has to do with effects of speech that have nothing to do with physical violence, in particular: (1) the social damage that comes from loss of reputation and (2) psychological damage.

---

[17] From among many possible examples, see, e.g., Meyer v. Grant, 486 U.S. 414 (1988).

[18] It is perhaps worth observing that such considerations can be "viewpoint-neutral," if you think they should be, if by that you mean that the state should not take sides on the truth-value of claims in a certain domain in deciding whether their expression is worth spending money to protect. Identifying speech as political does not require you to distinguish between those advocating a position and those advocating its contrary: You can think each of them entitled to protection if the other is. But I do not think that people who seek a public forum have to be offered protection – and allowed to speak if what they say would lead to violence if public resources were not devoted to it – if what they are saying is simply preposterous (which is not a matter of whether we like or dislike what they are saying, but a matter of evaluating its epistemic rationality). So I think that on a reasonable view, whether we ought to spend resources to make it possible for someone to speak without violence can depend not just on what it is about and whether it is relevant for public life, but also on whether it is a genuine contribution to discussion. Someone might object that we should not give the state the power to weigh such considerations because it will abuse that power. But that is a different question from whether there are such considerations to be weighed. (Threatening violence if someone speaks ought always to be a crime, of course. That is one way the law can help protect free expression.)

Reputation is clearly an important social asset, and depriving someone of a reputation can harm her socially and economically. To be sure, there are limits on our concern for loss of reputation. Most obviously, we want to protect people only from *unwarranted* loss of reputation. If the harm arises from the expression of the truth, we have a reason to protect expression, because knowing relevant truths about people helps all of us regulate our relationships with them. Truth ought, for this reason, to be a defense, especially, again, where the subject is of public importance; and even where what is said is not true, good faith ought to be mitigating. In any case, in this area, experience suggests that civil rather than criminal law provides the appropriate means of deterrence and redress.[19]

In addition, just as our moral concern in relation to physical violence depends on whether we think of it as reasonable (and therefore, as we say, provoked), so when it comes to psychological damage, we worry most about harm that arises from *normal* or *reasonable* responses to the insult. (Let us call this reason-grounded harm.) When someone's pain is the result of unusual or irrational sensitivities, we are not likely to want to protect her.[20]

But why should we care about the psychological discomfort that is caused by hearing yourself defamed at all? There are many sorts of negative psychological impact we do not protect people from. I am free to cause widespread aesthetic discomfort by painting my car in clashing colors that offend the sensitivities of many. I am free to deprive people of sources of pleasure: I may cut down the beautiful tree on my property that has given pleasure for generations to those who walk by. These consequences may cause more distress to some than a bloodied nose, which most people would want the law to prohibit. So one reason for trying to protect people from psychological harms is just that they are harms. It matters, generally speaking, when people are pained, especially when their pain is a normal or reasonable response to what others have done.

But the costs of legal protections from psychological harm are high. You cannot insulate people from the negative psychological effects of the speech of others except at the cost of severely limiting speech altogether. A world in which we were constantly trying to predict and avoid upset would be a world with much less communication, and many of the desirable consequences of a world rich in communication would have to be foregone. Identifying actual psychological harms is, in any case, a difficult exercise, one that we would be wise to avoid imposing on our courts. And making

---

[19] But we have also developed the idea that people are entitled to keep even certain *truths* about themselves from public knowledge; and so we have legal protections for privacy, which entail limiting expression. Achieving a balance here strikes me as a difficult and, therefore, interesting problem; I shall say little further about it here, however, because it does not seem to me relevant to defamation of religion.

[20] Peter Molnar asks me whether the special sensitivities of victims of discriminations, of survivors of genocides, which might appear as irrational to some or many, fall into the category of normal and reasonable. I think that sometimes they do.

any upset caused by speech or writing a legally cognizable harm incentivizes people to pretend to be upset to shut others up.

An alternative approach to one that seeks to identify actual harm would identify the harms a reasonable person would suffer when spoken of in defamatory ways, and aim to prohibit speech that would cause suffering to a reasonable person. Such an approach provides less incentive to those who might feign offense to get speech they do not care for banned by the state. But it faces the difficulty that whether it is reasonable to experience psychological pain on hearing speech that is defamatory of oneself (or those persons and things one cares about) is likely itself to be a function of what expression the law prohibits. Reasonable people adjust to their circumstances. The real question is what sorts of defamatory speech we should expect people to get used to. We need to decide which forms of psychological upset are reason-grounded.

To make progress with this question, we have to ask what it is in the speech of others that can cause us psychic discomfort or pain. A first form of discomfort is simply that caused by hearing people say things we wish they would not say. There are many reasons why we might not want someone to say (or write) something:

1.  It will lead others to believe things that we would rather they did not believe.
2.  It expresses a thought we wish they did not have.
3.  It is painful to see yourself represented in an unflattering light.
4.  It makes public what we would prefer to keep private.

More generally, we can be pained by words either because of the *beliefs* they express, true or false; or because of the *attitudes* they express, warranted or unwarranted, toward us and those people and things we care about.

We also have many reasons to care about the consequences of the expression of beliefs, including on our reputations and on the attitudes of others. But I want to focus now on the harms we suffer when someone says something defamatory and we are pained by the discovery of the state of mind it reveals, not on the further harms that their saying it may lead to.

Putting aside considerations of privacy, where it is the beliefs expressed that pain us, we are not generally entitled to protection if they are true; where they are false, we have the remedy of proffering arguments and evidence to refute them. Involving the criminal law in such disagreements does not generally seem likely to be productive; indeed, criminalizing the uttering of falsehoods that upset other people makes it less likely that they will be exposed as false in the marketplace of ideas. And reflection suggests, in any case, that it is not the fact that people have false beliefs but the fact that they are willing to express them that is usually most unsettling. If that is true, then it is the attitude expressed in the defamatory speech, not the false belief, that really pains us.[21]

---

[21]  To avoid a possible misunderstanding, let me underline that I am considering cases where we are pained by the mere fact that someone has a false belief about us. Of course, the expression of the belief may have lots of unpleasant downstream consequences for my reputation, which I care about.

As for the attitudes people express, we can be worried either about the attitude itself – where the words that pain us are evidence of that attitude – or about its expression. It seems to me that the law ought not to be in the business of attempting to prevent others from making their beliefs known to others; and, given that our attitudes are not normally under our voluntary control, it would be wrong to sanction us for having them.[22] So I conclude that the one sort of harm from expression that we might want to do something about is the harm that flows from the expression of the *attitude* of the author of defamatory speech. And here the most important source of pain derives from the fact that defamatory speech can deny us the respect of others, which is one of the greatest human goods: It is both as an act and as an expression of disrespect that defamatory speech causes pain. That is the essence of the third sort of argument for regulating defamatory speech.

## C. *Protecting Honor: Seeking to Enforce Respect*

This third line of argument would have recommended itself to earlier theorists of such matters – from Aristotle and Confucius on. But I suspect it would strike many contemporary people around the world as unfamiliar and implausible. It is exemplified in the Scottish Enlightenment by Adam Smith's discussion of the problem of dueling. We all have an interest in preserving our honor or dignity, Smith assumed. But dignitary assaults were, in his view, too lightly punished under the laws of Great Britain. So people dueled, Smith thought, because it was the only way to protect their honor from affronts. "The small punishment therefore which is incurred by these affronts according to our law is one great cause of dueling, and is to be accounted a *deficientia juris*."[23] Smith's assumption, then, was that we have a legitimate interest in our honor, that we are entitled to defend it, and that if the law provides inadequate means of defense, we will – and we should – pursue private options. If those private options are objectionable on public grounds, the civil magistrate needs to provide a satisfactory public substitute for them. If he does not, the deficiency is the state's, not the citizen's.

Criminalizing assaults on another person's honor could be motivated by the thought that *possessing* honor requires you to defend your honor from assault. If we believe that honor is something worth having and if a disposition to defend your honor is a requirement of being honorable, then failing to provide a legal mechanism for responding to such assaults will lead honorable people to seek redress outside the law. But whatever solution the law offers here, it cannot be a criminal one, for

---

[22] Among the attitudes that people do not have voluntary control over, of course, is belief. I gather that in American First Amendment jurisprudence, people are treated as having complete freedom of belief; and that Cantwell v. Connecticut, 310 U.S. 296 (1940), is one standard citation.

[23] Adam Smith, "Friday. January 21st. 1763," in *Lectures On Jurisprudence* (R. L. Meek, D. D. Raphael, & P. G. Stein eds., Liberty Fund 1982) (1762–1763), *available at* http://oll.libertyfund.org/title/196/55597.

it is part of the logic of honor that I can restore my honor from a dignitary assault only by doing something myself. The state cannot recover my honor for me; it can, at best, offer me the opportunity to redeem it for myself.

### D. *Summary of Reasons for Worrying about Defamation*

All these lines of thought focus on the law of defamation as preventing harms that attach to human individuals; the harms we worry about can be identified by finding those who have been (or might be) harmed and summing the harms they have (or might have) suffered. Even when a group is dishonored, the harm that occurs is harm to the members of the group, by way of the harm each of them suffers when an identity they share is defamed. And the harm I suffer when I am dishonored is not naturally understood as a subjective harm, the consequence of my being pained by being dishonored. How much it matters does not depend on how much it pains me; and, in particular, it can matter even if it does not pain me at all. For honor is, roughly speaking, an entitlement to respect; and if someone denies me what I am entitled to, I am harmed whether I care about it or not.

So defamation in the individual case risks at least five kinds of evil we might want to prevent:

1. violence from the insulted, in response to the insult, and the consequent public disorder;
2. violence against the insulted, incited by the insult;
3. unwarranted damage to the reputation of the insulted;[24]
4. emotional pain suffered by the insulted;
5. harm to the honor or dignity of the insulted.

With all of these, the harm that matters is suffered by individuals, and the total harm is the sum of these individual harms. I stress this point because, so far as I can see, the significance of the distinction between individual and collective insult is not in the harm it causes but in the scale of its likely effects. Group insult is much more likely to lead to affray or riot; and the greater significance of dignitary assaults on groups (as opposed to individuals) has to do with their capacity to harm (or enrage) large numbers of persons in a single act. Now, as I have argued elsewhere, people can be harmed when identities they share are subjected to disrespect.[25] So certain kinds of disrespectful speech harm very large numbers of people. But the correlation between the distinction between individual and collective defamation, on the one hand, and the scale of the threat, on the other, is imperfect. Defaming a beloved

---

[24] I mentioned invasion of privacy as a reason for limiting speech; it is not a particular problem of group defamation, however, so I ignore it here.

[25] Kwame Anthony Appiah, *The Ethics of Identity* 108–9 (Princeton University Press 2005); *see also* Kwame Anthony Appiah, *The Honor Code: How Moral Revolutions Happen* (W.W. Norton 2010).

religious or political leader can pose threats to public order as substantial as the defamation of a group.

## III. PSYCHIC HARMS

In the United States, we are used to the idea that violence and unwarranted loss of reputation are matters that concern the state. So items (1), (2), and (3) on the previous list will look like proper subjects for legal response. We are not inclined to think, however, that the state should seek to protect us from the psychic costs of hearing ourselves defamed, even though the pain caused can no doubt be greater and more long-lasting than the consequences of some physical assaults, which are nonetheless criminal. Where an insult has a propositional content, we are used to thinking, as I said earlier, that the pain matters only if the proposition is either false or an invasion of privacy. If it is true and appropriately public, the utterance of a fact about you is something you have to bear, however unpleasant.

Why should this be? The defenses of truth in libel and of public interest in privacy cases suggest that these rules derive from our thinking of expression as something that should be limited only for very good reasons. Reputation matters to its bearer in obvious ways. But we all also have an interest in the reputations of others being *warranted*, and therefore have good grounds for allowing truth as a defense when reputation is at stake. Privacy involves a complex collection of ideas; but if we are to limit the circulation of truth about people, again we need good reasons for doing so, and we then need to allow as a defense that there is a public interest at stake in the information we have made public.

The foregoing establishes that we need good reasons for limiting insulting speech. But given that people can be seriously harmed by insults, do we not have such reasons? Why should we not offer ourselves protections from these harms? I can think of two arguments. One is that the harm done by offensive speech is, in some sense, enabled by the victim. If what someone else says about me is true, then the harm that flows from public exposure (modulo privacy concerns) often begins with something I did. If it is false, then I can correct it. If it is insultingly expressed, I can only be upset if I care about being treated respectfully by the insulter: and why should I care what he or she says? If I do, my concerns are not reason-grounded. "Sticks and stones," my nanny used to say, "may break my bones, but words can never hurt me." The remedies need not involve the state, then, because they are all in my hands. Better if the state leaves them in my hands and I learn to deal with insults.

Despite having my nanny's authority, I do not find this argument all that compelling. A reasonable person will usually be angered by certain sorts of insult – those, in particular, that amount to displays of disrespect or contempt – and is entitled to expect others not to issue unmerited insults of those kinds. Whether the law should stand with the insultee or not, it surely has no reason to stand with the insulter. And if the fact that I am justifiably upset by an insult means that morality condemns the insulter – even if, in some sense, my upset is up to me – it is not immediately clear why the law should take my role in my anger as sufficient grounds to refuse me its protection.

A second objection to attempting to protect people from psychic harm is another problem of moral hazard. If you make language that causes pain criminal or civilly actionable, then, given the difficulty of actually discovering whether and how much pain has been caused, you motivate people to pretend to have been pained to discourage speech that they happen not to like.[26] (This is a version of the "heckler's veto" problem.[27]) Worse, you may actually encourage people to develop real sensitivities of this kind to restrain the speech of others. These are genuine costs to laws against insult, costs that mean that such laws need to achieve substantial benefits before they should even be entertained.

I think, however, that there is a deeper reason why these sorts of harms do not get much recognition in Anglo-American political or legal culture. We do not think of honor as something that the state should protect; and most of the pain caused by insult comes from the fact that an insult *dishonors* its victim. There are three major social mechanisms for the regulation of behavior: the market, which encourages with prospects of monetary reward; the law, which discourages with threats of civil and criminal penalties; and public opinion, which both encourages with the esteem of our fellow citizens and discourages with their contempt.[28] In the United States, we are inclined to see both economy and esteem as belonging to civil society and not to the state. I do not have room to develop this, but I am inclined to think that there are reasons, of roughly the sort that Adam Smith identified, for the state to protect individual honor, because I believe honor is a natural, proper, and inevitable preoccupation of normal human beings.[29]

## IV. WHAT DOES THIS MEAN FOR DEFAMATION OF RELIGION IN PARTICULAR?

As we saw, a legitimate concern for public order may justify the state in limiting speech in certain contexts where it risks provoking violence and maintaining public

---

[26] Both objections highlight the central difficulty created by the variability of people's responses to insult: in the first case because the damage caused is a feature of the victim's response; in the second because it is part of why it is so hard to tell what real damage has occurred.

[27] The term was coined by Harry Kalven, who pointed out, in the context of limits on speech that provokes a hostile, possibly violent, audience reaction, that "[i]f the police can silence the speaker, the law in effect acknowledges a veto power in hecklers who can, by being hostile enough, get the law to silence any speaker of whom they do not approve." Harry Kalven, Jr., *The Negro and the First Amendment* 140 (Ohio State University Press 1965).

[28] This point is well made in Geoffrey Brennan and Philip Pettit, *The Economy of Esteem: An Essay on Civil and Political Society* (Oxford University Press 2004).

[29] *See* Appiah, *The Honor Code, supra* note 25.

order while not banning the speech is either impossible or too expensive to be worth doing.[30] These arguments provide a rationale for the existing requirement in international law that states protect people from incitement to violence against them by virtue of their race, religion and so on. I can see no argument that creating a further special offense of defamation of religion is needed for this reason. So, if there is a justification for extending beyond current protections, it cannot be this.

That leaves us with three possible further reasons that derive from the general account, namely items (3), (4), and (5) from the last list: unwarranted damage to the reputation of the insulted; emotional pain for the insulted; and harm to the honor or dignity of the insulted.

Let us begin with the question of reputation.

## A. *Reputation*

The Resolution mentions the fact that, especially since 9/11, there have been frequent attempts in Europe and North America to associate Islam with terrorism.[31] This is a reputational problem that faces almost every Muslim with the possibility of being treated as a terrorist even though he or she is not. It is clear that there would be a genuine burden here, imposed on many, if speech and writing that contributes to the idea that each Muslim is likely to engage in terrorism were to be established in the minds of individual citizens or, more especially, of officials. Now truth, as we saw, is obviously relevant in discussing reputational harm. It matters to whether we should seek to prevent this sort of harm whether the claims made are false – as they clearly would be here – or true. There is, no doubt, much confusion in the minds of those who make such imputations. For example, even if a majority of those who pose terrorist threats in western countries are Muslims, it is a very, very small minority of Muslims who pose this threat. And the scale of the damage that has actually been wrought by Muslim terrorists in Europe and North America is, in my view, often overstated. On the other hand, discussion of the reasons why some people engage in terrorism in the name of Islam is an essential part of the response of all societies to helping face this danger. If someone engages in an act of terrorism in the name of Islam, it is hard to see how we can discuss the problem they pose for us without discussing whether they are right in believing that what they are doing is justified by the tenets or the traditions of Islam. And even if, as I believe, the answer here is a plain "No," we may want to consider what it is about the situation of particular

---

[30] The richer the community and the more effective its policing, no doubt, the less likely that cost will be a justified excuse. Once more, some might think that allowing the state the very possibility of this excuse will make it very likely that it will be abused. But, as I said in note 18, *supra*, the fact that a legitimate consideration may well be abused by the state does not undermine its legitimacy.

[31] *HRC Resolution, supra* note 1, at ¶ 7 (expressing "deep concern . . . that Islam is frequently and wrongly associated with human rights violations and terrorism").

Muslim communities that has made them home to such claims. Treating all such discussion as defamatory of Islam is simply wrong.

Would it be helpful, in these circumstances, to criminalize the speech of those who make false accusations about this matter to protect the reputation of Islam? I do not see that it would. Remember that I have conceded that where speech that is defamatory is a form of incitement to group hatred of the sort that threatens violence, it should be banned under existing international law. So I am focusing here only on the narrow question of reputational harms that do not lead to violence. I cannot see that such criminalization would help, and in some respects it would be counterproductive.

There is, to begin with, already a good deal of suspicion in many quarters that discussion of these issues is conducted without frankness out of a desire to avoid causing offense to the great majority of innocent Muslims. That suspicion would increase if those who spoke frankly risked not just being thought to be Islamophobic but also fines or imprisonment. If the governments of the world want to do something useful in this area, it is far better to respond to defamatory speech with information and a reminder of the desirability of respectful discussion of these matters. Or, more effectively yet, why not encourage the creation of fora within which such discussion can occur? This is surely more likely than the criminalization of a few bigots to effect change.

How are individual Muslims most likely to be harmed by the association of Muslims with terrorism? The answer, I suspect, is that the association makes them more likely to be mistreated by state officials, who "profile" individuals who pose no threat, delaying them at airports, stopping their cars, searching their homes and their property: Governments seriously worried about these harms should surely focus on these civil rights problems, especially where it is their own public officials who are causing it. Those of us who are enthusiasts for freedom of speech believe, however, that in most contexts the best response to unhelpful speech is helpful speech.[32]

This is especially so when the matter in question is one of public political concern. Where an individual's reputation is unjustly harmed, he or she may not have the resources to combat the slur in public without access to the courts. Where the harm is to members of large groups, there are significantly greater resources available in

---

[32]  The classic statement in American jurisprudence is from Justice Brandeis: "If there be time to expose through discussion the falsehood and fallacies, to avert the evil by the processes of education, the remedy to be applied is more speech, not enforced silence. Only an emergency can justify repression. Such must be the rule if authority is to be reconciled with freedom." Whitney v. California, 274 U.S. 357, 377 (1927) (Brandeis, J., concurring). Where a religious minority, like Muslims in many European countries, is disadvantaged and badly placed in the contest of arguments, this claim is likely to seem less compelling. But we should worry that a generalized criminalization of defamation of religion is as likely to be used against them as in their defense. And remember, the argument here is not meant to exclude the criminalization of incitement to violence, nor does anything I have said rule out strong legislation against discrimination in housing, employment, and public accommodations.

the public sphere; and the state, with its significant resources, can also play a role in correcting the misinformation. Criminalization, on the other hand, is an easy route to the creation of martyrs to the cause of their religion or to the cause of free speech.

There are other cases imaginable where a criminal remedy would be even less effective. Suppose I say that people of some faith follow a false god, then whether or not this is true is relevant, as usual, to the question whether their consequent loss of reputation (if I am believed) is unwarranted. It seems like a bad idea for courts to be in the business of adjudicating such claims. The most basic reason is that it is widely understood nowadays that there are no methods of settling such questions that are entitled to the universal assent of reasonable people.[33] And a court that has to use procedures that reasonable people have no reason to respect lacks an essential component of legitimacy.

## B. *Psychological Damage*

Emotional damage from speech that disparages one's religion is clearly something that one can reasonably hope to avoid in private. You are entitled to quiet enjoyment of your church or temple or mosque, and people who disrupt you are a public nuisance and can reasonably be punished, whether or not the disruption is defamatory. But the banning of the expression of disrespect for a religious idea in public fora would be a reasonable remedy only if the harm done were very substantial and the psychic discomfort were a reasonable response. In states with established religions or substantial majorities of one faith, chances are that the question whether the harm caused was substantial and, in this sense, reasonable would be very hard to adjudicate in ways that would look legitimate to religious minorities, whether the speech complained of was by or about them. The question is whether a legal regime could be crafted that genuinely advanced the interests of those who were in need of the greatest protection. I have my doubts.

There is an interesting analogy here with the treatment of pornography. Someone might argue that people are entitled to be protected from exposure to discussions of their religious life by others just as we are entitled to be protected in public from exposure to sexually explicit representations. Whatever psychic damage is caused in either case could be avoided by identifying images and writings that are potentially offensive to certain people and by warning people to avoid certain private spaces where expression that might be offensive is likely to occur. That way we can keep the public square free of pornography. Why not do the same for speech that is religiously offensive to some?

---

[33] *See* Kwame Anthony Appiah, "Causes of Quarrel: What's Special about Religious Disputes?," in *Religious Pluralism, Globalization, and World Politics* 41–64 (Tom Banchoff ed., Oxford University Press 2008).

The answer here, I think, is that it is not a plausible idea that speech about religious matters, like sexually arousing representations, should be confined to a private sphere. Religion is too important to too many people in ways that matter for our public life. Experience suggests that laws against speech that upsets religious sensibilities are bound to be used to keep people free from the possibility of challenge to their faith. And the trouble is that, whereas I, like you, currently think that my own religious view is correct, the possibility that we are in fact incorrect and that we are therefore living in a false belief – the possibility that serious people of all faiths have always entertained – is one that argues against this. That is why the freedom to evangelize is rightly regarded as one of the elements of religious freedom. And people of every religion, as well as of no religion, have a reason for wanting it to be possible to face other people with challenges to their faith, namely that this is the only way those people can be brought to see the truth. They are likely to think, too, that in a public debate conducted on terms of rough equality, their own view will emerge sustained rather than undermined, whereas the views of others risk being diminished. We also all have a higher-order interest in having the correct view; and if, as seems likely, the chances of our having the correct view are increased by vigorous free discussion, limitations of freedom of expression on religious matters are an especially serious threat to our interests. It is only if it is best to hold on to your religious view whether or not it is right that limiting discussion of such matters advances our interests. Most religious traditions would rightly not make that claim.

People who are not religious – or whose religion is, so to speak, postmodern – are likely to be skeptical of the importance of reasoning in the shaping of religious affiliation, even in the shaping of religious belief. I am not so skeptical myself. And, in any case, that skepticism is, as I have said, not one that most religious people should share. Given what they believe, they ought to be against the privatization of religion.

### C. *Practical Considerations*

So, as you see, even though I can imagine rationales for and practices of religious antidefamation law that would be defensible, I do not think such laws are a good idea in the real world. Let me end with two more such reasons that strike me as simple and compelling and that have to do with the likely effects of laws criminalizing defamation of religion. These are not knockdown arguments or arguments of high principle. But they are arguments nevertheless.

First, as the International Freedom of Expression Exchange (IFEX) has noted: "[T]he banning of forms of expression considered defamatory of a certain religion...is often used to discriminate against religious minorities...."[34] Where

---

[34] International Freedom of Expression Exchange, *supra* note 2.

people whip up hysteria against religious groups in ways that lead to violence, what they do is already covered by laws against incitement to violence: The only effect of special laws about religion is likely to be to allow the authorities to treat innocent behavior by minority religions as criminal, while failing to discourage the much more likely harm of violence by majorities (or the state itself) against religious minorities. In advocating for changes in the limited class of cases where current international human rights law recognizes exceptions to a broad right of free speech, one crucial consideration – as in the reasonable assessment of all proposals about criminal law – is whether such changes are likely to be abused by states.[35]

Second, so it seems to me, one thing we need above all in our world today is greater conversation across religious traditions. Of course, I believe that this is most likely to be productive if it is conducted respectfully, and I believe it should be conducted respectfully whether or not that will make it productive.[36] But the practical effect of laws singling out defamation of religion for special criminal sanction is most likely to be to discourage exactly that conversation. That is one thing, I suspect, that many of those who favor such laws are clear about. They want to protect their own faith from public discussion and scrutiny. I would simply urge them to display greater confidence in their faith and traditions . . . and commend to them the thought that if their faith will not survive debate and scrutiny, it may be the wrong faith.

Free expression matters for two fundamental reasons. One is that expression is central to who we humans are. That makes expression something that we should limit only where other substantial interests are at stake. A second is that a world rich with free expression is one in which we will learn more and learn faster. The state might intervene to advance these ends – arguing that compulsory good manners would improve the capacity of our conversation to produce truth – but once it enters into the regulation of expression, as we have seen over and over again, it tends mostly to do so to advance the interests of those who command the state. So even though I can imagine regimes of laws against defamation of religion that would advance religious understanding, I do not believe that actual laws against defamation of religion are likely to help secure that aim.

In any case, there are other things that it would be more useful to be doing, including developing, through education and in public discourse, a culture of mutual respect among citizens. I have tried to show that, although there are considerations

---

[35] As Toby Mendel shows, there are too many exceptions here already. *See* Toby Mendel, "Does International Law Provide for Consistent Rules on Hate Speech?," Chapter 22 herein. It has struck me often in listening to discussions of these matters that the expression "incitement to hatred or violence" brings together two very different sorts of wrong. It is bad to hate people who do not deserve it; and it is no doubt wrong to incite people to do what is bad. But if the hatred does not lead to violence or discrimination, then it is not obvious to me why it should be a matter of legal concern. And if it is violence and discrimination that matter, then why not target those directly?

[36] *See* Kwame Anthony Appiah, *Cosmopolitanism: Ethics in a World of Strangers* (W.W. Norton 2006).

in favor of criminalizing defamation of religion, they are generally outweighed by the considerations against. There is, I think, one second-order conclusion to be drawn from discussions like this one: Even if we could draft laws that were attentive to all the morally relevant distinctions, they would be extremely likely to do harm along with whatever good they did. And much of that harm would fall on those who are already the most disadvantaged.

# 10

# Responding to "Hate Speech" with Art, Education, and the Imminent Danger Test

*Peter Molnar*

"Racism is a weapon of mass destruction."
– Faithless, *Mass Destruction*[1]

## I. INTRODUCTION

The debate about responses to "hate speech"[2] is caught between vague generalizations, lack of information, and false accusations. In this discussion, the argument for freedom of speech often is misunderstood. Those who would protect the free-expression rights even of racists frequently are mischaracterized, and accused of sacrificing equality and the fight against racism and other prejudices on the altar of freedom of speech, disregarding the danger and harm that "hate speech"

---

[1] http://www.metacafe.com/watch/sy-25142307/faithless_mass_destruction_official_music_video/.

[2] As I wrote in the first note of a previous essay:

> When used in legal parlance, the colloquial expression "hate speech" seems to presuppose that the state can define with legal precision the particular forms of content that should be regulated as "hate speech." Because I regard this implicit assumption as questionable, I shall use "hate speech" only in quotation marks. I do not mean to imply that many clear instances of obvious "hate speech" cannot be identified; I mean only to stress that a reliable definition of this term, if possible at all, cannot be taken for granted.

> Peter Molnar, "Towards Better Law and Policy Against 'Hate Speech' – The 'Clear and Present Danger' Test in Hungary," in *Extreme Speech and Democracy* 237, 237 (Ivan Hare & James Weinstein eds., Oxford University Press 2009).

I would like to thank Michael Herz, Leslie Newman, Robert C. Post, Zelma Rios, and Todd Grabarsky for their helpful comments on this chapter, Jeremy Waldron for the opportunity to present part of this chapter in his workshop at NYU Law School on "hate speech" in fall 2009, the participants in that workshop and the colloquium and conference at Cardozo Law School in spring 2010 for their useful questions and comments, Tom Finkelpearl and Margaret Morton for information about the statue that I use as an example, and Stephanie Rosenblatt and Leslie Graifman for their work at the Institute of International Education, which allowed me as a Fulbright Fellow to see the play that called my attention to the statue.

can cause in order to further the abstract value of freedom of expression. Yet, the difference between competing viewpoints on the constitutional treatment of racist and other "hate" speech is not based on a qualitatively higher valuing of either equality or free speech. Rather, supporters and opponents of content-based prohibitions on speech diverge as to the most effective responses to "hate speech." They differ as to whether adoption or rejection of content-based bans on "hate speech" better serves equality and reduces the dangers and other harms caused by such speech.

This chapter suggests that we start a new phase in the discourse on responses to "hate speech." It proposes that discussion be based on a detailed understanding of the historical and cultural context of each country, region, or continent in which the "hate speech" is spoken. Further, this search must focus on the most effective law and policy against such speech. Instead of content-based bans, I suggest two, less explored, responses that are in my view the most helpful ones, and which have no or only marginal unintended side consequences.

Section II of this chapter does not comprehensively examine the many arguments for and against "hate speech" laws, which are content-based by definition – and are so ably analyzed by other contributors to this volume. Rather, as a means of explaining graphically my point, I use the example of a sculpture, the symbolism of which is deeply rooted[3] in U.S. history and culture, as described by Levy Lee Simon, an African-American playwright.[4] I argue that instead of content-based bans on "hate speech" we should rely on art and other educational responses, among other reasons because prohibitions cannot reach the roots of hatred or even its symptoms. I stress that art and education in the broadest sense are the most effective preventatives against "hate speech"; they can powerfully cure public discourse as they reach the roots of prejudice: ignorance, misunderstanding, and false beliefs.

Section III suggests that we need a better understanding of the circumstances under which speech can cause an imminent danger of violence. For example, I argue that we have to consider both the immediate and the broader social environment in which "hate speech" occurs. In inflammable social-political situations, the danger caused by "hate speech," depending on both its content and context, might justify limitations on freedom of expression under the "imminent danger" test if we consider not only the immediate environment of the speech but also the wider context of its possible effect. We have to examine the extent to which racism, homophobia, and other prejudices have gained momentum in a country, have become institutionalized through elected representation in national and local governments, and have acquired popular approval. All these aspects of the broader environment influence whether "hate speech" creates a clear and present danger of violence in specific situations. Considering these factors and other elements of a carefully

---

3  "Deeply rooted" "hate speech" is differentiated from other similar expression by Alon Harel in "Hate Speech and Comprehensive Forms of Life," Chapter 15 herein.

4  *See* Levy Lee Simon, *The Guest at Central Park West*, first produced at St. Philips Theatre, New York, NY (2007).

conceptualized "imminent danger" test[5] moves the reach of this test closer to the scope of narrowly tailored, well-intended "hate speech" laws that aim to cover only the most vicious instances of such speech, some of which might create imminent danger.[6]

Finally, I conclude that art and education in the broadest sense and the proper application of the "imminent danger" test, applied together, offer the best combination of responses to "hate speech" in all democracies.

## II. "HATE SPEECH" LAWS AND THE ROOTS OF HATRED

Writing about efforts to regulate racist and other "hate" speech on university campuses, Nadine Strossen argues that "if we are to understand and eradicate the complex root causes of racial discrimination, then we must think creatively as more than just lawyers."[7] She emphasizes that speech is only the tip of the iceberg: "To draft legal rules that address only one manifestation of these deeper problems of racial inequality is at best ineffective, and at worst counterproductive."[8] We need to think about the latent structures of racism, homophobia, and other similar prejudices. To fight "hate speech" effectively, we need to find and treat its deepest roots.

The ongoing debate on the constitutional treatment of "hate speech" is informed significantly by our beliefs about the connection between racist and other prejudiced expressions in the public sphere, as well as the structures of racism[9] and other prejudices in the deep, often hidden, layers of societies. It is understandable that many experts argue that "hate speech" reinforces stereotypes and humiliates, even silences, discriminated-against minorities, and that therefore it must be counteracted by content-based probations. A major line of this argument holds that the essential concern is how the targeted groups experience racist and similarly hateful verbal attacks. As four Critical Race Theorists observe, "[i]t is not a coincidence that the strongest sentiment for regulating hate speech has come from members of victimized communities."[10] Jeremy Waldron, although *not* a member of a victimized community, passionately argues:

> The harm that expressions of racial hatred do is harm in the first instance to the groups who are denounced or bestialized in pamphlets, billboards, talk radio, and blogs. It is not harm – if I can put it bluntly – to the white liberals who find the racist

---

[5] *See* Brandenburg v. Ohio, 395 U.S. 444 (1969).

[6] Many "hate speech" laws are created to suppress dissent. For examples, see *Striking a Balance: Hate Speech, Freedom of Expression and Non-discrimination* (Sandra Coliver ed., ARTICLE 19 and University of Essex 1992).

[7] Nadine Strossen, "Regulating Racist Speech on Campus: A Modest Proposal?," 1990 *Duke L.J.* 484, 495.

[8] *Id.*

[9] With regard to "structural racism," see, for example, the research of the Center for Social Inclusion, http://www.centerforsocialinclusion.org.

[10] Mari J. Matsuda et al., "Introduction," in *Words That Wound: Critical Race Theory, Assaultive Speech, and the First Amendment* 1, 1 (Westview Press 1993).

invective distasteful. Maybe we should admire some lawyer who says he hates what the racist says but defends to the death his right to say it, but this sort of intellectual resilience is not what's at issue. The question is about the direct targets of the abuse. Can their lives be led, can their children be brought up, can their hopes be maintained and their worst fears dispelled, in a social environment polluted by these materials? Those are the concerns that need to be answered when we defend the use of the First Amendment to strike down laws prohibiting the publication of racial hatred.[11]

I partially agree. We need to consider thoroughly the experience of and arguments from and for the communities that were exterminated, enslaved, persecuted, and discriminated against in the past, and often still are discriminated against in the present. One of the strongest reasons for a content-based ban on "hate speech" is that when directed at such communities – which are usually minorities – it does more than simply offend: it deeply damages both the targeted groups, and society as a whole, which must forgo the unrealized contributions of a disempowered group whose members cannot fully participate in the polity due to their ongoing subjugation. Indeed, arguably, "hate speech" significantly exacerbates the already disadvantaged situation of discriminated-against groups, and the political community as a whole has a responsibility to protect against this further debilitation. Those who are not directly subjected[12] to "hate speech," usually those who belong to the majority, must clearly express their solidarity with targeted communities and must join forces with them in order to find the most effective responses.

As a Central-European observer and participant in the heated discussions on "hate speech" and the First Amendment, I can add my home country, Hungary, to the list of places where terrible sufferings must be remembered when taking a stand for or against content-based bans of "hate speech." As I have written in another article,[13] the history of Hungary provides powerful reasons for such regulation through the criminal law without waiting for the clear and present danger of violence. Yet, as I discuss elsewhere,[14] I support the courts of the Republic of Hungary, which, led by our Constitutional Court, have followed largely the prevailing interpretation of the First Amendment of the U.S. Constitution,[15] which bars prohibiting

---

[11]  Jeremy Waldron, "Free Speech and the Menace of Hysteria," *N.Y. Rev. of Books*, May 29, 2008, *available at* http://www.nybooks.com/articles/21452.

[12]  Racism and other similar "hate speech" hurt not only the directly targeted group, but every humanistic individual and the political community as a whole.

[13]  Molnar, *supra* note 2. I hope that this article demonstrates that since the early 1990s, the American constitutional treatment of "hate speech" is not exceptional. There is at least one more country that follows the approach upheld under the First Amendment, and it is not a country with a particularly nice history in the twentieth century. It is one of the countries where the Holocaust was the most horrible and devastating. Notwithstanding the Hungarian Holocaust, courts in Hungary abide by the American approach.

[14]  *See* Molnar, *supra* note 2.

[15]  Largely, but not entirely. One of the exceptions is that in 2010 Hungary criminalized holocaust denial, making it punishable by up to three years in prison.

"hate speech" based on its content. This approach usually is characterized as an example of U.S. exceptionalism,[16] but since the first "hate speech" decision of the Hungarian Constitutional Court in 1992,[17] it can be more correctly labeled the American-Hungarian approach.

The Jewish community is divided on the constitutional treatment of "hate speech" both in the United States and in Hungary,[18] and Roma-Hungarians, the other traditional targets of wide-spread prejudice in Hungary, also differ in their opinions about it. Such disagreements, which perhaps involve equal parts strategy and principle, are long-standing. Samuel Walker describes, for example, how the National Association for the Advancement of Colored People (NAACP) – after clashing with the ACLU over such issues as banning D. W. Griffith's racist movie, *The Birth of a Nation* – reversed its position and opposed restricting racist content in the mails. Walker writes:

> The NAACP reversed itself on post office censorship in the 1940s because it now believed that constitutional litigation to protect individual rights was the most promising avenue for advancing African American rights. This shift by the leading civil rights organization in the country was a key indicator of the trend in American law and policy.[19]

As opposed to this approach, which advocates constitutional protection even for racist speech, Mari Matsuda argues that the "claim that a legal response to racist speech is required stems from a recognition of the structural reality of racism in America."[20] But the question is whether restricting speech, even though a natural emotional reaction to "hate speech" by at least most humanistic people, including myself, is the best legal response, or whether other legal options and extra-legal remedies are more effective. We must find the most efficient public policy responses to such speech, and avoid choices that would only bring an illusion of emotional comfort. We have to go below the surface to reach and deal with the roots of "hate speech": prejudice and ignorance.

Lawrence, Matsuda, Delgado, and Crenshaw include the following among the defining premises of Critical Race Theory: "Current inequalities and social/institutional practices are linked to earlier periods in which the intent and

---

[16] See Frederick Schauer, "The Exceptional First Amendment," in *American Exceptionalism and Human Rights* 29 (Michael Ignatieff ed., Princeton University Press 2005).

[17] HCC, 30/1992 (V. 26.) AB decision.

[18] According to a 1999 survey of Jewish Hungarians, 85 percent of those interviewed "consider it acceptable to place legal restrictions on the public expression of antisemitic views, while 59 per cent support such sanctions against Holocaust deniers." See *Jews and Jewry in contemporary Hungary: results of a sociological survey* 44 (András Kovács ed., Institute for Jewish Policy Research 2004).

[19] Samuel Walker, *Hate Speech: The History of an American Controversy* 24 (University of Nebraska Press 1994).

[20] Mari J. Matsuda, "Public Response to Racist Speech: Considering the Victim's Story," 87 *Mich. L. Rev.* 2320 (1989).

cultural meaning of such practices were clear."[21] As both links between these times
and present structures of discrimination may be – although not necessarily – subtle,
art has unique power to shed light on them, illuminating a nuanced understanding.
This quoted statement of Critical Race Theory can be exemplified and in regard the
implied subtleness of "current inequalities," to some extent challenged by a specific
piece of theater art, *The Guest at Central Park West*, the award-winning play by Levy
Lee Simon. The play ends with a dramatic scene in which all the characters, blacks
and whites together, are looking out the window of a Central Park West apartment,
and one of them, Terrence, a homeless African-American man, rails:

> [P]eople were put into slavery. A race of people were killed and their land
> stolen.... Now you take that statue out there, just one block from where we are
> now. You know the one I am talking about, the one with Teddy Roosevelt on a
> horse with a barefoot Indian on one side and a barefoot African slave on the other.
> That statue has sat in front of that museum since 1943. And all these years later
> it's still there. I remember first seeing that statue on a school trip when I was in
> the eighth grade and I remember feeling something was very wrong. I remember
> feeling weak, queasy, and embarrassed. I didn't understand all the reasons at that
> time but as I got older as I began to understand what it meant for me to live in
> this world, I came to understand the meaning of that statue and how evil it is. You
> see that statue is the symbol of the idea of white supremacy, manifest destiny. That
> statue, that just about every elementary and junior high school kid in New York and
> all over the country will see before they are twelve years old sits on a main street in
> the greatest city in the world. It's not sitting in front of some museum in Alabama
> with a confederate flag waving next to it. No, it is sitting in New York City, Central
> Park West, the melting pot, with a state and federal flag flying nearby, a symbol that
> reminds us that we are supposed to be inferior. A symbol that is more dangerous
> than any bomb anybody could drop. – Ain't that some shit. – Yeah, I came over
> here tonight with an agenda Charles. See when I leave here, I am crossing the
> street from Central Park to the Museum of Natural History and I am going to put
> these sticks of dynamite around that statue, light the fuse and blow that statue to
> smithereens!... That statue has caused me more pain and suffering than spending
> fifteen years of my life in prison because it's the idea of white supremacy that locked
> me away.[22]

The statue of Theodore Roosevelt,[23] as perceived by Simon, might or might not
fall within the prohibition of various "hate speech" laws. Simon certainly chose an
extremely forceful symbol, what one author has (accurately) described as "[t]hirty
tons of corroded bronze constitut[ing] a racial archetype – domination by the worthy

---

[21] Matsuda et al., *supra* note 10, at 6.
[22] Simon, *supra* note 4.
[23] For an analysis of how ideas of racial differences and supremacy influenced Theodore Roosevelt
from his childhood, see Joshua Hawley, *Theodore Roosevelt: Preacher of Righteousness* 32–47 (Yale
University Press 2008).

of the genetically unfit."[24] In my view, the Theodore Roosevelt statue could be a subject of constant, heated outrage,[25] were it not, like most publicly displayed statues, simply part of the unnoticed background for the overwhelming majority of people. But even if almost invisible to many, art discloses what is hidden, and we have to face the disturbing symbolism of this Theodore Roosevelt statue: It is a continuous expression of deeply rooted[26] subordination and discrimination against groups of people who were treated in horrible ways, the worst in the history of the United States, and are still subject to discrimination. If this sort of symbolic speech remains ignored, it undermines the credibility of American responses to what may be characterized as "hate speech," in addition to sustaining ongoing forms of such speech.

Any serious, multilayered policy that aims to respond effectively to "hate speech" must be able to address an issue such as is presented by the statue of Theodore Roosevelt at the edge of Central Park.[27] Otherwise, as Terrence says in Simon's play: "After civil wars and civil rights and world wars, they are still living by the same idea."[28]

Efforts to find effective remedies for "hate speech" often have focused on strengthening criminal prohibitions. Let us assume that New York State enacts a content-based statute to protect discriminated-against minorities from denigrating expressions. Of course, such a restriction of free speech could not stand under the First Amendment, but for the sake of this argument, let us assume that the courts uphold the law,[29] and some individuals and groups sue, urging the application of this anti–"hate speech" law to the Theodore Roosevelt sculpture. The Museum of Natural History is a private institution, and the sculpture itself is part of the Museum's collection and thus privately owned. But its buildings, as well as the land on which

---

[24] Gray Brechin, "Conserving the Race: Natural Aristocracies, Eugenics, and the U.S. Conservation Movement," 28 *Antipode* 229, 229 (1996). Brechin links the statue to the eugenically tinged ideas of Henry Fairfield Osborn, president of the American Museum of Natural History when the statue and the museum's Roosevelt wing were commissioned.

[25] I want to make it clear that I am not writing this sharply critical point with a sort of anti-American attitude. As a foreign observer, I love the United States. I consider New York the city in which I am most comfortable after my hometown, Budapest.

[26] Alon Harel defines deeply rooted "hate speech" as speech that is part of a comprehensive form of life. (As Harel writes, there is no clear line between deeply rooted and not deeply rooted hatred. Harel, *supra* note 3.) I disagree with Harel when he suggests that deeply rooted hatred should enjoy more constitutional protection than other "hate speech." In my view, deeply rooted "hate speech" can be the most dangerous of all "hate speech." But the notion of deeply rooted "hate speech" can help to develop specific policy responses to "hate speech" embedded in the mindset of families through generations as opposed to "hate speech" manifested under occasional influences.

[27] For a creative discussion of the constitutional symbolism of historic statues, see Sanford Levinson, *Written in Stone* (Duke University Press 1998).

[28] Simon, *supra* note 4.

[29] Note that this statute would protect only certain groups and not others, which is always hard and often impossible to accept politically (and legally, *see* R.A.V. v. City of St. Paul, 505 U.S. 377 [1992]) by many members of the majority.

they sit and the sidewalk in front of the buildings, are owned by the City of New York. The Museum enjoys a perpetual lease, rent-free.[30] It also receives meaningful financial support from the City (11 percent of its budget in 2009). Thus, the lawsuit would be against both the Museum and the City that tolerates, or supports, and subsidizes on its property a sculpture that denigrates discriminated-against minorities. Independent courts could hold that the City as well as the private institution are in violation of the hypothetical state law banning denigration of discriminated-against minorities. But as the sculpture is a historic piece of art,[31] the law, in order to cover it, would have to be so broad that it would gravely endanger freedom of speech and could be discriminatorily applied against the very minorities that have been discriminated against. Why, then, should a community that praises both equality and liberty resort to law instead of other available remedies?[32]

The alternative response is art and education in the broadest sense. The sculpture, as it stands now, is part of a national tradition. All national legacies have good and bad parts, and communities need to re-conceptualize their heritage once they recognize that one part of it should be condemned rather than celebrated, or that another should be highlighted as a particularly positive element. With the first African-American president of the United States now in office, time is very much up for re-conceptualizing the sculpture of his predecessor, who a century ago became the first president to invite an African-American, Booker T. Washington, for dinner at the White House.

---

[30] As the Museum's financial statement summarizes: "The buildings occupied by the Museum and the land on which they reside are owned by the City and are occupied by the Museum pursuant to an 1877 lease with the City. The lease grants to the Museum, free of rent, the exclusive use of the land and buildings erected and to be erected thereon for so long as the leased properties are used for purposes consistent with the Museum's charter."

[31] For an example of how art might enjoy particular constitutional protection, see Act XLV of 1993, On the amendment of Act IV of 1978 of the Criminal Code, which added the following provision to the Hungarian Criminal Code under the title "Use of Symbols of Despotism."

Section 269/B of the Criminal Code:

(1) Anyone who
   a) distributes;
   b) uses in front of a large public gathering;
   c) exhibits in public a swastika, the SS sign, an arrow-cross, the hammer and sickle, a five-pointed red star or a symbol depicting the above commits a misdemeanour – unless a graver crime is realised – and shall be punishable by fine.
(2) The person who commits an act defined in paragraph (1) for the purposes of disseminating knowledge, education, science, or art, or for the purpose of information about the events of history or the present time shall not be punishable.

The Constitutional Court took this provision as an exception, holding it constitutional with the thoroughly unconvincing argument that symbols are such special forms of expression that they can trigger specific criminal prohibition. Decision 14/2000 (V. 12.) AB, http://www.mkab.hu/content/en/en3/06079304.htm.

[32] For a superb analysis of speech subsidized by the state, see Robert Post, "Subsidized Speech," 106 *Yale L.J.* 151 (1996).

Shall the statue be removed from where it stands on the Museum's property off the sidewalk across the street from Central Park and placed in a special space inside the Museum, surrounded by a "translation" by art historians and historians that transforms its original and persistent meaning, where willing visitors, who should be provided with clear, critical explanations, can see it? Or should it stay in front of the Museum, accompanied by an additional sculpture as a response? There is no legal precedent to look to consider whether the City of New York has the authority to require the Museum of Natural History to remove the statue, or install an additional one. It is also not clear, whether the Museum could take either of these two steps without approval from the Art Commission of the City. Thus, the City and the Museum should join forces in order to determine the best solution, through a process that includes public discussions about the meaning of the statue that might be contested.[33] As a believer in the American tradition of "the-more-speech-the-better," I see adding a sculpture of an African-American and a Native-American who fought against discrimination, along with an accompanying exact, detailed history of the Theodore Roosevelt statue, as the best solution. This creative artistic-educational response to a symbol of a highly disturbing part of the American national heritage has to be supported by broad, nationwide efforts to examine all unexplored parts of related structures of subordination, both past and present.[34] Two wonderful documentary films provide recent examples of such work on closely related subjects, demonstrating how critics, historians, filmmakers, other artists, and educators can help re-conceptualize and translate the meaning of the statue.

*Faubourg Tremé: The Untold Story of Black New Orleans* depicts "arguably the oldest black neighborhood in America, the birthplace of the Civil Rights movement in the South and the home of jazz."[35] As the filmmakers' synopsis asks:

Who knew that in the early 1800's, while most African Americans were toiling on plantations, free black people in Tremé were publishing poetry and conducting symphonies? Who knew that long before Rosa Parks, Tremé leaders organized sit-ins and protests that successfully desegregated the city's streetcars and schools? Who

---

[33] The discussion could include comparison with the Memorial that depicts Robert Gould Shaw on a horse as he was leading Massachusetts 54th Regiment, with the soldiers of the first African-American regiment in the Civil War walking besides him. *See* Robert Gould Shaw and the 54th Regiment, http://www.nps.gov/boaf/historyculture/shaw.htm. In my view, it makes the Shaw Memorial fundamentally different from the Theodore Roosevelt Statue that Shaw and the African-American soldiers were fighting together for the abolishment of slavery, the Memorial obviously commemorates this joint effort in which Shaw died and as we can read on the website for the memorial, "[t]he artist was especially attentive to the depiction of the African-American soldiers." *See* http://www.nga.gov/feature/shaw/s4000.shtm

[34] Of course, the Theodore Roosevelt statue and the related tradition in the United States is only an example; other countries, starting with my own, Hungary, also have a lot to do in responding to the unacceptable parts of their national traditions.

[35] Web site for *Faubourg Tremé: The Untold Story of Black New Orleans* (Dawn Logsdon & Lolis Eric Elie directors; Serendipity Films 2008), http://www.tremedoc.com/synopsis/.

knew that jazz, the area's greatest gift to America, was born from the embers of this first American Civil Rights movement?[36]

The second film complements *Faubourg Tremé*. In *Traces of the Trade: A Story from the Deep North*, filmmaker Katrina Browne, with nine of her cousins, discovers the history of her own ancestors. As Stephen Holden wrote in the *New York Times*: "The implications of the film are devastating":[37]

Given the myth that the South is solely responsible for slavery, viewers will be surprised to learn that Browne's ancestors were Northerners. . . .

They sailed their ships from Bristol, Rhode Island to West Africa with rum to trade for African men, women and children. Captives were taken to plantations that the DeWolfs owned in Cuba or were sold at auction in such ports as Havana and Charleston. Sugar and molasses were then brought from Cuba to the family-owned rum distilleries in Bristol. Over the generations, the family owned 47 ships that transported thousands of Africans across the Middle Passage into slavery. They amassed an enormous fortune. By the end of his life, James DeWolf had been a U.S. Senator and was reportedly the second richest man in the United States.

The enslavement of Africans . . . was a cornerstone of Northern commercial life. The Triangle Trade drove the economy of many port cities (Rhode Island had the largest share in the trade of any state), and slavery itself existed in the North for over 200 years. . . . While the DeWolfs were one of only a few "slaving" dynasties, the network of commercial activities that they were tied to involved an enormous portion of the Northern population. Many citizens, for example, would buy shares in slave ships in order to make a profit.[38]

Documentary movies like these can contribute to an acknowledgment of the undeniably racist and subordinating message of the Theodore Roosevelt statue as it stands now on Central Park West. Other artistic and educational responses are similarly much more helpful than content-based bans on speech which, especially in the Internet era, seem like jumping on a shadow. Legal prohibition should be reserved for incitement that causes imminent danger. The sculpture causes imminent danger of violence in Simon's play, if blowing up a statue qualifies as violence. Is it otherwise a typical example of speech that begs and allows responses, but is not likely to create imminent danger? The answer to this question depends on the details of the surrounding circumstances. Therefore, we must explore these contextual elements.

[36] *Id.*

[37] Stephen Holden, "Courage to Bear Witness to Man's Infinite Cruelties," N.Y. *Times*, June 13, 2008, at E6.

[38] Web site for *Traces of the Trade: A Story from the Deep North* (Katrina Browne director 2008), http://www.tracesofthetrade.org/synopsis/.

## III. WHAT DANGER IS IMMINENT ENOUGH?

Whether danger caused by speech is imminent turns more on the context than the content of the speech. Shouting "Fire!" can be very helpful when it urges people to leave a burning building, but someone can create imminent danger by "falsely shouting fire in a crowded theater."[39] Justice Holmes's classic example well supports the decisive significance of context, but it is about a situation when people react to speech solely based on its immediate environment. Public discourse is different.

To determine whether speech causes imminent danger, thus justifying an exceptional prohibition of the respective communication, we have to take account of not only the immediately surrounding circumstances of the speech, but also its broader social environment, which obviously influences the immediate impact of speech that depending on its context can create a clear and present danger of violent action. If someone argues that the imminence of the danger caused by speech should be measured only by looking at the immediate surroundings, she or he also should conclude that the danger caused by a neo-Nazi march is the same regardless of whether the marchers form a marginalized group or one with significant support in the Parliament. This argument does not seem to have much strength. Realistically, the state of the whole society matters. "Hate speech" expressed in a village, town, or district of a city is more dangerous if people living there also hear such speech from politicians on television instead of hearing condemnation of it by those influential public figures.

Justice Black, in his concurrence in *New York Times Co. v. Sullivan*, provides an example of how wide-spread prejudices can affect the social meaning of public utterances, and so whether expressions cause a clear and present danger of violence. After describing the racist environment in Montgomery, Alabama, he writes: ."Viewed realistically, this record lends support to an inference that instead of being damaged Commissioner Sullivan's political, social, and financial prestige has likely been enhanced by the *Times*' publication."[40]

A march by hood-wearing Klansmen does not have the same meaning or impact in the North as in the South – or even in different parts of Manhattan. It is arguable that the KKK would cause more imminent danger in Harlem, although in 1999, some of the responses were violent in downtown Manhattan as well.

Yet, imminence is imminence. Or not? Anthony Lewis, a firm defender of First Amendment protections, writes:

> In an age when words have inspired acts of mass murder and terrorism, it is not
> as easy for me as it once was to believe that the only remedy for evil counsels, in

---

[39] Schenck v. United States, 249 U.S. 47, 52 (1919). The example may have been based on a real-life tragedy. *See* L. A. Powe, Jr., "Searching for the False Shout of 'Fire'," 19 *Constitutional Commentary* 345 (2002).

[40] New York Times Co. v. Sullivan, 376 U.S. 254, 294 (1964).

Brandeis's phrase, should be good ones. . . . [P]erhaps judges, and the rest of us, will be more on guard now for the rare act of expression – not the burning of a flag or the racist slang of an undergraduate – that is genuinely dangerous. I think we should be able to punish speech that urges terrorist violence to an audience some of whose members are ready to act on the urging. That is imminence enough.[41]

Lewis seems to relax the requirement of imminence. He suggests that the danger caused by speech that incites terrorist violence is imminent enough if it addresses a group of people in which there are some individuals who are ready to commit such violent acts. This argument comes close to eliminating the imminence requirement, at least in its narrowest sense; one might have expected a First Amendment enthusiast to point out that if the hearers cannot act in the very place where they are under the direct influence of the inciting speech, there is still opportunity to rely on counterspeech instead of prohibition by criminal law.

Earlier in this same essay, Lewis mentions examples of dangerous expressions, including "preaching to young Muslims in England that they should become suicide-bombers. (One worshipper who heard such sermons, Richard Reid, tried unsuccessfully to blow up an airliner with a bomb in his shoe.)"[42] Such sermonizing cannot meet a strict requirement of imminent danger. The targets of the terrorist attack are not present at the sermon where the possible perpetrators are urged to become suicide bombers. Even those audience members who are likely candidates to commit the suicidal terrorist act may return home from the sermon and watch a television program that may convince them that they should not commit such a terrible crime. But Lewis chooses his words carefully. He speaks of "terrorist violence" in particular, not violence in general. As a specific example of contextual detail that matters, terrorist activities are characteristically organized in a fanatic, highly conspiratorial way that leaves no opening for arguments from outside the world of the terrorist organization.[43] But even emphasizing this context would not effectively narrow Lewis's relaxation of the imminence requirement, as the possible suicide bomber/worshipper might not be a member of a terrorist organization.

Consider a fairly recent example of imminently dangerous incitement to violence from Hungary. Extreme right groups urged visitors to their Internet sites to attack the gay pride parade in Budapest on July 5, 2008. This was not mere "hate speech" directed against the participants in the parade, protected by the American and the

---

[41] Anthony Lewis, *Freedom for the Thought That We Hate: A Biography of the First Amendment* 166–7 (Basic Books 2008). *See also* C. Edwin Baker, *Human Liberty and Freedom of Speech* (Oxford University Press 1989); Kent Greenawalt, "'Clear and Present Danger' and Criminal Speech," in *Eternally Vigilant* 96–119 (Lee C. Bollinger and Geoffrey R. Stone eds., University of Chicago Press 2002).

[42] Lewis, *supra* note 41, at 166.

[43] The fanatic, highly conspiratorial way terrorist activities are organized seems to be different from communist activities although another firm defender of freedom of speech, Justice Jackson describes them similarly in his concurring opinion in Dennis v. United States, 341 U. S. 494 (1951) 533.

Hungarian constitutions. It was incitement to violent, lawless action at a specific event, and it was instrumental in producing actual physical attacks.[44]

At the parade, "counter-demonstrators" engaged in "hate speech" against peaceful demonstrators while many "counter-demonstrators" were holding and throwing stones and acid-filled eggs at the peaceful marchers and homemade bombs at the police. In such situations, instrumental incitement to violence on the Internet, even if somewhat remote and in advance (which, with the proliferation of mobile devices, it will not necessarily be[45]), coupled with "hate speech" *at* the demonstration, meets even the most demanding test for prohibiting only speech that creates – or directly and decisively contributes to the creation of – a clear and present danger of violence. As Robert Post writes, "the relationship between speech and action is always a contextual matter, never a matter just of the content of speech."[46] Incitement to violence on the Internet, even if practically targeted and instrumental, might be still more off the beaten track than "hate speech" live at a demonstration. Yet, although different in their content and context, both can create, or directly and decisively contribute to the creation of, imminent danger of violence.

It is important to mention that participants in the parade were badly hurt, although actual violence is not part of the imminent danger test. When would speech meet the *Brandenburg* test[47] or its Hungarian counterpart if not in the environment of the viciously attacked gay parade in Budapest? A significant difference between the American and the Hungarian "imminent danger" tests is that in the United States inciting speech can be restricted only if the imminent danger is *intended* by the speaker, while in Hungary it is enough if the speaker had to have known that his/her speech caused imminent danger of violence. Requiring intent is, of course, a very important safeguard to protect freedom of speech. But as the example of the 2008 gay pride parade in Budapest shows, there can be situations when, if the prevailing interpretation of the constitution has required that the prosecution establish intent as an element of the crime, courts should be able to infer intent.

Speech that causes imminent danger of violence is punishable and can be banned in advance, not because of the content of speech, but because of the circumstances

---

44  Considering the instrumental character of this incitement to violence, it has to be remembered that the most terrifying example of the directly instrumental use of modern communication tools to produce violence is the use of the radio during the genocide in Rwanda. Besides spreading hatred, Radio-Television Libre des Milles Collines provided continuous, well-targeted, practical information for the perpetrators to find their victims. Lewis also includes this example in his argument, between the two paragraphs from which I quoted. Lewis, *supra* note 41, at 166. *See* Enrique Armijo, *Building Open Societies: Freedom of the Press in Jordan and Rwanda*, 13 J. *Int'l Media & Ent. L.* 27 (2009); Yared Legesse Mengistu, "Shielding Marginalized Groups from Verbal Assaults without Abusing Hate Speech Laws," Chapter 19 herein.

45  It is at least imaginable that some of the "counter-demonstrators" at a gay pride parade look at the homophobic Internet sites on a regular basis, while others of them look at these sites right before going to the parade.

46  Email to the author.

47  Brandenburg v. Ohio, 395 U.S. 444 (1969).

under which even less vicious speech can create such danger. But even the most awful "hate speech" can be constitutionally protected if it does not occur under circumstances in which it causes imminent danger. If nobody is likely to engage in violence, then there cannot be a clear and present danger. But if there are many people, or at least someone, throwing stones and eggs and/or who are likely to commit another violent action, then speech against the targeted group seems to meet the *Brandenburg* test even if the "hate speech" is not expressly calling for violence, but is "only" expressed against the targeted group. Shouting "Eggs on the crowd" might be an unprotected solicitation to commit crime, besides incitement to violence. But yelling "rotten faggots" where many people are ready to commit violent acts also meets the *Brandenburg* test even though it does not call for action explicitly. It has to be stressed that in such a situation, crime can be committed by speech not because of the content of the speech in the first place, but because of the circumstances in which that content creates imminent danger. This is why it is better to use the term "incitement" instead of "hate speech" in this context, because using the term "hate speech" gives the impression that the whole argument is about banning and punishing speech for its content, although that is not the case.[48]

In short, the more inflammatory a situation, the less time is left for responses through art, education, political condemnation, or other forms of counterspeech[49] to marginalize speech that can incite violence, and the more communication is covered by the "imminent danger" test.

## IV. CONCLUSION

As the example of the Theodore Roosevelt statue shows, creative artistic and other educational responses to expressions, including art and symbolic speech, that can be labeled "hate speech" are much more effective than content-based laws, and do not put freedom of speech at risk in the way legal restrictions on public communication do.

In considering legal restriction of incitement that causes imminent danger, we need to take into account not only the immediately surrounding circumstances of the speech but also the broader environment, which moves the danger test closer to the content-based test. The strongest reason for having a "hate speech" law is that the social and political situation is so inflammable that it requires restricting speech based on its content to sustain peace. In such circumstances, however, limitations on free speech can also be justified under the imminent danger test, the conceptualization of which has to be further elaborated. Some elements of a carefully built, workable concept are: consideration of not only the narrow environment of

---

[48] I owe this idea to Adam Liptak, the Supreme Court correspondent of the *New York Times*.
[49] *See* Katharine Gelber, "Reconceptualizing Counterspeech in Hate-Speech Policy (with a Focus on Australia)," Chapter 11 herein.

"hate speech," but also its broader surroundings; examination of the connection between speech and the imminent danger of violent action, including whether the incitement to violence is so instrumental, or the situation is so inflammatory that relatively distant incitement to violence, or mere "hate speech," can cause imminent danger of violent action even if the speaker did not intend it, or alleges so; and clear understanding of how imminent the danger has to be in order to restrict freedom of speech.

Art and education in the broadest sense, combined with a careful application of the "imminent danger" test, provide useful remedies against "hate speech" in all democracies. One of these two responses should help in all situations. If expressions create a clear and present danger of violent action, they can be banned under the "imminent danger" test. Doing so carries some risk of unintended side effects, but significantly less than "hate speech" laws that prohibit communication based solely on its content. Such prohibitions can be always subject to the arbitrary judgment of the majority or the ruling group.[50] If "hate speech" does not cause an imminent threat of violence, then art, education, and other cultural activities, which have no or only limited risk of side effects, should be relied on to uproot prejudice and hatred.

[50]   This concern is prominent, for example, in the interview with Nadine Strossen in the present volume. *See* Chapter 20 herein.

# 11

# Reconceptualizing Counterspeech in Hate Speech Policy (with a Focus on Australia)

## Katharine Gelber

There is an aspect of the hate speech debate that tends to rest on common, yet unstated, assumptions, and that has profound implications for the progress of the debate and for the perceived dichotomous relationship between responding to the problem of hate speech and protecting freedom of expression. The "free speech versus hate speech" debate is infused by a conception of counterspeech that is, I will argue, unnecessarily narrow. Further, it is one that contributes to an unhelpful and ultimately futile polarization of positions with regard to what states, or governments, or communities ought to do in response to the problem of hate speech.

I will outline the nature and the implications of this shared conception for the hate speech debate both at a policy and a theoretical level. I will then present an argument for an alternative conception. This alternative is based on a reconceptualization of counterspeech located within Martha Nussbaum's capabilities theory, and it has significant implications for ideas about an appropriate response to speech that is perceived as harmful. I will make a seven-step argument for a new type of policy, one that is able to overcome the difficulties of the often unrecognized, but shared, dominant assumptions about counterspeech in the current debate.

## I. EXISTING POLICY RESPONSES

The common conceptualization that I will outline in this chapter manifests in a range of policy proposals and existing policy responses worldwide. It is worth noting them first here, to acknowledge the range that exists and to provide a context for the discussion that is to follow. Particular emphasis will be placed in this overview on

I wish to thank Michael Herz for inviting me to the hate speech conference at Cardozo Law School in November 2005, from which this chapter has been developed, Michael and Peter Molnar for helpful comments on the draft, and the participants at that conference for their perceptive comments.

the Australian position because it is somewhat unusual in world jurisprudence and it attempts to come to grips with the hate speech problem in an interesting way.

## A. *Criminalization*

Some advocates of hate-speech laws have suggested a criminal-law response.[1] Given the importance of freedom of expression generally, the prospect of jailing someone, or even imposing a criminal fine, for an expression of views raises obvious questions of the threshold of harm that must be passed for an expression to warrant incarceration of the speaker. Thus, criminal-law responses face particular theoretical challenges in the making of the argument.

Nevertheless, a criminal response is arguably endorsed by international human rights treaty provisions, including Article 4(a) of the International Convention on the Elimination of All Forms of Racial Discrimination (ICERD) and Article 20 of the International Covenant on Civil and Political Rights (ICCPR).[2] Many countries do have criminal laws relating to hate speech, including Canada[3] and Germany,[4] which survive constitutional free-speech challenges because they are regarded as appropriate and proportionate to the achievement of other constitutional values, such as protection from the harm of discrimination or the preservation of human dignity.

Australia has a federal system of government, with scope for the enactment of antivilification laws at both federal and State/Territory levels.[5] In Australia, criminal antivilification laws exist in only some jurisdictions. Although neither federal[6] nor Tasmanian[7] antivilification laws contain a criminal component, Western Australia has enacted *only* criminal antivilification provisions[8] and every other State[9] and the

---

[1] *See, e.g.,* Alexander Tsesis, *Destructive Messages: How Hate Speech Paves the Way for Harmful Social Movements* (NYU Press 2002); Mari Matsuda, "Public Response to Racist Speech: Considering the Victim's Story," in *Words That Wound: Critical Race Theory, Assaultive Speech, and the First Amendment* 17 (Mari Matsuda et al. eds., Westview Press 1993) [hereafter *Words that Wound*].

[2] G.A. Res. 2106 (XX), at 48, U.N. Doc. A/RES/2106 A (XX) (Dec. 21, 1965); G.A. Res. 2200A (XXI), at 55, U.N. Doc. A/RES/2200A (XXI) (Dec. 16, 1966); Simon Bronitt, "Hate Speech, Sedition and the War on Terror," in *Hate Speech and Freedom of Speech in Australia* 135–6 (Katharine Gelber & Adrienne Stone eds., Federation Press 2007) [hereinafter *Hate Speech in Australia*].

[3] Criminal Code, R.S.C. 1985, c. C-46, part VIII, §§ 318, 319.

[4] Gesetz über Urheberrecht und verwandte Schutzrechte STRAFGESETZBUCH [STGB] [PENAL CODE], Nov. 13, 1998, BGBL. I at 3322 §§86, 86A, 130.

[5] In Australia, Territories have been created by a law of the federal parliament. The self-governing Territories of the Northern Territory and the Australian Capital Territory do not possess the constitutional jurisdiction, and therefore the powers, of States.

[6] *Racial Discrimination Act* 1975 (Cth) §§ 18B-18F.

[7] *Anti-Discrimination Act* 1998 (Tas) § 19.

[8] *Criminal Code* 1913 (WA), pt. II, ch. XI, §§ 76–80H.

[9] *Anti-Discrimination Act* 1977 (NSW) §§ 20B-20D, 38R-38T, 49ZS-49ZTA, 49ZXA-49ZXC; *Anti-Discrimination Act* 1991 (Qld) §§ 124A, 131A; *Racial Vilification Act* 1996 (SA), *Civil Liability Act* 1936 (SA) § 73; *Racial and Religious Tolerance Act* 2001 (Vic).

Australian Capital Territory[10] have both criminal and civil antivilification laws. The ground for complaint common to all jurisdictions is race (further defined variously as inclusive of race, color, descent, ethnic origin, and national origin); other grounds covered in some, but not all, jurisdictions are religion, sexuality or homosexuality, disability, transgender or gender identity, and HIV/AIDS status.

Criminal provisions in Australia tend to have an understandably high threshold before a prosecution can be pursued. They usually require either a public act that incites, or is done with intention to incite, hatred, serious contempt, or severe ridicule of a person on the specified ground by means that threaten physical harm to person(s) or property; or that incite others to threaten physical harm to person(s) or property;[11] or that constitute a threatening act.[12] The link to actual or threatened violence leaves a great deal of hate speech beyond the statute's reach. Penalties include fines and imprisonment (varying from a minimum of six months to a maximum of three years). In the two and half decades since their enactment, not a single prosecution has been pursued under these provisions. Sometimes, where egregious examples of vilification have been accompanied by threats of physical manifestations of harm, prosecution under other criminal offenses has been pursued, which has rendered the criminal vilification provisions moot.[13] Additionally, there are procedural and threshold limitations on the referral of incidents for criminal prosecution that tend to result in a reluctance to pursue criminal-law options on the part of prosecutorial authorities.[14]

An exception to this relative consistency between many jurisdictions is Western Australia. In 1990, Western Australia enacted exclusively criminal provisions directly in response to activities of a white supremacist group. In 2004, the offenses were amended to expand their applicability[15] by creating two tiers of offenses based on the existence or absence of intent. The offenses include conduct intended to, or likely to, incite racial animosity or racial harassment; possession of material for dissemination with intent to, or likely to, incite racial animosity or racial harassment; conduct intended to, or likely to, racially harass, meaning to threaten, seriously and substantially abuse or severely ridicule; and possession of material for display with

---

[10] *Discrimination Act* 1991 (ACT) §§ 65–67. The Northern Territory does not have antivilification laws at this time.

[11] *Anti-Discrimination Act* 1977 (NSW) § 20D; *Anti-Discrimination Act* 1991 (Qld) § 131A; *Racial Vilification Act* 1996 (SA) § 4; *Civil Liability Act* 1936 (SA) § 73; *Racial and Religious Tolerance Act* 2001 (Vic) §§ 24–25.

[12] *Discrimination Act* 1991 (ACT) § 67.

[13] This occurred, for example, in four of the five Western Australian cases referred to in *infra* note 17.

[14] For example, in New South Wales, these include statutory time limits and a requirement to obtain the consent of the Director of Public Prosecutions (DPP) to pursue a prosecution, consent that has not been forthcoming because the DPP has tended to regard the incident as insufficient to overcome the threshold. Luke McNamara, *Regulating Racism: Racial Vilification Laws in Australia* 140–4, 243 (Sydney Institute of Criminology Monograph Series No. 16, 2002).

[15] Katharine Gelber, "Hate Speech and the Australian Legal and Political Landscape," in *Hate Speech in Australia, supra* note 2, at 7–8.

intent to, or likely to, racially harass.[16] Penalties include fines and a maximum of fourteen years imprisonment. The new WA provisions do not have as high a threshold as those in other states and territories and have resulted in the only successful prosecution under criminal antivilification laws in Australia to date.[17]

## B. *Civil Liability*

An alternative policy proposal is to call for a civil law response to hate speech. In the United States this has manifested, for example, in the form of a call for a tort cause of action for damages.[18] In Australia, although criminal laws exist, civil remedies are emphasized. On the one hand this has meant Australia has been subjected to criticism for non-compliance with Article 4 of the ICERD, as its federal hate speech laws lack a criminal component and are purely of a civil nature.[19] On the other hand, the emphasis on civil remedies in the Australian context means it is possible to argue that the Australian provisions are more able to deal comprehensively with a range of vilificatory expressions than more narrowly targeted criminal provisions.[20]

In Australia, antivilification laws in civil form have become an accepted and normal part of the Australian antidiscrimination framework at federal, state, and territory[21] levels. Typically these provisions make it an offense to "incite hatred towards, serious contempt for, or severe ridicule of a person or group of persons" on the specified ground/s.[22] The federal statute makes it unlawful to do an act if the act is reasonably likely to "offend, insult, humiliate or intimidate another person or group of people" on a specified ground.[23] The civil mechanisms usually provide for a person to lodge a complaint with a relevant authority such as an antidiscrimination commission. The number of claims dealt with under these mechanisms is modest, but significant in comparison to the lack of use of the criminal law. For example, in the

---

[16] *Criminal Code* (WA) §§ 76–80.
[17] Following a high-profile graffiti attack in which swastikas and slogans including "Hitler was right" and "Asians out" were painted on a synagogue and Chinese restaurant in July 2004, five men were successfully prosecuted for criminal damage. One of the men, Damon Paul Blaxall, was also charged with possession of racist material. In 2005, Blaxall was convicted on both counts and sentenced to eight months in jail for criminal damage and four months for possession of the racist material. Australian Associated Press, "Jail for race-hate graffiti," *The Australian*, May 20, 2005, at 3; Holly Nott, "WA; Three men sentenced for racist graffiti," *AAP General News*, Aug. 5, 2005; Peta Rasdien, "Green plea fails to save graffiti racist," *The West Australian*, Dec. 21, 2005, at 41.
[18] Richard Delgado, "Words That Wound: A Tort Action for Racial Insults," in *Words That Wound*, *supra* note 1, at 89.
[19] McNamara, *supra* note 14, at 21.
[20] Luke McNamara, "Criminalising Racial Hatred: Learning from the Canadian Experience," 1 *Australian J. Hum. Rts.* 198, 200, 206–8 (1994).
[21] The exception is the Northern Territory, which does not have antivilification laws at this time.
[22] *Anti-Discrimination Act 1977* (NSW) § 20C; *Anti-Discrimination Act 1991* (Qld) § 124A; *Civil Liability Act 1936* (SA) § 73; *Anti-Discrimination Act 1998* (Tas) § 19; *Racial and Religious Tolerance Act 2001* (Vic) § 7; *Discrimination Act 1991* (ACT) § 66.
[23] *Racial Discrimination Act 1975* (Cth) § 18C.

year 2008–2009, the New South Wales Anti-Discrimination Board received twenty-five vilification complaints, the Western Australian Anti-Discrimination Commission received nine, the Australian Capital Territory's Human Rights Commission received eleven, and the Tasmanian Anti-Discrimination Commission reported eighty-seven complaints of inciting hatred.[24] The authority then assesses the claim and, if it is substantiated, mediates a remedy that might include an apology, education in a workplace, publication of a retraction, or a commitment not to reoffend. Recalcitrant cases are referred to a Tribunal or, in the case of complaints under federal law, to the Federal Court, where possible remedies include an order to apologize or retract and/or a fine. An earlier study has shown that in approximately 20 percent of complaints lodged, these procedures resulted in a beneficial outcome in the sense of engendering an apology or retraction or commitment not to reoffend by the person/s against whom a complaint was made.[25] In South Australia a complainant can lodge a tort action for damages, and a court can award damages up to $40,000.[26] However, this provision has never been utilized.

## C. *Constitutional Limitations*

Antivilification laws are thus commonplace in Australia. They survive free-speech challenges for two related reasons: the historical mechanisms for speech protection and the laws' narrow scope and purpose.

With regard to the first, freedom of speech is not expressly protected in either the Australian Constitution or in federal statutory law.[27] The mechanisms that have been used to preserve and protect freedom of speech for most of Australia's post-settlement history are a common-law tradition that recognizes the place of freedom of speech in Australian political and legal culture, and mechanisms of responsible government inherited from the United Kingdom. Ideally, the Westminster model of responsible government is said to ensure that the executive is accountable to the legislature from which it is drawn, and the legislature in turn is accountable to the people. This

---

[24] New South Wales Anti-Discrimination Board, *Annual Report 2008–2009* 15 (ADB 2009); Western Australian Anti-Discrimination Commission, *Annual Report 2008–2009* 19 (ADC 2009); Australian Capital Territory Human Rights Commission, *Annual Report 2008–2009* 47 (HRC 2009); Tasmanian Anti-Discrimination Commission, *Annual Report 2008–2009* 20 (ADC 2009).

[25] Katharine Gelber, "Implementing Racial Anti-Vilification Laws in New South Wales 1989–1998: A Study," 59 *Australian J. Pub. Admin.* 16 (2000).

[26] *Civil Liability Act* 1936 (SA) § 73(4).

[27] More recently emerging State/Territory charters of rights have appeared to endorse the idea that anti-hate speech laws ought not to be overridden with free-speech protections. In the Australian Capital Territory's Human Rights Act of 2004, the right to freedom of expression expressed in § 16 is qualified by § 28, which allows for any right enunciated to be subject to reasonable and lawful limits such as are demonstrably justified in a free and democratic society. In the Victorian Charter of Human Rights and Responsibilities Act of 2006, the right to freedom of expression in § 15 is qualified by the acknowledgment of "special duties and responsibilities" that apply to that right, and to allow for the lawful restriction of some speech to, among other things, protect the rights of others.

mechanism of accountability is claimed to be able to protect fundamental rights,[28] although in practice, it often falls short.

These methods have been complemented, since 1992, by a High Court jurisprudence on freedom of political communication. The High Court of Australia has held that the representative form of government established by the Australian Constitution *implies* a freedom of communication on political matters, where none is actually stated. In the two 1992 landmark cases that established the freedom, the justices held that freedom of communication on political matters derived from constitutional provisions (§§ 7 & 24) that ensure that representatives are to be "directly chosen by the people."[29] Representative democracy was the foundation of the freedom because it required public participation in political discussion; indeed such discussion was "indispensable," "essential," "necessary," and "inherent" to it.[30] A unanimous decision in 1997 in *Lange v. Australian Broadcasting Corporation*[31] clarified the conception of political communication, in a manner consistently applied since that time.

The doctrine, however, is limited both in its scope and its application. In terms of its scope, it includes nonverbal forms of expression,[32] is not confined to election periods, and includes public servants and statutory authorities tasked with carrying out the policies of, and reporting to, the legislature or a Minister.[33] But political communication has been held to mean that communication "concerning political or government matters which enables the people to exercise a free and informed choice as electors"[34] in federal elections and referenda.[35] The exact parameters of this conception are unclear, but at the very least, the doctrine can be said not to cover the entire range of communications that might be considered "political" in a broader sense.

---

[28] Brian Galligan, A *Federal Republic: Australia's Constitutional System of Government* 139 (Cambridge University Press 1995). There are, of course, numerous criticisms of the effectiveness of the Westminster model of responsible government in protecting fundamental human rights, but there is no room to explore that here. *See, e.g.,* Katharine Gelber, "High Court Review 2004: Limits on the Judicial Protection of Rights," 49 *Australian J. Pol. Sci.* 307 (2005).

[29] Haig Patapan, *Judging Democracy: The New Politics of the High Court of Australia* 51–59 (Cambridge University Press 2000); Adrienne Stone, "Freedom of Political Communication, the Constitution and the Common Law," 26 *Fed. L. Rev.* 219 (1998); Adrienne Stone, "Rights, Personal Rights and Freedoms: The Nature of the Freedom of Political Communication," 25 *Melbourne U.L. Rev.* 374 (2001).

[30] Gerald Rosenberg and John Williams, "Do Not Go Gently Into That Good Right: The First Amendment in the High Court of Australia," 1997 *Sup. Ct. Rev.* 439, 448–50.

[31] Lange v. Australian Broadcasting Corp., 189 CLR 520 (1997).

[32] Levy v. Victoria, 189 CLR 579 (1997).

[33] *Lange,* 189 CLR at 561; *see also* Dan Meagher, "So Far so Good? A Critical Evaluation of Racial Vilification Laws in Australia," 32 *Fed. L. Rev.* 225 (2004).

[34] *Lange,* 189 CLR at 560.

[35] Michael Chesterman, "When is a communication 'political'?," 14 *Leg. Stud.* 5, 6–9 (2000); Meagher, *supra* note 33, at 450.

The doctrine is also limited in its application. Even where a communication can be determined to be in principle potentially subject to the protection afforded by the implied freedom, the High Court has permitted restrictions where they occur as a result of a law that is reasonably appropriate and adapted to serve a legitimate government end in a manner compatible with the maintenance of the constitutionally prescribed system of representative and responsible government.[36] Thus, the freedom is arguably relatively easily overridden where another legitimate purpose is to be achieved by a speech-restricting government policy. For example, it has been held that provisions in both State[37] and federal[38] legislation governing elections, which prohibit advocacy of voting in a manner contrary to the procedures specified in that legislation, are valid. In the federal jurisdiction, this was held to be the case despite the fact that the method of voting being advocated by a political activist at that time was valid and legal; it was merely its advocacy that was not.[39] In another example, a law prohibiting entry without a license into a duck-shooting area was held to be valid when used to prevent the activities of animal-rights protesters who wished to draw media attention to the area, because its purpose was to protect public safety and its restriction on political communication only a coincidental effect of the legislation.[40] A restriction on the ability of lawyers to advertise for personal injury services was upheld as valid on the ground that such communications were not concerned with government or political matters.[41] And a law prohibiting the use of "threatening, abusive or insulting words" to any person in a public place, and which was used to prosecute a political activist who accused police officers of corruption, was read to proscribe only those insulting words that are reasonably likely to provoke "unlawful physical retaliation." Thus narrowed, the provision was upheld.[42] The fragility of freedom of speech within this framework has been remarked on by scholars and described as a "delicate plant"[43] and "partial and unsatisfactory."[44]

In Australia, it has been held that principles of freedom of political communication do not extend to the protection of vilificatory comments because the right to "engage in a robust discussion"[45] is not an untrammeled or an absolute right. In this climate, antivilification laws have experienced little – if any – constitutional impairment. Unlike in the United States, where attempts to restrict racist speech

---

[36] Coleman v. Power, 220 CLR 1, 66 (2004) (adapting the *Lange* test). *See* Gelber, *supra* note 15, at 3.

[37] Muldowney v. South Australia, 186 CLR 352 (1996).

[38] Langer v. Commonwealth, 186 CLR 302 (1996).

[39] Katharine Gelber, "Citizens Engaging Government," in *Government Communication in Australia* 270, 280–2 (Cambridge University Press 2007).

[40] Levy v. Victoria, 189 CLR 579 (1997).

[41] APLA Ltd. v. Legal Services Commissioner (NSW), 219 ALR 403 (2005).

[42] *Coleman*, 220 CLR 1.

[43] Michael Chesterman, *Freedom of Speech in Australian Law* (Ashgate 2000).

[44] Katharine Gelber, "Pedestrian malls, local government and free speech policy in Australia," 22 *Pol'y & Soc'y: J. Pub., Foreign & Global Pol'y* 44 (2003).

[45] Islamic Council of Victoria, Inc. v. Catch the Fire Ministries, Inc., [2004] VCAT 2510, at 3.

have typically fallen foul of First Amendment strictures,[46] in Australia, antivilification laws have survived resistance from quarters emphasizing free-speech concerns. Even though some have argued that incidences of hate speech may constitute political communication as conceptualized under the implied constitutional freedom,[47] this does not render antivilification laws constitutionally invalid or inoperative so long as the laws themselves are regarded as reasonably and appropriately adapted to a legitimate government end – such as that of minimizing the attendant harms of vilification and discouraging its practice. Attempts by respondents to cite the constitutionally implied freedom of political communication in their defense in vilification cases[48] have tended to fail.

## D. *Beyond Regulating the Speaker*

Thus, in Australia, the mechanisms most commonly invoked to deal with vilification complaints are the civil, antidiscrimination mechanisms that emphasize mediation and conciliation. The criminal laws are almost never used. The civil mechanisms attempt to influence the behavior of the hate speaker, by encouraging them to agree to desist or to apologize, or, if that fails, by imposing fines. This stands in contrast to the approach of those jurisdictions, such as Germany, which emphasize the use of criminal laws.

Nevertheless it is arguable that all these approaches share a common characteristic essential to the discussion of counterspeech. Generally speaking, hate speech policies are designed to target the hate speakers and their behavior. Their ability to ameliorate the harms of hate speech and/or reduce its incidence is limited. This is particularly true of criminal-law responses. And although the nonpunitive, mediated remedies described in Australia go some way in attempting to provide assistance to the targets of hate speech, they are also premised on an attempt to change the speaker's behavior. The remedy that results often originates from the hate speaker, and it is by extension

---

[46] *See, e.g.*, R.A.V. v. City of St. Paul, 505 U.S. 377 (1992); Skokie v. National Socialist Party, 373 N.E.2d 21 (Ill. 1978). *See also* Robert Post, "Racist Speech, Democracy and the First Amendment," in *Speaking of Race, Speaking of Sex: Hate Speech, Civil Rights, and Civil Liberties* 115–17 (Henry Louis Gates et al. eds., NYU Press 1994). Note that in Virginia v. Black, 538 U.S. 343 (2003), the Supreme Court concluded that a state may, consistently with the First Amendment, ban cross burning carried out with the intent to intimidate, thus upholding the long-standing premise that "true" threats do not constitute protected speech. *See* Frederick Schauer, "Intentions, Conventions, and the First Amendment: The Case of Cross Burning," 2004 *Sup. Ct. Rev.* 197, 201, 210.

[47] Chesterman, *supra* note 43, at 16–18; Meagher, *supra* note 33, at 251–3.

[48] Examples include Toben v. Jones, 129 FCR 515 (2003), in which Federick Toben was found to have contravened federal antivilification laws by authoring material on a Web site hosted by the Adelaide Institute, which denied the Holocaust; and the *Catch the Fires Ministries* litigation, in which a complaint lodged by the Islamic Council of Victoria against a Christian organization that had described Muslims as rapists, terrorists, and prone to violence, was rejected. *Islamic Council of Victoria*, [2004] VCAT 2510, vacated and remanded by Catch the Fire Ministries, Inc. v. Islamic Council of Victoria [2006] VSCA 284. *See* Lawrence McNamara, "Salvation and the State: Religious Vilification Laws and Religious Speech," in *Hate Speech in Australia*, *supra* note 2, at 145.

(rather than directly) that the targets of hate speech are assisted. This leaves the larger question – of how hate speech policy might directly be brought to bear to assist the targets of hate speech themselves – unanswered. To try to address this issue, I turn now to the idea of counterspeech.

## II. COMMON CONCEPTUALIZATIONS OF COUNTERSPEECH

I want to return now to the assumption that, I argue, is often implicit and invisible to participants in this debate.[49] It turns on the conceptualization of counterspeech at play in the dominant hate speech arguments, both of free-speech defenders and of advocates of hate speech laws.

Free-speech defenders tend to argue that even if hate speech is harmful, even if it is abhorrent, governmental limits or restrictions on that speech are inappropriate.[50] A variety of alternative responses are invoked, prominent among which is the idea that the best response to hate speech is for its targets and the community more broadly to answer back, to engage in more speech to discuss, and counteract, the hate speakers' messages. This idea was famously encapsulated in *Whitney v. California*[51] – that "the remedy to be applied is more speech" – and is still strongly advocated. For example, the ACLU declares that, "where racist, sexist and homophobic speech is concerned, the ACLU believes that more speech – not less – is the best revenge."[52]

This reliance on more speech – which I will refer to here as counterspeech – contains within it two related, and often unstated, assumptions. These assumptions are that when it comes to engaging in more speech, (1) the response ought to be undertaken by the targeted individuals or groups themselves, and (2), what is implicit in the first, that those individuals and groups are up to the task. That is, a notion of *unsupported* counterspeech is at play in these arguments. Sometimes this call for an essentially unsupported notion of counterspeech is explicit. For example, Jonathan Rauch[53] asserts that those who are harmed by words "must be led to expect nothing as compensation." Instead, we must be "sensitive . . . to . . . the obligation to put up with criticism" and offense and "settle for responding with criticism or contempt" rather than requiring punishment or restitution for the offense. Similarly,

[49]  This is drawn from an extensive argument developed in Katharine Gelber, *Speaking Back: The Free Speech Versus Hate Speech Debate* (John Benjamins 2002), and updated by Katharine Gelber, "Free Speech, Hate Speech and the Argument from Democracy: The Transformative Contribution of Capabilities Theory," 9 *Contemp. Pol. Theory* 304 (2010).

[50]  There is no space here to discuss the many reasons *why* a restrictive government response is argued to be inappropriate. The interview with Nadine Strossen in the current volume, Chapter 20, sets out a classic exposition of these arguments.

[51]  274 U.S. 357, 373–9 (1927) (Brandeis, J., joined by Holmes, J., concurring).

[52]  American Civil Liberties Union, "Hate Speech on Campus" (Dec. 31, 1994), http://www.aclu.org/studentsrights/expression/12808pub19941231.html, accessed Aug. 1, 2008.

[53]  Jonathon Rauch, *Kindly Inquisitors: The New Attacks on Free Thought* 159 (University of Chicago Press 1993).

David A. J. Richards argues that a public "contest of...stereotypical" ideas is required, rather than state sanctioning of correct or incorrect views.[54] State censorship disempowers those who it is intended to protect and "stifles the empowering protests of individuals to that discourse through which they express, demand and define their individuality as persons against such stereotypical classifications." Here, Richards argues that a punitive response to hate speech limits what would otherwise be the freedom of targeted individuals and groups to respond to the claims of hate speakers. He argues that "hearing one's own voice in such protest" is crucial to empowerment. (Notably, he does not outline how such empowerment might occur, a question to which I shall return.)

Often in free-speech arguments, the assumption that targeted individuals will possess the ability to engage in an unsupported counterspeech is more implicit than in these two instances. For example, Magnet, in arguing against hate speech laws on the ground that they chill free speech,[55] opines that "more speech, not less" is needed to enable self-government, and that hate speech laws achieve the opposite of this. He adds that banning racist speech is likely to reduce opportunities for social mobilization to combat racism rather than to increase them.

Thus, such arguments are imbued with an implicit notion of counterspeech. This is a notion that counterspeech is an essentially private endeavor that is to be undertaken by individuals, or together by individuals acting as groups, themselves. In some instances, the anticipated responsive speech is from not only the targets of attack, but from others who support, identify with, or sympathize with them. So the targets might be "supported" by other individuals or groups.[56] But the expectation remains that the response will come unaided from other private speakers; that is, the counterspeech itself, whatever its source, is unsupported. This notion assumes that the onus for engaging in speech rests with the targets themselves, and/or with others who might wish to counteract the messages of the hate speakers. It assumes, or perhaps hopes, that these people will be able to respond if they only make the choice to do so. It assumes that choosing to respond is both a necessary and a sufficient condition for being able to respond.

This assumption is not surprising. It is part and parcel of the dominant conception of free speech in "negative" terms; as a liberty that most flourishes when it is free from government interference. Free speech, it is assumed, is best maintained by government not restraining individuals from speaking, as a liberty that "limits the authority

---

[54] David A. J. Richards, *Free Speech and the Politics of Identity* 135–6 (Oxford University Press, 1999).

[55] Joseph Magnet, "Hate Propaganda in Canada," in *Free Expression: Essays in Law and Philosophy* 248 (W. J. Waluchow ed., Oxford University Press 1994).

[56] In their contributions to the present volume, Nadine Strossen and Theodore Shaw both emphasize what they see as an obligation on the part of persons who are not themselves the target of hate speech to speak out against such speech and in support of its targets. *See* Chapters 20 and 21, respectively. In doing so, they seem implicitly to acknowledge that direct counterspeech by victims will often be ineffective and inadequate. They do not show, to my mind, that others either can or will contribute sufficiently to make unsupported counterspeech effective.

of government."[57] In an argument derived from John Stuart Mill, free speech is achieved by maximizing restraint on government (or, alternatively expressed, by government restraining itself from interfering), and it is this restraint on government interference that is the best means to allow individuals to participate in speech. The dominant arguments in defense of free speech emphasize the absence of restraint on individuals by government as the paramount goal. In the views of free-speech advocates, the goal of minimizing restraint on speech is directly counterposed to the policy goal of ameliorating the harms of hate speech via restrictive, limiting, or punitive measures on hate speakers.

Interestingly, the dominant arguments in favor of hate speech laws also assume that counterspeech (within the terms of the arguments they critique and reject) involves an unsupported, private response to hate speech. Examples here include Mari Matsuda's critique of the view that "private remedies – including counterspeech, social approbation, boycott and persuasion" – insufficiently recognize and respond to the problem of hate speech.[58] Similarly, Richard Delgado objects that the ordinary remedies, including that of "more speech," are inadequate, adding that "racial insults invite no discourse" in the sense of engagement with differing points of view in a constructive manner, and "no speech in response can cure the inflicted harm."[59] Catharine MacKinnon particularly decries the "lack of recognition that some people get a lot more speech than others" and argues that this inequality of speech renders the counterspeech of the subordinated less able to be heard.[60] Thus, these scholars argue that reliance on the counterspeech remedy is hopelessly wishful thinking.

Having dismissed counterspeech as an inadequate response to hate speech, these scholars propose an alternative range of measures designed to combat hate speech. In making such arguments, like their civil libertarian counterparts, advocates of hate speech laws tend to counterpose the two goals of preserving free-speech conditions and responding in a necessarily limiting, restrictive, or punitive manner to hate speech. They may draw the line at a different place in terms of where the "balance" between free speech and restriction ought to be drawn. But their arguments are still couched in this dichotomy: free speech versus hate speech, in a zero-sum game. Where one gains, the other must necessarily lose.

This is problematic, primarily because a reliance on a conception of counterspeech as an unsupported and private endeavor is unable to explain *how* participation in speech might become possible. To ignore how people might become able to speak is to overlook one of the central and most powerful arguments of advocates of hate speech laws – that hate speech can have tangible effects on its listeners, and that these effects may render it difficult or sometimes even impossible for them to

---

57  Eric Barendt, *Freedom of Speech* 30 (Oxford University Press, 2d ed. 2005).
58  Matsuda, *supra* note 1, at 36–7.
59  Delgado, *supra* note 18, at 95, 108.
60  Catharine MacKinnon, *Only Words* 72–3, 75–6 (Harvard University Press, 3d ed. 1996).

respond. As Owen Fiss notes, "[i]n this context, the classic remedy of more speech rings hollow."[61] An unsupported conception of counterspeech assumes that less regulation by government of individuals means more speech, and that somehow in this morass the speech of those who are being denigrated (or their supporters) will find a voice. This is at best an underestimation of what is required to be able to compete in the marketplace of ideas. At worst it is an abrogation of the responsibility of the state to protect those who suffer tangible harm.

This dilemma may be addressed by bringing into play an enlarged conception of counterspeech. In this enlarged conception, freedom is not merely an "opportunity," but an "exercise."[62] In this conception, individuals become "free" to speak when they are *able to exercise the capacity to speak*. Achieving the capacity to speak in response to hate speech requires thinking about speech in different ways. It cannot be achieved by thinking of freedom of speech in absence-of-restraint terms. Freedom of speech has to be conceived in broader ways, ways commensurate with other enlarged conceptions of freedom. Gibbs argues, for example, that freedom depends on an individual both attaining and being able to enjoy the goods they have chosen.[63] This is an obvious reference to the idea of positive freedoms, and of course the distinction between positive and negative conceptions of freedom is a difficult one.[64] Nevertheless, the distinction is relevant here for two reasons. First, it assists in the delineation of the type of speech I mean when I speak of "free" speech. In so doing, it differentiates this type sufficiently from the more common and dominant views of speech, that see "freedom of speech" in terms of an absence of constraint on speakers. Here, I am broadening the theoretical debate by adding a heuristic consideration in relation to policy. Secondly, the distinction is relevant here because it assists in illuminating that which is normally invisible in free-speech scholarship.

Thinking of freedom of speech in an enlarged, positive conception has considerable implications for considerations of hate speech policy. It enjoins us to consider *how* speech may be exercised. It implies that a policy goal of those who wish to see policy that can respond meaningfully to hate speech ought to be providing, or assisting to ensure, conditions conducive to ensuring that participation in speaking is possible. This links to other contributions to the literature; Owen Fiss, for example, argues that *fostering* full and open debate is a permissible role for the state.[65]

---

[61] Owen Fiss, *The Irony of Free Speech* 16 (Harvard University Press 1996).

[62] Quentin Skinner, "The Idea of Negative Liberty: Philosophical and Historical Perspectives," in *Philosophy in History: Essays on the Historiography of Philosophy* 196 (Richard Rorty et al. eds., Cambridge University Press 1984) (quoting Charles Taylor).

[63] Benjamin Gibbs, *Freedom and Liberation* 22 (Sussex University Press 1976).

[64] See in particular Eric Nelson, "Liberty: One Concept Too Many?" 33 *Pol. Theory* 58 (2005); John Christman, "Saving Positive Freedom," 33 *Pol. Theory* 79 (2005).

[65] Fiss, *supra* note 61, at 17.

## III. SUPPORTED COUNTERSPEECH: A SEVEN-STAGE ARGUMENT

With this alternative conceptualization at play, it is possible to construct an argument concerning a policy response to hate speech that overcomes the unnecessary and unhelpful polarization I referred to earlier. First, free-speech protections are usually justified in terms reliant on a consideration of *why* speech is important. Free speech is defended as instrumentally valuable because it contributes to self-development, or the search for truth, or self-governance; or it is described as a deontologically conceived right.[66] Yet whatever one's preferred justification for protecting (or privileging) freedom of speech, surely we must also consider *how* participation in speech might be achieved. The problem with the shared conception of counterspeech typically at play in the free-speech-versus-hate-speech debate is that the preoccupation with the *why* distracts us from the *how*. Free-speech theorizing is not helpful in answering *how* those who wish to counter hate speech might become capable of doing so. This is a vital, yet frequently overlooked, question.

Therefore secondly, to answer how targets of hate speech and their supporters might become capable of responding to hate speech, it is important and necessary to reconceptualize freedom of speech in participatory terms. The expansion of participation in speech by those previously prevented from so participating serves the free-speech cause arguably more comprehensively and thoroughly than does freedom of speech conceived in terms of a lack of restraint. The expansion of participation in speech in this way thus enhances the arguments in defense of free speech more generally. It enables these goals (self-development, self-governance, or the search for truth, for instance) to be realized more effectively.

Thirdly, a corollary to the idea that speech as participation will enhance the underlying reasons why free speech is considered important is the proposition that speech can do things "in and for" people's lives. This is an idea derived from the work of Martha Nussbaum,[67] who has elaborated a theory of ethics that posits central human functional capabilities as requisite for the pursuit of human flourishing. To ensure every citizen is able to enjoy and engage in activities conducive to human flourishing, lawgivers are required to make available to all individuals the concrete circumstances within which they may choose how to live, by becoming sufficiently

---

[66] *See, e.g.*, Barendt, *supra* note 57, at 6–23; Frederick Schauer, *Free Speech: A Philosophical Enquiry* (Cambridge University Press 1982); Ronald Dworkin, "The Coming Battles Over Free Speech," *New York Review of Books* (June 11, 1992), at 55; Robert Post, "Reconciling Theory and Doctrine in First Amendment Jurisprudence," 88 *Cal. L. Rev.* 2353 (2000).

[67] Nussbaum's version of capabilities theory has generated a copious literature, which it is not possible to analyze here. *See, e.g.*, Martha Nussbaum, "Women's Capabilities and Social Justice," 1 *J. Human Dev't* 219 (2000) [hereinafter Nussbaum, "Women's Capabilities"]; Martha Nussbaum, "Capabilities as Fundamental Entitlements: Sen and Social Justice," 9 *Feminist Economics* 33 (2003) [hereinafter Nussbaum, "Capabilities as Entitlements"]; Martha Nussbaum, "Reply: In Defence of Global Political Liberalism," 37 *Dev't & Change* 1313 (2006). Here I leave aside the controversy over Nussbaum's list of human functionings and debate concerning the universal applicability of her argument.

capable of choosing to live and function well. It is the role of the lawgiver to ensure the provision of adequate institutional, material, and educational support to make it possible for every individual to reach a capabilities threshold, so that they become capable of choosing how to live well and who to be.

The list of central human functional capabilities includes a number to which freedom of speech generally, and freedom of political speech in particular, is central.[68] With regard to "Senses, Imagination and Thought," Nussbaum argues the central capabilities are "being able to use the senses, to imagine, think and reason ... [and b]eing able to use one's mind in ways protected by guarantees of freedom of expression with respect to both political and artistic speech." With regard to "Practical Reason," she argues the central capabilities are "being able to form a conception of the good and to engage in critical reflection about the planning of one's life. (This entails protection for the liberty of conscience ... )." With regard to "Affiliation," she argues the central capabilities include "being able to ... engage in various forms of social interaction. ... (Protecting this capability means protecting institutions that constitute and nourish such forms of affiliation; and also protecting the freedom of assembly and political speech.)" With regard to "Control over one's Environment," she argues the central capabilities include "being able to participate effectively in political choices that govern one's life; having the right of political participation, protections of free speech and association." The prominence afforded freedom of speech generally, and freedom of political speech specifically, does not arise from a distinct argument about a "right" but rather from an acknowledgment of the constitutive role of speech in the formation of individual capabilities. Thus within the capabilities framework, speech, and political speech in particular, is regarded as vital, central, and inherent to the processes of thought, expression and interaction required to become capable of choosing to live well. This implies a particular, and robust, conception of the role of speech.

A corollary to the idea that speech is capable of doing things in and for people's lives is that (and this is the fourth stage of my argument) speech can do both good and bad things. Speech is able both to enhance the development of our capabilities and, under the right circumstances, to imperil the development of capabilities. This view is often supported by advocates of hate speech laws, but less often recognized by free-speech defenders, some of whom fail to appreciate the harms that speech can cause. Speech can do good things (such as making people feel appreciated and recognized, or congratulating a person for their achievements), and bad things

---

[68] Nussbaum, "Capabilities as Entitlements," *supra* note 67, at 41–2. Nussbaum's newer versions of her list give a more central place to "political liberties" than did earlier versions, although she argues these were always incorporated but had previously been granted less prominence. Nussbaum, "Women's Capabilities," *supra* note 67, at 231–3, 237. For earlier versions, see Martha Nussbaum, "Aristotelian Social Democracy," in *Liberalism and the Good* 203 (Gerald M. Mara et al. eds., Routledge 1990); Martha Nussbaum, "Non-Relative Virtues: An Aristotelian Approach," in *Quality of Life* 263–5 (Martha Nussbaum & Amartya Sen eds., Clarendon Press 1993).

as well (such as making people feel denigrated, attacking people's self-esteem and self-respect, causing psychological harm, marginalizing people from the broader community, instilling negative stereotypical ideas about members of a group, or inciting hatred).

Obvious historical examples exist of speech that hindered the realization of capabilities in some individuals. The clearest is the distorted language-use of the National Socialists in 1930s Germany, which contributed directly to the German people's capacity to murder Jews, people with disabilities, homosexuals, and others not considered worthy of consideration as human beings.[69] Holocaust denial can be described as hate speech (and not just an expression of one's opinion) because in the act of denying this historical truth, the deniers denigrate Jewish people and memories of historical occurrences, suggest that those who accept the truth of the Holocaust lie, and relativize the suffering incurred.[70] Thus, the act of Holocaust denial is not simply an expression of a belief in what did or did not happen historically, given that the Holocaust has been historically verified. It is an act of vilification that denigrates and harms.

A range of hate speech scholarship convincingly describes the harmful effects of hate speech on individual victims, target groups, and the community as a whole.[71] The range of harms said to be instigated includes creating the conditions for further and more egregious physical manifestations of harm, the enactment of discrimination in the very utterance of hate speech, psychic injury, disempowerment, marginalization, lack of affiliative opportunities, and silencing. It is often difficult to refute these aspects of the arguments made by hate speech law advocates. At the least, it is more difficult to refute these elements altogether than it is to question the linkage between these harms and appropriate policy responses. As an example of the latter, Robert Post makes an argument against hate speech laws on the ground that speech is vital to the functioning of democracy. He thus responds to a range of alleged harms by arguing not that they do not occur, but that they do not provide sufficient justification for restrictions on speech, when the importance of speech is conceptualized as central to opportunities for deliberative self-definition and thus democratic self-governance.[72] It is not my intention here to enter into this aspect of the debate further, but to acknowledge the vitality of the idea that hate speech can harm and the relevance of this argument to my own.

Of course, the argument that hate speakers either can do bad things, or mean to do bad things, to others with their words and the fact that sometimes they are successful

---

[69] *See* Victor Klemperer, *The Language of the Third Reich* (Martin Brady trans., Continuum 2002).

[70] Holocaust denial has other effects and methods. *See* Catriona McKinnon, *Toleration: A Critical Introduction* 153–71 (Routledge 2006).

[71] Tsesis, *supra* note 1; Delgado, *supra* note 18; Rae Langton, "Speech Acts and Unspeakable Acts," 22 *Phil. & Pub. Aff.* 293 (1993); Matsuda, *supra* note 1; *see also* L. W. Sumner, "Hate Propaganda and Charter Rights," in *Free Expression, supra* note 55, at 153–4, 170–1; Cass Sunstein, *Democracy and the Problem of Free Speech* 186 (The Free Press, 2d ed. 1995).

[72] Post, *supra* note 46.

should not be taken to mean either that a hate speaker must have intended to harm for an expression to constitute hate speech, or that a hate speaker's expression is necessarily or always successful in achieving the bad outcome. In relation to the first possibility, if harm is occasioned by the utterance then the existence of that harm (if not perhaps the degree) is what is to be measured in determining whether an expression constitutes hate speech, not whether the harm was intended or not. It is theoretically possible that a speaker might utter an expression that could be termed hate speech without realizing what they were doing or intending to harm. Examples include someone, particularly a child, who is heavily influenced by his or her peer group, but who does not really understand the messages he or she is perpetuating. In relation to the second possibility, it is undoubtedly true that some targets, even direct targets, of hate speech respond to those utterances by becoming angry or defiant or galvanized to act in defense of themselves and their community. Not all targets necessarily become victimized or disempowered or marginalized; on the contrary, some become activated. My argument is not weakened by this; rather my argument relies only on the viability of the idea that hate speech is capable of harming *some* of its listeners in particular ways. This, far more modest, claim appears viable given the extent of scholarship on this question, referred to earlier.

Fifthly, if some speech can do bad things, then there is a justification for some kind of a policy response to it. Nussbaum argues that some "freedoms" may "subvert core entitlements"; some freedoms "include injustice in their very definition."[73] We can make decisions as to which freedoms are good and which are bad, assessed against the list of central human functional capabilities. Hate speech can be defined, then, as speech that enacts harms that imperil the realization of central human functional capabilities by, among other things, disempowering, marginalizing, and silencing. These harms would ordinarily act to deter or perhaps even prevent a targeted person or community or their supporters from responding to the hate speech with (unsupported) counterspeech.

Sixthly, if one tries to construct a policy response to hate speech in the context of the idea that participation in speech is regarded as both important and a justifiable goal for speech policy, then a restrictive, limiting, or punitive focus on the hate speakers does not seem always appropriate. This is because the purpose of a policy designed to respond to hate speech ought to be, among other things, to respond to the harm occasioned, including the ways that hate speech can hinder participation in speech. Restriction, limitation, or punishment of aberrant speech is not directly helpful in ensuring participation in speech, because it is very difficult, if not impossible, to draw a causal link between restricting or punishing hate speakers and supporting the ability of their targets to speak in response.

The final and seventh stage of my argument, therefore, is to reconceive the appropriate policy response to hate speech, to allow for a *supported response* to

---

[73] Nussbaum, "Capabilities as Entitlements," *supra* note 67, at 45–6.

contradict the message contained within the hate speech and its effects, insofar as it includes silencing or marginalization or disempowerment that prevents targets, their communities, and their allies from speaking back. Even allies of the targets of hate speech can be silenced by a fear of association, or a potential fear of being targeted by those who might believe them to be a member of a specified group (in homophobic hate speech, for example). A supported policy response is not focused on the hate speakers. It is focused on the targets of hate speech themselves, and their allies and the community at large. I do not necessarily suggest this ought to be the sole component of a hate speech policy; indeed it is likely that this component would achieve its best results when used in tandem with other policy approaches, so that each approach could be adapted and used to benefit where the needs are greatest.

## IV. IMPLICATIONS FOR COUNTERSPEECH

It is a much enlarged conception of counterspeech that forms the core of my argument. Asking the state to intervene to provide conditions in which speech may be practiced, not simply asking the state to refrain from taking action and expecting people spontaneously to do so for themselves, becomes a policy goal in responding to hate speech. This would enhance participation in speech, thus overcoming one of the central concerns of advocates of laws against hate speech – that of the silencing, marginalizing, and disempowering effects of hate speech on its targets and their (broadly defined) affiliates and supporters. At the same time, this permits the recognition of the special and robust importance of free speech by ensuring efforts are devoted to enabling participation in speech, with all its benefits, and by conceiving of speech in a way that ensures its centrality to human endeavors.

The kinds of activities that might be supported through such a policy would need to be decided on the ground in the context of the specific incidents requiring a response and the needs of the affected communities. They might include a wide range of undertakings:

- the production and distribution of a community newsletter in response to a specific event to counteract misunderstandings causing, and/or perpetuated during, that event;
- the development of a new antiracism awareness program in a workplace; support for a community workshop to discuss the effects of vilifying language;
- assistance to draft and publish a reply in the press in response to an earlier article;
- the production and broadcast of radio or television advertisements or programs;
- subsidizing the creation of small-scale community art projects; or
- supporting the production of an online video by a group of marginalized youth.

In the United States, this proposal would likely not survive constitutional strictures against viewpoint discrimination, or against policies designed to enhance the ability to speak of those suffering an imbalance of speech opportunities.[74] However, it may well be that other countries (as discussed in this volume) would not face the same problems of application.

It is logical that the activities to be supported would be undertaken in response to manifestations of hate speech that had occurred in a given community in terms of scale, topic, and medium. If a hate speech incident occurred at a local sporting match, the communities involved in that sporting organization could be approached to see if some of their members would like to participate in organizing a pamphlet for local distribution or a local community multicultural event. If a hate speech incident occurred on a radio or television broadcast, the targeted communities could be encouraged and supported to request alternate coverage in some kind of current affairs program that would seek to counteract the negative stereotyping relied on in the first broadcast. Additionally, effort could be devoted to identifying existing grassroots, community-based interventions that would reflect this kind of policy but that lack resources, with a view to devoting public monies to their continuation and duplication in other areas and with other communities.

It is not necessary that those engaged in producing the response have been personally the targets of a hate speech incident. One of the characteristics of hate speech is that it targets groups that are identifiable as suffering prejudice and their affiliates, thus injuring entire communities and not just the individuals who are targeted by or within hearing of it. The response of members of targeted identities, or their affiliates, is capable of having the same potential effect over time as the counterspeech of targets themselves, and the objective of providing support to enable targets of hate speech to counteract the marginalizing and silencing effects of hate speech would still be achieved.

## V. CONCLUSION

Counterspeech ought to be conceived of as a supported, enabled response to hate speech, one that enables speakers both to contradict the messages contained within hate speech acts and to counteract the silencing and disempowering effects of hate speech acts. A supported counterspeech approach recognizes that speech is

---

[74] On the impermissibility of viewpoint discrimination, see the chapter by Michel Rosenfeld in this volume (Chapter 13), as well as Smith v. Collin, 439 U.S. 916 (1978) (Blackmun, J., dissenting from the denial of certiorari), and R.A.V. v. City of St. Paul, 505 U.S. 377 (1992). On the impermissibility of using policy to balance speech opportunities, see Miami Herald Publishing Co v. Tornillo 418 U.S. 241 (1974); CBS v. Democratic National Committee, 412 U.S. 94 (1973); Robert Post, "Subsidized Speech," 106 *Yale L.J.* 151 (1996). On the issue of the compatibility of the policy I propose with First Amendment doctrine, see Katharine Gelber, "'Speaking Back' – The Likely Fate of Hate Speech Policy in the United States and Australia," in *Speech and Harm: Controversies Over Free Speech* (Ishani Maitra & Mary Kate McGowan eds., Oxford University Press forthcoming 2012).

important and crucial and deserves protection. It also goes further in seeking to ensure that protection than the freedom-from-restraint arguments. It responds in a concrete way to the harms caused by hate speech on its targets. The policy I propose also does not counterpose the two goals of responding to the harms of hate speech and preserving freedom of speech. Instead, the two goals are mutually and collaboratively realized. Reconceptualizing counterspeech in this way thus may offer us a way out of the zero-sum game of the free-speech-versus-hate-speech debate.

# 12

# Hate Speech and Self-Restraint

## Arthur Jacobson and Bernhard Schlink

It is a truism of comparative constitutional law that the United States takes an absolutist position against the criminalization of hate speech, and that it is alone among
the constitutional democracies in taking this position.[1] The First Amendment, as
interpreted by the courts, bars states and the federal government from banning hate
speech just because it is hate speech and for no other reason. Other constitutional
democracies do ban hate speech just as hate speech, and for that reason alone. They
may justify the ban differently; they may differ on its extent and consequence. But
one way or the other, to one degree or another, they ban hate speech and the United
States does not.

The truism recognizes, of course, that the United States, in fact, does ban hate
speech. What the United States does not do – and constitutionally cannot do –
is ban hate speech *as such*. However, if hate speech falls within one of the well-
known exceptions to protected speech, then the First Amendment does not stop the
government from banning it. Possibly relevant exceptions include "fighting words"[2]
and words that create a "clear and present danger" of imminent lawlessness.[3] Yet the

[1] In 1992, Hungary started to follow the American approach. *See* Peter Molnar, "Towards Improved
Law and Policy on 'Hate Speech' – The 'Clear and Present Danger' Test in Hungary," in *Extreme
Speech and Democracy* 237 (Ivan Hare & James Weinstein eds., Oxford University Press 2009). Apart
from this recent exception, however, the truism remains true.

[2] *See* Chaplinsky v. New Hampshire, 315 U.S. 568 (1942), as limited by Cohen v. California, 403 U.S.
15 (1971).

[3] *See* Schenck v. United States, 249 U.S. 47, 52 (1919), as limited by Brandenburg v. Ohio, 395 U.S. 444
(1969). Those who know their First Amendment doubtless note that we have left group libel off the list
of exceptions, even though the Supreme Court put it on the list in Beauharnais v. Illinois, 343 U.S. 250
(1952). We do so because *Beauharnais* is of dubious current validity. Crucial to the Court's reasoning
was the assumption that statutes criminalizing libel enjoy complete immunity from First Amendment

The authors would like to thank Maria Matasar-Padilla for her invaluable assistance and Professor Mauro
Bussani of the Università degli Studi di Trieste, Professor Otto Pfersmann of the Université de Paris
I Panthéon-Sorbonne, and Professor Henner Wolter of Humboldt-Universität zu Berlin for easing the
doctrinal path.

exceptions are limited. They permit little more than the criminalization of words that are tantamount to an incipient assault, and neither of them permits the naked and unadorned criminalization of hate speech.

This striking difference in constitutional doctrine raises a difficult and, for constitutional democracies other than the United States, awkward series of questions. At the heart of democracy is free expression. Every constitutional democracy acknowledges that. And so, constitutional democracies limit free expression only in the name of defending democracy and human dignity, thus only in the interest of protecting free and respectful communication. Constitutional democracy, they say, cannot survive when hate speech flourishes.[4] Democracy requires a minimum, yet durable, measure of mutual respect among its citizens and between every group making its public presence felt. Hate speech corrodes the very core of mutual respect and threatens democracy itself.

So how is it that the United States can disable itself from banning hate speech, yet remain a constitutional democracy? Perhaps democracy does not require a minimum measure of mutual respect and constitutional democracies that ban hate speech do so gratuitously. Do such bans reflect a taste, or a historical obsession, rather than considered judgment about the requisites of democratic society? Alternatively, perhaps the United States *does* in fact restrain hate speech just like everyone else, but in a different way. Might the limited and backhanded way the United States restrains hate speech be adequate to the task of protecting mutual respect?

We understand why constitutional democracies regard restraining hate speech as essential to the maintenance of democracy. But we also understand why the United States, in its respect for freedom of expression, does not regard criminal law as a desirable way of restraining communication. One wonders, then, whether the United States has ways of restraining hate speech apart from criminal law. We thus have been led to investigate three areas to find out whether other mechanisms achieve the same purpose. These mechanisms are: workplace harassment claims,

---

restrictions. This assumption was destroyed in New York Times Co. v. Sullivan, 376 U.S. 254 (1964). The *Sullivan* case was effectively brought home to *Beauharnais* by the Seventh Circuit in Collin v. Smith, 578 F.2d 1197 (7th Cir. 1978) (permitting The National Socialist Party of America to march in the Village of Skokie, which had a sizeable population of Holocaust survivors, while displaying the swastika, despite an ordinance making it a misdemeanor to disseminate any material that promotes or incites racial or religious hatred), cert. denied, 439 U.S. 916 (1978). Were the Supreme Court to revisit the issue of criminal libel, these decisions would bode ill for *Beauharnais*.

4 *See, e.g.,* Regina v. Keegstra, [1990] 3 S.C.R. 697 (Can.) (Dickson, C.J.C.):

> I am aware that the use of strong language in political and social debate – indeed, perhaps even language intended to promote hatred – is an unavoidable part of the democratic process. Moreover, I recognize that hate propaganda is expression of a type which would generally be categorized as "political," thus putatively placing it at the very heart of the principle extolling freedom of expression as vital to the democratic process. Nonetheless, expression can work to undermine our commitment to democracy where employed to propagate ideas anathemic to democratic values. Hate propaganda works in just such a way....

standards and practices codes in the broadcast and cable media, and speech codes on college and university campuses. There are doubtless more.[5] But the three we study adequately reflect the variety of approaches to restraining hate speech in the United States. None of the three makes use of criminal sanctions. Two do not even draw directly on the resources of law. Nonetheless, they function as prohibitions or regulations of hate speech.[6] How effective they are in restraining hate speech, especially by comparison with criminalization, we cannot say. That is an empirical question, and a tricky one at that. We do know this, however. It is simply impossible to assess the quantum of restraint by focusing narrowly on constitutional doctrine, or on criminal law, or even on law altogether. One must look beyond external, legal restraints and also consider self-restraint in civil society. Only then is one ready to compare systems.

## I. WORKPLACE HARASSMENT CLAIMS

Title VII of the Civil Rights Act of 1964 makes it unlawful for an employer to "discriminate against any individual with respect to his compensation, terms, conditions, or privileges of employment, because of such individual's race, color, religion, sex, or national origin."[7] In 1986 in *Meritor Savings Bank, FSB v. Vinson*,[8] the Supreme Court held the sexual harassment of an employee by a supervisor to be actionable under Title VII. The Court required the harassment to be "sufficiently severe or pervasive 'to alter the conditions of [the victim's] employment and create an abusive working environment.'"[9] Before *Meritor*, circuit courts had held "hostile environment" harassment actionable when based on race, religion, and national origin as well as sex,[10] and after *Meritor* everyone assumed that the Supreme Court meant to do so as well.

The premise of hostile-environment harassment claims is a discriminatory difference in working conditions. It is not enough that behavior be offensive; it must

---

[5] David Bernstein offers a survey of laws in the United States restraining speech. *See* David E. Bernstein, *You Can't Say That!: The Growing Threat to Civil Liberties from Antidiscrimination Laws* (Cato Institute 2003).

[6] On the concept of functional equivalence in comparative law, see Ralf Michaels, "The Functional Method of Comparative Law," in *The Oxford Handbook of Comparative Law* 339–82 (Mathias Reimann & Reinhard Zimmermann eds., Oxford University Press 2006), and the sources cited therein.

[7] 42 U.S.C. § 2000e-2(a)(1). For the sake of simplicity, we focus on the categories protected in Title VII. Two similar statutes protect other categories: they are the Age Discrimination in Employment Act of 1967, 29 U.S.C. §§ 621–633a, and the Americans with Disabilities Act of 1990, 42 U.S.C. §§ 12101 et seq. Nothing in the analysis changes. We also consider workplace harassment claims at the federal level only, and equate the law at the federal level with the "American" model. States have their own, often different, antidiscrimination laws.

[8] 477 U.S. 57 (1986).

[9] *Id.* at 67.

[10] *See, e.g.*, Bundy v. Jackson, 641 F.2d 934 (D.C. Cir. 1981); Rogers v. EEOC, 454 F.2d 234 (5th Cir. 1971).

actually change the employee's working conditions: "Conduct that is not severe or pervasive enough to create an objectively hostile or abusive work environment – an environment that a reasonable person would find hostile or abusive – is beyond Title VII's purview."[11] And it is not enough that the behavior actually changes the employee's working conditions. It must also constitute unequal treatment "because of" a category protected by Title VII: "The critical issue, Title VII's text indicates, is whether members of one sex [or race, or religion, etc.] are exposed to disadvantageous terms or conditions of employment to which members of the other sex [or race, or religion, etc.] are not exposed."[12]

Hostile-environment harassment includes behavior that would be classified as hate speech in a jurisdiction where hate speech is an operative legal category. Of course, one must adjust for cultural, social, and political differences, yet it remains tolerably true that hate speech may be comprised and controlled by hostile-environment harassment claims. The only Title VII specific requirement is that the hate speech differentially affect the workplace conditions of a member or members of a protected category.

At the same time, actionable harassment also may, and often does, include behavior that does not come close to hate speech. This is especially true of sex discrimination, where the change in workplace conditions may be the result of behavior that runs the gamut from the merely offensive (unwelcome sexual advances,[13] distasteful or degrading remarks or behavior[14]) to the hatefully violent,[15] only some of which, some of the time, will be hate speech.

It is of decisive importance to the structure and operation of this mechanism of restraining hate speech that the harassment claim lies against the employer, not against the harasser. The harasser may be liable in tort under state law – intentional infliction of emotional distress, assault, outrage, even, in some states, the tort of

---

[11]  Harris v. Forklift Systems, Inc., 510 U.S. 17, 21 (1993).

[12]  *Id.* at 25 (Ginsburg, J., concurring). And so the courts of appeals have concluded, at least after Oncale v. Sundowner Offshore Services, Inc., 523 U.S. 75 (1998), repeated and elaborated *Harris*'s insistence on a finding of unequal treatment. Where, for example, a supervisor abuses members of both sexes equally, lower courts have found no disparate treatment of either sex. *See, e.g.,* Holman v. Indiana, 211 F.3d 399 (7th Cir. 2000), overruling McDonnell v. Cisneros, 84 F.3d 256 (7th Cir. 1996). However, courts have sometimes found that the same abuse may impact women more harshly, and thus be remediable under what is in effect a disparate impact theory. *See, e.g.,* EEOC v. National Educ. Ass'n, Alaska, 422 F.3d 840 (9th Cir. 2005); Steiner v. Showboat Operating Co., 25 F.3d 1459 (9th Cir. 1994).

[13]  *Meritor,* 477 U.S. at 68 ("The gravamen of any sexual harassment claim is that the alleged sexual advances were 'unwelcome.'").

[14]  *See, e.g.,* McLaughlin v. New York, 739 F.Supp. 97 (N.D.N.Y. 1990) (prima facie case of sexual harassment supported, in part, by distasteful and degrading comments).

[15]  *See, e.g.,* Little v. Windermere Relocation, Inc., 301 F.3d 958 (9th Cir. 2002) (holding that an employer's actions and inactions after the employee reported that she had been raped by a customer may form the basis of a hostile work environment claim).

harassment[16] – but not under Title VII.[17] Only the employer is liable.[18] And the employer must answer to the victim of the harassment, not to a prosecutor wielding the power of the state, with its own interests, its own agenda, its own inertia. All the differences between hate crime and workplace harassment claims flow from these two facts.

Consider three salient features of restraining hate speech through criminal law:

1. Hate crime statutes express and impose the will of the state, without the participation or contribution of any individual or of any institution mediating between the individual and the state.

2. The statutes address individuals primarily; they address institutions and organizations only secondarily, as aggregates of individuals.

3. The statutes threaten punishment as the state defines punishment, either imprisonment or fines; they do not seek compensation for victims or rely on methods of control other than punishment.

Restraining hate speech through workplace harassment claims differs in all three features. First, workplace harassment claims resemble criminal prosecution in that they express and impose the will of the state. This much is true of any regulation based on a statute. Unlike prosecution, however, a harassment claim may be initiated and prosecuted by an individual.[19] The individual decides whether to press the claim and

---

[16] *Cf.* Stevenson v. Precision Standard, Inc., 762 So.2d 820 (Ala. 1999) (an independent cause of action for sexual harassment does not exist under Alabama state law; instead, claims of sexual harassment are maintained under common law tort theories, such as assault and battery, invasion of privacy, negligent training and supervision, and outrage).

[17] *See, e.g.,* Lissau v. Southern Food Serv., 159 F.3d 177 (4th Cir. 1998).

[18] The standard for employer liability depends on the role of the employee who is doing the harassing. If the harasser is a co-employee of the victim, then the employer's liability is judged by a negligence standard; the employer is liable for a coworker's harassment if it "knows or should have known of the conduct, unless it can show that it took immediate and appropriate corrective action." 29 C.F.R. 1604.11(d) (from the EEOC's Guidelines on Discrimination Because of Sex, quoted approvingly in Faragher v. City of Boca Raton, 524 U.S. 775, 799, 800 (1998)). If, on the other hand, the harasser is "a supervisor with immediate (or successively higher) authority" over the victim, then the employer's liability depends on whether the supervisor's harassment "culminates in a tangible employment action, such as discharge, demotion, or undesirable reassignment." *Faragher*, 524 U.S. at 807, 808. If the harassment does culminate in a tangible employment action, then the employer is liable as if the supervisor were his agent. *Id.* at 790. If the harassment does not culminate in a tangible employment action – if all the supervisor has done is differentially alter the terms or conditions of the victim's employment – then the employer can avoid liability by proving an affirmative defense. The affirmative defense requires the employer to show "(a) that the employer exercised reasonable care to prevent and correct promptly any sexually harassing behavior, and (b) that the plaintiff employee unreasonably failed to take advantage of any preventive or corrective opportunities provided by the employer or to avoid harm otherwise." *Id.* at 807.

[19] The Equal Employment Opportunity Commission (EEOC) may initiate claims or intervene in claims initiated by individuals. 42 U.S.C. § 2000e-5(f). Typically, however, the EEOC leaves enforcement to individual claimants, taking on the role of attempting to conciliate disputes between employer and employee prior to the latter's filing in court. In some cases, the EEOC will also participate in

controls its timing, the remedies to pursue, and whether, when, and how to settle. The harassment claimant can also press the court to adopt new theories for claims or defenses or to drop old ones. The claimant shares with the state the enforcement and creation of the law. The victim of a hate speech crime, in contrast, is utterly dependent on the whim – or, to be kind, discretion – of the prosecutor. He cannot control enforcement (although he can influence it, at least negatively by refusing to cooperate). When hate speech comes to the attention of the prosecutor because the speech is in some way public – in a newspaper, on the television, at a rally – then the victim does not even need to play the role of reporting the crime to the authorities, does not even need to testify at the trial being prosecuted in the name of his or her benefit. The caption of the report of the trial – and captions are no small thing – reads "People v. Hate Speaker" rather than "Victim v. Hate Speaker."

Second, Title VII harassment claims do not address the harasser; they address the *employer* of the harasser. It is the employer, not the harasser, who has the burden of making sure that the workplace is free of harassment. The employer may or may not discipline the harasser, may or may not give the harasser an incentive to change his ways. Or, instead, the employer may plead with the harasser, warn the harasser, transfer the harasser to another office or another part of the factory floor where he is less likely to find himself in trouble. Only some employers, in some cases, will fire the harasser, make the harasser take a leave, or dock his pay. The employer's job is not to do justice; it is to manage the harasser, and management serves interests alien to the law.

Moreover, Title VII does not cover small employers, only large ones.[20] So far as federal law is concerned, mom-and-pop enterprises can engage in as much discrimination as they please without legal consequence. Employers large enough to be covered by the Act, therefore, are likely to be organizations or institutions, not individuals, because sole proprietors tend to seek the protection of limited liability when the number of employees to manage – and therefore lose track of – gets too large. The immediate, on-the-ground enforcers of federal antiharassment law, the ones who Title VII seeks to mobilize for the suppression of workplace harassment, are thus organizations or institutions, not the state and not individuals. The organizational or institutional employer becomes a private police force working gratis on behalf of the state to forestall and, if necessary, sanction behavior that the state wishes

---

fact investigation. *See* 42 U.S.C. § 2000e-5(b). The statute actually *requires* the EEOC to make an investigation, but the commission has long since rescinded its full investigation policy in favor of a three-tiered priority list. *See* 4 Lex K. Larson, *Employment Discrimination*, § 73.06, n. 2 (Matthew Bender).

[20] Title VII defines "employer" (and therefore the persons it covers) as "a person engaged in an industry affecting commerce who has fifteen or more employees for each working day in each of twenty or more calendar weeks in the current or preceding calendar year, and any agent of such a person." 42 U.S.C. § 2000e(b). Of course, "agent" is more likely to include individuals than "employer" since "agent" is not limited by the 15-person/20-week requirement, yet the fact of the matter is that one rarely if ever sees a claim against an individual.

would go away. The employee experiences the employer, not the government, as the normative and practical source of the policy; the law virtually requires the employer to feign, if it does not have, an authentic desire to banish harassment. (When an employer circulates its antiharassment policy, it does not say, "Government mandate requires Wonka Widgets to circulate this policy. Harassment violates Title VII and therefore, etc." It says, "Wonka Widgets strongly believes that harassment is wrong and will do everything in its power to stop it." Only by showing vigorous and credible efforts to stamp out harassment can the employer be sure of avoiding liability should harassment occur.)[21] Federal antiharassment law thus breaks the direct relationship between state and individual that criminalization imposes and requires.

Third, because the relationship between the state and the individual in federal antiharassment law is indirect, because Title VII interposes the employer between them, the sanction that the state wields in direct relationships with individuals – the criminal sanction – ceases to be appropriate. A hate speech statute addresses the perpetrator of the wrong. Title VII does not; it addresses the perpetrator's employer. A hate speech statute tells the perpetrator, "If you say hateful things, you are a criminal, and we will prosecute you and convict you for committing a crime." Can the state say anything like that to a harasser's employer? Can the state make the case that the harasser's employer is a criminal? The only wrong the employer has done is employing and then perhaps tolerating a harasser. Is it criminal to employ people who commit wrongs, even racist wrongs, even in the workplace? Is it criminal to tolerate their wrongful behavior? These are fair questions. They have no obvious or simple or universally correct answers. Far easier for the state to say to the employer: "We want to cut down on the amount of harassment in the workplace. We would like to enlist your help. Who better than you to give it? All we ask is that you make a decent effort to put a stop to harassment. We would like you to do what an employer can do to persuade employees not to harass each other. We know you don't have available to you the sanctions of criminal law. But you can educate, and you can impose your own sorts of sanctions. If all that fails, as it will upon occasion, we won't hold you responsible. But if you won't make the effort, then we will hold you responsible, but only for putting the victim of harassment in as good a position as he or she would have been in had the harasser behaved properly."

This is the deal that Title VII thrusts on employers.[22] It is a far more palatable deal than saddling employers with criminal liability for the behavior of persons over whom they have only partial control. But note the consequence. Instead of a single regime of criminal liability that punishes the harasser, Title VII is two different remedial regimes operating at two different levels. The first is a regime in which the

---

[21] See *supra* note 18.

[22] To be more precise, this is the deal Title VII imposes on employers when the harassment is not connected with a tangible employment action against the victim. If the harassment is connected with a tangible employment action, then the employer cannot avoid liability by exercising reasonable care to eliminate harassment. See *supra* note 18.

state forces the employer to compensate the harasser's victim, unless the employer can show that it tried to stop the harassment and the victim did not try to avoid it.[23] The harasser himself is exempt from making compensation. Nor does this first-level regime punish the harasser. It leaves dealing with him to the second level, in which the employer tries to shield itself from liability for a harasser's behavior by installing internal mechanisms designed to stop harassment or alleviate its consequences once it has occurred.

This bi-level regime created by Title VII resembles a delegation by the legislature to private entities of the administration of a portion of public law. It is in one respect no different from any delegation to any administrative agency: A statute loosely defines a goal or a subject matter or a problem and asks the delegate to do something to reach the goal or grapple with the subject matter or solve the problem. It allows people whom the delegation is designed to benefit to take the delegate to court for a determination of whether the delegate has honestly been trying to do its job. The statute requires only a good-faith effort, not absolute "success" (whoever defines success and however it may be defined). All the delegation does is deprive the delegate of the power to choose whether or not to make that effort. In this one respect, therefore, the employer is an arm of the state. In other respects, however, the task that Title VII thrusts on employers differs from delegation to an agency.

First, in the case of agencies, the delegation is to a single entity that performs the delegation in a unified and coherent way throughout an entire jurisdiction. Title VII, in contrast, speaks to *employers*, to multiple entities, each carrying out its task in its own way with its own intensity and variations. Of course, the efforts of employers to comply with Title VII do wind up following certain well-beaten paths, whether consciously or not, if not between industries then certainly within a single

---

[23] On the affirmative defense to a harassment claim outlined in *Faragher*, 524 U.S. 775, see *supra* note 18. We use the term "compensation" to indicate a remedial scheme whose complexities would take much patient exposition to thread. Here is a stark and simplistic summary. Since 1991, Title VII complaining parties have been able to seek compensatory and punitive damages. 42 U.S.C. § 1981a(a)(1). Prior to 1991, complainants could seek only equitable remedies, such as back-pay, reinstatement, and an injunction. Congress had initially envisioned the remedial powers of the court under Title VII to be those of a chancellor. But compensatory and punitive damages are available only if the employer engaged in unlawful intentional discrimination (and only if the complaining party cannot recover under 42 U.S.C. § 1981). Thus an employer that is liable under Title VII only for the discriminatory impact of a facially neutral employment practice but has not intentionally discriminated is subject to neither compensatory nor punitive damages; the victim may seek one of the equitable remedies provided in Title VII, as appropriate.

"Punitive damages" has a particular meaning in the Title VII context. The Civil Rights Act of 1991 provides that a Title VII complaining party may recover punitive damages against a respondent (other than a government, government agency, or political subdivision) "if the complaining party demonstrates that the respondent engaged in a discriminatory practice or discriminatory practices with malice or with reckless indifference to the federally protected rights of an aggrieved individual." 42 U.S.C. § 1981a(b)(1). The Supreme Court has rejected the equation of "punitive damages" under Title VII with "punitive damages" in ordinary tort law. *See* Kolstad v. American Dental Association, 527 U.S. 526 (malice or reckless disregard are not identical with egregious misconduct).

industry. Nonetheless, the responsibility for administering Title VII falls to many hands. A decision by one employer will have no necessary effect on decisions by other employers; ensuring one employer's compliance with Title VII will not assure compliance by others.

Second, an employer failing to do the job thrust on it by Congress must pay damages. An agency that does not do its job can be rebuked by a congressional committee or reviewed in court, its staff dismissed or reshuffled. But both Congress and the courts, with some exceptions, have been committed to the view that citizens have no recourse against agencies for neglect or failure of enforcement.[24]

Third, entrusting (at least) frontline Title VII enforcement to private entities rather than to an agency dramatically alters the possibilities of enforcement. An employer has at its disposal an entirely different toolbox for dealing with harassment. This is especially true in comparison with a prosecutor's office, the agency responsible for the prosecution of hate speech. Even though American jurisdictions are getting more creative these days in sentencing (specialized drug courts can order therapy, for example), the prevailing currency of criminal courts is still punishment. Employers always have "punishment" as an option (as employers punish). But scouring harassment from the employer's ranks is fundamentally a problem of management – of balancing costs and benefits, creating incentives and models, steering people in particular directions, seeing what works and what does not. It is also, therefore, in the end a problem of education, of training (or making sure that someone else has trained) the employee not to harass just as one trains him to do his job or to know his skill. Management demands trade-offs. At the level of management, antiharassment becomes one interest among many to be served. We pursue interests in the shadow of management – of ordinary business acumen and needs. In the first-level regime, the contact of state with employer, antiharassment constitutes a right to be pursued.[25] In the second-level regime, the contact of employer with harasser, it constitutes an interest to be served. The right to be free from harassment necessarily encounters and intertwines with practices, structures, and goals that from the law's perspective modulate the right. This, we suppose, is true of any legal phenomenon. But here the law intends for this to happen, for enforcement to appear as management and for liability to be deflected from the actual harasser.

Comparing the administration of hate speech sanctions with the broader remedial palette available in Title VII's bi-level enforcement regime, one is struck by what amounts to a quid pro quo. In the passage from hate crime to Title VII, the state gives up absolute control over the sanction and abandons recognition of its own interest

---

[24] *See, e.g.,* Heckler v. Chaney, 470 U.S. 821 (1985) (holding that an administrative agency's decision not to institute enforcement proceedings is presumptively not subject to judicial review).

[25] Even here one must notice a caveat (there is always a caveat in the law): Title VII requires the EEOC to attempt to "conciliate" disputes between employers and aggrieved employees. 42 U.S.C. § 2000e-(5)(b). Conciliation is an aggressive form of mediation. *See also* 29 C.F.R. § 1601.20. Here too interest makes its presence felt.

as paramount. What civil society gets, in return, is transmutation and adaptation of the state's interest to suit the interests, ways, and means of civil society. What Title VII accomplishes, in effect, is mobilization of the energy and effectiveness of civil society behind a hybrid of the state's and the victim's and the employer's objectives. Antiharassment law may perform the same function as statutes criminalizing hate speech, but it does so in a different way, reflecting different concerns yielding different consequences.

In the regulatory regime sponsored by Title VII, law plays a direct yet nonexclusive role. It takes on an ally in management. The regulation of hate speech in Title VII is thus Janus-faced. On the one side, it uses instruments of law – claims, regulations, corporate controls, and corporate equal employment opportunity officers – designed to fend off liability. On the other side, it hosts a grab bag of motives and methods. Management may indeed just be responding to the law, regulating hate speech just to reduce exposure to workplace harassment claims. But it may also be responding to ideal motives. It may be banning hate speech because it has a certain vision of corporate responsibility, not because – or not just because – it wants to reduce exposure. It may be banning hate speech because its shareholders want it banned. It may be banning it because of a fear of publicity, or because its customers will not patronize an enterprise that tolerates hate speech. Or it may have other motives, articulate or inarticulate.

The point is that one side of Title VII's face is management, and management, precisely because it is not the government and not subject to the constraints of the First Amendment, may, if it wishes, ban hate speech as such. Private actors in the United States may accomplish what is forbidden to the state. The typical antiharassment statement that an employer publicizes to its employees does not say, "You may harass any other employee you wish because of race, sex, etc., so long as the harassment doesn't change the employee's working conditions." Or, "You may harass any other employee you wish because of race, sex, etc., so long as you harass everyone equally." No, it says: "Don't harass any other employee because of race, sex, etc., and if you do all hell will break loose, whether you change their working conditions or not, whether you are an equal opportunity harasser or not." The employer does not care a whit for the jurisdictional premise that makes government action in the form of Title VII constitutionally tolerable. It is a private employer, not the government, and because of the generality of the typical antiharassment statement, private employers often wind up exceeding the government's constitutional powers. The government can honestly say, "We stand by our constitutional premise and when a workplace harassment claim comes to court we require a discriminatory change in working conditions. What the employer does in the course of partnering with us to regulate hate speech is not our business." But the fact is, the government's partner is banning hate speech.

We do not claim that mobilization of the resources of civil society in the interest of law is an innovation of Title VII. Certainly Title VII is a prominent example. But other examples are common. Nor do we claim that legal scholarship has neglected this mobilization. It surely has not. All we claim is that it is vitally important when comparing legal systems to look at the resources law mobilizes as well as the doctrines it propounds. Only then can one know what and how the law seeks to control.

## II. CIVIL SOCIETY

Once one recalls – for that is the correct word here – that civil society has instruments at its disposal for banning hate speech even if the government does not, then the puzzle with which this chapter began – how is it that United States can refrain from criminalizing hate speech and remain a constitutional democracy? – is solved. The *government's* refusal to ban hate speech does not stop civil society from banning it, and doing so as effectively as the criminal law.

We have chosen two institutions in civil society to consider, each of which covers a large and important tract of American life. These are the broadcast and cable industry and higher education. Both institutions commonly, even universally, ban hate speech. The first does this quietly, without drawing attention to the fact that it does. The second does so openly. The first constitutes what has long been the public square of American life. (Now it must share that role with the Internet.) The second conducts an education into public consciousness. Unlike the workplace, which vexes classification as either public or private, both these institutions play the role of the public reaching into and forming or educating the private. One of them comes into your home; the other becomes your home, at least for many, at least for a time. Unlike employers enforcing Title VII, however, neither institution forms an arm or agent of the government. Even though they represent the public, they are unabashedly private and aggressively lay claim to all the freedoms that privacy in America enjoys.[26] Hence regulating hate speech for them is, in large measure, if not entirely, an expression of freedom. It is what they wish or think they need to do. It is civil society regulating itself, restraining itself in its own way for its own reasons, as distant as can be from the model of regulation offered by criminal law.

### A. *Standards and Practices in Broadcast and Cable*[27]

Every broadcast and cable network in the United States has a censor. Every network pays the censor to do its job. The network hires the censor and fires the censor. The censor is not just one person. It is a *division*, typically known by the name "standards

---

[26] Of course, state-sponsored universities, at least in theory, do bear certain marks of the public. We shall see, however, that the differences between public and private universities are, in crucial respects and certainly in public perception, considerably less than meets the eye.

[27] We had the invaluable assistance in the preparation of this section of an attorney experienced in standards and practices in the broadcast and cable media. We shall refer to the conversation with this attorney as "private conversation."

and practices." Actually it is three separate divisions. One of them is devoted to regulating the content of commercials, another to monitoring news shows, and a third, entertainment. All of them ban hate speech.

It is hard to come by information about standards and practices. Networks guard their codes as proprietary information. The codes' existence is public;[28] their contents are not.[29] What little information there is often becomes public during a controversy, for example when a network is forced to defend a controversial news broadcast.[30] The codes are secret for a variety of reasons. First and foremost, code content is a target of special interest groups.[31] Networks can avoid negotiating with these groups over language if the groups do not know the language. Also, networks want to maintain

---

[28]  Bruce Linton, "Self-Regulation in Broadcasting Revisited," 64 *Journalism Quarterly* 483, 486 (1987) ("Stations do have guidelines.").

[29]  *Id.* at 487 n. 29 ("All of the manuals given to this writer by station managers . . . [were] provided in confidence and cannot be cited specifically as to the station.").

[30]  For example, the Thornburgh-Boccardi Report detailing the errors in the CBS 60 *Minutes Wednesday* Dan Rather segment, "For the Record," about George W. Bush's Texas Air National Guard Service, says simply that "CBS News established Standards for its News Division in 1976 and most recently revised those Standards in 1999. The Standards are set forth in an internally published CBS News Standards Manual covering four areas: personal standards; production standards – newsgathering; production standards – editing and production; and legal issues. As set forth in the Introduction to the Manual, most of the Standards 'come down to two essential principles: *accuracy* and *fairness*.'" Report of the Independent Review Panel, Dick Thornburgh and Louis D. Boccardi, *On the September 8, 2004 60 Minutes Wednesday Segment 'For the Record' Concerning President Bush's Texas Air National Guard Service* 41 (Jan. 5, 2005), *available at* http://www.cbsnews.com/htdocs/pdf/complete_report/ CBS_Report.pdf.

In testimony before Congress about a report she co-authored, "Television's Performance on Election Night 2000: A Report to CNN," Joan Konner, Professor and Dean Emerita of the Columbia University Graduate School of Journalism, said: "Public affairs journalism is the pursuit of truth in the public interest, and its major values are accuracy, fairness, balance, responsibility, accountability, independence, integrity and timeliness. Those are the standards that informed our judgment, and they are the standards that define professionalism, according to the written codes of most mainstream organizations and the journalists that work for them." Election Night Coverage by the Networks: Hearing Before the House Committee on Energy and Commerce, 107th Cong. 35 (2001) (statement of Joan Konner, Professor of Journalism and Dean Emerita, Graduate School of Journalism, Columbia University).

Bruce Linton's article, *supra* note 28, was written in the wake of the National Association of Broadcasters abandoning its code in 1982, when the Department of Justice won summary judgment in a suit against the NAB alleging that some of the advertising restrictions in its code violated the antitrust laws.

[31]  In the words of one industry participant, in a private conversation, standards and practices are a "flashpoint for advocacy interest groups," and these groups "are not always reasonable." "Pressure groups . . . are . . . organized and vocal." Linton, *supra* note 28, at 484. Alice Henderson and Helaine Doktori have written about their work in standards and practices: "We also meet with representatives of various recognized special interest groups who frequently offer insights to their specific areas of concern. Input from these organizations, our affiliated stations, and our viewing audience is given careful consideration in the formulation and application of CBS broadcast acceptance policy." Alice M. Henderson and Helaine Doktori, "How the Networks Monitor Program Content," in *Television as a Social Issue* 130, 130 (Stuart Oskamp ed., Sage Publications, 1988). *See also* Kathryn C. Montgomery, *Target: Prime Time: Advocacy Groups and the Struggle Over Entertainment Television* (Oxford University Press 1989).

maximum flexibility; they do not disclose restrictions explicitly so they can adapt as situations require. They believe that it is hard to be flexible if you are getting pressure to stick to language that you have already approved in writing saying what is acceptable and what is not.

If their content is hidden, the codes' motivations are clear. Prior to 1982, the National Association of Broadcasters (the "NAB") published a code, the dual purposes of which were to fend off government regulation and to minimize audience and advertiser dissatisfaction.[32] In 1982, the Department of Justice won a summary judgment motion in a suit against the NAB alleging that some of the advertising restrictions in the code violated the antitrust laws. The industry responded by withdrawing the *entire* code, not just the affected provisions. It did so because it felt that politically it did not need one given the then-prevailing antiregulatory climate.[33] But that put the question to the networks: If the government does not care, do you? Do you really want to live by a code or did you have a code to fend off government regulation? The answer was: Both. We really do want to live by a code: Our advertisers and viewers demand it *and* we always fear content-based regulation.

"Our standards address the 'mass audience' that watches us," says a statement of the CBS/Broadcast Group, "recognizing that, in the final analysis, it is the individual viewer that establishes his or her own standards, for it is in the viewer's power simply to change channels or turn us off."[34] As one person in the industry told us, "Standards and practices is about brand protection."[35] Others have said:

> One of the most important factors in our review is the audience's expectation. Not only does the viewing audience for individual programs vary ... but every individual viewer brings a different attitude and background. ... The editors in Program Practices are trained to review program material with a view toward meeting this enormously complex set of audience expectations.[36]

FCC regulation of content is rare and limited. It does regulate "indecency," but only in broadcast, not cable, and with the narrow goal of preventing content that parents would like to keep from their children while children are likely to be watching television.[37] Nevertheless, the possibility of more intrusive regulation always looms, and fear of that accompanies "brand protection" as a subsidiary impetus toward

---

[32] *See* Patricia Brosterhous, "United States v. National Association of Broadcasters: The Deregulation of Self-Regulation," 35 *Fed. Comm. L.J.* 313, 315 (1983).

[33] *See id.* at 341–5. The NAB replaced the code in October 1990 with an anodyne "Statement of Principles of Radio and Television Broadcasters." The Statement has little bark and no bite. *See* Mark M. MacCarthy, "Broadcast Self-Regulation: The NAB Codes, Family Viewing Hour, and Television Violence," 13 *Cardozo Arts & Ent. L.J.* 667 (1995)

[34] CBS/Broadcast Group, "Program Standards for the CBS Television Network," in *Television as a Social Issue, supra* note 31, at 132, 133.

[35] Private conversation.

[36] Henderson and Doktori, *supra* note 31, at 131.

[37] *See* Patricia Daza, "FCC Regulation: Indecency by Interest Groups," 2008 *Duke L. & Tech. Rev.* 3 (2008).

self-regulation. The networks have one eye cocked at the public, the other at the FCC.

Because the dominant aim of standards and practices is protection of the network against adverse public reaction, we can expect differences among codes. (Even if the language of two codes happens to be the same, there may be differences in application.) Some networks fish in the same waters. If "brand protection" is indeed the watchword of standards and practices, then these networks should make similar decisions about content. But other networks fish in other waters. Their standards-and-practices decisions should reflect the difference. And they do.[38] Even within a single network, individual stations make their own decisions about content, and stations in different parts of the country have different sensitivities and different thresholds of tolerance. Variation also exists within a network between different standards-and-practices divisions. News divisions have more flexibility in their standards and practices than do entertainment divisions. News standards and practices may permit the airing of a violent incident that entertainment standards and practices would prohibit. The word "nigger" is absolutely forbidden in entertainment but would probably be allowed in a documentary about the Ku Klux Klan.[39]

Standards and practices classifies hate speech under the code rubric of "offensive language," though "offensive language" is a broader term. It is regarded as "one of the more difficult areas." The actual standard depends on the context and content of the show. The offensive language standard is "thornier" than others. What is allowable – the actual standard – "develops over time" and is variable depending on the audience and advertisers of a particular program and the particular genre (news vs. entertainment).[40] In part, network standards-and-practices practitioners find the "offensive language" standard difficult because it presents them with a dilemma. On the one hand, they experience a sense of responsibility toward the clients, where the clients are the network's advertisers and audience. On the other hand, where the goal is entertainment, they do not want the end result to be bland. So it is that standards-and-practices practitioners find news and reality easier than fiction, because they do not present this dilemma. Nonetheless, they have "made peace" with the need to regulate offensive speech.[41]

Network standards-and-practices divisions are private censors. They represent their fraction of the public, their market niche, just as the government as a whole claims to represent the public as a whole. They pay tribute to those who must be feared. Unlike the government, however, they live under a perpetual referendum. The voters are

---

[38] Private conversation.

[39] Private conversation. Peter Molnar has pointed out that as a consequence a network would not air August Wilson's play, *Joe Turner's Come and Gone*, because characters say the word "nigger" (August Wilson, of course, is black); nor would it air an irreverent black stand-up comedian who uses the word.

[40] Private conversation.

[41] Private conversation. Alice Henderson and Helaine Doktori capture the dilemma unwittingly: "Generally speaking, our concerns in Program Clearance are that plots and characters be balanced in the presentation of ideas and issues and that sexual themes, violent action, and language be neither gratuitous nor exploitative." Henderson and Doktori, *supra* note 31, at 131. Enough said.

their viewers and advertisers. They vote by turning a show on or turning it off, by placing ads on it or not placing ads on it. But standards and practices "legislates" just for their fraction. The broadcast and cable industry censors the public sphere, but only in a patchwork fashion. They do not distil the common sense of the community as a whole. Indeed network audiences do not form a community of any sort. They are dispersed, anonymous. Like law, they dictate what will and what will not go on air. In their application they result in what are, effectively, adjudications. They govern behavior. Producers know what they say and adjust program content accordingly. They have teeth; if standards and practices will not approve content, it does not get aired. And whereas law reflects the morality of a community as a whole, they do reflect the morality of different groups of people – the network's audiences and its advertisers. So whereas law often just represents the moral minimum of different groups and strata of society, they reflect moral maxima of different groups and strata.

And the codes are secret, which diminishes them as law. They are known to and by those they regulate, but are invisible to the supposed regulatory beneficiaries or the larger society. They do not announce the practical morality to the very people from whom it has been drawn. They do not permit a people to be in conversation with itself. That is an essential – perhaps *the* essential – function of law. If a people cannot be shown its practical morality, then the people cannot know itself. It cannot know what it is endorsing because it cannot know what it is rejecting. It cannot know whether it approves or disapproves of what it has turned out to be. The most familiar of metaphors is best. Law holds up a mirror to a people. It permits a people to see who they are and who they wish to be. Standards-and-practices codes cater to our moral predilections but shield us from knowing what those predilections are and how they are recognized and enforced as rules. But without knowledge, we cannot take responsibility. We lose the power of progressive moral beings. We lose the gift of dissatisfaction. It is one thing to have a moral predilection, quite another to acknowledge that one has it. We might be satisfied to have a predilection, but not to see it as law.

Because standards-and-practices divisions operate in secret, they can reach more deeply and regulate more intensively than the state. Regulation in a constitutional democracy must always be public. It is therefore subject to law and political constraint. Standards and practices, in contrast, are as immune from scrutiny as Star Chamber. They need not accord either due process or equal protection to their suppliants. So long as they keep the state at bay, they need not answer to political demands. Beyond that, they know only the demands of the market – of *their* market and no other. If they are fair, it is because it pays to be fair and not because fairness is a public virtue. If they respond to a political demand, it is because the political demand has become an economic demand and is having an economic consequence, not because they must agree or disagree or come to terms with a political position. Their only job is to respect the prejudices of their segment of the market, which they may do without any of the burdens of governing all the segments of the market.

In these ways network standards and practices divisions differ from employers enforcing Title VII's mandate. But they differ in another way as well. Title VII's mandate constitutes a kind of delegation of enforcement. Employers are enforcing law and know that they are enforcing law; they know they are acting on behalf of, and in fulfillment of the purposes of, the state. Standards-and-practices divisions relate to the state in a subtler, less obtrusive way. Standards-and-practices administrators believe that they are satisfying a market, not that they are doing the state's bidding. Nevertheless, the state is not entirely absent. It looms in the background: To fend off the state, networks must satisfy a demand for censorship that the state would undoubtedly make if the networks did not do the job instead. So standards-and-practices divisions are promoting a public purpose in all but name. One may wonder, however, if they are not also endangering a public purpose. Their censorship is harsher than state regulation under the constitutionally protected freedom of expression could ever be.

## B. *Campus Speech Codes*

Standards-and-practices codes do have one enormous advantage: They allow Americans to hold on to a myth. They allow them to believe that they own a political culture in which the values of the First Amendment are paramount. By putting the suppression of hate speech under wraps, they permit Americans the conceit that their public discourse is freewheeling, no holds barred, a brawl. At least in the traditional media, it is not.[42] But myths are important, the myth of the First Amendment no less so than any other political origin myth. But there is another setting where Americans are not so shielded, where the constraints on discourse are overt and meant to be felt and understood as constraints.

Most colleges and universities in the United States have instituted what are in effect speech codes.[43] The codes contain rules governing what members of the college or university community may and may not say. Of course, Title VII applies to schools as employers of faculty and staff, and just like any other employer a school would be liable for tolerating the harassment of one of its employees by a

---

[42] Compared with the print media and broadcast and cable, the Internet has provided an unruly forum in which hate speech can flourish. But the Internet too, just like broadcast and cable, has come under political pressure to self-regulate. *See* Jeanne Pia Mifsud Bonnici, *Self-Regulation in Cyberspace* (T.M.C. Asser Press 2008); Monroe E. Price and Stefaan G. Verhulst, *Self-Regulation and the Internet* (Kluwer Law International 2005). For an optimistic view of its capacity to do so, see David R. Johnson et al., "The Accountable Net: Peer Production of Internet Governance," 9 *Va. J. L. Tech.* 9 (2004), *reprinted with* "The Accountable Net Roundtable" as *Floersheimer Center Occasional Paper #2, available at* http://www.cardozo.yu.edu/floersheimer.

[43] We say "in effect" because some campuses forbid certain types of speech as constituting "verbal harassment" at the same time that they pride themselves on not having a speech code. Martin Golding cites Duke as an example. *See* Martin P. Golding, *Free Speech on Campus* 49 (Rowman & Littlefield Publishers 2000).

co-employee or by a supervisor. But campus codes can (and many do) apply to everyone, student and employee alike.[44] They can threaten any member of the community who is accused of violating the code with discipline, including, in the extreme, expulsion from the community. Enforcement is not, in the first instance, in the hands of lawyers or courts – of trained legal personnel – but is the province of either the administration, or the faculty, or an elected council of students, or some mix of administration and faculty and students.

The purpose of the codes, broadly speaking, is to create an environment in which historically disadvantaged groups, as defined principally by race and gender, feel as free and as comfortable as historically advantaged groups to participate meaningfully in the educational and social life of the campus. The premise of the codes is that to achieve such an environment, university officials must impose restrictions on the speech of the historically advantaged.[45] The intellectual forebears of the codes thus wished to achieve actual equality and actual freedom under what they regarded as systemically unequal and factually unfree social conditions.[46]

The codes range widely in the speech they prohibit.[47] The narrower ones confine their prohibition to harassment. But even these can define harassment far more

---

[44] Timothy Shiell argues that Title VII harassment regulations should apply to everyone on campus, because drawing a distinction between harassment against a college or university employee, who is entitled to the protections of Title VII, and a student, who is not, makes no sense. Timothy C. Shiell, *Campus Hate Speech on Trial* 105–11 (University Press of Kansas 1998).

[45] *See* Alan Charles Kors and Harvey A. Silverglate, *The Shadow University: The Betrayal of Liberty on America's Campuses* 96 (The Free Press 1998).

[46] The intellectual foundation for the regulation of speech in the interest of equality was laid by Herbert Marcuse in his essay "Repressive Tolerance," in Robert Paul Wolff, Barrington Moore, Jr., and Herbert Marcuse, A *Critique of Pure Tolerance* 81 (Beacon Press 1965). The application of Marcuse's vision to campus life was by Richard Delgado, "Words That Wound: A Tort Action for Racial Insults, Epithets, and Name Calling," 17 *Harv. C. R.-C.L.L.R.* 133 (1982); Mari J. Matsuda, "Public Response to Racist Speech: Considering the Victim's Story," 87 *Mich. L.R.* 2320 (1989); Charles R. Lawrence III, "If He Hollers, Let Him Go: Regulating Racist Speech on Campus," 1990 *Duke L.J.* 431 (1990); and Thomas C. Grey, "Discriminatory Harassment and Free Speech," 14 *Harv. J. L. & Pub. Pol'y* 157 (1991). *See also* Stanley Fish, *There's No Such Thing as Free Speech, and It's a Good Thing Too* (Oxford University Press 1994).

[47] The Foundation for Individual Rights in Education (FIRE) keeps tabs on campus speech codes around the country. Their Web site may be found at http://www.thefire.org/. Fundamental is the distinction between public and private colleges and universities: Public institutions are subject to First Amendment limitations; private institutions are not. Robert O'Neil argues that the distinction between public and private institutions is overstated: Most public institutions get the bulk of their funds from private sources – fund-raising, endowment, and tuition – and most private institutions get substantial support from the state. Some private institutions have or originally had public charters, and most are supervised to some degree by state licensing. Robert M. O'Neil, *Free Speech in the College Community* 218–39 (Indiana University Press 1997). FIRE's survey of campus speech codes supports O'Neil's argument. In 2010, policies violating First Amendment standards were found in 71% of public universities and 70% of private universities. FIRE, "Spotlight on Speech Codes 2010: The State of Free Speech on Our Nation's Campuses" (2010), *available at* http://www.thefire.org/public/pdfs/9aed4643c95e93299724a350234a29d6.pdf?direct.

broadly than have the federal courts in the context of Title VII. For example, Duke University's Office for Institutional Equity states:

> Harassment of any individual for any reason is not acceptable at Duke University. Harassment may arise in situations unique to a given interpersonal relationship or in actions rooted in an attitude toward a group. Sexual harassment is perhaps the most commonly understood form of harassment but it is important to note that harassment on any demographic basis–including age, color, disability, ethnic or national origin, gender, race, religion, class, institutional status, or sexual orientation or gender identity–also occurs and is expressly forbidden.[48]

Title VII extends much more narrowly. It applies only to a discrete list of protected classes; the Duke policy applies to harassment on any basis, including three notably absent from the federal list: "class, institutional status, or sexual orientation or gender identity." Federal law also applies only to harassment of an individual *because* the individual is a member of a protected class; the Duke policy applies also to harassment of an individual for reasons arising out of "a given interpersonal relationship."

Indeed, the discrepancy is even greater than it seems. This is so for two reasons. First, the campus adjudicator may attach a much less precise and therefore broader meaning to the words of the policy. The policy does, in fact, go on to define harassment in a way that would be familiar to any lawyer conversant with federal law.[49] But that definition, once in the hands of a panel of administrators, or faculty, or

---

[48]  Duke University, "Harassment Policy and Procedures," *available at* http://www.duke.edu/web/equity/har_policy.htm. Duke's policy does, however, require that the "policy against harassment shall be applied in a manner that protects the academic freedom and freedom of expression of all parties to a complaint." *Id.* It is therefore considered to be one of the more speech-protective of such policies. Golding, *supra* note 43, at 88.

[49]  Duke's policy provides:

Harassment may take two forms:

The first form of harassment is verbal or physical conduct – which may or may not be sexual in nature – that, because of its severity and/or persistence, interferes significantly with an individual's work or education, or adversely affects an individual's living conditions.

The second form of harassment occurs if a person uses a position of authority to engage in unwelcome sexual advances, requests for sexual favors, or other verbal or physical conduct of a sexual nature when:

- submission to such conduct is explicitly or implicitly made a term or condition of an individual's employment or education; or
- submission to or rejection of such conduct is used as a basis for decisions affecting an individual's education or employment.

The conduct alleged to constitute harassment under this Policy shall be evaluated from the perspective of a reasonable person similarly situated to the complainant and in consideration of the context of the behavior.

Harassment must be distinguished from behavior that, even though unpleasant or disconcerting, is appropriate to the carrying out of certain instructional, advisory, or supervisory responsibilities.

students, or a mix of administrators and faculty and students, may have an operative meaning that is quite different from the operative meaning that federal judges attach to Title VII. This raises the second point. Colleges and universities are noticeably reticent to afford defendants in campus adjudications procedural protections that in federal and state courts are routine and necessary.[50] These include the right to counsel, the right to confront an accuser, the right to a trial record, the right to cross-examine hostile witnesses, and so forth. Procedure protects many interests. Among them is finding the truth. Denial of procedural protections makes it less likely that adjudication will result in truth, and therefore less likely that an accused can be confident that it will result in truth. Hence any subject of such a regime will be less concerned with ensuring that the truth in an adjudication will vindicate them than with avoiding adjudication altogether. A regime with procedural protections that punishes hate speech deters hate speech. A regime without procedural protections that punishes hate speech is in danger of deterring speech itself.[51]

Other codes are even broader in scope than Duke's. Haverford College requires its students to draft and ratify an Honor Code each academic year. The code applies only to students and is administered only by students. Section 3.04(b) of the 2008–2009 code addresses "social concerns":

> Our social relationships should be based on mutual respect and concern. We must consider how our words and actions may affect the sense of acceptance essential to an individual's or group's participation in the community. We strive to foster an environment that genuinely encourages respectful expression of values rather than unproductive self-censorship. Upon encountering actions or values that we find degrading to ourselves and to others, we should feel comfortable initiating dialogue with the mutual goal of increasing our understanding of each other. The social concerns of the Code extend to all forms of communication, including, but not limited to: spoken discussion, posted writing, and internet discussion forums. If a violation of the code occurs, it should be resolved via face to face confrontation.[52]

This paragraph is full of vague and difficult concepts. What is "mutual respect and concern"? When a student considers that his or her words and actions "may affect the sense of acceptance essential to an individual's or group's participation in the

---

Duke University, *supra* note 48.

    The major difference with federal law is that Duke's policy applies to "living conditions" as well as to the workplace. That is an obvious result of the difference in coverage. Otherwise, the language invites comparison with federal law.

[50] Kors and Silverglate, *supra* note 45, at 278, 289–311.

[51] For a pessimistic assessment of the prospects for academic freedom in the "postmodern" world, see Louis Menand, "The Limits of Academic Freedom," in *The Future of Academic Freedom* (Louis Menand, ed., University of Chicago Press 1996). For a different take, see Walter P. Metzger, "A Stroll along the New Frontiers of Academic Freedom," in *Unfettered Expression: Freedom in American Intellectual Life* 91 (Peggie J. Hollingsworth ed., University of Michigan Press 2000).

[52] The Honor Code: Article III of the Constitution of the Haverford College Students' Association, *available at* http://www.students.haverford.edu/code/honorcode2008.pdf.

community," must the student consider the subjective sense of acceptance of the *actual* fellow student, even if unreasonable and demanding, or is he entitled to consider the sense of acceptance of the *reasonable* fellow student? These are just the most obvious of a host of questions the paragraph poses.

But there is more. The very next section of the code, Section 3.05, has the following provision:

> As individuals who are also members of a community, we are obligated to examine our own actions as well as the actions of those around us in light of their effect on the community. If it becomes clear through self-reflection or through expressions of concern by others, that either our academic or social conduct represents a violation of community standards, we are obligated to report our own breach to Honor Council, even if doing so may result in a trial and the possibility of separation from the college.

Thus, if a student violates Section 3.04 of the code and is aware that he has violated Section 3.04, either because others have complained to him or because he has come to realize the violation on his own, that student has also violated Section 3.05 of the code if he fails to turn himself in to the Honor Council. He can be hauled before the Honor Council for that reason alone, just for failing to turn himself in, and punished just for that reason, quite apart from the predicate violation of Section 3.04. Any student can create a second violation of the Honor Code simply by complaining to the student who commits the predicate violation, and since Section 3.03(a) of the Honor Code requires students to engage in confrontation, any victim or potential victim must complain to the violator or potential violator lest he himself be in violation of the confrontation requirement.

Not every speech code in the United States circumscribes speech as narrowly as Duke's, not to mention Haverford's. Not every campus even has a code. But the vast majority do, and most circumscribe speech at least as narrowly as Duke's.[53] So it is fair to take Duke as representative of what passes for normative on campuses

---

[53] FIRE surveyed the 100 "Best National Universities" and the 50 "Best Liberal Arts Colleges" as rated in the 2008 "America's Best Colleges" issue of *U.S. News & World Report*. The report also surveyed 222 other major public universities. Of the 375 schools surveyed, FIRE declined to rate 8 schools on the grounds that the school stated clearly and consistently that it holds a set of values above a commitment to freedom of speech. FIRE rated the remaining 367 schools. It awarded schools either a "red light," a "yellow light," or a "green light." A "red light" school "has at least one policy that both clearly and substantially restricts freedom of speech." A "yellow light" school has policies "that could be interpreted to suppress protected speech or policies that, while restricting freedom of speech, restrict only narrow categories of speech." A "green light" indicates that FIRE has found "no policies that seriously imperil speech." FIRE, "Spotlight on Speech Codes 2010," *supra* note 47, at 5. FIRE gave a red-light rating to 266 schools (71%); it gave a yellow-light rating to 90 schools (24%), and a green-light rating to 11 schools (3%). Eight schools (2%) stated clearly and consistently that they held some set of values above a commitment to freedom of speech. *Id.* at 6.

Of course, FIRE's ratings are evaluative and thus subject to dispute. Also FIRE makes no bones about its mission, to restore "individual rights" to higher education in the United States, rights which it considers sorely abused.

in the United States today. And what is normative on campuses far exceeds what is normative in other spheres of American life or what we have seen of the workplace and of network broadcasting.

## III. PATTERNS OF FREEDOM AND RESTRAINT

### A. *Assessing the Three Regimes*

We can array the three institutions we have been considering – the workplace, standards-and-practices divisions in the broadcast media, and institutions of higher learning – along two axes: the breadth of the institution's circumscription of speech and the proximity of the institution to the tasks and interests of the state.

Of the three institutions, Title VII is the least restrictive. It condemns speech only when the speech rises to the level of harassment, and only when the harassment is because of membership in a limited number of specifically defined groups. It punishes the employer rather than the harasser. It punishes the employer only if the employer has not made reasonable efforts to prevent the harassment, and only when the harassment creates objectively unequal conditions of employment. Thus Title VII stops speech only by indirection, not by head-on attack. It can plausibly be described as not stopping speech at all, but rather preventing unequal working conditions. At the same time, of the three institutions, Title VII is the closest to the tasks and interests of the state. The employer that patrols the workplace for harassment is performing a task thrust on it by the state and knows that it is performing such a task. The state could perform that task directly, using the methods and facilities it uses to prevent countless other behaviors of which it disapproves. But the American state has chosen not to do that. It has chosen to distance itself from the prevention of harassment in the workplace by sharing the responsibility for prevention with the owner of the workplace. The sharing is overt, even if unadvertised. The employer knows that it has been entrusted with responsibility and makes sure that the employees know it. What Title VII accomplishes is to align the interests of the employer with the interests of the state. That is its purpose and its result.

Standards-and-practices codes circumscribe speech more broadly than does Title VII. The range of speech that a code may suppress is as broad as it needs to be to avoid offense to the market. What gives offense can vary widely, depending on the segment of the market to which the broadcaster pitches its programming. In approach, codes are always the same: Do not offend the market. In content – what exactly offends *this* broadcaster's market? – they will often be different. The codes labor under nothing like the conditions constraining Title VII. The broadcaster simply does what is in its interest and because it is in its interest. No legal finding of any sort is requisite. The broadcaster is not in the position of acting overtly and directly on behalf of the state. It is not restricting speech because the state has told it to restrict speech and is threatening it with harmful consequences if it does not. Instead it is the market that is threatening the broadcaster with harmful consequences. And so it is that the broadcaster, unlike the employer, is not the state's partner. If anything, it is the market's partner, and it is as the market's partner that it must keep the state at bay. But that is the irony of its position: To keep the state at bay, the broadcaster must go at least partway to what it surmises the state would tell it to do were it not already doing it. The only way to avoid looming regulation may be to regulate yourself.[54] But self-regulation is no less regulation simply because the state stays in the background. It may, of course, be that the broadcaster's segment of the market is offended by exactly what offends the state, so that self-regulation is simply an expression of the broadcaster's self-interest. But it may also not be. The broadcaster's segment of the market need not be coincident with the will of the entire market expressed politically. Often enough it is. But sometimes it is not, and that is when the political will of the state makes itself felt. Or not – the broadcaster's regulation for the segment of a market may go way beyond what the state would ever require.

From one perspective, standards-and-practices codes appear to be utterly unconstrained. No constitution, no law of any kind, limits the topics over which they may range. So long as it pays minimal attention to the demand for censorship by the body politic as a whole, the broadcaster is free to censor or not to censor. But from another perspective, broadcasters are severely constrained. They are not free to censor or not to censor when it comes to the wishes of their segment of the market. Of course, their market may be indifferent to certain matters, and in those matters the managers of a broadcaster are free to indulge their collective whim. But they are free only because their market tolerates their freedom, only because their regulator leaves them free within certain limits for a certain time. They are in fact not free; they are constrained, not by the state, but by the very source of power that frees them from the state.

Colleges and universities in the United States, in contrast, are constrained neither by the market, which constrains broadcasters, nor by the state, which constrains employers. With respect to the speech they govern, they are their own source of power and impose their own limits on that power.[55] They are free, within a wide compass, to determine what speech is acceptable on campus and what speech is not, and they exercise this freedom to restrict a broad range of speech.

Thus a pattern appears. The more an institution is its own source of power vis-à-vis the state and the less it is influenced by it, the narrower that institution's constraint tends to be. To the degree that the motivation for constraining speech has its origin in interests and ideals apart from the state – in standards-and-practices divisions it is the

---

[54] "The willingness of an industry to regulate itself is often dependent on the belief that there is, as famously put in the securities-regulation context, a 'shotgun behind the door.'" Gideon Parchomovsky and Philip J. Weiser, "Beyond Fair Use," 96 *Cornell L. Rev.* 91, 135 (2010), quoting Walter Werner, "The SEC as a Market Regulator," 70 *Virginia L. Rev.* 755, 764 (1984).

[55] In theory, the Constitution of the United States constrains public universities in their ability to regulate speech, but in practice they behave as if they are unconstrained, and nothing the courts do seems to stop them. *See supra* note 47.

market; in higher education it is a vision of political decency and ideal citizenship –
the constraint may be more vigorous. But even the workplace, the institution whose
constraints on speech are the most closely linked to the state, suppresses speech
more vigorously than the First Amendment would tolerate were the state carrying
out the employer's task directly, and that is because the workplace, like the broadcast
networks and higher education, has interests and ideals of its own, which share a
platform with the interests and ideals expressed in Title VII. The pattern illustrates
the two sides of the state. It threatens freedom and grants it.

## B. *An American Model*

An American model emerges. It suppresses hate speech only incidentally, only as
part of other purposes, not specifically and never by name. It relies primarily, if
not exclusively, on the energies and ambitions of institutions within civil society,
not on compulsion by the state. It does not make use of criminal law and all the
moral, administrative, and political baggage that criminal law brings in train. It
does not work throughout society as a whole; it works within the institutions – the
workplace, broadcast networks, the campus – in which speech is most relevant. It
reflects the interests, needs, and perspectives of those institutions, which mark and
modulate any stance toward hate speech the institution may take or any effect on
hate speech it may have. It is in every way opposite the countermodel, a model that
suppresses hate speech directly just because it is hate speech, ignores civil society,
uses criminal law exclusively, targets all of society, and rationally bends all efforts
toward the suppression of hate speech and hate speech only.

What then of the other constitutional democracies? Do they supply the countermodel? Do they rely exclusively on the criminal sanction, on the state, for the
suppression of hate speech? Do they ignore the astonishing force that civil society
can bring to bear against the individual – the education, discipline, economic incentives, shunning, honoring – by which civil society achieves concord and conformity
and against which criminal law appears as afterthought and as confession of failure?

The answer is that on the whole, with some exceptions, the other constitutional
democracies do indeed supply the countermodel. Surely some surprises await in
the data, but a look at three constitutional democracies – France, Germany, and
Italy – shows a sturdy allegiance to the state-driven countermodel and a fairly uniform disregard of the American model, having nothing resembling the systemic,
wholehearted, and largely voluntary American effort to discourage hate speech.

None of these countries have university speech codes. They certainly do not have
individual codes adopted singly by universities, as in the United States. But they also
do not have a state-mandated code applicable to all universities. Universities share
the laws and regulations limiting speech of the population in general. However,
nothing resembling the self-administered, locally generated speech codes that populate American campuses can be found. The absence of such codes makes perfect
sense in the context within which the universities in these countries function. A

weak tradition of university self-management and the presence of highly specific statutes criminalizing hate speech make universities in these countries extraordinarily unpromising candidates for homespun, home-run codes.

The results are similar for broadcast networks, with one modest exception. Neither France nor Germany has laws or codes limiting speech on broadcast networks. Italy has adopted a law limiting speech in radio and television broadcasting, but did so only in 2005. The law provides that no radio and television program shall violate fundamental rights of individuals, incite the audience to crime, violence, or intolerance, or harm children's physical and psychological development.[56] But this law is a *law*, an imposition by the state, not a network-by-network assessment of the market, resulting in network-specific and network-administered standards and practices codes. The law thus reflects no contribution from civil society, and the entwining of private purposes with a public purpose is the hallmark of the American model. The exception is that all major Italian broadcasting companies have adopted a code of conduct concerning television programming for juvenile viewers.

The results are similar for the workplace. It is true that the countries we are considering have more actively regulated workplace speech than speech in the broadcast media. That is because on June 29, 2000, the Council of the European Union adopted Directive 2000/43/EC "implementing the principle of equal treatment between persons irrespective of racial or ethnic origin," and on November 27, 2000, the Council adopted Directive 2000/78/EC "establishing a general framework for equal treatment in employment and occupation." These directives have been implemented throughout the EU – the workplace has more and more fallen under the jurisdiction of the EU. All its enactments follow the statist pattern.

## IV. CONCLUSION

Exploiting the resources of civil society is not logically inconsistent with the criminalization of hate speech. But criminalization is a statement about an orientation, a habit of mind, a judgment about what is politically desirable. It may be driven by fear – fear of another Holocaust, of revanchist and nationalistic atavisms – or it may be driven by political structures and traditions reaching back into the period of absolutist monarchy, a sense of what is the right way and what is the wrong way to set up a decent society. But it is not an accident, and it is not without consequence. The American way may, in fact, wind up suppressing more types of speech more effectively than occurs in the other constitutional democracies; having one's teachers and fellow students and employers and sources of news and entertainment all toeing a single line and vigilant against departures from the line can be a formidable deterrent to unwanted speech. That is the irony of the First Amendment. Routing

---

[56] Legislative Decree no. 177, July 31, 2005, art. 4(1), Gazz. Uff. n. 208 of Sept. 7, 2005. A similar development in France: On May 7, 2009, President Sarkozy asked a committee to draft a code for the mass media in France, but they have not yet issued a report.

the suppression of hate speech through civil society rather than the state preserves the formal integrity of the First Amendment without having to pay the price levied by its substance, the hateful speech that it allows.

The criminal law brings a level of harshness and rigidity of control into society and social life, to which the softer and more flexible regulations that society comes up with in and of itself may seem preferable. But the general and universal standards that the state sets are, if not for any other reason than because of their universality and generality, more tolerant and liberal than the group-oriented, strata-oriented social restrictions that set much higher and more petty and rigid moral and social standards than the state ever would. Of course, the American tradition of not distinguishing too precisely between the public and the private sphere leads to smoother social regulations instead of harsher state regulations, but also to more rigid and petty moral and social norms than the more universal and tolerant norms of the state.

In the end, however, these are not choices; we can no more choose our ethics and our politics than we can choose our genetic code. In the United States, recourse to civil society to achieve a certain political result seems natural and proper because in the United States, the boundary between the state and civil society is blurred and marked by countless interchanges. The three institutions we have been considering are the principal institutions in which this blurring of boundaries, this interchange between private and public, takes place. They form the "commanding heights" of a democratic public. Once the forces arrayed against hate speech have captured these institutions – the employers, the networks, the campus – they have effectively deprived hate speech of a meaningful public forum. They have turned the educative powers of these institutions against the First Amendment, at least against its position that hate speech ought not to be restrained. What is left for these forces to conquer? Where else is hate speech getting its purchase on the public?

These questions have answers. The quarantining of hate speech by civil society in the United States is by no means perfect or complete. The Internet has made a hole – how large we do not yet know – in the fences that all constitutional democracies have erected against political atavism. Apart from that, the forums that hate speech musters in the United States are, by and large, not significant forums. This could change in a flash. Nothing guarantees that the tyranny of the majority[57] in the United States will continue to be directed against hate speech. The scientific point, however, remains valid: It is possible to regulate hate speech through the self-restraint of civil society as effectively as through the restraint of criminal law.

[57] As Tocqueville describes the political system of the United States, in which "the power of the majority . . . [is] not just predominant but irresistible." 1 Alexis de Tocqueville, *Democracy in America* 284, 288 (Library of America 2004); *see generally id.* at Part II, chapter 7 ("On the Omnipotence of the Majority in the United States and its Effects").

# 13

# Hate Speech in Constitutional Jurisprudence

## A Comparative Analysis

### Michel Rosenfeld

### INTRODUCTION

Hate speech – that is, speech designed to promote hatred on the basis of race, religion, ethnicity, or national origin – poses vexing and complex problems for contemporary constitutional rights to freedom of expression.[1] The constitutional treatment of these problems, moreover, has been far from uniform as the boundaries between impermissible propagation of hatred and protected speech vary from one setting to the next. There is, however, a big divide between the United States and other western democracies. In the United States, hate speech is given wide constitutional protection, whereas under international human rights covenants[2] and in other western democracies, such as Canada,[3] Germany,[4] and the United Kingdom,[5] it is largely prohibited and subjected to criminal sanctions.

The contrasting approaches adopted by the United States and other western democracies afford a special opportunity to embark on a comparative analysis of the difficult problems posed by hate speech and of the various possible solutions to them. As we shall see, in the United States, hate speech and the best ways to cope with it are conceived differently than in most other western democracies. This is due, in part, to differences in social context, and, in part, to differences in approach. It may be tempting, therefore, to endorse a purely contextual approach to hate

---

[1] I use the term "constitutional rights" in a broad sense that encompasses both rights arising under national constitutions and those established by international human rights covenants, notwithstanding that, strictly speaking, the latter may be treaty-based rights rather than constitutional rights.

[2] See discussion *infra* Section IV.

[3] See discussion *infra* Subsection IIIA.

[4] See discussion *infra* Subsection IIIC.

[5] See discussion *infra* Subsection IIIB.

This chapter is drawn from Michel Rosenfeld, "Hate Speech in Constitutional Jurisprudence: A Comparative Analysis," 24 *Cardozo L. Rev.* 1523 (2003).

speech encompassing a broad array of diverse constitutional responses ranging from American *laissez faire* to German vigilance. Given the trend toward globalization and the instant transnational reach of the Internet, however, a purely contextual approach would seem insufficient, if not downright inadequate. For example, much neo-Nazi propaganda is now generated in California and transmitted through the Internet to countries like Canada or Germany where neo-Nazi groups have established a much more significant foothold than in the United States.[6] Inasmuch as such propaganda generally amounts to protected speech in the United States, there seems to be little that can be done to limit its spread beyond American soil. Does that justify calling for a change of constitutional jurisprudence in the United States? Or, more generally, do present circumstances warrant a systematic rethinking of constitutional approaches to hate speech?

In this chapter, I concentrate on these questions through a comparison of different existing constitutional approaches to hate speech. Before embarking on such a comparison, however, I provide in Section I a brief overview of some of the most salient issues surrounding the constitutional treatment of hate speech. In the next two sections, I examine the two principal contrasting constitutional approaches to hate speech. Section II focuses on the United States and analyzes hate speech within the broader free speech jurisprudence under the American Constitution. Section III deals with the alternative approach developed in other western democracies, and Section IV details how the latter approach is incorporated in the relevant international covenants. Section V addresses the difficult problems raised by religion-based hate speech through a consideration of the Danish cartoons controversy. Finally, Section VI compares the two contrasting approaches and explores how best to deal with hate speech as a problem for contemporary constitutional jurisprudence.

## I. HATE SPEECH AND FREEDOM OF EXPRESSION: ISSUES AND PROBLEMS

The regulation of hate speech is largely a post–World War II phenomenon.[7] Prompted by the obvious links between racist propaganda and the Holocaust, various

---

[6] *See* B'Nai B'Rith Anti-Defamation League, *The Skinhead International: A Worldwide Survey of Neo-Nazi Skinheads* (Irwin Suall ed., Anti-Defamation League 1995); Robert A. Jordan, "Spreading Hatred," *Boston Globe*, Nov. 26, 1988, at 25; Paul Geitner, "Noting Neo Nazi Material, Internet Blocks Site," *Chattanooga Times*, Jan. 27, 1996, at A8. *See also* UEJF & LICRA v. Yahoo!, Inc. & Yahoo! France, T.G.I. Paris, May 22, 2000 (holding that the display and auction of Nazi paraphernalia over the Internet in France amounts to criminal violation, and is not protected speech). The French court's order that Yahoo! pay plaintiffs 10,000 Francs and make it impossible for French Internet users to view Nazi items on Yahoo's auction site was held unenforceable in the United States on First Amendment grounds. Yahoo!, Inc. v. La Ligue Contre le Racisme et L'Antisemitisme, 169 F. Supp. 2d 1181, 1186 (N.D. Cal. 2001).

[7] *See* Friedrich Kübler, "How Much Freedom for Racist Speech? Transnational Aspects of a Conflict of Human Rights," 27 *Hofstra L. Rev.* 335, 336 (1998).

international covenants[8] as well as individual countries such as Germany[9] – and, in the decade immediately following the war, the United States[10] – excluded hate speech from the scope of constitutionally protected expression. Viewed from the particular perspective of a rejection of the Nazi experience and an attempt to prevent its resurgence, the suppression of hate speech seems both obvious and commendable.

Current encounters with hate speech, however, are for the most part far removed from the Nazi case. Whereas in Nazi Germany hate speech was perpetrated by the government as part of its official ideology and policy, in contemporary democracies, in spite of the increase of hate speech among more mainstream political and social actors in the aftermath of the 9/11 terrorist attacks, it is primarily opponents of the government and, in a majority of cases, members of marginalized groups with scant hope of achieving political power that engage in hate speech. Moreover, in some cases, those punished for engaging in hate speech have been members of groups long victimized by racist policies and rhetoric, prosecuted for uttering race-based invectives against those whom they perceive as their racist oppressors. Thus, for example, it is ironic that the first person convicted under the United Kingdom's Race Relations Law criminalizing hate speech was a black man who uttered a racial epithet against a white policeman.[11]

Like Nazi racist propaganda, some of the straightforward racist invectives heard today are crude and unambiguous. Contemporary hate speech cannot be confined, however, to racist insults. Precisely because of the strong post-Holocaust constraints against raw public expressions of racial hatred, present-day racists often feel compelled to couch their racist message in more subtle ways. For example, anti-Semites may engage in Holocaust denial or minimizing under the guise of weighing in on an ongoing historians' debate. Or they may attack Zionism to blur the boundaries between what might qualify as a genuine debate concerning political ideology and what is pure and simple anti-Semitism. Similarly, American racists have on occasion resorted to what appears to be a scientific debate or invoked certain statistics – such as those indicating that in the United States African Americans commit proportionately more crimes than whites – to promote their prejudices under the guise of formulating political positions informed by scientific fact or theory.

---

[8] *See, e.g.,* International Covenant on Civil and Political Rights, art. 20, ¶2, Mar. 23, 1976, 999 U.N.T.S. 171 ("Any advocacy of national, racial or religious hatred that constitutes incitement to discrimination, hostility or violence shall be prohibited by law.").

[9] For a discussion of the extensive German regulation against hate speech, see Kübler, *supra* note 7, at 340–7.

[10] *See* Beauharnais v. Illinois, 343 U.S. 250 (1952) (upholding the constitutionality of a statute criminalizing group defamation based on race or religion). Although *Beauharnais* has never been formally repudiated by the Supreme Court, it is fundamentally inconsistent with more recent decisions. *See* discussion *infra* Section II.

[11] *See* Anthony Skillen, "Freedom of Speech," in *Contemporary Political Philosophy: Radical Studies* 139, 142 (Keith Graham ed., Cambridge University Press 1982).

Even these few observations suffice to establish that not all contemporary instances of hate speech are alike. Any assessment of whether, how, or how much hate speech ought to be prohibited, therefore, must account for certain key variables, namely *who* and *what* are involved and *where* and *under what circumstances* these cases arise.

The *who* is always plural, for it encompasses not only the speaker who utters a statement that constitutes hate speech, but also the target of that statement and the audience to whom the statement in question is addressed – which may be limited to the target, may include both the target and others, or may be limited to an audience that does not include any member of the target group.[12] Moreover, as already mentioned, not all speakers are alike. This is not only because of group affiliation. Thus, in the context of dominant majority group's hate speech against a vulnerable and discriminated-against minority, the impact of the hate speech in question is likely to differ significantly depending on whether it is uttered by a high government official or an important opposition leader, or whether it is propaganda by a marginalized outsider group with no credibility.[13] Furthermore, even the same speaker may have to be treated differently, or at least may have a different impact, which ought to be considered legally relevant, depending on who the target of his or her hate message is. Assuming, for the sake of argument, that black hate speech against whites in the United States is not the equivalent of white hate speech against blacks, what about black anti-Semitism? Ought it be considered as another (albeit inappropriate) instance of black response to white oppression?[14] Or as an assault against a vulnerable minority? In other words, is black anti-Semitism but one aspect

---

[12] The identity of the audience involved may be relevant for a variety of reasons, including assessing the harm produced by hate speech and devising effective legal means to combat hate speech. For example, demeaning racist propaganda aimed at a nontarget audience may be a necessary step in the creation of a political environment wherein policies of genocide might plausibly be implemented. *See generally* Gordon W. Allport, *The Nature of Prejudice* (Addison-Wesley Publishing Co. 1954). Thus, the German people might never have countenanced the Nazi policy of extermination of the Jews had they not been desensitized through years of vicious anti-Semitic propaganda. *See* Franklyn S. Haiman, *Speech and Law in a Free Society* 87 (University of Chicago Press 1981). Consistent with this, hate speech directed at a nontarget audience might well be much more dangerous than if exclusively addressed to a target-group audience.

From the standpoint of devising workable legal responses, the differences between different speakers and different target-group audiences may also be very important. For example, in the United States where hate groups like the neo-Nazis and the Ku Klux Klan are relatively marginalized and lack major financial means, allowing private tort suits by affected members of the relevant target groups may lead to expensive verdicts with crippling effects on the hate group's ability to function. *See* "Klansmen Sued over Shooting at S.C. Nightclub," *Atlanta J. Const.*, Nov. 1, 1998, at 6A (reporting crippling effect on Ku Klux Klan of a $37.8 million verdict over a church fire).

[13] For example, neo-Nazis in the United States are so marginalized and discredited that virtually no one believes that they pose any realistic danger. In contrast, a statement (better described as anti-Semitic rather than as hate speech) to the effect that the Jews have too much influence in the United States because they control the media – which is in part true – and the banks – which is patently false – uttered by the country's highest military official caused quite an uproar and led to his resignation. *See* Editorial, "Counting the Jews," *Nation*, Oct. 3, 1988, at 257.

[14] Because of prevailing social and economic circumstances, it has often been the case that the whites with whom black ghetto dwellers have the most – often unpleasant – contacts, namely shopkeepers

of a comprehensible resentment harbored by blacks against whites? Or is it but a means for blacks to carve out a common ground with white non-Jews by casting the Jews as the common enemy? And does it matter if the dangers of anti-Semitism prove greater than those of undifferentiated anti-white hatred?

The *what*, or message uttered in the context of hate speech, also matters and may or may not, depending on its form and content, call for sanction or suppression. Obvious hate speech such as that involving crude racist insults or invectives can be characterized as "hate speech in form." In contrast, utterances such as Holocaust denials or other coded messages that do not explicitly convey insults, but are nonetheless designed to convey hatred or contempt, may be referred to as "hate speech in substance." At first glance, it may seem easy to justify banning hate speech in form but not hate speech in substance. Indeed, in the context of the latter, there appear to be potentially daunting line-drawing problems, as the boundary between genuine scholarly, scientific, or political debate and the veiled promotion of racial hatred may not always be easy to draw. Moreover, even hate speech in form may not be used in a demeaning way warranting suppression.[15]

Finally, *where* and *under what circumstances* hate speech is uttered also make a difference in terms of whether or not it should be prohibited. As already mentioned, "where" may make a difference depending on the country, society, or culture involved, which may justify flatly prohibiting all Nazi propaganda in Germany but not in the United States. "Where" may also matter within the same country or society. Thus, hate speech in an intracommunal setting may in some cases be less dangerous than if uttered in an intercommunal setting. Without minimizing the dangers of hate speech, it seems plausible to argue, for example, that hate speech directed against Germans at a Jewish community center comprising many Holocaust survivors, or a virulent antiwhite speech at an all-black social club in the United States, should not be subjected to the same sanctions as the very same utterance in an intercommunal setting, such as an open political rally in a town's central square.[16]

Circumstances also make a difference. For example, even if black hate speech against whites in the United States is deemed as pernicious as white hate speech against blacks, legal consequences arguably ought to differ depending on the circumstances. Thus, for example, black hate speech ought not be penalized – or at

---

and landlords, happen to be Jews. *See* Vince Beiser, "Surviving The Rage in Harlem," *Jerusalem Rep.*, Feb. 8, 1996, at 30.

[15] For example, in the United States, the word "nigger" is an insulting and demeaning word that is used to refer to a person who is black. When uttered by a white person to refer to a black person, it undoubtedly fits the label "hate speech in form." However, as used among blacks, it often is not at all hostile but instead connotes both intracommunal solidarity and implicit condemnation of white racism.

[16] What accounts for their difference is that the oppressed are in a different position than the oppressors. Reaction by the oppressed, even if tinged with hatred, should therefore arguably be somewhat more tolerated than hate messages by members of traditionally oppressor groups.

least not as much as otherwise – if it occurs in the course of a spontaneous reaction to a police shooting of an innocent black victim in a locality with widespread perceptions of racial bias within the police department.

More generally, which of the aforementioned differences ought to figure in the constitutional treatment of hate speech depends on the values sought to be promoted, on the perceived harms involved, and on the importance attributed to these harms. As already noted, the United States' approach to these issues differs markedly from those of other western democracies. Before embarking on a comparison of these contrasting approaches, however, it is necessary to specify two important points concerning the scope of the present inquiry: 1) there is no discussion of the advantages or disadvantages of various approaches to the regulation of hate speech, such as criminal versus civil liability; and 2) given that all the countries that are discussed in this chapter, including the United States, deny protection to hate speech that incites violence – or, to put it in terms of the relevant American jurisprudence, that poses "a clear and present danger"[17] of violence – what follows does not focus on such speech. Instead, the focus is on hate speech that incites racial hatred or hostility but that falls short of incitement to violence. Indeed, the key question is whether hate speech not likely to lead to immediate violence, but capable of producing more subtle and uncertain evils, albeit perhaps equally pernicious, ought to be suppressed or instead fought with more speech.

## II. HATE SPEECH AND THE JURISPRUDENCE OF FREE SPEECH IN THE UNITED STATES

Freedom of speech is not only the most cherished American constitutional right, but also one of America's foremost cultural symbols.[18] Moreover, the prominence of free speech in the United States is due to many different factors, including a strong preference for liberty over equality, commitment to individualism, and a natural-rights tradition derived from Locke, which champions freedom from the state – or negative freedom – over freedom through the state – or positive freedom.[19] In essence, free-speech rights in the United States are conceived as belonging to the individual against the state, and they are enshrined in the First Amendment to the Constitution as a prohibition against government interference, rather than as the imposition of a positive duty on government to guarantee the receipt and transmission of ideas among its citizens.[20]

---

[17]  *See* Schenck v. United States, 249 U.S. 47 (1919).

[18]  *See* Lee C. Bollinger, *The Tolerant Society: Freedom of Speech and Extremist Speech in America* 7 (Oxford University Press 1986).

[19]  For a thorough discussion of the distinction between positive and negative liberty, see Isaiah Berlin, *Four Essays on Liberty* 118–72 (Oxford University Press 1969).

[20]  The First Amendment provides, in relevant part, that "Congress shall make no law . . . abridging the freedom of speech, or of the press." U.S. Const. amend. 1.

Even beyond hate speech, freedom of speech is a much more pervasive constitutional right in the United States than in most other constitutional democracies.[21]
Indeed, Americans have a deep-seated belief in free speech as a virtually unlimited good and a strong fear that an active government in the area of speech will
much more likely result in harm than in good. In spite of this, however, there have
been significant discrepancies between theory and practice throughout the twentieth century, with the consequence that American protection of speech has been
less extensive than official rhetoric or popular belief would lead one to believe. For
example, although political speech has been widely recognized as the most worthy
of protection,[22] for much of the twentieth century, laws aimed at suppressing or criminalizing socialist and communist views were routinely upheld as constitutional.[23]
With respect to communist views, therefore, American protection of political speech
has been more limited than that afforded by most other western democracies.

American theory and practice relating to free speech is ultimately complex and
not always consistent. Accordingly, to better understand the American approach to
hate speech – which has itself changed over time[24] – it must be briefly placed in its
proper historical and theoretical context.

In the broadest terms, one can distinguish four different historical stages in which
the perceived principal function of free speech saw significant changes. On the
other hand, there have also been four principal philosophical justifications of free
speech, which have informed or explained the relevant constitutional jurisprudence.
Moreover, the philosophical justifications do not necessarily correspond to the historical stages, but rather intertwine and overlap with them. Nor do sharp boundaries
separate the four historical stages, which run into each other and in which free
speech fulfills various different functions. The principal marking point between
these various stages is a shift in the *dominant* function of free speech. All this makes
for a complex construct with a large number of possible permutations. Accordingly,
only the broadest outlines of the historical and theoretical context of American
free-speech jurisprudence will be considered in what follows.

Of the four historical stages of free speech, the first three have had definite – if
often only implicit – influences on the Supreme Court's free-speech jurisprudence.
In contrast, the fourth stage, which is much more recent, thus far has had little effect

---

[21] *See, e.g.*, Texas v. Johnson, 491 U.S. 397 (1989) (involving a flag burning at the 1984 Republican
National Convention in Dallas, Texas); Hustler Magazine, Inc. v. Falwell, 485 U.S. 46 (1988) (concerning a crude parody of a church leader); New York Times Co. v. United States, 403 U.S. 713
(1971) (involving the publication of classified diplomatic information susceptible of adversely affecting
sensitive peace negotiations). In each case, the Supreme Court held that the expression involved was
constitutionally protected.

[22] *See, e.g.*, Alexander Meiklejohn, *Free Speech and Its Relation to Self-Government* (Harper & Bros.
1948).

[23] *See, e.g.*, Dennis v. United States, 341 U.S. 494 (1951); Gitlow v. New York, 268 U.S. 652 (1925); Debs
v. United States, 249 U.S. 211 (1919).

[24] *See infra* notes 45–70 and accompanying text.

on the judicial approach to free-speech issues, although it has already made a clear imprint on certain legislators and scholars.[25] The first of these historical stages dates back to the 1776 War of Independence against Britain, and establishes protection of the people against the government as the principal purpose of free speech.[26] Once democracy had become firmly entrenched in the United States, however, the principal threat to free speech came not from the government but from the "tyranny of the majority." Accordingly, in stage two, free speech was meant above all to protect proponents of unpopular views against the wrath of the majority.[27] Stage three, which roughly covers the period between the mid-1950s and the 1980s, corresponds to a period in the United States in which many believed that there had been an end to ideology,[28] resulting in a widespread consensus on essential values.[29] Stage three is thus marked by pervasive conformity, and the principal function of free speech shifts from lifting restraints on *speakers* to ensuring that *listeners* remain open-minded.[30] Finally, beginning in the 1980s with the rapid expansion of feminist theory, critical race theory, and other alternative discourses – all of which attacked mainstream and official speech as inherently oppressive, white-male-dominated discourse – there emerged a strong belief in the pluralization and fragmentation of discourse. Consistent with that belief, the principal role of free speech in stage four becomes the protection of oppressed and marginalized discourses and their proponents against the hegemonic tendencies of the discourses of the powerful.[31]

Of these four stages, stage three affords the greatest justification for toleration of hate speech,[32] whereas stage four provides the strongest case for its suppression – at least to the extent that it targets racial or religious minorities. Stages one and two do not provide clear-cut answers as the perceived evils of hate speech are likely to fluctuate depending on the circumstances. Assuming in stage one that hate speech is not promoted by government, the magnitude of the harms associated with it would depend on the degree of sympathy or revulsion it produces in official circles. In stage two, on the other hand, even if those who engage in hate speech constitute but a very small minority of the population, the danger posed by hate speech would depend on whether political majorities tend to agree with that speech's underlying message,

---

[25] An example of legislation consistent with stage four is the ordinance held unconstitutional in R.A.V. v. City of St. Paul, 505 U.S. 377 (1992). For an example of scholarship informed by a stage-four perspective, see Mari J. Matsuda et al., *Words That Wound: Critical Race Theory, Assaultive Speech, and the First Amendment* (Westview Press 1993); Catherine A. Mackinnon, *Feminism Unmodified: Discourses on Life and Law* (Harvard University Press 1987).

[26] *See* Bollinger, *supra* note 18, at 144.

[27] *Id.*

[28] *See, e.g.,* Daniel Bell, *The End of Ideology: On the Exhaustion of Political Ideas in the Fifties* (The Free Press 1960).

[29] *See* Bollinger, *supra* note 18, at 143–4.

[30] *Id.*

[31] *See, e.g.,* Matsuda et al., *supra* note 25; Mackinnon, *supra* note 25.

[32] For an extended argument in favor of such toleration from a stage-three perspective, *see* Bollinger, *supra* note 18.

or whether they are seriously disturbed by it and firmly committed to combating the views it seeks to convey.

Assessment of how hate speech might fare under the four different historical stages is made much more difficult if the four main philosophical justifications for free speech in the United States are taken into proper account: the justification from democracy; the justification from social contract; the justification from the pursuit of the truth; and the justification from individual autonomy.[33] As we shall see, each of these justifications ascribes a different scope of legitimacy to free speech. Moreover, even different versions of the same justification lead to shifts in the boundaries between speech that requires protection and speech that may be constitutionally restricted, and such shifts are particularly important in the context of hate speech.

The justification from democracy is premised on the conviction that freedom of speech serves an indispensable function in the process of democratic self-government.[34] Without the freedom to convey and receive ideas, citizens cannot successfully carry out the task of democratic self-government. Accordingly, political speech needs to be protected, but not necessarily all political speech.[35] If the paramount objective is the preservation and promotion of democracy, then antidemocratic speech in general, and hate and political extremist speech in particular, would in all likelihood serve no useful purpose, and would therefore not warrant protection.[36]

The justification from social contract theory is in many ways similar to that from democracy, but the two do not necessarily call for protection of the same speech. Unlike the other three justifications, that from social contract theory is essentially procedural. Its premise is that political institutions must be justifiable in terms of an actual or hypothetical agreement among all members of the relevant society,[37] and significant changes in those institutions must be made only through such agreements. The necessary "consent of the governed" is meaningful, however, only if fully informed; rational social contractors would not consent to a regime that made its own decisions about what information they receive. Just as with justification from democracy, then, here too there is a need for free exchange and discussion of ideas. Unlike the justification from democracy, however, the social contract justification

---

[33] For an extensive discussion of philosophical justifications of free speech that both overlaps with, and differs from, the present discussion, see Frederick Schauer, *Free Speech: A Philosophical Enquiry* (Cambridge University Press 1982).

[34] The principal exponent of this view was Alexander Meiklejohn. *See* Meiklejohn, *supra* note 22.

[35] Meiklejohn himself had a broad view of political speech and advocated extensive protection of it.

[36] It is, of course, possible to maintain that toleration of extremist antidemocratic speech would tend to invigorate the proponents of democracy and hence ultimately strengthen rather than weaken democracy. Be that as it may, toleration of antidemocratic views is not logically required for purposes of advancing self-governing democracy. For example, advocacy of violent overthrow of democratically elected government and establishment of a dictatorship need not be protected to ensure vigorous debate on all plausible alternatives consistent with democracy.

[37] *See, e.g.*, John Rawls, *A Theory of Justice* 11–12 (Belknap Press of Harvard University Press 1971).

cannot permit *ex ante* exclusion of any views that, even though incompatible with democracy, might be relevant to a social contractor's decision to embrace the polity's fundamental institutions or to agree to any particular form of political organization. Accordingly, the justification from social contract seems to require some tolerance of hate speech, if not in form then at least in substance.

The justification from the pursuit of the truth originates in the utilitarian philosophy of John Stuart Mill. According to Mill, the discovery of truth is an incremental empirical process that relies on trial and error and requires uninhibited discussion.[38] Mill's justification for very broad freedom of expression was imported into American constitutional jurisprudence by Justice Oliver Wendell Holmes and became known as the justification based on the free marketplace of ideas.[39] This justification, which has been dominant in the United States ever since,[40] is premised on the firm belief that truth is more likely to prevail through open discussion (even if such discussion temporarily unwittingly promotes falsehoods) than through any other means bent on eradicating falsehoods outright.

Mill's strong endorsement of free speech was rooted in his optimistic belief in social progress. According to his view, truth would always ultimately best falsehood so long as discussion remained possible, and hence even potentially harmful speech should be tolerated as its potential evils could best be minimized through open debate. Accordingly, Mill advocated protection of all speech so long as it falls short of incitement to violence.

Although Holmes's *justification* of free expression is very similar to Mill's, his *reasons* for embracing the free marketplace of ideas differ. Unlike Mill, Holmes was driven by skepticism and pessimism and expressed grave doubts about the possibility of truth. Because of this, Holmes justified his free-marketplace approach on pragmatic grounds. Given that most strongly held views eventually prove false, any limitation on speech is most likely grounded in false ideas. Accordingly, Holmes was convinced that a free marketplace of ideas was likely to reduce harm in two distinct ways: it would lower the possibility that expression would be needlessly suppressed based on falsehoods; and it would encourage most people who tend stubbornly to hold on to harmful or worthless ideas to develop a healthy measure of self-doubt.[41]

Like Mill, Holmes did not endorse unlimited freedom of speech. For Holmes, speech should be protected unless it poses a "clear and present danger" to people, such as falsely shouting "fire" in a crowded theater and thereby causing panic.[42] Both Mill's and Holmes's justification from the pursuit of truth justify protection

---

[38] *See* John Stuart Mill, *On Liberty and Other Essays* (John Gray ed., Oxford University Press 1998) (1859).

[39] *See* Abrams v. United States, 250 U.S. 616, 630 (1919) (Holmes, J., dissenting).

[40] *See* Schauer, *supra* note 33, at 15–16.

[41] *See* Abrams, 250 U.S. at 630.

[42] *See* Schenck v. United States, 249 U.S. 47 (1919).

of hate speech that does not amount to incitement to violence. Indeed speech amounting to an "incitement to violence" is but one instance of speech that poses a "clear and present danger." In the end, whether speech incites to violence or creates another type of clear and present danger, it does not deserve protection – under the justification from the pursuit of truth – because it is much more likely to lead to harmful action than to more speech, and hence it undermines the functioning of the marketplace of ideas.

In the end, Mill and Holmes represent two sides of the same coin. Mill over-estimates the potential of rational discussion whereas Holmes underestimates the potential for serious harm of certain types of speech that fall short of the clear and present danger test. The justification from the pursuit of truth is, at its bottom, prag-matic. As we shall see later in the chapter, however, because both the Millian and Holmesian pragmatic reasons for the toleration of hate speech are based on dubious factual claims, they may in the end undermine rather than bolster any pragmatic justification of tolerance of hate speech that falls short of incitement to violence.[43]

Unlike the three preceding justifications, which are collective in nature, the fourth justification for free speech – that from autonomy – is primarily individual-regarding. Democracy, social peace and harmony through the social contract, and pursuit of the truth are collective goods designed to benefit society as a whole. In contrast, individual autonomy and well-being through self-expression are presumably always of benefit to the individual concerned, without in many cases necessarily producing any further societal good.

The justification from autonomy is based on the conviction that individual auton-omy and respect require protection of virtually unconstrained self-expression.[44] Accordingly, all kinds of utterances arguably linked to an individual's felt need for self-expression ought to be afforded constitutional protection. Consistent with this, the justification from autonomy clearly affords the broadest scope of protection for all types of speech.

As originally conceived, the justification from autonomy seemed exclusively con-cerned with the self-expression needs of speakers. Given that hate speech plausibly could contribute to the fulfillment of the self-expression needs of its proponents, it would seem to qualify for protection under the justification from autonomy.

Under a less individualistic – or at least less atomistic – conception of autonomy and self-respect, however, focusing exclusively on the standpoint of the speaker would seem insufficient. Indeed, if autonomy and self-respect are considered from the standpoint of listeners, then hate speech may well loom as prone to undermining

---

[43] For an extended critique of the use of pragmatism to justify free-speech protection of hate speech that does not pose a clear and present danger of violence, see Michel Rosenfeld, *Just Interpretations: Law Between Ethics and Politics* 150–96 (University of California Press 1998).

[44] *See* Ronald Dworkin, *Taking Rights Seriously* (Harvard University Press 1977); David A. J. Richards, "Free Speech and Obscenity Law: Toward a Moral Theory of the First Amendment," 123 *U. Pa. L. Rev.* 45 (1975).

the autonomy and self-respect of those whom it targets. This last observation becomes that much more urgent under a stage-four conception of the nature and scope of legitimate regulation of speech. Indeed, if the main threat of unconstrained speech is the hegemony of dominant discourses at the expense of the discourses of oppressed minorities, then self-expression of the powerful threatens the autonomy of those whose voices are being drowned, and hate speech against the latter can only exacerbate their humiliation and the denial of their dignity and autonomy.

As these last observations indicate, the possible intersections between the four historical stages and the four philosophical justifications are multiple and complex. Current American constitutional jurisprudence concerning hate speech, however, relies by and large on the justification from the pursuit of truth and tends to espouse implicitly a stage-three – or a combination of stage two and stage three – vision on the proper role of speech.

Judicial treatment of hate speech in the United States is of relatively recent vintage. Indeed, nearly sixty years ago, in *Beauharnais v. Illinois*,[45] the Supreme Court upheld a conviction for hate speech emphasizing that such speech amounted to group defamation, and reasoning that such defamation was in all relevant respects analogous to individual defamation, which had traditionally been excluded from free-speech protection. Beauharnais, a white supremacist, had distributed a leaflet accusing blacks of, among other things, rape, robbery, and other violent crimes. Although Beauharnais had urged whites to unite and protect themselves against the evils he attributed to blacks, he had not been found to have posed a "clear and present danger" of violence.

*Beauharnais* has never been explicitly repudiated, but it has been thoroughly undermined by subsequent decisions. Already the dissenting opinions in *Beauharnais* attacked the Court's majority's rationale by stressing that both the libel and the "fighting words"[46] exceptions to free speech involved utterances addressed to individuals, and were hence unlikely to have any significant impact on public debate. In contrast, group libel was a public, not private, matter and its prohibition would inhibit public debate.

The current constitutional standard, which draws the line at incitement to violence, was established in the 1969 *Brandenburg v. Ohio*[47] decision. *Brandenburg* involved a leader and several members of the Ku Klux Klan who in a rally staged for television (in front of only a few reporters) made several derogatory remarks mainly against blacks, but also some against Jews. In addition, while not threatening any imminent or direct violence, the speakers suggested that blacks should return to Africa and Jews to Israel, and announced that they would petition the government

---

[45] 343 U.S. 250 (1952).
[46] In Chaplinsky v. New Hampshire, 315 U.S. 568, 572 (1942), the Supreme Court held that insults addressed to an individual that were so offensive as to readily prompt a violent reaction did not fall within the ambit of constitutionally protected speech.
[47] 395 U.S. 444 (1969).

to act, but that if it refused they would have no other recourse than to take matters in their own hands. Selected portions of this rally were later broadcast on local and national television.

The Supreme Court in a unanimous decision set aside Brandenburg's criminal conviction, concluding that the Klan may have *advocated* violence but had not *incited* it. Significantly, in drawing the line between incitement and advocacy, the Court applied to hate speech a standard it had recently established to deal with communist speech involving advocacy of the forcible overthrow of the government.[48] In so doing, the Court's decision raises a question that remains beyond the scope of the present undertaking, namely whether hate speech ought to be equated with (politically) extremist speech.

If one case has come to symbolize the contemporary political and constitutional response to hate speech in the United States, it is the *Skokie* case from the late 1970s. This case arose out of a proposed march by neo-Nazis in full SS uniform with swastikas through Skokie, a suburb of Chicago with a large Jewish population, including thousands of Holocaust survivors. The local municipal authorities took measures – including enacting new legislation – designed to prevent the march, but both state and federal courts eventually invalidated the measures as violating the neo-Nazis' free-speech rights.[49]

The neo-Nazis made it clear that they chose Skokie for the march precisely to upset Jews through a direct confrontation with their message. The constitutional battle focused on whether the proposed march in Skokie would amount to an "incitement to violence." Based on the testimony of Holocaust survivors residing in Skokie, who asserted that exposure to the swastika might provoke them to violence, a lower state court determined that such a march could be prohibited.[50]

That appellate court reversed, finding that the proposed march had not met the "incitement to violence" requirement.[51] While acknowledging the intensity of the likely feelings of Holocaust survivors, the court held that they were not a sufficient ground on which to prohibit the proposed march.[52] The court did not specify what standard would have to be met to justify banning the display of the swastika. What if a Jew who was not a Holocaust survivor had testified that a neo-Nazi march with a swastika would have moved him to violence? What if a gentile had thus testified?

These uncertainties illustrate some of the difficulties associated with the "incitement to violence" standard, even if one assumes that it is the right standard. Be that as it may, the Skokie controversy ultimately fizzled. After their legal victories, the

---

[48] *See* Yates v. United States, 354 U.S. 298 (1957) (holding conviction for mere advocacy unconstitutional).
[49] *See* Smith v. Collin, 436 U.S. 953 (1978); Nat'l Socialist Party of Am. v. Vill. of Skokie, 432 U.S. 43 (1977).
[50] Vill. of Skokie v. Nat'l Socialist Party of Am., 373 N.E.2d. 21 (Ill. 1978).
[51] *Id.* at 24.
[52] *See id.*

neo-Nazis decided not to march in Skokie. Instead, they marched in Chicago, far from any Jewish neighborhood.[53] Because of their very marginality, and because they had no sway over the larger nontarget audience in the United States, the actual march by the neo-Nazis did much more to showcase their isolation and impotence than to advance their cause. Under those circumstances, allowing them to express their hate message probably contributed more to discrediting them than would have a judicial prohibition against their march.

Because of contextual factors prevalent in the United States during the late 1970s, the result in the *Skokie* case may appear to be pragmatically justified and to fit within a stage-three conception of free speech.[54] Indeed, inasmuch as the neo-Nazi message had no appeal, and reminded its listeners of past horrors as well as of the fact that the United States had to go to war against Hitler's Germany, it could conceivably be analogized to a vaccine against total complacency. Moreover, by the very falsehood of its ring, the utterance of the neo-Nazi message could well be interpreted as reinforcing the belief in a need for virtually unlimited free speech associated with the justification from the pursuit of the truth.[55]

Even if the *Skokie* case was rightly decided, the constitutional jurisprudence it helped shape has proved quite troubling when applied under less favorable circumstances. This conclusion becomes manifest from a consideration of two cases involving cross burning. The first of these, *R.A.V. v. City of St. Paul*,[56] concerned the burning of a cross inside the fenced yard of a black family by young white extremists.[57] The latter were convicted under a local criminal ordinance, which provided in relevant part that:

> Whoever places on public or private property a symbol, object, . . . but not limited to, a burning cross or Nazi swastika, which one knows . . . arouses anger, alarm or resentment in others on the basis of race, color, creed, religion or gender commits disorderly conduct. . . . [58]

In a unanimous decision, the U.S. Supreme Court reversed the conviction, holding the ordinance unconstitutional for two principal reasons. First, it targeted speech that would not amount to an incitement to violence. Second, even on the

---

53 *See* Smith v. Collin, 439 U.S. 916 (1978) (Blackmun, J., dissenting from denial of certiorori).

54 For an extended argument in support of the judicial handling of the *Skokie* case within the scope of a stage three conception, *see* Bollinger, *supra* note 18.

55 It is significant, consistent with these observations, that Jews were on both sides of the Skokie controversy, as civil rights organizations defended the Neo-Nazis' right to speak. For a further analysis of this fact, see Michel Rosenfeld, "Extremist Speech and the Paradox of Tolerance," 100 *Harv. L. Rev.* 1457, 1487 (1987) (book review).

56 505 U.S. 377 (1992).

57 The burning of a cross, long a practice of white supremacists, such as those belonging to the Ku Klux Klan, has been a symbol of virulent racism much like the display of the swastika has been associated with virulent anti-Semitism.

58 St. Paul Bias-Motivated Crime Ordinance (1990), *quoted in R.A.V.*, 505 U.S. at 380.

assumption that a burning cross qualified as unprotected "fighting words," by criminalizing some incitements but not others, the ordinance was based on impermissible viewpoint discrimination: Whereas the ordinance criminalized expression likely to incite violence on the basis of race or religion, it did not criminalize similar expression equally likely to incite violence on other bases, such as homosexuality.

Because of the pervasive nature of racism and the long history of oppression and violence against blacks in the United States, and given the frightening associations evoked by burning crosses, the situation in *R.A.V.* cannot be equated with that involved in the *Skokie* case. Of course, swastikas tend to inspire as much fear and anger in Jews as burning crosses do in blacks. The major difference between the *Skokie* case and *R.A.V.*, however, has to do not with the perniciousness of the respective symbols involved, but with the different factual and emotional impact of these symbols on the target and nontarget audiences before whom they were meant to be displayed.

Significantly, the Holocaust survivors who testified that the proposed neo-Nazi march in Skokie would lead them to violence emphasized that their reaction would be triggered by memories of the past. Moreover, although there was some anti-Semitism in the United States in the 1970s, the small, fringe neo-Nazis were so discredited that it seemed most unlikely that they would in any way, directly or indirectly, advance the cause of anti-Semitism.[59] In contrast, cross burning produced fears not only concerning the past but also the present and the future, and not based on events that had taken place across an ocean, but on events that had marked the sad history of race relations in the United States from the founding of the republic. Indeed, the cross burning in *R.A.V.* occurred in a racially mixed neighborhood, in an era in which several homes of black persons who had moved into white neighborhoods had been burned in efforts to dissuade members of a growing black middle class from moving into white neighborhoods.[60]

In sum, even though both the proposed march in *Skokie* and the cross burning in *R.A.V.* were meant to incite hatred on the basis of religion and race, respectively, their effects were quite different. The events surrounding *Skokie* mainly produced contempt for the marchers and a reminder that there was little danger of an embrace of Nazism in the United States. *R.A.V.*, on the other hand, played on pervasive, and to a significant degree justified, fears concerning race relations in America. Undoubtedly, cross burning itself is rejected as repugnant by the vast majority of

---

[59] This last observation may no longer hold true in view of certain more recent events, which have increased the profile of white supremacist extremists. For example, several children were shot at a Jewish day-care center in Los Angeles. *See* Terry McDermott, "Panic Pierces Illusion of Safety," *L.A. Times*, Aug. 11, 1999, at A1. In Chicago, a white supremacist went on a shooting spree that included the firing of many shots that did not cause any injuries near a synagogue. *See* "Suspect in Racial Shootings Had a Troubled Past," *Chron. of Higher Educ.*, July 16, 1999, at A8. During that same spree, however, that individual killed both a black and Asian person. *Id.*

[60] *See, e.g.,* "Second Racial Attack in Two Weeks," UPI, Nov. 20, 1984, Tuesday, AM Cycle; [untitled], UPI, Feb. 18, 1997, LEXIS, Nexis, Library, UPI File.

Americans. The underlying racism associated with it and the message that blacks should remain in their own segregated neighborhoods, however, unfortunately still have adherents among a non-negligible portion of whites in America.

The ultimate difference between the impact of the hate speech in *Skokie* and that in *R.A.V.* relates to the emotional reactions of the respective target and nontarget audiences involved. In *Skokie*, the vast majority of Jews felt no genuine present or future threat whereas the nontarget gentile audience felt mainly contempt and hostility toward the Nazi hate message. In *R.A.V.*, however, the target audience definitely experienced anger, fear, and concern, whereas the nontarget audience was split along a spectrum spanning from revulsion to mixed emotions to downright sympathy for the substance of the hate message if not for its form.

This latter conclusion is buttressed by a consideration of *Virginia v. Black*, decided by a divided U.S. Supreme Court in 2003,[61] which involved two cross-burning incidents, one at a Ku Klux Klan rally, the other by whites not affiliated with the Klan in the yard of an African-American neighbor. This second cross-burning case clearly illustrates that the fear, panic, and terror experienced by African Americans confronted with cross burnings is of an entirely different order of magnitude than the anger and revulsion experienced by American Holocaust survivors upon exposure to the Nazi military uniform and swastika worn by homegrown neo-Nazis. Furthermore, whereas *Black* formally adhered to the U.S. doctrinal approach, it also underscores the arbitrariness of drawing a bright line between incitement to hatred and incitement to violence in a context as marked by violence, injustice, and oppression as that of the historical relationship between whites and blacks in the United States.

The Virginia statute at stake in *Black* criminalized the burning of a cross with the intent to intimidate, and specified that the very act of burning amounted to *prima facie* intent to intimidate.[62] The Court held that criminalizing cross burning with an intent to intimidate was constitutional, but that drawing a *prima facie* inference that burning a cross evinced an intent to intimidate was unconstitutional. As an intent to intimidate need not entail an intent to cause violence – one may intimidate through threats of humiliation, exposure to ridicule, social ostracism, job loss, and so forth – it may seem, at first, that the Court in *Black* had deviated from its incitement to violence standard. This is dispelled, however, by Justice O'Connor who, in writing for the Court, noted that throughout the history of the Ku Klux Klan, "cross-burnings have been used to communicate . . . threats of violence. . . ."[63] Indeed, as cross burnings have frequently been followed by beatings, lynchings, shootings, and killings of African Americans, they either amount to incitements to violence or they create a reasonable fear in those who they target of becoming victims of impending violence.

---

[61] 538 U.S. 343 (2003).
[62] *Id.* at 348.
[63] *Id.* at 354.

Because of the particular historical context, the Ku Klux Klan's incitement to hatred seems inextricably intertwined with incitement to violence. But even in the case of the Klan, incitement to hatred cannot be simply equated with, or treated automatically as the cause of, incitement to violence. Significantly, the Klan rally at stake in *Black* involved a reunion among hooded members of the group for a ritualistic cross burning accompanied by the group's customary vicious rhetoric of extreme racial hatred. The rally in question was not meant for outsiders, being held on private property with the full accord of the owner, and only running afoul of the authorities because witnessed by a passing sheriff on a nearby road.[64] Moreover, this preaching of hatred among the converted, centered on a cross burning, amounted to communication of what Justice O'Connor characterized as "potent symbols of shared group identity and ideology."[65] As such, the particular cross burning at issue was adjudged by the Court to amount to constitutionally protected speech.

Concerning the cross burning by whites not members of the Klan in the yard of an African-American neighbor, on the other hand, the surrounding circumstances suggest an intent to intimidate,[66] as well as the use of means designed to convey a message of racial hatred.[67] It is by no means clear, however, that either the cross burners or their intended target had imminent violence in mind. Just as likely, consistent with the circumstances of the case, intimidation was meant to deter further complaints by the target to the police similar to a previous one regarding the shooting of firearms in the cross burner's own yard,[68] or was intended to prompt the targeted victim to leave the neighborhood to which he had moved recently,[69] based on race-based hostility perpetrated by his neighbors.

Whereas the confluence of incitement to hatred and incitement to violence stressed by the Court seems highly artificial in the context of *Black*, the continuum between the two is vividly illustrated in that case. Accordingly, in contexts in which such continuum is not trivial, in which violence follows often enough, but by no means always, messages of hatred, and in which the time span between the communication of hatred and the triggering of violence can often develop over an extended period of time, it would seem that the incitement-to-violence standard would fall short for purposes of achieving the aims entrusted to it by its proponents.

---

[64] *Id.* at 348.

[65] *Id.* at 356.

[66] Whereas the U.S. Supreme Court held that the *prima facie* inference of intent to intimidate involved in the trial of both cross burnings was unconstitutional, the relevant facts as recounted by the Court nevertheless seem consistent with an intent to intimidate, *see id.* at 350–3, and will be treated as such for the purpose of the present analysis.

[67] It is highly relevant in this respect that the neighbor of the targeted victim who was involved in the cross burning on the latter's yard had previously shot firearms in his own adjacent yard, thus disturbing, if not intimidating, his would-be victim. *See id.* at 350. Had the cross burner chosen instead to shoot a firearm to frighten his targeted neighbor, that might have been as intimidating as cross burning, but it would have not necessarily involved any communication of racial hatred.

[68] *See id.* at 350.

[69] *Id.*

By the same token, the Court's conclusion that the Klan's cross-burning rally in *Black* amounted to a constitutionally protected sharing of ideology also looms as shortsighted. Assuming the continuum described earlier, even preaching exclusively among the converted – including advocating violence as one speaker declared that "he would love to take a [gun] and just randomly shoot the blacks"[70] – seems closely woven together with the real possibility of subsequent intimidation and violence. As Klan members are predisposed by their ideology to contemplate perpetrating violence motivated by racial hatred, the ritualistic convening involving cross burning seem particularly apt to whip up the emotions, to exacerbate the hatred, and to dispel any lingering inhibitions to turn the shared hatred into violence. Again, the turn to violence may not be immediate, but the history of the Klan as outlined in Justice O'Connor's opinion in *Black* provides ample evidence of a multifaceted yet closely integrated cycle involving rallying the troops, intimidating the targets, and perpetrating various forms of violence against the latter. Finally, the Klan rally in *Black* appears to have only included those already converted to the cause. But what if it had also been intended for a nontarget audience of whites? Should that have been deemed a constitutionally protected attempt to spread ideology? Or, given the broader context carved out by the Klan's history, an effort to recruit more soldiers for the Klan's campaign of hatred and violence?

## III. THE TREATMENT OF HATE SPEECH IN THE CONSTITUTIONAL JURISPRUDENCE OF OTHER WESTERN DEMOCRACIES

Whereas free speech in the United States is shaped above all by individualism and libertarianism, collective concerns and other values such as honor and dignity lie at the heart of the conceptions of free speech that originate in international covenants and in the constitutional jurisprudence of other western democracies. Thus, for example, Canadian constitutional jurisprudence is more concerned with multiculturalism and group-regarding equality.[71] For its part, the German constitution sets the inviolability of human dignity as its paramount value[72] and specifically limits freedom of expression to the extent necessary to protect the young and the right to personal honor.[73]

These differences have had a profound impact on the treatment of hate speech. To better appreciate this, I briefly focus on salient developments in three countries: Canada, the United Kingdom, and Germany. In addition, I briefly consider the

---

[70] *Id.* at 349.
[71] *See* Kathleen Mahoney, "The Canadian Constitutional Approach to Freedom of Expression in Hate Propaganda and Pornography," 55 *Law & Contemp. Probs.* 77 (1992).
[72] Grundgesetz [GG] art. 1 (F.R.G.), *translated in The Constitution of the Federal Republic of Germany: Essays on the Basic Rights and Principles of the Basic Law With a Translation of the Basic Law* 227 (Ulrich Karpen ed., Nomos 1988).
[73] *Id.* art. 5(2).

paradoxical case of Hungary, a country that in context and culture seems much closer to Germany, but that has nonetheless developed a hate-speech jurisprudence much like that of the United States.

## A. *Canada*

It is particularly interesting to start with the contrast between the United States and Canada, neighboring countries that both were once British colonies and now are advanced industrialized democracies with large immigrant populations with roots in a vast array of countries and cultures. Moreover, although Canada has produced a constitutional jurisprudence that is clearly distinct from that of the United States, the Canadian Supreme Court has displayed great familiarity with American jurisprudence.[74]

Although both the United States and Canada are multiethnic and multicultural polities, the United States has embraced an assimilationist ideal symbolized by the metaphor of the "melting pot," whereas Canada has placed greater emphasis on cultural diversity and has promoted the ideal of an "ethnic mosaic."[75] Consistent with this difference, the Canadian Supreme Court has explicitly refused to follow the American approach to hate speech. In a closely divided decision, the Canadian Court upheld the criminal conviction of a high school teacher who had communicated anti-Semitic propaganda to his pupils in the leading case of *Regina v. Keegstra*.[76]

Keegstra told his pupils that Jews were "treacherous," "subversive," "sadistic," "money loving," "power hungry," and "child killers." He went on to say that the Jews "created the Holocaust to gain sympathy." He concluded that Jews were inherently evil and expected his students to reproduce his teachings on their exams to avoid bad grades.[77] The criminal statute under which Keegstra had been convicted prohibited the willful promotion of hatred against a group identifiable on the basis of color, race, religion, or ethnic origin.[78] The statute in question made no reference to incitement to violence, nor was there any evidence that Keegstra had any intent to lead his pupils to violence.

In examining the constitutionality of Keegstra's conviction, the Canadian Supreme Court referred to the following concerns as providing support for freedom of expression under the Canadian Charter:

(1) seeking and attaining truth is an inherently good activity; (2) participation in social and political decision-making is to be fostered and encouraged; and (3)

---

[74] One example is the thorough discussion of American decisions and rejection of the American approach in the majority opinion in Canada's leading hate speech case, Regina v. Keegstra, [1990] 3 S.C.R. 697.
[75] *See* Will Kymlicka, *Multicultural Citizenship: A Liberal Theory of Minority Rights* 14 (Oxford University Press 1995).
[76] [1990] 3 S.C.R. 687.
[77] *See id.* at 714.
[78] *See id.* at 713.

diversity in forms of individual self-fulfillment and human flourishing ought to be cultivated in a tolerant and welcoming environment for the sake of both those who convey a meaning and those to whom meaning is conveyed.[79]

Thus, the Canadian protection of freedom of expression, like the American one, relies on the justifications from democracy, from the pursuit of truth, and from autonomy. The Canadian conception of autonomy, however, is less individualistic than its American counterpart, as it seemingly places equal emphasis on the autonomy of listeners and speakers.

In spite of these affinities, the Canadian Supreme Court refused to follow the American lead and draw the line at incitement to violence. Stressing the Canadian Constitution's commitment to multicultural diversity, group identity, human dignity, and equality,[80] the Court adopted a nuanced approach designed to harmonize these values with freedom of expression. Based on this approach, the Court concluded that hate propaganda such as that promoted by Keegstra did not warrant protection as it did more to undermine mutual respect among diverse racial, religious, and cultural groups in Canada than to promote any genuine expression needs or values.

In reaching its conclusion, the Canadian Court considered the likely impact of hate propaganda on both the target-group and on nontarget-group audiences. Members of the target group are likely to be degraded and humiliated, to experience injuries to their sense of self-worth and acceptance in the larger society, and may as a consequence avoid contact with members of other groups within the polity.[81] Those who are not members of the target group, or society at large, on the other hand, may become gradually desensitized and may in the long run become accepting of messages of racial or religious inferiority.[82]

Not only does the Canadian approach to hate speech focus on gradual long-term effects likely to pose serious threats to social cohesion rather than merely on immediate threats to violence, but it also departs from its American counterpart in its assessment of the likely effects of speech. Contrary to the American assumption that truth will ultimately prevail, or that speech alone may not lead to truth but is unlikely to produce serious harm, the Canadian Supreme Court is mindful that hate propaganda can lead to great harm by bypassing reason and playing on the emotions. In support of this, the Court cited approvingly the following observations contained in a study conducted by a committee of the Canadian Parliament:

> The successes of modern advertising, the triumphs of impudent propaganda such as Hitler's, have qualified sharply our belief in the rationality of man. We know that under strain and pressure in times of irritation and frustration, the individual is

---

[79] *Id.* at 728.
[80] *See id.* at 736.
[81] *See id.* at 746.
[82] *See id.* at 747.

swayed and even swept away by hysterical, emotional appeals. We act irresponsibly if we ignore the way in which emotion can drive reason from the field.[83]

In short, the Canadian treatment of hate speech differs from its American counterpart in two principal respects. First, it is grounded in somewhat different normative priorities; second, the two countries differ in their practical assessments of the consequences of tolerating hate speech. Under the American view, there seems to be a greater likelihood of harm from suppression of hate speech that falls short of incitement to violence than from its toleration. From a Canadian perspective, on the other hand, dissemination of hate propaganda seems more dangerous than its suppression as it is seen as likely to produce enduring injuries to self-worth and to undermine social cohesion in the long run.[84]

## B. *The United Kingdom*

Unlike the United States and Canada, the United Kingdom does not have a written constitution. Nevertheless, it recognizes a right to freedom of expression through its adherence to international covenants, such as the European Convention on Human Rights, and through commitment to constitutional values inherent in its rule of law tradition.[85] Moreover, the United Kingdom has criminalized hate speech going back as far as the seventeenth century. The focus of British regulation of free speech has shifted over the years, starting with concern for reinforcing the security of the government, continuing with preoccupation with incitement to racial hatred among nontarget audiences, and culminating with the aim of protecting targets against racially motivated harassment. As we shall see, the results of British regulation have been mixed, with significant success against Fascists and Nazis, but with much less success in attempts to defuse racial animosity between whites and nonwhites.

The seventeenth-century offense of seditious libel punished the utterance or publication of statements with "an intention to bring into hatred or contempt, or to excite disaffection against the person of Her Majesty . . . or to promote feelings of ill-will and hostility between different classes . . . [her] subjects."[86] To the extent that seditious libel allows for punishment of political criticism of the government,

---

[83] *Id.*

[84] The Canadian Supreme Court reaffirmed the approach to hate speech developed in *Keegstra* in Regina v. Krymowski, [2005] 1 S.C.R. 101.

[85] *See* European Convention on Human Rights and Fundamental Freedoms [ECHR], Nov. 4, 1950, art. 10, 213 U.N.T.S. 221; Regina v. Sec'y of State for the Home Dep't, *ex parte* Brind, 1 A.C. 696 (1991) (holding that freedom of expression is considered a basic right under both written and unwritten constitutions). Furthermore, through adoption of the Human Rights Act of 1998, which became effective in October 2000, the United Kingdom has incorporated ECHR Article 10 into domestic law, thus making it directly applicable before British courts. *See* Thomas Morton, "Free Speech v. Racial Aggravation," 149 *New L.J.* 1198 (1999).

[86] Anthony Lester and Geoffrey Bindman, *Race and Law in Great Britain* 345 (Harvard University Press 1972).

it contravenes a core function of modern freedom-of-expression rights. Although seditious libel was primarily used to punish those perceived to pose a threat to the monarchy, occasionally, it was used in the context of what today is called "hate speech."[87] Thus, in *Regina v. Osborne*,[88] the publishers of a pamphlet that asserted that certain Jews had killed a woman and her child because the latter's father was a Christian were convicted of seditious libel. As a consequence of distribution of the pamphlet, some Jews were beaten and threatened with death.[89] As this case involved direct incitement to violence and a clear threat to the maintenance of public order, it may be best viewed as vindicating government dominance and control rather than as protecting the Jews from group defamation.

Because seditious libel can be used to frustrate criticism of government, it can pose a threat to the kind of vigorous debate that is indispensable in a working democracy. In the early twentieth century, seditious libel became rather ineffective as convictions could only be obtained upon proof of direct incitement to violence or breach of public order.[90] In 1936, Parliament adopted *The Public Order Act*.[91] This legislation, which proved useful in combating the rise of British fascism prior to and during World War II, relaxed the seditious libel standards in two critical respects: first, it allowed for punishment of speech "likely" to lead to violence even if it did not actually result in violence; second, it allowed for punishment of mere intent to provoke violence.[92]

After World War II, the United Kingdom enacted further laws against hate propaganda, consistent with its obligations under international covenants.[93] Thus, in 1965, the British Parliament enacted Section 6 of the Race Relations Act (RRA 1965), which made it a crime to utter in public or to publish words "which are threatening, abusive or insulting," and which are intended to incite hatred on the basis of race, color, or national origin.[94]

The RRA 1965 focuses on incitement to hatred rather than on incitement to violence, but it reintroduces proof of intent as a prerequisite to conviction. This makes prosecution more difficult, as evinced by the acquittal in the 1968 *Southern News* case.[95] The case involved a publication of the Racial Preservation Society, which advocated the "return of people of other races from this overcrowded island to their own countries." At trial, the publishers asserted that their paper addressed important

---

[87] *Id.*

[88] 2 Swanst. 503n (1732).

[89] *See* Lester and Bindman, *supra* note 86, at 345.

[90] *Id.* at 347.

[91] Public Order Act, 1936, 1 Geo. 6, c. 6 (Eng.).

[92] *See* Nathan Courtney, "British and U.S. Hate Speech Legislation: A Comparison," 19 *Brook. J. Int'l L.* 727, 731 (1993).

[93] *Id.* at 733.

[94] Race Relations Act, 1965, c. 73, § 6 (1) (Eng.).

[95] This is an unreported case discussed in the London *Times. See* "Race Act Not a Curb," *The Times* (London), Mar. 28, 1968, at 2.

social issues and that it did not attempt to incite hatred. Because of the prosecution's failure to establish the requisite intent, the net result of *Southern News* was the dissemination of its racist views in the mainstream press, and a judicial determination that its message was a legally protected expression of a political position rather than illegal promotion of hate speech.

The problem posed by *Southern News* was remedied by removal of the intent requirement in the Race Relations Act of 1976 (RRA 1976).[96] Moreover, the RRA 1965 did lead to convictions, but a number of these were obtained against leaders of the Black Liberation Movement in the late 1960s, raising disturbing questions, if not about the law itself, at least about its enforcement. For example, in *Regina v. Malik*,[97] the black defendant was convicted and sentenced to a year in prison for having asserted that whites are "vicious and nasty people" and for stating, *inter alia*,

> I saw in this country in 1952 white savages kicking black women. If you ever see a white man lay hands on a black woman, kill him immediately. If you love our brothers and sisters you will be willing to die for them.[98]

The defendant admitted that his speech was offensive to whites but argued that he had a right to respond to the evils that whites had perpetrated against blacks.[99] In another case, four blacks were convicted of incitement to racial hatred for a speech made at Hyde Park's Speakers' Corner in which they called on black nurses to give the wrong injection to white people.[100] The court was unswayed by the defendants' claim that they were expressing their frustrations as blacks who had to endure white racism.[101]

The laws discussed thus far have focused on threats to the public and on promotion of hatred through persuasion of nontarget audiences. In 1986, however, Parliament added Section 5 of the Public Order Act, which made hate speech punishable if it amounted to harassment of a target group or individual, and in 1997, it enacted the Protection from Harassment Act.[102] These provide more tools in the British legal arsenal against hate speech, but have not thus far led to any clearer or more definitive indication of the ultimate boundaries of punishable hate speech in the

---

[96] *See* Race Relations Act, 1976, c. 74, § 70 (Eng.), *quoted in* D.J. Walker and Michael J. Redman, *Racial Discrimination: A Simple Guide to the Provisions of the Race Relations Act of 1976*, at 215–16 (Shaw 1977).

[97] [1968] 1 All E.R. 582, 582 (C.A. 1967).

[98] "Bitter Attack on Whites," *The Times* (London), July 25, 1967, at 1.

[99] Although the previously cited passage urges violence if certain conditions are met, it clearly falls short of an "incitement" to violence. Actually, to the extent that it advocates violence to combat violence, it arguably preaches self-defense rather than mere aggression.

[100] *See* "Sentences Today on Four Coloured Men," *The Times* (London), Nov. 29, 1967, at 3.

[101] *Id.*

[102] *See* Public Order Act, 1986, c. 64, §§ 5–6 (Eng.); Protection From Harassment Act, 1997, c. 40, § 7 (Eng.).

United Kingdom. Thus, for example, there have been many allegations that the 1997 Act has been used by corporations to stifle legitimate protest.[103]

In 2006, the United Kingdom amended its hate-speech law through adoption of the Racial and Religious Hatred Act.[104] This Act prohibits threats that incite to religious hatred, but explicitly exempts religious criticism even if it involves "antipathy, dislike, ridicule, insult or abuse of particular religions or the beliefs or practices of their adherents.[105] The issue of hate speech targeting religion – highlighted by the worldwide controversy over the publication of the "Danish Cartoons" in 2005, which portrayed the prophet Muhammad in satirical and derogatory fashion and caused outrage among Muslims throughout the world – poses particularly thorny problems, some of the most salient of which will be briefly addressed later in the chapter.[106] Finally, in 2008, the United Kingdom added the incitement to hatred based on sexual orientation to the list of prohibited forms of expression.[107]

In the last analysis, the difficulties relating to hate speech regulation in the United Kingdom have to do less with the particular legal regime involved and more with the social and political context in which that regime is embedded. As already mentioned, British legislation has been much more successful in combating fascism and Nazism than in dealing with hatred between whites and nonwhites. Perhaps the reason for that difference is that a much greater consensus has prevailed in Britain concerning fascism than concerning the absorption and accommodation of the large, relatively recent influx of racial minorities.

## C. *Germany*

The contemporary German approach to hate speech is the product of two principal influences: the German Constitution's conception of freedom of expression as properly circumscribed by fundamental values such as human dignity and by constitutional interests such as honor and personality;[108] and the Third Reich's historical record against the Jews, especially its virulent hate propaganda and discrimination that culminated in the Holocaust.

Unlike the United States, and much like Canada, Germany treats freedom of expression as one constitutional right among many, rather than as paramount or even as first among equals. Whereas under the Canadian constitution, freedom of expression is limited by constitutionally mandated vindications of equality and

---

[103] *See* Edward Countryman, "Those behind the harassment law did not want it to stifle protest," *guardian.co.uk*, Jan. 7, 2009, *available at* http://www.guardian.co.uk/commentisfree/2009/jan/07/harrassment-law.

[104] Racial and Religious Hatred Act, 2006, c. 1 (U.K.).

[105] *Id.* at § 29J.

[106] *See infra* Section V.

[107] *See* Criminal Justice & Immigration Act, 2008, c. 4, sched. 16 (U.K.).

[108] *See supra* notes 72, 73.

multiculturalism, under the German Basic Law, freedom of expression must be balanced against the pursuit of dignity and group-regarding concerns.[109]

The contrast between the German approach and other approaches to freedom of speech, such as the American or the Canadian, is well captured in the following summary assessment of the German Constitutional Court's treatment of free speech claims:

> First, the value of personal honor always trumps the right to utter untrue statements of fact made with knowledge of their falsity. If, on the other hand, untrue statements are made about a person after an effort was made to check for accuracy, the court will balance the conflicting rights and decide accordingly. Second, if true statements of fact invade the intimate personal sphere of an individual, the right to personal honor trumps freedom of speech. But if such truths implicate the social sphere, the court once again resorts to balancing. Finally, if the expression of an opinion – as opposed to fact – constitutes a serious affront to the dignity of a person, the value of personal honor triumphs over speech. But if the damage to reputation is slight, then again the outcome of the case will depend on careful judicial balancing.[110]

In broad terms, freedom of speech, like other constitutional rights in Germany, is in part a negative right – that is, a right against government – and, in part a positive right – that is, a right to government sponsorship and encouragement of free speech.[111] In contrast to the Anglo-American approach, which in its Lockean tradition regards fundamental rights as inalienable and as preceding and transcending civil society, the German tradition regards fundamental rights as depending on the (constitutional) state for their establishment and support. Consistent with this, the more free-speech rights are conceived and treated as positive rights, the easier it becomes to pin on the state the responsibility for hate speech that it may find repugnant, but that it does not prohibit or punish. Furthermore, the German constitutional system is immersed in a normative framework that is more Kantian than Lockean, thus requiring a balancing of rights and duties not only on the side of the state, but also on that of the citizenry.[112]

As in the United States, in Germany freedom of speech is legitimated from the respective standpoints of the justification from democracy, from the pursuit of truth, and from autonomy. These justifications are conceived quite differently in Germany than in the United States, however, with the consequence that the nature and scope of free-speech rights in Germany stand in sharp contrast to their

---

[109] The values underlying the Basic Law's approach of freedom of expression were discussed by the German Constitutional Court in the landmark *Lüth* case, BverfGE 7, 198 (1958) (stating that the Basic Law "establishes an objective order of values . . . which centers upon dignity of the human personality developing freely within the social community") (translated in Donald Kommers, *The Constitutional Jurisprudence of the Federal Republic of Germany* 363 [Duke University Press, 2d. ed. 1997]).

[110] Kommers, *supra* note 109, at 424.

[111] *Id.* at 386.

[112] *See id.* at 298, 305.

American counterparts. Indeed, because of its constitutional commitment to "militant democracy,"[113] the German justification from democracy does not encompass extremist antidemocratic speech, including hate speech advocating denial of democratic or constitutional rights to its targets. The German justification from the pursuit of truth, on the other hand, does not embrace its American counterpart's Millian presuppositions. This emerges clearly from the German Constitutional Court's firm conviction that established falsehoods can be safely denied protection without hindrance to the pursuit of truth.[114] Finally, the German justification from autonomy is not centered on the autonomy of the speakers, as its American counterpart has proven to date. Instead, the German justification implies the need to strike a balance between rights and duties, between the individual and the community, and between the self-expression needs of speakers and the self-respect and dignity of listeners.

The contemporary German constitutional system is grounded in an order of objective values, including respect for human dignity and perpetual commitment to militant democracy.[115] As such, it excludes certain creeds and thus paves the way for content-based restrictions on freedom of speech that would be unacceptable under American free-speech jurisprudence.[116] Undoubtedly, the German Basic Law's adoption of certain values and the consequent legitimacy of content-based speech regulation originated in the deliberate commitment to repudiate the country's Nazi past and to prevent at all costs any possible resurgence of it in the future. Within this context, concern with protection of the Jewish community and with prevention of any rekindling of virulent anti-Semitism within the general population has left a definite imprint not only on the constitutional treatment of hate speech, but also on the evolution of free-speech doctrine more generally.

Evidence of this can be found in the Constitutional Court's landmark decision in the 1958 *Lüth Case*.[117] *Lüth* involved an appeal to boycott a postwar movie by a director who had been popular during the Nazi period as the producer of a notoriously anti-Semitic film. Lüth, who had advocated the boycott and who was an active member of a group seeking to heal the wounds between Christians and Jews, was enjoined by a Hamburg court from continuing his advocacy of a boycott. He

---

[113] *See* Grundgesetz [GG] art. 21 (F.R.G.), *translated in The Constitution of the Federal Republic of Germany: Essays on the Basic Rights and Principles of the Basic Law With a Translation of the Basic Law* 236 (Ulrich Karpen ed., Nomos 1988).

[114] *See, e.g.*, Holocaust Denial Case, 90 BVerfGE 241 (1994).

[115] Neither Article 1 of the Basic Law, which enshrines human dignity, nor Article 21, which establishes militant democracy, are subject to amendment and are thus made permanent fixtures of the German constitutional order.

[116] *See, e.g.*, R.A.V. v. City of St. Paul, 505 U.S. 377 (1992) (holding hate speech prohibition unconstitutional on ground that it promoted viewpoint discrimination by targeting racial hatred, but not hatred against homosexuals). See *supra* Section II and accompanying notes for a discussion of the R.A.V. case.

[117] BverfGE 7, 198 (1958).

filed a complaint with the Constitutional Court claiming a denial of his free-speech rights.

The Constitutional Court upheld Lüth's claim and voided the injunction against him, noting that he was motivated by apprehension that the reemergence of a film director who had been identified with Nazi anti-Semitic propaganda might be interpreted, especially abroad, "to mean that nothing had changed in German cultural life since the National Socialist period. . . . "[118] The Court went on to note that Lüth's concerns were very important for Germans as "[n]othing has damaged the German reputation as much as the cruel Nazi persecution of the Jews. A crucial interest exists, therefore, in assuring the world that the German people have abandoned this attitude. . . . "[119] Accordingly, in balancing Lüth's free-speech interests against the film director's professional and economic interests, the Court concluded that "[w]here the formation of public opinion on a matter important to the general welfare is concerned, private and especially individual economic interests must, in principle, yield."[120]

Germany has sought to curb hate speech with a broad array of legal tools. These include criminal and civil laws that protect against insult, defamation, and other forms of verbal assault, such as attacks against a person's honor or integrity, damage to reputation, and disparaging the memory of the dead.[121] Although the precise legal standards applicable to the regulation of hate speech have evolved over the years,[122] hate speech against groups, and anti-Semitic propaganda in particular, have been routinely curbed by the German courts. For example, spreading pamphlets charging "the Jews" with numerous crimes and conspiracies, and even putting a sticker only saying "Jew" on the election posters of a candidate running for office, were deemed properly punishable by the courts.[123]

Under current law, criminal liability can be imposed for incitement to hatred or for attacks on human dignity against individuals or groups determined by nationality, race, religion, or ethnic origin.[124] Some of these provisions require showing a threat to public peace, whereas others do not.[125] But even when such a showing is necessary, it imposes a standard that is easily met,[126] in sharp contrast to the American requirement of proof of an incitement to violence.

Perhaps the most notorious and controversial offshoot of Germany's attempts to combat hate speech relate to the prohibitions against denying the Holocaust, or – to use a literal translation of the German expression – to engage in the "Auschwitz

---

[118] Kommers, *supra* note 109, at 367.
[119] *Id.*
[120] *Id.*
[121] *See* Kübler, *supra* note 7, at 340.
[122] For an account of the most important changes, *see id.* at 340–7.
[123] *See id.* at 343–4.
[124] *See id.* at 344.
[125] *Id.* at 345.
[126] *See id.* at 344, n. 32.

lie."[127] Attempts to combat Holocaust denials raise difficult questions not only concerning the proper boundaries between fact and opinion, but also concerning the limits of academic freedom.

These issues came before the Constitutional Court in the *Holocaust Denial Case* in 1994.[128] This case arose as a consequence of an invitation to speak at a public meeting issued by a far-right political party to David Irving, a revisionist British historian who has argued that the mass extermination of Jews during the Third Reich never took place. The government conditioned permission for the meeting on assurance that Holocaust denial would not occur, stating that such denial would amount to "denigration of the memory of the dead, criminal agitation, and, most important, criminal insult, all of which are prohibited by the Criminal Code."[129] Thereupon, the far-right party brought a complaint alleging an infringement of its freedom-of-expression rights.

Relying on the distinction between fact and opinion and emphasizing that demonstrably false facts have no genuine role in opinion formation, the Constitutional Court upheld the lower court's rejection of the complaint. In so doing, the Court cited the following passage from the lower court's opinion:

> The historical fact itself, that human beings were singled out according to the criteria of the so-called "Nuremberg Laws" and robbed of their individuality for the purpose of extermination, puts Jews living in the Federal Republic in a special, personal relationship vis-à-vis their fellow citizens; what happened [then] is also present in this relationship today. It is part of their personal self-perception to be understood as part of a group of people who stand out by virtue of their fate and in relation to whom there is a special moral responsibility on the part of all others, and that this is part of their dignity. Respect for this self-perception, for each individual, is one of the guarantees against repetition of this kind of discrimination and forms a basic condition of their lives in the Federal Republic. Whoever seeks to deny these events denies vis-à-vis each individual the personal worth of [Jewish persons]. For the person concerned, this is continuing discrimination against the group to which he belongs and, as part of the group, against him.[130]

In short, given the special circumstances involved, Holocaust denial is seen as robbing the Jews in Germany of their individual and collective identity and dignity, and as threatening to undermine the rest of the population's duty to maintain a social and political environment in which Jews and the Jewish community can feel themselves to be an integral part.

Holocaust denial in relation to the Jews in Germany presents a very special case. But what about the fact/opinion distinction in other contexts? Or hate speech and insults against other individuals or groups?

[127] *Id.* at 344–6.
[128] 90 BVerfGE 241 (1994).
[129] Kommers, *supra* note 109, at 383.
[130] *Id.* at 386.

The Constitutional Court rendered a controversial decision bearing on the fact/opinion distinction in the *Historical Fabrication Case*.[131] That case involved a book claiming that Germany was not to be blamed for the outbreak of World War II, as that war was thrust on it by its enemies. The Court held that the book's claim amounted to an "opinion" – albeit a clearly unwarranted one – and was thus within the realm of protected speech.[132] Who is to blame for the outbreak of the war is clearly more a matter of opinion than whether or not the Holocaust took place, but the line between fact and opinion is by no means as neat as the Constitutional Court's jurisprudence suggests. For example, is admission of the Holocaust coupled with the claim that the Jews brought it on themselves a protected opinion or such a gross distortion of the facts as to warrant equating the "opinion" involved with assertion of patently false facts?

Insults linked to false statements targeting groups other than Jews was at the core of the Constitutional Court's decision in the *Tucholsky I Case*,[133] which dealt with the display of a bumper sticker on a car with the slogan "soldiers are murderers." The bumper sticker in question had been displayed by a social science teacher who was a pacifist and who objected to Germany's military role in the 1991 Gulf War. Moreover, this slogan had a long pedigree in German history as it was the creation of the writer Kurt Tucholsky, an anti-Nazi pacifist of the 1930s who was stripped of his German citizenship in 1933.

The lower court interpreting the slogan literally found it to be a defamatory incitement to hatred, which assaulted the human dignity of all soldiers. By asserting that all soldiers are murderers, the slogan cast them as unworthy members of the community. Based on this analysis, the social science teacher was fined for violating the criminal code's prohibition against incitement to hatred against an identifiable group within society.

The Constitutional Court, construing the slogan as an expression of opinion, held it to be constitutionally protected speech. In so doing, the Court asserted that the slogan should not be construed literally. Emphasizing that the slogan had been displayed next to a photograph from the Spanish Civil War showing a dying soldier who had been hit by a bullet accompanied by an inscription of the word "why?", the Court interpreted the message of the slogan as casting soldiers as much as victims as it had as killers. Accordingly, the slogan could be interpreted as an appeal to reject militarism, by asking why society forces soldiers – who are members of society as everyone else – to become potential murderers and to expose them to becoming victims of murder.

The Constitutional Court's decision provoked an angry reaction among politicians, journalists, and scholars.[134] The Court revisited the issue as it reviewed other

---

[131] 90 BVerfGE 1 (1994).
[132] *See* Kommers, *supra* note 109, at 387.
[133] 21 EuGRZ 463–65 (1994).
[134] *See* Kommers, *supra* note 109, at 392–3.

criminal convictions in cases involving statements claiming that "soldiers are murderers" or "soldiers are potential murderers," in its 1995 *Tucholsky II Case*.[135] Noting that the attacks involved were not against any particular soldier but against soldiers as agents of the government, the Court reiterated that the statements involved amounted to constitutionally protected expressions of opinion rather than to the spreading of false facts. The Court recognized that public institutions deserve protection from attacks that may undermine their social acceptance. Nonetheless, the Court concluded that the right to express political opinions critical or even insulting to political institutions, rather than to any segment of the population, outweighed the affected institutions' need for protection.

These two decisions illustrate some of the difficulties involved in drawing cogent lines between fact and opinion, and between acceptable – and in a democracy indispensable – political criticism and inflammatory excesses threatening the continued viability of public institutions. This notwithstanding, in Germany, the prohibitions against hate speech are firmly grounded. The only open questions concern their constitutional boundaries in cases that do not involve anti-Semitism or the Holocaust.


## D. *Hungary*

Hungary's hate-speech jurisprudence in the aftermath of its transition from socialism to constitutional democracy rests on a paradox or, more precisely, as will be briefly described later in the chapter, on a series of paradoxes. As already noted, from a historical standpoint, Hungary's experience relevant to hate speech is very much like that of Germany, its ally during World War II. Hungary took an active part in the Holocaust and most of its Jews outside of Budapest were exterminated in 1944.[136] Furthermore, Hungary currently has the largest Jewish population in Central Europe and a recent history of virulent anti-Semitic and anti-Roma rhetoric and intimidation.[137]

On the other hand, unlike West Germany, which became a thriving constitutional democracy only a few years after the end of World War II, Hungary went almost straight from Nazi to Soviet domination. Because of this, Hungary lacked any genuine opportunity to fully air its life under authoritarian rule before the end of

---

[135] *Id.* at 393.

[136] *See* Peter Molnar, "Towards Improved Law and Policy on 'Hate Speech' – The 'Clear and Present Danger' Test in Hungary," in *Extreme Speech & Democracy* 237, 244 (Ivan Hare & James Weinstein eds., Oxford University Press 2009).

[137] In the April 2010 Parliamentary elections, Jobbik, a neo-Nazi party with an open and virulent anti-Semitic and anti-Roma political agenda, obtained around 17% of the vote and, for the first time, seats in the Parliament. *See* Bruno Waterfield, "Hungary Elections: First Step to Power for Far-Right since Nazi Era," *Telegraph.co.uk*, Apr. 11, 2010, *available at* http://www.telegraph.co.uk/news/worldnews/europe/hungary/7578561/Hungary-elections-first-step-to-power-for-far-Right-since-Nazi-era.html.

the Soviet era.[138] Under these circumstances, it is understandable that after emerging from Soviet domination, Hungary should embrace a very broad conception of freedom of speech closer to that of the United States than to that of Germany.[139]

Specifically, the Hungarian Constitutional Court (HCC) has adopted a hate-speech jurisprudence that tracks that of the United States in substance, albeit not in form. From the beginning, the HCC found criminalization of incitement to hatred on the basis of national, ethnic, or religious identity to be constitutional while proclaiming that group defamation on the same grounds was constitutionally protected.[140] Notwithstanding its drawing a formal line at "incitement to hatred," the HCC in effect imposed an "incitement to violence" standard by requiring that actual incitement to hatred produce a "clear and present danger" of violence to become constitutionally subject to criminal sanction.[141] Relying on this interpretation, moreover, lower courts concluded that thousands chanting at football matches that "the trains are ready for Auschwitz" was not criminally actionable.[142] As this upset many in a country that had had Nuremberg-like race laws and a World War II government with a hand in the deportation of Jews to extermination camps, the government tried to tighten hate speech laws in the late 1990s and early 2000s. In 1999 and 2004, the HCC struck down these laws as unconstitutional for failure to impose a "clear and present danger" standard.[143]

Whereas one can understand the HCC turning to the United States rather than Germany in spite of Hungary's World War II experience, there is a further paradox that defies any straightforward explanation. The HCC and Hungarian free-speech jurisprudence have retreated somewhat from their initial distinctly liberal bent.[144] This can be easily explained by the inevitable disappointments of the postcommunist era and to increased nationalism after the lifting of Soviet antinationalist repression. What is harder to explain, however, is a tension within the HCC's decisions. In two cases decided on the same day in 2000, the HCC upheld (a) the criminalization of disparagement of national symbols and (b) a prohibition on totalitarian symbols.[145] With the exception of the latter decision, however, the Court's ultra-liberal protection of hate speech has continued unabated,[146] as evidenced by the 1999 and 2004 decisions mentioned earlier. It is quite significant in this regard that

---

[138] *See* Molnar, *supra* note 136, at 244.

[139] *See* Michel Rosenfeld and András Sajó, "Spreading Liberal Constitutionalism: An Inquiry into the Fate of Free Speech Rights in New Democracies," in *The Migration of Constitutional Ideas* 142, 162–3 (Sujit Choudhry ed., Cambridge University Press 2006).

[140] *Id.* at 161.

[141] *Id.* at 163.

[142] *Id.*

[143] HCC, Decision 18/2004 (V.25) AB hat; HCC, Decision 12/1999 (V.21.) AB hat.

[144] *See* Rosenfeld and Sajó, *supra* note 139, at 168–9.

[145] HCC, Decision 13/2000 (V. 12.) AB hat; HCC, Decision 14/2000 (V. 12.) AB hat. *See* Rosenfeld and Sajó, *supra* note 139, at 167.

[146] *See* Molnar, *supra* note 136, at 261–3. It is noteworthy that, in 2010, the Hungarian parliament criminalized holocaust denial. The HCC has not passed on the constitutionality of that law, however.

the HCC aligned itself explicitly with the widespread European prohibition against disparagement of national symbols.[147] In view of this, the HCC seems split in its free-speech jurisprudence: European in the context of attacks on symbols held dear by the country's majority; American in the context of expressions of hate against two minorities historically subject to discrimination, violence, and abuse. Is the former a concession to strong majoritarian impulses? Or is the latter a valiant – albeit perhaps misguided – attempt to preserve as much free-speech liberalism as possible in an increasingly conservative era?

## IV. THE TREATMENT OF HATE SPEECH UNDER INTERNATIONAL HUMAN RIGHTS NORMS

Freedom of speech is protected as a fundamental right under all the major international covenants on human rights adopted since the end of World War II, such as the 1948 UN Universal Declaration of Human Rights,[148] the 1966 UN Covenant on Civil and Political Rights (CCPR),[149] and the 1950 European Convention on Human Rights (ECHR).[150] These covenants, however, do not extend protection to all speech, and some, such as the CCPR, specifically condemn hate speech.[151] A particularly strong stand against hate speech, which includes a command to states to criminalize it, is promoted by Article 4 of the 1965 International Convention on the Elimination of All forms of Racial Discrimination (CERD). Article 4 provides, in relevant part, that States Parties:

> condemn all propaganda and all organizations which are based on ideas or theories of superiority of one race or group of persons of one colour or ethnic origin, or which attempt to justify or promote racial hatred and discrimination in any form . . . [;]
>
> [s]hall declare an offence punishable by law all dissemination of ideas based on racial superiority or hatred, incitement to racial discrimination . . . and also the provision of any assistance to racist activities, including the financing thereof; [and]
>
> [s]hall declare illegal and prohibit organizations . . . and all other propaganda activities, which promote and incite racial discrimination, and shall recognize participation in such organizations or activities as an offence punishable by law. . . . [152]

---

[147] Rosenfeld and Sajó, *supra* note 139, at 167.
[148] *See Basic Documents on Human Rights* 25 (Ian Brownlie, Q.C. ed., Oxford University Press, 3rd ed. 1992).
[149] International Covenant on Civil and Political Rights art. 19, Mar. 23, 1976, 999 U.N.T.S. 171.
[150] European Convention on Human Rights and Fundamental Freedoms [ECHR], Nov. 4, 1950, art. 10 ¶2, 213 U.N.T.S. 221.
[151] *See* International Covenant on Civil and Political Rights, *supra* note 149, at 20 ¶2.
[152] International Convention on the Elimination of All Forms of Racial Discrimination art. 4, Dec. 21, 1965, G.A. Res. 2106 A (XX), 660 U.N.T.S. 195 (1969).

The United States attached a reservation to its ratification of CERD, given that compliance with Article 4 would obviously contravene current American free-speech jurisprudence.[153]

International bodies charged with judicial review of hate-speech cases have, by and large, embraced positions that come much closer to those prevalent in Germany than to their U.S. counterpart. For example, in *Faurisson v. France*,[154] the UN Human Rights Committee upheld the conviction of Faurisson under France's "Gayssot Act," which makes it an offense to contest the existence of proven crimes against humanity. Faurisson, a French university professor, had promoted the view that the gas chambers at Auschwitz and other Nazi camps had not been used for the purposes of extermination, and claimed that all the people in France knew that "the myth of the gas chambers is a dishonest fabrication."

The Human Rights Committee decided that Faurisson's conviction for having violated the rights and reputation of others was consistent with the free-speech protection afforded by Article 19 of CCPR. Because Faurisson's statements were prone to foster anti-Semitism, their restriction served the legitimate purpose of furthering the Jewish community's right "to live free from fear of an atmosphere of anti-[S]emitism."

Notwithstanding its support for Faurisson's conviction, the Human Rights Committee noted that the Gayssot Act was overly broad inasmuch as it prohibited publication of bona fide historical research that would tend to contradict some of the conclusions arrived at the Nuremberg trials. Thus, whereas suppression of demonstrably false facts likely to kindle hatred is consistent with UN standards, suppression of plausible factual claims or of opinions based on such facts would not be justified even if it happened to lead to increased anti-Semitism.

The European Court of Human Rights has also upheld convictions for hate speech as consistent with the free-speech guarantees provided by Article 10 of the ECHR. An interesting case in point is *Jersild v. Denmark*.[155] The Danish courts had upheld the convictions of members of a racist youth group who had made derogatory and degrading remarks against immigrants, calling them, among other things, "niggers" and "animals," and that of a television journalist who had interviewed the youths in question and broadcast their views in the course of a television documentary that he had edited. The journalist appealed his conviction to the European Court, which unanimously stated that the convictions of the youths had been consistent

---

[153] *See* Kübler, *supra* note 7, at 357.

[154] U.N. GAOR, Hum. Rts. Comm., 58th Sess., Annex, U.N. Doc. CCPR/C/58/D/550/1993 (1996). The decision and related French prosecutions are discussed in Julie C. Suk, "Denying Experience: Holocaust Denial and the Free-Speech Theory of the State," Chapter 8 herein.

[155] App. No. 15890/89, 19 Eur. Ct. H.R. Rep. 1 (1995) (Commission report). *Jersild* and related decisions of the European Court of Human Rights are thoroughly canvassed in Tarlach McGonagle, "A Survey and Critical Analysis of Council of Europe Strategies for Countering 'Hate Speech'," Chapter 24 herein.

with ECHR standards, but which, by a twelve-to-seven vote, held that the journalist's conviction violated the standards in question.

The convictions of the youths for having treated a segment of the population as being less than human were consistent with the limitations on free speech for "the protection of the reputation or rights of others" imposed by Article 10 of the ECHR.[156] The conviction of the journalist for aiding and abetting the youths had been premised on the finding that the broadcast had given wide publicity to views that would otherwise have reached but a very small audience, thus exacerbating the harm against the targets of the hate message. The European Court's majority stressed that the journalist had not endorsed the message of his racist interviewees and had tried to expose them and their message in terms of their social milieu, their frustrations, their propensity to violence, and their criminal records as posing important questions of public concern. The Court concluded that the journalist's conviction had been disproportionate in relation to the permissible aim of protecting the rights and reputations of the target group, because the journalist had no intent of promoting hatred; the legitimacy of his conviction turned on a balancing of his expression rights in reporting facts and conveying opinions about them and the harms imposed by the hate message on its targets. Both the majority and the dissenters on the European Court agreed that balancing was the proper approach. They disagreed, however, on how much weight should be borne by the competing interests involved. From the standpoint of the dissenters, the majority placed too much weight on the journalist's expression rights and too little on the protection of the dignity of the victims of hatred. The dissenters emphasized the fact that the journalist had edited down the interviews to the point of principally highlighting the racial slurs, and that he had at no point in the documentary expressed disapproval or condemnation of the statements uttered by his interviewees.

In the end, the disagreements between the majority and the dissent in *Jersild* center on the proper interpretation to be given to the general tenor of the documentary and to the attitude displayed in it by the journalist through his interviews and reports. Accordingly, just as it became plain in the context of hate-speech regulation in Germany, prohibitions against crude insults and patently false statements of fact generally seem legally manageable. On the other hand, issues depending on opinions or on drawing the often elusive line between fact and opinion present much more troubling questions.

A recent opinion by the UN Committee on the Elimination of Racial Discrimination in interpreting the scope of CERD explores the deeply problematic relationship between race-based and religion-based hate speech. In a 2007 decision in the case of *A.W.R.A.P. v. Denmark*,[157] the committee confronted the question of whether

---

[156] *See* European Convention on Human Rights and Fundamental Freedoms [ECHR], Nov. 4, 1950, art. 10(2), 213 U.N.T.S. 221.

[157] Communication No. 37/2006, U.N. Doc. CERD/C/71/D/37/2006 (Aug. 8, 2007).

anti-Islamic statements made by a member of the Danish parliament amounted to prohibited racial discrimination under CERD. The statements at stake, made in Parliament and in interviews with the press, included the declaration that "according to Islam it is the right of the male to beat his children and wife yellow and blue. That form of violence . . . is of sadistic and brutal character."[158] The complainant, a Danish Muslim citizen, had requested that his country's authorities take action against the parliamentarian who had expressed the aforementioned views, and upon the Danish authorities' refusal to take action, he petitioned the CERD Committee. The latter refused to intervene, however, concluding that the statements complained of did not fall within the scope of CERD. In the Committee's view, these statements concern "perception of persons of a specific religion and of a religious doctrine but do not concern persons of a particular 'race, colour, descent, or national or ethnic origin' . . . [as] not all Muslims are of a particular ethnic origin . . . [or] of the same race."[159]

Whereas the Committee's conclusion is certainly literally accurate, it is nonetheless troubling. To a large extent, in many countries of immigration, religious minorities made up for the most part of immigrants, as is the case with Muslims in many European democracies, tend to be of different ethnic and national origin than the majority within their country of immigration. More generally, the equation of race-based and religion-based hate speech is highly questionable as there may be more disanalogies than analogies between them, as will be now summarily explored.

## V. THE SPECIAL PROBLEM OF RELIGION-BASED HATE SPEECH WITH EMPHASIS ON THE DANISH CARTOONS CONTROVERSY

In a nutshell, the special problem posed by religion-based hate speech stems principally from two separate but often in practice intertwined factors: first, as alluded earlier, sometimes religion is tied to ethnic and national origin, and sometimes it is not; second, disparaging *religion* cannot in many cases be equated with disparaging *the religious*.

Some religions, such as Judaism, are tied to a particular people, whereas others, such as Buddhism, Christianity, or Islam, are not. Significantly, anti-Semitism has been historically both religion and race-based. Whereas the Jew could for the most part overcome religion-based anti-Semitism by converting to the majority religion – for example, Christianity – religious conversion proved of no use to avoid extermination under Nazi race-based anti-Semitism, as it sufficed for that purpose to have one Jewish grandparent. Notwithstanding this difference, and as evinced by the previously described early seditious libel case that arose in the United Kingdom,[160] hate

---

[158] *Id.* at 2.3.
[159] *Id.* at 4.1.
[160] *See supra* notes 88 and 89 and accompanying text.

against the Jewish religion and hate against Jews often loom as fungible from the standpoint of hate speech. Indeed, there seems to be little difference between falsely claiming that the Jewish religion requires murdering Christian children for use of their blood in Passover rituals and defaming Jews by accusing them of stopping at nothing, including theft and murder, to further their quest for world domination.

Even in relation to religions that are universal in scope, there are circumstances in which hate directed at the religion largely overlaps with hate targeting adherents of the religion. Thus, in the context of a predominantly Christian European country with an Arab minority that is overwhelmingly Muslim, anti-Arab and anti-Muslim hate speech may largely overlap. Moreover, in cases where hate speech targeting a religion stands primarily as a proxy for hate speech targeting those who practice that religion on account of the latter's racial, ethnic, or national origin, it seems reasonable to treat religion-based hate speech much like its race-based counterpart.

In stark contrast, criticism of a particular religion itself, even if disparaging and highly offensive to those deeply committed to it, is an altogether different matter. Freedom to criticize religion is historically embedded at the very core of freedom of expression as it emerged during the period of the Enlightenment as encapsulated in Voltaire's famous battle cry "Écrasez L'Infâme" ("Crush the Infamous One") directed against the Catholic Church.[161] Indeed, freedom of expression was then perceived as crucial in the struggle against the authoritarian rule of the absolute monarch and against the stranglehold of the Church on public discourse and acceptable morals. Moreover, freedom to criticize religion – which should be broadly construed as also encompassing the freedom to criticize the rejection of religion – still remains central to contemporary freedom of speech. Religion is liberating to some, oppressive to others; an indispensable source of morality for some, an invariable source of prejudice and violence for others; the necessary glue for a just political society according to some, the greatest impediment to freedom and equality for all regardless of sex, gender, or sexual orientation, according to others. Also, because of these vivid splits, the discussion around religion often tends to be vigorous, pungent, and trenchant. It often turns to satire, caricature, ridicule, oversimplification, and distortion, and it is particularly prone to provoking feelings of anger, resentment, humiliation, and contempt.

Consistent with these observations, hatred toward religion (or nonreligion) or toward particular religions because of their dogmas or teachings would seem analogous to hatred toward particular ideologies or political agendas, and accordingly should be equally tolerated. Just as one should be free to expound virulently against communism, capitalism, colonialism, or excessive permissiveness, one should also be free to angrily denounce, caricature, or vilify a religion that one is convinced is

---

[161] See *Rousseau and L'Infâme: Religion, Toleration, and Fanaticism in the Age of Enlightenment* 9 (Ourida Mostefai & John T. Scott eds., Rodopi 2009).

homophobic or sexist, or atheism if one deems that godlessness leads to the moral disintegration of society.

When it comes to criticizing, negatively portraying, or satirizing religion, freedom of speech has been limited in many countries through application of blasphemy laws. Thus, for example, Austrian courts ordered seizure of a film deemed an abusive attack on the Catholic religion because of its provocative portrayal of God the Father, the Virgin Mary, and Jesus Christ. The seizure in question was challenged before the European Court of Human Rights. That court deferred to Austria, deeming that it had not acted disproportionately in its aim to ensure religious peace and to prevent believers from feeling the objects of attacks on account of their religious convictions in an unwarranted and offensive way.[162]

As Catholicism is the religion of a vast majority of Austrians, attacks on that religion through depictions such as those present in the film seized by Austrian authorities cannot be equated with race-based or national origin-based hatred. Although it is beyond the scope of this undertaking to examine the issue in any detail, "blasphemy" against a majority religion is best defined as any speech offensive to deeply held beliefs or ideological precepts prevalent through a polity. Blasphemy laws run deeply counter to liberal conceptions of free speech, but be that as it may, for present purposes, suffice it to stress that blasphemy standing alone need not be regarded as raising any significant hate-speech issue.

The matter may appear entirely different, however, when the religion attacked is a minority one practiced mainly by "outsiders" who are not smoothly integrated into the social fabric of the polity. This difference, however, is vividly illustrated by the Danish Cartoons controversy, where an attack on a religion was sought to be cast as conflating with a racist or ethnic-based attack on that religion's practitioners.

The controversy arose as a consequence of the publication in a Danish newspaper of a series of cartoons that were derogatory, satirical, and offensive from the standpoint of Islam. As one commentator observed:

> The cartoons themselves are rather uninteresting. Some simply depict a man wear-
> ing traditional Arab dress, while others present the Prophet [Muhammad] in a
> satirical context. For example, in one cartoon, the Prophet stands at the gates of
> heaven halting people from entering, saying "Stop, stop, we ran out of virgins." In
> another cartoon, perhaps the most provocative, a bearded Arab-looking man wears
> a bomb that looks like a turban, which has the Islamic declaration of faith written
> on it: "There is no god but Allah and Muhammad is the Messenger of God."[163]

Muslims worldwide saw the cartoons as an attack on their prophet, their religion, and their community, and Muslims' reaction to the cartoons ranged from a boycott

---

[162] *See* Otto-Preminger Institute v. Austria, 295 Eur. Ct. H. R. (Ser. A) (1994).

[163] Anver M. Emon, "On the Pope, Cartoons, and Apostates: Shari'a 2006," 22 *J.L. & Religion* 303, 308 (2006–2007).

of Danish goods to violent riots resulting in damages to European embassies.[164] Under the Shari'a, a Muslim who insults the prophet is guilty of apostasy and may be condemned to death.[165]

From a liberal standpoint, the cartoons are clearly protected speech similar to the disparaging depiction of God the Father, the Virgin Mary, and Jesus Christ in the film at the center of the *Preminger* case discussed earlier. In both cases, the proponents of the offensive depictions presumably used these to expose what they perceive as the oppressive and sanctimonious positions spread by Catholicism and Islam, respectively. Consistent with this, caricaturing and satirizing religion and venerated religious figures like Jesus or Muhammad seem analogous to doing the same with respect to political ideologies and their charismatic champions. Although ridiculing religions and religious figures may be more offensive to more people, from a liberal free-speech perspective, it ought to be deemed no different than caricaturing and satirizing Franklin Roosevelt and the New Deal, De Gaulle and his political vision for France, Margaret Thatcher and Thatcherism, or Ronald Reagan and his brand of political conservatism. In all these cases, the critics wish to take the larger-than-life figures involved off their pedestals as a step toward desacralizing their projects. In this context, a caricature may prove much more effective than a carefully reasoned expose of the shortcomings of the positions that the relevant critic stands against.

To transform the Danish cartoons from mere blasphemy to "racist" hate speech, it was necessary to transform an attack on a religion and on its most highly revered religious figure into an assault against the religious community that embraced that religion – a religious community that happens to constitute, moreover, a minority in Europe. As one observer puts it:

> Criticism of religion can be labeled "racist" through the following argumentative process. First, blasphemy is an attack on God, but it also aggresses believers. . . . Second[] such an attack . . . is racist in that, the argument goes, in order to attack a religious group in such a violent way, one necessarily must despise or hate "these people." The offender entertains a sort of irrational fear – a "phobia." The term "Islamophobia" was coined in that context.[166]

In short, by claiming violations of their freedom of religion, equality, and dignity rights, Muslims seek to turn criticism of certain forms of violent politics claimed by their proponents to be based on Islamic fundamentalist prescriptions into race-based, religion-based, and ethnic-origin-based hate speech.

The liberal repudiation of speech restrictions based on blasphemy would be sufficient to justify full free-speech protection to the Danish cartoons, but for two complicating factors. First, Islam in Europe is a minority religion; second, there is a question of whether the cartoons are directed against the Islamic religion or against

---

[164] *Id.* at 309.
[165] *Id.* at 312.
[166] Guy Haarscher, "Religious Revival and Pseudo-Secularism," 30 *Cardozo L. Rev.* 2799, 2809 (2009).

Muslims as a "race" or ethno-cultural group as opposed to those who embrace a creed perceived by its critics as being both undesirable and dangerous.

Blasphemy, particularly as expressed in films or cartoons, does not restrict the freedom of religion of those offended by them. They do not affect the belief, worship, or practice of spreading the religion they attack, and the religious by and large can avoid exposure to the offensive films or caricatures. Accordingly, in the case of the majority religion in a polity, the free-speech protection of blasphemy far outweighs whatever harm blasphemy may cause to the rights of those who are offended by it. The same, however, does not necessarily follow in the case of a minority religion. Suppose the Danish cartoons conveyed nothing negative against Muslims as a minority group, but only that Islam is a cruel and violent religion. Would a Muslim in Denmark be similarly situated to a Frenchman or Italian in their respective countries in the context of cartoons depicting Catholicism as a venal, power-hungry, and cruel religion? Arguably, the answer is in the negative as anti-Islam attitudes can easily and imperceptibly slip into anti-Muslim sentiments in a way that anti-Catholicism is not at all likely to degenerate into anti-French in France or anti-Italian in Italy. Therefore, it seems much more difficult to exclude slippage from antireligion speech to hate speech in the case of minority religions than in that of a majority religion.

Determining whether the message of the Danish cartoons is anti-Islam or anti-Muslim is even more difficult. One possible interpretation of the cartoons is that they ridicule jihadist Islamic fundamentalism such as that preached by Al Qaeda and all those who sympathize with it. Another plausible interpretation, however, is that all Arabs or all Muslims are violent and likely to become terrorists as even their prophet does not seem beyond planting bombs that would kill innocent bystanders in the pursuit of his community's hegemonic and domineering aims.

Denouncing all Muslims as would-be terrorists and suicide bombers bent on killing infidels constitutes hate speech similar to accusing Jews of killing Christian babies for use in Passover rituals. The Danish cartoons do not go that far by any means, but nonetheless pose difficult line-drawing problems. To the extent that they are criticisms of a religion, they ought to be fully protected; on the other hand, if they amount to group defamation against a minority community, they come within the ambit of hate speech. Ideally, courts could sift our criticism of religion from defamation of a religious group. In practice, however, that will often prove impossible. That leaves essentially three alternatives: (1) a blanket protection of all expression like that found in the Danish cartoons; (2) a blanket prohibition of all such expressions; or (3) use of a proportionality standard that would accord a strong presumption of protection to any utterance that can be plausibly understood as registering a genuine criticism of religion (including one that is caricatural or satiric in form) that could only be overcome in cases of demonstrable great palpable harm amounting to defamation on the basis of race, ethnic or national origin, or religious affiliation (as contrasted to religion). Under this latter standard, blood libel against

Jews and blanket portrayal of all Muslims as terrorists would clearly be actionable hate speech in countries that use an incitement-to-hatred standard. In contrast, the Danish cartoons would be protected in light of the plausibility of one of the two interpretations mentioned previously, namely that the cartoons deride the jihadist interpretation of Islam that has been advanced by certain fundamentalists such as those associated with Al Qaeda.[167]

## VI. CONFRONTING THE CHALLENGES OF HATE SPEECH IN CONTEMPORARY CONSTITUTIONAL DEMOCRACIES: OBSERVATIONS AND PROPOSALS

The preceding analysis reveals that both protection and prohibition of hate speech raise serious and difficult problems. Not all hate speech is alike, and its consequences may vary from one setting to another. Furthermore, to the extent that hate speech produces harms that are not immediate, these may be uncertain and hard to measure. The impact of hate speech also seems to depend to a significant extent on the medium of its communication. Thus, an oral communication to a relatively small audience at Speakers' Corner in London's Hyde Park should not be automatically lumped together with a posting on the Internet available worldwide.

The two contrasting approaches to hate speech adopted by the United States and by other western democracies each have advantages and drawbacks. The main advantage of the American approach is that it makes for relatively clear-cut boundaries between permissible and impermissible speech. And, at least in cases in which hate speech poses little threat to its targets and its message is repudiated by an overwhelming majority of its nontarget audience, as in the *Skokie* case, tolerance may be preferable. Indeed in that case, the dangers stemming from suppression and the possible spread underground of hate speech would seem to outweigh the harm from unconstrained communication. The same, however, may not be true for a country like Hungary where hate speech has much greater resonance for a significant portion of the nontarget audience.

The chief disadvantage of the American approach is that it is not attuned to potentially serious harms that may unfold gradually over time or have their greatest immediate impact in remote places. In addition, the American approach tends to remain blind to the considerable potential harm that hate speech can cause to the equality and dignity concerns of its victims or the attitudes and beliefs of nontarget audiences. The latter groups may reject the explicit appeal to hate but nonetheless

---

[167] Consistent with these observations, the various "defamation of religion" resolutions adopted by the United Nations, including the UN Human Rights Council Resolution 7/19 "Combating Defamation of Religions" ¶¶ 9,12, Rep. of the Human Rights Council A63/53, Mar. 27, 2008, would be objectionable inasmuch as they would inevitably unduly curtail legitimate freedom-of-speech rights.

be influenced by the more diffuse implicit message lurking beneath the surface of that appeal.[168]

The principal advantages to the approach to hate speech prevalent outside the United States are that it makes for unequivocal condemnation of it as morally repugnant, and at least in some cases, such as in the United Kingdom's efforts against the spread of fascist hate propaganda, it can play an important role in the struggle against extremist antidemocratic political movements. Furthermore, as exemplified by contemporary Germany's steadfast and continuous bans of anti-Semitic hate propaganda, vigorous prohibition and enforcement can bolster the security, dignity, autonomy, and well-being of the target community, while at the same time reminding nontarget groups and society at large that the hate message at stake is not only repugnant and unacceptable, but that it will not be tolerated, and that those who are bent on spreading it will be punished.

The principal disadvantages to the approach to hate speech under consideration, on the other hand, are: that it inevitably has to confront difficult line-drawing problems, such as that between fact and opinion in the context of the German scheme of regulation; that when prosecution of perpetrators of hate speech fails, such as in the British *Southern News* case,[169] regulation may unwittingly do more to legitimate and disseminate hate propaganda at issue than a complete absence of regulation would have;[170] that prosecutions may be too selective or too indiscriminate owing to (often unconscious) biases prevalent among law enforcement officials, as appears to have been the case in the prosecutions of certain black activists under the British Race Relations Act; and that because not all that may appear to be hate speech actually is hate speech – such as the documentary report involved in *Jersild v. Denmark* or a play in which a racist character engages in hate speech, but the dramatist intends to convey an antihate message – regulation of that speech may unwisely bestow powers of censorship over legitimate political, literary, and artistic expression on government officials and judges.

In the last analysis, none of the existing approaches to hate speech are ideal, but on balance, the American seems less satisfactory than its alternatives. Above all, the American approach seems significantly flawed in some of its assumptions, in its impact, and in the message it conveys concerning the evils surrounding hate speech. In terms of assumptions, the American approach either underestimates the potential for harm of hate speech that is short of incitement to violence, or it overestimates the

---

[168] This may have occurred for many whites in connection with the *R.A.V.* case. See *supra* Section II for a discussion of *R.A.V.* These whites most likely found the cross burning repugnant, but nonetheless did not want to live in a racially mixed neighborhood. They may even have hidden that belief from themselves by rationalizing that it is better to have a racially segregated neighborhood to avoid the kind of ugly violence exemplified by cross burning.

[169] See *supra* note 95.

[170] This disadvantage should not be overestimated, however. Indeed, if most prosecutions against a certain type of hate succeed and only a few fail, then conceivably prohibition may on the whole be preferable to freedom spread through lack of regulation.

potential of rational deliberation as a means to neutralize calls to hate. In terms of impact, given its long history of racial tensions, it is surprising that the United States does not exhibit greater concern for the injuries to security, dignity, autonomy, and well-being that officially tolerated hate speech causes to its black minority. Likewise, America's hate-speech approach seems to unduly discount the pernicious impact that racist hate speech may have on lingering or dormant racist sentiments still harbored by a non-negligible segment of the white population.[171] Furthermore, even if we discount the domestic impact of hate speech, given the worldwide spread of locally produced hate speech, such as in the case of American-manufactured neo-Nazi propaganda disseminated through the World Wide Web, a strong argument can be made that American courts should factor in the obvious and serious impact abroad of certain domestic hate speech in determining whether such speech should be entitled to constitutional protection. Finally, in terms of the message conveyed by refusing to curb most hate speech, the American approach is a double-edged sword. On the one hand, tolerance of hate speech in a country in which democracy has been solidly entrenched since independence more than two hundred years ago conveys a message of confidence against both the message and the prospects of those who endeavor to spread hate.[172] On the other hand, tolerance of hate speech in a country with serious and enduring race-relation problems may reinforce racism and hamper full integration of the victims of racism within the broader community.[173]

The argument in favor of opting for greater regulation of hate speech than that provided in the United States rests on several important considerations, some related to the place and function of free speech in contemporary constitutional democracies, and others to the dangers and problems surrounding hate speech. Contemporary constitutional democracies are increasingly diverse, multiracial, multicultural, multireligious, and multilingual. Because of this and because of increased migration, a commitment to pluralism and to respect of diversity seem inextricably linked to vindication of the most fundamental individual and collective rights. Increased diversity is prone to making social cohesion more precarious, thus, if anything, exacerbating the potential evils of hate speech. Contemporary democratic states, on the other hand, are less prone to curtailing free-speech rights than their predecessors either because of deeper implantation of the democratic ethos or because respect of

---

[171] In this connection, it is significant that following a steep rise in racist incidents involving hate speech on university campuses throughout the United States, several universities, including the University of Michigan and Stanford University, adopted regulations against hate speech. These were, however, struck down as unconstitutional by lower courts because they restricted speech falling short of the incitement to violence standard. *See* Doe v. Univ. of Mich., 721 F. Supp. 852 (E.D. Mich. 1989); Corry v. Stanford, No. 74039 (Cal. Super. Ct. Santa Clara Co. Feb. 27, 1995) (applying constitutional standard incorporated in state law and made applicable to private universities).

[172] This is the view defended in Bollinger, *supra* note 18.

[173] For a discussion of the uses of tolerance of hate speech to promote existing racism, see Rosenfeld, *supra* note 55, at 1457, 1487.

supranational norms has become inextricably linked to continued membership in supranational alliances that further vital national interests.

In these circumstances, contemporary democracies are more likely to find themselves in a situation like stage four in the context of the American experience with free speech rather than in one that more closely approximates a stage-one experience.[174] In other words, to drown out minority discourse seems a much greater threat than government-prompted censorship in contemporary constitutional democracies that are pluralistic. Actually, viewed more closely, contemporary pluralistic democracies tend to be in a situation that combines the main features of stage two and stage four. Thus, the main threats to full-fledged freedom of expression would seem to come primarily from the "tyranny of the majority" as reflected both within the government and without, and from the dominance of majority discourses at the expense of minority ones.

If it is true that majority conformity and the dominance of its discourse pose the greatest threat to uninhibited self-expression and unconstrained political debate in a contemporary pluralist polity, then significant regulation of hate speech seems justified. This is not only because hate speech obviously inhibits the self-expression and opportunity of inclusion of its victims, but also, less obviously, because hate speech tends to bear closer links to majority views than might initially appear. Indeed, in a multicultural society, although crude insults uttered by a member of the majority directed against a minority may be unequivocally rejected by almost all other members of the majority culture, the concerns that led to the hate message may be widely shared by the majority culture that regards other cultures as threats to its way of life. In those circumstances, hate speech might best be characterized as a pathological extension of majority feelings or beliefs.

So long as the pluralist contemporary state is committed to maintaining diversity, it cannot simply embrace a value-neutral mindset, and consequently it cannot legitimately avoid engaging in some minimum of viewpoint discrimination. This is made clear by the German example, and although the German experience has been unique, it is hard to imagine that any pluralist constitutional democracy would not be committed to a similar position, albeit to a lesser degree.[175] Accordingly, without adopting German free-speech jurisprudence, at a minimum, contemporary pluralist democracy ought to institutionalize viewpoint discrimination against the

---

[174] *See supra* notes 22–29 and accompanying text.

[175] This includes even the United States, which, for all its professed commitment to a free-speech jurisprudence anchored on viewpoint neutrality, has in certain cases upheld restrictions on speech that seem based on viewpoint bias. *See, e.g.,* Dennis v. United States, 341 U.S. 494, 544–45 (1951) (Frankfurter, J., concurring) (characterizing clearly political speech of members of the Communist Party advocating – but not inciting to violence or creating any imminent present danger of – the violent overthrow of the government as speech that ranks "low" "on any scale of values which we have hitherto recognized"). This confuses the *category* of speech involved, namely political speech, which has traditionally been ranked as the highest, and the content of the speech, which had been indeed rejected as repugnant by the vast majority of Americans.

crudest and most offensive expressions of racism, religious bigotry (as opposed to antagonism against religion), and virulent bias on the basis of ethnic or national origin.

Rejection of a content-neutral approach to speech does not contravene the four philosophical justifications of free speech discussed earlier, but it does somewhat alter the nature and scope of speech protected under some of them. In terms of the justification from democracy, whereas tolerating hate speech is not inherently at odds with maintaining a free-speech regime compatible with the flow of ideas required to sustain a well-functioning democracy, it is inconsistent with the smooth functioning of a democracy marked by an unswerving commitment to pluralism. Accordingly, the justification from democracy is either regarded as constrained by the need to sustain pluralism, or conceived as linked to a particular kind of democracy grounded in pluralism. In either case, in a polity committed to pluralism, hate speech could not conceivably contribute in any legitimate way to democracy.

A similar argument can be advanced in relation to the justification from social contract. Either commitment to pluralism is not subject to alteration through agreement, or it is assumed that preservation of basic individual and collective dignity is in the self-interest of every contractor, and thus not prone to being bargained away in the course of agreeing to any viable pact. Consequently, hate speech could be safely banned without affecting the integrity of the social contract justification.

In view of the earlier discussion of the justification from autonomy,[176] it is obvious that it goes hand in hand with a ban on hate speech so long as the autonomy of speakers and listeners is given equal weight. In other words, if autonomy is taken as requiring dignity and reciprocity, then it demands banning hate speech as an affront against the basic rights of its targets.

Unlike these justifications, the pursuit of truth does not depend on whether or not one embraces pluralism. Nevertheless, if one rejects the presumptions made by Mill and Holmes, the banning of hate speech can be amply reconciled with commitment to the pursuit of truth. The justification for rejecting the Millian and Holmesian presumptions has been persuasively made by the Canadian Supreme Court in the *Keegstra* case.[177] Moreover, banning definitively proven falsehoods, such as unequivocal denial of the Holocaust, cannot conceivably hinder pursuit of the truth.

Opinion-based hate speech may not be as convincingly dismissed, but it is difficult to see how hate speech in form could contribute to furthering the truth. The same cannot automatically be said about the broader message lurking beneath hate-based opinion. Thus a racist belief or opinion may be based on fears or concerns that may not themselves be worthless from the standpoint of pursuit of the truth. For example, sentiments against recent immigrants belonging to different races or cultures may

---

[176] *See supra* note 44 and accompanying text.
[177] *See supra* Subsection IIIA for a discussion of the *Keegstra* case.

stem from fears of challenges against one's economic security and cultural values. Whether and to what degree such fears may be warranted are certainly questions that ought to be freely discussed from the standpoint of pursuit of the truth. Consistent with this, special caution should be exercised when dealing with what appears to be hate speech in substance but is not hate speech in form.

From a theoretical standpoint, it is quite possible to draw a bright line between fears and concerns and racist animus. Arguing that immigration from a former colony should be curtailed because it will result in a loss of jobs among the natives and result in undesired changes in the local culture is certainly distinguishable from the hate message that the immigrants in question are "animals" who should be shipped back to their country of origin,[178] even if one recognizes that the former message is implicitly incorporated into the latter. Because of the ambiguity and openness to several inconsistent interpretations of some messages that may plausibly amount to hate speech in substance, the aforementioned line may not always be easy to draw in practice. As we shall examine later, that standing alone does not afford a good reason for tolerating all opinion-based hate speech. In short, whether couched as hate speech in form or as hate speech in substance, expressions of racial animus do not advance the search for the truth and thus do not call for protection from the standpoint of the justification from pursuit of the truth.[179]

Although consistent with the four philosophical justifications of freedom of speech, to become fully acceptable from a practical standpoint, regulation of hate speech must cope satisfactorily with the vexing problems identified in our review of current regulation outside the United States. The principal problems encountered involve line drawing, bias, difficulties in interpretation leading to suppression of speech deserving of protection and/or to toleration of certain hate messages, and facilitation of government- or majority-driven censorship.

Most of these problems are raised in the prevalent American criticism against regulation based on the so-called slippery-slope argument.[180] Pursuant to this argument, because it is impossible to draw neat lines imposing verifiable constraints on judges and legislators, once the door to regulation is open ever so slightly it is bound gradually to open wider, eventually allowing for censorship of all kinds of legitimate yet unpopular speech. Accordingly, failure to confront the slippery-slope problem may lead to dangerous erosion of free speech. Similarly, although the Danish cartoons may be interpreted variously as involving hatred of a religion, hatred of a religious minority, or hatred of those who misappropriate the same religion, it seems sufficiently clear that they should not qualify as actionable hate speech.

---

[178] *Cf.* Jersild v. Denmark, App. No. 15890/89, 19 Eur. Ct. H.R. Rep. 1 (1995) (Commission report). For a discussion of *Jersild*, see *supra* Section IV and accompanying notes.

[179] In this connection, it is important to distinguish between *expression* of racial animus and *reporting* such animus. Conveying information concerning whether one is a racist, as opposed to uttering racial epithets, can, of course, contribute to discovery of the truth.

[180] *See* Frederick Schauer, "Slippery Slopes," 99 *Harv. L. Rev.* 361 (1985).

Unless one adopts a Holmesian view of speech,[181] the slippery-slope argument is largely unpersuasive, and this seems particularly true in the context of hate speech. Indeed, in many cases, such as those involving Holocaust denial, cross burning, displaying swastikas, and calling immigrants "animals," there do not appear to be any line-drawing problems. These cases involve clearly recognizable expressions of hate that constitute patent assaults against the dignity of those whom they target, and that fly in the face of even a cursory commitment to pluralism. On the other hand, there are cases of statements that some groups may find objectionable or offensive, but that raise genuine factual or value-based issues, and that ought, therefore, to be granted protection. For example, strong criticism of the Pope for his opposition to contraception and to homosexual relationships as being "indifferent to human suffering caused by overpopulation and an enemy of human dignity for all" may be highly offensive to Catholics, but even in a country where Catholics are a religious minority should clearly not be officially censored, punished, or characterized as hate speech.

There is, of course, a gray area between these two fairly clear-cut areas, in which there are difficult line-drawing problems, as exemplified by the German controversy over the claim that "soldiers are murderers."[182] Line-drawing problems, however, are quite common in law as they tend to arise whenever a scheme of regulation attempts to balance competing objectives. Such problems may well be exacerbated when a fundamental right like free speech is involved, but that justifies, at most, deregulating the entire gray area, not tolerating all hate speech falling short of incitement to violence.

In the last analysis, the best way to deal with the problems likely to arise in connection with regulation of hate speech is to approach them consistently with a set of fundamental normative principles, and in light of key contextual variables. In other words, the standards of constitutionally permissible regulation of hate speech should conform to fundamental principles that transcend geographical, cultural, and historical differences,[183] and at the same time remain sufficiently open to accommodate highly relevant historical and cultural variables. The fixed principles involved are openness to pluralism and respect for the most elementary degree of autonomy, equality, dignity, and reciprocity.[184] The variables, on the other hand, include the

---

[181] *See supra* notes 39–42 and accompanying text.

[182] *See supra* notes 134–135 and accompanying text.

[183] That does not necessarily mean that these are universal, only that they ought to be common to contemporary pluralist constitutional democracies. For a more extended discussion of the question of universalism of human rights, see Michel Rosenfeld, "Can Human Rights Bridge the Gap Between Universalism and Cultural Relativism? A Pluralist Assessment Based on the Rights of Minorities," 30 *Colum. Hum. Rts. L. Rev.* 249 (1999).

[184] This standard establishes a bare minimum, which seems adequate in the context of speech regulation, but not in that of government policy. For example, this standard would allow for criticism of a particular religion on the grounds it is too restrictive, an enemy of progress, or indifferent to the rights of women. Although these statements may offend believers, it cannot be fairly said that they deprive them of the

particular history and nature of discrimination, status as minority or majority group, customs, common linguistic practices, and the relative power or powerlessness of speakers and their targets within the society involved.

To minimize difficulties and to reduce the possibility of bias, regulation of hate speech should focus on efforts to reconcile the fixed principles and the relevant variables. This focus should determine, among other things, how far within the gray area regulation should extend. Thus, for example, given their different historical experiences with anti-Semitism, it seems reasonable that Germany should go further than the United States in prohibiting anti-Semitic speech that falls within the gray area. Although American and German Jews are entitled to the same degree of dignity and inclusion within their respective societies, greater restrictions on anti-Semitism are required in Germany than in the United States to achieve comparable results.

Recourse to the aforementioned approach is also likely to minimize bias in the regulation of hate speech. One way in which this can be achieved is by taking into account historically significant differences between the proponents and intended targets of hate messages. Thus, racist speech by a member of a historically dominant race against members of an oppressed race is likely to have a more severe impact than racist speech by the racially oppressed against their oppressors. Even if this does not justify selective regulation of hate speech, it does call for greater leniency when the racially oppressed is at fault, and for taking into account as a mitigating factor the fact – found in some of the British cases discussed earlier[185] – that the racist speech of a member of an oppressed racial group was in response to the racism perpetrated by members of the oppressor race. Furthermore, if these contextual variables are properly accounted for, it becomes less likely that majority biases will dominate prosecutorial or judicial decisions.

## CONCLUSION

Hate speech raises difficult questions that test the limits of free speech. Although none of the constitutional regimes examined in these pages leaves hate speech unregulated, there are vast differences between the minimal regulation practiced in the United States and the much more extensive regulation typical of other countries and of international covenants. Both approaches are imperfect, but in a world that has witnessed the Holocaust, various other genocides, and ethnic cleansing, all of which were surrounded by abundant hate speech, the American way seems definitely less appealing than its alternatives. As hate speech can now almost instantaneously spread throughout the world, and as nations become increasingly socially, ethnically, religiously, and culturally diverse, the need for regulation becomes ever more urgent.

---

most elementary degree of dignity. However, a government policy attacking such religion, or making it difficult for its adherents to freely practice it would require meeting a much higher standard.

[185] *See supra* Subsection IIIB.

In view of these important changes, the state can no longer justify commitment to neutrality, but must embrace pluralism, guarantee autonomy and dignity, and strive for maintenance of a minimum of mutual respect. Commitment to these values requires states to conduct an active struggle against hate speech, while at the same time avoiding the pitfalls bound to be encountered in the pursuit of that struggle. It would, of course, be preferable if hate could be defeated by reason. Unfortunately, that has failed all too often, so there seems no alternative but to combat hate speech through regulation to secure a minimum of civility in the public arena.

# 14

# One Step Beyond Hate Speech

## *Post-Soviet Regulation of "Extremist" and "Terrorist" Speech in the Media*

### *Andrei Richter*

The "war on terror" in the wake of 9/11 has led to new restrictions on the freedom of the press worldwide. In the post-Soviet countries, political elites have twisted the war on terror into a fight against "extremism," a vague term that quickly expanded to encompass almost all forms of political dissent. Moreover, the numerous local wars in the post-Soviet world have come to be seen as a new front in the global fight against international terrorism – this was certainly true of the official approach to the events in Chechnya (Russia), the Trans-Dniester region (Moldova), South Ossetia, Abkhazia and Ajara (Georgia), Andijan (Uzbekistan), Kyrgyzstan, Tajikistan, and elsewhere. Because terrorism has roots in political extremism, to overcome terrorism and terrorist organizations, the state must suppress first and foremost extremism and extremist speech; such was the motivation of the governments. On this view, all combatants became "international terrorists," and journalists covering their illegal activity, however objectively, could be labeled extremists and accomplices to terrorists.

This chapter details the ways in which unjustified restrictions against "extremist" speech have been adopted in the name of the war on terror. These include, but are hardly limited to, expansive readings of prohibitions on hate speech.

## I. RUSSIAN RESTRICTIONS ON TERRORISM AND TERRORIST SPEECH

Russia's "war on terror" involves primarily Chechnya and the surrounding region of the North Caucasus. The first campaign, of 1994–1996, lacked the "counterterrorist" label. Subsequent conflicts, however, were called "counterterrorism operations," with far-reaching legal and political consequences, particularly for freedom of the

This chapter is updated and expanded from portions of Andrei Richter, *Post-Soviet Perspective on Censorship and Freedom of the Media* (UNESCO 2007).

press. From the outset of the current warfare in 1999, the authorities expected journalists and the media to support the counterterrorism line. They regarded the fight against terrorism as an ideological, social, and moral battle more than a military one. As Russia's acting Minister of the Interior put it in 2004: "[W]e must do battle as appropriate – applying force but also, to a significant extent, ideology and information. . . . We must deny to the terrorists any opportunity to sow fear among the public through the media. Reporting of acts of terrorism must be highly professional, without the unnecessary display of violent scenes."[1]

The political and legal framework for counterterrorism operations began with the federal statute "On the fight against terrorism," enacted in July 1998. Beginning in spring 2000, one sees references to this statute when restricting freedom of the mass media. Mikhail Seslavinsky, then First Deputy Minister for Press, Broadcasting and Mass Communications (and now head of the Federal Agency on the Press and Mass Communications), told the presidential Commission for Countering Political Extremism that "apart from the media statute we also have the terrorism statute, which will be applied henceforth when evaluating journalists' reports on Chechnya." Article 15 of the terrorism statute, which the government read to extend to the mass media, stated that the public should be informed of acts of terrorism in a form and extent to be decided by the head of the counterterrorism operation's command headquarters. The same article also banned the circulation of materials "serving to promote or justify terrorism and extremism." The newspapers *Kommersant* and *Novaya gazeta* were subsequently accused by the press ministry of violating this provision, for which they received official warnings, which could have led to their closure.[2]

However, the legal basis of the effort to apply the federal terrorism statute to the Chechen conflict was insecure. A March 2001 report from the Media Law and Policy Institute cast doubt on whether the statute applied to reports about Chechnya.[3] As for warning the newspapers, the sole legally indisputable ground for warning and, when appropriate, closing a media outlet is breach of article 4 of the Mass Media statute, titled "Inadmissibility of misuse of the freedom of mass communication." Although it has since been amended, at the time, article 4 contained no reference to or prohibition of the distribution of material supporting or justifying terrorism.[4]

---

[1] Statement by Rashid Nurgaliev, Acting Russian Minister of the Interior, at a meeting with Russian journalists, Jan. 13, 2004.

[2] *See generally* Russian Federation Law on Mass Media (1991), *reprinted in* 11 *Cardozo Arts & Ent. L.J.* 625 (1993) [hereinafter Russian Mass Media Law].

[3] "Interview with Terrorists: Press Ministry Issues Warnings without any Explanations," Commentary of the Media Law and Policy Institute // *Zakonodatelstvo i praktika mass media*, Issue n. 3, 2001.

[4] As originally enacted, article 4 provided:

> The mass media may not be used for purposes of performing criminally punishable acts, for publicizing information which comprises a state secret or other secret protected by law, for an appeal to seizure of power, violent change of the constitutional order and integrity of the state, for inciting national class, social, religious prejudice or intolerance, or for propaganda of war.

Russian Mass Media Law, *supra* note 2, art. 4.

Later events, particularly the Beslan tragedy,[5] showed that media legislation did not always ensure "proper conduct" by journalists in and around a counterterrorism operation; media coverage could jeopardize the safety of hostages and security personnel. The authorities complained that terrorists could learn of the movements of security forces by watching TV news and listening to the radio. Russian officials hastily got to work on new laws and self-regulation standards that would significantly tighten the rules for covering such incidents. In 2005, after a concerted campaign by journalists' organizations, the president amended pending legislative proposals that would have restricted the media's rights. These, he said, would have contravened article 1 of the Statute "On the Mass Media," which states that the right to seek, obtain, produce, and disseminate mass information shall not be limited except by provision of the Mass Media statute itself. As a result, the clauses in question were absent from the new counterterrorism statute enacted in 2006.

The journalists' victory was short-lived, however. The State Duma interpreted the president's objections as a hint as to what it really needed to change. Within months of passing a liberal counterterrorism statute, it passed a law entitled "On amendments to individual legislative instruments of the Russian Federation in connection with enactment of the Federal Statute 'On ratification of the Council of Europe Convention on the Prevention of Terrorism.'" This new statute made two crucial amendments to article 4 of the mass media statute that affect the way in which journalists can report acts of terrorism and counterterrorism operations. First, article 4 now provides: "The procedure for information-gathering by journalists within the boundaries (site) of a counterterrorism operation shall be determined by the operation's commander." Second, it prohibits "disseminating materials which contain public calls to terrorist activity or publicly justify terrorism, and other extremist materials." Terrorism, in turn, was defined as "the ideology of violence and the practice of influencing the decision making of state bodies, local municipal bodies or international organizations, involving intimidation of the population and (or) other forms of illegal violent action."[6]

## II. RUSSIAN RESTRICTIONS ON "EXTREMISM"

It is quite possible that the lack of effective antiterrorism legal tools for regulating the media that hampered the authorities led to the 2002 drafting and enactment, on the

---

[5] This was the September 1, 2004 takeover by terrorists of a school in North Ossetia during an opening ceremony for a new school year. It resulted in some 350 deaths, including pupils, parents, and teachers. For a general account, see Timothy Phillips, *Beslan: The Tragedy of School No. 1* (2007).

[6] For an overview and critique of this and related legislation, see Lev Levinson, "Governance as a Counter-Terrorist Operation: Notes on the Russian legislation against terrorism" (Jan. 2007) (submission to the Eminent Jurists Panel), *available at* ejp.icj.org/IMG/Levinson.pdf.

president's initiative, of the Federal Statute "On Countering Extremist Activity."[7] The statute's central purpose as regards the media was to prohibit their engaging in "extremism" or being used to spread "extremist" material. Article 13 prohibited the publication or dissemination of extremist materials. The penalties for violating the ban culminate in the closure of the media outlet.

The key issue for the mass media under this statute is in what circumstances their actions could be deemed "extremist." In part, the statute defined "extremism" by listing acts, specifically including those by the mass media, that were already offenses under Article 282 of the Russian Criminal Code, to which I will return. These included what might be classified as hate speech. Thus, extremism included acts by the mass media or individuals directed at "excitation of racial, national or religious strife, and also social hatred associated with violence or calls for violence," or "the abasement of national dignity," or "propaganda of the exclusiveness, superiority or deficiency of individuals on the basis of their attitude to religion, social, racial, national, religious or linguistic identity."[8] But the 2002 statute also added new types of prohibited communications, mostly by linking them to violence or calls to violence. Thus extremist activity also includes "planning, organizing, preparing and committing acts directed at the violent . . . violation of the Russian Federation's territorial integrity," "seizure or usurpation of power," "creation of illegal armed formations," and "perpetration of terrorist activities."[9] In 2003, Article 282 of the Criminal Code was expanded accordingly. The need to have overlapping norms can be explained by the impossibility of using the Criminal Code against legal entities such as public organizations or mass media outlets.

This list of extremist activities was again significantly expanded by amendments passed in July 2006. This time, most observers understand the motivation for the changes to have been the desire to shield the authorities from criticism and protest. As amended, Article 13 now prohibits spreading material that explains or justifies extremist activity, disseminating public calls to engage in such activity, and promoting or facilitating such activity through the media without a link of such activity to violence, or threat thereof, or to calls for violence. In addition, the definition of extremist activity was broadened to include "public slander of involvement in extremist activity directed toward figures fulfilling the state duties of the Russian Federation," as well as "interfering with the legal duties of organs of state authorities."[10]

A year later, the statute was broadened yet further. The new wording of article 13 provides that materials are deemed extremist once a court decision designating them

[7] Russian Federation Statute on Countering Extremist Activity, July 25, 2002, No. 114-FZ, available, unamended, in English at http://medialaw.ru/e_pages/laws/russian/extrimist.htm (hereinafter Russian Extremism Law).

[8] *Id.* art. 1 (defining "extremist activity [extremism]").

[9] *Id.*

[10] Committee to Protect Journalists, "President signs law labeling criticism of state officials "'extremism'" (July 28, 2006) (expressing "alarm" at the new law), *available at* http://cpj.org/2006/07/president-signs-law-labeling-criticism-of-state-of.php.

such enters into force. Such a decision is made on the motion of the prosecutor concerned or as part of a resolution of an administrative, civil, or criminal case in which such demand was made. The amended articles 9 and 10 concern the Federal Register of Extremist Organizations. The decision to add an organization to the Register will be taken by the Ministry of Justice and will be based on a court decision on the ground of the petition of the federal Ministry of Justice or by its regional agency. While the petition is under consideration, the activity of such an organization may be suspended by the decision of the Ministry of Justice agency.[11]

Extremist acts or dissemination of extremist content by the media can quickly lead to closure of the media outlet. The initial sanction under the extremism statute and under article 4 of the mass media statute is a warning by *Roskomnadzor* or one of its regional bodies.[12] In general, the warning is preceded by an independent expert appraisal of the allegedly problematic content. A media outlet that receives two warnings in a twelve-month period is subject to permanent closure by a court. In some cases of threats to public security, even the initial warning leads to suspension of dissemination of the offending material and/or mass media outlet and could be a step in the procedure for closure of the latter. Both the extremism statute and the mass media statute provide for warnings and closure, obtained from a court on request of public prosecution at any level – from the Prosecutor General all the way down to a district public prosecutor – in cases of using the media for extremist purposes. Prosecutors are free to suspend activity of a given media outlet, confiscate the circulation, and petition the court of law to shut it down even after the first warning. The extremism statute expressly prohibits the media to disseminate information on the activity of organizations whose functions are forbidden by a court decision and which are included in the Federal Register of Extremist Organizations, unless the report makes an appropriate reference to that status, as, for example, by stating "this organization is forbidden as an extremist one."

The extremism statute imposes significant restrictions on the freedom of mass information. Its most dangerous consequence is that not only may reporters and editors be penalized for spreading extremist material (including slander of state officials; see earlier discussion),[13] but editorial offices and broadcasting companies can also face sanctions up to and including closure.

---

[11] For a highly critical assessment of the 2007 amendments, see Fred Weir, "Russia Stretches 'Extremism' Laws," *Christian Science Monitor*, Aug. 9, 2007, *available at* http://www.csmonitor.com/2007/0809/p06s01-woeu.html.

[12] "Roskomnadzor" is a Russian abbreviation for the Federal Service for Supervision of Communications, Information Technologies and Mass Media, which is located in the Ministry of Communications and Mass Communications. It is the key governmental mass media agency; its functions include licensing of broadcasters, registration of the mass media outlets, and issuance of warnings for noncompliance with the mass media statute.

[13] For example, the Code of the Russian Federation On Administrative Offences, Dec. 30, 2001, No. 195-FZ, now has Article 20.29, which refers to the liability for the production and dissemination of extremist materials. It provides for high fines for persons and organizations found guilty of this offense. Similarly, the Russian Criminal Code, No. 63-FZ, and the Criminal Procedure Code, No. 174-FZ, impose liability for crimes committed with extremist and xenophobic motives. *See* Nadezhda Deeva,

Any media outlet that has received a warning has a right to seek judicial review. In most such appeals, the judges side with the prosecutors and/or *Roskomnadzor*.[14] One instance in which a warning to a media outlet was successfully challenged in court stands out. The 2×2 television channel, owned by a private Russian company, *ProfMedia*, broadcasts via cable networks throughout Russia and broadcasts in St. Petersburg over the air. Its twenty-four-hour-a-day programming consists of cartoons for adults. Critics view some of the cartoons as pornographic, encouraging violence and cruelty, and amounting to the crime of extremism in purposely promoting religious strife. The company has asserted that these critical attacks are insincere, motivated not by genuine concern with their legality but by competitors' interest in obtaining 2×2's precious frequency in St. Petersburg.

Reportedly spurred by public complaints, a Moscow district prosecutor's office in the Basmanny county obtained an expert opinion (from the Center of Legal Expertise of the North-Western District in St. Petersburg) that an episode of the "South Park" cartoon series entitled "Mr. Hankey's Christmas Classics" was extremist within the meaning of the extremism statute because it promoted hatred between religions. That served as the basis of a warning under the statute. In addition, in September 2008, the same prosecutor initiated a separate criminal investigation against the editor-in-chief of the TV channel on suspicion of excitement of religious strife. In a further motion, the prosecutors asked the court to declare the series to be extremist material that would justify criminal prosecution of those who disseminated it for violation of Article 282 of the Russian Criminal Code, which addresses "Incitement of Hatred or Enmity, as Well as Abasement of Human Dignity."[15]

"Russian Federation: Anti-extremism Amendments," 9 *IRIS: Legal Observations of the European Audiovisual Observatory* 19 (2007).

[14] Useful discussions can be found in a series of reports in English by Alexander Verkhovsky, including "Inappropriate enforcement of the anti-extremist legislation in Russia in 2009," available on the Web site of the SOVA Center for Information and Analysis. *See* http://www.sova-center.ru/en/misuse/reports-analyses/2010/04/d18482/.

[15] Article 282 provides:

   1. Actions, designed to incite hate or enmity as well as demean the dignity of a person or group of persons on the basis of sex, race, nationality, language, origin, relationship to religion as well as the affiliation to any social group, committed publicly or with the use of the mass media

   are punishable by a fine in the amount of one hundred thousand to three hundred thousand rubles or in the amount of the salary or other income of the perpetrator of one to two years, or in the loss of the right to occupy certain positions or engage in certain activities for a period of up to three years, or by mandatory work for a period of up to one hundred eighty hours, or by corrective work for a period up to one year, or by incarceration for a period of up to two years.

   2. The same actions, committed:
      a. with the use of violence or with the threat to use it
      b. by a person using his/her official position
      c. by an organized group

   are publishable by a fine in the amount of one hundred thousand to five hundred thousand rubles or in the amount of a salary or other income of the perpetrator for the period of one to three years, or by the loss of right to occupy certain positions or engage in certain activities for a period of up to five

After two new expert opinions were provided that concluded that the cartoons were not extremist, these latter efforts – the investigation and the court motion – were abandoned by the prosecutor's office.[16] However, it continued to defend the legality of the warning in court. On June 2, 2009, the Basmanny District Court in Moscow, relying on the expert opinions, overruled the warning. The District Court decision was appealed by the prosecutor's office in the Moscow City Court, which upheld the lower court's decision on August 28, 2009.[17] Accordingly, the 2×2 channel has retained its sought-after frequency in St. Petersburg.

## III. INTERVIEWS WITH "TERRORISTS" AND "EXTREMISTS"

Judging from its legislative and law-enforcement activity, the type of media content that most worries the government is that which can be labeled extremist. Of this, the subset that until recently incurred the greatest official wrath was interviews with Chechen separatist leaders. By today, however, this type of journalist material has been effectively eradicated. Let us consider the legal means of counteracting such interviews.

As the second Chechen conflict began in autumn 1999, the State Duma passed a resolution "On the situation in the Republic of Dagestan, and priority measures to ensure the national security of the Russian Federation and the fight against terrorism." The Resolution called for "the taking of all necessary steps to prevent appearances in the media by representatives of illegal armed formations," and for "failure to heed this demand to be treated as a serious offence, leading to the imposition of sanctions as contained in Russian Federation legislation up to and including withdrawal of broadcast license."

As regards actual law-enforcement practice, the figures on the press ministry's warnings to the media are of particular interest. During the four-year period from 2000 to the end of 2003, it handed out a total of forty-five warnings for abuse of freedom of mass information, of which thirty-five were for inciting interethnic enmity.[18] What most caught the government's attention here was interviews with

---

years or by mandatory work for the period of one hundred twenty to two hundred forty hours, or by corrective labor for a period of one to two years, or by incarceration for a period of up to five years.

Ugoloynyi Kodeks RF [UK] [Criminal Code] art. 282 (Russ.).

[16] These experts included the author of this article. Our opinion was based on the need to take into account the target audience, the context of the particular series, the cartoon's genre of satire, the absence of calls to violence against a religion or its followers, and the absence of special linguistic or other means to convey slanderous characteristics or negative emotional evaluations, negative frameworks in relation to a particular religion or its believers – in short, the cartoon could not be expected actually to provoke religious strife or conflict in Russia. *See* Andrei Richter, "TV extremism: Content analysis of the South Park cartoon series," *Mediascope* (Feb. 2009), http://mediascope.ru/node/396 (in Russian).

[17] Andrei Richter, "RU: Warning to broadcaster annulled," 8 *IRIS: Legal Observations of the European Audiovisual Observatory* 18 (2009).

[18] *See* http://www.lenizdat.ru/ao/ru/pm1/c.thtml?i=1016744&p=0#1 .

separatists. In contrast, according to the official report of *Roskomnadzor* for 2008,[19] during that year, the Federal Service issued forty-seven written warnings to various media outlets for violation of Article 4 ("Inadmissibility of abuse of the freedom of mass information") of the Statute "On the Mass Media." Of these, twenty-eight were for dissemination of extremist materials. In 2009 the ratio was sixty-seven total to thirty-three anti-extremism warnings.[20] These figures demonstrate a heavy increase of the emphasis for the government on fighting extremism from among other violations of the law by the mass media outlets.

Although not a statute, and thus not legally binding, the 1999 resolution amounted to a de facto ban on Chechen rebels in the Russian media. This occurred at the same time as the second conflict began. In August 1999, the press ministry sent a telegram to all the nationwide TV channels, gently advising them not to carry interviews with the rebels. In February 2000, the first deputy press minister, Mikhail Seslavinsky, cautioned *Radio Liberty* and *Ekho Moskvy* radio that "if any Chechen terrorist leader is allowed into the Russian media to air views that justify acts of terrorism of hostage-taking, there would be grounds for the ministry to investigate."

The ministry progressed from threats to action when it issued official warnings to the newspapers *Kommersant* and *Novaya gazeta* in April 2000 and *Nezavisimaya gazeta* in March 2001. In February 2005, *Kommersant* received another warning, this time from a new government body, *Rosokhrankultura*,[21] which alleged both an abuse of freedom of mass information and violation of the extremism statute.[22]

Of particular interest is a 2003 action against the newspaper *Zavtra*. In September of that year, the Ministry of Culture issued *Zavtra* an official warning for printing an interview by its editor-in-chief Aleksandr Prokhanov with "Maskhadov envoy" Akhmed Zakayev. The warning alleged violations of article 4 of the mass media statute and articles 1 and 8 of the extremism statute. The paper sought judicial review, and the Tverskoy intermunicipal court in Moscow set aside the warning in May 2003. The court relied on an analysis of the interview prepared for the ministry at the Russian Academy of Sciences' Miklukho-Maklay Institute of Ethnology and Anthropology – by a chief researcher who was also chairman of the coordinating council of Chechen cultural and public organizations in Moscow.[23] Shortly

---

[19]   The full text of the Report is available at http://www.rsoc.ru/main/about/960/.

[20]   The full text of the Report is available at http://rsoc.ru/docs/doc_530.pdf.

[21]   This agency, the Federal Surveillance Service for Compliance with the Legislation in Mass Media and Cultural Heritage Protection, was the predecessor to the *Roskomnadzor*.

[22]   All four warnings, incidentally, were prompted by interviews with Aslan Maskhadov. The ordinary procedure was for the press ministry to confer with experts and request expert opinion from the prosecutor-general's office and state academic institutions before it issued a warning for abuse of freedom of mass information. (As occurred, for example, in the warning issued to 2×2 discussed earlier.) But in these cases, interestingly, the prosecutor bypassed that process and acted on the day of publication or the following day. It is doubtful, therefore, that the offending articles received any kind of proper expert analysis.

[23]   *See* http://www.gazeta.ru/kz/more_business.shtml.

afterward, on May 21, 2003, then deputy press minister Valeriy Sirozhenko told a conference at the State Duma that *Zavtra* was about to be stripped of its registration permit without reference to the courts.[24] The threat was not carried out, but we should note that the extremism statute contains no such extrajudicial procedure.

Let us take a closer look at the *Zavtra* case. Strikingly, the warning simply asserted that article 4 of the mass media statute had been breached; it offered no reasoning or specific quotes to back up this conclusion. Had the ministry at least once highlighted the offending content, it would have helped editors to avoid repeats. Furthermore, no one in the media (with the possible exceptions of *Radio Liberty* and *Kommersant*) and no civil-liberties group examined the substance behind the charges or came to the defense of the accused journalists. So we will undertake our own review of the publication.

Prokhanov, the interviewer, himself says nothing objectionable. He was, of course, giving Zakayev publicity, but there is no sign in the text of the newspaper pursuing an extremist or separatist agenda or backing terrorism. In the interview, Prokhanov politely distances himself from his interviewee: "We . . . are on opposite ends of the spectrum as politicians and soldiers, and we both have our own vision of the truth." Elsewhere, in a passage about whether Chechnya should secede from Russia, Prokhanov says: "For Chechens, the only terms for peace are absolute sovereignty, Chechnya's absolute independence from Russia. But for modern-day Russia to accept these terms would amount to capitulation."

Later on he explains that the purpose of the interview is to look at individual aspects of the Chechen conflict by showing a man who holds separatist views but is very different from "the poverty-stricken slow-witted men of the mountains or the Moscow kebab peddlers." He apparently wants to hold up to public scrutiny, examine, and explain the conduct of Chechens who advocate the separatist cause: "It is important for me to understand your point of view. . . . [I]t seems that there are three Chechnyas. The one that you represent is grenade-launchers, landmines and terrorism. There is a second Chechnya, constructed by Moscow, which consists of Kadyrov and his administration, police, money and universities. And there is a third, which is the diaspora that has embedded itself within Russia, in Russia's world of business and its politics and culture."

Prokhanov counters Zakayev's separatism with this: "Do you not think that after they return from their exile in Kazakhstan, the Chechens embarked upon a new era of prosperity? Cities, industries, universities sprang up. A splendid intelligentsia of scholarship and the arts emerged. And all this was given to them by the empire." And again, further on: "Chechnya chose for itself the path of war, of suffering, of total resistance. But is war really better than development?"

Both Prokhanov and Zakayev condemn terrorism and speak of the amorality, danger, and illegality of propagating ethnic hatred or notions of ethnic supremacy.

---

[24] *See* http://www.i-news.org/viewnews/sng/4722.

Zakayev, for example, says this: "If someone were to say that there must be acts of terrorism in Russia, I would not understand him. They might be effective if Russia had a civic society that could through fear influence its rulers and force them to stop the war. But it has no such thing. As a result terrorism can only increase the number of casualties in the war; it cannot force any political outcome."

An open-minded review of the *Zavtra* interviews reveals that this was a serious, not sensational, piece of journalism intended for an informed readership. The authorities had no cause to intervene and the warning was unfounded.

Indeed, closure of a publication because of articles such as this could have been successfully challenged at the European Court of Human Rights. Interpreting the Convention for the Protection of Human Rights and Fundamental Freedoms in the well-known *Jersild* case, [25] that Court ruled that media restrictions of this nature, even if permitted by law, are not, as the Convention requires, "necessary in a democratic society."[26]

The Russian presidency's short-lived Judicial Chamber for Information Disputes, which was in existence from 1994 to 2000, arrived at a similar conclusion in 1995 when it examined a complaint from MPs against the VGRTK state broadcaster. The MPs argued that a program called *Newspaper Histories (Fascism in Russia – who?)* was provocative, inflammatory, and capable of inciting ethnic strife. But the Chamber rejected the claim, concluding that the program's title and content showed that it was an attempt to highlight fascism in Russia, the form it takes, and specific individuals behind its ideology and practice. For that reason, the program was timely and justified, it raised public concerns, and it prompted official action – which is, after all, a basic goal of investigative journalism.

This chapter addresses actions "beyond hate speech." That is not to ignore actual hate speech incidents and restrictions used to combat racist, chauvinistic, anti-Semitic, and other types of speech. For example, in 2007, Zyuzinsky district court in Moscow reached a verdict in the case of Aleksandr Aratov, the editor of the marginal *Russkaya pravda* newspaper. Investigation had proved that the articles published by Aratov incited national enmity, religious and racial hatred at large and specifically toward Jewish nation and Christianity. In addition, they contained information that called for violence against Chechen and Jewish ethnic groups. The journalist was found guilty, under Article 282 of the Criminal Code,[27] of incitement of hatred and enmity and of abasement of the honor and dignity of a person and groups of people by criteria of ethnicity and attitude to religion through the use of the mass media. Because these acts were committed through the journalist's official position,

---

[25] Jersild v. Denmark, 298 Eur. Ct. H.R. (ser. A) (1994).
[26] For a discussion of *Jersild* and the European Court of Human Rights free-speech jurisprudence in general, *see* Tarlach McGonagle, "A Survey and Critical Analysis of Council of Europe Strategies for Countering 'Hate Speech'," Chapter 24 herein.
[27] *See supra* note 15.

as editor of his own newspaper, the heavier sanction of imprisonment of three to five years was applicable. Aratov received a three-year suspended sentence, including a two-year probationary period. The verdict was appealed but upheld by the Moscow city court.

## IV. THE MOHAMMAD CARTOONS

The worldwide conflict caused by publishing Mohammad cartoons first in Danish and then other western newspapers had its echo in Russia, although it was a tiny one compared to clashes elsewhere. But it is emblematic of the limits of the free press here.

The cartoons have never appeared in the national or Moscow media. The reason usually given is that editors are extremely cautious about triggering the rage of the government. From the start of the controversy, the Russian government expressed a strong policy against publication of the cartoons. The head of the governmental service that oversees compliance with the media law has expressed concern that publication would incite violence – not violence in Russian cities, but in Arab capitals directed against Russian diplomats.

Before the firm government opposition became clear, however, the Mohammad cartoons were published by a handful of provincial media: on February 9, 2006, in Volgograd's *Gorodskie vesti* daily; on February 15, in Vologda's *Nash Region Plus* newspaper; in March, in *Bankfax*, an Internet news service in Altai; and the same month, on the Internet site Pravda.ru (a site unrelated to the newspaper *Pravda*). The immediate and firm government response is instructive and reveals a great deal about the relation between the government and the press in Russia. Consider the following elements:

- *Swift response.* The government reaction to the appearance of the cartoons in these obscure publications was firm and instantaneous. The federal service and/or prosecutor's office immediately issued warnings asserting that the publishers had excited religious strife, thus violating the anti-extremism statute, and threatening closure if violation of government policy continued. Such a swift reaction was quite unusual and can be equated only with the instances of interviews with Chechen separatists published in Russian papers in 2000–2005.
- *Damage control.* Every possible step was taken to erase from the historical record even the fact that these "harmful" materials were ever published. The newspapers in Vologda and Volgograd were both shut down by their owners, obviously under pressure from the top. Interestingly, the Volgograd newspaper was resurrected the next day by the same owner with the same journalists – but under a slightly different title. In Vologda, the owner closed the newspaper for good. (This would seem an act of purge if the owner were not the husband of the editor who had published the cartoon.) As for the two Internet postings, the

Federal Security Service did everything possible to block access to the pages in question within hours.

- *The rule of law.* Russia has not had a blasphemy law since 1917. (Prior to that date, such a law had a long tradition in Russia. Peter the Great enacted the first such prohibition, punishing blasphemy by chopping off lips and burning the tongue. More recently, in the early twentieth century, a person convicted of blasphemy in Russia merely faced imprisonment of up to six months. But modern Russia has a civilized Criminal Code). The editor in Vologda was prosecuted under Article 282 of the Criminal Code, which prohibits actions that incite religious enmity or abase human dignity. At the trial, a local Muslim leader testified that he had not even seen the cartoons that so offended him until the investigators showed them to him and asked him to come forward as a victim. Moreover, during the trial, it turned out that the particular cartoons shown to him had not in fact been reprinted in the newspaper. Despite these and other procedural flaws, the editor was fined 100,000 rubles (almost $4,000) – a substantial sum that would impress any provincial editor in Russia.
- *Learning from your neighbor.* The swift, harsh response from the government sent an unmistakable signal to editors and publishers nationwide, all of whom clearly got the message to stay away from any controversial materials that were so high on the official agenda. With the lesson well learned, peace has not been disturbed.
- *Team spirit.* Publishers and editors cannot but have learned another lesson: In dealing with the authorities, do not count on professional solidarity. In the first hours after the pressure was put on the Vologda newspaper, when it was not yet clear that the government was behind the displeasure of the prosecutors, national Media-Union, a professional organization of which the editor was not just a member but the regional branch leader, promised support and legal aid. But those promises were retracted the next day without explanation. The Russian Union of Journalists made a statement supportive of the editor but did not go any further. Once again individual news outlets faced the harsh reality that in a conflict with the authorities they could rely only on themselves. Indeed, the professional associations are presently at their weakest point in the post-Soviet period. To make things worse, for the first time in the same period, journalists cannot rely on public support.[28]
- *"Just don't take it personally."* In May 2006, an appeals court ruled that the Vologda editor did not have to pay the fine as the public danger had passed. And there was no public danger, the judge said, because the newspaper was shut down anyway.[29]

---

[28] *See generally* Andrei Richter, *Post-Soviet Perspective on Censorship and Freedom of the Media* 285–310 (UNESCO 2007).

[29] Article 14 of the Criminal Code, titled "The Concept of Crime," defines crimes as certain "socially dangerous act[s]," and specifies that to be a crime, such acts must cause harm or create a threat of damage to a person, society, or the state.

In sum, the story of the publication of the Mohammad cartoons in Russia demonstrates that the government holds strong views on what is appropriate and permissible for the press to publish and, even though it is probably unable to control all 100,000 registered media outlets, the government is quite capable of inducing compliance with those strong views.

## V. COUNTERTERRORISM RESTRICTIONS IN OTHER CIS STATES

Most Commonwealth of Independent States (CIS) countries' have adopted a version of the CIS Inter-Parliamentary Assembly's Model Statute "On the fight against terrorism," adopted December 8, 1998 and revised in 2009.[30] Model statutes, as their name implies, serve as examples that are recommended by the Inter-Parliamentary Assembly of the CIS, which is currently comprised of delegations of the parliaments of Armenia, Azerbaijan, Belarus, Kazakhstan, Kyrgyzstan, Moldova, Russian Federation, Tajikistan, and Ukraine to the national parliaments.

Article 21 of the model terrorism statute deals with restrictions on reporting. In particular, it bans the disclosure of special techniques and tactics used in counterterrorism operations, of any information that might impede a counterterrorism operation or endanger human life or health, or of details of special-forces personnel involved, or of other persons assisting. This provision (in various forms) can be found in most of the legislative instruments against terrorism currently in place in the former Soviet Union.[31] At the same time, however, each has its own particular features. Ukraine's statute adds to the list of prohibited publications any reports on devices that could be used for hi-tech terrorism or on calls to resist a counterterrorism operation. It also makes the release of information about persons assisting a counterterrorism operation conditional on their consent. Turkmenistan prohibits video recording and live radio and television broadcasts from the area of a counterterrorism operation – which is entirely sensible, given the tragic way in which the hostages were freed in the Moscow theater siege.[32]

---

[30] *See* Andrei Richter, "Commonwealth of Independent States: Model Statute to Fight Terrorism," 9 *IRIS: Legal Observations of the European Audiovisual Observatory* 1 (2010).

[31] E.g., article 15 of Belarus's statute of 2002; article 14 of Moldova's organic statute of 2001; article 17 of Ukraine's statute of 2003; article 16 of Turkmenistan's statute of 2003. The only exceptions are Kyrgyzstan's terrorism statute of 1999, which says nothing at all about regulating the media, and Kazakhstan's equivalent, also of 1999.

[32] Professor Kim Scheppele, who was in Moscow at the time, recalls:

In October 2002, about fifty Chechen terrorists stormed a Moscow theater where the popular Russian musical Nord-Ost (North-East) was in full swing. Heavily armed with guns and large bombs, the terrorists held everyone in the theater hostage – probably about 800 people, though an exact count has never been given – for three days. The siege was broken when the Russian special forces pumped a sleeping gas into the theater, knocking out both hostages and terrorists before the bombs could be detonated. Storming the building, the special forces shot all of the unconscious terrorists at point blank range and waited an impossibly long time before evacuating the unconscious hostages. In the end, about 130 of the hostages died, virtually all from reactions to the sleeping gas and the botched

The Turkmen law, incidentally, is the only one among those examined here that confers a special role on the media. In particular, clause 2 of article 11 says that the media, together with the relevant ministries, agencies, and public associations, should work in a nationwide and meaningful way to foster noble spiritual and moral ideals in Turkmenistan's citizens and instill in the younger generation a sense of national pride and loyalty to their traditions and nation, and constant readiness to lay down their lives for their beloved Fatherland to ensure its security and integrity. This has a practical effect as almost all Turkmen media are established by the office of the President of the country.

It is worth noting that the criminal codes of several of these countries make it an offense to use the media for advocating terrorism or spreading calls to commit acts of terrorism.[33]

## VI. RESTRICTIONS FOR COUNTERING EXTREMISM IN OTHER CIS STATES

The laws against extremism in former Soviet countries are generally less developed than those against terrorism. The first to enter into force was Russia's 2002 Statute "On countering extremist activity," discussed earlier. Moldova and Tajikistan passed similar statutes in 2003, Kazakhstan and Kyrgyzstan in 2005, and Belarus in 2007. The trend was even more solidified by the Commonwealth of Independent States (CIS) Interparliamentary Assembly which enacted on May 14, 2009 the Model Statute with the same title.[34]

Moldova's extremism statute deserves a closer look. It defines its subject matter as, in particular, media activities in the planning, organization, preparation, or commission of acts intended to:

- forcibly change the foundations of the constitutional order or violate the Republic of Moldova's territorial integrity;
- undermine the Republic of Moldova's security;
- seize state power or usurp the authority of an official;
- establish illegal armed groups;
- engage in terrorist activities;
- incite racial, ethnic, or religious enmity or social enmity with violence or calls to violence;

rescue. (Only two had been killed by the terrorists.) . . . [T]he whole event was broadcast live on television, including live audio of cell phone calls out of the theater from hostages and even a live television interview inside the theater during the stand-off with some of the terrorists.

Kim Lane Scheppele, "'We Forgot About the Ditches': Russian Constitutional Impatience and the Challenge of Terrorism," 53 *Drake L. Rev.* 963, 1009–10 (2005).

[33] *See, e.g.,* Kazakhstan, article 233–1.

[34] *See* Andrei Richter, "Commonwealth of Independent States: Model Statute to Fight Extremism," 9 *IRIS: Legal Observations of the European Audiovisual Observatory* 7 (2010).

- denigrate national dignity;
- provoke mass unrest, commit breaches of public order or acts of vandalism for reasons of ideological, political racial, ethnic or religious hatred or enmity, or of hatred or enmity toward any group in society;
- advocate exclusivity, superiority, or inferiority on grounds of religion or race, nationality, ethnicity, language, gender, opinions, political affiliation, property status, or social origin.

The statute authorizes a court of law to declare a media outlet an extremist organization if it engages in extremism or disseminates content of an extremist nature, meaning documents or information in various formats and including content that is anonymous, intended for publication, and designed to call for or justify extremist activity or justify war crimes or other crimes.

Article 7 of the statute sets out a detailed procedure for closing down an extremist media outlet. It begins with the registering authority or prosecutor-general (or subordinate prosecutors) issuing to the founder and/or editorial office (editor-in-chief) a written warning with details of the offenses. If the offenses can be remedied, a deadline is given of a maximum of one month from the date of the warning. We see the following problem here, however: No *minimum* deadline is specified, nor is it stated that the deadline should be reasonable, so there is potential for abuse. That said, a warning can be contested in court.

If a warning is not contested or if its legality is upheld, if no remedial action is taken by the given deadline, or if within twelve months of being warned a media outlet is again engaging in extremism or spreading extremist content, then the registering authority or prosecutor-general (or subordinate prosecutors) can apply to the courts for it to be shut down or suspended for up to one year. Of course if the offenses could be remedied but were not remedied within the stated period, the media outlet faced forced closure or suspension.

To prevent the continued distribution of extremist content, a court can suspend the sale of the relevant issues of a periodical, or the production run of an audiovisual medium, or the release of a television, radio, or video program in execution of a court ruling. A court may also order confiscation of the unsold part of a media production run with extremist content, from wholesale and retail premises.

The statute not only describes the procedure for halting extremism in the media but also gives the media a role in fighting extremism, the fundamental principles for which include, in particular, collaboration between the state and the media. One of the particular aims of the Moldova's anti-extremist legislation is a peculiar situation when part of the country is a de facto independent Trans-Dniester Moldovan Republic, which in the eyes of the Moldova's law presents in itself a hotbed of terrorism and, consequently, extremism. Thus the anti-extremism statute serves the interests of the political elite in Chisinau to limit free speech on the coexistence of the two parts of the country and shape it in the framework of a fight against "extremism."

Kazakhstan's extremism statute is generally similar to Moldova's, although during its passage through parliament, MPs managed to remove from its text all relevant clauses on media regulation. Also, the procedure for stopping the spread of extremist content is less detailed. Article 12 prohibits the use of communications networks and systems for extremism and also the publication and dissemination of extremist content. Whether content is extremist is decided by a court of law local to the media outlet in question, at the request of prosecutors; in the case of religious extremism, a court-appointed expert must review the material in question.

## VII. CONCLUSION

Authorities in some of the CIS countries are imposing restrictions on journalists that are not actually "necessary in a democratic society" as that phrase is used Article 10 of the European Convention on Human Rights. The wording of these countries' extremism and terrorism statutes is so broad and vague that they can be and are used to stifle debate in the media of issues of increasing public interest – such as the motivations underlying insurgency. The authorities could use these statutes and their clauses to suppress the views of radical political opponents. For the sake of democracy itself, it is crucial that the public, and the journalistic and academic communities, debate the "war on terror" restrictions on freedom of mass information. It is unfortunate that the state rarely seeks to balance the need to eradicate terrorism with respect for journalists' rights, preferring the easier path of curbing the flow of information and the circulation of opinions.

# 15

# Hate Speech and Comprehensive Forms of Life

*Alon Harel*

## I. INTRODUCTION

This chapter attempts to justify a differential treatment of hate speech in accordance with the discourse to which it belongs. More specifically, it argues that hate speech that constitutes an integral part of a comprehensive and valuable form of life (what I will call "deeply rooted" hate speech) should be protected more stringently than hate speech that is not "deeply rooted."

Two considerations justify greater respect for deeply rooted hate speech. First, when hate speech is part of a broader and more comprehensive and valuable form of life, its regulation expresses authoritative condemnation not only of the views or opinions censored, but also of the whole way of life of which they are a part.[1] This is because hate speech that is part of such a comprehensive way of life is typically related to other foundational components of the tradition. Second, direct prohibition of such speech is both less necessary and less likely to be effective than prohibition of hate speech that is not deeply rooted. When hate speech is part of a comprehensive and valuable form of life, it is understood by those who share this form of life as part of a more comprehensive worldview. Therefore, on the one hand, there are prospects of reinterpreting the tradition in new and benign ways – ways that will transform the discourse and eradicate the sentiments of hatred. And, on the other hand, external legal intervention is unlikely to succeed in eradicating such sentiments. When hate speech is deeply rooted in individuals' long-term customs, ways of life, and ideological commitments, when it is bound up with their identity,

---

[1] *See* Joseph Raz, "Free Expression and Personal Identification," in *Ethics in the Public Domain: Essays in the Morality of Law and Politics* 131, 141 (Clarendon Press 1994).

This chapter was presented at a conference on hate speech at the Cardozo Law School. I am grateful to the participants of the conference for their comments. I am also grateful for the very thorough and detailed comments of Peter Molnar on numerous drafts. Zelma Rios edited the chapter and provided excellent comments. I am grateful to her for her contribution to the completion of this chapter.

external direct intervention – in particular, criminal law, tort law, and other forms of coercive intervention – are unlikely to succeed in eradicating the sentiments of hatred.

Two limiting clarifications should be made at the outset. First, a benign interpretation of a tradition is feasible or likely only when the tradition in its entirety includes prominent humanistic components. Islam, Judaism, and Christianity fall into such a category. Nazism and the Ku Klux Klan do not. They are hatred-based traditions and, consequently, the argument is inapplicable to them.[2] The hate speech promulgated by these latter groups may be deeply rooted, but the tradition in which it is rooted is not a humanistic one and, consequently, the prospects of reinterpretation in benign ways are slim or nonexistent.

Second, I do not argue that the protection granted to deeply rooted hate speech is absolute. For instance, speech that is likely to cause imminent violence ought to be regulated even when it is deeply rooted.[3] Whether the speech is dangerous is a critical factor in determining the degree of protection of that speech.

The arguments in this chapter are ultimately grounded in empirical or quasi-empirical conjectures. No purely logical or conceptual arguments establish that deeply rooted hate speech ought to be protected more stringently than speech that is not deeply rooted. The ultimate test of the soundness of these arguments is the realities on the ground, and it is crucial, therefore, to examine whether the factual premises underlying the analysis are sound.

The distinction drawn in this chapter is relevant not only to hate speech, but also to other forms of discriminatory or harmful behavior that are part of a comprehensive form of life. Many harmful nonspeech activities are also integral to forms of life, and these nonspeech activities deserve greater protection when they are conducted as part of more comprehensive (and valuable) forms of life. Thus, this chapter examines hate speech not as part of free-speech jurisprudence, but as part of the discourse concerning multiculturalism and the regulation of cultural practices.[4]

Section II explains what comprehensive forms of life are and what it means to say that a practice is part of a comprehensive form of life. Section III defends the claim that regulation of deeply rooted hate speech typically is understood to express contempt not only toward the censored speech or the ideas contained in it, but also

---

[2] Of course, the question of whether a group belongs to a particular category is not always easy to answer. I explore this question later in the chapter.

[3] Some would argue that deeply rooted hate speech is more likely to be dangerous. This is an empirical question that I am not going to explore here.

[4] In an article that traces the fundamental differences between European hate-speech legislation and American hate-speech legislation, James Whitman demonstrates that not all western cultures conceptualize hate speech within the free-speech rubric. Germany regulates hate speech as part of intricate legislation governing civility. Civility includes the practices that involve showing respect to others. These practices include not only forms of address (the use of "Sir" and "Madam"), but also nonverbal activities such as yielding to one another on the street, forms of deportment, etc. James Q. Whitman, "Enforcing Civility and Respect: Three Societies," 109 *Yale L.J.* 1279 (2000).

toward the form of life of which it is a part. Section IV defends the claim that external legal regulation of hate speech is unlikely to be effective in the case of deeply rooted hate speech and that internal transformation is more likely to succeed in eradicating deeply rooted hatred. Section V investigates some institutional concerns that may be raised by differentiating hate speech that is deeply rooted from hate speech that is not. It argues that despite the difficulties in differentiating deeply rooted hate speech from other instances of hate speech, these determinations can be made, and, indeed, the legal system already uses them.

## II. HATE SPEECH AND VALUABLE COMPREHENSIVE FORMS OF LIFE

### A. *Challenging the Speech/Conduct Distinction*

Any doctrine of freedom of expression must face the following question: Why should society respect people's freedom to express false, worthless, degrading, or depraved views and opinions? It is bad opinions that ultimately need the protection of the principle of free speech. Typically, there is no reason to regulate the good ones.

Hate speech constitutes one of the most damaging forms of "bad speech." The most serious harms from hate speech are expressive and psychological injuries; prominent advocates of hate speech legislation often highlight the distinctive nature of these harms.[5] Other harms that, in the view of some, may justify regulation of hate speech include the risk of violence and the contribution of such speech to creating or sustaining and reinforcing a discriminatory or oppressive social environment.[6]

To address these concerns, legislatures can use two tests to identify and regulate hate speech. First, they can regulate hate speech on the basis of the evil intentions of the speaker or the evil content of the speech. Second, they can regulate hate speech on the basis of the potential harms it may cause. Under the intention/meaning test, an expression motivated by certain intentions, or an expression with certain meaning, is classified as an offense without an examination of whether the speech leads, or may lead, to harm. Under the test of materialization of harm, the courts ought to determine whether the expression was likely to cause actual harm on the basis of the concrete circumstances in which it was said. The well-known test of "near certainty" of serious harm is one of the tests used by judges to determine the justifiability of regulation.[7] One of the main debates in the jurisprudence of hate

---

[5] *See, e.g.*, Mari J. Matsuda, "Public Response to Racist Speech: Considering the Victim's Story," 87 *Mich. L. Rev.* 2320 (1989).

[6] Bhikhu Parekh's chapter in the present volume provides a useful overview. *See* Bhikhu Parekh, "Is There a Case for Banning Hate Speech?," Chapter 2 herein. *See also* Jean Stefancic and Richard Delgado, "A Shifting Balance: Freedom of Expression and Hate Speech Restriction," 78 *Iowa L. Rev.* 737 (1993) (book review).

[7] *See, e.g.*, Kahane v. Broadcasting Authority, 41 (3) P.D. 255, 295–6 (Isr. 1986) (upholding ban on march by followers of anti-Arab political leader because "a near certainty of real injury exists because of the

speech is the debate between the advocates of the intention/meaning test and the advocates of the materialization of harm test.[8]

The fact that hate speech generally both reflects evil meaning/intentions and causes grave harm (expressive or emotional harm and often incitement to violence) puts the burden of justification on those who would protect it. Opponents of hate-speech legislation address this challenge in two ways. Some free-speech advocates believe that bad speech (including hate speech) should be protected because of the institutional inability to distinguish bad speech from good speech. The primary aim of a free-speech doctrine is to guarantee the existence and flourishing of good speech. The well-known Millian belief in the "marketplace of ideas," with its "hidden hand" mechanism guaranteeing (in a fairy-tale manner) the ultimate victory of good speech, is the most influential version of such a theory.[9]

In contrast, other free-speech theorists believe that bad speech is valuable not as a means to guarantee the flourishing of good speech, but because of some redeeming features of speech as such (including bad speech). Under this view, speech *as such* – irrespective of its content or the intentions of the speakers – has some value. Perhaps the most influential theory of this latter type grounds protection of free speech in autonomy considerations. Under this theory, speech, including bad speech, is a means by which individuals exercise their autonomy. Its value is therefore a by-product of its being an expression or a manifestation of one's autonomy.[10] Other theorists of free speech have identified other important benefits of protecting bad speech (including hate speech).[11]

One feature characterizes all of the views mentioned earlier. They all share the view that hate speech ought to be classified as speech – though possibly speech that does not merit the protections generally accorded to speech. Under this view, activities are divided into speech activities and nonspeech activities. The former are more protected than the latter; the question is whether hate speech falls outside the

racist content of Petitioners' message" and "[a] near certainty that the feelings of a religious or ethnic minority be really and harshly hurt, by publication of a deviant speech, is enough to justify limiting that speech"); Kol-Haam v. Minister of Interior, 7 P.D. 871 (Isr. 1953) (holding that expression may be restricted for reasons of security and public order only when there is "near certainty" that a grave threat to such public interests will materialize).

8   For a discussion of these tests, see Alon Harel, "The Regulation of Speech: A Normative Investigation of Criminal Law Prohibitions of Speech," in *Freedom of Speech and Incitement against Democracy* 247 (David Kretzmer & Francine Kershman Hazan eds., Kluwer Law International 2000).

9   The Millian argument is dissected by Frederick Schauer in his chapter in the present volume. *See* Frederick Schauer, "Social Epistemology, Holocaust Denial, and the Post-Millian Calculus," Chapter 7 herein.

10  For an attempt to defend such a position, see C. Edwin Baker, *Human Liberty and Freedom of Speech* (Oxford University Press 1989). Professor Baker's chapter in the present volume articulates a preliminary autonomy-based justification for protecting hate speech. *See* C. Edwin Baker, "Hate Speech," Chapter 3 herein.

11  One of the more interesting theories is that toleration of speech is conducive to the flourishing of the virtue of toleration in general. *See* Lee C. Bollinger, *The Tolerant Society: Freedom of Speech and Extremist Speech in America* (Oxford University Press 1986).

general protection granted to speech. The most visible indication of the importance of classifying hate speech as a form of speech is the fact that advocates of regulating hate speech often claim that hate speech is *not* speech, but "speech acts," and therefore, its regulation ought not to be regarded as regulation of speech, but as the regulation of conduct.[12] Under this view, concluding that hate speech is not speech removes the most important barrier to its regulation.

These structural features of the debate concerning hate speech are predictable given the First Amendment doctrine. The First Amendment is itself "deeply rooted" in American constitutional history and in the national psyche, and the distinction between speech and conduct, or between expressive and nonexpressive conduct, is fundamental to American constitutional law. But political theory sometimes ought to transcend the doctrinal constraints of constitutional law,[13] and, it will be argued, the preoccupation of American constitutional law with communicative conduct is too narrow a frame for consideration of hate speech by the political theorist.

Speech (like conduct that is not speech) can be either part of a valuable comprehensive form of life or a relatively isolated expression. Hate speech may merit protection not because it is speech, but because it is an integral part of a comprehensive valuable form of life, such as religion. By investigating the role that hate speech plays within comprehensive forms of life, this chapter relocates the discussion of hate speech and transplants it in a new context – the context of the discourse concerning multiculturalism.

In arguing that sometimes hate speech ought to be protected because it is part of a comprehensive and valuable form of life, I equate hate speech not with other forms of bad speech, but with other protected illiberal or discriminatory practices. By regarding certain forms of hate speech as part of comprehensive valuable forms of life, this chapter bridges the gap between the literature concerning hate speech and the literature on multiculturalism, and, in particular, the literature concerning the boundaries of toleration for discriminatory and undesirable communal and cultural practices. Hate speech is conceptualized as one (undesirable) manifestation of cultural practices, on a par with sexist or racist practices that characterize certain religions or ethnic communities.

## B. *Comprehensive Forms of Life*

Let us first examine more carefully what a comprehensive form of life is. A comprehensive form of life is composed of a thick, interconnected network of values, beliefs,

---

[12] Numerous writers have made this argument. *See, e.g.,* Andrew Altman, "Liberalism and Campus Hate Speech: A Philosophical Examination," 103 *Ethics* 302 (1993); Rae Langton, "Speech Acts and Unspeakable Acts," reprinted in *The Problem of Pornography* 203 (Susan Dwyer ed., Wadsworth 1994).

[13] Scholars have pointed out that often doctrinal constitutional questions distort moral and political discourse. *See, e.g.,* Jeremy Waldron, "The Core of the Case Against Judicial Review," 115 *Yale L.J.* 1346, 1376–86 (2006).

conventions, practices, rituals, and ceremonies. By stating that these values, beliefs, practices, and so on are interconnected, I mean to assert that those who participate in these forms of life explain and justify some of the practices in terms of some of their values and beliefs, and vice versa. In other words, practices and rituals are perceived as tangible manifestations of values and beliefs, and values and beliefs are abstract formulations of the ideas embodied in the practices and rituals. There is, therefore, mutual interdependence and reinforcement between values, beliefs, and practices, which together form a comprehensive form of life. Values justify and rationalize practices; practices express and convey values, and thus help sustain them.

Religions typically form comprehensive forms of life. Often, however, religions provide the basis for practices and customs that extend beyond the boundaries of believers and provide a framework for the lives of nonbelievers. Other nonreligious long-term ideological and cultural commitments also can be characterized as "comprehensive forms of life."[14]

Typically, the participants in these forms of life are engaged in an ongoing process of deliberation concerning the justifiability of the content of their beliefs and values, as well as the nature and form of their rituals and ceremonies. The deliberation is perceived as a means of reinterpreting tradition and reformulating practices in light of the tradition's foundational values. Such a process of reinterpretation is one that involves shifts and changes in values, beliefs, and practices in light of what is described as a better and more authentic understanding or interpretation of the tradition. Often there are disagreements among the participants in the form of life – disagreements that may lead to the forming of subcommunities that diverge from the official understandings of the tradition. Their very identity as members of the community may sometimes be questioned, and the members of these subcommunities may sometimes depart from the community and establish a new separate tradition.

This description enables one to identify several important features of comprehensive forms of life. First, comprehensive forms of life typically are shared by a group – a community. It is difficult and perhaps even impossible to conceive of an individual developing by oneself, or for oneself, a comprehensive form of life. Second, a comprehensive form of life typically involves an intensive commitment by individuals – a commitment that is required to develop the form of life and to sustain it. The degree of commitment differs from one person to another, and different comprehensive forms of life may require different sorts of commitment. Nevertheless, sustaining a form of life requires the existence of a group of individuals who bear the burden (and share the benefits) of doing so. Last, it seems that a comprehensive form of life provides individuals with a sense of identity and belonging. It defines what they perceive is essential to their identity.

---

[14] For further clarification, see Raz, *supra* note 1; Alon Harel, "The Boundaries of Justifiable Tolerance: A Liberal Perspective," in *Toleration: An Elusive Virtue* 114, 116–18 (David Heyd ed., Princeton University Press 1996).

## C. *Regulation of Comprehensive Forms of Life*

The question then arises whether it should matter to the state that particular conduct or practices are integral to a comprehensive form of life. Liberal theory might address this question in two ways. First, it could be culture-blind, oblivious to the cultural context of the relevant speech. Precisely as some liberals advocate *color*-blindness in the racial context, so some liberals may be disposed to adopt *culture*-blindness in the regulatory context. Under this view, the regulation of conduct or speech ought not to be affected by its cultural context. Second, liberal theory could adopt more stringent or more lenient treatment of practices that form part of a valuable comprehensive form of life. Under the latter view, the fact that a practice is part of a valuable comprehensive form of life may provide reasons to regulate it, or, alternatively, to protect it. As will be shown later in this chapter, there are supporters for each of these views.

One influential conviction of liberals is that the beliefs, practices, and rituals of participants in a certain form of life are private matters, and therefore, the state ought to be culture-blind with respect to human conduct. Under this view, cultural practices are understood as instances of individual behavior whose permissibility should be judged independently of the fact that they are constitutive of forms of life. Therefore, when judging whether a certain practice ought to be regulated, one ought to abstract it from its context and judge it as if it was independent of the tradition in which it is rooted. John Locke was a primary advocate of such a view:

> The only business of the church is the salvation of souls; and it no way concerns the common-wealth, or any member of it, that this or the other ceremony be there made use of. Neither the use, nor the omission of any ceremonies, in those religious assemblies, does either advantage or prejudice the life, liberty, or estate of any man. For example, let it be granted, that the washing of an infant with water is in itself an indifferent thing: let it be granted also, that if the magistrate understand such washing to be profitable to the curing or preventing of any disease that the children are subject unto, and esteem the matter weighty enough to be taken care of by a law, in that case he may order it to be done. But will any one therefore say, that a magistrate has the same right to ordain, by law, that all children shall be baptized by priests, in the sacred font, in order to the purification of their souls?[15]

Locke continues:

> The sprinkling of water, and the use of bread and wine, are both in their own nature, and in the ordinary occasions of life, altogether indifferent. Will any man therefore say, that these things could have been introduced into religion, and made a part of divine worship, if not by divine institution? If any human authority or civil power

---

[15] John Locke, *A Letter Concerning Toleration* 35–6 (Halifax 1796) (1689).

could have done this, why might it not also enjoin the eating of fish, and drinking of ale, in the holy banquet, as a part of divine worship? Why not the sprinkling of the blood of beasts in churches, and expiations by water or fire, and abundance more of this kind?[16]

In Locke's view, the state ought to be indifferent to the fact that a practice is part of an interconnected network of values, beliefs, and practices. Each of the numerous acts of the participants in a practice is judged in isolation from the context in which it is performed. Modern legal systems almost never adopt such an extreme view. At times, the fact that a practice forms part of an interconnected network of values, beliefs, and practices provides a special reason to regulate the practice. Thus, for instance, the regulation of the wearing of the hijab in French schools is the result of the fact that the hijab is a component of a comprehensive form of life.[17] Were it not, the hijab could be considered to be just another article of clothing, like torn jeans. The regulation of the hijab is justified on the grounds that it is a manifestation of religion, and religion ought to be practiced only in private.[18] It is also justified on the grounds that wearing the hijab degrades women and disguises their sexuality.[19] In short, the hijab is regulated because of its *meaning*, and its meaning flows from the fact that it is part of a comprehensive form of life.

Many states have prohibited other practices precisely because these practices are part of comprehensive forms of life. The prohibition of female circumcision in various legal systems is based, of course, primarily on the physical harms resulting from this practice. But it is also based on the understanding that circumcision is not merely a form of mutilation. Its harmful effects are partly the result of the fact that circumcision is a traditional practice that expresses, sustains, or even enhances the inferior status of women within the relevant tradition.[20]

At other times, however, the fact that a certain practice is part of a comprehensive form of life provides a special reason to *protect* it. One of the more controversial

---

[16] *Id.* at 37.

[17] "The hijab" is not identical to "the veil," and its meaning is complex and varying. *See* Tabassum F. Ruby, "Listening to the Voices of Hijab," 29 *Women's Studies Internat'l Forum* 54, 56 (2006).

[18] For a discussion of the secular ideology underlying the opposition to the hijab, see Cécile Laborde, "Secular Philosophy and Muslim Headscarves in Schools," 13 *J. Polit. Phil.* 305 (2005).

[19] *See* Susan Moller Okin, "Is Multiculturalism Bad for Women?," in *Is Multiculturalism Bad for Women?* 7 (Joshua Cohen et al. eds., Princeton University Press 1999). For an excellent critical discussion of the conflicting considerations underlying the debate on headscarves, see Norma Claire Moruzzi, "A Problem with Headscarves: Contemporary Complexities of Political and Social Identity," 22 *Political Theory* 653 (1994).

[20] *See* Okin, *supra* note 19; Amnesty International, *What Is Female Genital Mutilation?* Act (1997), *available at* http://www.amnesty.org/en/library/asset/ACT77/006/1997/en/373c3381-e984-11dd-8224-a709898295f2/act770061997en.pdf. For a powerful critique of Okin, see Sander Gilman, "'Barbaric' Rituals?," *Boston Rev.*, Oct./Nov. 1997, *available at* http://www.bostonreview.net/BR22.5/gilman.html.

exceptions to the Israeli law prohibiting discriminatory provision of goods and services states that the law does not prohibit:

> The existence of separate spheres for men and women, when integration would prevent part of the public the provision of the good, or the public service, the entrance to the public place, or the provision of the space to the public space as long as the separation is justified given among others the nature of the good, the nature of the public service or the public place, its importance, the existence of reasonable alternatives, and the needs of the public that may be affected by separation.[21]

This complex provision is designed to deal with religious prohibitions on the intermingling of men and women. Under this provision, the practice of separating men and women in swimming pools located in ultraorthodox areas or buses serving the ultraorthodox community may be permissible (despite the general prohibition on gender discrimination) precisely on the grounds that such an intermingling is prohibited or frowned upon in the ultraorthodox community. This exception to the general prohibition on discriminatory provision of goods and services is based on the fact that the strict understanding of Jewish law or Jewish tradition is opposed to the intermingling of men and women, and the state is willing to tolerate separation only because it is part of the Jewish tradition.[22]

### D. Hate Speech and Comprehensive Forms of Life

In what ways does this observation bear upon hate speech? To better understand its relevance, one ought to recall the fact that hate speech is often part of a comprehensive form of life. Admittedly, some assertions that are classified as hate speech and the sentiments underlying these assertions are isolated phenomena – ones that do not constitute part of a comprehensive form of life. These assertions may represent prejudices that can be eradicated without transforming the speaker's identity, feelings of belonging, or foundational convictions. At other times, however, similar assertions and the sentiments underlying them are part of comprehensive forms of life. They are reflected in the community's practices and are legitimated by its doctrinal convictions.

The distinction between these two forms of hate speech is not always sharp. Consider the example of hate speech expressing antigay sentiments. Even when the proponent of antigay sentiments does not draw on foundational convictions in justifying his hatred, these sentiments often have deeper ideological roots. They

---

[21] Prohibition of Discriminatory Provision of Goods and Services, S.H. 2001, § 3(d)3(h), p. 54.

[22] For a more comprehensive discussion, see Alon Harel, "Benign Segregation? A Case Study of the Practice of Gender Separation in Buses in the Ultra-Orthodox Community," 20 S. Afr. J. Hum. Rts. 64 (2004) [hereinafter Harel, "Gender Separation"]; Alon Harel, "Regulating Modesty-Related Practices," 1 Law Ethics Hum. Rts. 213 (2007).

may, for instance, represent a macho attitude – one that respects masculine power and identifies gays with effeminacy; or they may reflect a conservative attachment to family values narrowly understood. Yet, it will be argued, the difficulty in drawing the distinction between hate speech that is deeply rooted in a comprehensive form of life and hate speech that is not deeply rooted is not a reason to abandon the distinction. Sometimes antigay sentiments are closely interconnected with other convictions, and at other times, they are relatively independent of one's broader and more foundational worldview. The difference between these two cases is a matter of a degree but has real normative ramifications.

To illustrate what I mean by "deeply rooted" hate speech, consider the traditional religious attitudes toward gays. Many religions endorse a strict prohibition of homosexual relationships grounded in biblical sources.[23] These sentiments are not independent of adherents' comprehensive convictions concerning family life, the sanctity of marriage, the importance of sexual chastity, and so on. Neither are they separated from sexual practices characterizing family life. They form an integral part of a comprehensive form of life.

Similarly, many religions endorse antipathy and sometimes even hatred toward those who do not belong to the religion. One of the more pernicious cases to reach the Israeli Supreme Court in recent years involved a Halakhic ruling, which held that the prohibition of murder does not apply to cases in which a Jew kills a gentile.[24] In the Israeli context, such a ruling could be understood by some religious zealots as permitting, or even encouraging, the murder of non-Jews. The antigentile sentiments that can be found among Jewish religious zealots are interconnected with the belief that Jews are the chosen nation and that they have a special metaphysical status. Indeed, this statement clearly qualifies as "deeply rooted" speech. Halakhic rulings are part of a long and important historical practice that has been central in the development of Jewish law. The identity of the speaker (a Rabbi), the style of discourse he chose, and, in particular, the characterization of what he wrote as a "Halakhic ruling" indicate that his speech is part of the Jewish tradition.

To provide a better understanding of the term "deeply rooted" hate speech, let me distinguish two cases in which speech can be regarded as "deeply rooted" in a tradition. Sometimes, as demonstrated by the example of the Rabbi arguing that the killing of non-Jews is not murder, the hateful statement is understood by the relevant community or presented by the speaker as an authoritative interpretation

[23] Indeed, several prominent hate-speech controversies have involved condemnations of homosexuality by religious figures. For example, in 2004, a Swedish pastor was convicted of violating that country's hate-speech statute and sentenced to a month in prison when he preached a sermon on the sinfulness of homosexuality, which he called a "cancerous tumor." The conviction was set aside by an appellate court. Keith B. Richburg, "Swedish Hate-Speech Verdict Reversed," *Wash. Post*, Feb. 12, 2005, at A16.

[24] Cr. A. 2831/95, Elba v. State of Israel, 50 (5) P.D. 221 (Isr. 1996). The Rabbi who issued the ruling was convicted of incitement to racism and incitement to violence; a panel of the Supreme Court upheld the conviction by a vote of 5 to 2. For a more thorough discussion of this and similar cases, see Harel, *supra* note 8.

of the tradition, or at least as a development in the spirit of the tradition. Within Judaism, "Halakhic rulings" are understood to be authoritative statements of this type. The censorship of such a statement will be understood to be a condemnation of the way of life of which this ruling purports to be a part.

Alternatively, the speaker might be a spiritual leader of a religious community, but his or her speech not purport to be an authoritative interpretation of the tradition. An example of hate speech of the latter type is a statement made by Rabbi Ovadia Yosef, a leading spiritual leader of the Sephardic religious community in Israel. Rabbi Ovadia Yosef condemned the Oslo agreements harshly and stated: "What kind of peace is this? Will you put them [the Arabs] beside us? You are bringing snakes beside us.... Will we make peace with a snake?"[25] Strictly speaking, this extremely distasteful statement was not presented as an authoritative interpretation of the Jewish tradition. Yet the fact that it was made by a spiritual leader who also happened to be associated with what was at the time Israel's third-largest political party, Shas, cannot be ignored. Censoring Rabbi Ovadia Yosef would be understood by his adherents as a condemnation of the community he represents. The fact that this community is a relatively poor community that suffers from discrimination would strengthen the sense that criminal law was being abused to promote sectarian or elitist interests.

Of course, the question of whether speech is deeply rooted in a tradition may often be controversial. A person or a group can present its ideas as belonging to a certain tradition (or present himself as a leader within a particular tradition) when most members of the tradition do not perceive it to be the case. Differentiating between deeply rooted speech and speech that is not deeply rooted requires one to identify the relevant communities to which the speakers belong. For instance, a radical religious sect that purports to act in the name of Islam might indeed be part of Islam, or its speech and practices might be so extreme that it ought to be understood as a separate sect. If it is characterized as a separate sect, it could perhaps be a sect whose form of life lacks value as most of its practices and values are hateful. If, on the other hand, it is classified as part of Islam, it would benefit from my proposal, as it is evident that Islam is indeed a valuable comprehensive form of life.

Determining whether a group belongs to a certain community requires piercing the veil of mere rhetoric. It is not sufficient that the relevant sect claims to be Islamic. It is also necessary that the group in fact shares the values embedded in Islam and is attentive to their interpretation in the rest of the Islamic community. What determines whether the sect is Islamic is the willingness of the relevant sect to be part of the Islamic community, and the willingness of the Islamic community as a whole to accept the sect as part of it and to communicate with its members.

---

[25] *See* Jack Katzenell, "Rabbi says Holocaust victims were reincarnations of sinners," *Independent* (Aug. 6, 2000), *available at* http://www.independent.co.uk/news/world/middle-east/rabbi-says-holocaust-victims-were-reincarnations-of-sinners-711547.html.

The fact that a pernicious belief or a discriminatory practice forms an integral part of a religion does not imply that it is uncontested within the religion. Many have argued, of course, that antigay sentiments do not "authentically" reflect this or that religious tradition, but are a distortion of the real meanings of the religious texts. The influential writings of John Boswell (on the history of Christianity)[26] and Daniel Boyarin (on Judaism)[27] purport to demonstrate that the condemnation of homosexuality within these traditions is "inauthentic." Boswell establishes his claim by showing that antigay sentiments developed in Christianity only in the Middle Ages and had not been part of ancient Christianity.[28] Although these are scholarly works, they are often used by progressive religious leaders calling for reinterpretations of their traditions. This attempt on the part of progressive religious thinkers is only an illustration of what was stated earlier. Comprehensive forms of life are typically arenas for battles over the "true" or "authentic" understanding of a tradition. They are not monolithic systems. They are re-understood, reinterpreted, and reconstructed through fierce debates; they are sustained through endless disagreements and argumentation. It is therefore to be expected that hate speech conducted within the framework of comprehensive forms of life would be regarded by the more enlightened participants in these forms of life as an inauthentic manifestation of their tradition. At the same time, "inauthentic" manifestations of a tradition, as well as accusations of inauthenticity, are themselves also part of the material on which an evolving tradition draws.

Some instances of hate speech form, therefore, an integral part of comprehensive forms of life. Such hate speech does not differ from discriminatory practices that are not speech-related. Furthermore, under the view advocated here, hate speech ought not to be treated as a single category. The legal system ought to differentiate between hate speech that is deeply rooted – that is, hate speech that belongs to a certain tradition – and hate speech that is not part of such a tradition. Identifying hate speech that is part of a comprehensive form of life therefore has important normative ramifications.

Before establishing this claim, let me reiterate an additional dichotomy. Some worldviews, such as the Nazi ideology, are founded on hatred, whereas in other ideologies, hatred is a peripheral (and often controversial) sentiment.[29] At times, as

---

[26] *See, e.g.,* John Boswell, *Christianity, Social Tolerance, and Homosexuality* (University of Chicago Press 1980).

[27] *See, e.g.,* Daniel Boyarin, *Unheroic Conduct: The Rise of Heterosexuality and the Invention of the Jewish Man* (University of California Press 1997).

[28] *See* Boswell, *supra* note 26.

[29] It is not always easy to draw the boundaries between worldviews in which hatred is the primary force and those in which it is peripheral. As is often noted by political theorists, some groups endorse hatred of other groups but, at the same time, reinforce and sustain solidarity among their members. In describing the Ku Klux Klan, Amy Gutmann writes: "Among its members, the Ku Klux Klan may cultivate solidarity and trust, reduce incentives for opportunism . . . [but] the associational premises of these solidaristic ties are hatred, degradation, and denigration of fellow citizens and fellow human

current developments demonstrate, hatred can intensify even within rich worldviews and become a potent and dangerous force. Yet, in the rich forms of life – the ones examined here – hatred is only one sentiment among many. Its peripheral nature within these traditions is often corroborated by the fact that the tradition tolerates opponents of sentiments of hatred – opponents who justify their opposition to these sentiments by using the tradition. The peripheral nature of the sentiments of hatred within rich traditions does not guarantee that the hatred will not intensify and be manifested in violence or other forms of pernicious conduct such as discrimination. It guarantees, however, that the tradition has the potential of transforming itself in a fresh and benign form.

## III. INDIVISIBILITY OF COMPREHENSIVE FORMS OF LIFE

Section II distinguished between two types of hate speech (or, more broadly, harmful practices). Some harmful practices involve isolated practices that are relatively independent of one's foundational values and convictions. In contrast, other harmful practices are deeply rooted in foundational values and convictions. Should the state treat these two forms of hate speech differently?

John Locke thought that it should not. In the paragraph quoted earlier in the chapter, Locke expressed his conviction that baptizing a child can be adequately perceived by the state as the practice of "washing an infant with water."[30] Baptism ought to be regulated, therefore, only if the practice of "washing infants with water" has a negative effect on their health.

Of course, devout Christians would reject such a description of baptism as radically incomplete. Baptizing, it would be argued, is different than washing an infant with water because it is bound up with numerous beliefs as to its spiritual significance. These beliefs are interconnected with other beliefs and practices of the Christian religion. The characterization of baptism in the *Catholic Encyclopedia* illustrates the interconnectedness of baptism with other practices and values:

> The Roman Catechism (Ad parochos, De bapt., 2, 2, 5) defines baptism thus: Baptism is the sacrament of regeneration by water in the word (per aquam in verbo). St. Thomas Aquinas (III:66:1) gives this definition: "Baptism is the external ablution of the body, performed with the prescribed form of words."
>
> Later theologians generally distinguish formally between the physical and the metaphysical defining of this sacrament. By the former they understand the formula expressing the action of ablution and the utterance of the invocation of the Trinity; by the latter, the definition: "Sacrament of regeneration" or that institution of Christ by which we are reborn to spiritual life.[31]

---

beings." Amy Gutmann, "Freedom of Association: An Introductory Essay," in *Freedom of Association* 3, 6 (1998).

[30] *See* Locke, *supra* note 15, at 36.

[31] "Baptism," in *The Catholic Encyclopedia, available at* http://www.catholic.org/encyclopedia/view .php?id=1463.

For the political theorist, the primary question is whether the state and, in particular, the legal system ought to accept Locke's position and abstract all cultural practices from their cultural setting, or whether, in deciding whether to regulate these practices, it should take into account their rich cultural significance. The answer to this question may have important implications not merely in the context of benign practices such as baptism, but with respect to deeply rooted harmful practices, including hate speech.

In this section, I argue against the Lockean position. Because comprehensive forms of life are indivisible wholes, the state cannot condemn a specific practice, tenet, or expression without condemning the form of life as a whole.

In the case of isolated instances of harmful conduct – ones that are not deeply rooted – censorship or criminal punishment expresses (justified) disapproval of the particular act of expression. Its condemnatory force targets the speech and only the speech. In contrast, if the speech is bound up and interconnected with other values and practices, censoring it condemns the whole tradition. The criminalization of hate speech conducted within the framework of rich traditions is therefore often perceived by the members of the group to be a condemnation of the way of life as such.[32] Comprehensive forms of life are indivisible wholes. Attempting to target specific norms or practices and criminalizing them often would be understood as condemning the tradition to which these norms or practices belong.

Indeed the rhetoric of established traditions is often indicative of the holistic aspects of the tradition. A clear indication can be found in the Catholic *Persona Humana: Declaration on Certain Questions Concerning Sexual Ethics*.[33] In this text, homosexuality is not simply condemned as immoral. Its immorality is grounded in "objective moral order." It is understood to be a part of a much broader and comprehensive view concerning personal relations and sexuality. The same document deals with practices as diverse as sexual union before marriage and masturbation, all of which are condemned on the basis of firm opposition to morality based *purely* on human deliberation – a morality that fails to acknowledge the importance of revelation. Opposition to the various sexual practices condemned by the Pope is grounded in the notion that human deliberation is limited and that there are truths that are revealed to the believer, which cannot be established in a rational manner. The condemnation of sexual practices cannot be detached from these convictions concerning the limitations of human reason.

A critic would raise the following objection. The state prohibits only the hateful speech and not other (benign) religious practices. The prohibition on hate speech condemns only what it prohibits, namely the hate speech; it does not condemn what it does not prohibit, namely other practices that form part of the religion. Why would such a prohibition be understood as condemning the religion as such?

---

[32] For a similar argument, see Raz, *supra* note 1.

[33] Pope Paul VI, "Persona Humana: Declaration on Certain Questions Concerning Sexual Ethics" (1975), *available at* http://www.vatican.va/roman_curia/congregations/cfaith/documents/rc_con_cfaith_doc_19751229_persona-humana_en.html.

The answer is that the state cannot determine unilaterally the social significance of the prohibition it issues. Of course, the state controls what it prohibits, but it does not control how its prohibitions are understood by those who are subject to them.[34] Given that harmful behavior, including hate speech, is interconnected with other practices and values, it is not surprising to find that the prohibition of deeply rooted harmful practices or the censorship of them are often understood to be condemnatory of the form of life in its entirety. The social meaning of the state's regulation is not determined exclusively by the state's own intentions, or even by the content of the state's prohibitions. The meaning is constructed in a dialogue between the state and the relevant cultural community. Let me provide a few examples establishing this conjecture. Regulation of the hijab has been resisted by many members of the Islamic community on the ground that it is a direct attack on Islam. Qur'anic verses as well as later interpretations of Islamic scholars are often invoked to establish the importance of the hijab;[35] women who wear the hijab regard it as central to their Muslim identity.[36] Interestingly, some human rights organizations have supported this view and have described the restriction as anti-Islamic.[37] The hijab is understood to be a "religious signifier" identifying women as Islamic and reinforcing their Islamic convictions.[38] Salma Yaqoob expressed eloquently the intimate interrelation between the hijab and foundational Islamic values:

> For many Muslim women wearing the hijab is an expression of Islamic notions of women's empowerment.... "Hijab" literally means "barrier." It flows from the emphasis on marriage in Islam – the Qur'an describes a husband and wife as each other's "garments" – giving each other intimacy, warmth and protection. The idea of hijab is to maintain the exclusivity of that relationship, such that the degree of physical intimacy and exposure is limited in all other interactions between men and women.[39]

The hijab, in other words, is not merely a garment; its significance is understood only in the context of Islamic conceptions of family life, marriage, modesty, and so forth.

---

[34] Peter Molnar argues that one also ought to take account of the way that *permission* to engage in hate speech is understood and interpreted by the targeted group – the victims of hate speech. However, such permission does not in itself indicate that the state agrees with or supports the speech. In a liberal state, permission to engage in speech does not imply any attitudes on the part of the state toward the speech; nonregulation is not the same as endorsement.

[35] *See* Ruby, *supra* note 17, at 56–7.

[36] *Id.* at 60–2.

[37] *See* Québec Human Rights Commission, "Religious Pluralism in Québec: A Social and Ethical Challenge" (Feb. 1995), *available at* http://www.cdpdj.qc.ca/en/publications/docs/hidjab_anglais.pdf.

[38] *See* Chouki El Hamel, "Muslim Diaspora in Western Europe: The Islamic Headscarf (Hijab), the Media and Muslims' Integration in France," 6 *Citizenship Studies* 293, 297 (2002).

[39] Salma Yaqoob, "Hijab: A Woman's Right to Choose," Address Before the European Social Forum (Oct. 16, 2004) (transcript available at http://www.whatnextjournal.co.uk/pages/latest/hijab.pdf).

Similarly, in Israel, religious parties, eminent Rabbis, and the religious communities describe and understand their strong opposition to the gay pride marches in Jerusalem as dictated by the real and authentic understanding of Judaism.[40] In a characteristic statement emphasizing the need to prevent the gay pride march, Rabbi David Batzri called on his followers to "be zealous towards the Lord, and to hate those that fail and the evil that they create. Zeal is atonement for all Israel."[41] There is no way to restrict the hate speech targeted at gays without also targeting convictions concerning what zealousness for God means within Judaism.

This observation also applies when the relevant community is a pluralistic one and some, or even many, of its members object to the hateful speech. Many community members would oppose external coercive intervention and perceive it as offensive to their tradition even when they themselves are opposed to the manifestations of hate embodied in practices within their own communities and regard these manifestations as inauthentic. There is a fundamental difference between external and internal critique of social practices. It is one thing to argue that the correct interpretation of the Bible requires tolerating gays and another thing willingly to accept government repression of hateful antigay speech – regulation grounded in a secular worldview. The debate on the hijab is a good illustration; many Muslims who oppose the hijab, including secular Muslims, are opposed to its regulation.[42]

Not every prohibition of deeply rooted hate speech will be understood as condemning the tradition as a whole. Such an understanding is especially likely when there are preexisting conflicts between secular elites, which control the legal system, and religious groups, which have little influence on the legal system. This is especially true when the secular elites belong to a different ethnic or cultural group than the religious minority. These contingencies may or may not exist in different societies. There is no logical or conceptual necessity that restrictions of hateful speech or hateful practices will be interpreted in this way. These observations and predictions are based on factual contingencies that depend on certain conditions. Unfortunately, however, these conditions prevail in many heterogeneous western societies.

To sum up, censoring deeply rooted hate speech is in many cases bound to be understood as a public condemnation of the speaker's form of life, and not merely of the expression itself. The more the hateful practice is understood to reflect deeply seated traditional values, the more its regulation is likely to raise such concerns. Dress codes that are often sexist are not merely dress codes; they are also manifestations

---

[40] Some of the statements made by eminent representatives of the orthodox community are reported in "Jerusalem Gets Gay Pride March Amid 'Holy War' Threat," *Pinknews*, Sep. 19, 2006, *available at* http://www.pinknews.co.uk/news/articles/2005-2505.html.

[41] Ronen Medzini, "Rabbis Against Pride Parade: God is Testing Us," *Ynet News*, June 17, 2008, *available at* http://www.ynetnews.com/articles/0,7340,L-3556576,00.html.

[42] *See* El Hamel, *supra* note 38, at 298.

of foundational values such as modesty and exclusivity of sexual relationships.[43] Hate speech directed against gays often is interrelated with traditional perceptions of family life, duties of reproduction, and so on. These practices do not float in isolation from the rest of the tradition; they are understood to reflect foundational values. It is natural therefore that their regulation is perceived to be offensive or dismissive of values fundamental to the tradition. To prevent such a perceived condemnation of forms of life, hate speech conducted within the framework of such a tradition ought to be tolerated in cases in which it does not cause the imminent danger of violence. The degree to which external intervention in the hateful practices is perceived to be a condemnation of the tradition as a whole depends on the nature of the hateful practice.

Arguably, the state need not worry about the fact that its prohibition is understood to be condemnatory of the tradition as a whole. Perhaps it could maintain that as long as it does not interfere with nonhateful speech, it ought not to worry about how its prohibition is understood by members of the relevant group.

This objection fails to appreciate the depth and intensity of the resentment generated by the perceived condemnatory stance of the state. It is one thing to condemn a particular belief; it is another to condemn one's whole worldview, especially when one's worldview as a whole is a valuable one. The radical confrontation following such a condemnation is not only dangerous; it undermines the sense of belongingness to the polity and therefore ought to be avoided at all costs.

Comprehensive forms of life typically consist of interconnected chains of beliefs and practices; they are perceived to be indivisible wholes. Regulation of deeply rooted hate speech often would be understood as condemnation of a form of life – a form of life that has noble aspects. This is true even when the tradition itself is ambivalent with respect to the relevant practice and even when some or many members of the community are opposed to the practice. Hence, it follows that the state ought to be particularly cautious in regulating deeply rooted hate speech.

## IV. THE POTENTIAL FOR INTERNAL AND EXTERNAL TRANSFORMATION

Understanding comprehensive forms of life as indivisible wholes provides one reason for greater restraint in regulating deeply rooted hate speech. Another reason is a more pragmatic one. An *external* effort to eradicate hatred by regulating it is less likely to succeed when the hatred is deeply rooted within a comprehensive form of life. Moreover, the chances for an *internal* eradication of hatred, or at least its transformation into ritualistic hatred, are better when the hatred is deeply rooted in a tradition (as long as the tradition in its entirety is a humanistic tradition).

It seems evident that an external effort to eradicate hatred is less likely to be effective when the hatred is deeply rooted. Let me elaborate therefore on the

---

43 See Harel, "Regulating Modesty-Related Practices," *supra* note 22.

second observation, namely the prospects of internal eradication of deeply rooted hatred.

The coexistence of sentiments of hatred and practices conveying hatred with other humanitarian sentiments makes possible an internal transformation of the tradition. The web of interconnected beliefs, values, and practices is not a simple aggregation of independent beliefs, convictions, and practices. Typically, beliefs and values are hierarchical; some are more foundational than others. At other times, beliefs, values, and practices are interrelated and interconnected. Consequently, comprehensive traditions have a potential for internal transformation. Some of the more peripheral beliefs can be eradicated or gradually transformed in light of other beliefs.[44] At other times, some of the practices are transformed in light of changes in the beliefs, and vice versa.

This dynamic influences discriminatory practices. Some of these practices can be transformed in benign ways. Even when some of the explicit racist statements are not eradicated from the practices of the tradition, they may become nothing more than rigid ritualistic gestures, thereby losing their potency.

Moreover, expressions of hatred are not necessarily a negative feature of comprehensive forms of life so long as they are peripheral beliefs and not founding values. Sometimes, hatred serves to solidify the group, strengthening the relationships among members of the community and reinforcing solidarity without threatening other groups.

One prominent example of these processes is the directive to blot out the remembrance of Amalek from under heaven. This directive is an integral part of the Jewish tradition. The Amalekite tribes opposed the Hebrews at certain formative points in early Jewish history and as a result became associated with ruthlessness.[45] Amalek is perceived in the Jewish tradition as the tangible manifestation of evil. But even though this hatred may, under certain circumstances, become dangerous (as when existing groups, for example, Palestinians, are identified as belonging to Amalek), the hatred of Amalek is generally a ritualistic hatred – hatred that has no real-life manifestations and the primary purpose of which is to remind Jews of the dangers of persecution. Most contemporary orthodox Jews believe that Amalek has been extinguished and consequently its significance is symbolic or metaphorical. Similarly, the concept of jihad is also interpreted by moderate Muslims in a benign way. The nonviolent jihad is based on the view that the greater jihad – jihad of the soul – is more important than the lesser jihad, understood as a battle.[46] Notions such as jihad or Amalek can sound dangerous to outsiders, and indeed they can be dangerous. But they often also are benign, and regulating them is not only unnecessary, but often is undesirable.

---

[44] For discussion of the potential for change by de-linking the discriminatory from its underlying values, see Harel, "Gender Separation," *supra* note 22, at 73–4.

[45] *See Exodus* 17:8–14.

[46] For discussion of what moderates believe to be the real meaning of jihad, see Omar Sacirbey, "Muslims Campaign to Reclaim 'Jihad' from Extremists" (May 13, 2008), *available at* http://pewforum .org/news/display.php?NewsID=15610.

To sum up, the interconnectedness of beliefs and practices has two important ramifications. First, state regulation is less likely to be successful given the deeper roots of hate speech. Second, the coexistence of sentiments of hatred with other opposing humanistic sentiments provides internal prospects for transforming the tradition. It is rare, although admittedly not impossible, in principle, that the state's regulation will reinforce the more humanistic interpretations of the tradition. It is also difficult at the time of regulation to know what its effects will be. Most characteristically, such a regulation is perceived as offensive by most community members, including those who are opposed to the religion's hateful manifestations. This description is reversed when the sentiments of hatred are not deeply rooted. In such settings, the speaker's overall commitments and ideological convictions are detached from the sentiments of hatred. Censorship or criminal sanctions can be effective. At the same time, without external intervention, in particular but not exclusively coercive interventions, the sentiments of hatred are not likely to disappear. There are no internal mechanisms based on conflicting humane values or convictions, which can overcome, weaken, or transform the sentiments of hatred. It seems therefore that state intervention in this case is both necessary (given the absence of internal mechanisms for change) and effective (given the superficial roots of hate speech which is not deeply rooted).

## V. INSTITUTIONAL CONCERNS

Differential treatment of speech in accordance with the principles discussed here would present an enormous challenge for the legal system. The differential treatment involves making normative judgments that are difficult and perhaps illegitimate. First, the legal system must decide whether a particular instance of hate speech is part of a comprehensive form of life. This judgment often will be difficult and controversial. Second, the legal system must judge whether the relevant comprehensive tradition is a valuable and worthwhile one, that is, whether the hatred embedded in that tradition is a peripheral aspect of the tradition or whether it is part of its essence. These judgments are also difficult to make, in particular given the incentives that such a scheme would provide to the advocates of hatred. Under such a legal system, advocates of hatred may seek to exploit the lenient and vague legal scheme by purporting to speak in the name of a comprehensive tradition even absent a real commitment to it.

It seems evident that such a system must rely on discretionary powers given to judges, which in turn, of course, poses dangers of its own, which ought to be addressed. Sometimes additional legal procedures are needed to address such dangers. For example, in Israel, any prosecution for speech-related offenses must be approved by the Attorney General.[47]

---

[47] *See, e.g.*, Penal Law Amend. No. 20, 1191 S.H. 219 (1986), § 144E (incitement to racial hatred); *see generally* Eliezer Lederman and Mala Tabory, "Criminalization of Racial Incitement in Israel," 24

So far I have shown that there are reasons why *ideal* institutions *should* differentiate between deeply rooted hate speech and hate speech that is not deeply rooted. To complete the argument, one ought to show that *real* institutions *can* make these differentiations accurately and in a way that does not undermine the legitimacy of these institutions.

This task is beyond the scope of this work. Yet, contemporary legal institutions do take into account these considerations more than they generally admit. Consider the famous case of *Wisconsin v. Yoder*, in which the U.S. Supreme Court held that the state of Wisconsin could not force Amish children to attend school after the eighth grade – compulsory education, thought by the Amish to undermine their way of life. The Court observed:

> Whatever their idiosyncrasies as seen by the majority, this record strongly shows that the Amish community has been a highly successful social unit within our society, even if apart from the conventional "mainstream." Its members are productive and very law-abiding members of society; they reject public welfare in any of its usual modern forms. The Congress itself recognized their self-sufficiency by authorizing exemption of such groups as the Amish from the obligation to pay social security taxes.[48]

Although I do not necessarily accept the Court's view that self-sufficiency is such an important criterion in determining the value of the Amish form of life, the case is nevertheless an indication that courts are sometimes engaged in making judgments about the value and comprehensiveness of forms of life. Another example of a legal system engaging in such reasoning is provided by the peculiar feature of speech-related prosecutions in Israel, noted earlier: Major speech offenses can be prosecuted only with the approval of the Attorney General. In general, criminal prosecutions are left to the discretion of lower officials, but speech offenses require specific approval of the highest official in the Ministry of Justice. This exceptional treatment of speech offenses is often justified on the grounds that freedom of speech is particularly valuable.[49] In my view, this special treatment also reflects, and is justified by, the fact that it is impossible to spell out in the criminal code itself the sort of considerations involved in making such a decision. Judgments of the type mentioned here are ones that can be taken into account by an official with broad discretionary powers, but not ones that can be included as part of the definition of the offense. These two examples demonstrate that although the legal system is naturally reluctant to acknowledge the relevance of considerations of the type discussed here, these considerations may play a role in the implementation of hate-speech provisions.

*Stan. J. Int'l L.* 55, 68 (1987). The same is true of hate-speech prosecutions in Canada. R.S.C., ch. C-46, § 319(6); *see also* R. v. Keegstra, 3 S.C.R. 697 (1990).

[48] Wisconsin v. Yoder, 406 U.S. 205, 222 (1972).

[49] *See, e.g.*, Lederman and Tabory, *supra* note 47, at 68 ("[R]ealizing that abuse of the new enactment [prohibiting racial incitement] could curtail both freedom of expression and association, the legislature justifiably restricted prosecutions under the new law to those to which the Attorney General consents in writing.").

## VI. CONCLUSION

This chapter has argued that hate speech should not be treated merely as a single and less valuable form of speech. I have focused attention on the role that particular hate speech has in the lives and worldviews of the speakers. This view implies that hate speech should not only be considered as part of free-speech jurisprudence, but also as part of the literature concerning multiculturalism and the toleration of communal practices. To be sure, there is another important aspect to hate speech, namely the impact that hate speech has on the targeted group. Although undeniably relevant, an examination of the effects of hate speech on the targeted group would not change my conclusion that the meaning and role of such speech for the speaker is critical and variable.[50]

Considered from this perspective, hate speech is not a single category. Some instances of hate speech are deeply rooted whereas others are not. As I have argued, hate speech belonging to these two categories should be treated differently.

The enlightened reader may be frustrated. Some forms of deeply rooted hate speech are so pernicious that the disposition to regulate them seems not only natural but almost irresistible. Can the state tolerate pernicious forms of hatred? Does tolerating it mean failing to acknowledge pains and agony of its victims – the targeted groups? Perhaps two comments may provide some consolation.

First, it is not my claim that deeply rooted hate speech can never be regulated, but merely that the burden required to justify its regulation is heavier. Second, the fact that hate speech cannot be regulated criminally does not mean that the state has no other tools to address it. The most effective remedy is counterspeech conducted within the tradition and disputing the status of the hate speech or of the hate speech speaker as authentic representations of the relevant tradition. The state may perhaps play an indirect role in encouraging and reinforcing such counterspeech. Its powers in regulating these forms of speech, however, are severely constrained.

---

[50] *See also supra* note 34.

# PART III

# Equality and Fear

# 16

# Hate Speech and Political Legitimacy

*Jeremy Waldron*

Proposals to ban hate speech are sometimes met with the objection that the restrictions on free speech that they envisage will undermine the legitimacy of the political system that imposes them. I have defended the idea of such restrictions elsewhere,[1] and in this chapter I consider whether this worry about legitimacy constitutes a serious objection.

There are a number of arguments in the literature that link the protection of free expression to the flourishing of self-government in a democracy. Some say little more than that, though they say it sonorously and at great length.[2] In a few of these arguments, however, the position is advanced beyond a general concern for the democratic process. It is sometimes said that a free and unrestricted public discourse is a *sine qua non* for political legitimacy in a democracy.[3] Robert Post makes this argument.[4] Some sharpen the point yet further, arguing that the political legitimacy of certain specific legal provisions and institutional arrangements may be imperiled by the enactment and enforcement of hate speech laws.

## I. DWORKIN ON LEGITIMACY

The most powerful argument of this kind is presented by Ronald Dworkin, in a "Foreword" he contributed to a large, recent, and valuable volume entitled *Extreme*

---

[1] *See* Jeremy Waldron, "Dignity and Defamation: The Visibility of Hate (2009 Oliver Wendell Holmes Lectures)," 123 *Harv. L. Rev.* 1596 (2010). The present chapter is drawn from Section III of that article.

[2] *See, e.g.*, Alexander Meiklejohn, *Free Speech and Its Relation to Self-Government* 26 (The Lawbook Exchange 2000) (1948) ("The principle of the freedom of speech springs from the necessities of the program of self-government.").

[3] *See, e.g.*, James Weinstein, "Extreme Speech, Public Order, and Democracy: Lessons from *The Masses*," in *Extreme Speech and Democracy* 28, 38 (Ivan Hare & James Weinstein eds., Oxford University Press 2009).

[4] Robert C. Post, "Racist Speech, Democracy, and the First Amendment," 32 *Wm. & Mary L. Rev.* 267, 279–83 (1991).

*Speech and Democracy*, edited by James Weinstein and Ivan Hare.[5] According to Professor Dworkin, freedom for hate speech or group defamation is the price we pay for enforcing the laws that the haters and defamers oppose (for example, laws forbidding discrimination). Here is how the argument goes.

Dworkin agrees that it is important for the law to protect people, particularly vulnerable minorities, from discrimination, from "unfairness and inequality in employment or education or housing . . . for example."[6] He is as committed to these laws as any proponent of racial equality. Like them, however, he acknowledges that if we adopt such laws, often it will have to be over the opposition of a few people who favor discrimination. Now, we usually say that it is enough that such laws be supported by a majority of voters or elected representatives, provided that the opponents of the bills are not disenfranchised from that process. But actually, says Dworkin, that is not all that is required:

> Fair democracy requires . . . that each citizen have not just a vote but a voice: a majority decision is not fair unless everyone has had a fair opportunity to express his or her attitudes or opinions or fears or tastes or presuppositions or prejudices or ideals, not just in the hope of influencing others (though that hope is crucially important), but also just to confirm his or her standing as a responsible agent in, rather than a passive victim of, collective action.[7]

Free expression, in other words, is part of the price we pay for political legitimacy: "The majority has no right to impose its will on someone who is forbidden to raise a voice in protest . . . before the decision is taken."[8] If we want *legitimate* laws against violence or discrimination, we must let their opponents speak. And *then* we can legitimize those laws by voting.

Now, some of the opponents of antidiscrimination laws will have no desire to express their opposition hatefully. But some may: For them, defaming the groups that these laws are supposed to protect is the essence of their opposition. Professor Dworkin's position is that it does not matter how foul and vicious the hatemongers' contribution is. They must be allowed their say. Otherwise no legitimacy will attach to the laws that are enacted over their opposition. It does not even matter that the hatemonger's speech is not couched as a formal contribution to political debate. A community's legislation and policy, says Dworkin, are determined as much by its moral and cultural environment, the mix of people's opinions and prejudices, as by stump political speeches.[9] It is as unfair to impose a collective decision on someone who has not been allowed to contribute to that moral environment by expressing one's social convictions or prejudices as on someone whose political

5  Ronald Dworkin, "Foreword" to *Extreme Speech and Democracy, supra* note 3, at v–ix.
6  *Id.* at viii.
7  *Id.* at vii.
8  *Id.*
9  *Id.* at viii.

pamphlets against the decision were destroyed by the police. Whether scrawled on the walls, smeared on a leaflet, painted up on a banner, spat out onto the Internet, or illuminated by the glare of a burning cross, even the most hateful message has to be allowed to make its presence felt in the maelstrom of messages that populate the marketplace of ideas.[10]

And so, Dworkin's legitimacy argument boils down to this. We want to protect people with laws against discrimination and violence, and it is natural to want to legislate also against the causes of discrimination and violence. (I should mention that Professor Dworkin has his doubts about some of the causal claims made by defenders of hate speech laws: "Many of these claims are inflated," he says, "and some are absurd."[11] But I shall leave that aside as a separate line of attack.) Yet even if the defenders of hate speech laws are right, and such speech does lead to despair and violence and discrimination, there is only so much we can do about speech with such consequences without forfeiting the legitimacy of the laws we most care about. We can legislate against direct incitement to imminent violence, but (says Dworkin):

> [W]e must not try to intervene further upstream, by forbidding any expression of the attitudes or prejudices that we think nourish . . . inequality, because if we intervene too soon in the process through which collective opinion is formed, we spoil the only democratic justification we have for insisting that everyone obey these laws, even those who hate and resent them.[12]

The structure of the position is interesting. Professor Dworkin notices that arguments about hate speech often involve two sorts of laws, not one. On the one hand, there are the hate speech laws themselves – or the proposals that people would like to see enacted – regulations restricting expressions of racial or religious hatred, group defamation, and so on. On the other hand, there are laws in place protecting the people who are supposedly also protected by hate speech laws – I mean laws against discrimination, laws against violence, and so on. Following Dworkin's metaphor, I am going to call these *upstream laws* and *downstream laws*, respectively.[13]

Those who support the upstream laws often say that they are necessary to address the causes of downstream laws – if we leave hate speech alone, then we are leaving alone the slow-acting poison that leads to violence and discrimination. Professor Dworkin turns the tables on this argument by saying that if we interfere coercively upstream, we undermine political legitimacy downstream. That, he thinks, is a cost that even the defenders of hate speech legislation should not be willing to incur.

---

[10]  *Id.*

[11]  *Id.* at vi. *See also* Ronald Dworkin, *Freedom's Law: The Moral Reading of the American Constitution* 230 (Oxford University Press 1996) (expressing similar skepticism about the empirical claims of feminist writers, such as Catherine MacKinnon, about the harms caused by pornography).

[12]  Dworkin, *supra* note 5, at viii.

[13]  *Id.*

## II. IS LEGITIMACY A MATTER OF DEGREE?

How should we respond to this argument? There is no doubt that Dworkin has drawn attention to a troubling consequence of legislation forbidding hate speech. But how serious are these consequences? It is difficult to tell because "legitimacy" is a vague term, and there is a question about what "spoiling" the legitimacy of these laws actually amounts to.[14] In social science, legitimacy often involves little more than the fact of popular support.[15] Professor Dworkin means it, however, as a normative property – either the existence of a political obligation to obey the laws or the appropriateness of using force to uphold them.[16] Whichever of these is meant, there is a question of how literally we should take the claim that legitimacy is spoiled by the enforcement of hate speech laws. For example, I know that Dworkin does not mean that racists are entitled to rise up in revolution against a society that enforces hate speech regulation: It is not a loss of legitimacy in that drastic sense.[17] A freely elected regime that enacts hate speech limits and then antidiscrimination laws is not illegitimate in the same way as (say) a military dictatorship that toppled a democratically elected government.

At worst, restrictions on hate speech lead to a loss of legitimacy in relation *to these particular laws* rather than a catastrophic loss of legitimacy for the political system generally. Even with that limitation, however, the position seems counterintuitive. In Britain, there are laws forbidding the expression of racial hatred.[18] There are also laws forbidding racial discrimination, not to mention laws forbidding racial and ethnic violence and intimidation,[19] and laws against criminal damage protecting mosques and synagogues from desecration.[20] These are the downstream laws, the laws whose legitimacy Dworkin believes is hostage to the enforcement of hate speech regulation. Should we really believe that in Britain citizens have no obligation to obey these downstream laws? Or should we really believe that the enforcement of these downstream laws is morally wrong and that the use of force to uphold them is just like any other illegitimate use of force?

For example: A wealthy landlord discriminates against English families of South Asian descent in violation of the Race Relations Act. Do we really want to say that he has no obligation to obey the antidiscrimination law and that no action should be taken against him, at least so long as the statute book also contains provisions banning him from publishing virulent anti-Pakistani views? Suppose some skinheads

---

[14]  It will be obvious in what follows that I am greatly indebted to Professor Dworkin for discussing with me the ideas in this part of the chapter.

[15]  *See, e.g.,* Max Weber, *Economy and Society* 212–15 (Guenther Roth & Claus Wittich eds., University of California Press 1978).

[16]  *See* Ronald Dworkin, *Law's Empire* 190–2 (Belknap Press of Harvard University Press 1986).

[17]  Email from Ronald Dworkin to the author (Oct. 4, 2009, 21:34 EST).

[18]  Public Order Act, 1986, c. 64, §§ 3, 3A.

[19]  Race Relations Act, 1976, c. 74, § 70.

[20]  I refer here to the basic criminal law prohibitions on damaging property.

beat up a Muslim minicab driver in the wake of the 7/7 atrocities. Is it wrong for the police to pursue, arrest, and indict these assailants because Britain has religious hate speech laws that deprive downstream laws forbidding this sort of assault of their legitimacy? Must they stand by and not intervene because any intervention would be wrong? On a literal account, that is what "deprived of legitimacy" means. It is not just Britain. Almost every advanced democracy has hate speech laws, which, according to Dworkin, spoil the legitimacy of any antidiscrimination laws that they have.[21] It would seem that the only advanced democracy entitled to have and enforce such laws is the United States. Can that be right? That is American exceptionalism with a vengeance!

I do not think Professor Dworkin really means us to take the phrase "spoil the only democratic justification we have for insisting that everyone obey" the downstream laws in this literal sense.[22] It is said that any argument will look silly if "it is pushed to an extreme."[23] So let us consider some more moderate possibilities. One possibility is that the enforcement of hate speech laws undermines the legitimacy of some downstream laws and not others: Perhaps it undermines the legitimacy of laws forbidding discrimination but not the legitimacy of laws forbidding racial violence or criminal damage. They, after all, have independent and more general support. Police intervention to stop violence or rescue people from attack may not need the sort of legitimation that the majoritarian political process is supposed to provide, or they may not need to be legitimated through a no-holds-barred society-wide discussion of race. But this position will be hard for Dworkin to maintain in light of his more holistic observations about the importance for legitimacy of speech that is just part of the cultural environment, although not intended as a contribution to formal discussion of any particular law.[24] Anyway, it still leaves us stuck with the unpalatable conclusion so far as antidiscrimination laws are concerned.

A second possibility (compatible with the first) is that the legitimacy of any given law is itself a matter of degree and that, on the moderate version of Dworkin's argument, the enforcement of hate speech laws *diminishes* the legitimacy of other laws without destroying it altogether. I will address this possibility in a moment.

A third possibility (also compatible with the other two) is that legitimacy is relative to persons. Robert Post has suggested a version of this: "If the state were to forbid the expression of a particular idea, the government would become, *with respect to individuals holding that idea*, heteronomous and nondemocratic."[25] In Dworkin's argument, one might say the downstream law becomes legitimately unenforceable

---

[21] *See* Dworkin, *supra* note 5, at viii.

[22] *Id.*

[23] *Cf.* John Stuart Mill, *On Liberty* 26 (Currin V. Shields ed., Liberal Arts Press 1956) (1859) ("Strange it is that men should admit the validity of the arguments for free discussion, but object to their being 'pushed to an extreme' not seeing that unless the reasons are good for an extreme case, they are not good for any case.").

[24] *See* Waldron, *supra* note 1, at 1641.

[25] Post, *supra* note 4, at 290 (emphasis added).

against the person silenced by the upstream law even though it may be legitimately enforceable against others. But this third possibility gets tangled up in issues about generality. Hate speech laws are presented in quite general terms: They forbid *anyone* from hateful defamation of racial, ethnic, and religious groups. Even if they only have to be enforced against a few isolated extremists, they have (and are intended to have) a chilling effect on everyone's speech. To the extent that this is so, it may be hard to identify the basis for the sort of narrowly focused *in personam* illegitimacy of the type that the third moderate possibility suggests.

The second moderate position seems the most plausible: Legitimacy is not an all-or-nothing matter; the existence of hate speech laws diminishes the legitimacy of downstream laws but does not eliminate it all together. Dworkin puts it this way:

> [T]here is something morally to regret when we enforce general nondiscrimination laws against racists who were not allowed to influence the formal and informal political culture as they wished to do. On balance Britain is entitled to enforce such laws, I think, but we are left with a deficit in legitimacy – something to regret under that title – because of the censorship.[26]

So it is all a matter of degree:[27] The "something to regret" might be more or less considerable; the "deficit in legitimacy" might be larger or smaller.

However, if we are going to recognize differences of degree, we should recognize them on the other side of the equation as well. Let me explain. An individual, X, may oppose something – say, an antidiscrimination law – for a range of reasons:

1. He may oppose it because he thinks it will make him worse off.
2. He may oppose it because he thinks it will generate perverse economic incentives, undermining economic efficiency or otherwise reducing the general welfare.
3. He may oppose it because he distrusts the bureaucracy necessary to administer it.
4. He may oppose it because he denies that the intended beneficiaries of the law are worthy of the protection that it offers them.

Let us focus particularly on (4). Position (4) may be expressed by its proponent in various ways:

4a. X may simply express his dissent from the broad abstract principle that individuals must show equal concern and respect to all members of the community.
4b. X may expound some racial theory that he thinks shows the inferiority, by certain measures, of certain lines of human descent.

---

[26] E-mail from Ronald Dworkin, *supra* note 17.

[27] For a more general acknowledgment that legitimacy is a matter of degree, see Ronald Dworkin, *Is Democracy Possible Here?* 97 (Princeton University Press 2006).

4c. X may express the view that those who are intended to be protected by the antidiscrimination law are no better than animals.

4d. X may say in a leaflet or on the radio that those who are intended to be protected by the antidiscrimination law are no better than the sort of animals we would normally seek to exterminate, like rats or cockroaches.

Out of all these various views and expressions, laws against hate speech and group defamation – of the kind we are familiar with in actually existing democracies – are almost certain to restrict (4d), quite likely to restrict (4c), and maybe they will restrict some versions of (4b), depending on how hatefully these views are expressed.

On the other hand, most such laws bend over backward to ensure that there is a lawful way of expressing something like the propositional content of views that become objectionable when expressed as vituperation. They try to define a legitimate mode of roughly equivalent expression, a sort of safe haven for the moderate expression of the gist of the view whose hateful or hate-inciting expression is prohibited. The most generous such provision of which I am aware is in the Australian Racial Hatred Act 1995 (that is a federal statute for the Australian Capital Territory, comprising the city of Canberra and its environs), which provides that its basic ban on actions that insult, humiliate, or intimidate a group of people done because of the race, color, or national or ethnic origin "does not render unlawful anything said or done reasonably and in good faith: . . . in the course of any statement, publication, discussion or debate made or held for any genuine academic, artistic or scientific purpose or any other genuine purpose in the public interest."[28] The purpose of these qualifications is precisely to limit the application of the restriction to the bottom end of something like a (4a)–(4d) spectrum.

Now if we accept the basic framework of Professor Dworkin's position, we may want to say that a law that prohibited the expression of (4a) and (4b) as well as (4c) and (4d) would have a worse effect on downstream legitimacy than a law that merely forbade something like (4d). It would – as I have argued – be a matter of degree. And if we had a law that was specifically tailored to prohibit only expression at the viciously vituperative end of this spectrum, it might be an open question whether it had anything more than a minimal effect on legitimacy.

Part of our estimation of the effect on legitimacy would surely also revolve around the reasonableness and importance of the objectives being sought by the restrictive upstream laws. We see this all the time with regard to *non*-content-based restrictions on speech (laws restricting time, place, and manner of political demonstrations, for example). If they are arbitrary or motivated by only very minor considerations of

---

[28] Racial Hatred Act, 1995, § 18D. See also section 18(1)(a) of the Public Order Act 1986 (UK), which prohibits the display of "any written material which is threatening, abusive or insulting" if its display is associated with an intention "to stir up racial hatred," but says that no offense is committed if the same material is not presented in a threatening, abusive, or insulting manner or if the person concerned "did not intend . . . the written material, to be, and was not aware that it might be, threatening, abusive or insulting."

public order, we might say that they gravely impair the legitimacy of collective decisions on the matters that the demonstrators wanted to address. But if the motivation is based on serious considerations of security, we might be more understanding. Something similar may be true in the case of hate speech laws. A motivation oriented purely to protect people's feelings against offense is one thing. But a restriction on hate speech oriented to protecting the basic social standing – the "elementary dignity," as I put it in the Holmes Lectures[29] – of members of vulnerable groups, and to maintaining the assurance they need to go about their lives in a secure and dignified manner – that may seem like a much more compelling objective. And complaints that attempts to secure it damage the legitimacy of other laws may be much less credible as a result.

## III. TIME AND SETTLEMENT

We would not do justice to Dworkin's argument without discussing one much more difficult and challenging response to it. What I want to say here is difficult and (I believe) thought-provoking, and because I am not at all sure about it, I want to appeal to the patience and consideration of my readers. Let me begin with a couple of reminders.

The concern for dignity and reputation that I think is at stake in the debate over hate speech engages the basics of justice and rights, not the contestable elements such as (for example) theories of economic equality.[30] If the proposal were to ban people from expressing contemptible views about welfare recipients or democratic socialists, then I think there would be a case to be made along the lines of Professor Dworkin's argument – to the effect that such suppression would put in question the legitimacy of our pursuit of policies based on premises that people were being fined or put in jail for (vituperatively) denying. But we are, as I said, talking about the fundamentals of justice, not the contestable elements. By the fundamentals of justice, I mean things like elementary racial equality, the basic equality of the sexes, the dignity of the human person, freedom from violence and intimidation, and the like. These matters are foundational in two senses. On the one hand, they represent things that people rely on comprehensively and diffusely in almost every aspect of their dealings with others. If one cannot exact respect for one's basic status as a rights-bearing individual, then almost everything is thrown into question. On the other hand, they are also fundamental in the sense that they represent relatively settled points or premises of modern social and legal organization.[31] I do not mean that there is literal unanimity about them – the hatemongers show *that*. Still, these matters are more or less settled in the laws and constitutions of most modern democracies,

---

[29] *See* Waldron, *supra* note 1, at 1605, 1646.
[30] *Cf. id.* at 1626–7.
[31] For a helpful characterization of this settlement – in relation to racial equality – see David Kretzmer, "Freedom of Speech and Racism," 8 *Cardozo L. Rev.* 445, 447 (1987).

and so it is not just morally necessary but also quite reasonable now for us to treat them as foundations for an awful lot else that we do. A debate can be over in the sense that intelligent opinion has settled the matter, and it is inconceivable that public policy could proceed on any other basis, even though there remain dangerous enclaves of politically powerless but socially destructive outliers who do what they can to undermine the furnishing of assurances to members of racial minorities based on these settlements. So banning hate speech should not be understood as a way of influencing a great national debate about racial or sexual equality or religious tolerance, nor should it be seen as a way of contributing to the ending of that debate (as though without the intervention of these laws the racists might win). As I argued in the Holmes Lectures, the evil that hate speech legislation seeks to remedy is not the evil of the racists' thinking or believing certain things. Rather, it is the evil of these racists' attempts to create the impression that the equal position of members of vulnerable minorities in a rights-respecting society is less secure than is implied by the society's actual foundational commitments.[32]

Maybe there was a time when modern democracies had to have a great national debate about *race* – about whether there were different kinds of human beings, inferior and superior lines of human descent, ranked in hierarchies of capability, responsibility, and authority.[33] But I think it is fatuous to suggest that we are in the throes of such a debate now – a vital and ongoing debate of a sort that requires us to endure the ugly invective of racial defamation as a contribution in our continuing of a more or less open question. There is a sense in which the debate about race is over – won, finished. There are outlying dissenters, but we are moving forward as a society as though this were no longer a matter of serious or considerable contestation. The basis on which we move forward is that the settling of this debate is fundamental to almost every aspect of the well-being, dignity, and security of formerly vulnerable minorities. On issues like affirmative action, we continue to debate ways of moving forward on the basis of the settled conviction that racism is wrong, but we are no longer in need of a continuing debate about the fundamental *premises* of that argument.

If anything like this is true, then there is something odd about Professor Dworkin's legitimacy argument. The impression he gives is that the discourse to which racist hatemongers offer their "contributions" is a living element of public debate, on which we divide temporarily into majorities and minorities, but in respect to which no majoritarian laws can be legitimate unless there is some provision for this important debate to continue on a no-holds-barred basis, so that the losers (the racist and the bigots) have a chance to persuade the majority of their position on these fundamentals the next time around. One can see what Dworkin means; I wonder,

---

[32]  *See* Waldron, *supra* note 1, at 1627–31.
[33]  *See, e.g.,* Ivan Hannaford, *Race: The History of an Idea in the West* 277–368 (Johns Hopkins University Press 1996).

however, if you share my sense of how *weird* his position is. It seems to assume that debates are timeless and that considerations of political legitimacy relative to public debate must be understood as necessarily impervious to progress.

Maybe you do not share my sense of the weird artificiality of this position. I understand the delicacy of any claim that a debate is over and finished, and that therefore attempts to throw in question a position that most of us have accepted should be suppressed. To clarify: This idea of a debate being *over* is used only with reference to this question of how seriously we should regard the Dworkinian alarm about political legitimacy, particularly in light of Professor Dworkin's own acknowledgment that the effect of hate speech laws on legitimacy is a matter of degree. The legitimacy impact of restricting debate about an issue that is live and open seems to me quite a different matter from the legitimacy impact of restricting continued debate about a foundational issue that was settled effectively decades ago. It is with regard to that, and that only, that I introduce this idea of certain debates being *over* into the discussion.

I am mindful of John Stuart Mill's point about the importance of sustaining a "living apprehension" of the truths on which our social system is organized, even when certain debates are, to all intents and purposes, settled.[34] Most of us, however, part company with Mill when he seems to suggest that it might be appropriate to cultivate racism, for instance, to enliven our egalitarian convictions.[35] I mean that most of us would agree with Mill when he says

> [a]s mankind improve[s], the number of doctrines which are no longer dis- puted . . . will be constantly on the increase; and the well-being of mankind may almost be measured by the number and gravity of the truths which have reached the point of being uncontested. The cessation, on one question after another, of serious controversy is . . . as salutary in the case of true opinions as it is dangerous and noxious when the opinions are erroneous.[36]

We can accept that without necessarily accepting his claim that this brings with it a certain cost – namely, "[t]he loss of so important an aid to the . . . living apprehension of a truth as is afforded by the necessity of . . . defending it against[] opponents."[37] Mill concedes that this is not sufficient to outweigh the benefit of the universal recognition of some truth, but he says it is "no trifling drawback."[38] He even suggests that if we did not have local racists to keep our egalitarianism alive and jumping, we might have to invent them.[39] Most people, I think, are very chary of that rather daft suggestion by Mill, particularly when the effect of manufacturing or empowering a

34  Mill, *supra* note 23, at 48–55.
35  *See id.* at 53–5.
36  *Id.* at 53.
37  *Id.*
38  *Id.*
39  *See id.* at 54.

"dissentient champion"[40] is not only to perpetuate an (already completed) debate but also – and recklessly or destructively – to do so at the expense of the dignity, security, and assurance of vulnerable members of society.[41]

Let me emphasize again that the argument of this section is developed, not as a freestanding position, but as a response to Professor Dworkin's argument about legitimacy. I think we are now past the stage where we are in need of such a robust debate about matters like race that we ought to bear the costs of what amount to attacks on the dignity of minority groups – or, more importantly, *require individuals and families within those groups* to bear the costs of such humiliating attacks on their dignity and social standing – in the interests of public discourse and political legitimacy. I believe we are well past the point where we would sacrifice the legitimacy of our antidiscrimination laws or the laws prohibiting racial violence by not permitting people to defame one another in these terms.

## IV. CALLING THE BLUFF

Legitimacy is not a straightforward concept, by any means. It is used loosely in ordinary speech, and its usage in political philosophy is also quite varied. As political philosophers, it is supposed to be our job to use this term carefully, with a good sense of what it entails and what its conditions are. I said at the beginning of this chapter that some arguments in the literature about the connection between hate speech laws and political legitimacy offer only the loosest and most platitudinous account of the connection. I focused on Professor Dworkin's argument because it seemed to be a little sharper than that – giving us a reasonably clear account of the reasons why we might say that enforcing hate speech laws diminishes political legitimacy elsewhere in the legal system. I hope I have done justice to Dworkin's claim.

Where his argument overreaches is in its failure to qualify the claims that are made about how serious the legitimacy loss might be (supposedly arising out of the operation of hate speech laws). As Professor Dworkin presented it in the "Foreword" to *Extreme Speech and Democracy*, the claim seemed to be that the legitimacy loss would be ruinous: "[W]e spoil the only democratic justification we have for insisting that everyone obey these laws [against discrimination], even those who hate and resent them."[42] Dworkin was content to leave it at that in the "Foreword," and those who share his opposition to hate speech laws seem happy to accept this claim at face value,[43] hoping presumably that people otherwise inclined to stand up for such

---

[40] *Id.*

[41] *See* Frederick Schauer, "Social Epistemology, Holocaust Denial, and the Post-Millian Calculus," Chapter 7 herein ("It is a serious omission of Mill's that he rarely, if ever, considers the possibility of suppression for reasons other than the alleged falsity of the suppressed view[,] ... neglecting the possibility that various non-epistemic benefits might be worth the cost of some epistemic loss ...").

[42] Dworkin, *supra* note 5, at viii.

[43] *See* Weinstein, *supra* note 3, at 28 n. 19.

laws will not examine it too closely. However, when the position is scrutinized, there is a precipitate retreat by its main proponent to a much more moderate claim – hate speech laws may diminish the legitimacy of downstream laws (or they may lead to something of a "deficit" in legitimacy) even though they do not "spoil" the legitimacy of these laws altogether. Indeed, under pressure, the retreat is to a claim that may be of vanishing significance in relation to laws of the kind that we are realistically considering and actual public debates of the sort in which such laws typically intervene. Think of this chapter, then, as an exercise in resistance to browbeating. There may be a case to be made against hate speech laws, but it needs to be made with greater care than this.

# 17

# Reply to Jeremy Waldron

*Ronald Dworkin*

Professor Waldron believes that I beat a "precipitate retreat" from an earlier position in an email to him commenting on an argument he made.[1] He has called my "bluff" and resisted my "browbeating." I did not intend the email for publication, but I cannot find any retreat there. I had said, in the "Foreword" Waldron cites, that a law criminalizing "hate" speech "spoils the democratic justification we have for insisting that everyone obey."[2] I said, in the email Waldron decided to quote, that such laws leave us with "something morally to regret" and with "a deficit in legitimacy." In an earlier book Waldron cites, I said that legitimacy is a matter of degree, and that not every law that is "spoiled" by a defective democratic process justifies citizen rebellion.[3] Claiming that an opponent has retreated is often a useful rhetorical device, but it seems unpersuasive in this case. We can hardly justify a defect in political legitimacy by arguing that it might have been worse.

Waldron appears to accept, at least in this essay, that it is indeed a defect in legitimacy to enforce legislation against those who were not permitted to speak in opposition during the political process that produced that legislation, that this does "spoil" the democratic pedigree of the legislation to some degree. If the legislation in question required everyone to carry health insurance, for example, then suppression of even "vituperative" dissent would put the legitimacy of that law "in question." He thinks hate speech different, apparently, for two reasons. One of these – that issues of racial dignity have been settled in mature democracies – is doubtful, and Waldron offers it with what seems great hesitation. Well he might: These issues seem much less settled now – in Germany and the Netherlands, for example, as well as in Britain and the United States – than they seemed decades earlier. The other reason Waldron

[1] *See* Jeremy Waldron, "Hate Speech and Political Legitimacy," Chapter 16 herein. All references to Waldron are to this chapter.

[2] Ronald Dworkin, "Foreword," in *Extreme Speech and Democracy* v (Ivan Hare & James Weinstein eds., Oxford University Press 2009).

[3] Ronald Dworkin, *Is Democracy Possible Here?* 97 (Princeton University Press 2006).

offers is interesting, however; it touches a very deep issue in political philosophy. What is the basis of the "equal concern and respect" that coercive government owes those who fall under its dominion?

Waldron seems to assume that *government* owes equal concern and respect to all members of the political community because every *member* of the community does, even as a private individual. He suggests that racists dissent "from the broad abstract principle that individuals must show equal concern and respect to all members of the community." Given that we ourselves accept that principle, Waldron argues, the phenomenon of hate speech requires balancing. On the one hand, government does compromise legitimacy – it fails to treat racists with the kind of respect any justification of democracy assumes – when it obstructs their participation, on their own terms, in the democratic process. In that sense, hate speech is like vituperative opposition to health care legislation: In both cases, censorship would compromise legitimacy. But hate speech is different because vituperative hate speech also denies some citizens – its targets – the equal concern and respect they are entitled to have *from other citizens*. So balancing is necessary: Censorship of the worst forms of hate speech, at least, is justified on balance because the damage such speech does to the respect owed its targets outweighs the damage done to racists by compromising their democratic rights.

But the "abstract principle" that supposedly grounds this argument is mistaken: It fails to notice the crucial difference between the rights and responsibilities of government – our responsibilities when acting collectively and coercively in politics – and our responsibilities as individuals operating within the structure of coercive law. Government must treat the fate of each citizen as of equal importance. But I need not: I do not owe you or your children the concern, when I act as an individual deploying my own resources, that I show to my own children or to myself. Government may not adopt any ethical conviction – any opinion about the true basis of human dignity – and enforce that view against dissenting citizens. It must recognize a right of ethical independence. But recognizing that right means that no individual citizen may be forced to accept any official ethical conviction or be prevented from expressing one's own dissenting convictions. It is a popular view, for instance, that atheists cannot be trusted because they have no beliefs that can ground a moral commitment. I find that opinion deeply offensive because it denies my status as a moral agent, and moral agency is a matter that, as Waldron puts it, "people rely on comprehensively and diffusely in almost every aspect of their dealings with others." No law would be acceptable, no matter how popular, that rested on that ethical opinion. But I have no right that others, who *do* believe I lack that basic dignity, not hold or express that conviction as individuals. Living in a just society – a society whose government respects human dignity – means that I must accept the right of others to hold me in contempt.

So regulating hate speech is not, after all, a matter of balancing. Government may not violate the rights of any citizen to the ethical independence from government that dignity requires. It is no excuse that it does so to enforce a particular collective opinion about what forms of respect individual human beings owe one another just as human beings; that "excuse" only confirms the mistake. I myself believe that one opinion about that latter issue is correct and others mistaken. But it does not lie within the powers of just government to try to identify and impose that truth.[4] To be sure, life would be more pleasant for some members of the community – and less pleasant for others – if government had that power. But a government is not fully legitimate that claims it.

I have some other, less central, comments about Waldron's essay. I agree with him, first, that my argument does not suppose that "laws against racial violence or criminal damage" are in any way compromised when expressions of racial hatred are banned. I do not, however, understand why he thinks they might be. He suggests, second, that censorship of "hate" speech is comparable to "time, place, and manner" restrictions on political demonstrations. But the latter are permissible only when they are, as constitutional lawyers put it, "content-neutral."[5] Justifications for time, place, and manner restrictions are not based on any judgment, as censorship of race speech must be, that the speech restricted is false or offensive.

I am surprised, third, that he seems to argue only for banning the crudest forms of hate speech: speech that declares that some people are no better than the animals "we would normally seek to exterminate, like rats or cockroaches." That is not the danger; no person or political party that hoped to attract support or attention would speak in that way. If Waldron's case for censorship of hate speech is to count in actual politics, it must reach what is actually said and feared. "The holocaust was invented by Jews for their own advantage." "Moslems are all terrorists who should be shunned." "Islam has contributed nothing of value to the world's culture." "The immigration of alien races will destroy the indigenous culture that we, who have developed and embraced that culture, have a right to protect." "They should all be sent back where they came from." None of these misbegotten declarations implies that any human being is no better than an animal or should be exterminated like a cockroach. None implies that anyone inherently lacks the status or dignity of a human being. Any argument that hopes to defend the hate speech laws actually in force in European countries must defend censorship of the kind of speech that is actually used to inspire hatred.

Europeans have said to me, on many occasions, that their history is different from and darker than that of the United States, and that if I had been born in Europe, I would share their opinion rather than the reflex First Amendment tic they think an

---

[4] In *Justice for Hedgehogs* (Harvard University Press 2011), I argue for what I take to be the correct account of what kind of respect people owe each other as individuals, and I describe what I believe to be the ethical, moral, and political consequences of that view. But I also argue there, at some length, for a right of personal independence from coercive government in the ethical as distinct from the moral sphere.

[5] E.g., Ward v. Rock Against Racism, 491 U.S. 781, 790–4 (1989).

American disease.[6] They may be right about the impact of history on conviction: A great many distinguished and otherwise liberal European political philosophers do support censorship in this area, although of course others do not. In any case, however, explanation of a conviction's genesis is not an argument for its truth.

---

[6]  Stephen Holmes's comments in this volume take something of the same view. *See* Stephen Holmes, "Waldron, Machiavelli, and Hate Speech," Chapter 18 herein.

# 18

# Waldron, Machiavelli, and Hate Speech

*Stephen Holmes*

I

I am not particularly knowledgeable about the subject of hate speech. I am not a philosopher at all. Yet Peter Molnar has pursued me persistently to contribute to this project. I could not understand why he kept calling me up and sending me emails telling me I should speak on a subject I know nothing about. I finally realized that the answer had to be that I once bumped into him at Washington Square Park and we had a conversation about hate speech.

That conversation took us back to the mid-1990s, when I heard Ronald Dworkin lecture in Budapest. Dworkin was speaking, of course, a few hundred miles away from the Balkan tragedy, where hundreds of thousands of people were killed on the basis of violent hate ideologies, and on a continent in which a hundred million people were killed in that century on the basis of violent hate ideologies. My recollection is that he argued for total freedom to express hatred of other people, without considering this context.

It does not take Sigmund Freud to understand that, if you have two continents, in one of which one hundred million people were killed on the basis of highly violent hate ideologies, accompanied and propelled by extreme hate speech, and in the other of which, at least by comparison, basically nothing happened, you will get different judicial traditions. This is not a *legal* point; it simply reflects the fact that what drives people most in their judgments is their own experience – or, to be precise, their remembered experience. When you forget about the Great Depression, then you say, "Well, government doesn't need to regulate the banks anymore." When you forget about the Vietnam War, you can say, "We should go over to Iraq." So, what you remember – your experience – is far more consequential than norms or philosophies.

This is a revised transcription of remarks delivered on March 25, 2009, at the Cardozo School of Law, largely as a response to a presentation by Jeremy Waldron based on his chapter in the current volume.

## II

I agree very much with Jeremy Waldron that there is a "weirdness"[1] to Dworkin's theories; they are so rigid, one's reaction is that it just cannot be right to be so absolutist. But what interests me is not so much the merits of Dworkin's position, but rather the question of *why* this position emerges. Free-speech absolutism is not unique to Ronald Dworkin; it is a whole tradition, and it is an entrenched way of thinking way beyond arguments – no matter how good your arguments in favor of a particular regulation of speech, you are not going to change the deep commitment to this idea.

I think Waldron needs to devote more attention to questions of cultural anthropology, in particular to explaining American exceptionalism. Why does this country not have universal health care? Where does our silly absolutism of free speech come from? What about the Second Amendment absolutism seen in America? That has nothing to do with the Constitution. People love their guns for other reasons – cultural; the mythology of the frontier; "you're not a man if you don't have a gun;" "on the street in the black community you've got to have a gun." There is a whole romance of the gun very much in evidence now; you have your gun when you go into Starbucks. But liberals are not in favor of it. There is no liberal support for Second Amendment absolutism. The exceptionalism that needs to be explained is why liberals support *free-speech* absolutism.

Partly, as I suggested in my opening, the answer lies in different historical experiences. On the European side, Nazism is the main issue. Here in the United States, liberals experienced the loyalty programs, commie hunting, McCarthy, the Smith Act, among other things. They were under incredible pressure – people looking at you, listening to every word, trying to find a reason to see you as a traitor. In a democratic society, that leads to what is essentially a bargain. Rather than leaving things to elites to solve, as in Europe, the two sides agree on absolute freedom of speech. This means freedom of speech for us liberals to say the things that have led to persecution and harassment, and it also means freedom for others to say, for example, the sort things they are saying against Obama on the streets around the White House. Absolute freedom of speech is one of those institutions that serves both parties in turn. It is like the filibuster, or federalism, or presidential power; these are institutions that obviously can and will be used against you, but you accept them because you will also be able to use them, over time. There could be a democratic argument for this approach, and, notably, a commitment to freedom of speech has never been at the forefront of a genocidal campaign.

---

[1] *See* Jeremy Waldron, "Libel and Legitimacy," Chapter 16 herein (referring to the "weirdness" and "weird artificiality" of Dworkin's position, which "seems to assume that debates are timeless and that considerations of political legitimacy relative to public debate must be understood as necessarily impervious to progress").

So, for liberals, historically the commitment to absolute protection of speech may have been strategic. It protected the speech of liberals who had vaguely socialist policies but did not want to be associated with the country's enemy, the Soviet Union – particularly in the context where the Soviets were repressing free speech, so you could stand up against such repression, which meant you were anti-Soviet even as your ideas were otherwise being accused of being pro-Soviet. Thus the Cold War context is very important.

Other strategic reasons come to mind. Shutting up one's opponents can be disastrously counterproductive. I do not want to make the profound error of turning Ann Coulter into a free-speech martyr. So that is a reason. And there are many others.

On the other hand, I think that *sociology* might be much more important than *reasons*. This obsession with free speech, like the obsession with allowing pornography, may be part of the left's caving in – the destruction of the real progressive movement that was about class politics, labor, redistribution, and other really important substantive issues. Instead, we worry about whether you can publish pornography, whether you can say bad things. I think this focus may be a kind of compromise of the American left, which makes its politics harmless to the class interests that are most powerful. This is a leftism that leaves the power structure untouched; because it is unthreatening, it is acceptable. Free-speech proponents can pretend to be champions of some great cause, but actually those who have control are and should be perfectly happy with this. That would be a different reason for the obsession with free speech; it seems quite plausible to me.

One way to read Waldron's very persuasive argument is that the difference between Americans on the one hand and Canadians and Europeans on the other lies in the relative intensity of the fear of regulation and the fear of the behavior to be regulated. If we Americans were rational, we would be convinced by the arguments for regulating hate speech. But the different focus, the selectivity of the fear, is not based on an evaluation of the consequences of these rules; it results from past experience, which gave liberals a reason to fear regulation more than speech. White liberals – I am talking about the ACLU, not the black movements' experience in America – being the targets of the hate, were focused on speech-restrictive laws that restricted speech that veered toward Communism; that is what it was about. That was something they could point to and say, "This is a danger." For them, that experience was seared and crystallized, hardened into a rule, one that is not open to argument. So First Amendment fetishism is very much path-dependent, experiential, and class-based.

Just a word here about one path in particular, in light of the Danish cartoons controversy and the European side of this. It is very irritating to realize that people just want to stick their finger in the eyes of a particular minority group; they want to humiliate them. That is all. They invoke freedom of speech as an excuse; they do not actually care about freedom of speech. (It is just like saying Americans went into Iraq "for democracy.") The hypocrisy is annoying. On the other hand, there is an argument that hypocrisy is civilizing. For example, in Holland, as well as other places in Europe, the extreme right, because it is so anti-Muslim, is beginning to defend gays. At the beginning, they do not really believe what they are saying; over time, however, the values they invoke – about gays, or women, or whatever – actually affect their thinking. Similarly, if you keep *saying* "freedom of speech!" even if what you really want to do is hurt somebody, over time it may change both your beliefs and your behavior.

III

Let me now turn to the arguments for and against restrictions on speech that is insulting, or worse.

Machiavelli's *Discourses*, in a section on mistakes in war, contains a whole chapter on hate speech, or vituperation.[2] Machiavelli explains that soldiers should not shout insults at the enemy because that just supercharges their energy against them; they should just let the other side come, without taunting. He also observes that when the Roman military leader Tiberius Gracchus had command over a bunch of soldiers who had been slaves, he made it a *capital offense* for anyone to denigrate them for their former servile condition because he was trying to create what he called a harmonious atmosphere in the military. The point is that dignity is not just a moral principle; it is also a psychological bomb that can explode if you put your finger in it.

Let us back up for a second. The different values in play could be formulated, at the individual level, as individual freedom of expression versus personal dignity. Protecting the one or the other has social consequences; emphasizing the first enhances the legitimacy of the political system; emphasizing the second enhances the harmony of the society. And there is no single way to reconcile them. Different societies reconcile them in different ways; how they do so depends very much on the experiences of the particular society.

So, rules might evolve – in this case, rules that Machiavelli offered as *realpolitik* rules – about limiting gratuitous insults because of their self-defeating character, the poisonous consequences for *you, the speaker*. Now, that limiting principle can only be taken so far. No society that has any life in it can extend the principle indefinitely, because all moral speech is potentially insulting. If I distinguish between good and bad, I am setting forth in front of you the conditions under which I will respect you or disrespect you, and that itself is a threat and can produce conflict. That is a problem with morality itself. You would not want an extreme version: "We will ban all speech that causes discontent and distress and so forth"; you need a stopping

---

[2]  Niccolò Machiavelli, *The Discourses*, Book II, ch. 26, entitled "Contempt and Insult Generate Hatred Against Those Who Employ Them, Without Any Usefulness to Them."

point. This is all about line drawing. And to an extent, I am making an argument for rules against harmful speech, but one that is slightly different than Waldron's. It reflects a more Machiavellian way of thinking.

The Machiavellian position reflects an acute awareness of the revenge instinct. That is very dangerous, and society has to deal with it.[3] One of the purposes of criminal law is to control the revenge instinct in society. The best proof of this is the law of attempt. If you try to murder me and fail, you are punished much less than if you succeed. That does not make sense from the point of view of deterrence theory or retribution. But it makes a lot of sense if the purpose of punishment is to absorb the revenge instincts of my relatives. Because I am not dead, they have no revenge instinct. So we create a legal system to tamp down, manage, and channel this very primordial emotion, which is mimetic or contagious violence.[4] Similarly, looking beyond criminal punishment, the ability to sue may be a way of civilizing and disciplining these impulses, producing a more legitimate political context. Waldron's basic argument is that there are *many* sources of political legitimacy, including a social context in which people feel respected. It is not *just* wide-open debate that produces political legitimacy.

Now consider the argument *against* restrictions on insulting speech. I think this is best understood if we get ourselves out of the Hobbesian metaphor. The Hobbesian metaphor assumes an absolute distinction between vertical threats and horizontal threats. That is, the state threatens us, or we threaten each other. It is obvious, however, that one citizen can use the state to harm another; horizontal threats can be carried out through vertical means. The Mafia can use the police to kill another Mafioso; the Afghan tribe can use the American drones to kill members of another tribe. The same is true with regard to freedom of expression. We should be very worried not about (or at least not only about) the official, petty or high, who determines what orthodoxy we should speak, but about private groups getting ahold of this power to decide what can be said. Justice Brennan famously wrote that public officials must be "men of fortitude, able to thrive in a hardy climate."[5] Perhaps; yet it is tempting to think that we could ameliorate that climate, at least a little. The

---

[3]  *See* Kenworthey Bilz, "The Puzzle of Delegated Revenge," 87 *B.U. L. Rev.* 1059, 1063 (2007) (citing numerous studies showing a universal, non–culturally specific urge for revenge).

[4]  Sir James Fitzjames Stephen offered a classic, if anachronistic, statement of this idea:

> The unqualified manner in which [revenge and hatred] have been denounced is in itself a proof that they are deeply rooted in human nature. No doubt they are peculiarly liable to abuse, and in some states of society are commonly in excess of what is desirable, and so require restraint rather than excitement, but unqualified denunciations of them are as ill-judged as unqualified denunciations of sexual passion. The forms in which deliberate anger and righteous disapprobation are expressed, and the execution of criminal justice is the most emphatic of those forms, stand to the one set of passions in the same relation in which marriage stands to the other.

Sir James Fitzjames Stephen, *A History of the Criminal Law of England* 82 (Macmillan 1883).

[5]  New York Times Co. v. Sullivan, 376 U.S. 254, 273 (1964).

liberal argument is that such temptation is dangerous. "Climate control" sounds good, but who is going to do the controlling? There is some advantage, some safety, in saying, "Hands off the thermostat. Everybody has to get their hands off it." That is certainly the way the thinking goes. I do not think it is just a cultural whim. There is an understanding that the kinds of people who stand outside the White House shouting "Obama is a monkey" will never actually get power; that is part of why we allow them to say these vile things and do not criminalize their behavior. It is sickening to watch. On the other hand, however, you do not want them to capture this thermostat. The challenge is figuring out a theory about the whos, whats, and hows of *private* control. I do not know what that theory is. But it seems inadequate, and certainly highlights the problems of legitimacy, to say that only responsible elites will control the thermostat.

## IV

Waldron states that certain limitations on speech do not raise concerns of political legitimacy, because the substantive debate at issue is over. In this setting, suppressing a viewpoint is much like suppressing a purely factual falsehood, and thus, relatively speaking, is less problematic.[6] This makes me uneasy.

It is awfully hard to say that a particular debate is truly over, dead and buried. After all, we all thought that the debate about torture was over. And *I* think that while there have been debates about the existence of God forever, that is over, there is no more debate. But, of course, most Americans do not think that at all, or they agree the debate is over and done with, but the outcome is different from what I think it is. So the best I can do as a secular person is say, "Well, it's an ongoing debate." I do not want to use the phrase, "the debate is over" – more strongly, I do not want that to be a permissible assertion – because I think that same phrase can be captured by another group.

Debates may appear to be over when they are not in another way as well; that is, when positions have been repressed. Yugoslavia is a very good example of repressing certain kinds of speech, and it turns out that it takes nothing to wake it up again. It is buried, but it is not dead. That sort of thing makes you worry a little bit about what is dead and what is alive. It looks on the surface as if a certain viewpoint or belief is not there, people are not talking about it, but in reality it is seething below the surface. Was that the case in Yugoslavia, or were historic views just manipulated into life again? But it is a good example of repression failing – there is a return of the repressed. You cannot rely on surface behavior. The same is true in Hungary, where the repression had been total.

---

[6] *See* Waldron, *supra* note 1 (suggesting that some debates – for example, those over racial equality or the value of human dignity – are over and no longer subject to contestation).

## V

Ours is a society of acoustical communities. Many have pointed to the existence of "information cocoons" on the Internet,[7] but this is not simply an online phenomenon. Perhaps the most segregated part of America is the Christian church. Let us think about Jeremiah Wright and "God damn America." Within the African-American churches, you have 160 years of the story that the blacks are the Jews, the Americans are the Romans, and they should be killed, every man, woman, and child. This is said in closed settings, in a certain space. It is quite provocative: "God damn America." One of the inspiring things about Barack Obama is that he could hear it. He could hear the anger. Why are middle-class blacks still angry at white people? They have all their legal freedoms. And Obama goes and hears it and understands it, then walks out and does not channel it at all. Then we saw an effort to peek in there to try to show something evil and dangerous is happening, but it was *not* dangerous – we did not even know about it.

This separation into acoustical communities has been going on forever. I think that is an important story, and that we need to consider how this acoustical separation affects the legitimacy of speech and the danger of speech.

---

7 *See, e.g.*, Thomas Nagel, "Information Cocoons," *London Rev. of Books*, July 5, 2001, at 24 (reviewing Cass Sunstein, *republic.com* [2001]).

# 19

# Shielding Marginalized Groups from Verbal Assaults Without Abusing Hate Speech Laws

*Yared Legesse Mengistu*

"Between the strong and the weak, between the rich and the poor, between master and servant, it is freedom that oppresses and the law that sets free. [Entre le fort et le faible, entre le riche et le pauvre, entre le maître et le serviteur, c'est la liberté qui opprime, et la loi qui affranchit.]"

> – Jean-Baptiste Henri Dominique Lacordaire (1802–1861)

"...and their word will consume like gangrene."

> – The Bible, 2 Timothy 2:17

## I. INTRODUCTION

In this chapter I argue that "the marketplace of ideas" metaphor for free speech perpetuates deep and built-in structural societal imbalances. I argue that substantive, or real, equality demands the prohibition of hate speech that targets historically nondominant and oppressed minority groups to enable these groups to renegotiate their status and power in society. An attempt to prohibit hate speech against *all* ethnic groups without regard to the ethnic dynamics in the country, however, tends to shut off a large amount of much-needed political debate. I will explore the cross-cutting issues of regulating hate speech and protecting minorities in richly diverse and deeply divided societies, in particular Ethiopia. I will show the difficulty of regulating speech that relates to ethnicity when ethnicity itself is a prime vehicle for political organization and mobilization. Finally, I will explore how hate speech regulation has been utilized in Ethiopia and other African countries as a pretext and tool to suppress opposition to the government and perpetuate the subordination of historically oppressed minorities.

Even as legal protections of ethnic minorities have become more robust, it has become evident that in many multiethnic societies, notwithstanding a thinly veiled claim of state neutrality regarding ethnicity, the state may privilege one or a few ethnic groups to the exclusion of a vast multitude of others. Indeed, in multilingual societies, the very *language* the state uses illustrates its affiliation with a majority who shares that language to the exclusion of others.

Because the state often is not a neutral arbiter of social relations, it is important that legal protections are in place to protect and strengthen the rights of minority groups. At the risk of oversimplification, one can argue that to provide this legal protection to minority groups, there is a need to acknowledge *groups* as constitutionally and politically relevant categories, for individuals cannot be empowered without first empowering the group to which they belong. Ethnic or national identity is a group identity in which individuals are so deeply embedded that such identity has to be accorded protection to protect the rights and dignity of the individual members.

Empirical findings and events unfolding throughout the world bear testimony to the fact that ethnicity is the strongest marker of group identities.[1] It is imperative that the state use ethnicity as a constitutional category to empower members of minority ethnic groups whose destiny and fate are tied up with their ethnic group. This chapter will attempt to show that the protection of such minority groups includes, among other things, shielding them from hate speech that perpetuates their inferior position in the social hierarchy.

Ethiopia is home to more than eighty nations/nationalities, and the interethnic relationships in the country always have been anything but just and even. After the Tigrayan Peoples' Liberation Front (TPLF), a liberation movement organized on the basis of ethnicity, had ousted the former military junta that led the country from 1974 to 1991, ethnicity became an integral part of political life in Ethiopia. The current Constitution of the Federal Democratic Republic of Ethiopia (FDRE), which was proposed in 1994 and adopted in 1995, divides the country into nine more or less ethnically based federal units. It proclaims that the authors of the Constitution,[2] and the ultimate sovereigns,[3] are the "nations, nationalities and peoples" of Ethiopia – a tectonic shift from the standard "we the people" formulation that decorates other constitutions.

In a further divergence from democratic constitutions the world over, the Ethiopian Constitution accords nations and nationalities the right to self-determination, *including by means of secession*. Indeed, Ethiopia is one of only a few countries that explicitly recognize a right to secession in their constitutions. The

---

[1] Mary Jane Rotheram-Borus, "Biculturalism Among Adolescents," in *Ethnic Identity: Formation and Transmission Among Hispanics and Other Minorities* 81, 92 (Martha E. Bernal & George P. Knight eds., SUNY Press 1993). Among many other current examples, the balkanization in the former Yugoslavia and many Eastern and Central European countries attests to the increased salience of ethnicity on the world stage.

[2] The opening words of the Constitution are: "We, the nations, nationalities and Peoples of Ethiopia...." FDRE Const., preamble.

[3] *Id.*, art. 8(1) ("Sovereignty resides in the nations, nationalities and peoples of Ethiopia.").

right to self-determination cannot be derogated from even in times of emergency, thereby elevating it to the level of a sort of domestic *jus cogens*.[4]

On the subconstitutional level, there is an attempt to mirror the country's ethno-linguistic diversity in appointments to civil service positions, including in the judiciary. Many of the political parties are ethnically based, although in recent years the opposition successfully has organized multiethnic parties and forged multiethnic coalitions. Indeed, the government has created many satellite political parties that are known by the common acronym of PDOs (Peoples' Democratic Organizations), which simply carry a prefix indicating the name of the members' ethnic group. Now many of the ethnic groups have their own such peoples' democratic organizations – Guraghe Peoples' Democratic Organization, Oromo Peoples' Democratic Organization, and so on. In sum, one can say that in Ethiopia, ethnicity is politicized and politics is ethnicized. In this setting, hate speech regulation is a very difficult enterprise.

The sweeping current Ethiopian law governing hate speech precludes much useful political debate because it attempts to prohibit any speech remotely insinuating to ethnic groups in the country from the scope of protected speech. In one court case, a journalist was convicted under hate speech regulations for criticizing ethnic discrimination ("apartheid"). By drawing from the conflict-prone nature of ethnic relations in the country, this chapter will argue that hate speech regulations should prohibit only speech that targets ethnic or national minorities who have historically and hitherto been removed from the mainstream political life of the country.

My argument rests on a notion of substantive equality[5] that demands taking into account relevant differences among the various groups in society. The substantive equality position supports the view that marginalized groups should be shielded from hate speech, because they continue to suffer the effects of past government-sanctioned discrimination and cannot otherwise easily surmount the biases in the marketplace of ideas. At the same time, it is at best unnecessary to extend hate speech regulation to protect powerful and dominant groups. From this vantage point, Ethiopia's superficially "even-handed" hate speech regulation ignores the country's ethnic dynamics and unjustifiably purports to extend protection to dominant and marginalized groups alike.

---

[4] In contrast, the current constitution provides that freedoms of expression, religion, and demonstration *are* derogable during a state of emergency. *See* FDRE Const., art. 93(4)(b) (providing that when a state of emergency has been declared, the "Council of Ministers shall have the power to suspend such political and democratic rights contained in this Constitution to the extent necessary to avert the conditions that required the declaration of a state of emergency").

[5] "A substantive equality approach recognizes that patterns of disadvantage and oppression exist in society and requires that law makers and government officials take this into account in their actions." Court Challenges Program of Canada, "Rights: Our Equality Rights in the Charter," *available at* http://www.ccppcj.ca/e/rights/rights-charter.shtml.

## II. HATE SPEECH REGULATION AND CONSTITUTIONAL EQUALITY: A THEORETICAL OVERVIEW

### A. *Speech and Equality*

Hate speech regulation can be taken as a setting where two constitutional ideals, namely freedom of speech and equality, conflict.[6] The conflict takes on a curious shape as the equality argument cuts both ways. Equality demands that one should not be discriminated against by the government on the basis of the content of one's speech (one's viewpoint), and substantive equality further demands due consideration of the differences in the distribution of social power. The constitutional protection of speech rightly presumes that the government does not have a "pipeline" or "privileged access" to (the) truth that justifies its engaging in viewpoint discrimination.[7] Viewpoint discrimination rests on epistemologically shaky ground. Instead, the marketplace-of-ideas argument assumes that, as long as all have equal access to the marketplace, it is the best determiner of truth and of the acceptability of ideas.

In the best-known judicial statement of this philosophy, Justice Holmes wrote in his dissent in *Abrams v. United States* that the best test of truth is the power of a thought to get itself accepted in the competition of the market.[8] This premise implies that the answer to problematic speech is more speech.[9] Thus, in the marketplace of ideas, there is no call for prohibition of certain categories of speech; more speech will be produced to neutralize the hate speech and undo the harm. Viewed from this angle, hate speech regulation only "puts the state in the censorship business" and on a slippery slope of unjustifiable content-based regulation of speech.

The marketplace of ideas is one of the firmest theoretical justifications for the protection of freedom of expression. But there is a gap between theory and the real world. In practice, hate speech can create a space where certain groups (oft-marginalized extremist groups such as neo-Nazis, the KKK, etc.) lash out at a historically disempowered segment of the population and plunge it into perpetual inferiority.

In the United States, critical race and feminist theories oppose the mainstream support for the constitutional protection of hate speech on substantive (real) equality

---

[6] The FDRE Constitution guarantees both equality and freedom of speech. *See* FDRE Const., arts. 25 ("All persons are equal before the law and are entitled without any discrimination to the equal protection of the law."), 29 ("Right of Thought, Opinion, and Expression").

[7] Even the seemingly simplest of propositions, such as "the earth revolves around the sun," is not inherently true; it is true because, like any other item in the market, many of us have "bought" it.

[8] Abrams v. United States, 250 U.S. 616, 630 (1919) (Holmes, J., dissenting). *See generally* Kevin O'Kelly, "War by Other Means: Oliver Wendell Holmes and the Law," 15 *Experience* 17, 17–18 (2004); Chris Demaske, "Modern Power and the First Amendment: Reassessing Hate Speech," 9 *Comm. L. & Pol'y* 273, 284–5 (2004).

[9] Reliance on counterspeech is endorsed wholeheartedly by Nadine Strossen, *see* Chapter 20 herein, and qualifiedly by Katharine Gelber, *see* Chapter 11 herein.

grounds. It is argued that hate speech is a breach of the ideal of egalitarianism, which holds that "all [persons] are created equal" and each person is an equal moral agent and is the cornerstone of the American moral and legal system. Traditional liberal theory, with its emphasis on individual autonomy, fails to address variations in societal power of various groups or individuals and speech's role in that power dynamic. That is precisely the focus of substantive equality.

## B. *Substantive Equality*

The principle of substantive equality provides a viable constitutional means to address deep-seated, subtle imbalances in social power dynamics. Substantive equality analysis exposes the culturally dominant norms that are disguised by facially, formally neutral laws.[10] In brief, the concept of substantive equality generally entails the "elimination of major disparities in people's material resources, well-being, opportunities, and political and social power. It also ideally seeks to minimize economic, social, and cultural oppression and exploitation."[11]

To achieve the goals of substantive equality, it is necessary to assess laws and regulations in the context of historical discrimination. Lamentably, the law, especially the common law, generally works on a fundamental, often unarticulated, assumption that individuals have equal power. However, law is better conceived in light of the historical circumstances surrounding intergroup relations; "law is a technique for the regulation of social power," which rests on many foundations including wealth, personal prestige, tradition, and sometimes physical force.[12]

Substantive equality analysis acknowledges that the law can either be used to mask the reality of inequality or as a tool to work toward equality. We should not pretend that history has not affected the relative power among groups in a society where there has been a history of slavery, apartheid, holocaust, ethnic cleansing, or ethnic marginalization. Hate speech regulation acknowledges this history and harnesses the potential of law to be an arbiter of social relations. Hate speech regulation posits itself at the center of social relations and life that are imbued with unequal power relations, and the law does justice if it treats people taking due account of their

---

[10] It is, however, a temporary measure until equality is achieved in decent measure. What John Hart Ely writes about affirmative action in the case of African Americans effectively sums up the temporal nature of affirmative and other remedial measures informed by substantive equality:

> Let us pray the day will come when we can agree that the need to pursue the [fourteenth] amendment's historic core purpose of protecting blacks is so obsolete it can be disregarded. It would take an extraordinary insensitivity, however, to suppose that today is that day.

John Hart Ely, *Democracy and Distrust* 152 (Harvard University Press 1980).

[11] Joel Bakan, *Just Words: Constitutional Rights and Social Wrongs* 9 (University of Toronto Press 1997). *See generally* Christopher Totten, "Constitutional Precommitments to Gender Affirmative Action in the European Union, Germany, Canada, and the United States: A Comparative Approach," 21 *Berkeley J. Int'l. L.* 27 (2003).

[12] Otto Kahn-Freund, *Labor and the Law* 4 (Stevens & Sons 1972).

starting point in life. To mistake the conceptual apparatus of the law for the image of society may produce a distorted view of the multifaceted relations in the society.[13]

There are many areas of the law that reflect concerns of substantive equality. The South African Constitution, among others, provides for "horizontal" application of the equal protection of the laws[14] to avoid the pitfall of entrenching "back door apartheid." The socioeconomic imbalances left behind by the legacy of centuries of white rule cannot be addressed with an impoverished understanding of the role of law.[15] Another prominent example is labor law, which directly addresses the inherent relation of subordination between the employer and the employee and works to overcome the inequality in bargaining power. The debate over affirmative action can be seen as a debate over the persuasiveness of concerns of substantive equality. The view that every race-based classification is constitutionally suspect,[16] which sounds in principles of formal equality, lacks a nuanced understanding of equality; substantive equality dictates that in light of the history of discrimination against people of color, affirmative action *for* racial minorities, who form "insular and discrete minorities,"[17] should not trigger the strict scrutiny that racial classifications disfavoring racial minorities receive.[18] And the substantive equality argument has also dominated nationalism studies (although it has had a lesser impact on the law itself). States' claims to neutrality are patently false when it comes to ethnicity. For all its claims of neutrality, the government speaks the language of the dominant group to the exclusion of others. Hence, substantive equality demands that the government candidly create separate democratic spaces where minority groups can advance their language and culture.

I argue later in the chapter that these principles of substantive equality should also be brought to bear in constructing hate speech regulations. On this view, hate speech directed at historically oppressed groups who lack equal footing in society is quite properly restricted. But across-the-board hate speech restrictions, through reflecting a formal equality, are prone to abuse and lead, in operation, to perpetuation of real-world inequalities.

---

[13] *Id.* at 16–17.

[14] Horizontal rights regulate the relations between private individuals; vertical rights control only government actors. *See generally* Stephen Gardbaum, "The 'Horizontal' Effect of Constitutional Rights," 102 *Mich. L. Rev.* 387 (2003).

[15] Horizontal rights have also been adopted in Canada, Ireland, Germany, and the European Union. *Id.* at 387.

[16] *See, e.g.*, Adarand Constructors, Inc. v. Pena, 515 U.S. 200 (1995) (holding that all race-based classifications, regardless of which groups are favored or disfavored, are constitutionally suspect and presumptively invalid).

[17] United States v. Carolene Products Co., 304 U.S. 144, 152, n. 4 (1938). For an extended elaboration of this idea, see Ely, *supra* note 10.

[18] The view that affirmative action should receive mid-level rather than strict scrutiny garnered four votes, but not five, in Regents of University of California v. Bakke, 438 U.S. 265, 358–62 (1978) (Brennan, White, Marshall, & Blackmun, JJ., concurring in the judgment in part and dissenting in part).

## C. *Toward a Governmental Role in the Marketplace of Ideas*

The very metaphor of the "marketplace of ideas" implies that government *should* regulate freedom of speech in certain circumstances, *viz.*, where "market failures" or irregularities exist. Principles of substantive equality point to a market failure requiring government intervention if one group cannot get its ideas heard in the marketplace not because of the merits of those ideas but because of structural imbalances in society. As the South African Constitutional Court has observed, the notion of a marketplace of ideas "presupposes that both the supply and demand side of the market will be unfettered."[19] Free speech can be a powerful instrument of social oppression in the hands of historically dominant groups. Social power sometimes coalesces with legal power while at other times it may crosscut it. A view of society that calls for state "neutrality" in the marketplace of ideas is tantamount to a myopic neglect of the fundamental reality of unequal distribution of power.

For all the considerable attention scholars have paid to the "marketplace of ideas," many have failed to extend the metaphor to include various accepted forms of economic regulation, notably antitrust law. The prohibition of hate speech is the equivalent of an antitrust law that removes from the marketplace a cartel and the resulting abuse of monopoly that squelches competition. Formal equality as enhanced by the concept of a free market masks the real inequality that exists between groups. Accordingly, there is a need for government regulation of the speech market:

> These arguments are parallel to arguments that minimum wage laws or antitrust decrees do not limit economic efficiency but rather facilitate the production decisions that would have resulted had conditions of perfect competition genuinely obtained in the first place.[20]

Like corresponding economic regulations, regulation of speech should correct market failures, break up speech monopolies, redistribute relative speaking power, and even protect us from our existing speech preferences or tastes.[21] Moving beyond shallow equality entails the "elimination of major disparities in people's material resources, well-being, opportunities, and political and social power."[22] It is necessary to address systemic inequality and asymmetry of social power by assessing laws and regulations in the context of historical discrimination and by keeping in mind the goal of reducing historically rooted oppression.[23]

---

[19]  Case and Another v. Minister of Safety and Security, 3 SA 617 (CC) (1996).
[20]  Kathleen M. Sullivan, "Free Speech and Unfree Markets," 42 *UCLA L. Rev.* 949, 956 (1995).
[21]  *Id.* at 957.
[22]  Bakan, *supra* note 11, at 9.
[23]  Martha Albertson Fineman, "The Social Foundations of Law," 54 *Emory L.J.* 201, 212 (2005).

Slogans such as "the marketplace of ideas," or "the answer to problematic speech is more speech," disguise the way in which (modern) social power operates.[24] Hate speech must be regulated in a measured way to protect historically disadvantaged minorities without violating the constitutional guarantee of equality. Substantive equality will be violated in two distinct situations: first, when hate speech is protected like any other speech, and second, when hate speech is prohibited across the board to protect dominant and marginalized groups alike. To avoid both these undesirable outcomes, hate speech regulation must take into account three essential considerations: (1) the character, nature, and scope of the speech restriction; (2) the historical context of the cultural or ethnic groups involved in the speech at issue; and (3) the power relation (private and social) between the speaker and target of the speech at the particular speech moment.

In short, freedom of speech must be balanced against another central constitutional value – equality. No right, including freedom of speech, is absolute; thus, it is inadequate simply to assert that freedom of speech always prevails over equality claims when the two cannot coexist. In *Romer v. Evans*, using a well-worn Supreme Court phrase, Justice Kennedy wrote that "equal protection of the laws is not achieved through indiscriminate imposition of inequalities."[25] He further affirmed that central to the idea of the rule of law and to the U.S. Constitution's guarantee of equal protection is the principle that government and each of its parts remain open on impartial terms to all who seek its assistance. As such, the equal protection of the laws requires rendering the necessary assistance taking into account relevant power differences pertaining to groups.

In ethno-linguistically diverse societies, the prohibition of hate speech is needed to address the monopoly that some groups wield over speech. This takes the form not only of a monopoly over literary skills, but, far more importantly, a monopoly over the dominant language. In multilingual countries, such as Ethiopia or many other African nations,[26] usually one or a few languages are used in the public forum in the negotiation over conflicting narratives, visions, and loyalties. Marginalized groups cannot use the dominant language with the same level of mastery and proficiency as the dominant group. "More speech" cannot suffice as a response to hate speech against minorities because mastery of the language of social negotiation is not equally accessible to them. By the same token, prohibiting hate speech directed against any and all ethnic or racial groups, including dominant groups, only promotes greater inequality and is indefensible from the substantive equality perspective.

---

[24] Demaske argues that "if power is both repressive and productive, then the 'proliferation of liberationist discourse' becomes a way to further mask domination." Demaske, *supra* note 8, at 279 (quoting Jana Sawicki, *Disciplining Foucault: Feminism, Power and the Body* 27 [Routledge 1991]).

[25] Romer v. Evans, 517 U.S. 620, 633 (1996) (quoting Sweatt v. Painter, 339 U.S. 629, 635 [1950] [quoting Shelley v. Kraemer, 334 U.S. 1, 22 (1948)]).

[26] Most African countries are very diverse ethnically; not a few have hundreds of ethnic groups.

### D. A Detour: Hate Speech and Genocide

Although my general argument is that hate speech prohibitions should be unidirectional, an across-the-board prohibition of hate speech may be justified in one setting, namely where hate speech might lead to genocide. Genocidal acts never spring up over night; they are a practical working out of a long process of accumulated hate speech. Racist expressions fostering hatred based on a group's ethnicity can become so ingrained in everyday language that victimization, marginalization, servitude, and ultimately the massacre of outgroups might appear as normal.[27] Racial and ethnic slurs pave the way for horrendous acts against minorities. Hate speech has a tendency to create a climate of impunity where the majority becomes complacent in the face of oppression of minorities. Then it becomes normal and acceptable for the majority "first to libel, then to discriminate, and finally to persecute outgroups."[28]

Alexander Tsesis recounts examples where hate speech and genocide have coincided. One leading and obvious example is Nazi Germany, in which hate speech – in whispers and in roars – led to the disenfranchisement, imprisonment, and genocide of Jews. Thus, when the Nuremberg Tribunal sentenced to death the publisher of an anti-Semitic weekly newsletter, it pointed out that he had been known as "Jew-Baiter Number One," and that his publications "infected the German mind with the virus of anti-Semitism and incited the German people to active persecution."[29] Tsesis's second example is the enslavement of Africans in the United States, which required "protracted socialization over a considerable period of time during which preachers, politicians, the media, and others made slavery socially and religiously acceptable and defined Africans as sub-humans and part of a cursed race."[30]

Hate speech and genocide can be interlinked in two ways. First, hate speech might precede and *cause* genocide. Second, hate speech might be used as a *means* to flare up hatred once genocide is already underway. Such was the case in Rwanda, which I discuss in greater depth below. The use of powerful metaphors to mischaracterize Tutsis as cockroaches that need to be eliminated and the invocation of physical characteristics – as in the calls over the radio to "cut the tall trees"[31] – demonstrate the role of hate speech in aggravating the atrocities. The role of the media in the

---

[27] Ziyad Motala, "The First Amendment and Hate Speech: An Illustration of Why the United States Supreme Court's Approach Represents an Anomaly," 46 *How. L.J.* 507, 508–9 (2003) (reviewing Alexander Tsesis, *Destructive Messages: How Hate Speech Paves the Way for Harmful Social Movements* [NYU Press 2002]). Tsesis gives the name "misethnicity" to a synthesis of prejudice, racism, and ethnocentrism. Tsesis, *Destructive Messages*, at 2, 81.

[28] *Id.* at 26.

[29] Judgment against Julius Streicher, 22 International Military Tribunal, Trial of the Major War Criminals, 218th Day (Oct. 1, 1946), at 547 (1948).

[30] Motala, *supra* note 27, at 509.

[31] "Cut the tall trees" was the crucial code phrase during the genocide. Unlike Hutus, Tutsis are usually considered as taller and having a brown complexion. The Tutsis were considered Ethiopians, and hence their corpses were thrown into the river so that the river could take them to Ethiopia – where, according to some, they belonged.

Rwandan genocide was immense, so much so that for the first time the UN Tribunal found that mass media hate speech can constitute "genocide, incitement to genocide, and crimes against humanity."[32]

There is an unsettling resemblance between the hate propaganda used during the Rwandan genocide and the hate campaign surrounding the May 2005 elections in Ethiopia. Fortunately, Ethiopia did not experience killings of genocidal proportions, although the election air was charged with hate, recrimination, and bloodshed. Indeed, the June and November 2005, government killings of peaceful demonstrators contesting the officially declared results of the May 2005 founding elections have genocidal dimensions. This is because the top echelons of the country's ruling party, who are predominantly of Tigrayan extract, believed that the Amharas were out to regain their long-held dominance of the political landscape. The predominantly Amhara major opposition coalition, the Coalition for Unity and Democracy (CUD), contributed to the creation of Amhara-Tigray battle imagery.

### E. *Leveling the Playing Field*

In deeply divided and diverse societies, multinational federalism is one way of protecting ethnic minorities if they are territorially concentrated and sufficiently numerous. It allows an equilibrium between the competing ideals of accommodating diversity and promoting unity. Promotion of unity requires a positive effort on the part of political actors to narrow the chasm that exists between ethnic groups by uniting the broken pieces in the society. Without concerted efforts to maintain and promote unity of the polity, territorial devolution of power to ethnic groups can be just a step shy of secession and total independence of the subnational units. Given that multinational federalism is anchored in a tacit pact between the central government and the substate units not to recentralize the polity on the part of the former and not to secede on the part of the latter, secession is unacceptable.[33]

Furthermore, if subnational units secede from the federation, exploiting the political capital they have acquired as a result of the territorial devolution of power, the international community may, if grudgingly, acknowledge the independence of such states, as exemplified by the international community's acceptance of the de facto statehood of former Yugoslavian republics. Therefore, unity is best guarded and nurtured at the domestic level.

It is against this backdrop that one has to consider the role of hate speech in deeply divided and diverse societies. Hate speech in such societies triggers a wide array of very complex issues that demand to be addressed cautiously. On the one

---

[32] Prosecutor v. Nahimana, Barayagwiza, & Ngeze (*The Media Case*), Case No. ICTR-99-52-T (Dec. 3, 2003).

[33] The FDRE Constitution includes an explicit right to secession. "Every Nation, Nationality and People in Ethiopia has an unconditional right to self-determination, including the right to secession." FDRE Const. art. 39(1). This stance seems contrary to the normative conception described here.

hand, speech cannot be readily restricted in deeply divided societies without a spiraling effect; speech plays a crucial role in fostering interethnic cooperation and understanding. Robust speech protection is thus crucial in deeply divided societies to enable people to actively explore commonalties through assembly and speech. It is only through dialogue and coming together that deeply divided societies can discover common interests that can transcend ethno-linguistic and other cleavages. In fact, it is the only viable means by which people can come out of their ethnic enclaves and niches and onto the democratic space in a common venture to reconcile their conflicting narratives, conflicting visions of statehood, and conflicting loyalties.

On the other hand, hate speech against the minority works against the ideal of promoting unity. Unrestricted hate speech might eat at the unity of a polity "like acid on metal," alienating minority groups from the mainstream society and thus nourishing irredentist and secessionist movements. When hate speech is allowed to enter the public realm, then, the cord of unity – already such a thin thread in deeply divided societies – may be severed.

Finally, these considerations shift over time. To the extent prohibition of hate speech is justified by the real or substantive equality argument, at some point – as in the case of affirmative action – the equality terrain will be crossed over and inequality sets in. (Of course, the exact moment of that transformation will be far from clear, and being alert to such subtle nuances is easier said than done.) Furthermore, in deeply divided societies, identity politics weighs heavily and what often matters most is not so much the content of policies or laws, but who gets to decide what. Hence, parties tend to organize along ethno-linguistic lines and only later on may shift to a more integrated political organization once the language problem is addressed.

Only by adopting a more contoured and textured approach can constitution writers and policy makers strike an optimal balance between these two competing and shifting considerations.

## III. AN OVERVIEW OF HATE SPEECH REGULATION IN AFRICA

This Part reviews the hate speech law and jurisprudence of three African countries, namely Ethiopia, Rwanda, and South Africa.

### A. *Ethiopia*

#### 1. Freedom of Expression under the FDRE Constitution

The FDRE Constitution incorporates a bundle of speech-related freedoms under the caption, "Right of Thought, Opinion and Expression." Article 29 reads, in relevant part:

> Everyone has the right to freedom of expression without any interference. This
> right shall include freedom to seek, receive and impart information and ideas of all

kinds, regardless of frontiers, either orally, in writing or in print, in the form of art, or through any media of his choice.[34]

Notwithstanding this seemingly generous protection, article 29 goes on to set out an elaborate set of limitations on the right to free expression on grounds, among others, of "the well-being of the youth, and the honor and reputation of individuals."[35] It even directly imposes a positive obligation on the state to prohibit by law "public propaganda of war" and "public expression that injures human dignity."[36]

## 2. Hate Speech Regulation

Hate speech regulation in Ethiopia is found scattered in many pieces of legislation. What follows is a brief description of the most important laws pertaining to hate speech regulation. As will be shown below, Ethiopia has adopted a "truth-based" approach to hate speech regulation. That is, it permits hate speech that is truthful, regardless of the harm it causes, in contrast to a consequence-based approach, which limits even truthful speech if its consequences are sufficiently severe.

A. THE CRIMINAL LAW. Ethiopia's Penal Code of 1957, now repealed, contained a number of provisions that can potentially be applied against certain types of hate speech, including prohibitions of defamation, offenses against national interest, offenses against law and order, and breaches of the peace. Most importantly, the Penal Code prohibited "false rumors and incitements to breach of the peace,"[37] a provision that is both vague and broad in that it has no requirement of imminent violence.[38] The Code also criminalized defamation.[39]

In 2004, Ethiopia replaced the 1957 Penal Code with a new Criminal Code.[40] The new Criminal Code includes an interesting provision that is of particular relevance to hate speech regulation. Article 486(b) provides that whoever "by whatever accusation or any other means foments dissension, arouses hatred, or stirs up acts of violence or

---

[34] FDRE Const. art. 29(2). The provision draws from, but is not identical to, article 10 of the European Convention on Human Rights, which is discussed by Toby Mendel, Tarlach McGonagle, and Eduardo Bertoni and Julio Rivera Jr. in, respectively, Chapters 22, 24, 25 herein.

[35] *Id.* art. 29(6).

[36] *Id.*

[37] FDRE Penal Code (1957), art. 480. This provision was quite commonly invoked against journalists in Ethiopia. *See* Article 19, *Observations on the Protection and Promotion of Freedom of Expression in Ethiopia* (Nov. 2000), *available at* http://www.article19.org/pdfs/publications/ethiopia-foe-submission.pdf. Interestingly, "in May 2000, the Zimbabwean Supreme Court declared that a virtually identical false news provision to that found in Ethiopia's Penal Code violated the constitutional guarantee of freedom of expression." *Id.* at 10, citing Chavunduka & Choto v. Minister of Home Affairs & Attorney General, Judgment No. S.C. 36/2000, Civil App. No. 156/99 (May 22, 2000).

[38] Article 19, *supra* note 37.

[39] FDRE Penal Code (1957), art. 580.

[40] Proclamation No. 414/2004.

political,[41] racial or religious disturbances" is guilty of a crime. This provision has not been tested in court, but one recent case has brought hate speech into a sharp focus. In *Public Prosecutor v. Hailu Shawel*,[42] which arose in the immediate aftermath of the May 2005 nationwide elections, the Public Prosecutor charged the leaders and members of CUD, human rights advocates, and journalists with "outrage against the constitution and the constitutional order," "inciting, organizing and leading armed rebellion," "obstruction of exercise of constitutional power," "impairing the defensive power of the state," and "genocide."

The charge of attempted genocide was particularly interesting because of its strong nexus with hate speech. The genocide charge was predicated primarily on utterances made by CUD's leaders and others. Particularly noteworthy was a statement made by a prominent opposition figure, Ato Bedru Adem, which was evidenced by a video recording of his speech delivered in Assela, a small town in the Oromia Regional State of Ethiopia. Adam stated that "the power of the Federal Government is totally in the hands of the Tigrayans and the EPRDF[43] should thus be shoved back to its former turf by the united power of the people." The Federal High Court ruled that this was merely "hate speech," and was not intended to destroy the target group in part or in whole. However, the Federal High Court does not possess jurisdiction over hate speech cases and the case was not re-heard before the court having competence.

Also of note is article 816 of the Criminal Code, which criminalizes blasphemous utterances or attitudes that are grossly offensive to the religious feelings or convictions of others or toward the Divine Being or the religious symbols, rites, or religious personages of others. However, Articles 486 and 816 of the new Criminal Code do not criminalize the criticism of a religion or belief of others if they are interpreted in a way consistent with international and regional human rights tribunals.

The new criminal Code retains the 1957 Penal Code's protections of government officials. Ethiopia is now a "Federal Democratic Republic,"[44] and the monarchical system has not been part of the political landscape since the popular revolution in 1974. Along with the monarchical system, the provisions of the 1957 Penal Code about the Emperor are long gone. However, the new Criminal Code does prohibit certain insults to the state, foreign states, and emblems. In addition to protecting the honor and reputation of "individuals" under Article 613, the Code prohibits the starting or spreading of "false rumors, suspicions or false charge against the government or the public authorities."[45]

---

[41] Political groups are left from the purview of Art. 20 (2) of the ICCPR on hate speech. Also, both the 1957 Penal Code's Art. 281 and the Criminal Code's Art. 269 prohibition of genocide include political groups.

[42] Federal High Court, File No.43246 (1999).

[43] The Tigrayan people are commonly understood as the nucleus of the EPRDF (Ethiopian Peoples' Revolutionary Democratic Front). EPRDF is a coalition of four main ethnically based political parties including the Tigrayan Peoples' Liberation Front (TPLF).

[44] FDRE const. art 1.

[45] Criminal Code art. 486(b).

B. THE 1960 CIVIL CODE. Ethiopian law also recognizes a civil cause of action for defamation; the plaintiff can obtain damages and/or an injunction. Although there is some overlap between antidefamation and anti–hate speech laws, hate speech laws protect groups *qua* groups, whereas defamation laws protect only individuals; only individuals, not groups, can obtain a civil remedy. In addition, the protection from hate speech that defamation laws offer is only partial. In particular, truth is a defense: "No defamation shall be deemed to have been committed where the defendant adduces proof of the accuracy of his charges."[46] (However, if the person acted "solely with intent to injure," the truth defense does not avail.[47])

Given these narrow limitations, many people have ethnic jokes on their cell phones and can circulate these jokes with absolute impunity because of lack of regulation of hate speech with regard to persons other than the press. In group defamation or hate speech cases, Ethiopian courts have largely left the consequence-based regulation of hate speech in favor of the truth-based one. In the cases decided by Ethiopian courts, truth seems to be an absolute defense, with some exception for "actual malice," which in Ethiopian parlance is called "intent to injure."

Truth-based regulation of (hate) speech is problematic constitutionally because it entails content-based scrutiny of the speech. Consequence-based regulation is less problematic, even if one cannot possibly gauge potential consequences without some form of content-based probe. Protection of groups through a truth-based approach is at least immensely difficult, if not morally outrageous. The Chinese in Indonesia are widely considered as locusts; Idi Amin labeled the Asians (whom he ordered to be expelled in seventy-two hours from Uganda) leaches; the Tutsis were called cockroaches and snakes; Jews were labeled vermin and rats in Germany before the Holocaust. How can a court possibly deal with these issues with the truth-based approach?

C. REGULATION OF THE PRESS. Although lacking a general hate speech law, Ethiopia has criminalized certain types of hate speech that stems from the media. Thus, hate speech law as such has pertained only to the press; in effect, it is an exception to freedom of the press rather than an exception to freedom of expression more broadly. Two laws, each applying to a certain part of the public sphere, are relevant here: laws regulating the press, which are discussed in this section, and Broadcasting Proclamation No. 178/1999, which is discussed in the following section.

Press Proclamation No. 34/1992, which was repealed in 2008, contained a number of provisions that were *protective* of the press, at least on paper.[48] However, article

---

[46] Civil Code, art. 2047(1).
[47] Civil Code, art. 2047(2).
[48] Prominent among them is article 3, which reads, in its entirety:

1. Freedom of the press is recognised and respected in Ethiopia.
2. Censorship of the press and any restriction of a similar nature are hereby prohibited.

10, entitled "Ensuring the Lawfulness of the Contents of Press Products," restricted publication of false and offensive information, incitement of ethnic hatred, or libel. In particular, article 10(2) provided that "any defamation or false accusation against nation/nationality, people" or "any criminal instigation of one nationality against another or incitement of conflict between peoples" was punishable with imprisonment up to three years and/or a fine of up to approximately $8,000. Criminal liability in such cases rested with the editor, journalist, or publisher. The NGO ARTICLE 19 rightly criticized this provision as overbroad in that it did not require a showing that the speaker intended to "incite *imminent* violence," or that the expression "was likely to incite imminent violence," or that "there was a direct and immediate connection between the expression and the likelihood of imminent violence."[49] Of course, it seems that the intention of the government in passing this law was precisely to punish the mere incitement to hatred, even if the speech in question is a far cry from inciting violence.

Under Press Proclamation No. 34/1992, journalists could be jailed on a wide array of charges, including criminal defamation, incitement to violence, spreading false information, and incitement to ethnic hatred. The use of this draconian press law, which conflicts with the constitutional guarantee of freedom of expression, coupled with the anti-press-freedom sentiment of the ruling party, led to the incarceration of many journalists on account of "inciting ethnic hatred."[50] A case in point is the sentence passed against the editor of a private monthly magazine who was ordered by a court to pay a fine of approximately $1,500 for "arousing hatred against the Tigrayan-speaking people."[51]

A draft press law, first introduced in 2003, ignited a fierce debate among scholars and politicians in Ethiopia and abroad. Various international organizations and individuals working in the field expressed concern over the draft's chilling impact on free expression.[52] The draft contained various criminal penalties as well as a "reminder" clause that provides that persons who violate other laws relating to the press will be penalized according to the provisions of those other laws. Some objected

---

[49] Article 19, *supra* note 37.

[50] *See, e.g.,* Freedom House International, Map of Press Freedom 2005, *available at* http://www.freedomhouse.org/template.cfm?page=251&year=2005 (reporting that Ethiopian "[a]uthorities frequently invoke the 1992 Law on the Press . . . to justify the arrest and detainment of journalists" and that in light of official detentions and harassment "reporters often practice self-censorship").

[51] Committee to Protect Journalists, 2000 *Country Report: Ethiopia, available at* http://www.cpj.org/attacks00/africa00/Ethiopia.html. It is beyond dispute that the Tigrayan people, through their vanguard party, The Tigrayan People's Liberation Front, form the nucleus of the governing coalition in the country. Among others, the U.S. Department of State has confirmed that whereas the military as a whole was ethnically diverse, "diversity was less common in the higher ranks among officer personnel, which was dominated by members of the Tigrayan ethnic group." U.S. Dep't of State, 2004 *Report on Ethiopia, available at* http://www.state.gov/g/drl/rls/hrrpt/2004/41603.htm.

[52] *See, e.g.,* Article 19, *Briefing Note on the Draft Ethiopian Proclamation to Provide for the Freedom of the Press* (June 2004), *available at* http://www.article19.org/pdfs/analysis/ethiopia-note-may-2004-draft-press-law.pdf.

to this double criminal warning, viewing it as harassment, given that there is no need to mention another statute criminalizing certain speech-related offenses.

The draft press statute's preamble mentioned the need to ensure accuracy of information and "constructive and responsible journalism" through regulation. The government thus was to possess wide latitude in regulating the content of speech and exercising viewpoint discrimination. In particular, Article 10 of the draft law provided:

1. Every [member of the] press has the duty to ensure that any press product it circulates is free from any content that can give rise to criminal and civil liability.
2. Without prejudice to the generality of sub-article 1 of this Article, any [member of the] press shall have the duty to ensure that any press product it issues or circulates is free from:
   a. Any criminal offence against the safety of the State or of the administration established in accordance with the Charter or of the national defense force;
   b. Any *defamation or false accusation against any individual, nation/ nationality, people* or organization;
   c. Any *criminal instigation of one nationality against another or incitement of conflict between peoples*; and
   d. Any agitation of war.[53]

The penalty for a breach relating to content, notwithstanding the liabilities and penalties under the Penal Code, was to be imprisonment for up to three years but not less than one year or a fine of between 5,000 and 10,000 Ethiopian Birr, or both imprisonment and a fine.[54]

Finally, the draft would have authorized the government to prohibit the importation, suspend the circulation, or delete any harmful content of printed matters of foreign origin if they contain material that instigates hatred based on race, national or ethnic origin, color, language, religious faith, or social background.[55] Regarding press of domestic origin, the draft provided that the press has to make sure that the content does not give rise to civil and criminal liability, a requirement that clearly would pave the way for viewpoint discrimination.

That the draft press law received, and in some quarters continues to receive, serious consideration indicates the precarious status of press freedom in Ethiopia. Happily, the version of the law that was enacted in 2008 does not contain the more sweeping regulatory provisions described above, and the preamble offers quite

---

[53] Draft Press Law art. 10.
[54] *Id.* art. 20(1).
[55] Draft Press Law art. 3. The draft did not define or set parameters for the phrase "social background," but it seems that the phrase was used as a catchall to protect groups that cannot be neatly categorized under any one of the other grounds listed in the provision.

speech-protective language.[56] However, the new law contains harshly criticized registration requirements,[57] as well as a defamation provision that, in the case of speech about government officials, permits prosecution even if the target of the defamation chooses not to press charges,[58] both of which could easily lend themselves to abuse.[59]

D. REGULATION OF BROADCASTERS. As first adopted, the 1992 Press Proclamation applied to all media, including broadcasting media. With the 1999 promulgation of the Broadcast Proclamation, Proclamation No. 178/1999, however, the press law applied only to the extent it does not contradict the Broadcast Proclamation. The Broadcast Proclamation applies a wide array of content-based restrictions on programs that do not reflect varying viewpoints, fail to verify the accuracy of their sources, violate the dignity and liberty of mankind or the rules of good behavior, undermine the beliefs of others, or commit a criminal offense relating to state security or defense or the constitutionally established government.[60] It has been underscored by the NGO Article 19 that these restrictions have a chilling effect because "they apply to every program broadcast, rather than to the overall programming of a particular broadcaster."[61]

The Proclamation also provides that political parties and religious organizations are not allowed to own broadcasting stations.[62] Most political parties remain primarily ethnically based with the exception of the opposition, which has recently managed to forge a national coalition across ethnic cleavages.[63] Thus, the prohibition of broadcasting licenses to political parties might be considered an effort to avoid potential conflicts among various ethnic groups in the country. However, it remains to be seen whether other ethnically based organizations, which do not fall under the category of political parties and religious organizations – the Mecha Tulema (Oromo self-help), or Tigray Development Association, or Amhara Development Association, to name three – can hold broadcasting licenses.

These restrictions have been the subject of harsh criticism from many corners for chilling constitutionally protected expression, religious practices, and association. The consistent response from the drafters of the Proclamation has been that in a country like Ethiopia, faced with the enormous challenge of intractable religious

---

[56] Freedom of the Mass Media and Access to Information Proclamation No. 590/2008.

[57] *Id.* art. 9.

[58] *Id.* art. 43(7).

[59] *See generally* Tracy J. Ross, "A Test of Democracy: Ethiopia's Mass Media and Freedom of Information Proclamation," 114 *Penn. State L. Rev.* 1047, 1054–8 (2010) (arguing that the law violates Article XIX of the Universal Declaration of Human Rights).

[60] Proc. No. 178/1999, art. 27.

[61] Article 19, *The Legal Framework for Freedom of Expression in Ethiopia* (Jan. 2003), *available at* http://www.article19.org/pdfs/publications/ethiopia-legal-framework-for-foe.pdf.

[62] Proc. No. 178/1999, art. 23.

[63] U.S. Dep't of State, *supra* note 51.

and political conflicts, broadcasting by such groups might exacerbate the already problematic interethnic tensions. The situation in Rwanda, where the media were a powerful tool for the genocidaires, has always been pointed to as a cautionary tale. Given the "powerful and immediate" effect of audio-visual media, the government seems to have been carried away by pragmatic considerations.

However, the Broadcast Proclamation does not evenhandedly address the volatile political situation. Before its promulgation, the government had established *Radio Fana* and *Radio Ethiopia,* which air what are essentially the programs of the ruling party, the Ethiopian People Revolutionary Democratic Front (EPRDF). Proclamation 6/1991 provides that Radio Ethiopia and Ethiopian Television, described as the "mass media," will remain state-owned under the control of the Ministry of Information (what is now the Office of Government Communication Affairs). As such, the Broadcast Proclamation at best serves the partisan interests of the ruling party of the day by circumventing broadcasting by the opposition.

E. PROCLAMATION TO ESTABLISH THE PROCEDURE FOR PEACEFUL DEMONSTRATION AND PUBLIC POLITICAL MEETING (PROCLAMATION NO. 3/1991). This law prohibits, under the pain of criminal liability, peaceful demonstrations or public political meetings held to further "discrimination based on race, color, region, sex or similar characteristics" or "racist promotion and provocation of ethnic mistrust and hatred among nations, nationalities and peoples."[64] As such, one cannot discuss ethnic injustices in public meetings and demonstrators cannot carry placards or shout slogans that may fan the embers of ethnic conflict and hatred.

## 3. Hate Speech Jurisprudence

The hate speech jurisprudence in Ethiopia has generally and increasingly focused on "accuracy" or truth. Thus one can write or say anything, regardless of the ensuing consequences, as long as it is true – although one must be able to back it up with concrete evidence, not just citations to sources. As a result, courts have disproportionately placed the onus of proving the accuracy of their writings on the shoulders of the press.

Not only is the existing law regulating speech in Ethiopia silencing, but the courts have also time and again mechanically emphasized (or, one might say, hidden behind) the letter of the law and have wandered far from the core ideals of freedom of speech in a democracy.

In a very interesting case, a weekly newspaper, *Mebrek,* had reported, under the title "Little Tigray," that the Rehabilitation Commission of the Transitional Government of Ethiopia was dominated by the Tigrayan ethnic group.[65] The vice

---

[64] Proc. No. 3/1991, art. 8 (1).
[65] Public Prosecutor v. Allula Yasin, File No. 10/1995.

editor-in-chief of the newspaper, among others, was charged with falsely reporting that the non-Tigrayan staff of the Commission had been forced to resign or had been fired and that the property of the Commission had been transferred to the Tigray region. The court held that because the report was based on truth, it could not convict under the 1992 press law. The Commission admitted that most of its top officials are indeed of Tigrayan descent; for the court, that ended the case – the report was factually accurate and thus protected. Yet even if true, the report was highly likely to cause ethnic strife between Tigrayans and non-Tigrayans. The court was so constrained by its dogmatic jurisprudence, however, that it paid not the scantest attention to the possible inflammatory consequence of the statement.

In another case, another private weekly newspaper reported, under the title "Apartheid in Region 4," that many hundreds of people belonging to the Amhara ethnic group had been murdered and that the regional government of Oromiya had done nothing to ensure the well-being of the Amharas. Here the court held that despite an attempt on the part of the reporter to back up his report by citing sources, he had not *actually* ensured the accuracy of his reports using concrete evidence. The court emphasized that the *raison d'être* of the press proclamation is not to ask newspapers to cite sources but rather to make sure that their reports contain factual and accurate statements.[66]

The courts' approach threatens to give an unbridled rein to inflammatory hate speech as long as it is based on fact. The cases mentioned above and other similar cases show that the courts have almost invariably adopted the near-impossible and imprudent project of truth-based analysis of press products.

## 4. Abuse of Hate Speech Regulation in Ethiopia

Ethiopia's history has been marked by mutual animosity and distrust between the different ethnic groups that comprise the polity. The many deadly ethnic conflicts have widened the rift between ethnic groups. The 2003 attack on the Anuak people in the Gambella Regional State,[67] allegedly orchestrated by the army, bears gruesome testimony to the fragile ethnic relationship prevailing in the country.[68] It is against this backdrop that the issue of regulation of hate speech has to be approached.

---

[66] Public Prosecutor v. Nike Kassaye & Yohannes Abebe, File No. 36/1995.

[67] This is one of the nine federal units of the country where two ethnic groups have an uneasy alliance in jointly administering the region.

[68] According to Genocide Watch, about 416 ethnic Anuaks were murdered in a genocide that was orchestrated by government troops and joined by people from the highlands. Also, 3,000–5,000 Anuaks have fled to neighboring Sudan. This report has been confirmed by other international organizations and the U.S. State Department. *See* Genocide Watch, *The Anuak of Ethiopia* (Jan. 2004), *available at* http://www.genocidewatch.org/THE%20ANUAK%20OF%20ETHIOPIA.htm. Human Rights Watch has also corroborated this finding: "ENDF forces have committed murder, torture and rape in the course of widespread and possibly systematic attacks directed against the Anuak civilian population in Gambella." Human Rights Watch, *Targeting the Anuak: Human Rights Violations and Crimes against Humanity in Ethiopia's Gambella Region* 56 (March 2005), *available at* http://hrw.org/reports/2005/ethiopia0305/.

As the preceding discussion attempted to show, the government of Ethiopia has on many occasions imprisoned members of the independent press and cracked down on the opposition. Because ethnicity is increasingly salient, any speech amounting to incitement of hatred against nations, nationalities, or peoples is punishable by a prison sentence. At the same time, the government itself has extensively engaged in hate speech against the opposition.

Thus, when we examine the regulation of hate speech in Ethiopia, the picture is a dispiriting one. The government abuses its power to silence and, even worse, decapitate the opposition while giving free rein to its own supporters. One glaring fact in Africa is that even when there is an effort to treat ethnicity the way sex is treated – that is, as a subject that is simply taboo and inappropriate for discussion in the public sphere – it has the habit of operating in the background and it takes only the least powerful of catalysts to resurface. In a country of ethnicized politics, talking about ethnic injustice is both inescapable and more likely to be punished as hate speech. Hence, what one observes under such circumstances is debate by proxy. Apparently neutral terms, such as "party platform," "ideology," "economic policy," "land policy," and the like, are in fact loaded terms, code words for particular ethnicities. In Ethiopia, for instance, one can have a rough idea of a person's ethnic identity by their political platform – ethnic sensitivity, for one, is very dear to most of the historically marginalized ethnic groups, whereas historically privileged ethnic groups opt for individual-based liberal democracy.

Ethiopia's hate speech regulation stifles important political debate. The country would be better served if matters of public debate were immune from hate speech regulations to enable democratic self-governance. Useful models exist. For example, Australia's hate speech law provides exemptions for fair reporting, academic and scientific research, artistic work, and matters of public debate.[69] Canada, while also adopting a truth-based approach to regulation of hate speech, specifies defenses that may extend constitutional protection to speech, including, among others, a reasonable belief on the part of the accused that his/her statements were relevant to a subject of public interest, the discussion of which was for the public benefit or showing that the statements were made for the purpose of pointing out and abolishing hateful sentiments toward an identifiable group in Canada.[70]

---

[69] Simon Rice, "Do Australians have equal protection against hate speech?," *available at* http://arts.anu.edu.au/democraticaudit/papers/200508_rice_hate_speech.pdf; *see also* Katharine Gelber, "Reconceptualizing Counterspeech in Hate-Speech Policy (with a Focus on Australia)," Chapter 11 herein.

[70] Stephen Brooks, "Hate Speech and the Rights Cultures of Canada and the United States," *49th Parallel*, no. 13 (2004), *available at* http://www.49thparallel.bham.ac.uk/back/issue13/brooks.htm. Canada's Supreme Court held that the content of speech could be considered so offensive as to place it outside the protection of § 2 of the Charter. The court reasoned that the "pain suffered by target group members," Canada's "international commitments to eradicate hate propaganda," "Canada's commitment to the values of equality and multiculturalism in §§ 15 and 27 of the Charter," and "historical knowledge of the potentially catastrophic effects of the promotion of hatred" combined to make § 319 (2) of the Criminal Code a reasonable limit on freedom of expression. *Id.*

In diverse and deeply divided countries, the heavy-handed criminalization of hate speech across the board does more than simply close down meaningful and vital public discourse. Perhaps more importantly, it violates the guarantee of equal application of the laws, which is at the heart of the constitutional architecture. Substantive equality demands that hate speech be prohibited to give breathing space to historically disadvantaged minorities. However, when such protection is extended to dominant groups, it crosses over to the realm of inequality. One can discuss interethnic or interracial relations without resorting to hate speech, but it might be difficult to draw a bright line between the two. Any useful debate aimed at destroying social oppression cannot avoid discussion of interethnic relations. If hate speech regulations put those topics off limits, democratic change and self-governance become impossible. Ethiopia unfortunately stands as a case study in the abuse of hate speech law and rhetoric to cement the dominance of power groups.

## B. *Rwanda's Hate Speech Regime*

In 1994, Rwanda suffered the worst genocide in modern times. Approximately 800,000 Rwandans were murdered in a span of 100 days, most of whom were ethnic Tutsis and moderate Hutus or Tutsi sympathizers. Radio Tele Libre Mille Collines (RTLM), a privately owned radio station, assisted in the genocide by broadcasting a barrage of anti-Tutsi propaganda.

In the "radio-based culture" of Rwanda, where people tune in for the entire day,[71] the role of the RTLM in instigating and fanning the genocide was immense. According to Roméo Dallaire, "The station encouraged its listeners to kill Tutsis and called for the death of moderate Hutus, calling them traitors."[72] Its broadcasts were also accompanied by hate music from popular singers with lyrics such as: "I hate Hutus, I hate Hutus, I hate Hutus who think that Tutsis are not snakes."[73] Many sources have now confirmed that once the genocide was underway, the station played the role of an army general rather than the traditional role of the media. As such, it engaged in "reading out the names and locations of those who must be killed."[74] RTLM, dubbed a "hate radio station,"[75] became infamous for its description of Tutsis as "cockroaches" and for broadcasting the names, license plate numbers, and

---

[71] Roméo Dallaire, *Shake Hands with the Devil: The Failure of Humanity in Rwanda* 227 (Carroll & Graff Pubs. 2004).

[72] *Id.* at 261.

[73] *Id.*

[74] *Id.* at 272. Lieutenant General Dallaire claims that his entreaties to shut down the RTLM, which was serving as "direct instrument in promoting genocide," fell on deaf ears, and that the United States, which had the technological capability to jam the station, refused to do so because of the exorbitant cost and legal hurdles involved. *Id.* at 375.

[75] *Id.* at xii.

whereabouts of Tutsi individuals and families to help Hutu militias hunt down and kill them.[76]

The role of RTLM has become indelibly imprinted on the nation's psyche; it has informed the substance and spirit of hate speech regulation and discourse in Rwanda and served as an impetus to set narrow parameters for freedom of expression.

Rwanda adopted a new Constitution in 2003. Articles 33 and 34 of the Constitution guarantee freedom of the press and freedom of information, but these protections are qualified in ways that reflect the country's troubled history:

### Article 33

Freedom of thought, opinion, conscience, religion, worship and the public manifestation thereof is guaranteed by the State in accordance with conditions determined by law.

Propagation of ethnic, regional, racial or discrimination or any other form of division is punishable by law.

### Article 34

Freedom of the press and freedom of information are recognized and guaranteed by the State.

Freedom of speech and freedom of information shall not prejudice public order and good morals, the right of every citizen to honour, good reputation and the privacy of personal and family life. It is also guaranteed so long as it does not prejudice the protection of the youth and minors.[77]

A number of laws restrict freedom of expression. Prominent among them are laws on criminal defamation. The Penal Code criminalizes "defamation" and "defamatory denunciation" with penalties of up to three years' imprisonment. In addition, the 2002 Press Law imposes a wide range of limitations on the media, prohibiting the "publication of false news, defamation and abuses," "contempt of the President," and "verbal assaults committed through the press to a Head of State and foreign diplomatic officials, defamations and abuses committed through the press towards the public authorities and forces availed to the Government to maintain law and order."[78] These offenses carry severe jail punishments under the Penal Code.[79]

It is reported that the law is used regularly against the media and the press that criticize the government. In 2002, the government adopted a law criminalizing

---

[76] ACE Electoral Knowledge Network, *Rwanda: Hate Speech, available at* http://aceproject.org/ero-en/topics/parties-and-candidates/rwandahatespeech.

[77] Rwanda Const. arts. 33, 34.

[78] Law 18/2002 of 11/05/2002 Governing the Press, Republic of Rwanda, art. 84.

[79] Under the Press Law, "vendors, distributors or managers of poster display firms" may be held responsible for offenses committed by the printed press even though they have had no involvement in the content of a publication. *Id.* art. 88(5). They can be imprisoned if the journalist or other individual responsible for a publication cannot be found, under a hierarchy of penal liability. *See id.* art. 88.

every act considered to encourage "divisionism" or "sectarianism." In the absence of a precise definition of "divisionism" or "sectarianism," the law is subject to various interpretations and potential abuses by the government. Indeed, the government often has used this provision to muzzle press criticism of the government. The general climate for the press is foggy. Criticism of the government has often led to beatings, incarcerations, and finally to summary closing of some private newspapers.[80] In addition, criticism of the Tutsi-dominated government often is considered as anti-Tutsi propaganda. In 2007, army spokesman Major Jill Rutaremara and other top government officials accused critical media of collusion with "negative forces," which is a code name for opponents of Rwanda's Tutsi-dominated government, including Hutu rebels in neighboring Democratic Republic of Congo and exiled dissidents.[81]

The Committee to Protect Journalists has reported: "The government continued to invoke vaguely worded laws against ethnic divisionism and genocidal ideology to quiet dissenting views on sensitive topics such as the 1994 genocide, interethnic relations, and the trial of genocide suspects in 'gacaca' courts."[82] During Genocide Remembrance Week in 2007, a radio interview of a Hutu Christian priest claiming to have saved the lives of 104 people led authorities to charge host John Williams Ntwali of private City Radio in Kigali with promoting "genocidal ideology."[83]

Similarly, newspapers critical of the government are often accused of inciting ethnic hatred. The government does not tolerate criticism and uses "incitement of ethnic hatred" and "avoidance or recurrence of genocide" to repress its critics in the media. For example, in January 2007 the director of a bimonthly journal *Umurabyo*, was charged with "divisionism, sectarianism and libel." Agnès Nkusi-Uwimana, who had allowed publication of a reader's letter that compared ethnic killings during President Kagame's administration with those of the 1994 Hutu regime, was given a US$760 fine and a prison sentence of five years, reduced to one year.

In short, the same pattern appears in Rwanda as in Ethiopia: Hate speech regulations are manipulated to serve the interests of the government and suppress dissent.

## C. *South Africa's Hate Speech Regime*

Just as Rwanda's hate speech regulation is heavily influenced by the 1994 genocide, so South Africa's regulation of hate speech is overwhelmingly informed by the

---

[80] The High Council of the Press (also known as the National Press Council) is the State media regulator; it is established by the Constitution but "its functions, organization and operation" are to be determined by law. Rwanda Const. art. 34. Under Rwanda's Press law, the Council has the exclusive mandate to issue disciplinary recommendations against media outlets, but the details of its operations are determined by Presidential decree. Law 18/2002, *supra* note 78, arts. 73–75.

[81] Committee to Protect Journalists, *Attacks on the Press 2007: Rwanda* (quoting *The New Times*), *available at* http://www.cpj.org/2008/02/attacks-on-the-press-2007-rwanda.php.

[82] *Id.*

[83] Committee to Protect Journalists, "Radio host detained for 10 days, charged over 1994 genocide story" (May 11, 2007), http://cpj.org/2007/05/rwanda-radio-host-detained-for-10-days-charged-ove.php.

apartheid policy that was in force before 1993.[84] South Africa's regulation of hate speech is intertwined with the principle of dignity, which is the central, all-pervading constitutional principle. Hate speech regulation is aimed at restoring lost dignity and rehumanizing freedom of expression.

South Africa is another outlier in its hate speech regulation because it explicitly excludes hate speech from constitutional protection. Section 16 of the 1996 Constitution provides:

1.  Everyone has the right to freedom of expression, which includes –
    a.  freedom of the press and other media;
    b.  freedom to receive or impart information or ideas;
    c.  freedom of artistic creativity; and
    d.  academic freedom and freedom of scientific research.
2.  The right in subsection (1) does not extend to:
    a.  propaganda for war;
    b.  incitement of imminent violence; or
    c.  advocacy of hatred that is based on race, ethnicity, gender or religion, and that constitutes incitement to cause harm.

Section 16(2) thus explicitly places "hate speech" that is based on race, ethnicity, gender, or religion, and that constitutes incitement to cause harm outside freedom of expression, and removes it from the ambit of constitutional protection. Freedom of expression does not extend to those categories of speech "which have in advance been singled out by the framers of the South African Constitution as not deserving constitutional protection, since they have, among other things, the potential to impinge adversely on the dignity (one of the core values of the Constitution) of others and cause them harm."[85]

The category of unprotected speech is limited, however. First, as noted, only certain types of hate speech fall within section 16(2)(c). In addition, because that section is an exception to freedom of expression, it must be interpreted restrictively. It is submitted that the specifically enumerated grounds constitute an exhaustive list, so that analogous forms of hate speech, such as homophobic and perhaps even xenophobic speech, *are* protected under section 16(1).[86] Similarly, under the

---

[84] A useful overview of South Africa's hate speech regime is Christa Van Wyk, *The Constitutional Treatment of Hate Speech in South Africa* (2002), *available at* http://www.stopracism.ca/content/hate-speech-south-africa.

[85] *Id.*

[86] *See* Johan De Waal, Iain Currie, and Gerhard Erasmus, *The Bill of Rights Handbook* 319 (Juta & Co., 3d ed. 2000). This reading is in accordance with the view that exceptions, such as section 16(2), are to be restrictively interpreted. *See* Islamic Unity Convention v. Independent Broadcasting Auth. (CCT36/01) [2002] ZACC 3. At the same time, however, the Court in *Islamic Unity Convention* emphasized the interest of the state in regulating hate speech because such speech can harm the constitutionally mandated objective of building a nonracist and nonsexist society based on human dignity and equality.

constitution, the very definition of hate speech contemplates a consequence of incitement to cause harm.

In short, no *constitutional* challenge can be mounted against anti–hate speech legislation unless the legislation broadens the constitutional definition. Thus a person accused of hate speech can exonerate himself only if he could prove that the words in question do not constitute hate speech within the meaning of the Constitution.

However, hate speech that does *not* fall within the section 16(2) exclusion also can be and is regulated, as authorized by the Constitution's general limitations clause, section 36.[87] Accordingly, freedom of expression is limited by common-law rules such as the law of defamation to the extent that these are consistent with the Constitution's Bill of Rights, and, like other freedoms and rights, by general restriction grounds such as national security, public order, the constitutional order, the pursuit of national unity and reconciliation, public safety, public health, public morals, and democratic values. Freedom of expression is also limited by the rights of others, and conflicting rights often have to be balanced. Freedom of expression in South African law does not automatically trump the right to human dignity or the right to equality.

These competing considerations collide in South Africa's 2003 Promotion of Equality and Prevention of Unfair Discrimination Act (PEPUDA). Section 10 of that legislation contains a rather sweeping hate speech provision[88] that seems to extend far beyond the scope of section 16(2)(c).

[87] Section 36 permits limitations effected by a law of general application, which are "reasonable and justifiable" in a "democratic society based on human dignity, equality and freedom," taking into account a number of enumerated factors. *See generally* Van Wyk, *supra* note 84.

[88] The Act provides:
Prohibition on hate speech

(1) Subject to the proviso in section 12, no person may punish, propagate, advocate or communicate words based on one or more of the prohibited grounds, against any person, that could reasonably be construed to demonstrate a clear intention to –
(a) be hurtful
(b) be harmful or to incite harm;
(c) promote or propagate hatred;
(2) Without prejudice to any remedies of a civil nature under this Act, the court may, in accordance with section 21(2) and where appropriate, refer any case dealing with the publication, advocacy, propagation or communication of hate speech as contemplated in subsection (1), to the Director of Public Prosecutions having jurisdiction for the institution of criminal proceedings in terms of the common law or relevant legislation.

The proviso referred to in section 10(1) states:
Prohibition of dissemination and publication of information that unfairly discriminates

12. No person may –
(a) disseminate or broadcast any information;
(b) publish or display any advertisement or notice,

that could reasonably be construed or reasonably be understood to demonstrate a clear intention to unfairly discriminate against any person: Provided that bona fide engagement in artistic creativity, academic and scientific inquiry, fair and accurate reporting in the public interest or publication of

Whereas South Africa's constitution includes an express hate speech provision, Ethiopia and other countries[89] have incorporated general limitation clauses in their Bill of Rights while hate speech provisions are enacted in various criminal and civil statutes. Robust protection of speech requires a wider margin of error for media and individual defendants in defamation and hate speech cases.

## IV. CONCLUSION

There is immense difficulty in regulating hate speech on the ground of ethnicity when ethnicity is a prime vehicle for political organization and mobilization. On the one hand, substantive (real) equality demands that certain marginalized ethnic groups be shielded from hate speech in order to have any chance of successfully renegotiating and reclaiming the places they have lost in the society. On the other hand, hate speech regulation should not be used as a pretext for perpetuation of ethnic hierarchies and criminalization of dissent. If the solution is not clear, the Ethiopian example at least casts light on the curious tension between the two sides of the equality paradox.

---

any information, advertisement or notice in accordance with section 16 of the Constitution, is not precluded by this section.

[89] *See, e.g.*, Canadian Charter of Rights & Freedoms, § 1 (providing that rights and freedoms are "subject only to such reasonable limits prescribed by law as can be demonstrably justified in a free and democratic society").

## 20

# Interview with Nadine Strossen

**Peter Molnar:** One of the most common justifications for regulating "hate speech" is to prevent grave harms to marginalized groups. According to this argument such speech stigmatizes and demoralizes members of such groups and prevents them from achieving full equality in society.[1] Do you agree?

**Nadine Strossen:** I totally disagree with the factual premise. And even if I agreed with the premise, I still think that suppressing hate speech would not be an effective solution to the alleged problem.

So, first, I completely dismiss the claim that some people making nasty racist, sexist, or other discriminatory comments necessarily has a severe adverse impact on the individuals who are described. All of us have the ability to reject ideas that are conveyed by various expressions. I speak from experience. I have been the subject of anti-Semitic comments, antifemale comments, anti–civil libertarian comments, personally defamatory comments, and defamatory comments about an organization near and dear to me – and none of it affects my view of myself. It affects my view of the speakers, and of the speakers' ideas. Quite frankly, to suggest that there is inevitably a direct negative impact on the person who is insulted, I think, is insulting. It suggests that that person doesn't have enough self-confidence, doesn't have enough critical capacity. We are not somehow automatically diminished just because some bigot says something negative about us.

With regard to the fear that hate speech will encourage hatred and discrimination in society as a whole, we are *constantly* hearing problematic ideas, and, even if some groups accept them, most people reject them. And we don't have to use flagrant hate speech as a hypothetical, for in a somewhat camouflaged fashion you get hate

---

[1] *See, e.g.*, the contributions to the present volume by Bhikhu Parekh and Jeremy Waldron, Chapters 2 and 16, respectively.

This interview was conducted in New York City on November 4, 2009. Professor Strossen subsequently revised and expanded her remarks. Eds.

speech coming from certain media pundits and certain very respected politicians all the time. Sometimes it's cloaked in different terminology. When Ronald Reagan was running for president, he talked about "welfare queens"; that was a code word for a poor African-American woman who was taking advantage of the system.[2] Did that gain great traction in society? Yes, with some people; no, with a lot of other people. So it is kind of insulting to suggest that we lack critical capacity to evaluate and reject ideas and it is particularly paternalistic to suggest that members of minority groups need some special protection against speech that is critical or insulting toward them. The rest of us are supposed to just have a stiff upper lip and respond with more speech, to respond by turning away – but for some reason these individuals are not capable of doing that.

**PM:** The counterargument is that different groups might have different capacity to respond, and often the groups who are the targets of racist or other "hate" speech, precisely because of the systemic racism or another sort of prejudice that oft-times underlies such speech, will be in less of a position to respond effectively. Someone might put this counterargument especially provocatively by saying that not everyone has the education and, as a result, the critical capacity of, say, a white lawyer.

**NS:** That's such an elitist statement. Unbelievable! That position suggests that only a white, liberal lawyer has the capacity (a) to reject a biased idea and (b) to respond to it. I think that's one of the most insulting ideas that I've heard. Of course, though, I defend anyone's right to make that point! As a civil libertarian, I treat people as individuals. And I would never generalize that because someone is a member of a certain demographic group that person is less capable of responding. Henry Louis Gates is African American; he is one of the most eloquent, articulate people I know. Of course, we can all name countless members of racial minority groups who are brilliant and articulate, starting with the President of the United States. I mention Skip Gates in particular because he has powerfully written and spoken out against hate speech codes, starting early on when many liberals (especially white liberals) were a bit afraid of doing that, for fear of being accused of being soft on racism.[3]

Now, if the point is that it takes a certain amount of education to be able to respond effectively to hate speech with counterspeech, that would suggest a different understanding of which targets of hate speech must be protected, one that I would totally reject as well. It would say that we should protect only people who lack a certain intelligence, a certain language facility, a certain verbal ability, a certain self-confidence. If these are going to be the criteria, which I don't think they should

---

[2] *See generally* Wahneema Lubiano, "Black Ladies, Welfare Queens, and State Minstrels: Ideological War by Narrative Means," in *Race-ing Justice, En-gendering Power: Essays on Anita Hill, Clarence Thomas, and the Construction of Social Reality* 323, 330–40 (Toni Morrison ed., Pantheon 1992) (discussing the "welfare queen" and black women as welfare icons).

[3] *See* Henry Louis Gates, Jr., "Let Them Talk: Why Civil Liberties Pose No Threat to Civil Rights," *The New Republic*, Sep. 20, 1993, at 37.

be, this approach will not dovetail nicely with traditionally discriminated-against minority groups because, believe me, I know a lot of white liberal lawyers who get tongue-tied and don't speak well in pressured situations.

Finally, let's assume for the sake of argument that a disproportionately high number of individuals at whom hate speech is aimed are unable to respond effectively for various reasons. *They have other advocates.* They have human rights groups – domestically and internationally – who are responding to the hate speech. They have the media. They have political leaders, cultural and educational leaders. It's not as if the only person who can respond is the direct target of the hatred. I have seen many situations in which the person who is attacked initially cannot respond (and, by the way, that applies to liberal, well-educated lawyers – if you are personally insulted, it's a shocking experience and you may find yourself not able to respond for a while), but somebody else jumps into the fray and speaks out, and that empowers and encourages the targeted individual victim. So I do think that it is *very* important, especially for people who are in positions of leadership, to respond to hate speech immediately and strongly, to denounce it, and to say that it does not reflect the views of our society and our institutions. Whether it be a nation's political leaders, or the president of a university, or religious leaders, or whoever, I think it is very, very important to use speech to marginalize the ideas of the hate speakers.

**PM:** Let me give an example from Central Europe, though we could bring in similar American examples as well. Consider the situation of the Roma. The argument is not that there are *no* people in the Roma population who have critical capacity; the argument is that large parts of such groups, groups that have been discriminated against and disadvantaged in multiple ways by disproportionately high unemployment, discrimination in. . . .

**NS:** But *that's* the problem. You've got to address *the discrimination*.

That brings me to my second point regarding your initial question. Even assuming for the sake of argument that there's some special harm from hate speech (which I reject, and I'll come back to that in a moment), suppressing hate speech is not an effective way to deal with the problem. In fact, it's a distraction. Faced with a social problem, policy makers repeatedly scapegoat expression as the subject of regulation, but expression is always only a manifestation of a deeper problem. Attacking expression does not deal with the root causes of the problem and does not deal with its concrete manifestations in terms of conduct. If there is unemployment, let's address that. If there is discrimination, let's rectify that. If there is violence, let's prevent and remedy it; let's punish the perpetrators. Let's bring everybody to a position where everyone has security – in terms of basic safety, in terms of basic economic needs, in terms of educational opportunity, and in terms of job opportunity. Then everyone will be in a position to respond. I am not aware of any actual research on this, but I would be surprised if the targets victims of hate speech care as much about insulting words as they do about their actual status and opportunities in society.

The point is not merely that regulating speech focuses on the less important problem. It is also at best a distraction from, and sometimes an obstacle to, efforts to grapple with the real, concrete problems. We saw this, for example, in the development and then the reaction to campus speech codes. Minority student groups, who had initially sought such codes, later turned against them, objecting that they were symbolic only.[4] A university would enact a hate speech code and then they'd say "we've done it," and they'd abandon affirmative action programs; they'd abandon special scholarship programs for minority students; they'd abandon multicultural studies programs. So it became symbolism, or tokenism, rather than something real to promote actual equality in terms of treatment within society.

And it's so easy for politicians to regulate expression, because it doesn't cost anything. They don't have to raise taxes to censor speech. I'll only use the United States as an example, although I'm sure that the same temptations and incentives and disincentives exist for politicians in other countries as well. In response to unacceptable levels of violence in society, what is targeted in this country? Violence in the media. We have too few serious efforts to regulate handguns, but when we have an episode of a school shooting, members of Congress immediately rush to introduce bills to prohibit violent imagery in mass media. Look at all the legislation that is aimed at protecting children from the harm allegedly caused by certain kinds of media expression, sexually oriented and violent expression in particular. But when it comes to actually devoting resources to improving education and helping poor children, nobody wants to raise taxes to do it. Just as voting for the Child On-Line Protection Act[5] comes to count as "doing something for children," so voting to regulate hate speech could be counted as "doing something for racial equality." In both cases, however, this "something" is largely, if not completely, symbolic and fails to address the actual problem.

**PM:** But is there not reason to be concerned about the silencing effect of "hate speech"? Even if we don't assume that many members of discriminated-against minorities are less able to respond to such speech, members of these groups may feel some uncertainty, reinforced also by ongoing discrimination, as to whether they are equal members of the society. . . .

**NS:** They *are not* equal members of the society. But not because people are saying insulting things about them. Because they lack equal opportunity for education, equal opportunity for employment, and so on.

---

4  Azhar Majeed, "Defying the Constitution: The Rise, Persistence, and Prevalence of Campus Speech Codes," 7 *Geo. J. L. Pub. Pol'y* 481, 487 nn. 27–29 (2009).

5  Pub. L. No. 105–277, 112 Stat. 2681 (Oct. 21, 1998), codified at 47 U.S.C. § 231 (making it a crime to post on the internet "for commercial purpose" material that is "harmful to minors"). Enforcement of the Act was enjoined on First Amendment grounds in Ashcroft v. ACLU, 542 U.S. 656 (2004).

Now if you receive a disproportionately high number of insults because a disproportionately high number of people dislike you because of your race, does that
marginally add to the burdens that you suffer from entrenched discrimination in
terms of access to opportunities? Perhaps. But I think the real problem is the underlying discrimination. The government should not only eliminate discrimination,
but, I very strongly believe, require carefully designed affirmative action programs
to redress ongoing discrimination or ongoing effects of past discrimination. Here
I part company with many people on the right in the United States who oppose
hate speech codes, but that's it; they don't support a positive agenda for rectifying
the ongoing problems of racial discrimination or discrimination against members
of other relatively disempowered groups. I think there is a special responsibility for
those of us who reject hate speech regulation as merely symbolic to advocate some
*real* measures to counteract discrimination, and that would include appropriately
tailored affirmative action to specifically single out those groups.

People have negative attitudes and stereotypes; discrimination exists in both the
public and private sectors. Given all of those problems, is there some benefit to
prohibiting expression of negative attitudes through *words*, as opposed to expressing
them through *actions*? I want to emphasize that those of us who oppose censoring
hate speech don't have a "do-nothing" attitude. I think that the attitudes that are
expressed through hate speech are very problematic, and the government policies
and private-sector policies that reflect or are influenced by those attitudes are very
problematic. I don't think that those problems are addressed in *any* way by stopping
the people who have the bias and the hatred from expressing it verbally.

Finally, there are important practical considerations. On the one hand, suppressing expression is going to do more harm than good. The prejudiced attitudes and
hate speech just go underground; the ideas fester.

**PM:** Though some, such as Bhikhu Parekh, argue that if banning "hate speech"
drive racists and others with similar prejudices underground, so much the better;
that is the place they belong.[6]

**NS:** It makes them into free-speech martyrs, and everybody comes to their defense
in terms of free-speech principles, as opposed to emphasizing to them: Your message
is wrong, you have a right to think and say these things, but we're going to explain
to you why you shouldn't.

Perhaps most important, if speech is suppressed, there is no opportunity for a
public response. We have seen that an episode of hate speech on a campus, especially
on a campus that prides itself on being liberal and open-minded and tolerant, is a very
traumatic but ultimately cathartic and empowering experience. In particular, the
responsive outpourings – which, to the best of my knowledge, *always* occur – both

---

[6] Bhikhu Parekh, "Is There a Case for Banning Hate Speech?," Chapter 2 herein.

from the grassroots up and from the top down, galvanize people, who otherwise would never have addressed these issues, to speak out against racism, against homophobia. I've seen all kinds of creative, constructive responses on college campuses. For example, there was an incident at Swarthmore involving some homophobic chalking on a sidewalk (this being a favorite way for college students to communicate). In response to the initial message, other students organized to cover every single square inch of campus with rainbows and messages of equality. They would never have done this had the initial homophobic chalking not occurred; the episode galvanized them to work for equality in education and employment, and equality in marriage, understanding that there's a real problem here.

And on the other hand, even assuming that it was desirable to suppress expressions of hatred, you can't do it. Even the most ardent proponent of anti–hate speech laws would not say that you could outlaw the subtlety, the nuance, the innuendo. I don't know anybody that would go that far. That's why I use the example of Ronald Reagan and welfare queens. Would any advocates of suppressing hate speech go so far as to punish that kind of expression? As Henry Louis Gates memorably put it, it is a mistake "to spend more time worrying about speech codes than coded speech."[7] The more subtle, veiled, and nuanced the expression is, the more powerful it's going to be. Blatant expressions of racism, or anti-Roma prejudice, or homophobia, you name it, tend to be rejected in our societies. Such sentiments don't carry much credence with most people. Rather, the most effective expression in persuading people is the more subtle and more nuanced. So if you're going to control the expression that does the most harm – whether in its impact on people's attitudes toward minority groups or, perhaps, minority groups' attitudes toward themselves – it will not be the crude blatant expressions. What you need to worry about are these more veiled innuendoes. Thus, the government would have to probe beneath the surface, regulating a discriminatory or hateful subtext. But if we accept a code broad enough to reach that kind of expression, then we really are giving the government an enormous amount of power to suppress legitimate political discourse.

**PM:** Even a very broad regulation will probably not reach lots of coded speech.

**NS:** That's right. People who have those attitudes are going to express them, whether directly or subtly. Moreover, they will express those attitudes in words and deeds – and I'm *much* more concerned about the deeds.

The standard argument in favor of censoring hate speech is appealingly simple: These are bad ideas and we don't want the ideas to be implemented – with which I

---

7   Henry Louis Gates, Jr., "War of Words: Critical Race Theory and the First Amendment," in *Speaking of Race, Speaking of Sex: Hate Speech, Civil Rights, and Civil Liberties* 17, 47 (NYU Press 1994). Gates also offers the following "rule of thumb": "in American society today, the real power commanded by the racist is likely to vary inversely with the vulgarity with which it is expressed. . . . The circles of power have long since switched to a vocabulary of indirection." *Id.*

totally agree – *therefore* we should suppress the expression – and that's where I part company. I don't think "therefore" follows at all; as always, you have to balance the potential benefits against the potential harms. Here the potential benefits of reducing a narrow slice of racist or hateful expressions are ever so slight. Even assuming that suppressing the ideas would do any good, you're only touching the tip of the iceberg, by definition. Against which must be balanced enormous harms.

**PM:** Is your position that although allowing "hate speech" to be freely expressed does significant harm, we should bear that cost for the sake of having the advantages of free discussion? Or do you think that banning "hate speech" serves no purpose, and may even be counterproductive because such speech can alert the community to the existence of underlying prejudice and prompt a response?

**NS:** There definitely is a cost to allowing hate speech. Particularly if the expression is directly targeted at an individual, it causes hurt feelings and psychological and emotional harm. That is true of so much expression that we protect. We protect defamation; we protect insults; we protect offensive speech. I don't at all mean to minimize hurt feelings. Indeed, by virtue of public leadership positions I have held, and my advocacy on behalf of controversial causes, I have endured more than the average number of negative expressions, including threats, that are intended to instill fear and chill my expressions and actions. But there is a balancing test. Even from the point of view of the targeted individual – again you're going to say I'm a white liberal lawyer, but there are people in other demographic groups who would agree – if the speaker has that attitude, I would rather know about it than not know about it. So, yes, there's a harm in learning, even in being shocked, that this person has that idea about me, but (1) it's valuable information to me, (2) it gives me and others an opportunity to respond, and (3) it highlights some attitudinal issues that can be addressed in other ways, for example, through education. (I hasten to say that those three points do not exhaust the reasons not to suppress the speech; I mention them only to identify some actual benefits from the speech.)

**PM:** Let me put the counterargument in a different way. Both of us are in a position where we can speak; we can answer. Whether to respond is up to us; when and whether to write an article, when and whether to spend the time to formulate a response is all up to us. But let's imagine for the sake of thinking through this problem, that we are....

**NS:** But be very concrete. Who is saying what to whom?

**PM:** Let's imagine that we are members of a disadvantaged minority that has been discriminated against over a longer period.

**NS:** And what is the hate speech? Are you talking about Rush Limbaugh or Lou Dobbs on TV saying "All these people should..."?

**PM:** Let's imagine we are Roma people. We grew up studying in segregated schools – and let's add that human rights NGOs were encouraging parents in our community to challenge this arrangement in the courts, but the parents, including our parents, feared the consequences and didn't want to get in trouble, so they did not accept that offered help. If we are men, we have a higher chance of going to prison, and we are discriminated against in the workplace. Then let's say our country does not ban publication of racist newspaper articles and other public speech arguing that Roma are criminals, are a huge problem for the society, and so on and so forth. And, of course, the objection to not banning such speech is that it pushes us even further down, communicating and confirming the message of Roma inferiority and inequality. And here I am troubled. You know that I am a free-speech advocate and I have always supported the courts in Hungary as they have followed the American First Amendment approach on this issue.[8] But I am troubled that in a situation like this, speech that vilely attacks a discriminated-against group will worsen an already bad status.

**NS:** It might. A lot of wrong ideas have bad effects. Politicians lie. People in the media lie. Members of the public are constantly being fed wrongheaded opinions and inaccurate "facts." You have to depend on and nurture a critical analytical facility on the part of people who are media consumers.

Let's distinguish two separate harms. One is the direct harmful impact on the group that is targeted by the speech, in terms of their own self-esteem. The other is the indirect negative impact that results from speech that fuels, fosters, and reinforces negative stereotypes believed by other people in society. And I just don't think that in either case you can say that people are like sponges, that they just uncritically absorb and accept whatever they are told. It is incredibly important that those of us who are repelled by those ideas exercise counterspeech very vigorously. I want to emphasize again that my position is not passive; it is not "do nothing." Everyone has a *responsibility* to respond, to disagree, to denounce, to castigate, to marginalize the people who are spouting that kind of discriminatory idea. That is the effective response; I don't think it does any real good just to say "OK, we know that these influential media folks have these ideas and we are just not going to let them express them in certain words." (And again I have to emphasize the "in certain words," because we're never going to be able to stop them from expressing the same idea in *other* words.)

In addition, it is important in terms of public policy to be able to discuss troubling issues frankly and openly. What explains racial disparities in certain settings, such

---

[8] *See generally* Peter Molnar, "Responding to 'Hate Speech' with Art, Education, and the Imminent Danger Test," Chapter 10 herein.

as incarceration rates? Some will say, "It's because blacks are more criminal." But that statement gives the opportunity to the ACLU and others to do the relevant statistical analysis and demonstrate that in fact it has to do with discrimination in law enforcement. And so the hostile speech becomes an occasion for smoking out and, in many cases, changing attitudes. If there's no such discussion, if people are too polite, or too cowed, to articulate the stereotypes they hold, those stereotypes are never questioned or challenged.

**PM:** So you are saying that, instead of trying to manufacture a so-called decent social environment in which denigrating "hate speech" is suppressed, the society as a whole – including through a collaboration of sorts between disadvantaged groups, their organizations, and other human rights groups – must deal with the "hate speech" publicly, and by doing so can better address the deeper structural problems.

**NS:** And society can and must deal with the problem of *hate*. To me, hate speech is not an independent problem. To the contrary, it's potentially a tool for addressing the underlying problem, which is the hatred and the hateful conduct. It's like the question whether it should be a crime to advertise, promote, or engage in other expression about illegal services and products. The expression actually helps law enforcement officials uncover and track the illegal activity.[9] And, to me, it's an exact analogy. It is morally wrong, and in most cases it is legally wrong, or should be, to engage in discrimination; and hate speech flags where that discriminatory conduct is occurring or where it's being fueled. It helps diagnose the problem, which is an essential prerequisite for meaningfully addressing it.

**PM:** So allowing "hate speech" has several significant advantages, which makes it worth paying the price of the harm it causes, even if that harm includes some sort of silencing effect on those who have suffered segregation and other discrimination, into whose shoes I was trying to put us. Even if some targets of "hate speech" might have been silenced, allowing such speech might still be beneficial.

---

[9]  For example, this was one argument raised against a federal law that criminalized certain depictions of illegal treatment of animals, including dogfighting videos, which the Supreme Court struck down in *United States v. Stevens*, 130 S. Ct. 1577 (2010). Because such videos provide identifying information about the depicted animal abuse, they can be valuable aids for law enforcement officials in prosecuting and deterring such abuse. *See* Adam Ezra Schulman, "Animal-cruelty videos & free speech: some observations from data," *available at* http://archive.firstamendmentcenter.org/analysis.aspx?id=21814 (July 7, 2009) ("Prosecutors seem more willing to go forward when there is videotape evidence, and juries seem more willing to convict in such cases."). *See also* Bruce Lambert, "As Prostitutes Turn to Craigslist, Law Enforcement Takes Notice," *N.Y. Times*, Sep. 5, 2007, at A1 (describing how police around the United States are using online ads, on popular Web site Craigslist, to target and arrest prostitutes and their clients; also noting that the police have "turned to Craigslist to trace stolen goods offered for sale or make drug arrests").

**NS:** My view is that allowing such speech will have a net "amplifying" effect because it will trigger responses from community members who might not have felt angered or impassioned until they heard the speech – indeed, who might not have realized there was a problem until they heard it – and then a ripple effect follows. Some community leaders speak out first, then others do, and hopefully that emboldens the person who felt too chilled to speak out in the first place. But if no one hears the discriminatory expression, there's *no* opportunity to respond. By definition, there will be no response if there is nothing to respond to. So you have more opportunity to respond if you don't suppress the hate speech.

I don't think any silencing that hate speech might cause is nearly as powerful as the statements we have heard, for example, from university presidents who have responded to hate speech incidents on their campuses by extolling freedom of speech and saying: "However, this idea is wrong, this idea is dangerous, this idea is counter to everything this university stands for." To me, that's much more powerful and persuasive. Acknowledging the speaker's undeniable right to say what he or she wishes takes an argument away from the other side.

**PM:** But one more counterargument. If the government does not regulate the sort of speech we are talking about (setting aside the huge definitional problem), that can give the impression to both the targeted minority and all others that such speech and the ideas behind it are all fine; it could be understood as an implicit endorsement.

**NS:** That's why I said that it is very important for the government to respond with counterspeech. I would argue that the government certainly has a moral obligation to do so – I wouldn't go so far as to say it has a legal obligation. We have many examples where that has occurred. During the Clinton administration, there were some really bad examples of very strong antigovernment, anti-Clinton speech heard on right-wing talk radio; it was like hatred for the whole system. The Clintons were the immediate target, but they were being attacked, in significant part, because of their support for racial minorities. And the critics' attacks supported and mobilized the right-wing militia groups that were then gaining traction in parts of this country. Therefore, of course, there were some calls for censoring or punishing this speech out of concern that it might lead to violence, including against racial minorities, but also against the government, which was seen as being supportive of racial minorities. (By the way, no hate speech code that I've seen proposed would have encompassed that expression, and I doubt that even the most ardent proponents of such codes would extend them this far, to criticism of government officials and policies, which is the lifeblood of a democracy.) In the wake of the Oklahoma City bombing, Bill Clinton gave a *very* powerful speech, stating that these critics have a First Amendment right to express these ideas, but all of us, from the President of the United States on down, have a really important responsibility to respond to counteract those ideas.[10]

There have been a couple of very good examples on college campuses where the presidents have issued statements following episodes of anti–racial minority or sexist expression, statements that clearly defend the speakers' right to say what they did while absolutely rejecting and repudiating the ideas put forth and reaffirming prohibitions on conduct consistent with those ideas.[11] So I don't think government should be passive. It must adopt antidiscrimination and appropriately tailored

---

[10]  William Clinton, "Address to the American Association of Community Colleges" (Minneapolis, MN, April 24, 1995). An excerpt follows:

> In this country we cherish and guard the right of free speech. We know we love it when we put up with people saying things we absolutely deplore. And we must always be willing to defend their right to say things we deplore to the nth degree. . . .
>
> Well, people like that who want to share our freedoms must know that their bitter words can have consequences, and that freedom has endured in this country for more than two centuries because it was coupled with an enormous sense of responsibility on the part of the American people.
>
> If we are to have freedom to speak, freedom to assemble, and yes, the freedom to bear arms, we must have responsibility as well. And to those of us who do not agree with the purveyors of hatred and division, with the promoters of paranoia, I remind you that we have freedom of speech, too. And we have responsibilities, too. And some of us have not discharged our responsibilities. It is time we all stood up and spoke against that kind of reckless speech and behavior.
>
> If they insist on being irresponsible with our common liberties, then we must be all the more responsible with our liberties. When they talk of hatred, we must stand against them. When they talk of violence, we must stand against them. When they say things that are irresponsible, that may have egregious consequences, we must call them on it. The exercise of their freedom of speech makes our silence all the more unforgivable. So exercise yours, my fellow Americans.

Id., quoted in Jack B. Coffman, "Clinton Urges Outcry Against Words of Hate," *St. Paul Pioneer Press,* Apr. 25, 1995, at 1A.

[11]  One good example of this kind of statement was provided in 1985 by the then-president of Harvard University, Derek Bok, who circulated a letter to the entire Harvard community in response to a sexist flyer distributed by an undergraduate fraternity. He wrote:

> The wording of the letter was so extreme and derogatory to women that I wanted to communicate my disapproval publicly, if only to make sure that no one could gain the false impression that the Harvard administration harbored any sympathy or complacency toward the tone and substance of the letter. Such action does not infringe on free speech. Indeed, statements of disagreement are part and parcel of the open debate that freedom of speech is meant to encourage; the right to condemn a point of view is as protected as the right to express it. Of course, I recognize that even verbal disapproval by persons in positions of authority may have inhibiting effects on students. Nevertheless, this possibility is not sufficient to outweigh the need for officials to speak out on matters of significance to the community – provided, of course, that they take no action to penalize the speech of others.

Derek C. Bok, "Reflections on Free Speech: An Open Letter to the Harvard Community," *Harvard University Gazette,* Sep. 21, 1984, reprinted in *Educ. Rec.* (Winter 1985), at 4, 6. Likewise, six years later, when some Harvard students displayed Confederate flags – usually viewed as a racist symbol, particularly offensive to African Americans – and another displayed a swastika in response, President Bok responded with another thoughtful statement strongly criticizing the displays but equally strongly defending free-speech principles. He wrote, in part:

affirmative action measures, punish and protect against violence, and engage in counterspeech.

**PM:** That approach might work in the United States, or on college campuses, but what about countries with governments and public officials who are reluctant, or more than reluctant, to engage in counterspeech?

**NS:** *That* – the refusal to take a stand – is the problem. Here's an analogy. I oppose the V-chip, which will censor violent imagery on TV, because that's a job for parents. People will say to me: "But what about a family where the parents are absent?" Well, *that's* the problem. The problem is not the images the kids are seeing on TV; the problem is the absence of the parents. And if the problem is a government that is not enforcing antidiscrimination laws or affirmative action laws, that problem is not going to be redressed by the Band-Aid of prohibiting people from saying mean, nasty things. The real problem will remain unredressed. Moreover, the chances of it being redressed are reduced if those in power can hide behind the fig-leaf solution

To begin with, it is important to distinguish clearly between the appropriateness of such communications and their status under the First Amendment. The fact that speech is protected by the First Amendment does not necessarily mean that it is right, proper, or civil. In this case, I believe that the vast majority in this community believes that hanging a Confederate flag in public view – or displaying a swastika in response – is insensitive and unwise . . . because any satisfaction it gives to the students who display these symbols is far outweighed by the discomfort it causes to many others. I agree with this view and regret that the Harvard students involved saw fit to behave in this fashion . . . .

One reason why the power of censorship is so dangerous is that it is extremely difficult to decide when a particular communication is offensive enough to warrant prohibition or to weigh the degree of offensiveness against the potential value of the communication. If we begin to forbid flags, it is only a short step to prohibiting offensive speakers. Do we really want Harvard officials (or anyone else) to begin deciding whether Louis Farrakhan or Yasser Arafat or David Duke or anyone else should be allowed to speak on this campus? Those who are still unconvinced should remember the long, sorry history of preventing Dick Gregory and others from speaking at Southern universities on grounds that they might prove "disruptive" or "offensive" to the campus community, not to mention the earlier exclusion of suspected communists for fear that they would corrupt students' minds.

In addition, I suspect that no community can expect to become humane and caring by restricting what its members can say. The worst offenders will simply find other ways to irritate and insult. Those who are not malicious but merely insensitive are not likely to learn by having their flags or their posters torn down. Once we start to declare certain things "offensive," with all the excitement and attention that will follow, I fear that . . . the resulting publicity will eventually attract more attention to the offensive material than would ever have occurred otherwise . . . .

In conclusion, then, our concern for free speech may keep the University from forcibly removing the offensive flags, but it should not prevent us from urging the students involved to take more account of the feelings and sensibilities of others. Most of the time, I suspect, we will succeed in this endeavor. By so doing, I believe that we will have acted in the manner most consistent with our ideals as an educational institution and most likely to help us create a truly understanding, supportive community.

"Bok Issues Free Speech Statement," *Harvard University Gazette*, March 15, 1991, at 1, 4.

of saying, "Oh, look, we stopped people from saying nasty things, so we will continue to be passive and spineless when it comes to real reform and real protection."

**PM:** Yes, but part of the counterargument that I just brought up is that in countries where public officials are reluctant or fail to respond to racist and other "hate" speech with counterspeech, it might be harder for those officials to argue against outlawing such speech, just because that can be viewed as what most democracies do. It might be harder to block either the legislation or the application of the prohibition of "hate speech" than to ignore the need for counterspeech, and if so, it poses a tough choice for free-speech advocates in many countries where the public officials are disinclined to speak out against racist and other "hate" speech.

**NS:** I understand that. That's so ironic though. You posit a society where it is accepted that certain speech can be suppressed on the assumption that it causes so much harm; if indeed that is the assumption, doesn't that impose a greater moral obligation on the part of leaders of the society, either elected officials or other community leaders, to speak out against it and denounce it?

**PM:** It should, but unfortunately – and this is what makes it so hard – usually in such situations the majority is prejudiced; the majority is certainly prejudiced against Roma people in Hungary and other Central European and Eastern European countries. Then the challenge for human rights advocates who are advocating freedom of speech is how to foster the social norm of rejecting racism where racial prejudice is hammered into the minds of many people, where it is expressed in all sorts of ways, and the messages people hear are absorbed, perhaps without the listeners fully realizing their meaning. Wouldn't a prohibition on "hate speech" be beneficial in such a context?

**NS:** But if the government doesn't have the will to counteract those attitudes, how is the government going to have the will to pass an anti–hate speech statute or to enforce it?

To me, it's the same conundrum that I came up against with respect to antipornography laws.[12] In the hate speech context, the paradox is this: Confronted with a government and a society that is inherently racist, prejudiced, and discriminatory, we set out to cure that problem by handing over to this discriminatory, prejudiced, stereotype-reinforcing government and society and majority this enormous discretionary power to pick and choose which expression to punish. It just doesn't compute. If you don't trust the government, and you don't trust the majority, on these issues, why are you handing them an open-ended discretionary power they can use *at best* not in a helpful way and *at worst* in a terrible way. And you look at how hate speech laws have actually been enforced and it is always disproportionately to the direct

---

[12] *See generally* Nadine Strossen, *Defending Pornography: Free Speech, Sex, and the Fight for Women's Rights* (NYU Press 2000).

disadvantage of those very groups that are supposed to be protected and benefited by the laws.[13]

**PM:** I certainly share that concern, which is a huge one. It's a really troublesome paradox that the more prejudice exists in a society, the more that society might need well-constructed laws against speech that expresses those prejudices, but the less chance that society will have to have such laws on the books.

**NS:** Not only is there less chance to have such laws on the books; even if they are on the books, there is less chance that they will be enforced in a way that actually helps the minority groups they supposedly benefit. You've seen the historic and current examples: The British law is enforced against union activists, and the South African hate speech law during apartheid was enforced against anti-apartheid activists and communists. In the United States, the enforcement record of hate speech codes, as with everything, is disproportionately against young minority men.

It seems to me hard to believe that in a society where the opinions expressed in prohibited speech are in fact shared by a substantial portion of society, where criminal prosecutors are elected officials, where juries represent cross-sections of the community, and where judges are either elected directly or appointed by elected officials, that these laws will be enforced in ways that are protective of despised minorities.

**PM:** I fully agree that the paradoxical connection between the level of prejudice in society and the chances of its having well-constructed "hate speech" laws also applies to the enforcement of such regulations. But Julie Suk argues that in France after the war, restoring the antiracist regulation that had existed prior to the Vichy regime was essential to the legitimacy of the newly established republic, which had to demonstrate a clear break with the regime that collaborated with Nazi Germany.[14] She emphasizes the *expressive*, or communicative, function of such laws.

**NS:** I think a far more powerful and effective message is expressed through antidiscrimination laws, through civil rights laws, and through affirmative action programs. Those are not symbolic; they are substantive and meaningful.

If lawmakers want to make a symbolic statement that other people should not engage in racist speech, let them pass a resolution saying: "We believe that people should not engage in racist speech and we denounce the ideas expressed by such speech." If you're saying that they don't feel emboldened to do that individually, they need to do it through some collective action; of course they can act collectively

---

[13] *See* Martha Minow, "Regulating Hatred: Whose Speech, Whose Crimes, Whose Power?," in *Breaking the Cycles of Hatred: Memory, Law, and Repair* 31, 41 (Nancy L. Rosenblum ed., Princeton University Press 2002); Nadine Strossen, "Incitement to Hatred: Should There Be a Limit?," 25 *S. Ill. U.L.J.* 243, 266 (2001).

[14] Julie C. Suk, "Denying Experience: Holocaust Denial and the Free-Speech Theory of the State," Chapter 8 herein.

by resolution. But it should not have the force of law behind it, making it a crime for an individual to express a different opinion.

If what you're engaging in is symbolism, let's keep it at the symbolic level.

**PM:** But a resolution carries less weight.

**NS:** And I think that suppressing hate speech also carries less weight. To me, it's another form of tokenism that is ineffective at best, and I continue to believe is really counterproductive because, as I've said, it lets the legislature off the hook.

**PM:** I asked a Romanian scholar whether his country's "hate speech" law was working, and he said "No." But when I asked him whether it was still worth having on the books, he answered, "Yes, because of the message of the law."

**NS:** But if all you're talking about is the *message* of the law, you can accomplish that without the pretext of criminal punishment. To go back to one of the points that you threw at me earlier: Isn't it conveying a negative message to these discriminated-against minorities for society to pass a law and then, hypocritically, not enforce it? Isn't that saying: "We don't really take this problem seriously. We pay lip service to the problem through passing this law, but then we don't enforce it."

**PM:** Is it not possible that a person or a family with traditional prejudices against certain minorities and with some sort of authoritarian mindset in the sense of high respect for state authority might be unmoved by a resolution, but influenced or convinced that racism and other similar prejudices are wrong because the state says so if that judgment was actually embedded in the substantive criminal law?

**NS:** I doubt it. Looking at the United States, there are so many things that are in the criminal code but are not enforced, and people would never see those things as socially stigmatized. Sexual practices are the most obvious example. Many state criminal codes outlaw adultery, premarital sex, sex outside of marriage, kissing in public, masturbation, and the use of vibrators, and people just scoff at them. They are not enforced. Legislators are embarrassed to vote them off the books, but prosecutors are embarrassed to enforce them. That undermines the rule of law and, in the case of a merely symbolic law that purports to punish speech expressing discriminatory attitudes, having it on the books but not enforcing it undermines the seriousness of the problem of discrimination.

**PM:** Do you think the state has a role to play in empowering targets of "hate speech" to answer effectively?[15]

---

[15] Katharine Gelber argues in her contribution to the present volume that the state has such a role. *See* Katharine Gelber, "Reconceptualizing Counterspeech in Hate-Speech Policy (with a Focus on Australia)," Chapter 11 herein.

**NS:** Indirectly, for sure; that is, there should be appropriately designed affirmative action measures, education, job opportunities – absolutely. Additionally, the government itself should speak out, which is empowering and encouraging, and the government should encourage other people to speak out. This is not a burden that should fall just on the targeted minority groups themselves, but also on society as a whole.

**PM:** It seems that, despite the standard narrative of strong First Amendment protection for "hate speech," in reality, significant restrictions on such speech do exist in the United States. Arthur Jacobson and Bernhard Schlink point to limits on harassment in the workplace under Title VII, campus speech codes, and self-imposed codes governing broadcast and cable television stations.[16] So, in fact, there is a lot of regulation of "hate speech" in the United States as well.

**NS:** There certainly is, and I would not support it in any context, although I would support creating a culture where it becomes taboo to say certain things. I completely oppose broad-gauged workplace, campus, or other regulation. I qualify with the word "broad-gauged" because there is one distinction that we haven't talked about explicitly. If the speech is targeted at an individual or a small group of individuals, especially if there is an unbalanced power relationship (as, for example, between a professor and a student or between an employer and an employee), then certain speech – including, but not limited to, racist, homophobic, and misogynist speech – is harassment and it is unprotected. But for all the reasons I have already discussed, I oppose general restrictions on racist comments in the workplace, or on campus, and other places. However, I *do* think those are incredibly important venues to serve the educative, counterspeech, countereducational, antidiscriminatory, pro–affirmative action functions that I've been talking about. These are settings where the tone is set through rules of *conduct*, through leadership, and through the formation of a local culture in which discriminatory attitudes are strongly frowned upon, so you are embarrassed to say those things. I reject legal restrictions, but I welcome taboos against making such statements – I welcome the creation of social and cultural pressure against discriminatory ideas and against the expression of discriminatory ideas. It should be seen as impolite. But such a culture should not be enforced through law; it should be enforced through social sanctions.

Here is where I part company with many in the United States on the right who argue that this is a climate of what they denigrate as "political correctness." They claim that it's awful if you can't say certain things because they are "politically incorrect." I see no tension in there being some things that you have a complete legal right to say, but the articulation of which will have social consequences. There's absolutely nothing wrong with us using *our* free-speech rights to create a climate in

---

[16] *See* Arthur Jacobson and Bernhard Schlink, "Hate Speech and Self-Restraint," Chapter 12 herein.

which there are some propositions that, while anyone has the right to express them, we think are wrong; we think are evil; we think are dangerous; we think anyone should be ashamed to hold and embarrassed to express – in short, ideas that we think no one *should* express. But we should not penalize such expression through law. To make it a crime or subject it to any kind of university or employment discipline has many negative consequences, one of which is to create a free-speech martyr. "Oh, look at me! Come to my defense!" And then the speaker will indeed garner defense for the abstract right to say those things.

**PM:** There's a strong argument that in a free debate – even if we are skeptical about the outcome depending on the context – in a Millian way, "hate speech" challenges those who reject it, compelling them to be defiant against it, and that without such engagement the rejection of hatred would become inert dogma.

**NS:** One of the many negative outcomes of suppressing the expression of hate speech is that people become afraid to discuss the related issues at all. Even well-intentioned people become afraid of saying something that might unwittingly offend a member of a minority group, that might unwittingly be seen as conveying a racist idea when that's not what they intended. So then we engage in this huge self-censorship. It's like the saying about the elephant in the room. It's such an important subject in this society and, I'm sure, in every society, and yet we don't talk about it enough. It is so valuable to confront what the stereotypes are, to confront the facts, to confront the disparities, to confront different theories about what the explanations are.

To use another example: I thought the attack on Larry Summers, leading to his resignation as president of Harvard University, was really unfortunate. Speaking to a group of scientists in January 2005, he said that we have to figure out why women are so underrepresented in the sciences and threw out several hypotheses, and they were only hypotheses, including the possibility that innate differences between men and women were involved. That was an appropriate and important discussion to have. Yet people jumped on him as if it were sexist to even raise these issues.[17] That's really sad. It seems to me, if we are to really overcome racism and sexism, we have to feel free to engage in honest, frank, candid discussion that acknowledges racial and gender disparities and then try to figure out what accounts for them.

**PM:** Alon Harel suggests that "hate speech" that is "deeply rooted" in "comprehensive forms of life" (and the examples he gives involve religious groups), should be less restricted than other "hate speech". He argues that if "hate speech" reflects deeply

---

[17] *See, e.g.*, Sam Dillon and Sara Rimer, "No Break in the Storm Over Harvard President's Words," *N.Y. Times*, Jan. 19, 2005, at A14. The Summers affair has been widely covered and discussed. For one useful collection of articles addressing both the controversy over his remarks and the underlying question of underrepresentation, see "Symposium: Innate Differences: Responses to the Remarks by Lawrence H. Summers," 11 *Cardozo Women's L.J.* 497–598 (2005).

held beliefs that constitute a comprehensive way of life, the prohibition of such speech is problematic in a special way because it would amount to a condemnation not only of the respective speech but of the whole way of life of the group in which the "hate speech" has been embedded.[18]

**NS:** That's so interesting. I understand why, coming from Israel, he is making that argument. It points to a more general problem. One person's hate speech is another person's deeply held religious belief. It could also be someone's deeply held political belief, but religious beliefs are the most interesting example because they are as central to some people's sense of identity as ethnicity, gender, and sexual orientation are to other people's sense of identity. Some people's deeply held religious beliefs, which define who they are and dictate how they have to live their lives, condemn homosexuality as evil, as a sin, and impose a responsibility on believers to try to save others from eternal damnation by letting them know that it's a sin. When they do so, straightforwardly and forcefully in what they believe to be a positive spirit, they are accused of hate speech.

I so strongly disagree with members of the Christian right on so many civil liberties issues, but I also believe there is an enormous amount of ignorant, negative, discriminatory prejudice against and stereotypes about members of the Christian right, fundamentalist Christians, who are, after all, a minority in the United States as a whole. So under standard understandings of which groups should be considered vulnerable minorities meriting protection against hate speech, they are a classic example. There have been cases arising in high schools with hate speech codes in which Christian kids have been disciplined for wearing T-Shirts that quote a Bible verse that condemns homosexuality as a sin.[19] And yet it's not considered to be hate speech to denounce their deeply held religious belief in this Biblical message and, moreover, to expel them for expressing it.

**PM:** But you would not provide *more* protection for what Alon Harel conceptualizes as deeply rooted "hate speech"?

**NS:** I would not provide more. I would protect everybody. How are you going to decide whom to protect and whom not to? To me, that's a specific example of a general problem: Once you permit suppression of certain ideas because they convey prejudice against particular groups, you end up having to suppress seemingly limitless amounts of expression, because all of us are, in some way, a despised minority, whether it be political, religious, or demographic.

---

[18] *See* Alon Harel, "Hate Speech and Comprehensive Forms of Life," Chapter 15 herein.

[19] *See, e.g.,* Harper v. Poway Unified School Dist., 445 F.3d 1166 (9th Cir. 2006) (upholding disciplining of student who wore a t-shirt reading "BE ASHAMED, OUR SCHOOL EMBRACED WHAT GOD HAS CONDEMNED" on the front and "HOMOSEXUALITY IS SHAMEFUL 'Romans 1:27'" on the back).

**PM:** How do you understand the *Brandenburg*[20] test? How imminent must the danger be, and would you require intent to justify restricting speech?

**NS:** I think there has to be intent. I don't think there should be punishment for speech that negligently causes harm. I suppose that recklessness would satisfy the requirement of intent, as under N.Y. *Times v. Sullivan*.[21]

**PM:** Consider this situation. There is a gay pride parade, at which homophobes are shouting antihomosexual statements, and some are throwing rocks and acid-filled eggs at the parade participants. So some people are acting violently already, but others might be hesitant to do so. Those speakers who themselves do not act violently but engage in "hate speech" claim that they did not intend to incite or provoke violence. Is it enough that they are reckless in the sense that in that context – and contextuality is very important of course – they should have realized, they should have known, there is no way they didn't know, that they were directly and potentially decisively contributing to the imminent danger of violence.

**NS:** "Should have known" sounds like negligence; it's a lower standard. *Brandenburg* used the phrase "*directed to* inciting or producing imminent lawless action,"[22] whereas in N.Y. *Times v. Sullivan*, the standard is intentionally *or* recklessly. My mind would be open; it could descend down to recklessness. But what you described is negligence. You reasonably should have known; that's negligence, and that's not enough.

**PM:** I don't mean negligence. In a situation where someone holding an egg, or a rock, is standing next to a speaker. . . .

**NS:** I think we agree conceptually that it can be more than negligence and less than specific intent. I haven't thought about that as much as you, but my mind is certainly open to that. Imminence is necessarily defined functionally and contextually. There is a reason why *Brandenburg* referred to "imminent" lawless action without imposing a specific time limit. Similarly, the Holmes and Brandeis dissents in which the concept of imminent violence as a prerequisite for suppressing speech is born also take a very functional approach; they ask whether the harm will occur before it can be counteracted through either counterspeech or protection against the violence by law enforcement actions.[23] You have to look at any particular context. Is the

[20]  Brandenburg v. Ohio, 395 U.S. 444, 447 (1969) (holding that a state cannot "forbid or proscribe advocacy of the use of force or of law violation except where such advocacy is directed to inciting or producing imminent lawless action and is likely to incite or produce such action").

[21]  376 U.S. 254 (1964) (allowing an award of damages for libel to a public figure only if the defamatory statement was made with knowledge of its falsity or "reckless disregard" for its truth or falsity).

[22]  *Brandenburg*, 395 U.S. at 447 (emphasis added).

[23]  *See, e.g.*, Whitney v. California, 274 U.S. 357, 377 (1927) (Brandeis, J., joined by Holmes, J., concurring) ("If there be time to expose through discussion the falsehood and fallacies, to avert the evil by the

least restrictive alternative to preventing the violence shutting down the speaker? Or is there time to dissuade the audience from following the speaker? Is there time for police to arrest them before they actually engage in the violent conduct? You only suppress the speech or punish the speaker as a last resort, if that's the only way to prevent the violence. There's not so much a time limitation as there is a context-specific functional limitation. Anti-Islamic or anti-Hindu speech, or the Mohammed cartoons, in Pakistan or India could likely be very different, in terms of the likelihood of imminent violence, than the same publication in the United States or in Denmark.

**PM:** Let me give you another concrete example. Suppose during a soccer match, drunken hooligans in the stands are shouting anti-Semitic slogans and insults, such as "the train should go to Auschwitz" and similarly ugly stuff. In the stadium itself, barriers separate different groups of spectators, and there are sufficient police to prevent violence in the stadium. But right after the game, people are still drunk and the streets are crowded. At that point, there is imminent danger of violence against at least some of the people that the racists might consider to be Jewish. It's half an hour after the racist slogans were shouted, outside the stadium. The speech was inside the stadium. Would that speech meet the *Brandenburg* test?

**NS:** All I would ask is that the decision maker, whether it be a jury or a judge, applies the correct standard, and that there be evidence that that standard is satisfied in that particular situation. There was an example in the United States a while ago of a racist publication in California that specifically incited a particular individual to kill African immigrants.[24] The ACLU organizationally, and I, individually as a civil libertarian, did not take a position on the facts – that's up to the fact finder. We just insisted on the speech-protective standard: If you find that the facts satisfied the *Brandenburg* test, that there is no less restrictive alternative to suppressing the speech, that this is the only way to prevent violence in those particular circumstances, then – but only then – can you punish the speaker. Law enforcement officials have a responsibility to marshal all resources to protect against violence, and not just absent themselves and say, "Oh, we're going to punish the speaker because that's easier than protecting the speaker or others against violence." And whether the danger be in the form of inciting your followers to go out and commit mayhem or whether it be that the speaker is going to be attacked by those who disagree with the speaker, suppressing the speech should be a last resort. But if it is truly the only way to protect against imminent danger, then it has to be used.

processes of education, the remedy to be applied is more speech, not enforced silence."); Gitlow v. New York, 268 U.S. 652, 672 (1925) (Holmes, J., joined by Brandeis, J., dissenting); Abrams v. United States, 250 U.S. 616, 624 (1919) (Holmes, J., joined by Brandeis, J., dissenting).

24 *See* Berhanu v. Metzger, 850 P.2d 373, 375–6 (Or. Ct. App. 1993) (describing ACLU memorandum of law and oral argument).

**PM:** In that sense, the heart of the contextual analysis is this functional element; the length of time between the speech and the imminent danger that the speech causes or directly and decisively contributes to is relevant but is far from the only consideration. So it's not simply whether it is only five minutes or one hour or even one day.

**NS:** But one would hope that in a developed society it would functionally be a very small window of time. In fact, the U.S. Supreme Court has never found that this standard was actually satisfied, including in important cases that upheld First Amendment protection for provocative expression by political dissidents[25] and NAACP leaders.[26] These rulings illustrate one of my major reasons for protecting freedom of speech, even for speech that conveys provocative messages about race and other sensitive, controversial subjects. This robust freedom of speech is especially important for members of minority groups, an essential underpinning of their efforts to achieve equality and justice.

**PM:** Thank you so much for the interview.

**NS:** You are so welcome; thank you for your excellent questions.

---

[25]  *See* Hess v. Indiana, 414 U.S. 105 (1973) (overturning disorderly conduct conviction of leader of demonstration, who said, "We'll take the fucking street later," after the police had cleared the demonstrators from the street). The Court stressed that the *Brandenburg* test was not satisfied because there was "no evidence . . . that his words were intended to produce, and likely to produce, *imminent* disorder. . . ." *Id.* at 109 (emphasis in original).

[26]  *See* NAACP v. Claiborne Hardware Co., 458 U.S. 886 (1982) (overturning judgment against the NAACP for a boycott of white-owned businesses that it accused of racial discrimination). The Court held that the following statement by an NAACP official was protected speech, and did not satisfy *Brandenburg's* standards for unprotected incitement: "If we catch any of you going in any of them racist stores, we're gonna break your damn neck." *Id.* at 902–3. Notably, following this statement, acts of violence were committed against individuals who were not participating in the boycott. *Id.* at 904–5.

# 21

# Interview with Theodore Shaw

**Peter Molnar:** You have had extensive experience litigating civil rights cases. Let's begin with some questions about the ways, if any, in which free-speech protections that cover even "hate speech" might have affected your litigating efforts. Do you think the way "hate speech" is "free" in the United States made it harder for you to litigate discrimination and segregation in any way?

**Theodore Shaw:** In fact, nothing comes to mind. Thinking over the many school desegregation cases I've litigated, the Voting Rights litigation, a capital punishment case I did in Louisiana many years ago, the housing discrimination cases that I've done – I'd have to struggle to think of an example of how constitutionally protected hate speech really interfered with my ability to litigate cases. My answer would have to be right now, "No."

That does not mean that I have not been exposed to hate speech in my work. For example, I've done many school desegregation cases, and I took it for granted that some of the opponents to school desegregation would say hateful things. And they did. I remember being at the Justice Department early in my career, and we would have to respond to citizen mail. Some of the mail that came in criticizing the school desegregation cases we filed was very racist and hateful. But I can't say that that really got in the way of the actual litigation of the cases.

That noneffect may reflect the depth of the commitment in this country to an understanding that speech is highly protected and valued even if that speech at times is of low value or even hateful. So we're used to that; we understand that; we work in that environment.

On the other hand, I can think of an example cutting the other way. The first case I worked on after law school was a housing discrimination case. A leading elected official of Parma, Ohio said in a public meeting: "We don't want Negroes in Parma."

This interview was conducted on November 4, 2009, in New York City and subsequently revised. Eds.

That became an important piece of evidence in proving racial discriminatory intent on the part of city officials. Somebody could have said – I think they did say – that that was a statement protected by the First Amendment. Yes, it is. But that does not mean that it cannot be used to show discriminatory intent on the part of a governmental official.

**PM:** So racist speech on the part of public officials who engage in discrimination might actually help prove that they acted with discriminatory intent?

**TS:** That's right. To prevail on a claim of racial discrimination under the equal protection clause, *Washington v. Davis*[1] requires plaintiffs to prove discriminatory intent. That is very difficult to do, because most people are not as candid about their motivations if they are racist motivations. But when you get a public official making a statement that is indicative of racial discriminatory intent, that helps in terms of proving a Fourteenth Amendment claim. Most public officials are not going to be so clumsy as to do that.[2] But when they are, that's the kind of evidence you would like.

So there is an interesting dichotomy between, for example, EU systems, in which the plaintiffs in discrimination cases might not have to prove intent and hate speech is illegal, and the American system, in which plaintiffs have to prove discriminatory intent, but hate speech is not illegal. Maybe this is more than a dichotomy; maybe it's a reverse image that we see when we hold up those two systems and compare them to one another.

If we were to ban hate speech here, and people were prosecuted because of hate speech, it would probably drive even further underground the kind of speech that would be one of the strongest indicators of discriminatory intent for purposes of proving a Fourteenth Amendment violation.

**PM:** This might be an example of the advantages of the constitutional ban on content-based restriction of "hate speech"; allowing such expression makes it easier for litigants to prove discriminatory intent.

**TS:** Let me be clear. It is difficult even now to prove discriminatory intent, for the American courts are skeptical, if not hostile, when it comes to those kinds of claims. Within American law, there are a series of cases that we could point to in which the Court effectively has made policy choices. For example, do you have to prove discriminatory intent or is effect enough? *Washington v. Davis* says you have to prove intent. The Courts have said in cases like *Feeney*[3] that you have to prove that an

---

[1]   426 U.S. 229 (1976).
[2]   Public officials did not always see the need for such self-censorship. *See, e.g.*, Hunter v. Underwood, 471 U.S. 222 (1985).
[3]   Personnel Administrator of Massachusetts v. Feeney, 442 U.S. 256 (1979).

actor took an action that is allegedly discriminatory *because of,* rather than *in spite of,* race; if there are multiple reasons why an actor may have engaged in certain conduct, proving consciousness of racial impact is not sufficient; you have to show that in fact they acted *because of* race and not some other factor.[4] That is a very high bar.

**PM:** Could "hate speech" perhaps hamper your litigation indirectly? To some extent courts reflect public opinion, and judges are also in a sense members of the public. If public opinion is influenced by "hate speech," by the dialogue it creates, or by the message communicated by banning "hate speech," this could influence the courts.

**TS:** An indirect effect on judges might occur, but it would be very hard to measure; ultimately it's an empirical question and probably an unanswerable one. Certainly the biggest barrier to litigating these cases has been hostile judges – judges who simply came to these cases with some sort of predisposition against them. That has been more of a problem than hate speech or First Amendment issues.

So I'm not sure I see much of a connection between hate speech and judges' hostility to civil rights claims. I say that because when judges are hostile to civil rights claims and race cases, I cannot get inside their minds and say what is motivating them, because they aren't making racist statements. We are long past that point. Any judge who does that is asking for a quick end to his or her career. Does that mean that any individual judge could not have racial biases or prejudices? No, it doesn't mean that. But if they do have those biases and prejudices, it is probably much more subconscious. And if it isn't subconscious, it is never going to be articulated. So how does a civil rights lawyer discern what is motivating those judges? I don't think one can say, in the absence of an explicit statement that reveals racial bias, that these judges are acting out of racial bias. It may be that their view of the world and of the jurisprudence is so conservative that it leads them consistently to rule against African Americans, Latinos, and other minorities. I think that that should tell somebody something. But what it tells them is very much up for debate. If there were anti–hate speech laws in this country, I think the only effect that would have on judges is that they would have to adjudicate anti–hate speech cases. I don't think that it would have much of a discernable effect in terms of how they handle other civil rights claims.

**PM:** Moving beyond the narrow question of judicial attitudes, do you think there might be a positive social dynamic resulting from allowing "hate speech" to occur? Free discussion of such expression, even including ugly, racist views, might enable the public to reach, or reinforce, enlightened opinions and to work toward actual responses to underlying prejudices.

---

[4] *Id.* at 279.

**TS:** Yes, and that is one of a number of ways in which *allowing* hate speech might advance the cause of those opposed to the message being allowed. There is an argument that when you suppress speech you make martyrs out of the speakers who effectively portray themselves as victimized because they've been silenced. A related line of argument is that if you bring all of these vile thoughts and ideas into the open, let hate speech enter the public forum, it makes even more clear the fact that these views are still very much alive these days and that there are people who say and do hateful things, that racism is not a thing of the past. And of course there is the idea, central to American free-speech jurisprudence, that allowing the expression of misguided or harmful opinions exposes their flaws and leads to effective counterspeech, so such ideas are more potent when *unexpressed*.

On the other hand, I think about *Virginia v. Black,*[5] in which the Supreme Court held that a state can ban burning a cross with intent to intimidate, but struck down a provision that allowed the requisite intent to be inferred from the mere fact of burning the cross itself. Justice Thomas dissented.[6] Part of his point was that cross burning is conduct, not speech, so the First Amendment simply was not implicated. Even if it was, Justice Thomas had no problem with inferring intent to intimidate from the very act of burning a cross. Thomas wrote very clearly about what a burning cross means. Everybody in the black community and most people in the white community know exactly what a burning cross means. It is more than speech. It is meant to intimidate. Everybody knows that what comes next after the cross burns on the lawn is some act of violence to get people to move out, to try to scare them away. Now, in the United States system, we would say: "OK, that may be true, but if so, you prosecute based on the *act*, not on the thought or the word." Sometimes those things may be so close together that there is very little daylight between them, and it appears that what you are doing is prosecuting speech. But there is a sliver of daylight between those two things. Prosecuting someone for burning a cross on private property is not the same thing as prosecuting someone for hate speech. Similarly, if you prosecute someone for arson, that's not the same thing as prosecuting them for hate speech. So under our system, we've tried to balance these things, and have drawn some very fine lines that hold up better in some settings than others.

There is this passage from Robert Bolt's play, *A Man for All Seasons,* in which Sir Thomas More refers to giving "the Devil the benefit of law, for my own safety's sake."[7] The notion is that even those who express evil ideas get the protection of the law, because once you begin to prosecute people based on ideas, where do you stop? In our system, we have not been able to answer that question in a way that draws a bright line. Yet almost every other country does criminalize hate speech. So the United

---

[5] 538 U.S. 343 (2003).
[6] *Id.* at 388.
[7] Robert Bolt, *A Man for All Seasons,* Act I, p. 66 (Vintage Books 1962) (1960). The passage is quoted by the Supreme Court in TVA v. Hill, 437 U.S. 153, 195 (1978).

States may be peculiar in its way. We have a culture of the First Amendment and freedom of speech that goes beyond the First Amendment's language itself. The First Amendment applies, strictly speaking, only to governmental actors, and yet we act as if freedom of speech is a value that applies even in the context of private actors. So if private colleges and universities were to quash speech and penalize the expression of ideas, students and faculty would rise up and revolt, even though technically speaking the First Amendment does not apply to those institutions. Because it's a value that has been incorporated throughout the country, many people think that the First Amendment applies in the context of private employers. But again, the First Amendment does not literally apply in the context of private employment. It's a value that has been so incorporated in so many people's minds that it has become ubiquitous.

**PM:** You mentioned the value of ensuring that people do not mistakenly view racism as a problem of the past. If racist speech were suppressed, would it be harder for the society to perceive and acknowledge its existing problems of racism?

**TS:** If hate speech were made completely illegal, what would happen, I think, is the intensification of what we already have, which is a denial of the continued significance or salience of race. This denial is present in many settings, including judicial doctrine. The requirement of establishing discriminatory intent is one example. It is really a judicial policy choice, and one that allows discrimination to continue to live in the interstitial spaces of the law, as opposed to an all-out assault on all kinds of racial discrimination. The whole body of case law that countenances so-called de facto segregation[8] preserves these spaces within the law, this interstitial space, in which discrimination and racism live in this country, and cannot be attacked under our system. That's, in my view, a gratuitous choice, a policy choice. This issue is much larger than the question of hate speech. But I do think that an effective prohibition of hate speech would drive racism further underground and allow judges and others more freedom to deny its existence and relevance.

The counterargument is that if you make hate speech illegal you are sending another message about society's values and norms, you make it even less acceptable, you don't allow racism to live in these interstitial areas, these spaces between the law, because you are filling in some of these spaces with anti–hate speech legislation that would make it illegal.

The problem is that to accomplish that, it would have to be statutory or it would have to be because of the complete change in Supreme Court jurisprudence on this issue. I don't see the Court changing on that issue any time soon, if ever. Any statutory change would run directly into the First Amendment; there are constitutional issues, and a statutory prohibition would probably be struck down – it would have to give

---

[8] *See, e.g., Parents Involved in Community Schools v. Seattle School District No. 1*, 551 U.S. 701 (2007).

way to the First Amendment. It's an interesting theoretical debate, but as a practical matter I don't see it happening.

**PM:** That may be so, but if there could be a chance to change it, would you do so? Would you support such a change?

**TS:** I am going to give you a lawyer's answer. The lawyer's answer is, "It depends" or "I am of two minds on that." Let me explain what I mean by that.

I do think there is some speech that is without value. And we do regulate speech despite the First Amendment. The classic example, of course, is that you can't falsely yell "fire" in a crowded theater. There is regulation of certain forms of pornography in certain places, even though pornographers say that that's a form of speech. Not all speech is protected at all times and in all places. So given that we've carved out other areas, I think there's a strong argument that can be made that racist speech, hateful speech, ought also to be unprotected. (When I say "racist" I am conscious of the fact that we are not only talking about racism in its classic form, which was initially and primarily between white Americans and African Americans, or exclusively about racism at all. Hate speech also manifests along lines of gender and along lines of sexual orientation; we must also be concerned about anti-Semitism and Islamophobia, and so on. In referring to race and hate speech I am using shorthand.) What is the value of pure hate speech? Why pretend that hate speech does not do damage to the larger society as well as the individuals to whom it's directed? We won't let you yell "fire" in a crowded theater, but we do allow you to engage in certain kinds of hate speech that is setting fire to the fabric of the entire society.

But I think that if I have to come down on one side or the other, I will live with hate speech. First, I believe that when you have an infection of some kind, an illness, a disease, the better thing to do is to open up the body and expose the infection and to attack it with whatever surgery or treatment is necessary, rather than to deny that it's there and allow it quietly to fester.

Second, I would be very concerned about how a ban on hate speech would operate and be applied in practice. For example, the Nation of Islam taught that the white man was the devil. That message was preached by Malcolm X and other adherents of the Nation of Islam on street corners in black neighborhoods across this country. If you had hate speech laws, all of them would be prosecuted and sent to jail for what they said, and for what they thought. Now, I do not agree with many of the teachings of the Nation of Islam, and certainly not the assertion that each individual white man is the devil. I may think that during the era of slavery and the era of Jim Crow many white Americans, and white America in general, did devilish things, but to say that each individual white man is the devil sounds like hate speech to me. Yet that assertion was a reaction to the discrimination and racism that black people had experienced in this country. There were and may still be a lot of angry black folk around. There were and may still be a lot of angry Native Americans. When they begin to talk about the government, or what white folks did to them, a lot of that speech could fall into the banned category. Should they be prosecuted? One of the default assumptions in our race jurisprudence is that there is symmetry between minority groups who have been historically discriminated against and subjugated to white supremacy, on the one hand, and the discriminating group, on the other. The Supreme Court's application of strict scrutiny to affirmative action is the most obvious example.[9] I do not think that such symmetry is appropriate. That's not to say that black folks ought to be able to discriminate against white people but white people can't discriminate against black people. But there is an asymmetrical *reality* that gets lost or ignored, or denied, in our jurisprudence. Ignoring that asymmetry could have consequences for hate speech prosecutions that would be deeply problematic. The Black Panthers, back in the 1960s, said a lot of things that would have subjected them to prosecution if we had had hate speech legislation. What about Reverend Jeremiah Wright making statements from the pulpit that were widely publicized and deemed by some to be racist during the last presidential campaign? Should he be prosecuted? How does one define what hate speech is? It is *such* a slippery slope. It opens up all kinds of dangers.

Third, even with regard to white supremacists who say hateful, vile things, I don't want to prosecute them for what they think. I want to stop them from *acting* in harmful ways that may be motivated by their hateful thoughts. What I would want more than anything else is to change their *minds*. But when we begin to criminalize what they think and write, that's a slippery slope, and maybe a short road to a kind of – I don't want to say totalitarianism, because that would not be fair to those jurisdictions that do regulate hate speech – but it would potentially take us to a place that is very dangerous.

Again, it's this notion of giving the Devil the benefit of the law for my own safety's sake. I think I believe in that; I'm pretty sure I do. Even still, I don't mean to disrespect other systems that have made other choices and still seem to have avoided the road to perdition.

**PM:** You have spoken about the asymmetry in the situation of those who have historically discriminated and those who have been historically discriminated against. Many supporters of restrictions on "hate speech" emphasize that difference. They argue that racist and other "hate" speech puts discriminated-against and marginalized minorities into a very bad situation. This is for several reasons, among them that such speech has a silencing effect and denies equal membership in society. In light of what you said, what about the counterargument that if we make a choice to live

---

9 *See, e.g.,* Grutter v. Bollinger, 539 U.S. 306, 326 (2003) ("We apply strict scrutiny to all racial classifications. . . . "); Adarand Constructors, Inc. v. Pena, 515 U.S. 200, 227 (1995) (noting that Fourteenth Amendment "protect[s] *persons,* not *groups*" and therefore all "governmental action based on race – a *group* classification long recognized as 'in most circumstances irrelevant and therefore prohibited' – should be subjected to detailed judicial inquiry") (emphases original).

with "hate speech," it might mean that discriminated-against minorities are further marginalized by such speech?

**TS:** I certainly know, believe, and understand that hate speech can marginalize minority group members and individuals and can do great harm. My gut reaction is that where that is true, I don't want to see people marginalized and unprotected. The answer I would like to give is the classic answer: The antidote to hate speech is more speech. The truth is that counterspeech works most effectively when minority group members who are subjected to hate speech are not the only ones who respond to the hate speech. This is not a necessity, but it does make counterspeech most effective. In a society where the overwhelming majority of people hold values that are inconsistent with those that are expressed by hate speech, one would expect that people would come to the aid and protection of the minority-group individuals at whom the hate speech is being directed. But that isn't always true.

I remember – I don't know if I've told you this story, Peter – but I remember being on the subway years ago in Brooklyn. It took me a moment to get oriented to what was going on, but it seemed that there was a dispute going on. What was happening was that there were about four Caucasian adults who were screaming and yelling at two men who were orthodox Jews and were dressed in traditional orthodox Jewish garb. I don't know what started the dispute, but they were screaming at them, and they were saying: "you're filthy, you stink" and all kinds of other hateful things. And nobody on the subway car was saying anything. And it came into my mind: What must these two men think? Do they assume that the silence of everybody on the subway car meant that the people were shocked and appalled at what was being said, to such an extent that they didn't say anything because they were so shocked? Do they assume that the other passsengers disagreed with the people who were saying these things? Or did they feel like the people on the subway who were silent *agreed*, and didn't say anything to the contrary. I thought to myself, what do I do? Do I get into a physical confrontation with these people? But I felt like I had to say something. All I could think of to say was, "Shame on you." And they turned to me and they asked what I had said, and I said "shame on you"; it's all I could think of to say. But I have often thought about that incident afterward, and thought about what those two orthodox Jewish men must have felt. Certainly they could feel marginalized. And a lot of damage can be done; when you think about the whole history of anti-Semitism, you can't begin to underestimate how much of an effect that can have. Similarly, Roma in Central Europe and Eastern Europe are marginalized. If someone is shouting hateful epithets at them, it's one thing if people come to their defense and another if people are silent.

I guess what I'm trying to say, in an awkward way – and maybe this sounds too academic, maybe it *is* too academic – but I think that the deal ought to be that if we allow hate speech, if we tolerate hate speech, then the social compact ought to be that when people hear hate speech that they respond to it and condemn it; no matter to whom it's directed, they have to respond to it. That's the price I think we ought to pay for tolerating hate speech. If we are not going to condemn it, whenever we see it or hear it, then we need to rethink whether we should tolerate it, because of the impact it has.

What does that mean in real life? I don't know what it means beyond what I said; that is, to me as an individual. I would say that other individuals have the same obligation; whenever you see it, as uncomfortable as it may be, you have to condemn it, *on the spot, right there.* You have to let those minority group members to whom it's directed know, you have to make clear, that it's not tolerated, that we don't agree with it, and so on. I know as an African-American man that that doesn't always happen. But I think that that's the way it ought to work. I don't begin to suggest how it ought to work in other countries. I think certainly in the United States that's how I see it ought to work.

**PM:** When you said "shame on you" on the subway, what was their reaction?

**TS:** They turned on me and started cursing at me. Now, it got their attention off of these two men for a moment. And perhaps I should have done more. But I got to the subway stop where I had to get off and they were still yelling. That's what happened. Now, if they had gotten physical with these individuals, then I think it would be incumbent on people to come to their aid. Did my saying "shame on them" change the experience for these two men? I can't tell you that.

**PM:** I believe it did; and I think it's very important that you spoke up. That is a helpful example of what we need to do, although there may be circumstances in which those expressing "hate speech" are so ready to act violently that it is the lesser of two evils to avoid violence by not getting into a discussion with them at all.

**TS:** Let me just add something else. I think in candor I have to ask the question: What did I do in the many instances in which I was somewhere within the African-American community in which black people were railing against white folks? To be honest, I didn't always see it in the same way. I understood what was going on on those occasions as a venting of a certain kind of frustration. More to the point, maybe no white people were there at all; if they were, they were reporters or something like that, covering the event. If somebody was directly threatened as an individual, I think I would have done something similar to what I did on the subway. But the expression of anger and frustration, and sometimes even hatred for white people, in parts of the black community, has not been something that has always prompted me to get up and say, "I object."

But to press that a little further. I remember when an African-American man, now deceased, who was a member of the Nation of Islam, gave a controversial and virulently anti-Semitic speech at Kean College in New Jersey in 1993.[10] Khalid Abdul Muhammed was his name. At that time a board member of the NAACP Legal Defense and Educational Fund who happened to be Jewish – maybe he didn't "happen to be" Jewish, since the fact that he was Jewish is directly relevant to what happened – came to me, as Deputy Director Counsel of the Fund, and to the then-Director Counsel, Elaine Jones, and basically told us that he thought that we should condemn Khalid Muhammed's speech and he would make a contribution to the Legal Defense Fund. Well, that was insulting. I didn't want to be bought and paid for. So we didn't do it. We were not dancing at the end of somebody's string.[11] At the same time, I already had planned to and did get a copy of the speech. I listened to the speech. It was vile, hateful stuff. I felt compelled to write something in response to it, and I did.[12]

What one does in these settings will vary from individual to individual. It depends on what one believes. Certainly as a matter of law, Khalid Muhammed was entitled to say the things he did. I think that that speech was vile. If it incited people to do hateful things that were violent, then it would have crossed a line; but even if it did not, it merited a response because it was hate speech.

**PM:** Suppose the circumstances are reversed. What if a white person engages in public "hate speech" directed at black people?

**TS:** I've never been at a KKK rally, and I'm not going to be. What should white folks do if they are in a situation where they hear racist speech directed at minorities? Well, I leave that to them to figure out. I know what I think they should do. But some of this is a question of how one sees one's place in a larger society and what one's values are with respect to speech and ideas and discrimination and hatred. Ultimately, I am opposed to any kind of hatred. But that doesn't mean that I think you should prosecute people for saying hateful things.

**PM:** There seems to be a very strong argument that there is a difference, at least in some situations, between angry, frustrated expressions, even "hate speech," by people who belong to discriminated-against groups, on the one hand, and such speech by members of the groups that have discriminated against them, on the other.

**TS:** That's right. Part of it has to do with a power dynamic. Imagine Malcolm X or Louis Farrakhan standing on the corner of 125th Street and 7th Avenue in Harlem.

---

[10] The speech became a cause célèbre and led to resolutions of condemnation by both the House and the Senate. For a contemporary account of the speech, see Jon Nordheimer, "Divided by a Diatribe; College Speech Ignites Furor Over Race," *N.Y. Times,* Dec. 22, 1993, at B6.

[11] Similar exchanges regarding the speech, leading to similar standoffs, occurred between African-American and Jewish leaders from many other organizations as well. *See* Jack Salzman, "Introduction," in *Struggles in the Promised Land: Towards a History of Black-Jewish Relations in the United States* 3–4 (Jack Salzman & Cornel West eds., Oxford University Press 1997).

[12] *See* Elaine R. Jones, "Bigotry Is Immoral, No Matter Who Expresses It," *L.A. Times,* Jan. 28, 1994, at F7.

No matter what they said, the truth of the matter is that they were not much of an immediate threat to most, if any, white folks. On the other hand, white folks were engaging in a kind of systematic and systemic discrimination against black folks every day. So what you heard was a kind of frustration and anger in response to that. When you heard black folks speaking in anger, it was generally in reaction to the subjugation and discrimination they had experienced. White folks' racist statements came from another place. It was not that white people were being discriminated against. Any individual white person can say, "somebody black did something to me, and that's why I. . . . " But even that reaction is a racist reaction.

**PM:** I wonder whether you consider the civil rights litigation you have been involved with to be an indirect measure against "hate speech." Charles Lawrence has emphasized the *communicative* element of *Brown v. Board of Education*[13] and school desegregation.[14] A society's decision to permit or prohibit segregation and other discriminatory practices, in addition to its obvious practical consequences, communicates a message. Do you think that fighting segregation and other forms of discrimination is actually a way to fight "hate speech" itself?

**TS:** Yes, segregation is communicative. There is a message sent. The act, or even the reality of segregation (even what is called in this country de facto segregation, although in my view there is virtually no such thing as de facto segregation), communicates something. And therefore litigating against segregation sends the opposite message.

You mention *Brown v. Board of Education*. The truth is, and I have said many times and continue to say, that we honor *Brown* more in principle than we do in practice. And I have also said many times that *Brown* is now hallowed, but also hollowed. In the United States, we are schizophrenic when it comes to racism and how we deal with racism. I do not mean that in all instances it is dishonest. Schizophrenics probably are very sincere about going in two different directions. So we say that we are opposed to racism and we want to be a color-blind society, and yet we tolerate, countenance, and in some ways even promote racism or at least its effects.

But does that lead me back to a place where I would say that I would support legislation that just outlaws the expression of racist thoughts and racist speech? No. Could I be convinced that there are some instances in which racist speech or hate speech should not be legal? I *might* be convinced that there are some instances in which that is so, but I think we have to be very, very careful about that, for the

[13] 347 U.S. 483 (1954).
[14] Indeed, Lawrence states that because what made segregated schools unacceptable was at bottom the *message* that segregation communicated – *viz.*, "that black children are an untouchable caste, unfit to be educated with white children" – "*Brown* may be read as regulating the content of racist speech." Charles R. Lawrence III, "If He Hollers Let Him Go: Regulating Racist Speech on Campus," 1990 *Duke L.J.* 431, 439–40.

reasons that I expressed before. But I don't put hate speech in the same place as I do other kinds of speech that are more thoughtful and respectful of the humanity of every human being. The only reason to protect it is to protect ourselves, to protect all of us.

**PM:** You mentioned that perhaps in some instances "hate speech" could be prohibited. What instances are those? When such speech creates imminent danger?

**TS:** Yes. Where there's some kind of imminent danger. That's probably where I would begin to consider some regulation.

**PM:** How imminent must the danger be?

**TS:** I don't have a good answer for that. But I basically agree with the *Brandenburg* standard. If somebody is calling for people to rise up and attack individuals, or calling for a race war or an attack on somebody because he or she is gay or lesbian, or even saying that gays and lesbians ought to be subjected to violence, I'd be willing to consider that. But imminence and likelihood of violence matter, and those depend on context. I think back on some of the rallies or meetings that I went to in my youth of the Nation of Islam or the Black Panther Party, and there were things that were said there that were pretty rough. Did I think that they were actually about to happen? Well, the Black Panthers did engage in some violence, although they would and did say it was in self defense. They were also subjected to violence by governmental forces. Did I think the Nation of Islam posed an imminent threat to white America? I didn't think so. I don't think it would have been appropriate to punish the Nation of Islam for advocating racial separation at that time.

**PM:** Do you agree with the intent requirement in *Brandenburg*?

**TS:** When somebody puts someone else in imminent danger because of who or what they are, along the lines of race or religion or sexual orientation or gender, and the like, intent is inherently a part of what they are saying and doing. It's not hard to prove. I don't know how they might suggest that people be harmed on that basis without having the intent to do it. Maybe somebody can explain that to me. But I think intent is inherently part of it.

**PM:** Let me give you the example of the annual gay pride parade in Budapest. In 2007 and 2008, some "counter-demonstrators" were acting violently while others were shouting antigay and anti-Semitic slogans. If those who were shouting are prosecuted for inciting violence, what if they claim, "I just wanted to express my views, and I did not intend to incite to violence."

**TS:** What were they shouting?

**PM:** If they were shouting for example "rotten faggots," but didn't call for action.

**TS:** So they weren't explicitly calling for violence; they were just calling them names. That's a closer call. As reprehensible as that speech is, I think it has to be contextualized; intent could be clear in context. Maybe what I would do is impose a "knew or should have known" standard. I might be comfortable in some contexts, including that one in particular, with that approach. You know that if you're yelling things at people and the atmosphere is such that there's hostility, and other people may be saying things that are calling for violence, and then you say something and you yell and shout and call them names, you know or should know that it could lead to violence. To be precise, such a standard would involve knowledge as opposed to intent, and knowledge could be actual ("knew") or constructive ("should have known"). Maybe I could live with that standard.

**PM:** Part of the literature on "hate speech" describes a conflict between liberty and equality. Do you think there is such a conflict?

**TS:** I don't accept that those two things are, or ought to be, inherently in tension with one another. I can't imagine the Civil Rights Movement of the 1960s, or the gay rights movement of more recent years, or the women's rights movement, or *any* movement, being possible without free speech, given the way those movements were carried out. Free speech is essential for minority group members who are challenging systems of subordination, segregation, discrimination, particularly if they are attacking the complicity of government in creating and maintaining those systems of subordination. If we lose rights to free speech, the ground on which we stand with respect to other civil and human rights becomes quicksand.

It's not that I elevate speech above all other rights, or elevate all forms of speech at all times and in all places above all other rights. There are times when speech can be in tension with equality rights or principles. Those tensions have to be resolved on a contextual basis. But I don't believe that it is either/or, speech or equality.

**PM:** Does a country have to prioritize and focus on *either* fighting discrimination, including segregation, *or* "hate speech"?

**TS:** No. It is possible, however, that if a country focuses on regulating hate speech, which in and of itself might be very controversial, that might be where the energy and effort goes. As a consequence, other forms of discrimination might receive less attention. I would, of course, prefer to see systemic and systematic inequality and discrimination attacked in all of the places where they exist. So in the context of Roma, for example, I would prefer to see a focus on protecting Roma from violence that is directed at them, whether by individuals or by state actors such as the police. I would prefer to see housing discrimination and employment discrimination and education discrimination attacked. Those efforts need not be to the exclusion of protection against speech that provokes violence. But I would not want to see a focus on hate speech legislation result in ignoring all these other issues. That would only drive underground any *expression* of discrimination and hatred, without remedying or reducing the discrimination and hatred itself. I would rather see antidiscrimination efforts than anti-hate speech efforts.

Having said that, we don't have it right in this country. I want to be clear on that. We allow racial discrimination and racism to exist in these interstitial places, at the same time as we say that speech, including hate speech, is protected. So we don't have the balance right in this country either. We tolerate a lot of racial discrimination and racism in this country in ways that we shouldn't.

**PM:** Katharine Gelber argues that the state should facilitate counterspeech.[15] The argument is that it's not enough just to say that more speech is better. Often, members of discriminated-against minorities will not be in a position to answer forcefully enough. The Roma minority in Central European and Eastern European countries, including Hungary, is a good example, as they lack, for example, sufficient access to mass media. Are there useful measures the state can undertake to equip targets of "hate speech" to respond powerfully?

**TS:** I would need to read her work to have a fully formed response. What comes to mind first is the obligation I mentioned earlier of people who are *not* the targets to speak out against hate speech whenever it occurs. But I also think of what Frederick Douglass said many, many years ago: "Who would be free, themselves must strike the blow."[16] I believe deeply that minority group members who are discriminated against, who are subordinated and oppressed, have the obligation and responsibility – and whether they have it theoretically or not, as a practical matter the burden falls on them – to struggle and speak on their own behalf. Now, if they speak alone and nobody comes to their aid and support, that's a problem, and it violates the social contract I have referred to.

**PM:** But does this social contract include not *restriction* of "hate speech," but some sort of obligation on the state to empower members of disadvantaged minority groups, in order to better enable them to respond, to give them an effective voice they would otherwise lack?

**TS:** Perhaps. Think about equal protection law as it developed in the 1930s in the United States, and in particular judicial suspicion of laws that burdened "discrete

---

[15] *See* Katharine Gelber, "Reconceptualizing Counterspeech in Hate-Speech Policy (with a Focus on Australia)," Chapter 11 herein.

[16] Douglass was fond of this exhortation, and it is frequently attributed to him, but the line comes from Byron's *Childe Harold's Pilgrimage*. *See* George Gordon, Lord Byron, *Childe Harold's Pilgrimage*, canto II, stanza LXXVI (1812) ("Hereditary bondsmen! Know ye not/Who would be free themselves must strike the blow?/By their right arms the conquest must be wrought!/Will Gaul or Muscovite redress thee? No!"). *See, e.g.,* Frederick Douglass, *The Life and Times of Frederick Douglass* 98 (DeWolfe & Fiske Co. 1892) (Dover reprint 2003) (quoting the first two lines of the Byron excerpt).

and insular minorities."[17] That principle was asymmetrical; courts gave heightened scrutiny to classifications that burdened discrete and insular minorities. Now, of course, the case law has developed so that discreteness and insularity are not really part of the equation any more. Again, this shift is most prominent in so-called reverse discrimination cases, where the Court applies the same test to all racial classifications, regardless of whether they benefit majority white folks or minorities who have been discriminated against and subordinated in the past. That has led to a whole body of jurisprudence that is misdirected. So I do believe that the government may interact with minority-group members who cannot protect themselves in order to equip them to do so. To me, stricter scrutiny of laws that are disempowering and direct measures to empower members of disadvantaged minorities are on a single continuum. The state might go too far down that road, and one would have to know the context in which this principle was being applied. But in theory, yes, I agree with appropriateness of such measures.

**PM:** It seems that, as you say, antidiscrimination efforts themselves put the disadvantaged minority in a better position to speak and to respond to "hate speech."

Thank you so much for the interview.

**TS:** Thank you, Peter.

---

[17] United States v. Carolene Products Co., 304 U.S. 144, 152 n.4 (1938).

# PART IV

# International Law

**22**

# Does International Law Provide for Consistent Rules on Hate Speech?

*Toby Mendel*

This chapter addresses the difficult question of whether international law calls on states to adopt consistent criminal prohibitions on hate speech.[1] The concern is with the specific question of criminal hate speech rather than the much broader question of hate speech policies (which include, among other things, criminal, civil, and administrative rules, as well as a host of promotional measures to counter hate speech). The central focus is on whether a global legal framework exists that promotes a consistent[2] and coherent balance between the interests hate speech laws are designed to promote – equality and public order – and the right to freedom of expression.

This chapter argues that the International Covenant on Civil and Political Rights (ICCPR) does indeed provide sensible standards, at least in relation to criminal prohibitions on hate speech, and that these standards are precise and coherent. At the same time, the chapter recognizes that international courts have in key respects failed to provide a clear interpretive framework for the hate speech rules in the ICCPR, leaving states some discretion as to the hate speech rules they adopt. However, it argues that this is a challenge that could, and should, be overcome. The chapter also counters two of the more important critiques of these international standards, namely that the hate speech laws they envisage may be abused and that they are not effective.

---

[1] It may be noted that "hate speech" is not a term of art and it is used here generically to refer to speech that promotes racism and/or racially motivated acts.

[2] The term "consistent" is used here to signify a set of clear, precise, and uniform rules regarding what should be prohibited as hate speech.

## I. INTERNATIONAL STANDARDS

### A. *Key Standards: The ICCPR*

This chapter takes as its starting point international law, and specifically the International Covenant on Civil and Political Rights (ICCPR).[3] The ICCPR is not quite universal but, as of April 2010, it had been ratified by some 165 states, located in all regions of the world, and representing 75 percent of the world's states and a far greater proportion of those that could make a colorable claim to being democratic.

International law contains numerous other rules relevant to hate speech. Perhaps the most important is Article 4 of the International Convention on the Elimination of all Forms of Racial Discrimination (ICERD).[4] Regional treaties, such as the American Convention on Human Rights (ACHR),[5] also have a bearing on states' obligations regarding hate speech. This chapter does not address the difficult question of the consistency of these various obligations in the area of hate speech or how states should address apparent inconsistencies.[6]

Article 19 of the ICCPR guarantees the right to freedom of expression, although not in absolute terms.[7] Restrictions are permitted, but only where they are set out in law and where they are necessary to protect the public and private interests listed in that article, including public order and the rights of others. Article 20(2), on the other hand, *requires* States Parties to prohibit "advocacy of national, racial or religious hatred that constitutes incitement to discrimination, hostility or violence."[8]

---

[3] Adopted and opened for signature, ratification and accession by G.A. Res. 2200A (XXI), 999 U.N.T.S. 171 (Dec. 16, 1966) (entered into force Jan. 3, 1976).

[4] G.A. Res. 2106A (XX) (Dec. 21, 1965), 660 U.N.T.S. 195 (entered into force Jan. 4, 1969). There were 173 Parties to ICERD as of March 2010.

[5] Adopted Nov. 22, 1969, entered into force July 18, 1978. The American Convention is the subject of Eduardo Bertoni and Julio Rivera Jr., "The American Convention on Human Rights: Regulation of Hate Speech and Similar Expression," Chapter 25 herein.

[6] Based on their text, the extent of these obligations does appear to vary. ICERD, for example, defines the scope of hate speech that states are required to ban much more broadly than the ICCPR, whereas the ACHR defines it more narrowly.

[7] The relevant provisions of Article 19 are as follows:

> 2. Everyone shall have the right to freedom of expression; this right shall include freedom to seek, receive and impart information and ideas of all kinds, regardless of frontiers, either orally, in writing or in print, in the form of art, or through any other media of his choice.
> 3. The exercise of the rights provided for in paragraph 2 of this article carries with it special duties and responsibilities. It may therefore be subject to certain restrictions, but these shall only be such as are provided by law and are necessary:
>     a. For respect of the rights or reputations of others;
>     b. For the protection of national security or of public order (ordre public), or of public health or morals.

[8] Article 20(2) specifically states:

> 2. Any advocacy of national, racial or religious hatred that constitutes incitement to discrimination, hostility or violence shall be prohibited by law.

The *travaux préparatoires* of the ICCPR indicate that the drafters were fully aware of the potential tension between these articles and were careful to craft the provisions in a manner that was internally coherent.[9] It is clear from the careful wording of the texts of each provision that coherent interpretation is possible.[10] For obvious reasons, those officially tasked with interpreting these provisions, namely the UN Human Rights Committee (HRC) – a creature of the ICCPR – must do so in a manner that gives effect to both provisions.

We can thus conclude that the ICCPR regime requires states to put in place hate speech laws that meet the standards of Article 20(2) and that such laws must also conform to the requirements of Article 19. This provides the beginnings of a consistent set of international rules on hate speech laws.[11]

## B. *The Relationship between Articles 19 and 20*

This consistency, in terms of what hate speech laws states are required to adopt, might be defeated in three ways. First, if Article 19 permitted greater restrictions on hate speech than Article 20(2) required, a patchwork of different hate speech laws might still be in accordance with this regime, some conforming closely to Article 20(2) and others going beyond it, but still respecting Article 19. Second, if the scope of interpretation of Article 19 and/or Article 20(2) were wide, it would allow states to adopt different hate speech laws while still respecting the ICCPR legal framework. Third, the fact that assessment of the legitimacy of a restriction on freedom of expression is normally context-dependent might lead to rules that rest on consistent principles but are quite different in their specifics in light of varying contexts. I address these three possibilities in this and the following two sections.

Addressing the first possible route to inconsistency, it is submitted that Articles 19 and 20(2) are, if not fully legally contiguous, at least very nearly so. The drafting

---

[9] *See* Mark Bossuyt, *Guide to the "Travaux Préparatoires" of the International Covenant on Civil and Political Rights* 398–411 (Martinus Nijhoff Publishers 1987).

[10] *See, e.g.,* Dominic McGoldrick and Thésèe O'Donnell, "Hate-speech laws: consistency with national and international human rights law," 18 *Legal Studies* 453 (1998); Jean-Francois Gaudreault-DesBiens, "From Sisyphus's Dilemma to Sisyphus's Duty? A Meditation on the Regulation of Hate Propaganda in Relation to Hate Crimes and Genocide," 46 *McGill L.J.* 121 (2000); Thomas Jones, *Human Rights: Group Defamation, Freedom of Expression and the Law of Nations* (Kluwer Law Int'l 1998).

[11] It must be noted that the ICERD, *supra* note 4, complicates the international-standards picture. Article 4(a) of the ICERD imposes an obligation on states to ban a number of categories of statements, including "ideas based on racial superiority." This lacks any intent requirement, does not require advocacy of hatred, does not require there to be any incitement to a proscribed result, such as violence, discrimination, or hatred, and indeed, does not even refer to a proscribed result. It is, therefore, far broader than Article 20(2) of the ICCPR. As a result, if the preceding analysis is correct, namely that Articles 19 and 20(2) of the ICCPR are legally contiguous or nearly so, then Article 4(a) of ICERD must by definition be in conflict with Article 19 of the ICCPR. This conclusion is also warranted from a direct examination of the legal principles that underpin Article 19 of the ICCPR and, in particular, that only restrictions that are necessary can be justified.

history of Article 20(2) suggests that it was carefully crafted so as to prohibit as much harmful speech as possible while still respecting freedom of expression as defined by Article 19. While proposals to restrict Article 20(2) to incitement to violence were rejected, so were proposals to extend it – for example to include "racial exclusiveness" – on the basis of concern about free speech.[12] This suggests that the obligations of Article 20(2) are extremely close to the permissions of 19(3), leaving little scope for restrictions on freedom of expression over and beyond the terms of Article 20(2).

The HRC reached essentially the same conclusion in *Faurisson v. France*,[13] a case involving a challenge to a hate speech conviction for Holocaust denial. The Committee upheld Faurisson's conviction, relying on the "respect of the rights or reputations of others" ground listed in Article 19(3) and stating that the law served to protect the right of "the Jewish community to live free from fear of an atmosphere of anti-Semitism."[14] The individual opinion of Elizabeth Evatt and David Kretzmer, cosigned by Eckart Klein, stated:

> [T]here may be circumstances in which the right of a person to be free from incitement to discrimination on grounds of race, religion or national origins cannot be fully protected *by a narrow, explicit law on incitement that falls precisely within the boundaries of article 20, paragraph 2.* This is the case where . . . statements that do not meet the strict legal criteria of incitement can be shown to constitute part of a *pattern* of incitement against a given racial, religious or national group, or where those interested in spreading hostility and hatred adopt sophisticated forms of speech that are not punishable under the law against racial incitement, even though their effect may be as pernicious as explicit incitement, if not more so.[15]

Their point may be understood as advocating for an extremely narrow and precise interpretation of incitement in Article 20(2), alongside a recognition that there may be exceptional cases where statements which do not, of themselves, fall within the scope of this very narrow interpretation may still legitimately be prohibited because, in context and alongside other statements, they in fact do constitute incitement. It is also arguable, however, that their point really concerns the issue of how the term "incitement" is to be interpreted, rather than going outside of the boundaries of Article 20(2) per se. Either way, their holding supports the view that, in the area of hate speech, Articles 19(3) and 20(2) are legally contiguous or very nearly so.

This conclusion is further confirmed by the jurisprudence of the European Court of Human Rights. The jurisprudence of the European Court, interpreting the European Convention on Human Rights (ECHR), is not directly legally relevant to the scope of the ICCPR. At the same time, the guarantees of freedom of expression

---

[12]   *See* Bossuyt, *supra* note 9, at 404–5, 408.
[13]   Nov. 8, 1986, Communication No. 550/1993.
[14]   *Id.* ¶ 9.6.
[15]   *Id.*, individual opinion of Evatt and Kretzmer, ¶ 4 (emphasis added).

in the two instruments are very similar in nature, and so the jurisprudence of the European Court can be taken as highly authoritative guidance as to the scope of freedom of expression under the ICCPR.

The ECHR,[16] unlike the ICCPR, does not require States Parties to adopt hate speech legislation but it does include provisions ruling out both discrimination in the enjoyment of rights (Article 14) and reliance on rights to justify actions that are aimed at the destruction or undue limitation of other human rights (Article 17). In a series of cases, the European Commission and Court relied on these provisions, operating in tandem, to rule inadmissible various appeals from national decisions imposing restrictions on hate speech.[17]

Few of these cases elaborate on the relationship between the various ECHR articles they reference. In *Lehideux and Isorni v. France*, however, the Court did shed a bit of light on this issue. That case involved a prosecution for contesting the legitimacy of the conviction of the French leader Marshal Pétain for collusion with the enemy during World War II, involving the same law under which Faurisson had been convicted. The Court noted that the Commission[18] had held that Article 17 could not prevent the applicants from relying on Article 10. The Court implicitly agreed, as it analyzed the case through the filter of Article 10,[19] finding France to be in breach of its obligations, because the conviction was not a reasonable limitation on freedom of expression. This again suggests close legal proximity between what may be required to protect the rights of others and what is permitted as a restriction on freedom of expression. Similar accommodation between these two interests is found in the Council of Europe Recommendation on Hate Speech, which refers to instances of hate speech that do not enjoy the protection of Article 10 because they are aimed at the destruction of rights and freedoms recognized by the ECHR, that is, which breach Article 17.[20]

---

[16] Adopted Nov. 4, 1950, E.T.S. No. 5, entered into force Sep. 3, 1953. Article 10 of the European Convention, guaranteeing freedom of expression, states:

1. Everyone has the right to freedom of expression. This right shall include freedom to hold opinions and to receive and impart information and ideas without interference by public authority and regardless of frontiers. This Article shall not prevent States from requiring the licensing of broadcasting, television or cinema enterprises.

2. The exercise of these freedoms, since it carries with it duties and responsibilities, may be subject to such formalities, conditions, restrictions or penalties as are prescribed by law and are necessary in a democratic society, in the interests of national security, territorial integrity of public safety, for the prevention of disorder or crime, for the protection of health or morals, for the protection of the reputation or rights of others, for preventing the disclosure of information received in confidence, or for maintaining the authority and impartiality of the judiciary.

[17] The Court's decisions in this area are thoroughly canvassed in Tarlach McGonagle, "A Survey and Critical Analysis of Council of Europe Strategies for Countering 'Hate Speech'," Chapter 24 herein.

[18] At that time, cases went first to the Commission and then on appeal to the Court.

[19] Lehideux and Isorni v. France, Sep. 23, 1998, Application No. 24662/94, ¶¶ 34–35.

[20] Recommendation R(97)20 of the Committee of Ministers of the Council of Europe on "Hate Speech," Oct. 30, 1997, Appendix, Principle 4.

## C. *Interpretive Discretion*

The second way in which the ICCPR's internal consistency could be defeated would be if there were a wide scope to interpret Article 19 and/or Article 20(2), so that states could adopt different hate speech laws while still respecting their provisions. The ECHR, for example, has articulated the doctrine of "margin of appreciation," which allocates some discretion to States Parties in the application of rights, taking into account local context. The scope of this margin varies; whereas it is very limited in relation to political speech,[21] it is relatively wider when it comes to issues such as respect for religion[22] or incitement to violence.[23]

Neither the HRC nor the European Court has made it clear in their hate speech cases whether they consider such speech to be political. It seems obvious that hate speech is by its very nature political speech, inasmuch as it ventures an opinion on social organization and relations.[24] Sometimes, it is far more overtly political in the sense of being used as a rallying call explicitly within the political arena.[25] Neither the HRC nor the ECHR have addressed this question properly.

In practice, regardless of the margin-of-appreciation doctrine, the ECHR and, to a lesser extent, the HRC generally do not go through a strict legal analysis of the test for restrictions on freedom of expression when assessing whether a hate speech law conforms to the requirements of, respectively, Article 10 of the ECHR and Article 19 of the ICCPR.[26] In those cases in which the European Commission or Court has approved a hate speech conviction, they often spend very little time analyzing the impugned speech itself, providing little legal analysis for their holdings. It sometimes appears that the decision hinges primarily on whether the content and intent of the speech in question appears to be of a racist character, rather than on the application of a legal test (i.e., for restrictions on freedom of expression). On the other hand, where the Court deems the speech to be protected, this result often appears to be based on its subjective appreciation of the speech as nonracist (in either content

---

[21] *See, e.g.*, Refah Partisi et al. v. Turkey, Feb. 13, 2003, Application Nos. 41340/98, 41342/98, 41343/98 and 41344/98, ¶ 81.

[22] *See, e.g.*, Wingrove v. United Kingdom, Nov. 25, 1996, Application No. 17419/90, ¶ 58.

[23] *See, e.g.*, Gerger v. Turkey, July 8, 1999, Application No. 24919/94, ¶ 48.

[24] *See, e.g.*, R. v. Keegstra, [1990] 3 S.C.R. 697 (Can.) (Dickson, C.J.) (part VII(D)(i)).

[25] Note, for example, the Feb. 2, 2006 acquittal of British National Party leader Nick Griffin on charges of hate speech. *See* "BNP leader faces trial," *The Guardian*, Feb. 2, 2006, *available at* http://www.guardian.co.uk/farright/story/0,1700810,00.html. *See also* Glimmerveen and Hagenbeek v. Netherlands, Oct. 11 1979, Application No. 8406/78 (Eur. Comm'n on H.R.).

[26] An example from the European Court is Garaudy v. France, July 7, 2003, Application No. 65831/01 (European Court). Examples from the European Commission include *Glimmerveen and Hagenbeek*, *supra* note 25; Kühnen v. Germany, May 12, 1988, Application No. 12194/86; B.H., M.W., H.P. and G.K. v. Austria, Oct. 12, 1989, Application No. 12774/87; Ochensberger v. Austria, Sep. 2, 1994, Application No. 21318/93; and Nationaldemokratische Partei Deutschlands, Bezirksverband München-Oberbayern v. Germany, Nov. 29, 1995, Application No. 25992/94. The *Faurisson* case, *see supra* note 13 and accompanying text, is perhaps an exception. Interestingly, there has not yet been a case alleging a failure to comply with Article 20 on the basis that a country's hate speech laws are too *permissive*.

or intent), again rather than on the application of the ICCPR or ECHR test for restrictions on freedom of expression.[27]

It is thus the case that, in practice, under both the ICCPR and ECHR regimes, states enjoy quite a lot of discretion as to how they formulate and apply their hate speech laws, as long as these laws are directed only toward speech that is, in the view of the oversight bodies, actually racist in nature. This, however, is not an inherent characteristic of the legal regime established by the ICCPR and ECHR. To the contrary, it reflects shortcomings in its application. These international oversight bodies could and should impose much more careful supervision over both the text and application of national hate speech laws. In particular, both "hatred" and "incitement" in Article 20(2) of the ICCPR should be subject to much more refined and precise legal definition, as I discuss later in the chapter.

## D. *The Role of Context*

The third potential source of inconsistency results from the fact that the analysis of whether a restriction on freedom of expression is legitimate is almost always context-dependent. This is perhaps particularly true in the case of hate speech laws. Context often has a bearing on whether a particular statement is or is not likely to incite to violence, discrimination, or hatred – the standard imposed by Article 20(2) of the ICCPR. The European Court of Human Rights has often pointed to the context when analyzing hate speech laws. In *Lehideux and Isorni*, for example, the Court noted the passage of time as a consideration to be taken into account in relation to a law prohibiting the denial of crimes against humanity, as established by the Nuremburg Tribunal.[28] Specifically, the Court stated that due to the passage of time, it could not be claimed that France was not ready to deal with its history of collaboration in World War II.

At first blush, context-dependence may appear difficult to reconcile with the notion of universal human rights, key characteristics of which are inalienability and applicability regardless of the particular circumstances. However, international, and most constitutional, guarantees of free speech provide for a balancing between freedom of expression and other key public and private interests, which inevitably depends at least to some extent on context.[29] Whether certain words are protected depends on their meaning and impact; meaning and impact in turn depend importantly on context. Protecting similar language in one setting and not in another is

---

[27]  *See, e.g.*, Giniewski v. France, Jan. 31, 2006, Application No. 64016/00.

[28]  *Lehideux*, *supra* note 19, ¶ 55. The European Court held that the conviction was a breach of the applicants' right to freedom of expression. Although this was not a hate speech or genocide denial case, the point about context remains pertinent (and the law in question does serve as France's Holocaust denial law).

[29]  The famous "falsely shouting fire in a theater" example is one illustration of this. *See* Schenck v. United States, 249 U.S. 47, 52 (1919).

inconsistent only on the surface. What does not depend on context, however, is the presumption in favor of free speech, along with an established set of rules for overcoming that presumption. This is really the essence of the right to freedom of expression under international law and most national constitutions. Whereas the outcomes of particular cases will be affected by the context in which a given sort of speech occurs, the rules themselves are consistent.

It thus is submitted that, on its face, the ICCPR does establish a potentially consistent framework, at least of policy principles relating to hate speech laws. If the framework has not, in practice, been applied in a legally precise and hence consistent manner, this is a result of lax interpretation of the rules rather than the rules per se.[30]

## II. CRITIQUES OF THE INTERNATIONAL FRAMEWORK

### A. *Abuse of Hate Speech Laws*

Assuming that Articles 19 and 20(2) of the ICCPR do constitute some sort of consistent policy framework for hate speech laws, this framework may be critiqued at two different levels. First, one may accept as appropriate the language of these provisions but argue that international courts have gotten the balancing between the various interests – free speech, equality, public order – wrong. This is not fatal to the theory that these articles present a consistent policy regarding hate speech; there will always be debate on the precise interpretive balance to be achieved.[31]

Second, and posing a more serious challenge, are substantive critiques, in particular the objection that hate speech that does not constitute incitement to racist *acts*, for example of violence or discrimination, should never be restricted. Proponents of this view often point to the abuse of hate speech laws as a justification for their position.[32] Although superficially satisfying, this is in fact logically incoherent. The fallacy of this position is immediately apparent when an analogy is made with other restrictions on freedom of expression, such as defamation law, laws protecting privacy and national security, rules against obscene material, and so on. All of these can be, and many often are, abused. Experience indicates that, outside of the very most repressive countries, which exercise direct control over public communication

---

[30] It might be argued that the rules are applied in a socially consistent manner because, as noted earlier, hate speech prohibitions are approved by international courts only where they target speech that is actually racist in nature. This does not, however, serve as a legally consistent set of rules, among other things because it is dependent on what is ultimately a subjective view of what constitutes racist speech.

[31] If by a consistent policy is meant unanimous agreement on the precise standards, then this is clearly not an achievable social goal and the original question is superficial.

[32] I understand by abuse the application of such laws for goals for which they were not intended, such as to silence political criticism, rather than merely overbroad interpretation of these laws based on a lack of understanding of the principles of freedom of expression. Abuse here would also include the adoption of laws that are intended to be abused, rather than to protect against harmful speech.

systems, defamation law is the weapon of choice to silence legitimate speech. Yet it would be strange indeed to call for the abolition of defamation laws because of this. By comparison, historic abuse of hate speech laws is a far less serious, although certainly not negligible, threat to freedom of expression.[33]

The proper response to abuse of laws restricting freedom of expression, which address a legitimate social goal, is to address the cause of that abuse, not to remove protection for that social goal. If defamation laws are overly broad, they should be redrafted in more narrow and precise terms, although this alone can rarely be expected to bring the abuse to an end.[34] The same approach is warranted in respect to hate speech laws.

Closely related to this objection is the slippery-slope argument, which holds that if one opens the door to content-based restrictions on speech, overly broad application of such restrictions becomes inevitable. Once again, this argument has little merit; indeed, its legitimacy as an argumentative technique may be questioned.[35] More importantly, there is no evidence to support this argument. While there are cases of overbroad hate speech laws being abused, there are no examples of well-drafted laws gradually leading to greater restrictions on free speech. Democracies around the world have been applying hate speech laws for decades and, while the rate of prosecutions may fluctuate in different countries and at different times, there has been no general trend toward greater and broader application of these laws.[36] This argument is also unconvincing politically and legally. Courts in democracies are capable of interpreting hate speech laws reasonably consistently.

## B. *Are Hate Speech Laws Effective?*

A more serious objection is that hate speech laws are ineffective in combating racism and in promoting equality. Prosecutions, the argument goes, are as likely to create martyrs and to provide a powerful platform for the dissemination of racist ideas as they are actually to reduce the level and potency of racist speech.[37] Proper examination of this question takes us into an area of social science research that is beyond the scope of this chapter.

Two comments are, however, relevant. First, it is necessary to be clear as to the social evil, or evils, that hate speech laws purport to address before we can

---

[33] A review of the statements protesting undue restrictions on freedom of expression found on IFEX (www.ifex.org), the leading Internet site for such statements, demonstrates this.

[34] Normally, a range of problems underpin abuse of laws, such as an absence of the rule of law.

[35] Jean-Francois Gaudreault-DesBiens describes the slippery slope and similar arguments as "intellectual sponges," draining complexity from the analysis. Gaudreault-DesBiens, *supra* note 10, at 132.

[36] *See, e.g., Striking a Balance: Hate Speech, Freedom of Expression and Non-discrimination* (Sandra Coliver ed., ARTICLE 19 and University of Essex 1992).

[37] A possible example of this was the conviction in Austria in 2006 of David Irving, a well-known Holocaust denier. His conviction generated a vibrant discussion on the Internet, including through racist Web sites.

assess whether or not they are effective. It would appear to be uncontroversial that the social evils go beyond violence or racist acts; even those who would limit restrictions on speech to incitement to those results would acknowledge as much. Although governments must take steps to address racist physical attacks and acts of discrimination, the impact of hate speech is far more extensive than that.

Racism seriously undermines substantive equality in a host of different, and sometimes subtle, ways. The invidiousness of someone from a racial group being exposed to virulent hate speech, and the impact of this on that person's ability to enjoy equality in society, are among the targets of hate speech laws. Such speech is grossly degrading and represents a direct attack on the very humanity of its targets. Indeed, being targeted by hate speech is arguably more harmful than invasions of privacy or personal defamations. As a result, if hate speech laws do in fact limit the prevalence and scope of hate speech, that is in itself an important social good. When assessing the effectiveness of hate speech laws, we must also assess whether they contribute positively to protect equality in this more profound sense rather than just preventing racist attacks. The very act of social condemnation of such speech – a form of support and solidarity with the victims – helps mitigate the negative impacts of such speech on them.

Second, criminal hate speech laws serve as a normative statement of our collective values. They stand for the proposition that the society that has adopted them considers expressions of racial hatred to be an attack on equality, which undermines the ability of the target group to attain full equality, and which will not, therefore, be tolerated. It represents a moral statement of what we as a society believe in and is an expression of solidarity with the targets of hate speech. As Kretzmer argues, a society committed to equality cannot remain silent in the face of such attacks on equality.[38]

## III. A CRITIQUE OF INTERPRETATION BY INTERNATIONAL COURTS

The final section of this chapter assesses problem areas in the balancing of Articles 19 and 20(2) of the ICCPR, and their regional analogues, by international courts and others. As noted earlier, two interpretive problems are prominent, relating, respectively, to hate speech itself (or, more properly, to hatred) and to incitement.

### A. *What Is Hatred?*

What actually constitutes hatred has received very little attention from international courts or in authoritative standard-setting statements.[39] This is not a simple matter.

---

[38] David Kretzmer, "Freedom of Speech and Racism," 8 *Cardozo L. Rev.* 445, 456 (1987).

[39] Article 20 actually refers to "hostility" as the proscribed result, along with violence and discrimination, but this may be because it employs the term "hatred" earlier on to qualify the type of advocacy covered. Regardless, I treat these as closely related notions.

Attitudes potentially falling within its scope range from soft negative stereotypes, which most of us harbor in one form or another, to active dislike based on race, to the more extreme emotions that we normally associate with the word "hatred." Where, exactly, on this spectrum the emotion becomes hatred, for purposes of international law, is far from clear.

Most of the relevant instruments, including the ICCPR, do not define the term. Some do include a definition, but one that is circular. For example, the Council of the European Union's draft Proposal for a Framework Decision on Combating Certain Forms and Expressions of Racism and Xenophobia by Means of Criminal Law defines "hatred" as: "hatred based on race, colour, religion, descent or national or ethnic origin."[40] For the most part, international courts simply do not discuss the issue at all.[41] One exception is the International Criminal Tribunal for Rwanda, which, in *Prosecutor v. Nahimana, Barayagwiz and Ngeze*, defined hate speech as "stereotyping of ethnicity combined with its denigration."[42] The combination of these two elements – stereotyping and denigration – is probably necessary but clearly not sufficient to describe hate speech. Indeed, the Tribunal itself gives an example of a statement – that 70 percent of Rwandan taxis were owned by Tutsis – which would probably qualify as both stereotypical and derogatory, at least in that context, which was characterized by a high degree of ethnic tension, but which the Tribunal specifically recognized as not being hate speech. More generally, identification of stereotypical cultural characteristics of various groups, both positive and negative, is often a perfectly legitimate exercise of free speech. An example is the popular jokes about cultures or races, which, although sometimes in bad taste, are universally understood to be protected speech.

It is perfectly possible to formulate a better definition of what constitutes hatred. For example, the Canadian Supreme Court has defined it as follows:

> Hatred is predicated on destruction, and hatred against identifiable groups and therefore thrives on insensitivity, bigotry and destruction of both the target group and of the values of our society. Hatred in this sense is a most extreme emotion that belies reason; an emotion that, if exercised against members of an identifiable

---

[40]  Decision 2008/913/JHA of Nov. 28, 2008. Preamble, ¶ 9. Recommendation No. R(97)20 of the Committee of Ministers of the Council of Europe on "Hate Speech," Oct. 30, 1997, is slightly more satisfactory, defining "hate speech" as "all forms of expression which spread, incite, promote or justify racial hatred, xenophobia, antisemitism or other forms of hatred based on intolerance, including: intolerance expressed by aggressive nationalism and ethnocentrism, discrimination and hostility against minorities, migrants and people of immigrant origin." *Id.*, Appendix, under Scope.

[41]  Technically, they are often not required to. For example, when cases come before them alleging a breach of the right to freedom of expression, they are required to assess the restriction, which may be justified by reference to equality or public order needs, rather than define "hatred." At the same time, given the necessary implications of Article 20 in such cases, at least for the UN Human Rights Committee, it seems odd that the term should not have received more attention.

[42]  Dec. 3, 2003, ICTR-99–52-T (Trial Chamber), ¶ 1021.

group, implies that those individuals are to be despised, scorned, denied respect and made subject to ill-treatment on the basis of group affiliation.[43]

A better definition of hate speech would help promote more consistent application of Article 20(2) (and hence Article 19 in relevant cases). It would also require courts to be more rigorous in their analysis in such cases, leading to more careful reasoning and probably greater protection for freedom of expression, because currently these courts appear to rely on a very wide definition of hatred.

### B. *What is Incitement?*

International courts, with some exceptions, have also failed to elaborate on the meaning of incitement. Instead, they have tended to refer selectively to a hodgepodge of notions such as intent, tone or style, and truth. In doing so, they often appear to be establishing that they understand the speech in question to be racist, not that it qualified as incitement. They do sometimes refer to the likelihood of a given statement promoting a proscribed result, such as anti-Semitism, but normally only in the most general way, rather than undertaking a specific assessment of whether or not it incited that result.

It is perfectly possible to define incitement, and to define it narrowly as requiring a close nexus between the statements and the engendering of the proscribed result, which, pursuant to Article 20(2) of the ICCPR, is violence, discrimination, or hostility. Courts have successfully done this in other contexts, such as public disorder, crime, or violence. In *Brandenburg v. Ohio*, for example, the U.S. Supreme Court held that the First Amendment prohibits restrictions on advocacy of crime, "except where such advocacy is directed to inciting or producing imminent lawless action and is likely to incite or produce such action."[44] Similar standards on what constitutes incitement could also be applied in the context of hate speech.

### IV. CONCLUSION

This chapter has not addressed the political question of whether it is possible to get states to agree on consistent criminal prohibitions of hate speech. That would clearly represent a huge, perhaps insurmountable, challenge. But it answers the antecedent questions – whether international law provides a consistent policy framework in this area and, if so, whether this framework can withstand some of the critiques that may be leveled at it – with a tentative "yes."

The answer is yes because the language of Articles 19 and 20(2), on their face, do provide for a potentially consistent framework, which would address some of the

---

[43] *Keegstra*, *supra* note 24, Part VII(D)(iii)(a) (Dickson, C.J.).
[44] 395 U.S. 444, 447 (1969).

concerns about the impact of hate speech laws on freedom of expression. The "yes" is tentative for a number of reasons, including the fact that international courts have not yet developed a legally consistent interpretive approach that appropriately reconciles the goals of Article 20(2) and those of Article 19. So, a consistent international-law framework for hate speech laws is possible but has, so far, proven to be elusive.

# 23

# State-Sanctioned Incitement to Genocide

## *The Responsibility to Prevent*

### *Irwin Cotler*

Genocide is the most destructive threat known to humankind. It is the ultimate crime against humanity – the unspeakable crime whose name one should shudder to mention; a horrific and unspeakable act whereby incitement – often sanctioned and effected by state officials themselves – transforms hatred into catastrophe.

Universal condemnation of genocide brought the international community together in 1948 to draft the Convention on the Prevention and Punishment of the Crime of Genocide.[1] To this day, the *Genocide Convention* holds a unique place in international law. Its prohibition of genocide and related international obligations are recognized as compelling and overriding law, binding all states in the international community regardless of whether they signed and ratified the Convention itself or not (*jus cogens*). Indeed, the Convention articulates and establishes obligations owed by all members of the international community to all members of the international community (*obligatio erga omnes*).[2] The objective of the Convention is as clear as it is compelling: that State Parties to the Convention are obliged to prevent and to punish genocide – the pinnacle of human criminality.[3] The obligation to punish genocide does not extend simply to the physical acts of carrying out genocide, but also to the acts involved in the orchestration and organization of genocide – acts that create the climate of hatred necessary for the genocide to take place. Accordingly, Article 3(c) of the Convention expressly prohibits direct and public incitement to genocide. With this prohibition, the international community has recognized that incitement is both precondition to, and indicator of, genocide. Targeting incitement in the *Genocide Convention* speaks to both intertwined principles of a *responsibility to prevent* and a *responsibility to punish* genocide.

---

[1] Convention on the Prevention and Punishment of the Crime of Genocide, G.A. Res. 260 (III) A, U.N. GAOR, Dec. 9, 1948, hereinafter cited as *Genocide Convention*.

[2] *See* Reservations to the Convention on Genocide, Advisory Opinion: 1951 I.C.J. Reports 15, 23. *See also* Re Barcelona Traction, Light and Power Co. Ltd., 1970 I.C.J. Reports 3, ¶¶ 33–34.

[3] *Genocide Convention, supra* note 1, art. 1.

Tragically, in the decades since that Convention was signed, the world has been witness two further genocides in the Balkans and in Rwanda, in addition to the genocide by attrition in Darfur, where the first genocide of the twenty-first century continues to this day. The ultimate horror of these unspeakable genocides is that they were preventable. Nobody could say that we did not know; we knew but we did not act.

Indeed, the enduring lesson of the Holocaust and the genocides since is that genocide occurs not simply because of the machinery of death, but because of the state-sanctioned incitement to hate. It is this teaching of contempt, this demonizing of the "other" – this is where it all begins. As the Supreme Court of Canada recognized:

> The repetition of the loathsome messages of Nazi propaganda led in cruel and rapid succession from the breaking of the shop windows of Jewish merchants to the dispossession of the Jews from their property and their professions, to the establishment of concentration camps and gas chambers. The genocidal horrors of the Holocaust were made possible by the deliberate incitement of hatred against the Jewish and other minority peoples.[4]

After the genocides in Rwanda and the former Yugoslavia, the International Criminal Tribunal for Rwanda (ICTR) and the International Criminal Tribunal for the former Yugoslavia (ICTY) were established to hold accountable those individuals who were responsible for these horrific human tragedies. These tribunals have echoed the words of the Supreme Court of Canada in recognizing that *genocide begins with words*: The founding statutes of both the ICTR and the ICTY make direct and public incitement to genocide punishable as an offense in its own right.[5] Moreover, these statutes recognize the unique *jus cogens* and *obligation erga omnes* characteristics of the prohibition against genocide and its incitement by removing any possible head-of-state immunity for these crimes. Nonetheless, because such international tribunals are created to mete out justice once genocide has already occurred, they remain incapable of addressing genocidal threats before their destructive effects are wrought.

The preventative measures available through the *Genocide Convention* and the *Charter of the United Nations* are established in international law and ought not remain ignored in practice. Indeed, more than a half-century before the Security Council recognized the Responsibility to Protect (R2P) principle,[6] the *Genocide Convention* had already confirmed a responsibility to prevent principle with respect to genocide.[7]

---

4   *See* R. v. Andrews, [1990] 3 S.C.R. 870, 1990 CanLII 25 (S.C.C.), at 14.
5   Statute of the International Tribunal for Rwanda art. 2(3)(c), Nov. 8, 1994; Statute of the International Criminal Tribunal for the former Yugoslavia art. 4(3)(c), amended May 17, 2002.
6   *See* S.C. Res. 1674 ¶ 4, U.N. SCOR, 5430th meeting, (Apr. 28, 2006).
7   *Genocide Convention, supra* note 1.

For these instruments of justice – and not after-the-fact prosecutions, however important they may be – are the ones that will save lives before they are taken. As the UN High Commissioner for Human Rights, Navanethem Pillay, lamented, the *Genocide Convention* – along with the *Universal Declaration of Human Rights* – "grew out of the Holocaust, but we have yet to learn the lesson of the Holocaust, as genocide continues."[8] Indeed, the UN General Assembly was told bluntly, in September 2008:

> The [Genocide] Convention was born out of the desire to prevent recurrence of genocide, yet it failed to achieve this purpose on several occasions thereafter. The rallying cry "Never again!" can only be used so often before it loses credibility.[9]

In this context, the present article reviews the legal approaches to preventing genocide by addressing incitement to genocide, including: first, from an evidentiary perspective, the role that incitement plays in the genocide-fostering process is analyzed; second, from a juridical perspective, the mechanisms that exist in international law to take action against genocide are considered; third, specific legal principles and international and domestic jurisprudence confirming the specific evil – and criminality – of genocidal incitement are presented; and finally, the state-sanctioned incitement to genocide that emerges from contemporary Iran is provided as a case study in illegal hate speech – a case study that both highlights the impunity with which the legal prohibition on incitement to genocide is presently ignored and underscores the necessity to act.

## INCITEMENT TO GENOCIDE AS A COMPONENT
## OF THE GENOCIDAL PROCESS

Genocide is a crime almost unfathomable in its cruelty and its scale. As defined in the *Genocide Convention*, "genocide" covers five acts:[10]

1. killing members of a group;
2. causing serious bodily or mental harm to members of a group;
3. deliberately inflicting on a group conditions of life calculated to bring about its physical destruction in whole or in part;
4. imposing measures intended to prevent births within a group;
5. forcibly transferring children of a group to another group.

---

[8] "New UN rights chief stresses need to tackle discrimination, prevent genocide," *UN News Centre*, Sept. 8 2008, *available at* http://www.un.org/apps/news/story.asp?NewsID=27963&Cr=Pillay&Cr1.

[9] "Tackling impunity key to success of International Criminal Court – Liechtenstein," *UN News Centre*, Sept. 29, 2008, *available at* http://www.un.org/apps/news/story.asp?NewsID=28348&Cr=General+Assembly&Cr1=debate&Kw1=tackling+impunity&Kw2=&Kw3=#.

[10] *Genocide Convention, supra* note 1, art. 2.

As heinous as these acts are in themselves, the defining feature of genocide comes from its mental element: that the acts are "committed with intent to destroy, in whole or in part, a national, ethnical, racial or religious group."[11]

Genocide, then, is not at all indiscriminate. To the contrary, it is calculated. It involves the conscious and deliberate will to annihilate – to exterminate – a people.

As such, genocide is effectively impossible to perpetrate against victims that appear, to the *genocidaires*, as *human* – as moral entities deserving of life. Genocide scholar Helen Fein notes that potential victims of genocide must be seen in the minds of the *genocidaires* as beyond "the boundaries of the universe of obligation."[12]

Moreover, for a genocide to be effectively carried out, this psychological element must be present in a sufficient number of people to actively perpetrate the physical acts of genocide, as well as a sufficient number of people to acquiesce in the genocide's occurrence. It therefore is sensible to speak of a "genocidal process" through which a society's capacity to engage in genocide is fostered. Genocide is not a spontaneous discrete act. As former U.S. Secretary of State Madeleine Albright and former U.S. Secretary of Defense William Cohen note: "Genocide is not the inevitable result of 'ancient hatreds' or irrational leaders. It requires planning and is carried out systematically."[13]

In this context, addressing incitement to hatred as it leads into incitement to genocide becomes a form of genocide prevention. Albright and Cohen have drafted a "blueprint" for American policy makers on preventing genocide in which they observe that both state-led discrimination and exclusionary ideology have been identified as factors associated with an increased risk of genocide or mass atrocities.[14]

Professor Gregory Stanton develops this idea even further, devising a template of the eight stages of genocide. The initial steps are classifying the victim group as an "other" and developing a system to symbolize such difference. The third step, dehumanization, has a transformative impact:

Classification and symbolization are fundamental operations in all cultures. They become steps of genocide only when combined with dehumanization. Denial of the humanity of others is the step that permits killing with impunity. The universal human abhorrence of murder of members of one's own group is overcome by treating the victims as less than human. In incitements to genocide the target groups are called disgusting animal names – Nazi propaganda called Jews "rats" or "vermin"; Rwandan Hutu hate radio referred to Tutsis as "cockroaches." The

---

[11] *Id.*

[12] Helen Fein, *Accounting for Genocide* 33 (Free Press 1979).

[13] Madeleine Albright and William Cohen, "Leadership key to preventing genocide," *CNN.com*, Dec. 10, 2008, *available at* http://edition.cnn.com/2008/WORLD/europe/12/01/sbm.albright.cohen. commentary.

[14] Madeleine Albright and William Cohen, *Preventing Genocide: A Blueprint for U.S. Policymakers* 25 (United States Holocaust Memorial Museum 2008), *available at* http://www.ushmm.org/conscience/ taskforce/pdf/report.pdf.

targeted group is often likened to a "disease," "microbes," "infections" or a "cancer" in the body politic.[15]

This insight – and the horrific history of genocide that testifies to its truth – has led former Secretary-General of the United Nations, Kofi Annan, to exhort: "We must attack the *roots of violence and genocide*. These are intolerance, racism, tyranny, and the dehumanizing public discourse that denies whole groups of people their dignity and rights."[16]

The former Secretary-General's remarks underscore the fact that as offensive and inflammatory as intolerance, racism, and dehumanizing public discourse are, they also serve as warning signs – early indicators of a genocidal process that can still be stopped.

In this genocidal process, through stereotyping and singling out, dehumanization and demonization, would-be victims of genocide are identified, segregated, and targeted. In the context of these precursors to genocide, genocidal incitement emerges as almost commonplace rather than offensive. The banality of evil is thus set in motion. In turn, the calls themselves become more and more inflammatory. The destruction of the victim population is made to seem natural – even preordained.

Although the genocidal process does not require state support, dehumanization and demonization is arguably most pernicious in its state-sanctioned form. Operating under the cover of the state, the genocidal process obtains an aura of legitimacy as it gains in effectiveness. Few institutions boast the influence, media capabilities, and brute power of the modern state. Incitement to hatred recognized by its audience as being approved by the state – either because it is promulgated through state officials and networks, or because government agencies themselves participate in acts of dehumanization and demonization – demands special concern. Indeed, such "state-sanctioned incitement" has two particular features that make it particularly relevant to the present discussion: first, owing to the massive resources available to the state, state-sanctioned incitement makes genocide a more real threat; second, owing to the *jus cogens* and *erga omnes* character of the prohibition against genocide, state-sanctioned incitement cannot possibly be regarded as an internal matter with which the international community should not interfere. State-sanctioned incitement thus possesses practical and juridical characteristics that distinguish it from non-state-sanctioned incitement, and make the imperative to stop it all the more compelling.

During the period that the genocidal process is ignored or dismissed as mere rhetoric, the would-be *genocidaires* exploit the opportunity to accumulate the means to carry out genocide. Indeed, as Professor Stanton notes, the stage of

---

[15] Gregory H. Stanton, "The Eight Stages of Genocide" (Yale Program in Genocide Studies 1998), *available at* http://www.genocidewatch.org/images/8StagesBriefingpaper.pdf.

[16] Press Release, "Genocide is Threat to Peace Requiring Strong, United Action, Secretary-General tells Stockholm International Forum," SG/SM/9126 (Jan. 26 2004), *available at* http://www.preventgenocide.org/prevent/UNdocs/KofiAnnanStockholmGenocideProposals26Jan2004.htm (emphasis added).

dehumanization comes even before the *genocidaires* plan and organize the genocide. It is success during the stage of dehumanization that effectively empowers the *genocidaires* to continue the process: "Impunity breeds contempt for law, and emboldens genocidists, who can literally get away with murder."[17]

Despite the elaborate effort to orchestrate the genocide, would-be *genocidaires* are equally consistent in establishing a narrative that denies the intent or imminence of widespread destruction.[18] Indeed, with all other conditions in place, the would-be *genocidaires* thus deny the reality that they have started down the road to genocide, implicitly recognizing that the international community that is outside the dehumanizing and demonizing process – the genocidal web of hate – would vehemently object to such genocidal intentions. Accordingly, the world finds itself duped into complicity until it is too late.

For the international community, the psychological effect of this protracted genocide-fostering process is that genocide never appears to be imminent. A false sense of security takes hold, as despite the objective warnings, it always feels as if no preventative action need be taken immediately. The would-be *genocidaires'* constant denials prey on this false hope, offering the world a reason to stand back. The seeds of hate, planted years ago, are ignored, sanitized, or dismissed as unimportant, even though they will soon morph into tragedy; the physical threat of harm, which is proceeding apace, is dismissed as a fiction precisely because it has not yet materialized. Indeed, because the genocide has not occurred, the international community continues to proclaim there is no genocide – thus ignoring the genocidal path that has been embarked on and the responsibility to prevent before it is too late.

It is during this genocide-fostering period that the possibility of genocide transforms into reality. At a certain point, the *genocidaires'* incitement to hatred will have rendered the victims' dehumanization and demonization so natural to the general population that overt incitement to genocide can follow without much notice. The stage will be set for physical violence.

Incitement to genocide can therefore be regarded as the "port of last call" for the *genocidaires* before they arrive at the physical genocide itself. It marks the transition between the genocide-fostering process and the carrying out of genocide. As such, it is rightly the object of prohibition in the *Genocide Convention* because it is not mere background noise to the genocide – it is its opening stage.

The problem arises when one is asked to dissect the transition from incitement to hatred (which is part of the genocide-fostering process and is the object of prohibition *qua* hate propaganda in international treaties,[19] but is not prohibited in the *Genocide*

---

[17] Stanton, *supra* note 15.

[18] Professor Stanton explains that "[e]very genocide is followed by denial." *Id.* The events in Darfur, however, where the horror of genocide has been drawn out for more than five years under the world's watch, confirm that denial does not only take place after the genocide is over.

[19] *See* International Convention on the Elimination of All Forms of Racial Discrimination art. 4; International Covenant on Civil and Political Rights art. 20(2).

*Convention* itself) and incitement to genocide. Even in retrospect, such analysis is difficult because of the seamless transition from one stage of the genocidal process to the next. This difficulty, however, does not make the exercise any less necessary, as genocidal incitement is a unique crime in international law that straddles the line between punishing genocide and preventing its occurrence.

Indeed, after the genocide-fostering process is complete, the only remaining step is for the tragedy to actually unfold. It is during this developmental stage that the international community must learn to act. Once the genocide-fostering process nears an end, solutions short of military intervention will be almost impossible to implement.[20] Toward this end, the present article covers both the academic and practical aspects of prevention: The following two sections elaborate the juridical imperative to prevent genocide and to punish incitement in international law, respectively; the final section uses the example of contemporary Iran to illustrate the subtle transition from incitement to hate to incitement to genocide, and to call on the international community to act.

## PREVENTING GENOCIDE IN INTERNATIONAL LAW

After sixty years, the *Genocide Convention* remains the bedrock international legal treaty on preventing genocide. The First Article of the Convention attaches legal significance to the moral imperative of preventing genocide by stating: "The Contracting Parties confirm that *genocide*, whether committed in time of peace or in time of war, *is a crime under international law which they undertake to prevent* and to punish."[21]

The *Genocide Convention* thus declared that the international community could no longer acquiesce in genocide. It expressly imposed the obligation on its signatories to take action to prevent genocide. As then-High Commissioner for Human Rights Louise Arbour stated:

> [U]nder the Genocide Convention and its norms, which have been incorporated into international customary law, *States have a duty to prevent genocide.* . . .
>
> *[T]he prevention of genocide is a legal obligation*, and it is a justiciable obligation that one State effectively owes to the citizens of another State, outside its own territory.[22]

The effect of Article 1 extends beyond even the impressive list of State Parties to the Convention itself. Indeed, the preventative purpose of Article 1 has been elevated to a peremptory norm of international law – *jus cogens* – with the effect that no State,

[20] As Professor Stanton states, once the preparation stage is over, "[e]xtermination whether carried out by governments or by patterned mob violence, can only be stopped by force." Stanton, *supra* note 15.
[21] *Genocide Convention, supra* note 1 (emphasis added).
[22] Louise Arbour, UN High Commissioner for Human Rights, "The Responsibility to Protect as a Duty of Care in International Law and Practice," Address at Trinity College, Dublin (Nov. 23, 2007) (transcript available at http://www.unhchr.ch/huricane/huricane.nsf/o/ 5F1298CB9E6043BEC125739C0058FB02?opendocument).

whether signatory to the *Genocide Convention* or not, may ignore its mandatory nature.[23]

The obligation to take action to prevent genocide is also recognized as an obligation *erga omnes*: It is a responsibility owed to all members of the international community.[24] The combination of the *jus cogens* and *erga omnes* principles implies that the obligation to take action to prevent genocide in international law is overriding. Every state must prevent genocide, it must do so on behalf of every potential victim, and every state in the community of nations can hold its neighbors to account for their failure to join in upholding this obligation.

The International Court of Justice has explained that the "obligation on each contracting State to prevent genocide is both normative and compelling."[25] It elaborated that this obligation means that state parties must "employ all means reasonably available to them, so as to prevent genocide so far as possible."[26] Further, this obligation – "and the corresponding duty to act" – will arise not simply when genocide is on the cusp of materializing, but rather "at the instant that the State learns of, or should normally have learned of, the existence of a serious risk that genocide will be committed."[27]

The obligation to prevent genocide in the *Genocide Convention* dovetails with more recent international efforts to confirm the responsibility that all States have in the family of nations. The R2P movement, for instance, moves states away from the absolute paradigm of state sovereignty and toward a more nuanced one that recognizes their obligations to their own populations and, more generally, to those at risk of mass-atrocity crimes elsewhere.[28]

United Nations Secretary-General Ban Ki-moon describes R2P as "the obligation accepted by all States to act collectively, through the Security Council, when a population is threatened with genocide, ethnic cleansing or crimes against humanity."[29] Indeed, by its reference to the 2005 World Summit Outcome Document, the Security Council has confirmed not only the responsibility of states to take action to prevent genocide, but also its own responsibility to prevent the incitement that is a condition and indicator of genocide:

> Each individual State has the responsibility to protect its populations from genocide, war crimes, ethnic cleansing and crimes against humanity. *This responsibility entails the prevention of such crimes, including their incitement, through appropriate and*

---

[23] *See Reservations to the Convention on Genocide, supra* note 2; *see also* J.-Maurice Arbour, *Droit international public* 36 (Éditions Yvon Blais, 3rd ed. 1997).

[24] *Barcelona Traction, Light and Power Co., supra* note 2.

[25] Application of the Convention on the Prevention and Punishment of the Crime of Genocide (Bosn. & Herz v. Serb. & Montenegro), 1996 I.C.J. 595 (case no. 91), ¶ 427 (Feb. 26, 2007).

[26] *Id.* at ¶ 430.

[27] *Id.* at ¶ 431.

[28] *See* Gareth Evans, "A strong and principled basis for response," *Globe and Mail*, Nov. 29, 2008, *available at* http://www.theglobeandmail.com/news/opinions/article725070.ece.

[29] Ban Ki-moon, U.N. Secretary-General, SG/SM/11495, AFR/1674, Apr. 4, 2008, *available at* http://www.un.org/News/Press/docs/2008/sgsm11495.doc.htm.

*necessary means.* We accept that responsibility and will act in accordance with it. *The international community should, as appropriate, encourage and help States to exercise this responsibility and support the United Nations in establishing an early warning capability.*[30]

The responsibility to protect is particularly compelling and accentuated where the danger of indifference and inaction is greatest – as in the case of genocide – and where the probability of the danger materializing is most pronounced. As the leading expert on the responsibility to protect, Gareth Evans, has explained, a true "R2P situation" is one "where genocide, or ethnic cleansing, or other crimes against humanity, or war crimes were either actually occurring or could foreseeably occur at some time in the future – immediate, medium term or long term – unless appropriate preventive measures are taken."[31]

The responsibility to prevent genocide is therefore underpinned not only by the text of the *Genocide Convention* – itself elevated to a *jus cogens* norm of international law – but also by the emerging R2P doctrine as endorsed by the Security Council. Yet the problem in preventing genocide has never been the argument that this obligation does not exist; it has been the practical difficulty in convincing state actors to respond to their acknowledged legal and moral imperative. For that reason, the corpus of international law is replete with jurisprudence condemning genocidal incitement in the context of genocidal murder – but is silent on the application of these anti-incitement principles as mechanisms of prevention.

## INCITEMENT TO GENOCIDE IN INTERNATIONAL LAW

The legal basis for prohibiting and prosecuting incitement to genocide in international law is well-established. True to its ideal of both preventing and punishing genocide, the *Genocide Convention* was the first international treaty to prohibit "[d]irect and public incitement to commit genocide."[32]

Notably, the unqualified wording of the Convention makes it clear that direct and public incitement to genocide is punishable whether or not it can be shown to have caused the commission of genocide. This wording was specifically deliberated on by the drafters of the Convention and accords with the preventative purpose elaborated in Article 1 thereof. The international community does not need to wait for actual genocide to transpire before taking action to respond to its warning signs, including incitement.[33] The crime of "incitement" therefore contrasts specifically

---

[30] Referenced in S/RES 1674 (2006) (emphasis added).

[31] Gareth Evans, "Preventing Mass Atrocities: Making the Responsibility to Protect a Reality," Keynote Address to the United Nations University/International Crisis Group Conference on "Prevention of Mass Atrocities: From Mandate to Realisation" (Oct. 10, 2007) (transcript available at http://www.gevans.org/speeches/speech241.html).

[32] *Genocide Convention, supra* note 1, art. 3.

[33] *See Bosn. & Herz v. Serb. & Montenegro, supra* note 25, at ¶ 431.

with "instigation" in international law, the latter being punishable only when it leads to the actual commission of the offense intended by the instigator.[34]

Direct and public incitement to genocide has formed the basis of criminal convictions at the ICTR, pursuant to Article 2(3)(c) and 6(1) of the ICTR Statute, and the tribunal's treatment of these cases is largely responsible for building the edifice of modern international legal jurisprudence on the subject.[35] This jurisprudence emphasizes the gravity with which this offense is to be treated, even if there is no evidence that the incitement led to any loss of life. The mere potential for genocide, as intended by the inciter, suffices to justify the criminalization of incitement per se: "[G]enocide clearly falls within the category of crimes so serious that direct and public incitement to commit such a crime must be punished as such, even where such incitement failed to produce the result expected by the perpetrator."[36]

The foundational decision is the *Akayesu* case,[37] the source of the preceding quote. Jean-Paul Akayesu, a commune bourgmestre (equivalent to a mayor) and former teacher in Rwanda, was charged with incitement to genocide. On April 19, 1994, Akayesu led a gathering of more than 100 people assembled around the dead body of a young Hutu. He urged the population to unite in order to eliminate the Tutsi, which he referred to using a derogatory term and called the sole enemy. Akayesu even read out a list of names of individuals, whom he identified as being accomplices of the Rwandan Patriotic Front (which defended the Tutsi).

In analyzing the crime of incitement to genocide, the trial chamber specifically noted the role that such speech plays in the genocide-fostering process:

> At the time the Convention on Genocide was adopted, the delegates agreed to expressly spell out direct and public incitement to commit genocide as a specific crime, in particular, *because of its critical role in the planning of a genocide*, with the delegate from the USSR stating in this regard that, "It was impossible that hundreds of thousands of people should commit so many crimes unless they had been incited to do so and unless the crimes had been premeditated and carefully organized."[38]

The ICTR found Akayesu guilty of inciting to genocide and, in so doing, elaborated three necessary components to the crime of incitement to genocide: the *mens*

---

[34] *See* The Prosecutor v. Ferdinand Nahimana, Jean-Bosco Barayagwiza, Hassan Ngeze, Case No. ICTR-99–52-A, Appeals Judgment, ¶ 678 (Nov. 28 2007). *See also* Wibke K. Timmerman, "Incitement in International Criminal Law," 88 *Int'l Rev. of the Red Cross* 823, 832–40 (2006).

[35] Note, however, that the concept of punishing those who engage in direct and public incitement to genocide pre-dates the ICTR significantly. *See, e.g.*, the Case of Julius Streicher, 22 Nuremberg Proceedings 502, *available at* http://avalon.law.yale.edu/imt/09-30-46.asp.

[36] Prosecutor v. Akayesu, Case no. ICTR-96–4-T, Judgment, ¶ 562 (Sept. 2, 1998).

[37] The *Akayesu* trial judgment was affirmed on appeal, June 1, 2001. The Trial Chamber decision remains a cornerstone precedent in international incitement law: *see, e.g.*, Mugesera v. Canada (Minister of Citizenship and Immigration), [2005] 2 S.C.R. 100, ¶¶ 84, 86, 88 (Can.); Prosecutor v. Bikindi, Case no. ICTR-01–72-T, Judgment, ¶ 387 (Dec. 2, 2008).

[38] *Akayesu, supra* note 36, at ¶ 151 (emphasis added).

*rea* element, the "public" element, and the "directness" element. Hateful speech not satisfying these elements, though potentially heinous and inflammatory, is not covered by the prohibition in the ICTR Statute.

The *mens rea* element of the crime immediately distinguishes it from protected speech. Indeed, the mental component of incitement to genocide alone suffices to ensure that legitimate expression will not be caught by the prohibition. The Trial Chamber explained that:

> The mens rea required for the crime of direct and public incitement to commit genocide lies in the intent to directly prompt or provoke another to commit genocide. It implies a desire on the part of the perpetrator to create by his actions a particular state of mind necessary to commit such a crime in the minds of the person(s) he is so engaging. That is to say that *the person who is inciting to commit genocide must have himself the specific intent to commit genocide*, namely, to destroy, in whole or in part, a national, ethnical, racial or religious group, as such.[39]

The "public" element of the speech depends in large part on the forum in which the comments are aired. The Trial Chamber referred to a line of authority that interpreted "public" to mean spoken in a public place, as well as the International Law Commission characterization of "public incitement" as occurring where there is "a call for criminal action to a number of individuals in a public place or to members of the general public at large by such means as the mass media, for example, radio or television."[40]

Finally, the "directness" element is satisfied where the incitement "specifically provoke[s] another," as contrasted with "mere vague or indirect suggestion."[41] The Trial Chamber took care to emphasize that the incitement must be viewed "in the light of its cultural and linguistic content," and that it would determine this question by "focusing mainly on the issue of whether the persons for whom the message was intended immediately grasped the implication thereof."[42]

Later case law also stressed the need to understand comments in context to determine whether they constitute "incitement." The ICTR has explained that context alone can define the line between hateful rhetoric and illegal incitement:

> A statement of ethnic generalization provoking resentment against members of that ethnicity would have a heightened impact in the context of a genocidal environment. It would be more likely to lead to violence. At the same time the environment would be an indicator that incitement to violence was the intent of the statement.[43]

---

[39] *Id.* ¶ 560 (emphasis added).
[40] *Id.* ¶ 556.
[41] *Id.* ¶ 557.
[42] *Id.* ¶¶ 557–558.
[43] Prosecutor v. Nahimana, Barayagwiza and Ngeze (*Media Case*), Case No. ICTR-99–62-T, Judgment and Sentence, ¶1022 (Dec. 3, 2003). The Appeals Chamber affirmed the importance of context in evaluating incitement in its judgment in the same case ¶¶ 697, 701 and 703 (Nov. 28, 2007).

Accordingly, just as incitement contributes to the genocidal process as described previously, the existence of this larger process will inform the legal analysis of the incitement.

In the *Ruggiu* case,[44] context was analyzed for a slightly different purpose – not to understand its intended impact, but simply to understand its intended meaning. This inquiry was necessary because of the accused's use of euphemism. In rendering its decision after Georges Ruggiu pled guilty to incitement to genocide, the Trial Chamber explained not only how Ruggiu's phrases were spoken, but, more importantly, how they were understood. Notably, the tribunal alluded to how the meaning of phrases could change over time:

> The accused acknowledges that the widespread use of the term "Inyenzi" conferred the de facto meaning of "persons to be killed." Within the context of the civil war in 1994, the term "Inyenzi" became synonymous with the term "Tutsi." The accused acknowledges that the word "Inyenzi," as used in a socio-political context, came to designate the Tutsis as "persons to be killed." . . .
>
> The accused admits that as part of the move to appeal for, or encourage, "civil defence," he made a public broadcast to the population on several occasions to "go to work." The phrase "go to work" is a literal translation of the Rwandan expression that Phocas Habimana, Manager of the RTLM, expressly instructed the accused to use during his broadcasts. With time, this expression came to clearly signify "go fight against members of the RPF and their accomplices." With the passage of time, the expression came to mean, "go kill the Tutsis and Hutu political opponents of the interim government."[45]

The principle that euphemism cannot exculpate a *genocidaire* was again affirmed in what has become known as the *Media Case*.[46] In this decision, the ICTR elaborated the analysis to pursue in determining whether hateful speech regarding race, ethnicity, and nationality falls under the banner of legitimate expression or criminal advocacy. Professor Gregory Gordon has distilled from the tribunal's decision four specific elements useful in analyzing allegedly inciteful content: purpose, text, context, and the relation of the speaker to the subject.[47]

With regard to purpose, the determining factor is whether the intent "in publicly transmitting the material was of a *bona fide* nature (e.g., historical research, the dissemination of news and information, the public accountability of government authorities)."[48] For instance, the tribunal reviewed case law to the effect that when an interviewer takes care to distance himself from the remarks of his interview

[44] Prosecutor v. Ruggiu, Case No. ICTR-97–21-I, Judgment and Sentence (June, 1, 2000).

[45] *Id.* ¶¶ 44(iii)–(iv).

[46] *Media Case, supra* note 43.

[47] *See* Gregory Gordon, "From Incitement to Indictment?: Prosecuting Iran's President for Advocating Israel's Destruction and Piecing Together Incitement Law's Emerging Analytical Framework," 98 *J. Crim. L. & Criminology* 853, 874–8 (2008).

[48] *Media Case, supra* note 43, ¶ 1001.

subject, it operates as an indicator that the purpose in question was to disseminate news rather than to propagate racist views.[49]

With regard to text, the ICTR referred back to the *Faurisson* case,[50] a decision involving a Holocaust denier in which the UN Human Rights Committee considered the meaning of the term "incitement" at Article 20(2) of the *International Covenant on Civil and Political Rights*.[51] The ICTR noted how the Committee focused on the use of the term "magic gas chamber" in determining that Faurisson was motivated by anti-Semitism and not the pursuit of historical truth.[52]

Examination of context involves analysis of how such language operates in the immediate as well as the historical context. On this point, the tribunal referred to jurisprudence from the European Court of Human Rights emphasizing how a general statement about massacres needs to be understood in the context of the massacres taking place at that time. The ICTR quoted the European Court's statement that, understood as such, the speaker's words were "likely to exacerbate an already explosive situation."[53]

Professor Gordon's fourth factor – the relationship of the speaker to the subject – is based on the Trial Chamber's recognition that "special protections" have been developed in jurisprudence to take into account "the power dynamic inherent in the circumstances that make minority groups and political opposition vulnerable to the exercise of power by the majority or by the government."[54] In other words, a tribunal may be more lax in analyzing a member of a minority group's criticism of the government than a state official criticizing a minority group. Although the Appeals Chamber understandably appeared concerned about the implications of a rule expressed as such,[55] it did ultimately agree with the Trial Chamber's overall analysis.[56]

Two final ICTR decisions on incitement to genocide are noteworthy in the context of the present review. The *Kambanda* case[57] implicated the leader of Rwanda's

---

[49] *Id.* The case being referenced by the Trial Chamber is the *Jersild* case, decided by the European Court of Human Rights: Jersild v. Denmark, 19 Eur. Ct. H.R. 1, 27 (1995).

[50] Faurisson v. France, U.N. Doc. CCPR/C/58/D/550/1993 (1996).

[51] G.A. res. 2200A (XXI), 21 U.N. GAOR Supp. (No. 16) at 52, U.N. Doc. A/6316 (1966), 999 U.N.T.S. 171.

[52] *Media Case, supra* note 43, ¶ 1001.

[53] *Id.,* ¶ 1004. The case being referenced by the Trial Chamber is Zana v. Turkey, 1997-VII Eur. Ct. H. R. 57.

[54] *Media Case, supra* note 43, ¶ 1008.

[55] "The Appeals Chamber has a certain difficulty with these paragraphs. It notes, on the one hand, that the relevant issue is not whether the author of the speech is from the majority ethnic group or supports the government's agenda (and by implication, whether it is necessary to apply a stricter standard), but rather whether the speech in question constitutes direct incitement to commit genocide. On the other hand, it recognises that the political or community affiliation of the author of a speech may be regarded as a contextual element which can assist in its interpretation." *Media Case, supra* note 43, ¶ 713.

[56] *Id.,* ¶ 715.

[57] Prosecutor v. Kambanda, Case No. ICTR 97-23-S, Judgment and Sentence (Sept. 4, 1998).

caretaker government during the genocide (Jean Kambanda) and stands for the principle that nobody – not even heads of state – is above the law against incitement to genocide. Indeed, Kambanda's conviction marked the first conviction in history of a head of state for this crime. Kambanda pled guilty to directly and publicly inciting genocide (among other crimes); the acts for which he was convicted on this charge included encouraging – while on-air himself – a radio station to continue inciting violence, specifically calling it an "indispensable weapon in the fight against the enemy." Kambanda also congratulated individuals who already killed victims, and encouraged massacre when speaking before different audiences.

One judgment that is presently on appeal – the *Bikindi* decision[58] – marks a more recent application of incitement principles by the ICTR. Simon Bikindi was a popular singer in Rwanda and his charge of direct and public incitement to genocide was based both on his songs, which the prosecution argued in themselves satisfied the elements of the crime, and on two speeches he gave over a vehicle's loudspeaker while traveling. The Trial Chamber determined that Bikindi's songs were not illegal incitement per se, but his two speeches were.[59] Interestingly, the Trial Chamber reached this conclusion despite Bikindi's positive personal relationships with Tutsi:

> In reaching its conclusion, the Chamber has considered the evidence that Bikindi's second wife was Tutsi, and that he lived and worked with Tutsi on good terms. It has also considered the evidence that Bikindi assisted some Tutsi during the genocide while in Nyundo and supported some Tutsi while in exile in Zaire. However, the Chamber is of the view that Bikindi's direct and public address on the Kivumu-Kayove road leaves no doubt as to his genocidal intent at the time. Bikindi could not have been unaware of the targeting of Tutsi throughout Rwanda, including Gisenyi préfecture, at the time, a targeting that he had encouraged in the past by exhorting people to kill Tutsi in 1993 in Kivumu. Likewise, he could not have been unaware of the impact that his words would have on the audience, the words of a well-known and popular artist, an authoritative figure for the *Interahamwe* and a man perceived as an influential member of the [National Revolutionary Movement for Development].[60]

---

[58] *Bikindi, supra* note 37.

[59] On the songs, the Trial Chamber held that they "characterised Tutsi as Hutu enslavers, enemies or enemy accomplices, blamed the enemy for the problems in Rwanda, encouraged Hutu solidarity against a common foe, the Tutsi, and finally supported the spirit of the Bahutu Ten Commandments published in *Kangura*." *Id.* ¶ 254. However, despite the finding that the songs were "deployed in a propaganda campaign in 1994 in Rwanda to incite people to attack and kill Tutsi," it did not find "sufficient evidence to conclude beyond reasonable doubt that Bikindi composed these songs with the specific intention to incite such attacks and killings." *Id.* ¶¶ 255 and 421. On the loudspeaker statements, the Trial Chamber wrote: "Bikindi's call on 'the majority' to 'rise up and look everywhere possible' and not to 'spare anybody' immediately referring to the Tutsi as the minority unequivocally constitutes a direct call to destroy the Tutsi ethnic group. Similarly, the Chamber considers that Bikindi's address to the population on his way back from Kayove, asking 'Have you killed the Tutsis here?' and whether they had killed the 'snakes' is a direct call to kill Tutsi, pejoratively referred to as snakes." *Id.* ¶ 423.

[60] *Id.* ¶ 425.

The *Bikindi* case also raised explicitly a tension that underlies many judgments on incitement to genocide: the appropriate balance between freedom of expression and the criminalization of genocidal incitement. Recognizing the right to freedom of expression, the Trial Chamber explained:

> However, this right is not absolute. It is restricted by the very same conventions and international instruments that provide for it. For example, the [*Universal Declaration of Human Rights*] states that everyone should be free from incitement to discrimination. Similarly, the [*International Covenant on Civil and Political Rights*] prohibits war propaganda, as well as the advocacy of national, racial or religious hatred that constitutes incitement to discrimination, hostility, or violence, and the [*International Convention on the Elimination of All Forms of Racial Discrimination*] aims to outlaw all forms of expression that explicitly lead to discrimination. Each of the regional conventions mentioned above also restrict the freedom of expression: the [*European Convention on Human Rights*] recognises that there are "duties and responsibilities" that accompany the freedom of expression and thus limit its application; the [*American Convention on Human Rights*] allows for legal liability regarding acts that harm the rights or reputations of others, or that threaten the protection of national security, public order, or public health or morals and considers as offences punishable by law any propaganda for war and advocacy of national, racial or religious hatred that constitute incitements to lawless violence; and the [*African Charter on Human and People's Rights*] restricts the right to that which is "within the law." The Chamber notes that the restrictions on this right have been interpreted in the jurisprudence of the various adjudicating bodies created from the international and regional instruments above. The Chamber also notes that a large number of countries have banned the advocacy of discriminatory hate in their domestic legislation.[61]

In fact, among those countries banning the advocacy of discriminatory hate in their domestic legislation is Canada. The Canadian laws on hate propaganda have passed scrutiny under the *Charter of Rights and Freedoms* by the Supreme Court of Canada.[62] And recently, the Supreme Court had the opportunity to examine the offense of incitement to genocide directly.

In the watershed *Mugesera* decision (in which I was involved as then Minister of Justice and Attorney General of Canada),[63] the Supreme Court considered the validity of a deportation order issued against Léon Mugesera. Mugesera was a formerly active member of a hard-line Hutu political party who incited to murder, genocide, and hatred in a speech to 1,000 people; after fleeing from Rwanda, Mugesera successfully applied for Canadian permanent residency. The Supreme Court

---

[61] *Id.* ¶ 380.
[62] *See* R. v. Keegstra, [1990] 3 S.C.R. 697 (Can.); *Andrews, supra* note 4; Canada (Human Rights Commission) v. Taylor, [1990] 3 S.C.R. 892 (Can.).
[63] *Mugesera, supra* note 37.

upheld the deportation order that was issued against Mugesera when the government discovered his past incitement, holding that his speech rendered him inadmissible to Canada.

Relying substantially on international jurisprudence, the Court in *Mugesera* lent its support to the principles on incitement to genocide established by the ICTR, including the proposition that it is not necessary to establish a causal link between the incitement and genocidal acts that followed (if any).[64] This point is crucial not only to the prosecution of past incidents of incitement to genocide, but equally in the prevention of future cases of genocide. The bottom line – echoed now in both Canadian and international legal jurisprudence – is that the world need not wait until genocide has occurred to take action against those who seek to provoke it. To the contrary, through the dual obligations to prevent genocide and punish incitement to genocide, international law mandates juridical action even before any physical acts of genocide have begun.

Holding those who incite to genocide responsible for their crimes under international law, even before the genocides they preach have materialized, has the potential to be an effective juridical tool in combating genocide. This insight finds particular application in the case of contemporary Iran.

## IRAN: A CASE STUDY IN STATE-SANCTIONED INCITEMENT TO GENOCIDE

In President Mahmoud Ahmadinejad's Iran,[65] one finds the toxic convergence of the advocacy of the most horrific of crimes embedded in the most virulent of hatreds. It is dramatized by the parading in the streets of Teheran of a Shihab-3 missile draped in the words "Israel must be wiped off the map"[66] while the assembled thousands are exhorted to chants of "Death to Israel."[67] Moreover, Ahmadinejad's Iran increasingly resorts to incendiary and demonizing language, including epidemiological metaphors reminiscent of Nazi and Rwandan incitement. As one involved as Minister of Justice in Canada in the prosecution of Rwandan incitement, I am well placed to observe that the evidence of incitement in the Iranian case – as detailed in what

---

[64] *Id.* ¶¶ 84–85.

[65] From the outset, it should be noted that the comments herein on Iran refer uniquely to the current regime, embodied most notably by Supreme Leader Ayatollah Ali Khamenei and President Mahmoud Ahmadinejad. In particular, the present regime must be distinguished from the peoples of Iran who are themselves increasingly the target of massive human rights repression, as will be discussed in further detail later.

[66] *See* Benjamin Weinthal, "German official was at anti-Israel rally," *Jerusalem Post*, Oct. 15, 2008, *available at* http://www.jpost.com/Home/Article.aspx?id=117264.

[67] Video evidence of numerous "Death to Israel" chants is available online through the Middle East Media Research Institute, *available at* http://www.memritv.org/content/en/search.htm.

follows – is even clearer than the comparable evidence available to the international community in the period preceding the genocide in Rwanda. In the sections that follow, the early stages of a genocidal process can be discerned, as Iran engages in dehumanization, demonization, and incitement to genocide against Jews and Israel.

### *Delegitimization*

Iran has started the delegitimization process by impugning the legitimacy of Israel as a nation, and Israelis and Jews as a people, and singling them out for opprobrium and enmity warranting their demise. In segregating out these intended victims from the Iranian population, the government of Iran has framed this relationship as a zero-sum game, in which inherently competing interests can never be reconciled, a peaceful co-existence cannot be imagined, and the only solution is the elimination of the adversarial enemy: "There is only one solution to the Middle East problem, namely the annihilation and destruction of the Jewish state."[68]

In this artificial dialectic, Israel is wrongly portrayed as being the antithesis to "Muslims," a broad group in no way represented by the contemporary Iranian leadership. The consequence is that the issue becomes falsely framed as a clash of civilizations, where none, in truth, exists:

> Who are Israelis? They are responsible for usurping houses, territory, farmlands and businesses. They are combatants at the disposal of Zionist operatives. A Muslim nation cannot remain indifferent vis-a-vis such people who are stooges at the service of the arch-foes of the Muslim world.[69]
>
> Death to America and death to Israel are not only words written on paper, but a symbolic approach that reflects the desire of all the Muslim nations.[70]

This delegitimating paradigm finds further expression in the rhetoric treating Israel as a foreign and alien entity that has no rightful place in the Middle East. Indeed, Israel is often referred to simply as the "Zionist regime" – a convenient euphemism that avoids any implicit recognition of the State and is itself utilized as a means of delegitimation. Accordingly, Foreign Minister Manouchehr Mottaki has

---

[68] Reported in the *Daily Telegraph*, Jan. 1, 2000, *available at* http://www.frontpagemag.com/Articles/Printable.asp?ID=23841.

[69] Ramin Mostaghim and Borzou Daragahi, "Ayatollah Ali Khamenei says Iran, Israel on 'collision course,'" *L.A. Times*, Sep. 20, 2008, *available at* http://www.latimes.com/news/nationworld/world/la-fg-iran20-2008sep20,0,554272.story.

[70] Hossein Shariatmadari, a close confidant of Supreme Leader Ayatollah Ali Khamenei, in a speech on Oct. 4, 2007. *See* Joshua Teitelbaum, *What Iranian Leaders Really Say About Doing Away with Israel* 15 (Jerusalem Center for Public Affairs 2008), *available at* http://www.jcpa.org/text/ ahmadinejad2-words.pdf.

stated: "The West has tried to impose a fabricated regime on the Middle East, but even after 60 years, the Zionist regime has neither gained any legitimacy nor played any role in this region."[71]

President Mahmoud Ahmadinejad has frequently – and publicly – referred to the illegitimate "other" – Israel and its people – in a similar manner. For example, on a visit to Rome, he called Israel a "false regime."[72] And in front of the UN General Assembly, he labeled Israel a "criminal" and "forged" regime of "murderers" that "invade[s]" and "assassinate[s]," the whole created on "other people's land by displacing, detaining, and killing the true owners of that land."[73]

This exclusionary rhetoric underpins the antimony that Ahmadinejad's Iran seeks to promulgate: between the false Israel "other," seen as a Zionist western regime that was artificially placed in the Middle East; and between Muslims, held out as not only the rightful inhabitants of the region, but also as a group usurped by this alien "other." As the words of Supreme Leader Ayatollah Ali Khamenei demonstrate, this basic distinction provides the foundation on which the edifice of hatred is constructed, underpinned by ugly anti-Semitic tropes:

> What are you? A forged government and a false nation. They gathered wicked people from all over the world and made something called the Israeli nation. Is that a nation? All the malevolent and evil Jews have gathered there.... Those [Jews] who went to Israel were malevolent, evil, greedy thieves and murderers.[74]

### From Delegitimization to Dehumanization

Against this context of the singling out and delegitimization of the alien "other" Israel, the next genocidal precursor is the dehumanization of Israelis and Jews through the use of epidemiological metaphors reminiscent of the dehumanization of the Jews during the Holocaust and the dehumanization of Tutsi during the genocide in Rwanda. Indeed, in the genocide-fostering process, biological euphemisms are not just rhetorical tools; they seek to preclude the intended victims from even being considered human to begin with. Thus, just as Jews were labeled as "vermin" by the

---

71 "Tehran: Israel has neither legitimacy nor any role in the Middle East," *Ha'aretz*, Feb. 18, 2008, *available at* http://www.haaretz.com/hasen/objects/pages/PrintArticleEn.jhtml?itemNo=955417.

72 Phil Stewart, "Ahmadinejad calls Israel 'false regime' of Zionists," *Reuters*, June 3, 2008, *available at* http://uk.reuters.com/article/idUKL0369980720080603.

73 President Mahmoud Ahmadinejad, Address at the United Nations General Assembly (Sep. 23, 2008) (transcript available at: http://www.haaretz.com/hasen/objects/pages/PrintArticleEn .jhtml?itemNo=1024097 [translated by the Presidency of the Islamic Republic of Iran News Service]).

74 *Radio Iran*, July 20, 1994 (Foreign Broadcast Information Service Daily Reports [FBIS-DR]), *quoted in* Meir Litvak, "The Islamic Republic of Iran and the Holocaust: Anti-Semitism and Anti-Zionism," 25 *J. Israeli History* 267, 271 (2006).

Nazis and the Tutsi were labeled as "cockroaches" in Rwanda, so too have Israelis and Jews been dehumanized and labeled in Iran as:

1. a "filthy germ" and "savage beast";[75]
2. a "cancerous tumour";[76]
3. a "stain of disgrace" on the "garment of the world of Islam";[77]
4. a "stinking corpse";[78]
5. a "cancerous bacterium";[79]
6. stuck in a "cesspool created by itself and its supporters";[80]
7. "like cattle – nay, more misguided";[81]
8. a "rotten, dried tree";[82] and
9. an "unclean regime."[83]

### From Dehumanization to Demonization

Related to the dehumanization process is the demonizing process: The would-be victims of genocide are portrayed as inspirations of the devil. Dehumanization coupled with demonization accomplishes the dual purpose of making the would-be victim appear not only to be less than human (if not subhuman), but also to appear more threatening, thereby providing a warrant for genocide.

---

[75] President Mahmoud Ahmadinejad, in a speech on Feb. 20, 2008. *See* "UN Chief: Ahmadinejad's verbal attacks on Israel intolerable," *Ha'aretz*, Feb. 21, 200, *available at* http://www.haaretz.com/hasen/spages/ 956306.html. Note that the "filthy germ" quote has also been translated as a "black and filthy microbe": *See* Joshua Teitelbaum, "Analysis: Iran's talk of destroying Israel must not get lost in translation," *Jerusalem Post*, June 22, 2008, *available at* http://www.jpost.com/servlet/Satellite?cid= 1213794295236&pagename=JPost%2FJPArticle%2FPrinter.

[76] Ayatollah Ali Khamenei, Supreme Leader of Iran, quoted in "Iran leader urges destruction of 'cancerous' Israel," *Reuters*, Dec. 15, 2000, *available at* http://archives.cnn.com/2000/WORLD/meast/12/ 15/mideast.iran.reut.

[77] President Mahmoud Ahmadinejad, in a speech on Oct. 26, 2005. *See* Teitelbaum, *supra* note 75.

[78] President Mahmoud Ahmadinejad, speaking on the occasion of the sixtieth anniversary of Israel's founding, May 8, 2008. *See* "Ahmadinejad calls Zionist regime a 'stinking corpse,'" *Islamic Republic News Agency* (IRNA), May 8, 2008, *available at* http://www2.irna.ir/en/news/view/line-203/ 0805083448175250.htm.

[79] General Mohammad-Ali Jaafari, Commander of the Islamic Revolutionary Guard Corps, in a letter made public Feb. 18, 2008. *See* Dudi Cohen, "Iran: Cancerous Israel to be destroyed by Hizbullah," *Ynetnews*, Feb. 18, 2008, *available at* http://www.ynetnews.com/articles/0,7340,L-3508176,00.html.

[80] President Mahmoud Ahmadinejad, speaking to the United Nations General Assembly, Sept. 23 2008. *See* Claudia Parsons, "Ahmadinejad rails against Zionists, U.S. bullying," *Reuters*, Sept. 23, 2008, *available at* http://www.washingtonpost.com/wp-dyn/content/article/2008/09/23/ AR2008092303093_pf.html.

[81] President Mahmoud Ahmadinejad. Reported by the *Iranian News Channel* (IRINN), Aug. 1, 2006, *available at* http://www.memritv.org/clip_transcript/en/1216.htm.

[82] President Mahmoud Ahmadinejad, speaking at the opening of a conference, Apr. 14, 2006. *See* "Iran: Israel Facing 'Annihilation,'" *Associated Press*, Apr. 14, 2006, *available at* http://www.cbsnews.com/ stories/2006/04/14/world/main1499824.shtml.

[83] General Yahya Rahim Safavi, founder of the Islamic Revolutionary Guards Corps and advisor to Supreme Leader Ayatolla Ali Khamenei, Feb. 23, 2008. *See* Teitelbaum, *supra* note 70, at 14.

Indeed, demonization of Israel and Jews is frequent in Ahmadinejad's Iran. In this vein, President Mahmoud Ahmadinejad:

1.  has stated that "Zionists are the true manifestation of Satan,"[84] and that the "Zionist regime" is the "flag of Satan";[85]
2.  has remarked that "[n]ext to them, all the criminals of the world seem righteous";[86]
3.  has called Israelis "bloodthirsty barbarians,"[87] stated that they have "no boundaries, limits, or taboos when it comes to killing human beings,"[88] that Israel is "fighting a war against humanity,"[89] and that Zionism is the main cause of all corruption and wickedness in the contemporary era;[90]
4.  has further referred to Israel as a "criminal and terrorist Zionist regime which has 60 years of plundering, aggression and crimes in its file";[91] and
5.  builds on this demonic paradigm using different adjectives and metaphors in his speeches, referring, for instance, to Israel as the "epitome of perversion."[92]

He has elaborated:

Today, it has been proven that the Zionists are not opposed only to Islam and the Muslims. They are opposed to humanity as a whole. They want to dominate the entire world. They would even sacrifice the Western regimes for their own sake. I have said in Tehran, and I say it again here – I say to the leaders of some Western countries: Stop supporting these corrupt people. Behold, the rage of the Muslim peoples is accumulating. The rage of the Muslim peoples may soon reach the point of explosion. If that day comes, they must know that the waves of this explosion will not be restricted to the boundaries of our region. They will definitely reach the corrupt forces that support this fake regime.[93]

[84] "Zionist regime offspring of Britain, nurtured by US – Ahmadinejad," *Islamic Republic News Agency* (IRNA), Mar. 1, 2007, *available at* http://www2.irna.ir/en/news/view/line-20/0703015352005938.htm.

[85] Quoted by the *Islamic Republic News Agency* (IRNA) in "Ahmadinejad: Israel is 'flag of Satan,' may face disintegration," *Reuters*, Aug. 18, 2007, *available at* http://www.haaretz.com/hasen/spages/894744.html.

[86] Statement made during a speech broadcast on the *Iranian News Channel* (IRINN), Aug. 1, 2006, *available at* http://www.memritv.org/ clip_transcript/en/1216.htm.

[87] Speech broadcast on the *Iranian News Channel* (IRINN), Aug. 1, 2006, *available at* http://www.memritv.org/clip_transcript/en/1216.htm.

[88] *Id.*

[89] Patrick Bishop and Sebastian Berger, "'Eliminate' Israel to solve the crisis, says Iranian president," *Daily Telegraph,* Aug. 4, 2006, *available at* http://www.telegraph.co.uk/news/1525591/Eliminate-Israel-to-solve-the-crisis-says-Iranian-president.html.

[90] "Ahmadinejad: Zionist regime to be dismantled soon," *Islamic Republic News Agency* (IRNA), Aug. 20, 2008, *available at* http://www1.irna.ir/en/news/view/line-17/0808207991171114.htm.

[91] Phil Stewart, "Ahmadinejad calls Israel 'false regime' of Zionists," *Reuters*, June 3, 2008, *available at* http://www.reuters.com/ articlePrint?articleId=USL0369980720080603.

[92] Hossein Jaseb and Fredrik Dahl, "Ahmadinejad says Israel will 'disappear,'" *Reuters*, June 2, 2008, *available at* http://www.reuters.com/articlePrint?articleId=USL0261250620080602.

[93] Speech by President Mahmoud Ahmadinejad, reported on the *Iranian News Channel* (IRINN), July 11, 2006, *available at* http://www.memritv.org/clip_transcript/en/1187.htm (emphasis added).

The demonization of Jews in Ahmadinejad's Iran often fits within the traditional anti-Semitic canard of a small cabal of Jews running the world:

> The dignity, integrity and rights of the American and European people are being played with by *a small but deceitful number of people called Zionists*. Although they are a miniscule minority, they have been *dominating an important portion of the financial and monetary centers as well as the political decision-making centers of some European countries and the US in a deceitful, complex and furtive manner*. It is deeply disastrous to witness that some presidential or premiere nominees in some big countries have to visit these people, take part in their gatherings, swear their allegiance and commitment to their interests in order to attain financial or media support.
>
> This means that the great people of America and various nations of Europe need to obey *the demands and wishes of a small number of acquisitive and invasive people*. These nations are spending their dignity and resources on the crimes and occupations and the threats of the Zionist network against their will.[94]

Iranian presidential advisor Ali Ramin has even resurrected the historic falsehood of dirty Jews poisoning Christian wells – a pernicious and demonizing myth used to fuel anti-Semitism in the Middle Ages:

> But among the Jews there have always been those who killed God's prophets and who opposed justice and righteousness. Throughout history, this religious group has inflicted the most damage on the human race, while some groups within it engaged in plotting against other nations and ethnic groups to cause cruelty, malice and wickedness. Historically, there are many accusations against the Jews. For example, it was said that they were the source for such deadly diseases as the plague and typhus. This is because the Jews are very filthy people. For a time people also said that they poisoned water wells belonging to Christians and thus killed them.[95]

Supreme Leader Ali Khamenei has combined these two images – of Jews conspiring against the world and of Jews waging covert war on a people – in elaborating to his audience what he saw as the "satanic design":

> [T]he occupation of Palestine [by the Jews] is part of a satanic design by the world domineering powers, perpetrated by the British in the past and being carried out today by the United States to weaken the solidarity of the Islamic world and to sow the seeds of disunity among us.[96]

94  Ahmadinejad, *supra* note 73 (emphasis added).
95  *See* "Iranian Presidential Advisor Mohammad Ali Ramin: 'The Resolution of the Holocaust Issue Will End in the Destruction of Israel,'" Middle East Media Research Institute, Special Dispatch Series no. 1186, June 15, 2006, *available at* http://www.memri.org/report/en/0/0/0/0/0/0/1717.htm.
96  Ayatollah Khamenei, Address on the Occasion of the International Conference on Palestinian Intifada (Apr. 24 2001) (transcript available at http://www.radioislam.org/tehranconference/eng.htm). *See also* Litvak, *supra* note 74, at 270.

Ultimately, the strategy of demonization seamlessly leads to prophecy – and incitement:

> A Zionist organization with 2,000 [members] and with 7,000 or 8,000 activists have brought the world to a state of confusion. Let me tell them that if they themselves do not wrap up Zionism, *the strong arm of the peoples will wipe these germs of corruption off the face of the earth.*[97]

## From Incitement to Hate to Incitement to Genocide

Empowered by the culture of hate it has planted with impunity, Ahmadinejad's Iran feels no need to leave its genocidal intentions as an unspoken conclusion. To the contrary, the calls for Israel's destruction by Iranian officials are explicit and without ambiguity. Thus, President Mahmoud Ahmadinejad has publicly called for Israel to be "wiped off the map."[98]

The context of this comment is important, lest its clear message be somehow misunderstood. When President Ahmadinejad called for Israel to be "wiped off the map," he was speaking to thousands of students at a conference entitled the "World Without Zionism." Indeed, President Ahmadinejad hosted this conference in Tehran. Despite international condemnation,[99] when given the opportunity to retract his statement, President Ahmadinejad chose instead to add to their weight, remarking: "My words are the Iranian nation's words."[100]

In his call for annihilation, President Ahmadinejad referenced the former Iranian Supreme Leader Ayatollah Ruhollah Khomeini. On June 2, 2008, speaking at the shrine where the Ayatollah is buried, President Ahmadinejad repeated:

> [Ayatollah Khomeini's] ideal is about to be materialized today.... The Zionist regime is in a total dead end and, God willing, this desire will soon be realized and the epitome of perversion will disappear off the face of the world.[101]

---

[97] Text of a statement made by President Ahmadinejad as broadcast on the *Iranian News Channel* (IRINN), Sept. 23, 2008, *available at* http://www.memritv.org/clip_transcript/en/1868.htm (emphasis added).

[98] *See* Nazila Fathi, "Wipe Israel 'off the map' Iranian says," *International Herald Tribune*, Oct. 27, 2005, *available at* http://www.iht.com/articles/ 2005/10/26/news/iran.php.

[99] Mary Jordan and Karl Vick, "World Leaders Condemn Iranian's Call to Wipe Israel 'Off the Map,'" *Wash. Post*, Oct. 27, 2008, *available at* http://www.washingtonpost.com/wp-dyn/content/article/2005/ 10/27/ AR2005102702221.html.

[100] Nazila Fathi, "Iranian President Stands by Call to Wipe Israel Off Map," *New York Times*, Oct. 29, 2005.

[101] Jaseb and Dahl, *supra* note 92. This quote has also been translated as ending "this germ of corruption will be wiped off." *See, e.g.,* http://www.memritv.org/clip_transcript/en/1784.htm (Middle East Media Research Institute).

President Ahmadinejad has repeated this call for genocide many other times as well. To cite a few occasions:

> Israel's days are numbered.... [T]he people of the region would not miss the narrowest opportunity to annihilate this false regime.[102]
>
> [T]he Zionist regime is heading toward annihilation.[103]
>
> The region and the world are prepared for great changes and for being cleansed of Satanic enemies.[104]
>
> God willing, in the near future we will witness the destruction of the corrupt occupier regime.[105]
>
> This [Zionist] regime is on the verge of death, and we advise you to start thinking about your long-term interest and long-term relations with the peoples of the region. At the end of the day, these are all ultimatums.[106]
>
> [T]oday, the occupier regime [Israel] – whose philosophy is based on threats, massacre and invasion – has reached its finishing line.[107]
>
> [T]his fake regime [Israel] cannot logically continue to live.[108]

It is not only President Ahmadinejad who calls for the annihilation of Israel. The Supreme Leader of Iran, Ayatollah Ali Khamenei, makes it clear that this is the basic premise on which the State operates:

> It is the mission of the Islamic Republic of Iran to erase Israel from the map of the region.[109]

---

[102] From a speech delivered in Gorgan, northern Iran, quoted on *Press TV* and *Aftab*, May 14, 2008. *See* Y. Mansharof and A. Savyon, "Ahmadinejad: Israel Is a 'Dead Fish' and a 'Stinking Corpse'; 'The Zionist Regime Will Be Wiped Off'; 'The European Governments Do Not Want the Zionists Living in Europe,'" Middle East Media Research Institute, Inquiry and Analysis Series no. 447, June 6, 2008, *available at* http://memri.org/bin/ articles.cgi?Page=archives&Area=ia&ID=IA44708.

[103] Ahmadinejad, *supra* note 82.

[104] Speech at a military parade, April 17, 2008. *See* Alan Johnson, "Iran and Oran," *Progress Online*, *available at* http://www.progressonline.org.uk/ columns/column.asp?c=120. *See also* Teitelbaum, *supra* note 75.

[105] Speech to foreign guests marking the eighteenth anniversary of the death of Ayatollah Ruhollah Homeini, June 3, 2007. *See* "Ahmadinejad says destruction of Israel is close," *Associated Press*, June 3, 2007, *available at* http://chinadaily.com.cn/world/2007–06/03/content_886021.htm.

[106] Speech broadcast on *Jaam-e Jam 1 TV*, Oct. 20, 2006, *available at* http://www.memritv.org/clip_transcript/en/1301.htm.

[107] Statement from July 23, 2006. *See* "Iran: Israel doomed to 'destruction,'" *Associated Press*, July 23, 2006, *available at* http://www.jpost.com/servlet/Satellite?cid=1153291976348&pagename=JPost%2FJPArticle%2FPrinter.

[108] Statement from Apr. 24, 2006. *See* Angus McDowall, "Iranian President insists 'Israel cannot continue to live,'" *The Independent*, Apr. 25, 2006, *available at* http://www.independent.co.uk/news/world/middle-east/iranian-president-insists-israel-cannot-continue-to-live-475496.html.

[109] Kasra Naji, *Ahmadinejad: The Secret History of Iran's Radical Leader* 144 (University of California Press 2008). This quote has also been translated as stating that "the perpetual subject of Iran is the elimination of Israel from the region." *See* Teitelbaum, *supra* note 75.

Iran's stance has always been clear on this ugly phenomenon [Israel]. We have repeatedly said that this cancerous tumour of a state should be removed from the region.[110]

There is only one solution to the Middle East problem, namely the annihilation and destruction of the Jewish state.[111]

[W]e are on a collision course with the occupiers of Palestine and the occupiers are the Zionist regime. This is the position of our regime, our revolution and our people.[112]

Nor is this core state principle dependent on the vicissitudes of short-term foreign policy objectives. For example, in the context of the 2006 Lebanon War, President Mahmoud Ahmadinejad advocated an "immediate cease-fire" while also emphasizing that "the main solution is for the elimination of the Zionist regime."[113]

Repeated calls for the destruction of Israel, and "prophecies" of its demise, all work to normalize the idea of genocide to the Iranian population. Articulated in the context of demonizing rhetoric implying a clash of civilizations, calls for the annihilation of the Jewish State begin to appear not only moral and justifiable, but natural as well.

Such "normalization" is especially important where the intended genocide would be carried out by a single blow[114] from the state itself (i.e., a military missile strike)[115] rather than the comparatively slower process of having the population systematically murder victims themselves. Indeed, one may surmise that the psychological hurdle of acquiescing in a government's genocidal attack on a victim population is comparatively lower than the psychological hurdle of committing the acts of murder oneself.

Chillingly, all this incitement appears to be sinking into the popular consciousness. President Ahmadinejad's audience responds to his words instantly with chants

---

[110] "Iran leader urges destruction of 'cancerous' Israel," *Reuters*, Dec. 15, 2000, *available at* http://archives. cnn.com/2000/WORLD/meast/12/15/mideast.iran.reut. This quote has also been translated as ending "the cancerous tumour called Israel must be uprooted from the region." *See* Teitelbaum, *supra* note 75.

[111] Reported in the *Daily Telegraph*, Jan. 1, 2000, *available at* http://www.frontpagemag.com/Articles/ Printable.asp?ID=23841.

[112] Mostaghim and Daragahi, *supra* note 69.

[113] "Ahmadinejad's Mideast Solution: Destroy Israel," *Associated Press*, Aug. 3, 2006, *available at* http:// www.foxnews.com/story/0,2933,206823,00.html.

[114] *See* Ahmadinejad, *supra* note 82 (the "Zionist regime . . . will be eliminated by one storm").

[115] See the comments of former Iranian President Ayatollah Akbar Hashemi Rafsanjani: "If one day, a very important day of course, the Islamic world will also be equipped with the weapons available to Israel now, the imperialist strategy will reach an impasse, because the employment of even one atomic bomb inside Israel will wipe it off the face of the earth, but would only do damage to the Islamic world." Quoted in Teitelbaum, *supra* note 75. A slightly different translation, obtained from Iranian newspaper reports of the speech, is available in "Former Iranian President Rafsanjani on Using a Nuclear Bomb Against Israel," Middle East Media Research Institute, Special Dispatch Series no. 325, Jan. 3, 2002, *available at* http://www.memri.org/bin/articles.cgi?Area=sd&ID=SP32502.

of "Death to Israel."[116] And media commentary has followed the government's lead in inciting genocide as well. For instance, on October 22, 2006, *Resalat*, an Iranian newspaper, mirroring an Qods (Jerusalem) Day speech by President Mahmoud Ahmadinejad, wrote in an editorial: "The nation of Muslims must prepare for the great war, so as to completely wipe out the Zionist regime, and remove this cancerous growth. Like the Imam [Ayatollah] Khomeini said: 'Israel must collapse.'"[117]

## CONCLUSION

State-sanctioned incitement to genocide is a singular and unique threat to international peace and security. While more than sixty years have passed since the international community sought to address it by prohibiting genocidal incitement, this juridical response – absent tangible action to enforce it – has proven manifestly inadequate. We continue to be haunted by the recent preventable genocides in Rwanda and the former Yugoslavia, while our collective failure to end genocide in Darfur results in more lives lost on a daily basis. Meanwhile, Ahmadinejad's Iran has emerged as the world's first realistic threat – albeit still a nascent one – of a nuclear genocide.

Such incitement should not be allowed to continue with impunity. Indeed, there is a moral and legal imperative to stop it. Among the many remedies available to the international community are the following:

- The incitement to genocide by Ahmadinejad and other Iranian leaders could be referred to the appropriate UN agencies. For instance, such referral may be accomplished pursuant to the Secretary-General's authority under Article 99 of the *Charter of the United Nations* or by any state party to the *Genocide Convention* pursuant to its Article 8.
- The situation of genocidal incitement by Ahmadinejad and other Iranian leaders could be referred by the UN Security Council to the Prosecutor of the International Criminal Court for investigation and possible prosecution.[118]
- State parties to the *Genocide Convention* could initiate an interstate complaint against Iran before the International Court of Justice for its "direct and public incitement to commit genocide" in violation of the *Genocide Convention*, to which Iran is also a state party.[119]
- Sanctions from the international community could be targeted not only against Iran's illegal nuclear program, but its illegal genocidal incitement as well. The

---

[116] Middle East Media Research Institute, *supra* note 67.

[117] *See* "Qods (Jerusalem) Day in Iran: 'The Nation of Muslims Must Prepare for the Great War So As to Completely Wipe Out the Zionist Regime and to Remove This Cancerous Growth,'" Middle East Media Research Institute, Special Dispatch Series no. 1357, Nov. 15, 2006, *available at* http://www.memri.org/bin/articles.cgi?Page=countries&Area=iran&ID=SP135706.

[118] *See* Rome Statute of the International Criminal Court art. 13(b), U.N. Doc. A/CONF.183/9*.

[119] *Genocide Convention, supra* note 1, arts. 3(c) and 9.

nuclear program represents merely the means to carry out genocidal intentions; the international community ought to be focused on the genocidal ends as well.

A group of prominent international jurists, genocide experts, and survivors has already united to call attention to Iran's illegal genocidal incitement, and to call for action from state parties to the *Genocide Convention*, the United Nations, and the international community in general in response.[120] If genocide prevention is to have any meaning, the ubiquitous incitement to genocide of Ahmadinejad's Iran must not be allowed to continue with impunity.

The legal apparatus for effectively preventing genocide exists. The jurisprudence, which both articulates the criteria of incitement to genocide and documents its harm, has been written. What remains is for preventative action to be taken on the basis of these already established principles. As we have learned all too well, the cost of ignoring our responsibility to prevent is incalculable.

---

[120] *See The Danger of a Genocidal and Nuclear Iran: The Responsibility to Prevent*, a petition released by the author and signed by leading jurists, genocide experts, and genocide survivors from around the world, calling on State Parties to the *Genocide Convention*, among others, to take action to prevent genocide. It is available online at http://www.irwincotler.parl.gc.ca/documents/081209_petition.pdf.

# 24

## A Survey and Critical Analysis of Council of Europe Strategies for Countering "Hate Speech"

*Tarlach McGonagle*

### I. INTRODUCTION

The Council of Europe is a regional intergovernmental organization committed to ensuring respect for human rights, democracy, and the rule of law throughout Europe. Its current membership is forty-seven states. Its primary aim, as set out in its statute, is to "achieve a greater unity between its members for the purpose of safeguarding and realizing the ideals and principles which are their common heritage and facilitating their economic and social progress."[1] It pursues this aim "through the organs of the Council by discussion of questions of common concern and by agreements and common action in economic, social, cultural, scientific, legal and administrative matters and in the maintenance and further realization of human rights and fundamental freedoms."[2]

The Council employs a number of concurrent strategies to counter "hate speech." These strategies have been developed pursuant to the Council's various treaties and other standard-setting and monitoring initiatives. While they are broadly congruent in terms of their overall objectives and approaches, each initiative is characterized by its own priorities, emphases, and procedural possibilities. This has resulted in considerable diversity in the range of strategies devised by the Council to combat "hate speech." They include: the denial or reduction of legal protection for "hate speech"; the facilitation and creation of expressive opportunities (especially access to the media) for minorities; and the promotion of intercultural dialogue and understanding at the societal level.

This chapter scrutinizes the aforementioned strategies for tackling "hate speech," as well as the normative standards, jurisprudence, and monitoring practices on which

[1]  Statute of the Council of Europe, art. 1(a), May 5, 1949, E.T.S. No. 1 (as amended).
[2]  *Id.*, art. 1(b).

The author would like to thank the editors of this volume for their very helpful comments on a previous draft.

they are based. It assesses their individual and collective impact and ultimately argues that the aggregated approach of the Council of Europe offers depth in its diversity and is conducive to proactive and effective engagement with several of the root causes of "hate speech."

Before commencing this examination, the scope of the term "hate speech" must be explored and its various possible meanings explained. The term first came to lexical prominence within the Council of Europe in 1997, when the Committee of Ministers adopted a Recommendation on the topic. The European Court of Human Rights first used the term – without attempting to define it or explaining its introduction – in 1999. Since then, the term has gained currency in relevant case law of the Court and miscellaneous activities across the Council of Europe. In the absence of any legally binding or otherwise authoritative definition of the term,[3] it is susceptible to interpretations which are either over- or underinclusive. "Hate speech" can refer to a whole spectrum of negative discourse stretching from incitement to hatred to abuse, vilification, insults, offensive words, epithets, and, arguably, to extreme examples of prejudice and bias.[4]

The problems arising from such definitional uncertainty can have far-reaching practical consequences. For instance, recommendations to blanket-ban "hate speech" are unhelpful (and often unworkable) because of their failure to recognize that "hate speech" is essentially a shorthand, catchall term for a range of specific types of expression, which vary in terms of their intensity and abusiveness. Although, intuitively, "hate speech" is "objectionable for both intrinsic and instrumental reasons, for what it is and what it does,"[5] the shift from its moral condemnation to legal regulation (or prohibition) inevitably calls for greater definitional refinement than has hitherto been provided by any international, legally binding treaty or related adjudicative authority. In other words, the scope of the term needs to be clarified and different kinds of "hate speech" need to be distinguished. This is because:

> The multiple forms of anti-egalitarian expression that exist are neither equally harmful nor performative; we must not, therefore, lose sight of the link between the norm that the state is drafting and the broader public policies involved when identifing [sic] the specific forms of anti-egalitarian expressions to discourage.[6]

This kind of thinking informs, and indeed characterizes, the Council of Europe's diversified strategies for countering "hate speech," as is demonstrated in this

---

[3]  The aforementioned Committee of Ministers' Recommendation on "hate speech" (discussed in detail later in the chapter) proposes a definition of the term for the purposes of the Recommendation; the definition is not legally binding on Member States of the Council of Europe.

[4]  James B. Jacobs and Kimberly Potter, *Hate Crimes: Criminal Law and Identity Politics* 11 (Oxford University Press 1998).

[5]  Bhikhu Parekh, "Is There a Case for Banning Hate Speech?," Chapter 2 herein.

[6]  Jean-François Gaudreault-DesBiens, "From Sisyphus's Dilemma to Sisyphus's Duty? A Meditation on the Regulation of Hate Propaganda in Relation to Hate Crimes and Genocide," 46 *McGill L.J.* 121, 133 (2000); *see also* Parekh, *supra* note 5.

| Treaties | Articles |
|---|---|
| European Convention on Human Rights (ECHR) | 10, 14, 17, Protocol 12 |
| Framework Convention for the Protection of National Minorities (FCNM) | 6, 9 |
| European Convention on Transfrontier Television (ECTT) | 7(1) |
| Additional Protocol to Convention on Cybercrime | esp. 1–6 |

FIGURE 24.1. Tabular summary of the Council of Europe's most relevant treaty provisions on "hate speech."

chapter. The chapter begins with the Council of Europe's most relevant treaties: the European Convention on Human Rights, the Framework Convention for the Protection of National Minorities, the Additional Protocol to the Convention on Cybercrime, concerning the criminalization of acts of a racist and xenophobic nature committed through computer systems, and the European Convention on Transfrontier Television (see Figure 24.1). It then turns to approaches which are not treaty-based, principally, standard-setting texts adopted by the Committee of Ministers and the Parliamentary Assembly – the Council's executive and deliberative organs, respectively. Part IV considers the monitoring and standard-setting work of the European Commission against Racism and Intolerance. Finally, Part V focuses on periodic, media-specific policy-making conferences at the inter-ministerial level, and pertinent legal analyses prepared by the Commission for Democracy through Law (Venice Commission) – the Council of Europe's advisory body on constitutional matters.

## II. TREATIES

### A. *The European Convention on Human Rights*

#### 1. Key Provisions of the Convention

The Council of Europe's flagship treaty and the centerpiece of human rights protection in Europe is the Convention for the Protection of Human Rights and Fundamental Freedoms, more commonly known as the European Convention on Human Rights, or ECHR.[7] The ECHR's key provision dealing with freedom of expression is Article 10:

1. Everyone has the right to freedom of expression. This right shall include freedom to hold opinions and to receive and impart information and ideas without interference by public authority and regardless of frontiers. This article

---

[7] Convention for the Protection of Human Rights and Fundamental Freedoms, Nov. 4, 1950, 213 U.N.T.S. 221, E.T.S. No. 5. Since 1989, membership in the Council of Europe has been contingent on being a Party to the ECHR. As of this writing, there are forty-seven States Parties to the ECHR. For relevant details and analysis, see Florence Benoît-Rohmer and Heinrich Klebes, *Council of Europe Law: Towards a Pan-european Legal Area* 31–2 (Council of Europe Publishing 2005).

shall not prevent States from requiring the licensing of broadcasting, television or cinema enterprises.

2. The exercise of these freedoms, since it carries with it duties and responsibilities, may be subject to such formalities, conditions, restrictions or penalties as are prescribed by law and are necessary in a democratic society, in the interests of national security, territorial integrity or public safety, for the prevention of disorder or crime, for the protection of health or morals, for the protection of the reputation or rights of others, for preventing the disclosure of information received in confidence, or for maintaining the authority and impartiality of the judiciary.

Thus, Article 10(1) sets out the right to freedom of expression as a compound right comprising three main elements: the right to hold opinions; the right to receive information and ideas; and the right to impart information and ideas. Article 10(2) then proceeds to trammel the core right set out in the preceding paragraph, enumerating a number of grounds based on which the right may be restricted, provided that the restrictions are prescribed by law and are *necessary in a democratic society*. It justifies this approach by linking the permissibility of restricting the right to freedom of expression with the existence of duties and responsibilities that govern the right's exercise. The European Court of Human Rights has interpreted the criterion, "necessary in a democratic society," as "corresponding to a pressing social need."[8] Furthermore, any measure restricting the right to freedom of expression must also be proportionate to the legitimate aim pursued.[9]

In addition, the right to freedom of expression may be limited on the basis of Article 17 of the ECHR.[10] Entitled "Prohibition of abuse of rights," it reads:

Nothing in this Convention may be interpreted as implying for any State, group or person any right to engage in any activity or perform any act aimed at the destruction of any of the rights and freedoms set forth herein or at their limitation to a greater extent than is provided for in the Convention.

Article 17 can be regarded as a safety mechanism designed to prevent the ECHR from being misused or abused by those whose intentions are contrary to the letter and spirit of the Convention.

### 2. Judgments and Decisions of the European Court of Human Rights

In its seminal 1976 ruling in *Handyside v. United Kingdom*,[11] a case involving restrictions on freedom of expression to protect morals,[12] the European Court of Human

---

[8] *See, e.g.*, Handyside v. United Kingdom, 24 Eur. Ct. H.R. (ser. A) at 23, ¶ 48 (1976).

[9] *See, e.g., id.*, ¶ 49.

[10] For general commentary, see David Harris et al., *Law of the European Convention on Human Rights* 648–52 (Oxford University Press, 2d ed. 2009).

[11] 24 Eur. Ct. H.R. (ser. A) at 23 (1976).

[12] The case concerned the criminal conviction of the publisher of the *Little Red Schoolbook* and the seizure, forfeiture, and destruction of hundreds of copies of the book by the British authorities. The

Rights affirmed that freedom of expression "is applicable not only to 'information' or 'ideas' that are favourably received or regarded as inoffensive or as a matter of indifference, but also to those that offend, shock or disturb the State or any sector of the population. Such are the demands of that pluralism, tolerance and broadmindedness without which there would be no democratic society."[13] The *Handyside* judgment recognized that a democratic society must allow space for public discussion and debate. Since *Handyside*, the Court regularly has emphasized the importance of ensuring that individual and minority viewpoints are heard, so that public debate does not become the preserve of majoritarian, mainstream, and orthodox opinion.[14] This points to the need for public debate and the fora in which it is conducted to be designed in ways that facilitate the participation of diverse groups in society.[15] However, democratic society is not without its rough edges, and pluralistic public debate necessarily involves disagreement and confrontation between opposing viewpoints. Such disagreement and confrontation – even when expressed in strong terms (because Article 10 protects not only the substance of information and ideas, but also the form in which they are conveyed) – ordinarily come within the scope of the protection offered by Article 10.

The Court also has recognized the crucial role played by the media as facilitators of, and participants in, public debate. *Jersild v. Denmark* stands as a *locus classicus* for media freedom and it remains a central reference point for the Council of Europe's standard-setting activities concerning freedom of expression, the media, and "hate speech."[16] *Jersild* involved the conviction of a Danish journalist for aiding and abetting in the dissemination of racist statements in a televised interview he had conducted. The statements in question were uttered by members of an extreme right-wing group known as the "Greenjackets," and the journalist was convicted largely because he had failed to contradict or distance himself from the statements

book was aimed at adolescents and contained extensive information about sex and sexuality. The measures against the publisher and book were taken pursuant to the Obscene Publications Act, in which the notion of a tendency "to deprave and corrupt" was central. In concluding that the authorities had not violated Article 10, the European Court of Human Rights placed considerable store by its "margin of appreciation" doctrine, according to which a certain amount of discretion is afforded states in how they regulate free expression. The extent of the discretion, which is subject to supervision by the Court, varies. States have a narrow margin of appreciation in respect of political speech and a wider one in respect of public morals (as in the present case), decency, and religion. This is usually explained (again, as in the present case) by the absence of a European consensus on whether or how matters such as morality should be regulated. *In casu*, the European Court of Human Rights found the English courts' decisions – taken "in the light of the case as a whole" – to be "relevant and sufficient" for the purposes of Article 10(2) of the ECHR.

13  *Handyside*, 24 Eur. Ct. H.R. (ser. A) at 23, ¶ 49.
14  *See, e.g.*, Young, James & Webster v. United Kingdom, 44 Eur. Ct. H.R. (ser. A) at 25, ¶ 63 (1981); Chassagnou v. France, 1999-III Eur. Ct. H.R. 21, ¶ 112; Steel & Morris v. United Kingdom 2005-II Eur. Ct. H.R. 1, ¶ 89 (2005). For a case specifically concerning "hate speech" in which this principle was implicit, see Gündüz v. Turkey, discussed *infra* note 37.
15  *See, e.g.*, Appleby v. United Kingdom, 2003-VI Eur. Ct. H.R. 189.
16  Jersild v. Denmark, 298 Eur. Ct. H.R. (ser. A) (1994).

of the interviewees. The Court held that Jersild's conviction was not "necessary in a democratic society" and that it therefore violated his rights under Article 10. This conclusion rested largely on considerations of context in (news) reporting and the importance of journalistic autonomy for the functioning of democracy. The European Court of Human Rights held that the journalist's right to freedom of expression had been infringed, *inter alia*, because it was not for the courts to determine which journalistic techniques (e.g., "the methods of objective and balanced reporting") should be used.[17]

The space and tolerance for robust debate recognized in *Handyside* and subsequent cases do not extend so far as to protect most types of "hate speech." The Court consistently has relied on Article 17 to deny Article 10 protection to racist, xenophobic, or anti-Semitic speech; statements denying, disputing, minimizing, or condoning the Holocaust; and neo-Nazi ideas. Such cases are routinely declared "inadmissible"; that is, the application seeking a finding that the ECHR has been violated is rejected.

For example, in *Seurot v. France*,[18] a teacher was sanctioned for a text published in a school bulletin in which he deplored – as he put it – the overrunning of France by "hordes of Muslims"[19] from North Africa. This was found not to violate his right to freedom of expression under Article 10 because of the undeniably racist tone of the article and the duties and responsibilities of the applicant in his capacity as a teacher.

In *Norwood v. United Kingdom*,[20] the applicant, a regional organizer for the British National Party (a far-right political party), displayed in the window of his flat a poster depicting the Twin Towers in flames, the words "Islam out of Britain – Protect the British People," and a symbol of a crescent and star in a prohibition sign. He was convicted by the domestic courts of a public order offense. The European Court of Human Rights agreed with the assessment of the domestic courts and concluded that his conviction did not breach Article 10 because

> the words and images on the poster amounted to a public expression of attack on all Muslims in the United Kingdom. Such a general, vehement attack against a religious group, linking the group as a whole with a grave act of terrorism, is incompatible with the values proclaimed and guaranteed by the Convention, notably tolerance, social peace and non-discrimination.[21]

In *Ivanov v. Russia*,[22] the applicant had written and published a series of articles that the European Court of Human Rights found to have a "markedly anti-Semitic

---

[17] *Id.* at ¶ 31.
[18] Seurot v. France (dec.), Eur. Ct. H.R. (Second Section) (May 18, 2004) No. 57383/00.
[19] *Id.* at 2 (Author's translation, decision only available in French).
[20] Norwood v. United Kingdom (dec.), 2004-XI Eur. Ct. H., No. 23131/03.
[21] *Id.* at 4.
[22] Ivanov v. Russia (dec.), Eur. Ct. H.R. (First Section) (February 20, 2007) No. 35222/04.

tenor."[23] It agreed "with the assessment made by the domestic courts that he sought through his publications to incite hatred towards the Jewish people."[24] Following *Norwood*, the Court found that "[s]uch a general and vehement attack on one ethnic group is in contradiction with the Convention's underlying values, notably tolerance, social peace and non-discrimination,"[25] and accordingly rejected the claim that penalizing this speech violated the ECHR.

The Court took its most trenchant stance against hate speech to date in the *Garaudy v. France* case,[26] which involved a challenge to the French courts' conviction of the applicant for the denial of crimes against humanity, the publication of racially defamatory statements, and incitement to racial hatred.[27] The European Court of Human Rights held:

> There can be no doubt that denying the reality of clearly established historical facts, such as the Holocaust, as the applicant does in his book, does not constitute historical research akin to a quest for the truth. The aim and the result of that approach are completely different, the real purpose being to rehabilitate the National-Socialist regime and, as a consequence, accuse the victims themselves of falsifying history. Denying crimes against humanity is therefore one of the most serious forms of racial defamation of Jews and of incitement to hatred of them. The denial or rewriting of this type of historical fact undermines the values on which the fight against racism and anti-Semitism are based and constitutes a serious threat to public order. Such acts are incompatible with democracy and human rights because they infringe the rights of others. Its proponents indisputably have designs that fall into the category of aims prohibited by Article 17 of the Convention.
>
> The Court considers that the main content and general tenor of the applicant's book, and thus its aim, are markedly revisionist and therefore run counter to the fundamental values of the Convention, as expressed in its Preamble, namely justice and peace.[28]

A less clear-cut case, perhaps, as far as the boundaries of freedom of expression are concerned, was *Lehideux & Isorni v. France*.[29] The case concerned an advertisement

---

[23]  *Id.* at 4.

[24]  *Id.*

[25]  *Id.*

[26]  Garaudy v. France (dec.), Eur. Ct. H.R. (Fourth Section) (June 24, 2003) No. 65831/01. *See generally* Tarlach McGonagle, "Wresting (Racial) Equality from Tolerance of Hate Speech," 23 *Dublin Univ. L.J.* 21 (2001).

[27]  Garaudy was convicted pursuant to the Press Freedom Act of 29 July 1881, as amended, *inter alia*, by the Act for the Suppression of All Racist, Anti-Semitic or Xenophobic Acts, No. 90–615 of 13 July 1990 (the so-called Gayssot Law). For details and analysis of relevant legislative provisions, see generally Julie C. Suk, "Denying Experience: Holocaust Denial and the Free-Speech Theory of the State," Chapter 8 herein.

[28]  *Garaudy*, at 23 (official English translation).

[29]  Lehideux & Isorni v. France, 1998-VII Eur. Ct. H.R. 2864. For further analysis of this case, see Toby Mendel, "Does International Law Provide for Consistent Rules on Hate Speech?," Chapter 22 herein.

in a national newspaper, *Le Monde*, which was part of a campaign for the rehabilitation of the memory of General Philippe Pétain. The advertisement presented the General's life in a selective and positive manner, with certain dark chapters of the General's life during World War II being conspicuous by the absence of any reference thereto. In this case, the European Court acknowledged that protection would be withheld from speech that it deemed contrary to the core values of the Convention,[30] but found that the impugned advertisement did not amount to Holocaust denial or any other type of expression that would deprive it of protection in accordance with Article 17. The Court readily acknowledged the polemical nature of the advertisement (*viz.*, a biased and consequently contested portrayal of a controversial national figure in the broader context of ongoing historical debate), but reiterated that Article 10 "protects not only the substance of the ideas and information expressed but also the form in which they are conveyed."[31]

Elements of Nazi ideology or activities inspired by Nazism have figured strongly in many inadmissibility decisions.[32] The extent to which Nazism is incompatible with the ECHR can be gauged from the oft-quoted pronouncement of the now-defunct European Commission of Human Rights[33] in *H., W., P. & K. v. Austria*: "National Socialism is a totalitarian doctrine incompatible with democracy and human rights and [that] its adherents undoubtedly pursue aims of the kind referred to in Article 17."[34]

The actual term "hate speech" does not appear in the ECHR, and it was not used by the Court (or the European Commission of Human Rights) until 1999.[35] Prior to that, the vocabulary was different, even if the targeted mischief was the same.[36] The Court has not yet defined the term and it sometimes places it in (scare)

---

[30] *Id.* at ¶ 53; *see also* Jersild v. Denmark, 298 Eur. Ct. H.R. (ser. A) at ¶ 35 (1994).

[31] *Id.* at ¶¶ 52, 55.

[32] For a detailed overview of relevant ECHR case law, see McGonagle, *supra* note 26; Tarlach McGonagle, "Protection of Human Dignity, Distribution of Racist Content (Hate Speech)," in *Co-Regulation of the Media in Europe*, IRIS Special 43, 46 (Susanne Nikoltchev ed., European Audiovisual Observatory 2003).

[33] The European Commission of Human Rights was a body of independent experts charged with determining whether cases should be admitted for consideration on merits by the European Court of Human Rights. It was disbanded on November 1, 1998 upon entry into force of Protocol No. 11 to the Convention for the Protection of Human Rights and Fundamental Freedoms, which restructured the control machinery established by the Convention, E.T.S. No. 155, May 11, 1994. *See also id.* art. 5.

[34] H., W., P. & K. v. Austria (dec.), Eur. Comm'n H.R., No. 12774/87, 62 DR 216, 220–1 (1989).

[35] It would appear that the term was first used in four judgments of the European Court of Human Rights, all handed down on July 8, 1999: Sürek v. Turkey (No. 1), ¶ 62; Sürek & Özdemir v. Turkey, ¶ 63; Sürek v. Turkey (No. 4), ¶ 60; and Erdogdu & Ince v. Turkey, ¶ 54.

[36] For details of relevant case law, see Anne Weber, *Manual on Hate Speech* (Council of Europe 2009); Anne Weber, "The case-law of the European Court of Human Rights on Article 10 ECHR relevant for combating racism and intolerance," in European Commission against Racism and Intolerance (ECRI), *Combating racism while respecting freedom of expression* (Council of Europe 2007); Mario Oetheimer, "Protecting Freedom of Expression: The Challenge of Hate Speech in the European Court of Human Rights Case Law," 17 *Cardozo J. Int'l & Comp. L.* 427 (2009).

quotes.[37] This may indicate an unease with the *concept* of hate speech or perhaps the difficulty of defining the *term* in a clear way that would facilitate its application in case law. The difficulty of integrating the term, "hate speech," into a well-established body of jurisprudence based on recognized terminology has been apparent from the beginning. In *Sürek v. Turkey (No. 1)*, the Court reiterated that "the mere fact that 'information' or 'ideas' offend, shock or disturb does not suffice to justify" an interference with the right to freedom of expression, but then stipulated: "What is in issue in the instant case, however, is hate speech and the glorification of violence."[38] The significance of this stipulation is that the Court seems to be suggesting that "hate speech" is qualitatively different from speech that (merely) offends, shocks, or disturbs. To the extent the term is used to distinguish between categories of expression that enjoy presumptive protection under Article 10 and those that do not, the need to define it with precision becomes much more urgent. If a particular category of expression is to be denied Article 10 protection, it is of the utmost importance, not least from the perspective of legal certainty and foreseeability, that the Court would provide a clear sense of what the concept/category actually entails.

It should be noted that the Court does not use the term "hate speech" systematically. For instance, the term does not appear in *Norwood*, even though the type of expression at issue could be regarded as a typical example of "hate speech." Nor does the Court use the term consistently: It remains somewhat unclear whether incitement to violence or discrimination is an essential definitional element of the term. This uncertainty is prompted by the Court's judgment in *Gündüz v. Turkey*. The case arose out of the participation of the applicant – the leader of an Islamic sect – in a live studio debate on topics such as women's clothing, Islam, secularism, and democracy. The applicant was convicted by the Turkish courts for incitement to hatred and hostility on the basis of a distinction founded on religion. However, the European Court of Human Rights held:

> Admittedly, there is no doubt that, like any other remark directed against the Convention's underlying values, expressions that seek to spread, incite or justify hatred based on intolerance, including religious intolerance, do not enjoy the protection afforded by Article 10 of the Convention. However, the Court considers that the mere fact of defending sharia, without calling for violence to establish it, cannot be regarded as "hate speech." Moreover, the applicant's case should be seen in a very particular context. Firstly, as has already been noted . . . the aim of the programme in question was to present the sect of which the applicant was the leader; secondly, the applicant's extremist views were already known and had been discussed in the public arena and, in particular, were counterbalanced by the intervention of the other participants in the programme; and lastly, they were

---

[37] *See, e.g.*, Gündüz v. Turkey, Eur. Ct. H.R. (First Section) (December 4, 2003) at ¶ 51. The term "hate speech" is also enclosed by quotation marks in the Committee of Ministers' eponymously titled Recommendation No. R (97) 20, on which more below.

[38] *Sürek v. Turkey*, at ¶ 62.

expressed in the course of a pluralistic debate in which the applicant was actively taking part. Accordingly, the Court considers that in the instant case the need for the restriction in issue has not been established convincingly.[39]

Whereas the Court's use of the term "hate speech" is unclear, this is also true – at a more fundamental level – of its engagement of the interface between freedom of expression and various hues of racist and intolerant discourse. This is illustrated clearly by the controversial case of *Féret v. Belgium*.[40] The case arose from the conviction of a Belgian politician for incitement to hatred, discrimination, and violence due to the racist and xenophobic content of party political tracts distributed in the context of an electoral campaign. At the operative time, Daniel Féret was chairman of the far-right Belgian political party, Front National, editor-in-chief of the party's political publications, owner of the party's Web site (which was also used to distribute the impugned political tracts), and a member of the Belgian House of Representatives. To institute criminal proceedings against him, the Belgian prosecuting authorities lifted Féret's parliamentary immunity. He was ultimately found guilty of the aforementioned offenses and sentenced to 250 hours of community service relating to the integration of foreign nationals in Belgium, together with a 10-month suspended prison sentence. Furthermore, he was ruled ineligible to stand for parliamentary elections for a 10-year period and ordered to pay a provisional sum of 1 Euro to each of the civil parties involved.

The European Court of Human Rights found that the applicant's right to freedom of expression had not been violated, *inter alia*, because of the volatility of racist or xenophobic expression during electoral periods[41] and the duty of politicians "to refrain from using or advocating racial discrimination and recourse to words or attitudes which are vexatious or humiliating because such behavior risks fostering reactions among the public which are incompatible with a peaceful social climate and could erode confidence in democratic institutions."[42] In light of the civil nature of the sanctions and the suspended nature of the prison sentence, the Court found the sanctions not to be excessive.[43] The controversial nature of this judgment and the extent to which relevant questions persist can be gleaned from the Joint Dissenting Opinion to the judgment, which examines, *inter alia*, the relationship between heated political invective and racist expression, as well as the speculative nature of the link between the impugned expression and the harms it could cause.[44]

It is perhaps still too early to say what added value or clarity the introduction of the term "hate speech" has brought to the Court's jurisprudence relating to Articles 10 and 17 – at least in the absence of its own definition of the term. The Court

---

[39] *Gündüz v. Turkey*, at ¶ 51.
[40] Féret v. Belgium, Eur. Ct. H.R. (Second Section) (July 16 2009).
[41] *Id.* at ¶ 76.
[42] *Id.* at ¶ 77 (author's translation).
[43] *Id.* at ¶ 80.
[44] *Id.* (Sajo, J. dissenting, joined by Zagrebelsky & Tsotsoria, JJ).

sometimes refers to the Council of Europe's Committee of Ministers' Recommendation (97) 20 on "Hate Speech," which describes the term (albeit for the purposes of the application of the principles set out in the Appendix to the Recommendation) as "covering all forms of expression which spread, incite, promote or justify racial hatred, xenophobia, antisemitism or other forms of hatred based on intolerance, including: intolerance expressed by aggressive nationalism and ethnocentrism, discrimination and hostility against minorities, migrants and people of immigrant origin."[45] This description is helpful, but only in a limited way, because (1) the Recommendation is not legally binding on states, and (2) it has yet to feature either frequently or prominently in relevant case law of the European Court of Human Rights, thereby denying it the extra legitimization that would accrue from the same.[46] Nevertheless, the gradual development and consolidation of relevant jurisprudence help further our understanding of the term, or at least of the Court's interpretation of the term.

"Hate speech" is not going to go away, so it is imperative that the Court prepare itself for protracted engagement with the underlying issues and – as long as it continues to use the term in a way relevant for interpretive purposes – also the meaning and scope of the term itself. This will require, first and foremost, considerable definitional dissection. The task will demand careful refinement of the Court's key principles and a more systematic approach to how it applies those principles to specific factual circumstances. The Court will have to examine, in the specifics of each case, whether sufficient consideration has been given to factors such as the intent of the speaker, "contextual variables,"[47] and the demonstrably harmful impact of the impugned expression. Ascertainment of the intent or motivation of a speaker can reveal whether the impugned expression has been fueled by animus. Contextual variables could include the nature and impact of the medium used to convey the expression, audience-related considerations, sociopolitical factors, the nature and severity of the sanction imposed, and so on. The requirement of a demonstrably harmful impact insists on the establishment of a clear causal connection between the impugned expression and the alleged resultant harm to others.[48] To date, the Court's reliance on Article 17 to deny protection to certain broad categories of

---

45 Council of Eur., Comm. of Ministers, Recommendation No. R (97) 20 to Member States on "Hate Speech," 607th meeting (Oct. 30, 1997), Appendix, *available at* http://www.coe.int/t/dghl/standardsetting/media/Doc/CM/Rec(1997)020 &ExpMem_en.asp#TopOfPage.

46 Gündüz v. Turkey, Eur. Ct. H.R. (First Section) (December 4, 2003), is an example of a case in which the Recommendation was referred to by the Court (see ¶ 21 and especially ¶ 22 of the judgment) under the heading "Relevant international instruments." However, its subsequent engagement with the Recommendation is indirect – it merely refers to the aforementioned relevant international instruments *en bloc. Id.* at ¶ 40. In *Féret,* however, the Court's engagement with relevant Committee of Ministers' Recommendations and relevant work by ECRI is more explicit. *See Féret* at ¶ 72.

47 Michel Rosenfeld, "Hate Speech in Constitutional Jurisprudence: A Comparative Analysis," Chapter 13 herein.

48 For further discussion on the question of causality and the prevention of harm in free speech theory, see Frederick Schauer, "Is It Better to Be Safe Than Sorry?: Free Speech and the Precautionary Principle," 36 *Pepp. L. Rev.* 301 (2009).

expression has been routine and, on occasion, reflexive. The need for clarification of the relationship between Articles 10 and 17 is becoming increasingly urgent, as illustrated by a couple of recent cases involving political expression with a racist or intolerant character.[49]

## B. *Framework Convention for the Protection of National Minorities*

The 1995 Framework Convention for the Protection of National Minorities (FCNM)[50] sets out a range of rights to be enjoyed by persons belonging to national minorities, including:

- equality and nondiscrimination (Article 4)
- culture, identity, and nonassimilation (Article 5)
- freedom of religion or belief (Article 8)
- freedom of expression (Article 9)
- use of own language in public and in private and (in certain circumstances) in dealings with administrative authorities (Article 10)
- use of names (personal and geographical) in own language (Article 11)
- education (Articles 12 and 13)
- language learning (Article 14)
- effective participation in cultural, social, and economic life and in public affairs (Article 15).

As its title indicates, the FCNM is a *framework* convention. Accordingly, States Parties have some leeway in the honoring of their commitments under the Convention. States may implement the programmatic provisions of the Convention in such a way as to reflect relevant *couleur locale*. The rights that the FCNM purports to safeguard are not justiciable under the treaty itself. Rather, the implementation of the FCNM at the national level is assessed in the context of a system of state-reporting. Ultimate control and responsibility for monitoring the implementation of the FCNM rests with the Committee of Ministers of the Council of Europe and an Advisory Committee (AC) that assists it in this regard. The AC does the lion's share of the work, even though its role is formally described as one of "assistance."[51]

---

[49] Féret v. Belgium and Le Pen v. France, (dec.), Eur. Ct. H.R. (Fifth Section) (Apr. 20 2010), App. No. 18788/09.

[50] E.T.S. No. 157 (entered into force Feb. 1, 1998). As of this writing, thirty-nine Council of Europe Member States have ratified (or otherwise acceded to) the FCNM.

[51] The Advisory Committee currently comprises eighteen independent experts, who are appointed by the Committee of Ministers for periods of four years. Members of the Advisory Committee must have "recognised expertise in the field of the protection of national minorities." Members are required to serve in their individual capacities and discharge their functions in an independent, impartial, and efficient manner. *See also* Resolution (97)10, Rules adopted by the Committee of Ministers on the monitoring arrangements under Articles 24 to 26 of the Framework Convention for the Protection of National Minorities (Sep. 17, 1997).

The FCNM regards the creation of expressive and dialogical opportunities as being of crucial importance for safeguarding pluralism and tolerance in a democratic society. Its most important provisions in this respect are Articles 6 and 9. The former reads:

1.  The Parties shall encourage a spirit of tolerance and intercultural dialogue and take effective measures to promote mutual respect and understanding and co-operation among all persons living on their territory, irrespective of those persons' ethnic, cultural, linguistic or religious identity, in particular in the fields of education, culture and the media.
2.  The Parties undertake to take appropriate measures to protect persons who may be subject to threats or acts of discrimination, hostility or violence as a result of their ethnic, cultural, linguistic or religious identity.

Article 9 of the FCNM, for its part, expands slightly on the scope of Article 10, ECHR (on which it was modeled):

1.  The Parties undertake to recognise that the right to freedom of expression of every person belonging to a national minority includes freedom to hold opinions and to receive and impart information and ideas in the minority language, without interference by public authorities and regardless of frontiers. The Parties shall ensure, within the framework of their legal systems, that persons belonging to a national minority are not discriminated against in their access to the media.
2.  Paragraph 1 shall not prevent Parties from requiring the licensing, without discrimination and based on objective criteria, of sound radio and television broadcasting, or cinema enterprises.
3.  The Parties shall not hinder the creation and the use of printed media by persons belonging to national minorities. In the legal framework of sound radio and television broadcasting, they shall ensure, as far as possible, and taking into account the provisions of paragraph 1, that persons belonging to national minorities are granted the possibility of creating and using their own media.
4.  In the framework of their legal systems, the Parties shall adopt adequate measures in order to facilitate access to the media for persons belonging to national minorities and in order to promote tolerance and permit cultural pluralism.

The FCNM's strategies for countering "hate speech" stem from the synergistic interaction of these two articles. They seek to address the problem of "hate speech" before it actually spawns, by emphasizing the need to foster, including via the media, improved interethnic and intercultural understanding and tolerance through the development of dialogical relationships between communities. These strategies are informed by recognition that the media are capable of contributing to the promotion of tolerance and intercultural understanding, as well as to the elimination of negative stereotyping and negative portrayal of minorities.

Communicative engagement is essential to building intergroup awareness and understanding. This implies a need to share information and perspectives. Opportunities for self-definition and public representation are crucial for minorities, especially given the corrective potential of such opportunities vis-à-vis dominant or prevalent societal attitudes regarding them. The transmission of minority-centered programs can expose wider *tranches* of society to minority perspectives and cultures, thereby raising the profile of minority cultures and their prestige outside of minority groups themselves. The nature and extent of media coverage are related to, but also logically prior to, the problem of negative reporting on, and stereotyping of, minorities. These arguments, which inform Article 9(4), are important for the transmission and legitimization of minority cultures. The FCNM displays a conviction that "more speech" can be an effective, preemptive strategy against hate speech.[52] And the approach goes beyond traditional counterspeech, which is responsive and corrective; "more speech" can also be anticipatory and preemptive.

The AC has proposed various responses to the problem of negative reporting, many of which center on the promotion of balanced and accurate reporting[53] and adherence to journalistic codes of ethics and standards, among other things.[54] The AC has consistently emphasized the importance of special training and programs for journalists on minority issues.[55] The goal is to familiarize journalists with minority issues and sensitivities likely to arise in the course of their coverage of those issues. Exchange programs for journalists have also been considered, with the same goals in mind.[56] Related strategies include the establishment of ethnically diverse training courses in journalism,[57] with a view to increasing the number of persons from

---

[52] *See also* Katharine Gelber, *Speaking Back: The Free Speech Versus Hate Speech Debate* (John Benjamins Publishing 2002); Katharine Gelber, "Reconceptualizing Counterspeech in Hate-Speech Policy (with a Focus on Australia)," Chapter 11 herein.

[53] *See, e.g.,* AC's Opinion on Slovakia (Sep. 22, 2000) (Section: "In respect of Article 6"), *available at* http://www.coe.int/t/dghl/monitoring/minorities/3_FCNMdocs/PDF_1st_OP_SlovakRepublic_en.pdf.

[54] Of particular importance in this connection is the practice of only mentioning the ethnic origin of subjects of reporting when strictly relevant. *See, e.g.,* AC's Opinion on the United Kingdom (Nov. 30, 2001), ¶ 53, *available at* http://www.coe.int/t/dghl/monitoring/minorities/3_FCNMdocs/PDF_1st_OP_UK_en.pdf.

[55] *See, e.g.,* AC's Opinions on Albania (Sep. 12, 2002), ¶ 98, *available at* http://www.coe.int/t/dghl/monitoring/minorities/3_FCNMdocs/PDF_1st_OP_Albania_en.pdf; Lithuania (Feb. 21, 2003), ¶ 45, *available at* http://www.coe.int/t/dghl/monitoring/minorities/3_FCNMdocs/PDF_1st_OP_Lithuania_en.pdf; Spain (Nov. 27, 2003), ¶ 63, *available at* http://www.coe.int/t/dghl/monitoring/minorities/3_FCNMdocs/PDF_1st_OP_Spain_en.pdf; Sweden (Feb. 20, 2003), ¶¶ 34, 78, *available at* http://www.coe.int/t/dghl/monitoring/minorities/3_FCNMdocs/PDF_1st_OP_Sweden_en.pdf; Ukraine (March 1, 2002), ¶ 39, *available at* http://www.coe.int/t/dghl/monitoring/minorities/3_FCNMdocs/PDF_1st_OP_Ukraine_en.pdf.

[56] AC's Opinion on Slovakia, *supra* note 53.

[57] AC's Second Opinion on Denmark (Dec. 9, 2004), ¶ 95, *available at* http://www.coe.int/t/dghl/monitoring/minorities/3_FCNMdocs/PDF_2nd_OP_Denmark_en.pdf.

different ethnic, religious, and other groups entering the media sector in professional capacities.[58] These emphases form a rather comprehensive approach to countering negative reporting.[59]

The AC often calls for vigilance by state authorities toward negative reporting as a countermeasure to the same. However, those calls are accompanied by standard reminders of the need to show deference to the principle of (editorial) independence of the media, and also, on occasion, by reminders of the need to observe overarching principles of freedom of expression as well.[60]

## C. *Additional Protocol to the Convention on Cybercrime*

The 2001 Convention on Cybercrime[61] sought to pursue a common policy to protect society against cybercrime. After critics argued that it failed to address racism and xenophobia,[62] it was supplemented in 2003 by an Additional Protocol "concerning the criminalisation of acts of a racist and xenophobic nature committed through computer systems."[63] The central aims of the Additional Protocol are to harmonize "substantive criminal law in the fight against racism and xenophobia on the Internet," and to improve "international co-operation in this area."[64]

Article 3 of the Additional Protocol requires states to "adopt such legislative and other measures as may be necessary to establish as criminal offences under its domestic law, when committed intentionally and without right, the following conduct: distributing, or otherwise making available, racist and xenophobic material to the public through a computer system."[65] "Racist and xenophobic material" is defined as

---

[58] *Id.* at ¶ 103.

[59] AC's Opinion on the Russian Federation (Sep. 13, 2002), ¶ 135, *available at* http://www.coe.int/t/dghl/monitoring/minorities/3_FCNMdocs/PDF_1st_OP_RussianFederation_en.pdf.

[60] AC's Second Opinion on Italy (Feb. 24, 2005), ¶ 82, *available at* http://www.coe.int/t/dghl/monitoring/minorities/3_FCNMdocs/PDF_2nd_OP_Italy_en.pdf.

[61] E.T.S. No. 185, entered into force July 1, 2004. As of this writing, the Convention has been ratified (or otherwise acceded to) by thirty Council of Europe Member States and one non-Member State (the United States).

[62] *See, e.g.*, the following Parliamentary Assembly of the Council of Europe texts: Opinion No. 226 (2001), "Draft convention on cybercrime" (Apr. 24, 2001); Recommendation 1543 (2001), "Racism and xenophobia in cyberspace" (Nov. 8, 2001); Opinion No. 240 (2002), "Draft additional protocol to the Convention on Cybercrime concerning the criminalisation of acts of a racist and xenophobic nature committed through computer systems" (Sep. 27, 2002).

[63] E.T.S. No. 189, entered into force March 1, 2006 [hereinafter *Cybercrime Additional Protocol*]. As of this writing, the Additional Protocol has been ratified or otherwise acceded to by eighteen Council of Europe Member States and no non-Member States. *See also* Explanatory Report to the Additional Protocol to the Convention on cybercrime, concerning the criminalization of acts of a racist or xenophobic nature committed through computer systems (Nov. 7, 2002), ¶ 9 [hereinafter *Cybercrime Explanatory Report*].

[64] *Id.*, ¶ 3.

[65] *Cybercrime Additional Protocol*, *supra* note 63, art. 3(1).

any written material, any image or any other representation of ideas or theories, which advocates, promotes or incites hatred, discrimination or violence, against any individual or group of individuals, based on race, colour, descent or national or ethnic origin, as well as religion if used as a pretext for any of these factors.[66]

The breadth of Article 3 is largely determined by three main qualifications. First, and of central importance, is the requirement that intent or *mens rea* be present for activity to be criminal. A corollary of this requirement is that an Internet Service Provider (ISP) is not liable for the dissemination of material where it has acted merely as conduit, cache, or host for such material.[67]

Second, offenses must be committed "without right" – a term that recurs in other provisions of the Additional Protocol. The Additional Protocol's Explanatory Report makes a not entirely satisfying attempt to clarify the meaning of this term, stating that conduct taken "without right" can refer to "conduct undertaken without authority (whether legislative, executive, administrative, judicial, contractual or consensual)" or to "conduct that is otherwise not covered by established legal defences, excuses, justifications or relevant principles under domestic law."[68]

Third, Article 3(2) allows states not to criminalize relevant acts if the material "advocates, promotes or incites discrimination that is not associated with hatred or violence, *provided that other effective remedies are available*."[69] Such remedies would typically be of a "civil or administrative" nature.[70] This could be taken as an important endorsement of the efficacy and value of, for example, self- and co-regulatory complaints and sanctioning mechanisms. Nevertheless, neither the Additional Protocol nor its Explanatory Report explores the range of potentially effective remedies.

Whereas Article 3 concerns mere dissemination of racist material, Article 4 addresses actual threats. It requires States Parties to criminalize the following conduct when it is committed "intentionally and without right":

> threatening, through a computer system, with the commission of a serious criminal offence as defined under its domestic law, (i) persons for the reason that they belong to a group, distinguished by race, colour, descent or national or ethnic origin, as well as religion, if used as a pretext for any of these factors, or (ii) a group of persons which is distinguished by any of these characteristics.[71]

---

[66] *See also Cybercrime Explanatory Report, supra* note 63, at ¶¶ 10–22.

[67] *Id.*, ¶ 25. Similarly, Article 7 shields ISPs from aiding and abetting liability in the outlined circumstances. *Id.*, ¶ 45.

[68] *Id.*, ¶ 24.

[69] *Cybercrime Additional Protocol, supra* note 63, art. 3(2) (emphasis added). "Violence" refers to "the unlawful use of force" and "hatred" to "intense dislike or enmity." *Cybercrime Explanatory Report, supra* note 63, ¶ 15. The definitional approach to the notion of discrimination is *broadly* congruent with the approach taken by the European Court of Human Rights in respect of the European Convention on Human Rights. For further details and nuances, see *id.*, ¶¶ 16–21. However, no interpretive guidance is given on what *association* with hatred or violence could concretely entail.

[70] *Id.*, ¶ 32.

[71] *Cybercrime Additional Protocol, supra* note 63, art. 4.

This spans both public and private communications, unlike the target of the similarly worded Article 5 ("Racist and xenophobic motivated insult"), which is only concerned with public communications. Article 5 requires states to criminalize "insulting publicly, through a computer system, (i) persons for the reason that they belong to a group distinguished by race, colour, descent or national or ethnic origin, as well as religion, if used as a pretext for any of these factors; or (ii) a group of persons which is distinguished by any of these characteristics."[72] A requirement for states to criminalize racial insults could seems in real tension with relevant case law of the European Court of Human Rights. At first glance, the threshold for "insult" could appear rather low and thus potentially open to abuse. The Explanatory Report to the Additional Protocol states that the "notion of 'insult'" refers to "any offensive, contemptuous or invective expression which prejudices the honour or the dignity of a person," where it is clear that "the insult is directly connected with the insulted person's belonging to the group."[73] Yet, under the seminal principle laid down in *Handyside* (and consistently followed by the Court ever since), freedom of expression extends "not only to 'information' or 'ideas' that are favourably received or regarded as inoffensive or as a matter of indifference, but also to those that offend, shock or disturb the State or any sector of the population."[74] In specific cases, the intensity of the "insult" is necessarily determinative, but the presence of the racist element is clearly transformative: Racist insults are regarded as being qualitatively different to insults without a racist character.

Finally, Article 6 of the Additional Protocol ("Denial, gross minimisation, approval or justification of genocide or crimes against humanity") is a first in international human rights law in that it applies the offense of genocide denial to genocides other than the Holocaust. Article 6 reads:

1.  Each Party shall adopt such legislative measures as may be necessary to establish the following conduct as criminal offences under its domestic law, when committed intentionally and without right:

distributing or otherwise making available, through a computer system to the public, material which denies, grossly minimises, approves or justifies acts constituting genocide or crimes against humanity, as defined by international law and recognised as such by final and binding decisions of the International Military Tribunal, established by the London Agreement of 8 August 1945, or of any other international court established by relevant international instruments and whose jurisdiction is recognised by that Party.

---

[72] *Id.*, art. 5.
[73] *Cybercrime Explanatory Report, supra* note 63, ¶ 36.
[74] Handyside v. United Kingdom, 24 Eur. Ct. H.R. (ser. A) at 23, ¶ 49 (1976).

2. A Party may either
   (a) require that the denial or the gross minimisation referred to in paragraph 1 of this article is committed with the intent to incite hatred, discrimination or violence against any individual or group of individuals, based on race, colour, descent or national or ethnic origin, as well as religion if used as a pretext for any of these factors, or otherwise
   (b) reserve the right not to apply, in whole or in part, paragraph 1 of this article.[75]

This provision was drafted in response to a growing incidence of court cases at the national level concerning the denial or minimization of genocide or crimes against humanity (especially the Holocaust) and an awareness of the underlying racist or xenophobic motivation for such denial or minimization and its potentially nefarious impact on racist and xenophobic groups.[76] The inclusion of genocides other than the Holocaust was prompted by the realization that more recent genocides and crimes against humanity have been recognized by international courts and tribunals since the Nuremburg Tribunal and that others may be recognized in the future.[77] The Explanatory Report to the Additional Protocol links Article 6 to the conclusion of the European Court of Human Rights in the *Lehideux & Isorni* case, that the "negation or revision" of "clearly established historical facts – such as the Holocaust . . . would be removed from the protection of Article 10 by Article 17 [ECHR]."[78]

## D. *European Convention on Transfrontier Television*

The 1989 European Convention on Transfrontier Television (ECTT) sets out to "facilitate, among the Parties, the transfrontier transmission and the retransmission of television programme services."[79] Article 7(1) is entitled "Responsibilities of the broadcaster." Its *chapeau* paragraph insists that broadcast material must, in its presentation and content, "respect the dignity of the human being and the fundamental rights of others." The provision explicitly applies to "all items of programme services" – that is, "programmes, advertising, programmes trailers, public

---

[75] The Explanatory Report clarifies that art. 6(2)(a) can be achieved by a Party entering a declaration to the Protocol, and that art. 6(2)(b) can be achieved by a Party entering a reservation to the Protocol. *Cybercrime Explanatory Report, supra* note 63, ¶ 43.

[76] *Id.,* ¶ 39.

[77] *Id.,* ¶ 40. See generally Irwin Cotler, "State-Sanctioned Incitement to Genocide: The Responsibility to Prevent," Chapter 23 herein.

[78] *Cybercrime Explanatory Report, supra* note 63, ¶ 42, citing Lehideux & Isorni v. France, 1998-VII Eur. Ct. H.R. 2864, ¶ 47.

[79] E.T.S. No. 132 (entered into force May 1, 1993), as amended by a Protocol thereto, E.T.S. No. 171, (entered into force March 1, 2002), art. 1. As of this writing, thirty Member States of the Council of Europe have ratified (or otherwise acceded to) the ECTT, as well as one non-Member State (The Holy See).

announcements" and other such elements.[80] Article 7(1)(b) further states that programs shall not "give undue prominence to violence or be likely to incite to racial hatred." A Party shall communicate an alleged violation of the ECTT in the first instance to the transmitting Party. "If the alleged violation is of a manifest, serious and grave nature which raises important public issues" and concerns, *inter alia*, Article 7(1) and "if it persists within two weeks following the communication, the receiving Party may suspend provisionally the retransmission of the incriminated programme service."[81]

## III. REGULATION OF "HATE SPEECH" OUTSIDE THE TREATY FRAMEWORK

The Council of Europe engages in a wide range of standard-setting activities not based on specific treaties. An important preliminary caveat is in order. The standard-setting texts adopted by the Council of Europe's Committee of Ministers, Parliamentary Assembly, and European Commission against Racism and Intolerance may be politically persuasive, but they are not legally binding on Member States. They generally serve to indicate either the normative status quo in relation to their subject matter or the direction in which the body in question would like future law and policy to develop. Nevertheless, awareness of these standard-setting texts is growing and, as a result, so too is their impact. For instance, the European Court of Human Rights refers increasingly to the Committee of Ministers' Recommendation on "Hate Speech" (see below) in its judgments.[82]

### A. *Committee of Ministers*

The Committee of Ministers is the executive organ of the Council of Europe. It is empowered to issue, *inter alia*, Recommendations to Member States of the Council of Europe and general Declarations.[83] As their names suggest, Recommendations advocate particular courses of action, whereas Declarations are declaratory of particular (legal) situations or themes.

### 1. Resolution 68(30)

An early example of the Committee of Ministers' engagement with what could be classified as "hate speech" is its Resolution 68(30), entitled "Measures to be taken

---

[80] Explanatory Report to the European Convention on Transfrontier Television, as amended, ¶ 155, *available at* http://conventions.coe.int/treaty/en/Reports/Html/132.htm.

[81] E.T.S. No. 132, art. 24.

[82] It usually does so in the recurrent section, "Relevant International Instruments." *See, e.g.,* Féret v. Belgium, Eur. Ct. H.R. (Second Section) (July 16 2009) ¶¶ 44, 72; Gündüz v. Turkey, Eur. Ct. H.R. (First Section) (December 4, 2003) ¶ 22.

[83] Prior to 1979, Recommendations to Member States were known as Resolutions.

against incitement to racial, national and religious hatred."[84] Its primary aim is to press Member States of the Council of Europe to sign, ratify, and subsequently give domestic legal effect to the International Convention on the Elimination of All Forms of Racial Discrimination (ICERD).[85] It asks governments to "review their legislation in order to ensure that it provides for effective measures on the matter of prohibition of racial discrimination as well as on the related question of the elimination of all forms of intolerance and discrimination based on religion or belief."

## 2. Recommendation 97(20)

The Committee of Ministers' most extensive engagement with "hate speech" came in 1997, with the adoption of Recommendations on "hate speech"[86] and on the media and the promotion of a culture of tolerance.[87]

The recommendation on "hate speech," number 97(20), defines "hate speech" to cover

> all forms of expression which spread, incite, promote or justify racial hatred, xeno-phobia, antisemitism or other forms of hatred based on intolerance, including: intolerance expressed by aggressive nationalism and ethnocentrism, discrimination and hostility against minorities, migrants and people of immigrant origin.[88]

It is clear from the Preamble to the Recommendation that it is anchored in the prevailing standards of international law as regards both freedom of expression and antiracism. It acknowledges the need to grapple with "all forms of expression which incite to racial hatred, xenophobia, antisemitism and all forms of intolerance, since they undermine democratic security, cultural cohesion and pluralism." It also recognizes and draws attention to a number of the central paradoxes involved, for example, that the dissemination of such forms of expression via the media can lead to their having "a greater and more damaging impact," but that there is nevertheless

---

[84]  Adopted by the Ministers' Deputies on October 31, 1968.

[85]  *Id.*, ¶ A.1.

[86]  Council of Eur., Comm. of Ministers, Recommendation No. R (97)20 to Member States on "Hate Speech," 607th meeting (Oct. 30, 1997).

[87]  Council of Eur., Comm. of Ministers, Recommendation No. R (97)21 to Member States on the Media and the Promotion of a Culture of Tolerance, 607th meeting (Oct. 30, 1997).

[88]  Recommendation No. R (97)20, *supra* note 86. The drafting process of the Recommendations can be traced to the Summit of Heads of State and Government of the Council of Europe Member States held in Vienna in 1993. The Summit concluded with the adoption of, *inter alia*, a Declaration and Action Plan on combating racism, xenophobia, anti-Semitism, and intolerance. That Declaration set out the parameters for the work that was to follow. This is the formal explanation for why the resulting Recommendation (97) 20 on "hate speech" does not cover all forms of intolerance (e.g., "intolerance on grounds of sex, sexual orientation, age, handicap, etc."). Explanatory Memorandum to Recommendation No. R (97)20 on "Hate Speech," ¶ 22, *available at* http://www.coe.int/t/dghl/standardsetting/media/doc/cm/rec%281997%29020&expmem_EN.asp.

a need to "respect fully the editorial independence and autonomy of the media." These are circles that are not easily squared in the abstract, hence the aim of the Recommendation to provide "elements" of guidance for application in specific cases.

The operative part of the Recommendation calls on national governments to take appropriate steps to implement the principles annexed to the Recommendation; "ensure that such steps form part of a comprehensive approach to the phenomenon, which also targets its social, economic, political, cultural and other root causes"; where states have not already done so, "sign, ratify and effectively implement" ICERD in their domestic legal orders; and "review their domestic legislation and practice in order to ensure that they comply with the principles" appended to the Recommendation.[89]

The principles in question address a wide range of issues. Principle 1 points out that public officials are under a special responsibility to refrain from making statements – particularly to the media – that could be understood as, or have the effect of, hate speech. Furthermore, it calls for such statements to be "prohibited and publicly disavowed whenever they occur." According to Principle 2, states' authorities should "establish or maintain a sound legal framework consisting of civil, criminal and administrative law provisions on hate speech which enable administrative and judicial authorities to reconcile in each case respect for freedom of expression with respect for human dignity and the protection of the reputation or rights of others." It suggests detailed ways and means of achieving such ends. Principle 3 stresses that states' authorities should ensure that within their legal frameworks, "interferences with freedom of expression are narrowly circumscribed and applied in a lawful and non-arbitrary manner on the basis of objective criteria."

Principle 4 affirms that some particularly virulent strains of hate speech might not warrant any protection whatsoever under Article 10, ECHR. This is a reference to the import of Article 17, ECHR, and to existing case law on the interaction of Articles 10 and 17. Principle 5 highlights the need for a guarantee of proportionality whenever criminal sanctions are imposed on persons convicted of hate speech offenses.

Whereas the Recommendation as a whole is redolent of the *Jersild* case generally,[90] Principle 6 specifically harks back to one of the Court's key findings in the case: It calls for national law and practice to distinguish "between the responsibility of the author of expressions of hate speech on the one hand and any responsibility of the media and media professionals contributing to their dissemination as part of their mission to communicate information and ideas on matters of public interest on the other hand." The reasoning behind this Principle is that "it would unduly hamper the role of the media if the mere fact that they assisted in the dissemination of the statements engaged their legal responsibility or that of the media professional

---

[89] Recommendation No. R (97)20, *supra* note 86.
[90] *See* Explanatory Memorandum to the Recommendation, *supra* note 88, ¶¶ 19, 30, 38, 46 *et seq.*

concerned."[91] Principle 7 develops this reasoning by stating that national law and practice should take into account that:

- reporting on racism, xenophobia, anti-Semitism, or other forms of intolerance is fully protected by Article 10(1), ECHR, and may only be restricted in accordance with Article 10(2), ECHR;
- when examining the necessity of restrictions on freedom of expression, national authorities must have proper regard for relevant case law of the European Court of Human Rights, including the consideration afforded therein to "the manner, contents, context and purpose of the reporting;" and
- "respect for journalistic freedoms also implies that it is not for the courts or the public authorities to impose their views on the media as to the types of reporting techniques to be adopted by journalists."[92]

### 3. Recommendation 97(21)

Whereas combating hate speech may be considered a defensive or reactive battle, the promotion of tolerance – an objective to which it is intimately linked – is more proactive.[93] Recommendation (97)21 on the Media and the Promotion of a Culture of Tolerance was conceived of as the logical complement to the Recommendation on "Hate Speech." The main justification for preparing a separate Recommendation dealing with the positive contribution which the media can make to countering hate speech was:

> As concerns the propagation of racism and intolerance there is, in principle, scope for imposing legally binding standards without violating freedom of expression and the principle of editorial independence. However, as concerns the promotion of a positive contribution by the media, great care needs to be taken so as not to interfere with these principles. This area calls for measures of encouragement rather than legal measures.[94]

The Recommendation urges Member States to raise awareness of the media practices they promote in all sections of the media and to remain open to supporting initiatives that would further the objectives of the Recommendation. It is suggested that initial and further training programs could do more to sensitize (future) media professionals to issues of multiculturalism, tolerance, and intolerance. Reflection on such issues is called for among the general public, but crucially also within media enterprises

---

[91] *Id.*, ¶ 38.

[92] Recommendation No. R (97)20, *supra* note 86, appendix; Principle 7.

[93] It should also be mentioned that the European Commission against Racism and Intolerance frequently refers to the need to assure minority groups effective access to the media, *inter alia*, to counter negative stereotypes of their cultures and lifestyles, and more generally to promote intercommunity understanding and tolerance.

[94] Explanatory Memorandum to Recommendation No. R (97)20, *supra* note 88, ¶ 12.

themselves. It is also pointed out that it would be desirable for representative bodies of media professionals to undertake "action programmes or practical initiatives for the promotion of a culture of tolerance," and that such measures viably could be complemented by codes of conduct.

Broadcasters, especially those with public-service mandates, are encouraged to "make adequate provision for programme services, also at popular viewing times, which help promote the integration of all individuals, groups and communities as well as proportionate amounts of airtime for the various ethnic, religious and other communities." They also are encouraged to promote the values of multicultural-ism in their programming, especially in their program offerings targeting children. Finally, the Recommendation mentions the benefits of codes of conduct in the advertising sector, which prohibit discrimination and negative stereotyping. It also flags the usefulness of advertising campaigns promoting tolerance.

Together, the twin Recommendations on "hate speech" and on the media and the promotion of a culture of tolerance serve as an influential reference point among standard-setting texts adopted by the Committee of Ministers. They are frequently invoked in other Recommendations and Declarations. For instance, they – or their underlying principles, such as the protection of human dignity – have informed the Committee of Ministers' approaches to freedom of political debate, the fight against terrorism, the promotion of intercultural dialogue, the safeguarding of human rights in a digital environment, and the protection of minors, especially in an online context. These topics will now be summarily dealt with in turn.

## 4. Declaration on Freedom of Political Debate

The central aims of the 2004 Declaration on Freedom of Political Debate in the Media[95] were to "send a strong political signal to condemn" practices such as the persecution of journalists because of their criticism of politicians or public authorities and to "reaffirm the Council of Europe's attachment to the fundamental value of free political debate."[96] The Preamble to the Declaration recalls the Recommendation on "Hate Speech" and emphasizes "that freedom of political debate does not include freedom to express racist opinions or opinions which are an incitement to hatred, xenophobia, antisemitism and all forms of intolerance." The substantive part of

---

[95] Council of Eur., Comm. of Ministers, Declaration on Freedom of Political Debate in the Media, 872d Mtg. (Feb. 12, 2004) [hereinafter Declaration on Freedom of Political Debate].

[96] Páll Thórhallsson, "Freedom of Political Debate and the Council of Europe," in *IRIS Special: Political Debate and the Role of the Media – The Fragility of Free Speech* 53 (Susanne Nikoltchev ed., European Audiovisual Observatory 2006). Thórhallsson explains that the decision to issue a Declaration on this topic was taken as early as 1998 when it emerged from monitoring exercises within the Council of Europe that journalists were being persecuted for political criticism in many Member States. *Id.*

the Declaration – under the heading "Remedies against violations by the media" – states:

> Defamation or insult by the media should not lead to imprisonment, unless the seriousness of the violation of the rights or reputation of others makes it a strictly necessary and proportionate penalty, especially where other fundamental rights have been seriously violated through defamatory or insulting statements in the media, such as hate speech.[97]

As such, the Declaration reiterates that racist expressions amounting to incitement to specific types of hatred are beyond the pale of protection offered by Article 10, ECHR. This is an accurate representation of the case law surrounding Article 10. However, the implication of the quoted sentence is that hate speech is always an example of the most serious sort of defamation or insult, and thus one for which imprisonment is always an appropriate sanction. Given the severity and chilling effect of imprisonment as a sanction, and given also the potentially wide definitional embrace of the term "hate speech," it would have been both more accurate and more strategically sound to have referred to only the most serious or invidious types of "hate speech."

## 5. The Fight Against Terrorism

The 2005 Declaration on Freedom of Expression and Information in the Media in the Context of the Fight Against Terrorism[98] "invites" media professionals "to consider" suggestions such as:

- to bear in mind the significant role that they can play in preventing "hate speech" and incitement to violence, as well as in promoting mutual understanding;
- to be aware of the risk the media and journalists can unintentionally serve as a vehicle for the expression of racist or xenophobic feelings or hatred;
- to bear in mind the importance of distinguishing between suspected or convicted terrorists and the group (national, ethnic, religious, or ideological) to which they belong or to which they claim to subscribe; and
- to set up training courses, in collaboration with their professional organizations, for journalists and other media professionals who report on terrorism, on their safety and the historical, cultural, religious, and geopolitical context of the scenes they cover, and to invite journalists to follow these courses.

The perennial question of how to devise effective and appropriate counterterrorism strategies is highly sensitive, which increases the risk of emotionally laden

---

97 Declaration on Freedom of Political Debate, *supra* note 95, art. 8.
98 Council of Eur. Comm. of Ministers, Declaration on Freedom of Expression and Information in the Media in the Context of the Fight Against Terrorism, 917d Mtg. (March 2, 2005).

political debate and general media coverage. Hence the importance of specific provisions aiming to ensure that the depiction of certain groups remain within the bounds of the temperate. Responsible, value-sensitive journalism is the lodestar here, but the Declaration favors a noncoercive approach toward the media, thereby respecting the principle of media autonomy. The Declaration's promotion of responsible journalism concerns professional practice and training programs: This is evidence of a simultaneous commitment to the immediate and longer-term goals of countering "hate speech."

### 6. Promotion of Intercultural Dialogue

Without explicitly mentioning "hate speech," a number of recent texts adopted by the Committee of Ministers seek to promote intercultural communication and thereby pursue an aim that can prove effective in preempting "hate speech." The Committee of Ministers' 2007 Recommendation on media pluralism and diversity of media content, for instance, recognizes the "crucial contribution of the media in fostering public debate, political pluralism and awareness of diverse opinions, notably by providing different groups in society – including cultural, linguistic, ethnic, religious or other minorities – with an opportunity to receive and impart information, to express themselves and to exchange ideas."[99] It notes the capacity of community, local, minority, and social media to provide "a space for dialogue."[100] It further recommends that Member States "encourage the media to contribute to intercultural and inter-religious dialogue, so as to promote mutual respect and tolerance and to prevent potential conflicts through discussions."[101]

The Committee of Ministers' Recommendation on the Remit of Public Service Media in the Information Society articulates a number of insightful reflections on the goal of public service media to be inclusive vis-à-vis all groups in society and to therefore ensure that their services and structures are appropriately accessible to all.[102] Similar reflections about the suitability and diversity of public service media content are also provided.[103] Importantly for the present analysis, the Recommendation states that public service media should harness new digital and online technologies to "actively promote a culture of tolerance and mutual understanding."[104]

---

[99] Council of Eur., Committee of Ministers, Recommendation (2007)2 to Member States on Media Pluralism and Diversity of Media Content, 985th meeting (Jan. 31, 2007), Preamble, *available at* https://wcd.coe.int/wcd/ViewDoc.jsp?id=1089699.

[100] *Id.*, § I, ¶ 4.

[101] *Id.*, § II, ¶ 2.2. To achieve this aim, it suggests promoting minority participation in organizational structures and to exploit the potential of digital media literacy for bridging the digital divide.

[102] Council of Eur., Comm. of Ministers, Recommendation (2007)3 to Member States on the Remit of Public Service Media in the Information Society, 985th meeting (Jan. 31, 2007), ¶¶ 8–10, *available at* https://wcd.coe.int/wcd/ViewDoc.jsp?id=1089759.

[103] *Id.*, ¶¶ 23–24.

[104] *Id.*, ¶ 16.

The Committee of Ministers' Declaration on the role of community media in promoting social cohesion and intercultural dialogue recognizes community media as a distinct media sector and proposes various regulatory, technical, and capacity-building measures to promote its further development.[105] The Declaration explicitly acknowledges the "important role" that community media can play in "promoting social cohesion, intercultural dialogue and tolerance." More specifically, it recognizes

> the contribution of community media in fostering public debate, political pluralism and awareness of diverse opinions, notably by providing various groups in society – including cultural, linguistic, ethnic, religious or other minorities – with an opportunity to receive and impart information, to express themselves and to exchange ideas.[106]

### 7. Safeguarding Human Rights in a Digital Environment

Two of the foundational premises of the Committee of Ministers' approach to human rights questions in a digital environment are: (1) all human rights and "essential public interest objectives" should be afforded the same level of protection as in the off-line world;[107] and (2) a willingness to explore new regulatory models (i.e., including self- and co-regulatory models), technical standards and systems, codes of ethics and conduct, and other measures is key to safeguarding human rights and public interests.[108] Freedom of expression and information, the protection of human dignity, and protection from racial and other forms of discrimination are recurrently mentioned as meriting priority attention in this connection.[109]

These premises are set out in some detail in the Committee of Ministers' Declaration on Human Rights and the Rule of Law in the Information Society (2005).[110]

---

[105] Council of Eur., Comm. of Ministers, Declaration on the Role of Community Media in Promoting Social Cohesion and Intercultural Dialogue, 1048th meeting (Feb. 11, 2009), *available at* http://www.commedia.org.uk/wp-content/uploads/2009/02/declaration-community-media-adopted-11-02-09.pdf.

[106] *Id.*, Preamble.

[107] Council of Eur., Comm. of Ministers, Recommendation (2003)9 to Member States on Measures to Promote the Democratic and Social Contribution of Digital Broadcasting, 840th meeting (May 28, 2003), *available at* http://www.ebu.ch/CMSimages/en/leg_ref_coe_r2003_9_digital_broadcasting_280503_tcm6–5032.pdf.

[108] Council of Eur., Comm. of Ministers, Declaration on a European Policy for New Information Technologies, 104th Sess. (May 7, 1999), § (v), *available at* https://wcd.coe.int/wcd/ViewDoc.jsp?id=448133 ("With respect to Protection of rights and freedoms").

[109] *See, e.g.*, Council of Eur., Comm. of Ministers, Recommendation (2007)11 to Member States on Promoting Freedom of Expression and Information in the New Information and Communications Environment, 1005th meeting (Sept. 26, 2007), *available at* https://wcd.coe.int/wcd/ViewDoc.jsp?id=1188541; Council of Eur., Comm. of Ministers, Declaration on Freedom of Communication on the Internet, 840th meeting (May 28, 2003), *available at* https://wcd.coe.int/wcd/ViewDoc.jsp?id=37031.

[110] Council of Eur., Comm. of Ministers, Declaration on Human Rights and the Rule of Law in the Information Society, 926th Meeting (May 13, 2005), *available at* https://wcd.coe.int/wcd/ViewDoc

The first section of the Declaration is entitled "Human rights in the Information Society." Its treatment of "the right to freedom of expression, information and communication" includes the assertion that existing standards of protection should apply in digital and nondigital environments alike and that any restrictions on the right should not exceed those provided for in Article 10 of the ECHR. It calls for the prevention of state and private forms of censorship and for the scope of national measures combating illegal content (e.g., racism, racial discrimination, and child pornography) to include offenses committed using information and communications technologies (ICTs). In this connection, greater compliance with the Additional Protocol to the Cybercrime Convention is also urged. The second section of the Declaration puts forward a "multi-stakeholder governance approach for building the information society," urging private sector actors to "address in a decisive manner" issues such as "hate speech, racism and xenophobia and incitation to violence in a digital environment such as the Internet."

### 8. Protection of Minors, Especially in an Online Environment

The Committee of Ministers' standard-setting texts aiming to protect children in an online environment tend not to employ the term "hate speech." Nevertheless, they do acknowledge the need to protect the dignity of children and to equip them with the skills to deal with the harms that result from, *inter alia*, racism and discrimination in an online environment. These acknowledgments are cursory and often merely preambular and do not lead to detailed or substantive engagement with relevant issues, except to occasionally link them to the right to freedom of expression.[111] The Committee of Ministers' Recommendation (92) 19 on video games with racist content is an exception. One of its two main points is that states' authorities

---

.jsp?id=849061. The Declaration was submitted as a Council of Europe contribution to the Tunis Phase of the World Summit on the Information Society (WSIS) in November 2005. The WSIS was an initiative organized by the International Telecommunication Union (ITU), a UN agency under the auspices of which "governments and the private sector coordinate global telecom networks and services." The Summit was held in two phases: the first took place in Geneva in 2003 and the second took place in Tunis in 2005. *See also* World Summit on the Information Society, http://www.itu.int/wsis/.

[111] *See generally* Council of Eur., Comm. of Ministers, Recommendation (2009)5 to Member States on Measures to Protect Children Against Harmful Content and Behaviour and to Promote Their Active Participation in the New Information and Communications Environment, 1063d meeting (July 8, 2009) *available at* https://wcd.coe.int/wcd/ViewDoc.jsp?id=1470045 &Site=CM; Council of Eur., Comm. of Ministers, Recommendation (2008)6 to Member States on Measures to Promote the Respect for Freedom of Expression and Information with Regard to Internet Filters, 1022d meeting (Mar. 26, 2008), *available at* https://wcd.coe.int/wcd/ViewDoc.jsp?id=1266285 &Site=CM; Council of Eur., Comm. of Ministers, Declaration on Protecting the Dignity, Security and Privacy of Children on the Internet, 1018th meeting (Feb. 20, 2008), *available at* https://wcd.coe.int/wcd/ViewDoc.jsp?id=1252427 &Site=CM;Council of Eur., Comm. of Ministers, Recommendation (2006)12 to Member States on Empowering Children in the New Information and Communications Environment, 974th meeting (Sept. 27, 2006), *available at* https://wcd.coe.int/wcd/ViewDoc.jsp?id=1041181.

should "review the scope of their legislation in the fields of racial discrimination and hatred, violence and the protection of young people, in order to ensure that it applies without restriction to the production and distribution of video games with a racist content."[112]

In conclusion, notwithstanding the fact that the various standard-setting texts discussed previously are not legally binding on states, it is important to underscore their political relevance. They seek to address the problem of "hate speech" in a preventive and responsive manner, often from specific thematic angles. As already mentioned, in the past, these texts have tended to target racism, xenophobia, anti-Semitism and intolerance, and not, for example, "hate speech" focusing on gender identity, sexual orientation, age, handicap, and so forth.[113] The traditional scope of the Committee of Ministers' approach was expanded in 2010 with the adoption of a Recommendation on measures to combat discrimination on grounds of sexual orientation or gender identity.[114] The Recommendation comprises a substantive part with five recommendations and an appendix that sets out a range of relevant "principles and measures" intended as a source of guidance for member states "in their legislation, policies and practice." In respect of "hate speech," the Appendix recommends that "Member states should take appropriate measures to combat all forms of expression, including in the media and on the Internet, which may be reasonably understood as likely to produce the effect of inciting, spreading or promoting hatred or other forms of discrimination against lesbian, gay, bisexual and transgender persons." Those measures should be in accordance with Article 10 of the ECHR and relevant case law of the European Court of Human Rights.

---

[112] Council of Eur., Comm. of Ministers, Recommendation (92)19 to Member States on Video Games with a Racist Content, 482d meeting, (Oct. 19, 1992), ¶ a, *available at* https://wcd.coe.int/wcd/com.instranet.InstraServlet?command=com.instranet.CmdBlobGet &InstranetImage=574903 &SecMode=1 &DocId=605194 &Usage=. *See also* Council of Eur., Comm. of Ministers, Recommendation (2001)8 to Member States on Self-Regulation Concerning Cyber Content (Self-Regulation and User Protection Against Illegal or Harmful Content on New Communications and Information Services), 762d meeting, (Sept. 5, 2001), *available at* https://wcd.coe.int/wcd/ViewDoc.jsp?id=220387 &Site=CM. Although Recommendation (2001)8 does not contain any provisions dealing specifically with racism or racist speech, its Preamble recalls the relevance of such issues to self-regulation of online content. It refers to, *inter alia*, Recommendation (92)19 on video games with a racist content, Recommendation (97)20 on "Hate Speech" and Article 4, ICERD.

[113] This is explained by political considerations. *See supra* note 96.

[114] Council of Eur., Comm. of Ministers, Recommendation (2010)5 to Member States on Measures to Combat Discrimination on Grounds of Sexual Orientation or Gender Identity, 1081st meeting (Mar. 31, 2010), *available at* https://wcd.coe.int/wcd/ViewDoc.jsp?id=1606669. It is noteworthy that the Parliamentary Assembly of the Council of Europe has followed the lead of the Committee of Ministers in this respect. *See* Eur. Parl. Ass., "Discrimination on the Basis of Sexual Orientation and Gender Identity," Resolution 1728 (Apr. 29, 2010), *available at* http://assembly.coe.int/Main.asp?link=/Documents/WorkingDocs/Doc09/EDOC12087.htm; Eur. Parl. Ass., "Discrimination on the Basis of Sexual Orientation and Gender Identity," Recommendation 1915 (Apr. 29, 2010), *available at* http://assembly.coe.int/main.asp?Link=/documents/adoptedtext/ta10/erec1915.htm.

## B. *Parliamentary Assembly*

The Parliamentary Assembly of the Council of Europe (PACE) – the organization's deliberative organ[115] – has, since 2005, adopted a range of texts focusing on specific issues that arise in the fraught relationship between the rights to freedom of expression and freedom of religion and "hate speech."[116] This sustained focus could be seen as a response to highly visible political controversies. In particular, it has coincided with the fallout from the controversial publication – initially by a Danish newspaper, *Jyllands-Posten*, on September 30, 2005 and subsequently elsewhere – of twelve cartoons that included caricatures of the Prophet Mohammed.[117] The impact of the cartoons controversy on some of the PACE's recommendations is often palpable, for example, in its call on states' authorities to officially condemn "any death threats and incitements to violence by religious leaders and groups issued against persons for having exercised their right to freedom of expression about religious matters."[118] However, the cartoons controversy was neither the initial nor sole stimulus for this focus; the groundwork for at least one of the relevant PACE texts had begun earlier – with the tabling of a Motion for a Resolution on blasphemy, religious insults, and hate speech against persons on grounds of their religion in June 2005.[119]

All of the texts in question are anchored (explicitly) in relevant provisions of the ECHR[120] and distil or draw on principles elaborated in case law of the European Court of Human Rights.[121] The essence of relevant doctrine is captured as follows:

[I]n a democratic society, religious groups must tolerate, as must other groups, critical public statements and debate about their activities, teachings and beliefs, provided that such criticism does not amount to intentional and gratuitous insult

---

[115] Statute of the Council of Europe, art. 22, May 5, 1949, E.T.S. No. 1 (as amended).

[116] *See, e.g.*, Eur. Parl. Ass., Recommendation 1706 on Media and Terrorism (2005); Eur. Parl. Ass., Resolution 1495 on Combating the Resurrection of Nazi Ideology (2006); Eur. Parl. Ass., Resolution 1510 on Freedom of Expression and Respect for Religious Beliefs (2006); Eur. Parl. Ass., Recommendation 1768 on the Image of Asylum Seekers, Migrants and Refugees in the Media (2006); Eur. Parl. Ass., Resolution 1563 on Combating Anti-Semitism in Europe (2007); Eur. Parl. Ass., Recommendation 1804 on State, Religion, Secularity and Human Rights (2007); Eur. Parl. Ass., Recommendation 1805 on Blasphemy, Religious Insults and Hate Speech Against Persons on Grounds of Their Religion (2007).

[117] The details of that fallout – spin-doctoring, waves of protests, threats, violence, and diplomatic and political maneuvering – have been widely reported and will not be rehearsed again here. For overviews and analysis, see *Transnational Media Events: The Mohammed Cartoons and the Imagined Clash of Civilizations* (Elisabeth Eide et al. eds., Nordicom 2008); Kevin Boyle, "The Danish Cartoons," 24 *Netherlands Q. Hum. Rts.* 185 (2006); Robert Post, "Religion and Freedom of Speech: Portraits of Muhammad," 14 *Constellations* 72 (2007); David Keane, "Cartoon Violence and Freedom of Expression," 30 *Hum. Rts. Q.* 845 (2008).

[118] Eur. Parl. Ass., Recommendation 1805 on Blasphemy, Religious Insults and Hate Speech Against Persons on Grounds of Their Religion (2007), ¶ 17.7.

[119] Explanatory memorandum to Eur. Parl. Ass., "Freedom of Expression and Respect for Religious Beliefs," Doc. No. 10970, (2006), ¶ 1.

[120] Given the religious component to most of these texts, relevant provisions are Articles 9 ("Freedom of Thought, Conscience and Religion) and 10, ECHR. *See, e.g.*, PACE Resolution 1510, *supra* note 116; PACE Recommendation 1768, *supra* note 116; PACE Recommendation 1805, *supra* note 116.

[121] By way of example, see PACE Resolution 1510, *supra* note 116.

or hate speech and does not constitute incitement to disturb the public peace or to violence and discrimination against adherents of a particular religion. Public debate, dialogue and improved communication skills of religious groups and the media should be used in order to lower sensitivity when it exceeds reasonable levels.[122]

In its attempt to map and navigate the intersections of freedom of expression, freedom of religion, and "hate speech," the PACE notes that "critical dispute" and artistic freedom have traditionally helped stimulate individual and social progress: "Critical dispute, satire, humour and artistic expression should, therefore, enjoy a wider degree of freedom of expression and recourse to exaggeration should not be seen as provocation."[123] Whereas political expression and the discussion of matters of public interest may be subjected only to narrow restrictions, States enjoy a wider margin of appreciation when regulating expression that is "liable to offend intimate personal moral convictions or religion." In addition, "[w]hat is likely to cause substantial offence to persons of a particular religious persuasion will vary significantly from time to time and from place to place."[124]

All of the foregoing observations inform the PACE's most important message: Freedom of expression, as guaranteed by Article 10, ECHR, "should not be further restricted to meet increasing sensitivities of certain religious groups," but "hate speech against any religious group is not compatible with the fundamental rights and freedoms guaranteed by the Convention and the case law of the Court."[125] This statement seeks to prevent the dilution – based on subjective religious sensitivities – of existing legal protections of freedom of expression.[126] It posits that restrictions on expression may be justified when "hate speech" is at issue, but not merely on the basis of increasing religious sensitivities. Here again, the absence of a clear and binding definition of "hate speech" is regrettable: If "hate speech" is to be deemed incompatible with everything the Convention stands for (as the PACE maintains), then it is imperative that the precise meaning of that term be fully and formally established.

The PACE's strategies to counter "hate speech" mirror those of other bodies of the Council of Europe. That is, a central feature of the PACE's approach is also the bifurcation between preventive and prohibitive measures on the one hand and promotional and facilitative measures on the other hand.

Relevant PACE texts clearly emphasize the importance of effective enforcement of national legislation prohibiting incitement to hatred, violence, or discrimination

---

[122] PACE Recommendation 1805, *supra* note 116, ¶ 5.
[123] Resolution 1510, *supra* note 116, ¶ 11.
[124] *Id.*, ¶ 11.
[125] *Id.*, ¶ 12; *see also* PACE Recommendation 1768, *supra* note 116; PACE Recommendation 1804, *supra* note 116; PACE Recommendation 1805, *supra* note 116.
[126] This position has been further explicated as follows: "While we have an acknowledged duty to respect others and must discourage gratuitous insults, freedom of expression cannot, needless to say, be restricted out of deference to certain dogmas or the beliefs of a particular religious community." PACE Recommendation 1804, *supra* note 116, ¶ 19.

(and to first adopt such legislation where it does not already exist). Member States are also invited to "adopt and implement penal legislation against, *inter alia*, the public dissemination or public distribution, or the production or storage of material with a racist content or purpose."[127] The PACE similarly prioritizes the effective enforcement of (national) legislation "criminalising anti-Semitic and other hate speech;" the prosecution of political parties that promote anti-Semitic ideas; the criminalization of racially motivated public denials of crimes of genocide, crimes against humanity, or war crimes; and the strengthening of legislative provisions making anti-Semitic motivation an aggravating factor in criminal cases.[128] In its Resolution, "Towards Decriminalisation of Defamation," the PACE takes its cue from General Policy Recommendation No. 7 of the European Commission against Racism and Intolerance (ECRI, see further *infra*) and calls on Member States to "make it a criminal offence to publicly incite to violence, hatred or discrimination, or to threaten an individual or group of persons, for reasons of race, colour, language, religion, nationality or national or ethnic origin where those acts are deliberate."[129] It then calls for "only incitement to violence, hate speech and promotion of negationism" to be made "punishable by imprisonment."[130]

These calls to criminalize hate speech are very worrying, given the potentially wide scope of "hate speech." In the absence of a clear and authoritative legal definition of the term at the level of the Council of Europe, Member States are likely to determine its scope as they see fit. It is not implausible that this call could legitimate national provisions for prison sentences for "lesser" forms of "hate speech." The call also sits uneasily with other passages in the Resolution "Towards Decriminalisation of Defamation," which alert to the dangers of abusive restrictions on freedom of expression.[131] Furthermore, it jars with the position taken by the PACE elsewhere, for example when it has stressed the need for "penal laws" against incitement to hatred to respect the right to freedom of expression, or insisted that any penalties imposed *be necess*ary and proportionate, or called for media law and practice *to be changed* whenever "politically motivated application of such laws can be implied from the frequency and intensity of the penalties imposed."[132]

Relevant PACE texts also emphasize the importance of a range of nonprescriptive measures, in particular those aimed at fostering (structured) communicative opportunities. The promotion of dialogic interaction between religious groups is routinely encouraged, and a specific role for the media in furtherance of such interaction has

---

[127] PACE Recommendation 1768, *supra* note 116. In the same Recommendation, PACE also invites Member States to "adopt and implement legislation penalising leaders of groups promoting racism, and suppress public financing of organisations carrying out or supporting such activities."

[128] PACE Resolution 1563, *supra* note 116.

[129] Eur. Parl. Ass., Resolution 1577, "Towards Decriminalisation of Defamation" (2007), ¶ 17.4, *available at* http://assembly.coe.int/Main.asp?link=/Documents/AdoptedText/ta07/ERES1577.htm.

[130] *Id.* at ¶ 17.5.

[131] *Id.* at ¶¶ 12–15.

[132] Eur. Parl. Ass., Resolution 1636, "Indicators for Media in a Democracy" (2008), ¶ 8.3.

been identified.[133] Repeated references are made to the need for media codes of conduct/ethics to include specific guidelines for tackling stereotyping and intolerance.[134] In this regard, the PACE advocates responsible reporting that generally protects vulnerable minorities, migrants, and refugees from negative stereotyping and promotes positive media representations of such groups, as well as their participation in media activities.[135] Several capacity-building measures have been suggested with respect to the latter: training, funding, and other promotional measures concerning the production and broadcasting of programs featuring minorities, including in mainstream television programs and at peak viewing times.

Flowing from its emphasis on good media practices in respect of sensitive intercultural relations, the PACE has also regularly called for media complaints bodies to be adequately equipped to deal effectively with instances of "offences to religious persuasions";[136] "intolerant, racist or xenophobic attitudes towards migrants, asylum seekers or refugees";[137] and "anti-Semitism and other forms of hate speech."[138]

Another relevant aspect of media reporting concerns the fight against terrorism. In its Recommendation, "Media and Terrorism," the PACE "invites media professionals" *inter alia* to "avoid aggravating, through their news and comments, the societal tensions underlying terrorism, and in particular to refrain from disseminating any kind of hate speech."[139]

## IV. EUROPEAN COMMISSION AGAINST RACISM AND INTOLERANCE

The European Commission Against Racism and Intolerance (ECRI) was established in 1993 as a specialized monitoring body of the Council of Europe.[140] ECRI's work has three main focuses: its so-called country-by-country approach (which involves

---

[133] PACE Resolution 1510, *supra* note 116, ¶¶ 14, 16 (referring to the role of the media); PACE Resolution 1563, *supra* note 116; PACE Recommendation 1804, *supra* note 116.

[134] PACE Resolution 1510, *supra* note 116, ¶ 15; PACE Recommendation 1768, *supra* note 116; PACE Recommendation 1563, *supra* note 116 (specifically in respect of anti-Semitic stereotypes and prejudices).

[135] PACE Recommendation 1768, *supra* note 116.

[136] PACE Resolution 1510, *supra* note 116, ¶ 15.

[137] PACE Recommendation 1768, *supra* note 116.

[138] PACE Resolution 1563, *supra* note 116, ¶ 12.14.

[139] PACE Recommendation 1706, *supra* note 116, ¶ 8(vi).

[140] "ECRI was established by the first Summit of Heads of State and Government of the member States of the Council of Europe. The decision of its establishment is contained in the Vienna Declaration which the Summit adopted on October 9, 1993. The second Summit in Strasbourg on October 10–11, 1997 strengthened ECRI's action and on 13 June 2002 the Committee of Ministers adopted an autonomous Statute for ECRI, thereby consolidating its role as an independent human rights monitoring body." *ECRI in brief* 3 (Council of Europe, 2009), *available at* http://www.coe.int/t/dghl/ monitoring/ecri/activities/Ecri_inbrief_en.pdf.

the ongoing monitoring of relevant issues in Member States),[141] work on general themes (which includes the elaboration of general policy recommendations, as well as the collection and promotion of examples of "good practice" in the struggle against racism), and engagement with civil society.[142] The challenge of combating racism and intolerance in a way that is duly respectful of the right to freedom of expression is a recurrent issue in both ECRI's country-monitoring work and its work on general themes.[143]

## A. *Country Monitoring*

All Member States of the Council of Europe are subject to ECRI's country-by-country monitoring. Each year, ECRI prepares reports on approximately ten countries, relying on documentary analyses, a visit to the country in question, and confidential dialogue with the relevant State authorities.[144] The monitoring work is divided into five-year cycles, the fourth of which began in January 2008.

In the first monitoring cycle, the primary aim was to document and analyze relevant issues and make pertinent recommendations for perceived shortcomings. In the second monitoring cycle, the emphasis was on follow-up to the proposals made in the first cycle, updating relevant information, and providing more in-depth analysis of selected issues of particular interest per country. The third cycle contained an explicit focus on "implementation" – that is, an examination of the extent to which ECRI's recommendations in previous reports have been effectively "followed and implemented." The third cycle also included a focus on "specific issues" per country, which were examined in more depth. Finally, the fourth cycle prioritizes "implementation and evaluation" and "new developments." Thus, alongside scrutiny for the extent to which earlier recommendations have been implemented, the policies adopted and measures taken toward those ends are also being evaluated. No (formal) sanctions arise from a failure by Member States to implement any of ECRI's recommendations. However, political pressure can be exerted in the context of confidential dialogue with states' authorities or can result from repeated negative references in the country reports.

ECRI espouses a proactive and reactive approach to countering "hate speech," similar to that pursued by the Advisory Committee on the FCNM, while remaining

---

[141] This system is based on country reports drawn up by ECRI on the situation regarding racism and intolerance in each of the Council of Europe Member States.

[142] For further detail, see Appendix to Resolution (2002)8, Statute of the European Commission against Racism and Intolerance (ECRI), art. I. For commentary, see Lanna Hollo, *The European Commission against Racism and Intolerance (ECRI): Its First 15 Years* (Council of Europe 2009).

[143] *ECRI Expert Seminar: Combating Racism While Respecting Freedom of Expression* 1 (November 16–17, 2006), *available at* http://www.coe.int/t/dghl/monitoring/ecri/activities/22-freedom_of_expression_seminar_2006/NSBR2006_proceedings_en.pdf.

[144] Further information about the methodology employed can be gleaned from the standard foreword to all reports adopted in the context of the Fourth Monitoring Cycle.

mindful of the importance of the right to freedom of expression and the differentiated roles of the media in this context. The overall pattern that emerged from the country reports in the third cycle includes recommendations for both punitive and preventive measures.

In terms of punitive measures, a recurrent recommendation is that states' authorities strengthen existing legislation prohibiting incitement to hatred[145] or ensure that existing provisions are vigorously implemented.[146] ECRI regularly recommends particular vigilance in identifying and prosecuting cases of incitement to or dissemination of hatred by media professionals.[147] ECRI often calls for the prosecution and punishment of the authors or publishers of racist articles.[148] Some of the recommendations for punitive measures specifically concern racist and xenophobic material on the Internet.[149] The specificity of such a focus demonstrates the growing nature of the problem, yet such recommendations are by no means systematic in ECRI's country reports. This begs the question of whether, first, the problem exists to the same extent in all states, and second, whether the problem is perceived as being equally pressing in all states.

Alongside its recommendations for prosecution and punishment in a system built around legislation and the courts, other recommendations call for the adoption[150] and/or implementation[151] by the media sector of self-regulatory codes that would include provisions on racism, discrimination, and responsible reporting on minorities. The frequency of such recommendations indicates ECRI's awareness of, and deference to, the principle of media autonomy, which is a central principle of the Council of Europe's approach to freedom of expression. ECRI's commitment to this principle is even more obvious in its regular encouragement of the state authorities to "impress on the media, without encroaching on their editorial independence, the need to ensure that reporting does not contribute to creating an atmosphere of hostility and rejection towards members of any minority groups."[152] This recommendation usually includes an important corollary, namely that the state's authorities "engage in a debate with the media and members of other relevant civil society groups on how this could best be achieved."[153]

---

[145] *See, e.g.,* Denmark, ¶ 92; Norway, ¶ 101; Former Yugoslav Republic of Macedonia, ¶ 95.

[146] *See, e.g.,* Denmark, ¶¶ 20, 86, 87, 107; Latvia, ¶ 106; Lithuania, ¶ 62; Russia, ¶ 120.

[147] Czech Republic, ¶ 65; Luxembourg, ¶ 77; Romania, ¶ 113; Russia, ¶ 120; Sweden, ¶ 9.

[148] Bulgaria, ¶ 63; Croatia, ¶ 82; Estonia, ¶ 115 (the phrase, "duly prosecuted," is used here instead of the reference to "prosecute and punish"); Greece, ¶ 98; Poland, ¶ 79; Turkey, ¶ 100.

[149] Finland, ¶ 91; France, ¶ 107; Germany, ¶ 111; Lithuania, ¶ 64; Portugal, ¶ 92; Sweden, ¶ 83.

[150] Albania, ¶ 70; Austria, ¶ 73; Czech Republic, ¶ 65; Germany, ¶ 78; Turkey, ¶ 100.

[151] Austria, ¶ 73; Belgium, ¶ 59; Germany, ¶ 78; Hungary, ¶ 85; Norway, ¶ 80; Former Yugoslav Republic of Macedonia, ¶ 94.

[152] *See, e.g.,* Cyprus, ¶ 90; Finland, ¶ 90; Italy, ¶ 79; Latvia, ¶ 108; Lithuania, ¶ 63; Russia, ¶ 121; Spain, ¶ 86; Ukraine, ¶ 104.

[153] *See, e.g.,* Cyprus, ¶ 90; Finland, ¶ 90; Italy, ¶ 79; Latvia, ¶ 108; Lithuania, ¶ 63; the Netherlands, ¶ 97; Russia, ¶ 121; Spain, ¶ 86.

ECRI also has sought to harness the potential role that freedom of expression can play in countering racist speech by encouraging (rather than prescribing, again out of deference to the principle of media autonomy) more and better media coverage of minority issues.[154] To this end, it has recommended more state support for training schemes for media professionals on issues such as reporting in a diverse society,[155] human rights, racism, racial discrimination,[156] and anti-Semitism.[157] The ECRI also recommends greater representation of persons from immigrant backgrounds in the media profession.[158] This approach is based explicitly on the assumption that the enhanced representation of immigrants in media structures will have a positive impact on the representation of immigrants in media output.

ECRI also underscores the general importance of access to electronic and print media for persons belonging to minorities,[159] as well as the specific importance of ensuring the "adequate availability of electronic media in the language of national minorities."[160] The promotion via the media of minority identities[161] and of "an atmosphere of appreciation of diversity"[162] is also recommended, as is the creation of a shared forum in which separate linguistic communities can receive the same information, with a view to strengthening intergroup relations.[163]

## B. *Work on General Themes*

ECRI's General Policy Recommendations (GPRs) are the mainstay of its work on general themes. It has issued twelve GPRs:

1. Combating racism, xenophobia, antisemitism and intolerance (1996)
2. Specialised bodies to combat racism, xenophobia, antisemitism and intolerance at national level (1997)
3. Combating racism and intolerance against Roma/Gypsies (1998)
4. National surveys on the experience and perception of discrimination and racism from the point of view of potential victims (1998)
5. Combating intolerance and discrimination against Muslims (2000)

---

[154] Albania, ¶ 71; Austria, ¶ 74; Former Yugoslav Republic of Macedonia, ¶ 137.
[155] Austria, ¶ 73; Germany, ¶ 78.
[156] Denmark, ¶ 108; Estonia, ¶ 115; Romania, ¶ 112 ("national and local media training courses on combating discrimination"); Slovakia, ¶ 91 (this provision is directed at "professionals," presumably including, although without specifying, "media" professionals).
[157] Luxembourg, ¶ 77.
[158] Austria, ¶ 73; Belgium, ¶ 60; France, ¶ 105 (and see also ¶ 104 for details of a positive initiative in this connection); Germany, ¶ 78; Norway, ¶ 80. In these examples, references to "the press" are presumably expansive, i.e., to the press as an institution. It is submitted here that "the media" would have been a more suitable term.
[159] Albania, ¶ 72.
[160] Austria, ¶ 74.
[161] Slovenia, ¶¶ 73–74.
[162] Albania, ¶ 70.
[163] Estonia, ¶ 114.

6. Combating the dissemination of racist, xenophobic, and antisemitic material via the Internet (2000)
7. On national legislation to combat racism and racial discrimination (2002)
8. On combating racism while fighting terrorism (2004)
9. On the fight against antisemitism (2004)
10. On combating racism and racial discrimination in and through school education (2006)
11. On combating racism and racial discrimination in policing (2007)
12. On combating racism and racial discrimination in the field of sport (2008)

The first obvious strength of ECRI's thematic approach is the opportunity it affords to identify particular issues and grapple with their specifics in a detailed and rigorous fashion. For example, some of GPR No. 12's specific recommendations to combat racism and racial discrimination in sport are directed at various parties, including legislative and other authorities, police, sports organizations, athletes, coaches, referees, supporters' organizations, politicians, the media, and sponsors and advertisers.[164] In this context, recommended measures concerning the media are nonprescriptive, thereby respecting the principle of media autonomy. Member States are called on to "encourage the media"

a) to abstain from reproducing racist stereotypes in their reporting;
b) to pay the necessary attention to the image that they convey of minority groups in sports; and
c) to report on racist incidents taking place during sport events and to give publicity to sanctions incurred by racist offenders.

GPR No. 12 also contains provisions involving other freedom-of-expression issues. For instance, the police are requested to "identify and remove racist, antisemitic or discriminatory leaflets, symbols and banners." Similarly, sports federations and clubs are invited to "refuse access to sport grounds to persons who distribute or carry with them racist, antisemitic or discriminatory leaflets, symbols or banners." Supporters' organizations are encouraged to "be vigilant about possible racist content on their websites and fanzines." For their part, sponsors and advertisers are encouraged, *inter alia*, to "avoid giving a stereotyped picture of athletes from minority backgrounds." These last-named examples are largely self-regulatory in character insofar as they seek to promote a sense of responsibility within various organizations and promote practical measures/remedies as opposed to prescribing courses of action.

Unfortunately, ECRI's GPRs sometimes fail to identify and affirm the necessary linkage between equality/nondiscrimination provisions of European and international human rights standards and protections of other human rights, most notably

---

[164] Eur. Comm. Against Racism and Intolerance, General Policy Recommendation No. 12 on Combating Racism and Racial Discrimination in the Field of Sport, Doc. No. CRI (2009)5 (March 19, 2009).

freedom of expression and association. In GPR No. 6, for instance, ECRI's pursuit of the elimination of racist and xenophobic content online is fails adequately to acknowledge and weigh freedom of expression interests. The GPR's preamble invokes GPR No. 1:

> Recalling that, in its general policy recommendation No 1, ECRI called on the governments of Council of Europe member States to ensure that national criminal, civil and administrative law expressly and specifically counters racism, xenophobia, antisemitism and intolerance.
>
> Stressing that, in the same recommendation, ECRI asked for the aforementioned law to provide in particular that oral, written, audio-visual expressions and other forms of expression, including the electronic media, inciting to hatred, discrimination or violence against racial, ethnic, national or religious groups or against their members on the grounds that they belong to such a group are legally categorised as a criminal offence, which should also cover the production, the distribution and the storage for distribution of the material in question.

This citation of GPR No. 1 is abridged, however, although no indication is given that this is the case. In fact, GPR No. 1 only countenanced criminalization of these types of expression "in conformity with the obligations assumed by States under relevant international instruments and in particular with Articles 10 and 11 of the European Convention on Human Rights." The omission of this caveat – a departure from the language used in its own standards – suggests that in GPR No. 6, the ECRI has overlooked the importance of Articles 10 and 11 (Freedom of assembly and association) of the ECHR in its combat against dissemination of racist, xenophobic, and anti-Semitic material via the Internet. More concretely, the omission removed all reference to the key legally binding provisions that could be invoked to specify the safeguards required for the criminalization of certain types of expressive activity to be considered legitimate.

Admittedly, GPR No. 6 does acknowledge the Internet's potential for combating racism, *inter alia*, through self-regulatory measures, the transfrontier sharing of information concerning "human rights issues related to anti-discrimination," and the (further) development of educational and awareness-raising networks. Nevertheless, the absence of references to ECHR guarantees of freedom of expression and other pertinent rights conveys the impression of a document that is disappointingly selective in terms of the range of its sources of inspiration. Closer conceptual and linguistic alignment with the ECHR would have pointed to a body of relevant judicial pronouncements, thereby offering authoritative interpretative consistency and clarity.

A second strength of ECRI's thematic approach is that it enables more generous attention to be given to specific groups, for example those groups that have traditionally suffered – and continue to suffer – from racist discrimination. This is illustrated by the GPRs focusing on the Roma/Gypsies, Muslims, and anti-Semitism. These policy recommendations are very important as they address the root causes of racism and not merely its concrete manifestations. As such, they look at situational and systemic discrimination and explore ways of countering and eliminating the same.

The third strength of the thematic approach to combating racism is that it has provided ECRI with a very useful means to address policy, institutional, and methodological/procedural questions. GPR No. 1, entitled "Combating racism, xenophobia, antisemitism and intolerance,"[165] stands out among other GPRs for its recognition that international law is the backdrop to the struggle against racism, and that the obligations imposed on states by international law must remain salient. GPR No. 7 – on national legislation to combat racism and racial discrimination[166] – is somewhat weaker in that regard, but its shortcomings are offset to some extent by its accompanying Explanatory Memorandum, which offers useful explanatory detail on the recommendations concerning constitutional, civil and administrative, and criminal law.[167]

When assessing ECRI's thematic work at the macro level, two main points should be made. The thematic approach pursued by ECRI very importantly allows it to be responsive to changing agendas of racism and racial discrimination. By setting its own thematic agenda, ECRI has also managed to be proactive in its decisions to pursue certain topics. This is conducive to fostering dynamic working methods. However, the GPRs do not always reflect the letter of international-law provisions. Nor do they always manage to achieve the desirable, and indeed necessary, respect for other fundamental rights.

## V. MINISTERIAL CONFERENCES ON MASS MEDIA POLICY

European Ministerial Conferences on Mass Media Policy have been held periodically since the mid-1980s. These conferences involve the participation of ministers (or their delegates) with relevant portfolios at the national level. As such, the Ministerial Conferences can be distinguished from the day-to-day activities of the Council of Europe. Their relevance stems from their purpose to map out future European media policy, supplemented by action plans for its implementation. The preparation of these Conferences and the implementation of resultant Action Plans are overseen by the Council of Europe's Steering Committee on Media and New Communication Services (CDMC) – an expert body comprising members nominated

[165] Eur. Comm. Against Racism & Intolerance, General Policy Recommendation no. 1 on Combating Racism, Xenophobia, Antisemitism and Intolerance, Doc No. CRI(96)43 rev. (October 4, 1996).
[166] Eur. Comm. Against Racism & Intolerance, General Policy Recommendation No. 7 on National Legislation to Combat Racism and Racial Discrimination, Doc. No. CRI(2003)8 (December 13, 2002).
[167] For further commentary, see Giancarlo Cardinale, "The Preparation of ECRI General Policy Recommendation No 7 on National Legislation to Combat Racism and Racial Discrimination," in Jan Niessen and Isabelle Chopin, Eds., *The Development of Legal Instruments to Combat Racism in a Diverse Europe* 81–92 (Martinus Nijhoff 2004).

by Member States of the Council of Europe.[168] To reflect changing notions of the
media, the most recent conference was calibrated differently – as the "1st Council of
Europe Conference of Ministers responsible for Media and New Communication
Services."[169]

Of the seven Conferences on Mass Media Policy, the fourth, fifth, and seventh
have most directly engaged with the issues of "hate speech" or tolerance and intolerance in the media. Two texts adopted at the fourth European Ministerial Conference
on Mass Media Policy,[170] held in 1994, are relevant. In Resolution No. 2: Journalistic Freedoms and Human Rights, Principle 7(f) sets out generally that the "practice
of journalism in a genuine democracy" implies "avoiding the promotion of any
violence, hatred, intolerance or discrimination based, in particular, on race, sex, sexual orientation, language, religion, politics or other opinions, national or regional
origin, or social origin." In the Declaration on media in a democratic society, the
ministers of participating states condemn, "in line with the Vienna Declaration, all
forms of expression which incite to racial hatred, xenophobia, anti-Semitism and all
forms of intolerance, since they undermine democratic security, cultural cohesion
and pluralism."[171] They also affirm "that the media can assist in building mutual
understanding and tolerance among persons, groups and countries and in the attain-
ment of the objectives of democratic, social and cultural cohesion announced in the
Vienna Declaration."[172] These two principles again reflect the conceptual bifurcation between curbing hate speech and promoting understanding and tolerance – a
distinction that (by and large) consistently has been adhered to throughout relevant
Council of Europe instruments. Relatedly, in the Action Plan adopted at the Conference, it was proposed that the Committee of Ministers of the Council of Europe
"[s]tudy, in close consultation with media professionals and regulatory authorities,
possible guidelines which could assist media professionals in addressing intolerance
in all its forms."[173] This proposal provided important impetus to the process that led
to the drafting of the Committee of Ministers' Recommendations on "hate speech"
and on the media and the promotion of a culture of tolerance.[174]

---

[168] Terms of Reference of the Steering Committee on Media and New Communication Services
(CDMC), n.d., *available at* http://www.coe.int/t/dghl/standardsetting/media/CDMC/default_en.asp,
¶ 4(iv).

[169] *A New Notion of Media?*, May 28–29, 2009, Reykjavik, Iceland, http://www.coe.int/t/dc/files/
ministerial_conferences/2009_media_communication/default_en.asp.

[170] *The Media in a Democratic Society*, Dec. 7–8, 1994, Prague, http://www.ebu.ch/CMSimages/en/
leg_ref_coe_mcm_resolution_psb_07_081294_tcm6–4274.pdf.

[171] *Id.*, Principle 7.

[172] *Id.*, Principle 8.

[173] Action Plan setting out strategies for the promotion of media in a democratic society addressed
to the Committee of Ministers of the Council of Europe (Feb. 1, 1995), Point 6: "Media
and intolerance," *available at* http://www.coe.int/t/dghl/monitoring/minorities/6_resources/PDF_
CAHMIN(95)3_en.pdf.

[174] As mentioned *supra*, that process was initiated at the Vienna Summit of Heads of State and Government of the Council of Europe Member States in 1993.

The fifth European Ministerial Conference on Mass Media Policy,[175] held in 1997, paid the greatest attention to issues related to hate speech. Paragraphs 11 and 12 of the Political Declaration adopted at that Conference refer in general terms to the potential and risks of new communications and information services. In a similar vein, Resolution No. 1: The impact of New Communication Technologies on Human Rights and Democratic Values, emphasizes the ministers' condemnation of the use of new technologies and services "for spreading any ideology, or carrying out any activity, which is contrary to human rights, human dignity, and democratic values," as well as their resolve to "combat such use."[176]

Resolution No. 2: Rethinking the Regulatory Framework for the Media, calls on participating states to give domestic effect to the principles enshrined in the Committee of Ministers' Recommendations on, *inter alia*, "hate speech" and on the media and the promotion of a culture of tolerance.[177] It also calls on states' authorities "to ensure that measures for combating the dissemination of opinions and ideas which incite to racial hatred, xenophobia, anti-Semitism and all forms of intolerance through the new communications and information services duly respect freedom of expression and, where applicable, the secrecy of correspondence."[178] The reinforcement of cooperation within the Council of Europe, while liaising with other IGOs and "interested professional organisations," is also advocated.[179] Such cooperation should have standard-setting aspirations, initially for Europe and later more widely. The suggested focus is on "problems of delimiting public and private forms of communication, liability, jurisdiction and conflict of laws in regard to hate speech disseminated through the new communications and information services."[180]

The Conference's Action Plan calls for study of "the practical and legal difficulties in combating the dissemination of hate speech, violence and pornography via the new communications and information services, with a view to taking appropriate initiatives in a common pan-European framework." As already mentioned, it also calls for the "periodical evaluation" of Member States' "follow-up" to the Committee of Ministers' Recommendations on, *inter alia*, "hate speech" and on the media and the promotion of a culture of tolerance. In addition, it seeks a periodical evaluation of the implementation of Article 7, European Convention on Transfrontier Television, by Member States, particularly as regards the "responsibilities of broadcasters with regard to the content and presentation of their programme services." Finally, it provides for an examination – "as appropriate" – of the "advisability of preparing in addition other binding or non-binding instruments."[181]

---

[175] *The Information Society: A Challenge for Europe* (Dec. 11–12, 1997), http://www.coe.int/t/dghl/standardsetting/media/doc/DH-MM(2006)004_en.pdf.

[176] *Id.*, Resolution No. 1, ¶ 9; *see also id.*, ¶ 19(i) (reiterating these points in very similar language).

[177] *Id.*, Resolution No. 2, ¶ 8(i).

[178] *Id.*, ¶ 8(ii).

[179] *Id.*, ¶ 8(iii).

[180] *Id.*, ¶ 8(iii).

[181] *Id.*, Action Plan, ¶¶ 1–7.

At the seventh European Ministerial Conference on Mass Media Policy, held in March 2005, the ministers undertook, *inter alia*, to "step up their efforts to combat the use of the new communication services for disseminating content prohibited by the Cybercrime Convention and its additional Protocol concerning the criminalisation of acts of a racist and xenophobic nature committed through computer systems."[182]

Finally, it should be noted that the political texts adopted at the first Council of Europe Conference of Ministers Responsible for Media and New Communication Services – "A new notion of media?" – pay minimal attention to "hate speech." This is difficult to explain, given that (1) there is a real resurgence of "hate speech" in a new media context, which poses considerable regulatory challenges, and (2) the purpose of the Conference was to map out priorities in European media policy to be addressed by the Council of Europe in the coming years.

## VI. THE VENICE COMMISSION

In October 2008, the European Commission for Democracy through Law (the Venice Commission, i.e., the Council of Europe's advisory body on constitutional matters), issued a report on the relationship between freedom of expression and freedom of religion generally and the regulation and prosecution of blasphemy, religious insult, and incitement to religious hatred in particular.[183] Noting that national legislation in one country or another prohibits the disturbance of religious practice, blasphemy, religious insult, negationism, discrimination (including on religious grounds), and incitement to hatred, the report addresses three main issues.

The first concerns the scope of prohibitions. The Commission found that incitement to hatred, including religious hatred, is properly the object of criminal sanctions in almost all European states. In contrast, "it is neither necessary nor desirable to create an offence of religious insult (that is, insult to religious feelings) simpliciter, without the element of incitement to hatred as an essential component."[184] Similarly, the offense of blasphemy should be abolished and not be reintroduced.[185]

The second issue concerns criminal punishment. The report concluded that "criminal sanctions are only appropriate in respect of incitement to hatred (unless

---

[182] 7th European Ministerial Conference on Mass Media Policy (Mar. 10–11, 2005), Resolution No. 3, "Human rights and regulation of the media and new communication services in the Information Society," ¶ 18; *see also* Tarlach McGonagle, "Ministerial Conference on Mass Media Policy," 7 *IRIS – Legal Observations of the European Audiovisual Observatory* 2 (2005).

[183] European Commission for Democracy through Law (Venice Commission), Report on the Relationship Between Freedom of Expression and Freedom of Religion: The Issue of Regulation and Prosecution of Blasphemy, Religious Insult and Incitement to Religious Hatred, Doc. No. CDL-AD(2008)026 (Oct. 17–18, 2008), *available at* http://www.venice.coe.int/docs/2008/CDL-AD%282008%29026-e.asp. The Report was produced in response to a request from the PACE following its adoption of Resolution 1510, described earlier. *See supra* note 116 and accompanying text.

[184] European Commission for Democracy through Law (Venice Commission), *supra* note 183, ¶ 89(b).

[185] *Id.*, ¶ 89(c).

public order offences are appropriate),"[186] and that "criminal sanctions are inappropriate in respect of insult to religious feelings and, even more so, in respect of blasphemy."[187]

Finally, regarding alternatives to criminal sanctions, the Commission referred to a "new ethic of responsible intercultural relations in Europe and in the rest of the world" and stressed values such as tolerance, diversity, mutual understanding, and open debate.[188] It pointed to the relevance of dialogue, education, and relevant PACE Recommendations and those of the European Commission against Racism and Intolerance (ECRI) for the promotion of such values.

## VII. CONCLUSIONS

To summarize a very expansive set of standards and concomitant strategies, it can be said that the three main prongs to the Council of Europe's approach to countering "hate speech" are: (1) the prevention/prohibition/punishment of certain types of expression (e.g., incitement to hatred, racist expression); (2) the facilitation and creation of expressive and communicative opportunities for minorities; and relatedly, (3) the promotion of tolerance, understanding, and intergroup/intercultural dialogue. By virtue of their agenda-setting and forum-providing capacities, the media are specifically implicated in many of the strategies employed, but in a way that is deferential to their operational autonomy.

All of the Council of Europe standards share the ECHR as their central reference point. The scope of Articles 10 and 17 of the Convention and the interplay between them shape the European Court of Human Rights' approach to "hate speech." The Court's future engagement with the term will be crucial for the clarification of the term's scope and the consolidation of its case law dealing with relevant issues. In the absence of a legally binding definition of the term "hate speech," or a clear and consistent set of evaluation criteria for types of expression that could potentially amount to "hate speech," the scope and content of the term remain uncertain. This uncertainty has very practical (legal) consequences. Certain types of expression may be highly objectionable from a moral point of view, without actually triggering restrictions on, or prohibitions of, expression in accordance with recognized international human rights standards. Moreover, not all types of highly objectionable expression occasion, or are likely to occasion, similarly grave harms. Thus, legally binding approaches to "hate speech" ought to duly recognize the variety of types of expression and resultant harms that "hate speech" could be taken to signify.

---

[186] *Id.,* ¶ 91.
[187] *Id.,* ¶ 92.
[188] *Id.,* ¶¶ 95 *et seq.*

The selection of legal remedies for "hate speech" should be based, therefore, on principled assessments of the nature of any impugned expression, a range of relevant contextualizing factors, and the specific harms to be prevented or minimized. These arguments are also applicable, *mutatis mutandis*, to nonlegal remedies. In the context of the Council of Europe, it is imperative that the requisite differentiation be reflected in the case law of the European Court of Human Rights, precisely because the Court's interpretation of the ECHR is the point of inspirational departure for all the Council of Europe's other strategies for tackling "hate speech." Even though the preparation and implementation of the Council of Europe's standards and strategies against "hate speech" are not formally coordinated, they are broadly congruent. This can be attributed to their common provenance. Glitches in their overall congruence will inevitably persist, but greater clarity and consistency in the relevant case law of the Court would likely reduce the incidence of the same.

Finally, the foregoing criticism of the definitional and interpretive shortcomings of the Court should not detract from the merits of the Council of Europe's overall approach, which boasts an array of diverse standards and strategies against "hate speech." The diversity of approaches offers the various organs of the Council of Europe ample scope to simultaneously address the problem of "hate speech" in both a preventive and a responsive fashion. This makes for effective engagement with the range of fundamental *issues* involved. Nevertheless, the effectiveness of measures that are not legally binding is largely contingent on the goodwill of the states' authorities or other actors (e.g., the media) to which they are addressed. Addressing this challenge will therefore remain a work in progress for some time to come.

# 25

# The American Convention on Human Rights

## Regulation of Hate Speech and Similar Expression

### Eduardo Bertoni and Julio Rivera Jr.

Hate speech is defined by both its intent and its target. With respect to intent, hate speech is speech designed to intimidate, oppress, or incite hatred or violence on the basis of characteristics such as race, religion, nationality, gender, sexual orientation, or disability. With respect to its target, it is speech directed against a person or group based on such characteristics. Historically, hate speech has known no boundaries of time or place. It has been used by officials and others in Nazi Germany, by the Ku Klux Klan in the United States, by a full range of actors in Bosnia during the 1990s, and during the 1994 Rwandan genocide. But hate speech has a common thread: It is used to harass, to persecute, and to justify the deprivation of human rights. At its most extreme, hate speech can be used even to rationalize murder, as the world saw just a few years ago in Rwanda.

In the wake of the German Holocaust, and with the rise of the Internet and other media that can spread hate speech almost instantaneously, many governments and intergovernmental bodies have tried to limit the harmful effects of hate speech. Around the world, countries have criminalized incitement to hatred or violence; degrading, defamatory, or insulting speech;[1] the display of discriminatory symbols

---

[1] For example, the German penal code provides:
   Whosoever, in a manner capable of disturbing the public peace,

   1. incites hatred against segments of the population or calls for violent or arbitrary measures against them; or
   2. assaults the human dignity of others by insulting, maliciously maligning, or defaming segments of the population, shall be liable to imprisonment from three months to five years.

   shall be liable to imprisonment from three months to five years.
   Strafgesetzbuch [Stgb] [Penal Code], Nov. 13, 1998, BGBl. I § 130(1).

This chapter draws in part on Eduardo Bertoni, "Hate Speech Under The American Convention On Human Rights," 12 *ILSA Journal of International & Comparative Law* 569 (2006), which was a revision of oral remarks presented at the International Law Weekend 2005, held at the Association of the Bar of the City of New York, October 20–22, 2005. Those remarks were in turn based in part on chapter VII of the 2004 *Annual Report of the Office of the Special Rapporteur for Freedom of Expression*, Inter-American Commission on Human Rights, Organization of American States.

or emblems;[2] the possession and distribution of discriminatory materials;[3] and the approval or justification of genocide or crimes against humanity.[4] Some of these criminal prohibitions also reach new forms of hate speech, such as genocide denial or minimization and religious defamation.[5]

Although widely prohibited, hate speech cannot be casually dismissed as harmful expression with little or no value. Often, it is also a form of political speech, containing views on, and participating in a discussion of, contested issues such as immigration and asylum policy, terrorism, the role and the extent of the influence of religion in the society, international conflicts, and historical events. Accordingly, criminal punishment of this type of speech entails placing certain points of view on matters of public concern beyond political challenge or public debate. This is self-evidently problematic under generally accepted principles of freedom of expression.[6]

The regulation of *political* speech must be closely scrutinized. At times, the regulation of "hate speech" may conflict with treaties, constitutions, and domestic laws that guarantee the right to freedom of expression. The purpose of this chapter

---

[2] In Italy, it is a crime to show, display or manifestation of emblems or symbols of organizations, associations, movements, or groups inciting to discrimination or violence on racial, ethnic, national, or religious grounds. Decreto Legge 26 Aprile 1993, n. 122.

[3] Britain's Public Order Act provides:

A person who has in his possession written material which is threatening, abusive or insulting, or a recording of visual images or sounds which are threatening, abusive or insulting, with a view to –

(a) in the case of written material, its being displayed, published, distributed, or included in a cable programme service, whether by himself or another, or

(b) in the case of a recording, its being distributed, shown, played, or included in a cable programme service, whether by himself or another,

is guilty of an offence if he intends racial hatred to be stirred up thereby or, having regard to all the circumstances, racial hatred is likely to be stirred up thereby.

Public Order Act (1986), § 23(1) (Gr. Brit.).

[4] *See* Strafgesetzbuch [StGB] [Penal Code], Nov. 13, 1998, BGBl. I § 130(3) ("Whosoever publicly or in a meeting approves of, denies or downplays an act committed under the rule of National Socialism of the kind indicated in section 6(1) of the Code of International Criminal Law, in a manner capable of disturbing the public peace shall be liable to imprisonment of not more than five years or a fine."); Law of Mar. 23, 1995, art. 1 Moniteur Belge [M.B.] [Official Gazette of Belgium], Mar. 30, 1995, 7996 (making it a crime publicly to "deny, play down, justify or approve of the genocide committed by the German National Socialist regime during the Second World War").

[5] The problems surrounding freedom of expression standards and the idea of "defamation of religion" are outside the scope of this paper. On this issue, see the joint declaration of the UN Special Rapporteur on Freedom of Opinion and Expression, the OSCE Representative on Freedom of the Media, the OAS Special Rapporteur on Freedom of Expression, and the ACHPR (African Commission on Human and Peoples' Rights) Special Rapporteur on *Freedom of Expression and Access to Information, available at* http://www.cidh.oas.org/relatoria/showarticle.asp?artID=736 &lID=1.

[6] *See* Stefan Braun, *Democracy Off Balance: Freedom of Expression and Hate Propaganda Law in Canada* 89 (University of Toronto Press 2004). Braun's book is a sustained attack on what he calls "hate censorship"; here he contends that those who favor restrictions on hate speech are, as a rule, abandoning or contradicting their general assumption that "[p]oints of view on matters that touch vitally on the well-being of society and polity cannot be put beyond political challenge or public debate." *Id.*

is to examine one such potential conflict, reviewing the treatment of hate speech under the American Convention on Human Rights (the "American Convention").

## I. THE AMERICAN CONVENTION ON HUMAN RIGHTS

The 1969 American Convention on Human Rights,[7] along with the American Declaration of the Rights and Duties of Man,[8] are the two principal instruments through which the Inter-American system protects human rights. The Convention enumerates the rights and freedoms to be protected by States Parties and defines the functions and procedures of two organs with respect to the fulfillment of these international obligations: the Inter-American Commission on Human Rights (established in 1959), located in Washington, DC,[9] and the Inter-American Court of Human Rights (established in 1979), located in San José, Costa Rica.[10]

Modeled on similar international conventions, the American Convention lists twenty-three substantive rights and freedoms.[11] Individuals, groups, and nongovernmental organizations who have exhausted their domestic remedies may lodge petitions charging state violations with the Inter-American Commission. If the Commission fails to reach a friendly settlement with the state concerned, it may publish the case or submit it to the Inter-American Court, which consists of seven justices who are selected by the General Assembly of the Organization of American States (OAS) and serve six-year terms. The Commission may submit a case to the Court only if the state charged with violating the Convention both has ratified the Convention and has recognized the competence of the Court either (1) by submitting a declaration pursuant to Article 62 of the Convention or (2) by a special agreement.[12] Members of the OAS also may submit cases to the Commission and Court, provided they

---

7 Organization of American States [OAS], *American Convention on Human Rights*, "*Pact of San José, Costa Rica*," art. 13, OAS Treaty Ser. No. 36, Nov. 22, 1969, 1144 U.N.T.S. 123, *reprinted in Basic Documents Pertaining to Human Rights in the Inter-American System*, OEA/Ser.L.V/II.82 doc.6 rev.1 at 25 (1992) [hereinafter *American Convention*].

8 *American Declaration of the Rights and Duties of Man*, OAS Res. XXX, adopted by the Ninth International Conference of American States, April 1948, *reprinted in Basic Documents Pertaining to Human Rights in the Inter-American System*, OAS/Ser.L/V/1.4 Rev. 9 (2003).

9 *American Convention, supra* note 7, arts. 33, 34–51.

10 *Id.* arts. 33, 52–69.

11 These include the right to life (art. 4), the right to humane treatment (art. 5), freedom from slavery (art. 6), the right to personal liberty (art. 7), the right to privacy (art. 11), freedom of thought and expression (art. 13), freedom of association (art. 16), the rights of the family (art. 17), the rights of the child (art. 19), the right to equal protection (art. 24), the right to judicial protection (art. 25), and the right to progressive development of economic, social, and cultural rights (art. 26).

12 *Id.* art. 62. Twenty-one States Parties have accepted the compulsory jurisdiction of the Court. They are: Costa Rica, Peru, Venezuela, Honduras, Ecuador, Argentina, Uruguay, Colombia, Guatemala, Suriname, Panama, Chile, Nicaragua, Paraguay, Bolivia, El Salvador, Haiti, Brazil, Mexico, the Dominican Republic and Barbados. *See* Inter-Am. Comm'n H.R., 2009 *Annual Report, available at* http://www.corteidh.or.cr/docs/informes/eng_2009.pdf.

accept the competence of each as set forth in Articles 45 and 62 of the Convention.[13] The Inter-American Court also issues advisory opinions on the interpretation of the American Convention and other treaties.[14]

## II. ARTICLE 13 OF THE AMERICAN CONVENTION

Article 13 of the American Convention reads as follows:

1. Everyone has the right to freedom of thought and expression. This right includes freedom to seek, receive, and impart information and ideas of all kinds, regardless of frontiers, either orally, in writing, in print, in the form of art, or through any other medium of one's choice.
2. The exercise of the right provided for in the foregoing paragraph shall not be subject to prior censorship but shall be subject to subsequent imposition of liability, which shall be expressly established by law to the extent necessary to ensure:[15]
    a. respect for the rights or reputations of others; or
    b. the protection of national security, public order, or public health or morals.
3. The right of expression may not be restricted by indirect methods or means, such as the abuse of government or private controls over newsprint, radio broadcasting frequencies, or equipment used in the dissemination of information, or by any other means tending to impede the communication and circulation of ideas and opinions.
4. Notwithstanding the provisions of paragraph 2 above, public entertainments may be subject by law to prior censorship for the sole purpose of regulating access to them for the moral protection of childhood and adolescence.
5. Any propaganda for war and any advocacy of national, racial, or religious hatred that constitute incitements to lawless violence or to any other similar illegal action against any person or group of persons on any grounds including those of race, color, religion, language, or national origin shall be considered as offenses punishable by law.

---

[13] The Commission may admit petitions by only those States Parties that have submitted a declaration recognizing the competence of the Commission as per Article 45 of the Convention. In addition, the Commission may admit petitions by States Parties against only those States Parties that have made a declaration recognizing the competence of the Commission.

[14] *American Convention, supra* note 7, arts. 44–51, 61–64. For a general overview, see *The Inter-American System of Human Rights* (David J. Harris & Scott Livingstone eds., Oxford University Press 1998, reprinted 2004).

[15] The Inter-American Court has said that the English text of this provision mistranslates the original Spanish text. Rather than "to the extent necessary to ensure," the phrase should read "and be necessary to ensure." *See* Compulsory Membership in an Association Prescribed by Law for the Practice of Journalism (Arts. 13 and 29, American Convention on Human Rights), Advisory Opinion OC-5/85, ¶ 29 (Inter-Am. Ct. H.R., November 13, 1985), *available at* http://www.corteidh.or.cr/docs/opiniones/seriea_05_ing1.doc. [Authors' footnote].

As the Inter-American Court of Human Rights has explained, this Article

> shows the extremely high value that the [American] Convention places on free-
> dom of expression. A comparison of Article 13 with the relevant provisions of the
> European Convention[16] (Article 10) and the International Covenant on Civil and
> Political Rights[17] (Article 19) indicates clearly that the guarantees contained in
> the American Convention regarding freedom of expression were designed to be
> more generous and to reduce to a bare minimum restrictions impeding the free
> circulation of ideas.[18]

Still, the Convention's broad mantle of freedom of expression is not absolute. In the
first place, Article 13(2) explicitly permits some restrictions on freedom of expression,
endorsing subsequent liability for abuse of this right in limited circumstances. In
addition, like many international and regional agreements, Article 13(5) specifically
*requires* States Parties to make certain hate speech – that which "constitute[s] incitements to lawless violence or to any other similar illegal action" – a crime punishable
by law.[19] We argue that any such bar on hate speech remains subject to paragraph
2's general prohibition of prior censorship; however, as we discuss below, because of
the different language used in the English and the Spanish versions of Article 13(5),
that issue requires further analysis.

Neither the Inter-American Commission nor the Inter-American Court has yet
reviewed any restrictions on hate speech. Accordingly, these provisions have received
no authoritative interpretation in this context. The Commission's Office of the
Special Rapporteur for Freedom of Expression[20] did undertake an extensive study
of this topic, publishing its findings in its 2004 Annual Report.[21]

The report highlights that Article 13(5) of the American Convention diverges
from the International Covenant on Civil and Political Rights (the "ICCPR") and
the European Convention for the Protection of Human Rights and Fundamental

---

[16] European Convention for the Protection of Human Rights and Fundamental Freedoms, Nov. 4, 1950, 312 U.N.T.S. 221.

[17] International Covenant on Civil and Political Rights, art. 19, Dec. 16, 1966, 999 U.N.T.S. 171 [here-inafter ICCPR].

[18] *Compulsory Membership, supra* note 15, at ¶ 50.

[19] The English text of article 13(5) could be read to provide that states can, but need not, criminalize the covered hate speech, which it refers to as "punishable." However, in practice it is always read as *requiring* the criminal prohibition of covered hate speech, a reading which is clearer in the non-English versions of the Convention.

[20] The Office of the Special Rapporteur for Freedom of Expression was created by the Inter-American Commission on Human Rights in October 1997, during its ninety-seventh regular session. Since then, the Rapporteurship has had backing not only from the IACHR but from states, civil society organizations in the hemisphere, media, journalists, and, above all, from the victims of violations of freedom of expression who see the Rapporteurship as offering important support to restore the guarantees needed in order to exercise their rights or to ensure fair settlement of their claims.

[21] *See* Inter-Am. Comm'n H.R., Office of the Special Rapporteur for Freedom of Expression, *2004 Annual Report* 150–79, *available at* http://www.cidh.oas.org/relatoria/showarticle.asp?artID=459&lID=1 [here-inafter *2004 Report*].

Freedoms (the "European Convention") on some key points. The text of Article 13(5) requires prohibition of hate speech only in relation to incitement of "lawless violence" or "any other similar action." This is a significant restriction; neither the ICCPR nor the European Convention is so limited in the speech that it requires to be prohibited.[22] The ICCPR requires states to outlaw speech inciting "discrimination, hostility *or* violence,"[23] which suggests it covers a broader range of speech. The European Convention does not explicitly require states to ban hate speech, but permits those restrictions on free speech that are "necessary in a democratic society" and then lists a number of ends justifying these limits, such as national security and public safety.[24]

The limited scope of Article 13(5), in comparison with the ICCPR and the European Convention, has been attributed to the influence of the U.S. delegation in the negotiations. The Americans sought to avoid any inconsistency between the Convention and the U.S. Supreme Court's interpretation of the First Amendment in *Brandenburg v. Ohio*.[25]

---

[22] This difference has also been noted by scholars. *See* Elizabeth F. Defeis, "Freedom of Speech and International Norms: A Response to Hate Speech," 29 *Stan. J. Int'l L.* 57, 112 (1992); Joanna Oyediran, "Article 13(5) of the American Convention on Human Rights," in *Striking a Balance: Hate Speech, Freedom of Expression and Non-discrimination* 33 (Sandra Coliver ed., ARTICLE 19 & University of Essex 1992).

[23] ICCPR, *supra* note 17, at art. 19 (emphasis added). Article 19 provides:

   1. Everyone shall have the right to hold opinions without interference.
   2. Everyone shall have the right to freedom of expression; this right shall include freedom to seek, receive and impart information and ideas of all kinds, regardless of frontiers, either orally, in writing or in print, in the form of art, or through any other media of his choice.
   3. The exercise of the rights provided for in paragraph 2 of this article carries with it special duties and responsibilities. It may therefore be subject to certain restrictions, but these shall only be such as are provided by law and are necessary:
      a. For respect of the rights or reputations of others;
      b. For the protection of national security or of public order (ordre public), or of public health or morals.

[24] European Convention on Human Rights, art. 10, Nov. 4, 1950, E.T.S. No. 5, 213 U.N.T.S. 221 [hereinafter ECHR]. The relevant provision reads in full:

   1. Everyone has the right to freedom of expression. This right shall include freedom to hold opinions and to receive and impart information and ideas without interference by public authority and regardless of frontiers. This article shall not prevent States from requiring the licensing of broadcasting, television or cinema enterprises.
   2. The exercise of these freedoms, since it carries with it duties and responsibilities, may be subject to such formalities, conditions, restrictions or penalties as are prescribed by law and are necessary in a democratic society, in the interests of national security, territorial integrity or public safety, for the prevention of disorder or crime, for the protection of health or morals, for the protection of the reputation or rights of others, for preventing the disclosure of information received in confidence, or for maintaining the authority and impartiality of the judiciary.

[25] Brandenburg v. Ohio, 395 U.S. 444 (1969). *See generally* Stephanie Farrior, "Holding the Matrix: The Historical and Theoretical Foundations of International Law Concerning Hate Speech," 14 *Berkeley J. Int'l L.* 1, 80 (1996); Oyediran, *supra* note 22, at 33. In *Brandenburg*, the U.S. Supreme Court held that the First Amendment does not permit "a State to forbid or proscribe advocacy of the use of force or of

Article 13(5) also diverges from Article 4(a) of the International Convention on the Elimination of All Forms of Racial Discrimination (the "CERD"), which requires States Parties to criminalize "all dissemination of ideas based on racial superiority or hatred," even if the speech does not amount to incitement to racial discrimination or to violence.[26] By contrast, under the American Convention, the advocacy of hatred must constitute *"incitement,"* which may be defined as "strong encouragement," to commit acts of violence.[27]

Finally, two important clarifications should be made with regard to the scope of Article 13(5). Firstly, and following standards set by the UN Human Rights Committee, it could be concluded that Article 13(5)'s narrow definition of proscribed hate speech only applies to speech occurring in the *public discourse*.[28] The States Parties have much more leeway to regulate hate speech in other settings, such as the workplace, schools, or courtrooms.[29] For instance, with regard to discriminatory speech in school settings, the UN Human Rights Committee has stressed that "the influence exerted by school teachers may justify restraints in order to ensure that legitimacy is not given by the school system to the expression of views which are discriminatory."[30] In the UN Human Rights Committee's view, "the exercise of the right to freedom of expression carries with it special duties and responsibilities" that

---

law violation except where such advocacy is directed to inciting or producing imminent lawless action and is likely to incite or produce such action." 395 U.S. at 447. However, it should be mentioned that the text of Article 13(5) does simply reproduce the *Brandenburg* test.

[26] International Convention on the Elimination of All Forms of Racial Discrimination, art. 4(a), Jan. 4, 1969, 660 U.N.T.S. 195 ("[States Parties] [s]hall declare an offence punishable by law all dissemination of ideas based on racial superiority or hatred, incitement to racial discrimination, as well as all acts of violence or incitement to such acts against any race or group of persons of another colour or ethnic origin, and also the provision of any assistance to racist activities, including the financing thereof").

[27] With regard to interpretation of the term "incitement" in connection with hate speech, see Scott J. Catlin, "A Proposal for Regulation Hate Speech in the United States: Balancing Rights under the International Covenant on Civil and Political Rights," 69 *Notre Dame L. Rev.* 771, 798 (1994); Karl Josef Partsch, "Freedom of Conscience and Expression, and Political Freedoms," in *The International Bill of Rights: The Covenant on Civil and Political Rights* 209, 228 (Louis Henkin ed., Columbia University Press 1981).

[28] In referring to *public discourse*, we adopt James Weinstein's definition: "expression on matters of public concern occurring in settings dedicated or essential to public communication, such as books, magazines, films, the Internet, or in 'public forums' such as the speaker's corner of a park." James Weinstein, "Hate Speech, Viewpoint Neutrality, and the American Concept of Democracy," in *The Boundaries of Freedom of Expression and Order in American Democracy* 146, 149 (Thomas R. Hensley ed., Kent State University Press 2001).

[29] As Weinstein explains, when "the primary purpose of a particular setting is something other than public discourse, such as the effectuation of government programs in the government work place, instruction in the public school classroom, or the administration of justice in the courtroom, government has considerable more leeway to regulate speech." *Id.* Robert Post's interview in the present volume elaborates on this distinction, though his definition of "public discourse" has more to do with the *nature* of particular speech, whereas Weinstein's definition goes more to its *location*. The two are related but not identical. *See* Chapter 1 herein.

[30] Malcolm Ross v. Canada, ¶ 11.6, U.N. Doc. CCPR/C/70/D/736/1997, U.N. Human Rights Committee (HRC), (Oct. 26, 2000).

are "of particular relevance within the school system, especially with regard to the teaching of young students."[31] Secondly, Article 13(5) does not encompass insulting, degrading, or threatening speech directed against a *specific individual*, which could be restricted even if the speech does not amount to incitement to violence.[32]

## III. DECISIONS OF OTHER INTERNATIONAL TRIBUNALS

Given these significant textual differences between the American Convention, on the one hand, and the European Convention, the ICCPR, and the CERD, on the other hand, it can be concluded that although the decisions on hate speech from the European Court of Human Rights, the UN Human Rights Committee, or the Committee on the Elimination of Racial Discrimination can serve as guidance, not every example found by these systems to be hate speech would qualify as hate speech under Article 13(5) of the American Convention. We therefore must be careful to apply the lessons of international tribunals only insofar as they are consistent with the narrower textual limits of the American Convention. As the 2004 Annual Report of the Special Rapporteur for Freedom of Expression states, "the U.N. and European jurisprudence should be used not as limitations on freedom of expression, but as minimum standards."[33]

Nonetheless, despite these textual differences, the case law of the United Nations, the European Court of Human Rights, and other international tribunals can help illuminate the interpretation of this right in the Inter-American system. Some of the principles set forth by these tribunals can serve as guideposts in determining how far hate speech can be restricted under the American Convention.

First, the European Court of Human Rights has held that "freedom of expression is applicable not only to 'information' and 'ideas' that are favorably received or regarded as inoffensive or as a matter of indifference, but also to those that offend, shock or disturb."[34] According to this principle, which has also been mentioned by

---

[31] *Id.*

[32] As Frederick Schauer has observed, "when we think about those factors that mark the archetypal free speech setting, the attempt to persuade or to inform large audiences stands in the foreground of our understanding." Frederick Schauer, "Mrs. Palsgraf and the First Amendment," 47 *Wash. & Lee L. Rev.* 161, 168 (1990). Therefore, some distinction should be made between "what is simultaneously broadcast to a large audience" and "what is communicated person–to-person and essentially face-to-face." *Id.*

[33] *See 2004 Report, supra* note 21, at 178–9, par. 45.

[34] *See* Lehideux and Isorni v. France, (No. 92), 1998-VII Eur. Ct. H.R. ¶ 55 (1998); Giniewski v. France, 2006-I Eur. Ct. H.R. ¶ 52 (2006). Or, as U.S. Supreme Court Justice Oliver Wendell Holmes put it with typical pungency: "[I]f there is any principle of the Constitution that more imperatively calls for attachment than any other it is the principle of free thought – not free thought for those who agree with us but freedom for the thought that we hate." United States v. Schwimmer, 279 U.S. 644, 654–655 (1929) (Holmes, J. dissenting).

the Inter-American Court,[35] the mere fact that certain ideas or opinions might be regarded as extremely offensive or provocative by some groups within the society is not a valid justification for their restriction.[36] The rationale behind the principle is clear: No robust public debate on issues of public concern could take place if *offensiveness* was the standard under which the legality of political speech would be evaluated.

Another key principle found in legal systems outside the Americas is the relevance of the *purpose* of the speech.[37] Legitimate purposes can include the search for historical truth or the dissemination of news and information. For instance, in *Jersild v. Denmark*,[38] the European Court held that the criminal conviction of a journalist for assisting in the dissemination of racist statements made by another person during an interview constituted a breach of the European Convention. The Court stressed that the purpose of the journalist was not to propagate racist ideas but to expose, analyze, and explain the racist views of a group of youths frustrated by their social condition.[39] A similar principle was applied by the Inter-American Court in *Herrera Ulloa v. Costa Rica*,[40] which concerned the reproduction of defamatory statements, originally published in foreign newspapers, about Costa Rica's representative to the International Atomic Energy Agency. Quoting the European Court, the Inter-American Court held that "punishment of a journalist for assisting in the dissemination of statements made by another person . . . would seriously hamper the contribution of the press to discussion of matters of public interest."[41] Although the Inter-American Court has not yet dealt with a case concerning the report of racist views held by other persons, its decision in *Herrera Ulloa* indicates that it would

---

[35] *See* Kimel v. Argentina, Inter-Am. Ct. H.R., (ser. C) No. 177, ¶ 88 (2008), *available at* http://www.corteidh.or.cr/docs/casos/articulos/seriec_177_ing.doc; Herrera Ulloa v. Costa Rica, Inter-Am. Ct. H.R. (ser. C) No. 107, ¶ 113 (2004), available at http://www.corteidh.or.cr/docs/casos/articulos/seriec_107_ing.doc. For a summary of the Inter-American Court's freedom-of-expression case law, see Eduardo Bertoni, "The Inter-American Court of Human Rights and the European Court of Human Rights: A Dialogue on Freedom of Expression Standards," 2009 *Eur. Human Rights L. Rev.* 332.

[36] A similar principle has been articulated by some Justices of the Argentine Supreme Court. In the *Amarilla* case, Justices Petracchi and Bossert, relying on the U.S. Supreme Court's decision in Terminiello v. Chicago, 337 U.S.1, 4 (1949), observed that one of the main functions of free expression is "to invite dispute" and "it may indeed best serve its high purpose when it induces a condition of unrest, creates dissatisfaction with conditions as they are, or even stirs people to anger." Juan H. Amarilla, 321 Fallos 2558, 2578 (1998) (Petracchi and Bossert, JJ., concurring).

[37] To determine purpose, tribunals have looked to the actual language of the speech at issue. In one case, the UN Human Rights Committee found that the use of the words "magic gas chamber" in relation to Nazi Germany indicated the speaker was motivated by racism, not the search for historical truth, and thus the speech was not protected. *See* Faurisson v. France, ¶ 6 U.N. Doc. CCPR/C/58?D/550/1993, UN Human Rights Committee (HRC), (1993) (Individual Opinion by Evatt and Kretzmer).

[38] Jersild v. Denmark, App. No. 15890/89, 298 Eur. Ct. H.R. (ser. A) (1994).

[39] *Id.* at ¶ 33.

[40] Herrera Ulloa v. Costa Rica, Inter-Am. Ct. H.R. (ser. C) No. 107, ¶ 113 (July 2, 2004), *available at* http://www.corteidh.or.cr/docs/casos/articulos/seriec_107_ing.doc.

[41] *Id.* at ¶ 134.

likely follow the approach taken by the European Court in *Jersild v. Denmark*. It is extremely important to protect the rights of journalists to decide how best to communicate information and ideas to the public, nowhere more so than when they are reporting on racism and intolerance.[42]

A third principle that can be taken from international jurisprudence concerns *causation*: International jurisprudence has not required demonstration of a direct link between the expression at issue and the ultimate harm. The International Criminal Tribunal for Rwanda summarized prevailing principles in its decision in what is generally referred to as *The Media Case*.[43] The trial court in that case

> pointed to causation as an important principle. The ICTR noted that international jurisprudence has not required specific causation connecting "the expression at issue with the demonstration of a direct effect." In the *Streicher* case from Nazi Germany, for example, the publication of anti-Jewish statements was not alleged to have had ties to "any particular violence." Likewise, in the Turkish cases considered by the European Court, the expressions at issue were not stated to be causes of particular violence. Instead, the ICTR noted that the "question considered is what the likely impact might be, recognizing that causation in this context might be relatively indirect."[44]

Some have predicted that the Inter-American Court is not likely to read Article 13(5) to contain *Brandenburg's* requirement of imminent lawless action.[45] However, it should be borne in mind, as has already been explained, that the American Convention requires incitement to *violence* for speech to be proscribed as hateful. Consequently, discriminatory speech that does not amount to direct incitement to lawless violence – or other similar violent illegal action – against certain groups is not outlawed by the American Convention. The fact that such speech might contribute, in the long run, to an environment more prone to violence would not

---

[42] Under Argentine constitutional law, this would be the logical consequence of the "*Campillay* doctrine," pursuant to which a journalist may not be held liable for the content of a news story when it is attributed to an individualized source. Campillay v. La Razón, 308 Fallos 789 (1986).

[43] Prosecutor v. Nahimana, Barayagwiza and Ngeze ("*The Media Case*"), Case No. ICTR-99–52-T, ¶¶ 1001–07 (Int'l Crim. Trib. for Rwanda Dec. 3, 2003), *aff'd in relevant part*, Case No. ICTR-99–52-A, Appeals Chamber Judgment (Nov. 28, 2007).

[44] 2004 *Report, supra* note 21, at 178, ¶ 43 (citations omitted). For a review of the ECHR cases, see Tarlach McGonagle, "A Survey and Critical Analysis of Council of Europe Strategies for Countering 'Hate Speech'," Chapter 24 herein.

[45] *See, e.g.*, Defeis, *supra* note 22, at 112 & n. 281. As previously explained, the U.S. Supreme Court held in *Brandenburg v. Ohio* that the First Amendment does not allow "a State to forbid or proscribe advocacy of the use of force or of law violation except where such advocacy is directed to inciting or producing imminent lawless action and is likely to incite or produce such action." 395 U.S. 444, 447 (1969). This requirement of likely imminent lawless action requires an objective evaluation of the causal link between speech and harm. *See* Frederick M. Lawrence, "Violence-Conducive Speech: Punishable Verbal Assault or Protected Political Speech?," in *Freedom of Speech and Incitement Against Democracy* 11, 23 (David Kretzmer & Francine Kershman Hazan eds., Kluwer Law International 2000).

be a valid justification to restrict it under Article 13(5).[46] Otherwise, the significant textual differences between the American Convention and the other international conventions would be totally diluted.

A final principle of international jurisprudence is the relevance of the *context* of the speech. In *Zana v. Turkey*, for example, the European Court held that a Turkish mayor's comments about massacres were hate speech because they were made at a time when massacres were taking place, and thus were likely to "exacerbate an already explosive situation."[47] The European Court has also considered whether the speech at issue occurred in the realm of political expression, including criticism of the government, because this area enjoys greater protection.[48] By contrast, the European Court has held that national security issues have a wider "margin of appreciation" for authorities to restrict freedom of expression.[49]

## IV. HATE SPEECH AND PRIOR CENSORSHIP

Article 13(2) imposes an across-the-board ban on "prior censorship" while allowing "subsequent imposition of liability" in limited circumstances. Article 13(5) then requires the prohibition of hate speech that constitutes incitement to lawless violence. Having these provisions within the same article raises the question whether the prohibition on hate speech required by paragraph 5 is subject to the bar on prior prohibitions set out in paragraph 2. That is, although (limited) prohibition of hate speech is required, can that prohibition take the form of "prior censorship," or must hate speech limits, like other limits on expression, only be in the form of "subsequent imposition of liability"?

The answer is complicated by the fact that there is a discrepancy between the English and Spanish versions of Article 13(5). In English, the text notes that incidents of hate speech "shall be considered as offenses punishable by law." This suggests that hate speech can only be regulated through subsequent imposition of liability,

---

[46] That is why criminal laws that punish incitement to discrimination, group defamation, or genocide denial may be inconsistent with freedom of expression, as recognized by the American Convention.

[47] Zana v. Turkey, (No. 57), 1997-VII Eur. Ct. H.R. ¶ 60 (1997). *Context* has also been taken into account by Argentine courts. For example, in a case concerning hate speech against Muslims by a journalist, a Federal Criminal Court of Appeal deemed relevant that that the speech took place only five days after the terrorist attack on the World Trade Center in New York City. Given this context, the Criminal Court considered that the speech was more likely to incite persecution and hatred against the Muslim community. The journalist had compared Muslims with Nazis and said that, just as had happened with the Nazis during World War II, the Islamic people should be destroyed and democracy should be built by force on their ashes. Cherasnhy, G. s/ procesamiento, CNCrim y Correc Fed, Judgment (Sep. 10, 2004).

[48] *See* Lingens v. Austria, App. No. 9815/82, 103 Eur. Ct. H.R. (ser. A) ¶ 42 (1986); Castells v. Spain, App. No. 11798/85, 236 Eur. Ct. H.R. (ser. A) ¶ 46 (1992); Arslan v. Turkey, App. No. 23462/94, Eur. Ct. H.R. ¶ 46 (1999).

[49] The European Court has held that national authorities should be granted a wider margin of appreciation in connection with national security issues. *See, e.g.*, Brannigan and McBride v. United Kingdom, App. No. 14553/89 & 14554/89, Eur. Ct. H.R., ¶ 43 (1993).

as "punishment" occurs after the fact. In Spanish, however, the text uses the word "prohibir," meaning that hate speech is to be *prohibited* by law. This suggests that prior censorship of hate speech might be possible.[50]

If the full text of Article 13 is considered, it seems clear that paragraph 5 is indeed governed by paragraph 2's allowance of only subsequent liability. In both the Spanish and English versions of the American Convention, paragraph 4 of Article 13 states that public entertainment may be subject to prior censorship only for the moral protection of children, "[n]otwithstanding the provisions of paragraph 2." This reference to paragraph 2 makes clear that paragraph 4 was meant to be an exception to paragraph 2. Given that paragraph 5 makes no similar exception to paragraph 2 in either Spanish or English, it follows that hate speech is governed by paragraph 2's limitation to subsequent liability.

This reading is supported by the Inter-American Court's decision in *Olmedo-Bustos v. Chile*, which held that Chile's prohibition of the exhibition of the film *The Last Temptation of Christ* constituted prior censorship in violation of Article.[51] The Court stated that:

> Article 13(4) of the Convention establishes an exception to prior censorship, since it allows it in the case of public entertainment, but *only* in order to regulate access for the moral protection of children and adolescents. *In all other cases*, any preventive measure implies the impairment of freedom of thought and expression.[52]

As is emphasized in the 2004 Annual Report of the Special Rapporteur for Freedom of Expression, the Inter-American Court "made no reference, either explicit or implicit, to hate speech and paragraph 5 as ground for possible censorship, underscoring that hate speech should be regulated like the other areas of expression provided for in paragraph 2."[53]

The decision in *Olmedo-Bustos* represents a significant departure from the jurisprudence of the European Court, which held in *Otto-Preminger-Institut v.*

---

[50]  This interpretation of Article 13 (5) in Spanish is very common. It has been made, for example, by one of Argentina's leading constitutional scholars. *See* Néstor Pedro Sagüés, *Censura Judicial y Derecho a Replica* 91 (Astrea 2008). We understand that language and the local understanding of some legal terms might contribute to confusion and disagreement. In conversation, Michael Herz has pointed out that if something is *punished* after occurring, one hopes that it was *prohibited* before it occurred. Otherwise there is a huge retroactivity/ex post facto problem. On this view, the tension between the English and the Spanish does not seem very great. States have to prohibit certain kinds of hate speech, but that does not mean that they can impose prior restraints; it just means that there is a law on the books that can be enforced, and it will be enforced by punishing the speech after it occurs.

[51]  Olmedo-Bustos v. Chile, Inter-Am. Ct. H.R. (ser. C) No. 73 (2001) (emphases added), *available at* http://www.corteidh.or.cr/docs/casos/articulos/seriec_73_ing.doc. The prior censorship imposed on the film was justified on the grounds that the portrayal of Jesus in the film affected those who believed in him or considered him a model for their way of life; the prohibition to project the film ordered by the Chilean Court was based on "the alleged defense of the right to honor and reputation of Jesus Christ." *Id.* at 23, ¶ 61(g) (summarizing the Commission's arguments).

[52]  *Id.* at ¶ 70.

[53]  2004 *Report, supra* note 21, at 176, ¶ 38.

*Austria* that the seizure and forfeiture of an apparently "anti-Catholic" film did not violate the European Convention.[54] This departure can be attributed to the text of the American Convention, which, as has already been said, offers a much fuller protection of free expression.

## V. FREEDOM FROM *EX POST FACTO* LAWS AND FREEDOM OF EXPRESSION

The Inter-American Court has emphasized that restrictions on all human rights, including freedom of expression, must be "established by law."[55] In this regard, the Court explained that when a regulation is of a criminal nature, it is essential that it be "formulated previously, in an express, accurate and restrictive manner" to comply with the principle of *nullum crimen nulla poena sine lege praevia* ["there is no crime, or punishment, without a law"].[56] In the Inter-American Court's view, "[a]mbiguity in the formulation of criminal definitions generates doubts and opens the door to the discretion of the authorities, particularly undesirable where the criminal liability of a person is to be determined and punished with sanctions which severely affect fundamental rights, such as life or freedom."[57] For example, in *Kimel v. Argentina*, the Inter-American Court held that the lack of sufficient accuracy in the Argentine criminal legislation punishing defamatory statements constituted a violation of Articles 9 (freedom from *ex post facto* law) and 13 (freedom of expression).[58]

Against this background, it should be pointed out that any restriction on freedom of expression made pursuant to Article 13(5) should be formulated in a clear and accurate manner so as to afford legal certainty to the individuals. One of the most serious flaws of some criminal laws that punish certain forms of hate speech is their vagueness, which makes it very difficult to ascertain which speech is prohibited.[59]

---

[54] *See* Otto Preminger-Institut v. Austria, App. No. 13470/87 Eur. Ct. H.R. (1994). In this case, the European Court held that the seizure and forfeiture of the film was necessary to ensure religious peace and to prevent some people feeling themselves to be the object of offensive attacks on their religious beliefs. *Id.* at ¶ 56.

[55] Compulsory Membership in an Association Prescribed by Law for the Practice of Journalism. Advisory Opinion OC-5/85 Inter-Am. Ct. H.R. (ser. A) No. 5 ¶ 89 (1985).

[56] Kimel v. Argentina, Inter-Am. Ct. H.R. (ser. C) No. 177, ¶ 63 (2008).

[57] *Id.*

[58] *Id.* at ¶ 67.

[59] For instance, the term "hatred" – used in most criminal hate speech legislation – is a very elusive and subjective term. As a Canadian Supreme Court Justice observed, "[t]he subjective and emotional nature of the concept of promoting hatred compounds the difficulty of ensuring that only cases meriting prosecution are pursued." R. v. Keegstra, 3 S.C.R. 697, 856 (Can. 1990) (McLachlin dissenting). The problems raised by subjective standards in the area of political speech have also been highlighted by the U.S. Supreme Court. *See* Hustler Magazine Inc. v. Falwell, 485 U.S. 46 (1988) ("'Outrageousness' in the area of political and social discourse has an inherent subjectiveness about it which would allow a jury to impose liability on the basis of the jurors' tastes or views, or perhaps on the basis of their dislike of a particular expression"). A recent instance that supports McLachlin's doubts is

## VI. THE PRINCIPLE OF PROPORTIONALITY

The Inter-American Court has indicated that restrictions on the rights enshrined in the Convention should go no further than is "strictly necessary in a democratic society."[60] To determine if a certain restriction is "necessary in a democratic society," the Court has analyzed whether the restriction is strictly proportional, "so that the sacrifice inherent in the restriction of the right to liberty is not exaggerated or excessive compared to the advantages obtained from this restriction and the achievement of the purpose sought."[61] In *Kimel v. Argentina*, the Inter-American Court stated that it does not consider all criminal punishment of expression to be per se inconsistent with the Convention. However, the Court has warned that criminal sanctions "should be carefully analyzed, pondering the extreme seriousness of the conduct of the individual who expressed the opinion, his actual malice, the characteristics of the unfair damage caused, and other information which shows the absolute necessity to resort to criminal proceedings as an exception."[62]

Therefore, the subsequent imposition of criminal liability for hate speech should be carefully evaluated. Although criminal regulation may be consistent with the Convention, it should be considered whether imprisonment would constitute a *proportionate* punishment for hate speech.

## VII. CONCLUSION

It should come as no surprise that the American Convention offers such strong protection of freedom of expression. The Convention was born in a historical context characterized by the existence of authoritarian governments that criminalized political speech and prosecuted dissent to an unimaginable extent. If constitutionalism and human rights conventions may be analogized to Ulysses' strategy for resisting the singing of the Sirens, the generous protection of freedom of expression in the American Convention should be understood as an American strategy to avoid the

---

the 2010 decision by a Moscow Court that convicted and fined two art curators for "inciting hatred or enmity" and "denigration of human dignity." The curators had staged an exhibition entitled "Forbidden Art 2006"which had included, among other things, a set of paintings of Biblical scenes in which Jesus Christ was depicted as Mickey Mouse. The decision is described and criticized by the NGO Article XIX in "Russia: ARTICLE 19 Condemns Conviction of Art Curators" (July 12, 2010) (press release). For a description of the relevant Russian law, see Andrei Richter, "One Step Beyond Hate Speech: Post-Soviet Regulation of 'Extremist' and 'Terrorist' Speech in the Media," Chapter 14 herein.

[60] Ricardo Canese v. Paraguay, Inter-Am. Ct. H.R. (ser. C) No. 111 ¶ 95 (2004), *available at* http://www.corteidh.or.cr/docs/casos/articulos/seriec_111_ing.doc.

[61] *See* Chaparro Álvarez y Lapo Iñiguez v. Ecuador, Inter-Am. Ct. H.R. (ser. C) No. 170 ¶ 93 (2007), *available at* http://www.corteidh.or.cr/docs/casos/articulos/seriec_170_ing.doc.

[62] Kimel v. Argentina, Inter-Am. Ct. H.R. (ser. C) No. 177, ¶ 78 (2008).

serious mistakes of the past.[63] The Sirens whose singing we must resist are the recurring temptations to prosecute dissent in the name of some elusive and undefined public good.

---

[63] In this regard, Argentine Supreme Court Justice Petracchi has emphasized that the strong protection against prior censorship is a Latin American constitutional tradition. *See* V.S. v. D.A.M., 324 Fallos 975, 1061 (2001) (Petracchi, J., dissenting).

# 26

# Orbiting Hate? Satellite Transponders and Free Expression

## Monroe E. Price

## I. INTRODUCTION

In this chapter, I deal with the consequences of two significant changes: an expansion – a rather substantial one – in the categorization of various kinds of expression under the loose rubric of "hate speech" and simultaneously the increasing use of satellites to hurl this speech around the world. I examine a series of case studies dealing with programming transmitted by satellite that is connected to division and conflict – in these cases, conflict mostly related to societies in the Middle East.

One might anticipate that regulatory crises occur when organized and often status quo-disruptive senders shape a persistent and effective set of messages to be transmitted within a society and/or across national boundaries as part of an overall effort to gain substantial influence on target populations. As the case studies will show, when such messages have been transmitted by satellites, they have produced decisions by governments and powerful groups that have been almost invisible and exist outside a clear legal framework of articulated norms and transparent processes. One feature is paramount: Formal regulation of the content of satellite transmissions, including of speech with alleged attributes of hate, with few exceptions, rarely has been an effective theater for playing out governmental interests in satellite signal diffusion. There is also a lack of scholarly literature on the ways in which governments seek to control or affect the functioning of satellite services and their transnational distributions. In a sense, this underscores a major point: Decisions to allow or prohibit distribution of satellite signals have been treated more as strategic business decisions than as an interplay between national interests and free-expression values. Having these decisions take the form of leasing and subleasing of transponders, they become mere economic transactions, underplaying their role as modes of intervening in

Versions or portions of this chapter appeared in *Comp. Media L.J.*, No. 16, p. 127 (July–Dec. 2010), as "Satellite Transponders and Free Expression," 27 *Cardozo Arts & Ent. L.J.* 1 (2009), and as "Governance, Globalism and Satellites," 4 *Global Media & Comm.* 245 (2008).

national public spheres. In addition, because there is a relative absence of judicial decisions or similar official documents, observers must rely largely on reportorial and journalistic accounts and on information gleaned from Web sites and other unofficial sources.

The challenge is to extract from the anecdotal a better understanding of the strategic decisions being made, of what amounts to a "common law" of what kinds of content states informally ban on satellite and, even more specifically, of the interactions between content and the instruments of power. Instead of a deliberate system, there exists a hodgepodge of practices and efforts, often desperate, by states or regional and international entities to intervene when a crisis occurs or is perceived to occur.[1] As I shall note, there is the beginning of a tendency to render these decisions more formal. Only then will there be the possibility of a rule-of-law analysis of the quality and defensibility of state decisions.

The international debate over how and whether to regulate satellite transmissions has gone through several phases, starting with an extensive effort (that ended in tatters) in the United Nations to design a system of international standards.[2] Ownership and control have affected the debate in all its phases, and strategic considerations have played a role in the ownership structure of satellites from the outset. Initially, satellites were in transnational hands or controlled by the United States. The creation of Intelsat as a public entity was a way of acknowledging the conditions of control that might accompany an entirely new mode of transmitting information.[3] It was hardly an implementation of unfettered access to transponders. Privatization of satellites and competition removed one of the more automatic modes of control.[4] Now, in the post-9/11 world, after the industry has grown, and as the world seems more preoccupied with the role of mediated expression in the battle for hearts and minds, there are renewed attempts at regulation and control, using "hate speech" like labels as justification. The considerations that informed the first stage – the

---

[1] Given the magnitude of the subject, the scope of the discussion is limited in this chapter. For example, the International Telecommunications Union and governance in terms of the allocation or assignment of orbital slots is addressed. The debate there concerning equitable distribution of orbital positions and first come–first served, has been often told. This chapter will focus on a line of questioning arising out of an earlier work, Monroe Price, "Satellite Broadcasting as Trade Routes in the Sky," in *In Search of Boundaries: Communication, Nation States and Cultural Identities* 146 (Joseph M. Chan & Bryce T. McIntyre eds., Ablex Publishing 2002). The question raised there is whether, rather than looking for a universal or global governance scheme, we can identify different regional themes, different forms of state intervention that turn on particular satellites, particular footprints, or particular content. Put in metaphorical terms, does the law governing this trade depend on the ship, the port of call, the freight, or some combination thereof?

[2] *See* Kathryn M. Queeney, *Direct Broadcast Satellites and the United Nations* (Sijthoff & Noordhoff 1978).

[3] *See* Leland L. Johnson, *The Future of INTELSAT in a Competitive Environment* (Rand Corp. 1988); Kenneth Katkin, "Communication Breakdown?: The Future of Global Connectivity after the Privatization of INTELSAT," 38 *Vand. J. Transnat'l L.* 1323 (2005).

[4] *See* Katkin, *supra* note 3.

UN debate – are present again, but the geopolitical considerations mean different positions for key players.[5]

## II. THE UNITED NATIONS, THE PRIOR CONSENT DEBATE, AND THE ARTICULATION OF ISSUES

"Freedom of expression" norms and their application to hate speech arose at an early stage at the UN. Almost as soon as the extraordinary science-fiction laden prospect of direct-to-home satellite communication became widely seen as actually possible, the UN took up the question of whether international regulation would be desirable. After all, the sending of a signal from one country into the territory of another could be seen either as a triumph of free expression or as a potential violation of national sovereignty (or both).[6] Indeed, most terrestrial broadcasting regulation, at least on the multilateral level, had been established on the idea that in medium- and long-wave there should be some sort of agreement for the management of broadcasting signals so that national borders were respected and what might be called "intended spillover" was minimized.[7] A similar idea – requiring prior consent before a satellite signal is sent transnationally – was debated in both the UN and the UN Education, Scientific and Cultural Organization ("UNESCO") from the late 1960s to the early 1980s.[8]

---

[5] For example, Canada's novel mode of determining whether Al Jazeera could be carried on cable services; the application of the U.S. Terrorism Exclusion list in the case of Al Manar; and domestic informal and formal pressures related to the difficulty of Al Jazeera International in gaining shelf space on U.S. cable systems.

[6] *See* Colby C. Nuttall, "Defining International Satellite Communications as Weapons of Mass Destruction: The First Step in a Compromise Between National Sovereignty and the Free Flow of Ideas," 27 *Hous. J. Int'l L.* 389 (2005) (discussing the framing of the debate as conflicting perspectives of governing principles, with some states supporting a "free flow of information" and other states supporting "national sovereignty").

[7] For most of the twentieth century, the international consensus was that radio transmissions should be contained primarily within the boundaries of one nation; the international function, performed mainly through the International Telecommunications Union ("ITU"), was to dispense frequencies so as to assure that conditions of market division along national borders could be realized and enforced. Between the world wars, there were bilateral and multilateral agreements to control propaganda subversive to the state system. For example, the League of Nations sponsored the International Convention Concerning the Use of Broadcasting in the Cause of Peace, which provided:

> The High Contracting Parties mutually undertake to prohibit and, if occasion arises, to stop without delay the broadcasting within their respective territories of any transmission which to the detriment of good international understanding is of such a character as to incite the population of any territory to acts incompatible with the internal order or the security of a territory of a High Contracting Party.

International Convention Concerning the Use of Broadcasting in the Cause of Peace, Sep. 23, 1936, 186 L.N.T.S. 301 art. 1 (1936) (highlighting states' continuing "struggle with the question of whether to use law to protect transnational systems or to enhance international freedom to communicate").

[8] For details of debates on the prior consent requirement in particular and regulation of direct broadcasting by satellite in general, see Queeney, *supra* note 2; *National Sovereignty and International*

The main forum for this debate was the UN Committee on the Peaceful Uses of Outer Space ("COPUOS"),[9] which was established in 1958 and was responsible for creating the five major treaties that regulate activities in space. These treaties concern: the use and exploration of space; the rescue and return of astronauts and objects launched into space; liability for damage caused by space objects; registration of objects launched into space; and the use and exploitation of the moon.[10] Members of COPUOS's working group argued for "a prohibition on broadcasts beamed from satellites by one State to others without the explicit prior consent of the Government concerned through bilateral or multilateral agreements."[11] Quite quickly, the debate became a forum for rehearsing Cold War feints and parries, and for consideration of the relationship of satellite transmissions to spheres of influence. The Soviet Union, supported by many developing countries, fought for a prior-consent requirement (the USSR claiming it desired to limit political propaganda and hate-oriented speech, others more concerned with the impact on economic development and cultural heritage). Arguments over what were called direct broadcasting services were linked closely to debates on the free flow of information and agitation for the "New World Information and Communication Order."[12] The United States, along with several allies, opposed all restrictions, asserting a commitment to principles of free expression.[13] The debates stretched back to long-standing information strategies of West and East, and the framing of political ideologies in the specific context of the free flow of information.

The result of this conflict was failure to pass a binding international treaty on the regulation of direct broadcast satellites. Rather, in 1982, the UN General Assembly

---

*Communication* (Kaarle Nordenstreng & Herbert I. Schiller eds., Ablex Publishing 1979); Jon T. Powell, *International Broadcasting by Satellite: Issues of Regulation, Barriers to Communication* (Quorum Books 1985).

[9]   Nuttall, *supra* note 6, at 394 (describing UN's creation of the Committee on the Peaceful Uses of Outer Space ("COPUOS") in 1958 to acknowledge "the international challenges that space exploration [and satellite communications] could present" and the committee's focus "on developing workable international standards, policy, and law that t[ook] into account these new and developing challenges and their potential threat to international peace").

[10]   Alexandra M. Field, "INTELSAT at a Crossroads," 25 *Law & Pol'y Int'l Bus.* 1335 (1994).

[11]   U.N. GAOR, Comm. on the Peaceful Uses of Outer Space, Working Group On Direct Broadcast Satellites, "Report of the Second Session of the Working Group," ¶ 7 U.N. Doc. A/AC.105/66 (Aug. 12, 1969); *see also* U.N. GAOR Comm. on Peaceful Uses of Outer Space, "Broadcasting from Satellites, Working Paper Submitted by France to the Second Session of the Working Group on Direct Broadcast Satellites," 32–34, U.N. Doc. A/AC.105/PV.62 (June 30, 1969) (discussing Soviet position); Marika N. Taishoff, *State Responsibility and the Direct Broadcast Satellite* 34 (Pinter 1987) (describing Soviet fear of harmful propaganda).

[12]   *See, e.g.*, Thomas L. McPhail, *Electronic Colonialism: The Future of International Broadcasting and Communication* 162 (Sage Publications 1987); Seán Ó. Siochrú and Bruce Girard, *Global Media Governance: A Beginner's Guide* 77 (Rowman & Littlefield 2002).

[13]   *See* Frank Stanton, "Will they Stop our Satellites," *N.Y. Times*, Oct. 22, 1972, at D23; *see also* Nuttall, *supra* note 6 (discussing the United States' ardent support of the free flow of information and objection to virtually any interference with the right to impart information through any media form).

adopted Resolution 37/92, Principles Governing the Use by States of Artificial Earth Satellites for International Direct Television Broadcasting.[14] The explicit principle of requiring "prior consent" of the receiving countries was abandoned,[15] but paragraph 8 of the nonbinding document provided "States should bear international responsibility for activities in the field of international direct television broadcasting by satellite carried out by them or under their jurisdiction."[16] This reflected the alternative approach developed during the UN and UNESCO debates: a set of internationally agreed-on standards with the originating country being responsible for ensuring that no signal emanating from its territory would violate such standards, including those related to hate speech norms.[17]

As we shall see, the basic issues that guided national strategies in the UN debate continue to guide decisions concerning satellite communications today. The prior consent principle – granting that a state, even in the face of the right of an individual to receive and impart information,[18] should have some say over the receipt of satellite signals within its borders – lurks. So too does the alternative principle, namely that there should be common standards (global, regional, or national) determining the content of what is transmitted or received using satellite platforms. These approaches exist as artifacts that find their way into contemporary actions and debates, albeit not as universal principles and very seldom with reference to their

---

[14]  G.A. Res. 2916, U.N. GAOR, 37th Sess., Supp. No. 92, 100th meeting, U.N. Doc A/Res/37/92 (1982), http://www.un.org/documents/ga/res/37/a37r092.htm (107 countries voted for the resolution, 13 voted against, and 13 abstained); *see also* Nuttall, *supra* note 6, at 395 ("Of the declarations of principles proposed by COPUOS and adopted by the United Nations, the Principles Governing the Use by States of Artificial Earth Satellites for International Direct Television Broadcasting [Principles on TV Broadcasting] provides the most focused look at the potential influence the United Nations expected satellite broadcasts to exert across international boundaries.").

[15]  *See* G.A. Res. 2916, *supra* note 14. Section J of the Resolution concerns "Consultations and agreements between States." Paragraph 13 reads: "A State which intends to establish or authorize the establishment of an international direct television broadcasting satellite service shall without delay notify the proposed receiving State or States of such intention and shall promptly enter into consultation with any of those States which so requests." Paragraph 14 reads: "An international direct television broadcasting satellite service shall only be established after the conditions set forth in paragraph 13 above have been met and on the basis of agreement and/or agreements in conformity with the relevant instruments of International Telecommunication Union and in accordance with these principles."

[16]  *Id.* at ¶ 8.

[17]  *See* Comm. on the Peaceful Uses of Outer Space, Legal Subcomm. Rep. on its 17th Sess., Annex 2, at 6, U.N. Doc. A/AC.105/218 (1978) (containing draft principles on direct television broadcasting). There was also an effort to encourage consultation: "For that purpose a State which proposes to establish or authorize the establishment of a direct television broadcasting service by means of artificial earth satellites specifically directed at a foreign State shall without delay notify that State of such intention and shall promptly enter into consultations with that State if the latter so requests." *Id.*

[18]  *See* International Covenant on Civil and Political Rights, art. 19(2), Dec. 16, 1966, 999 U.N.T.S. 171 ("Everyone shall have the right to freedom of expression; this right shall include freedom to seek, receive and impart information and ideas of all kinds, regardless of frontiers, either orally, in writing or in print, in the form of art, or through any other media of his choice.").

historical antecedents.[19] As one way to look at emerging patterns, one could say that in the absence of an agreed international approach, there are states that have adapted some versions of these principles, coming as close to a prior-consent principle or to the standards-related alternative as they technologically and politically can.

## III. "INFORMAL" GOVERNANCE AND INFLUENCE

By and large, prior to the end of the 1990s and 9/11, the lack of an overarching international system to govern the distribution of satellite programming was of little significance.[20] Global players had not, as part of their communications strategy, fixed on transnational satellite programming, although some such efforts were nascent. Evangelical religious groups had begun to show the effectiveness of transnational broadcasting to affect allegiances.[21] Diasporic movements began to find the technology hospitable, followed by states seeking to link more closely with their nonresident populations. One such case involving the Kurdish community – and MED-TV, discussed later in the chapter – raised the major issues of how a set of focused satellite signals could reinforce a national identity among a geographically dispersed group, and what dangers that might pose to territorial integrity. Problems of regulation remained in the background because authoritarian countries could ban satellite dishes or otherwise control the receipt of information. To the extent that there were transnational broadcasting issues of political moment, they involved the residual short-wave radio efforts of the Cold War. These diminished in significance during the 1990s, with a few idiosyncratic and intense exceptions such as Radio Marti and Radio Free Asia.

Then, with the founding and broadcasting of Al Jazeera in 1996[22] and the NATO bombing campaign of 1999 (and with it a focus on the effort of Serbia to reach Serbians worldwide), the regional and global political impact of satellite transmissions began to attract renewed attention. As a result, internationally, states over the last

[19]  *See* Nuttall, *supra* note 6, at 404 (noting that "advocates of economic growth that support the expansion of the satellite market to promote competition" view regulation as necessary "to transform the telecommunications markets from monopolies into freely competing markets").

[20]  *See* John Tusa, "International Satellite Television – Good Neighbor or Global Intruder?,"7 *Eur. Bus. J.* 45 (1995) (discussing insufficiently developed satellite networks, in which numerous major players today "were scarcely in operation, their impact on societies and world events not yet fully felt or clearly demonstrated").

[21]  *See* Michael Serazio, "Media Power, Politics and Proselytizing: The Global Gospel of American Christian Broadcasting," *J. Media and Religion* (2006), *available at* http://www.global.asc.upenn.edu/docs/GlobalGospel.pdf (discussing the soft-power implications of American Christian broadcasting as it competes in the international marketplace for loyalties); *see also* Michael Serazio, "Geopolitical Proselytizing in the Marketplace for Loyalties: Rethinking the Global Gospel of American Christian Broadcasting," Paper presented at the annual meeting of the NCA 94th Annual Convention, San Diego, CA (Nov. 21, 2008).

[22]  Marc Lynch, *Voices of the New Arab Public: Iraq, Al-Jazeera, and Middle East Politics Today* (Columbia University Press 2006).

decade have begun groping again for some accommodation with the issues and positions put forward in the UN debate of the 1970s. There is not (and most likely never will be) an international agreement that involves the prior consent approach or a set of enforceable international standards. But unilaterally, bilaterally, and multilaterally, states will seek similar considerations, where they consider it important. And, frequently, the efforts to do so will be informal, nonobvious, almost impermeable. Decisions will be pragmatic (with some recognition of standards and obligations of speech-related human rights). Inferring from past experience, the justification for these formal and informal efforts include maintaining a balance of loyalties in the receiving country; protecting the business status quo of video providers; decreasing "terrorist" related programming; and maintaining standards of morality. The efforts deal with modes of production, transmission, and reception.

This section uses particular cases to demonstrate how these actions reflect the communications goals of the sender, and how restrictions reflect the counterstrategy of the receiving states.

## A. MED-TV

The case of MED-TV was one of the first in which the multilateral and informal aspects of satellite regulation significantly surfaced and the complexity of arrangements came to the fore. In 1994, MED-TV, a satellite service targeting Kurdish populations worldwide, was granted a ten-year license by the United Kingdom's Independent Television Commission (the "ITC").[23] MED-TV especially sought to reach Kurdish minorities in Turkey, Iran, and Iraq. The United Kingdom was its locus of licensing because it was "established"[24] there, but its programming was produced in large part in Belgium. To some, the satellite feed was a culturally enriching mix of news, entertainment, and education aimed at a historically diasporic community of 35 million people engaged in rediscovering and redefining Kurdish nationhood and reaffirming its language and culture. Naomi Sakr captured this view, calling MED-TV a "kind of Kurdistan in space,"[25] as it provided a culturally unifying function despite the lack of a Kurdish homeland or single territorial base. In sharp contrast, Turkish officials claimed that MED-TV was the media arm of the PKK, the separatist Kurdish force that has been engaged in armed conflict with Turkish government troops and is considered by Turkey to be a significant threat to

---

[23] Which, before being merged into a new entity, OFCOM, regulated commercial TV broadcasts in the United Kingdom (whether terrestrial or satellite). Indeed, the United Kingdom became home to a variety of satellite services seeking to reach groups or populations abroad and operate with the legitimization of a British license.

[24] The organization "established" itself in the United Kingdom, a technical term that meant that they were qualified to receive a license from the UK's Independent Television Commission.

[25] Naomi Sakr, *Satellite Realms: Transnational Television, Globalization and the Middle East* 62 (I. B. Taurus 2001).

the integrity and unity of the country.[26] For Turkey, MED-TV was a foreign intrusion, disturbing the local forms of regulation, and seeking to foment instability and violence. The Turkish government contended that MED-TV was fostering extremist claims and stirring up animosity among the Turkish population.

The Turkish government sought to suppress the receipt of the channels, for example, by attempting to ban the purchase and mounting of satellite dishes that could obtain the signals.[27] When this effort failed, Turkey sought to deny MED-TV leasing rights on government-controlled transponders on Eutelsat and mounted a campaign to pressure the British government to withdraw MED-TV's license.[28]

The location and ownership of the transponders on the Eutelsat system that were used by MED-TV were politically significant. Under Eutelsat's internal rules, the satellite's transponders were (loosely) controlled by public agencies; the states that controlled those agencies had good bilateral relations with Turkey. Stories were told of MED-TV securing time on a Slovakian-controlled slot on a satellite only to have the Turkish Foreign Minister obtain a cancelation through bilateral discussions. MED-TV was unceremoniously bounced from various transponders on Eutelsat and its contracts for access canceled or left to expire. One of the features of such informal negotiations and decisions was the absence of any requirement that the reasons behind the decision be published or justified.

One solace, an anchor, as it were, was MED-TV's British license. Whatever the station's political goals, the choice of a relatively secure legal and political system that would govern the delivery of its information seemed to be one of MED-TV's most important achievements and was a vital part of the strategy for obtaining transponder space to reach the relevant audience. Its establishment in the United Kingdom resulted in MED-TV's being subject to the ITC's content standards. Receiving a British permit allowed MED-TV to claim that it met those standards. This was seen as a means for increasing the chances that its programming would be subject only to legal, as opposed to extralegal, constraints.[29] Thus, Turkish officials

---

[26] *See* "Turkey Calls on USA to End MED-TV Broadcasts," BBC *Summary of World Broadcasts*, Aug. 30, 1996; "MED-TV Off the Air After UK, Belgian Police Raids," BBC *Summary of World Broadcasts*, Sep. 27, 1996; "Turkish Premier Discusses MED-TV With Tony Blair," BBC *Summary of World Broadcasts*, Dec. 19, 1997; Amir Hassanpour, "Med-TV, Britain, and the Turkish State: A Stateless Nation's Quest for Sovereignty in the Sky" (unpublished paper presented at the Freie Universitat Berlin, Nov. 7, 1995).

[27] For example, its transmission was originally on a satellite that directed its signal from a different location from the more commonly viewed Eutelsat satellites. MED-TV viewers had to turn their satellite dishes in a different direction from those receiving the Eutelsat original satellite, one that carried traditional Turkish entertainment channel services. The authorities could see the difference in the attitude of the dish and could use that information to harass the MED-TV viewers. To protect its viewers, MED-TV had to shift, therefore, to the more commonly viewed bird in the sky.

[28] Peter Feuilherade, "Med-TV: 'Kurdistan in the Sky'," BBC *News* (Mar. 23, 1999), *available at* http://news.bbc.co.uk/2/hi/world/monitoring/280616.stm.

[29] *See* Price, *supra* note 1 ("At the danger of pushing the metaphor too far, the MED-TV decision to obtain a license in the United Kingdom could be perceived as a rough equivalent of flying the British flag on the main mast.").

mounted an extensive campaign to pressure the British government to withdraw MED-TV's license and close down the producer. As part of this campaign, the Turkish government contended, with some informal proffer of evidence, that MED-TV was a "political organization" linked to the PKK and therefore, under UK legislation, precluded from obtaining a British license.

In February 1998, the ITC, charged with supervision of licensed entities in Britain, penalized MED-TV for three broadcasts, for a total fine of approximately $150,000.[30] According to the Commission, despite formal warnings, MED-TV violated the impartiality requirements of ITC's programming code. In one breach, according to the ITC, a "40 minute long programme consisted entirely of a political rally organized by the PKK." The violation was that "[n]o context was supplied and there was no balancing material." In a second breach of impartiality requirements, MED-TV "seemingly endorsed" the on-camera condemnation of a U.S. list of terrorist organizations that included the PKK. A third transgression involved "'personal comments' from a MED-TV journalist in the field, namely a description of the more pro-government Kurdish Democratic Party as 'treacherous and murderous.'" Finally, in 1999, the ITC withdrew MED-TV's license, finding that the station had too often violated standards of objectivity and impartiality. At the time, Sir Robin Biggam, the ITC's chair, defended the decision, using an argument that was not within the terms of the decision itself: "Whatever sympathy there may be in the United Kingdom for the Kurdish people, it is not in the public interest to have any broadcaster use the UK as a platform for broadcasts which incite people to violence."[31]

Soon thereafter, MED-TV closed down.[32] The project, however, was only temporarily blocked; given the complex, robust, and many-sourced bazaar for transponder rentals, versions have cropped up, albeit always and continuously subject to pressures on national hosts, in France and elsewhere, to curtail the service.[33] Despite

---

[30] This history is recounted in Monroe E. Price, "What Price Fairness?" 12 *Media Studs. J.* 82 (1998), from which this paragraph draws.

[31] *See* "UK Regulator Revokes Kurdish Med TV's License," *BBC News* (Apr. 23, 299), *available at* http://news.bbc.co.uk/2/hi/world/monitoring/326883.stm("Whatever sympathy there may be in the United Kingdom for the Kurdish people, it is not in the public interest to have any broadcaster use the UK as a platform for broadcasts which incite people to violence. Med TV have been given many opportunities to be a peaceful voice for their community; to allow them to continue broadcasting after such serious breaches would be to condone the misuse of the UK's system for licensing broadcasters.") (quoting ITC chair Sir Robin Biggam).

[32] David Romano, *The Kurdish Nationalist Movement: Opportunity, Mobilization, and Identity* 157 (Cambridge University Press 2006).

[33] *See* "New Kurdish TV Station Medya TV," *BBC Monitoring* (July 30, 1999 to Aug. 3, 1999). A successor, Medya-TV, opened in the summer of 1999, but under different legal circumstances:

> A new Paris-based Kurdish satellite television station identifying itself as Medya TV has been observed since 30th Jul. It broadcasts via the Eutelsat Hot Bird 4 satellite at 13 degrees east (10853 MHz vertical polarization, audio subcarrier 6.65 MHz). This transponder also carries Kurdish and Christian programming from the UK-based CTV (Cultural TV).... News bulletins formerly carried on CTV appear to have transferred to Medya TV along with some of the presenters.... Medya TV carried a live relay of its official launch ceremony in Paris. The

the legal efforts, MED-TV and its successors have persisted in finding ways to deliver some content to its dispersed audiences.

## B. *Islah*

The case of MED-TV is atypical because of the formality of the proceedings involving its content. Far more typical was the informal regulation of content in the instance of Islah or Reform Radio.[34] The Islah case involved Abdulzazis Alkhamis, former head of the London-based Saudi Center for Human Rights. As part of a strategy of dissenting civil society, Alkhamis sought to open up a space for speech in Saudi Arabia that arguably promoted greater public participation and democracy (although there could be other characterizations of the content).[35] In 2002, he contacted Saad Al Fagih, head of the Movement for Islamic Reform in Arabia, as a potential partner for a radio channel they named "Islah," or "Reform," Radio.[36] (To illustrate the tenuousness of characterizations, Al Fagih was first referred to in the *Wall Street Journal* as a "dissident," but later described by the U.S. government with the harsh and conclusory label "terrorist" or "aider and abettor" of terrorists.) With a plan to use media to reach into Saudi Arabia with a "democracy"-related message, the next question was a technical one: How to have a signal reach Saudi Arabia and become available to Saudis so that Alkhamis and Al Fagih's message could be heard. They searched out individuals who were experienced in helping outside groups,

> ceremony was held in a hall with the Medya logo depicted in laser lights as the stage backdrop. Two large screens on either side of the stage showed the musicians and the announcers, who spoke in Kurdish. What appeared to be a message marking the launching of the station by Kurdish National Congress President Serif Canli was carried at 1710 GMT. It was followed by a similar message in Kurdish from Yasar Kaya, president of the Kurdish parliament-in-exile.

*Id.* Medya TV's license was revoked by the French authorities on February 13, 2004. "Kurdish Medya TV Shuts Down," Clandestine Radio Watch (Feb. 13, 2004), *available at* http://www.clandestineradio. com/crw/news.php?id=211&stn=684&news=318.

[34] *See* Movement of Islamic Reform in Arabia (MIRA), *available at* http://www.islah.info/index.php?/english/empp11/.

[35] *See* David Crawford, "A Battle for Ears and Minds: As Technology Gives New Voice to Dissent, a Saudi Vies to Be Heard," *Wall St. J.*, Feb. 4, 2004 (discussing Islah's claimed purposes and innovative techniques). The BBC reported:

> Radio stations run by opposition groups are a rare occurrence in the Arab world, and the launch marks a dramatic breakthrough in a region where public broadcasting is tightly regulated by governments. The new satellite station Sawt Al-Islah – which means Voice of Reform – is using the latest internet technology to help disgruntled Saudis voice their criticism of the royal family. A spokesman for the Movement for Islamic Reform In Arabia told the BBC that by using an internet phone service – known as Paltalk – listeners can take part in the programme and say what they like without risking arrest or harassment. Saad al-Fagih said the bulk of the station's schedule was talk shows. The topics discussed, he said, included lack of transparency in the Saudi system, corruption, poverty and failure to implement Islamic law.

Magdi Abdelhadi, "Saudi opposition gets radio voice," BBC News – World Edition (Dec. 9, 2002), *available at* http://news.bbc.co.uk/2/hi/middle_east/2560313.stm.

[36] Crawford, *supra* note 35.

including church groups, state-sponsored international broadcasters, and splinter political groups, gain access across borders. They hired Ludo Maes, a Belgian short-wave specialist, who helped Islah gain access to short-wave transmitters located in Lithuania that were left over from short-wave broadcasts during the Cold War.[37] With Maes' counsel, Islah also contracted to be broadcast over the Hotbird satellite, owned by Eutelsat. Deutsche Telekom was the lessee of bandwidth on the satellite and provided Islah uplink facilities. Reform Radio began broadcasting over satellite and short-wave in December 2002, encouraging listeners "to speak out against corruption and for a moderate Islamic government in Saudi Arabia."[38]

Intervention and difficulty began almost immediately. First, the short-wave signal was jammed by a powerful opposing transmitter (set up to transmit on the same frequency).[39] In addition, Maes received a formal communication from a lawyer representing the Saudi Embassy in Belgium threatening legal action to halt the broadcasts, accusing the project of inciting terrorism through the broadcasting of propaganda. With short-wave jammed, Islah relied on its satellite broadcasts (with the shortcoming that the radio broadcasts only could be received on Saudi television sets). For this and other reasons, Reform Radio established a satellite television station and set up an uplink in Croatia.[40] David Crawford continues the story:

> A week later, the phone rang at the Usingen Earth Station near Frankfurt, where T-Systems, a Deutsche Telekom subsidiary, controls and monitors television, radio and data beamed to satellites. On the line was an anonymous caller. "Stop broadcasting Reform Radio or we will jam you," he said, according to someone involved in the incident. About the same time, a powerful jamming beam turned the video monitor in the office to static.
>
> The jamming affected five TV programs broadcast via the same transponder, including several small commercial channels. When Deutsche Telekom stopped

---

[37] *See* National Association of Shortwave Broadcasters, Inc., http://www.shortwave.org/ (demonstrating some of the variety of users, though emphasizing religious broadcasters); Clandestine Radio Stations broadcasting to Kurdistan, http://www.schoechi.de/cl-kur.html (describing 2005 efforts by Maes relating to Kurdistan TDP Shortwave Transmitter Airtime QSL-Cards); http://www.airtime.be/qsl.html (Maes' Transmitter Documentation Project); "hard-core-dx info" (Oct. 21, 2001), http://www.hard-core-dx.com/archives/oct2001.html ("'My hunch, and it is only that, about the reason for TDP secrecy on actual transmitter sites, is that some of this business is under-the-table, i.e. technicians at certain under-used sites are paid to put the programs on the air without full knowledge or authorization by the governmental agencies owning them,' writes Glenn Hauser in an issue of DX Listeners Digest. Ludo Maes has responded with dismay to these 'lies and serious accusations', adding: 'Don't we have a right for not publishing transmitter sites?'"); TDP Clandestine and Opposition Shortwave Radio Stations and International Broadcasters, http://www.shortwave.be/cla.html (listing opposition stations using short wave).

[38] Crawford, *supra* note 35.

[39] The ability to jam short-wave signals is far greater than the ability to jam satellite signals.

[40] *See* Crawford, *supra* note 35 ("Mr. Fagih, liberal by Saudi standards but still orthodox on most religious issues, prohibited music for moral reasons. Mr. Alkhamis had no budget for video programming. Instead, he broadcast a picture of the Reform logo, along with text information scrolling across the screen. The audio was from the radio broadcast.").

broadcasting Reform briefly, the jamming was stopped. A new anonymous phone call would then warn Deutsche Telekom not to resume broadcasting. On Oct. 25, Deutsche Telekom canceled its contract with Reform Radio.[41]

But this was hardly the end of the station's difficulties. In December 2004, the United States added Al Fagih to the State Department's list of terrorists; shortly thereafter, Al-Fagih was put on the UN's Consolidated List of terrorists. The Movement for Islamic Reform in Arabia was added to the State Department's list in July 2005.[42]

For present purposes, the importance of this story is the variety of informal arrangements implicated in the contested effort by these interests to enter the Saudi "market for loyalties." To fathom what occurred, it is important to understand the structure of access to short-wave and satellite transponders, the technical aspects of jamming; the modes of informal threats to intermediaries, the techniques of states bringing pressure to bear on other states to alter modes of diffusion, the modes of affecting financing (through terror lists and other means), and the interrelationship of technologies. There are elements that are difficult to retrieve, including how foreign dissenting channels are actually received, how reception fits in with constraints and policing that occurs in Saudi Arabia, and our current understanding, for example, what modes of formal and informal surveillance serve as barriers to reception.

## C. Al Zawraa

The case of Al Zawraa provides additional insights into the questions of informal pressure, this time involving a state that is neither the receiver nor the sender of the signal, namely the United States. Al Zawraa started as a broadcast channel in Iraq, with an audience-pleasing entertainment format. Owned by Mishan Al Jaburi, leader of the Sunni Arab Front for Reconciliation and Liberation, the channel over time became more politicized, reflecting the owner's decision to run for the Iraqi parliament. More importantly, it morphed into what Ibrahim Al Marashi and others have called insurrectionist television,[43] playing, among other things, repeated videos of jihadist bombings with footage of attacks against multinational forces. In November 2006, the Iraqi government ordered the station to be terminated and its offices in Iraq closed on charges of "inciting violence and murder."[44]

---

[41] *Id.*

[42] "U.S. Treasury Designates Two Individuals with Ties to al Qaida, UBL Former BIF Leader and al-Qaida Associate Named Under E.O. 13224" (Dec. 21, 2004) (press release), *available at* http://www.treasury.gov/press-center/press-releases/Pages/js2164.aspx.

[43] Ibrahim Al Marashi, "The Dynamics of Iraq's Media: Ethno-Sectarian Violence, Political Islam, Public Advocacy, and Globalization," 25 *Cardozo Arts & Ent. L.J.* 95 (2007).

[44] Andy Sennitt, "Iraq: US Blacklists Al-Zawraa TV," *BBC Monitoring* (Jan. 10, 2008), *available at* http://blogs.rnw.nl/medianetwork/iraq-us-blacklists-al-zawraa-tv.

Banned from using transmitters in Iraq, Al Jaburi staked his future on a satellite strategy, leasing channels on Egyptian-owned Nilesat. The channel's campaign against the U.S.-supported Iraqi government intensified – broadcasting "a blend of pro-insurgent propaganda, video clips of attacks on Coalition forces and calls for violence against Iraqi Shi'is and the Iraqi government"[45] and "audio messages from the Islamic Army of Iraq, an insurgent group dominated by the Iraqi Ba'th Party loyal to former president Saddam Husayn."[46] An influential American blogger described showing the Al Zawraa feed to U.S. soldiers and Iraqis:

> The soldiers and terps [(interpreters)] described the meaning of the images, music and voiceovers. There were songs about the Iraqi "victims" of the "U.S. occupiers." The violence in Iraq is squarely placed on the shoulders of the Americans. The images include destroyed mosques, dead women and children, women weeping of the death of their family, bloodstained floors, the destruction of U.S. humvees and armored vehicles, and insurgents firing mortars, RPGs, rockets and AK-47s. Juba, the mythical Iraqi sniper, was featured prominently (the Iraqi soldiers believe he is a composite of multiple snipers.). The "mujahideen" are portrayed as "freedom fighters," and are seen going through "boot camp training." Attacks from across the country were shown, including in Abu Ghraib, Ramadi, Fallujah, Baiji, Baghdad and elsewhere. The soldiers are seasoned veterans from the 1st Iraqi Army Division, and have served throughout Iraq. Most of the footage was popular, rehashed videos widely distributed on the Internet and in jihadi forums. I recognized many of the videos. The soldiers were angry at the images before them. "They destroyed my country," said Staff Sergeant Riad."[47]

The U.S. government began discussions with the Egyptian government to terminate the Al Zawraa transponder lease on Nilesat. Closing Al-Zawraa became a preferred alternative for Iraqi and U.S. officials. A report on Cairo's *Al-Misriyun* newspaper Web site in early 2007 said the U.S. ambassador in Cairo had asked Egyptian Information Minister Anas al-Fiqi to

> pull the plug on the channel, on the pretext that it constituted the last weapon in the hands of those he described as the Sunni "rebels" in Iraq. The minister, however, declined to respond to the ambassador's request initially, affirming that the broadcasting of the channel was purely a business transaction that had nothing to do with politics. The operational costs of the Egyptian satellite required the

---

45 Peter Feuilherade, "Egypt Row Brews Over Iraqi Sunni Channel Al-Zawraa on Nilesat," *BBC Monitoring*, Jan. 9, 2007.

46 *Id.*

47 Bill Roggio, "Al-Zawraa: Muj TV," *The Long War Journal* (Dec. 10, 2006), http://www.longwarjournal. org/archives/2006/12/muj_tv.php. For Al Jaburi's response to Roggio's article, see Bill Roggio, "Al-Zawraa Responds to Muj TV," *The Long War Journal* (Dec. 25, 2006), http://www.longwarjournal.org/ archives/2006/12/alzawraa_responds_to.php (demonstrating Aljabouri's efforts to distinguish al-Zawraa from al Qaeda).

renting of unoccupied channels. But threats made by supporters of the Shi'i Al-Mahdi Army affiliated with Muqtada al-Sadr to attack and kill members of the Egyptian diplomatic mission in Baghdad constituted pressure that drove Egypt to backtrack on its stand in this regard.[48]

There were dissenting voices (albeit not predominantly on free speech grounds):

This is [a] major dilemma in the modern age of information warfare. On [the] one hand, programs like al-Zawraa provide ready and effective propaganda and recruiting material for the insurgency and al Qaeda, while demoralizing both Western and Middle Eastern allies. On the other, the intelligence gleaned from these operations is deemed too valuable to turn off the tap.[49]

Superficially, Nilesat officials resisted the pressure and indicated that carriage was merely a contractual matter. The Nilesat chair was reported as saying, in *Al-Misri Al-Yawm*, that "satellites do not monitor the channels they are carrying. Accordingly, the Egyptian satellite should not be part of the dispute regarding the channel. It is the right of whoever is hurt by the material broadcast by Al-Zawraa to respond through their channels or media."[50]

With the threat of being ejected from Nilesat, Al Jaburi claimed the station soon would be carried "on three satellites from European countries."[51] He refrained from identifying the satellites "because we are really afraid of American pressures. But after we transmit [from Europe] there will be no fear anymore because we will be on the air."[52] By late January, Al-Zawraa was observed to be broadcasting via the Saudi-owned Arabsat and France-based Eutelsat.[53] In February, the Nilesat transmission was closed after Nilesat accused the station of "interference" with other channels;[54] in April, the French regulator required Eutelsat to stop transmission, claiming that the station's broadcasting of propaganda was in breach of the September 30, 1986 law prohibiting stations from incitement to hate and violence for reasons of religion or nationality, and the 1881 law of freedom of the press.[55]

---

[48] Feuilherade, *supra* note 45.

[49] Roggio, *supra* note 47.

[50] Feuilherade, *supra* note 45.

[51] Lawrence Pintak, "War of Ideas: Insurgent Channel Coming to a Satellite Near You," USC Center on Public Diplomacy (Jan. 10, 2007), http://uscpublicdiplomacy.com/index.php/newsroom/pdblog_detail/070110_war_of_ideas_insurgent_channel_coming_to_a_satellite_near_you/.

[52] *Id.*

[53] *See* "Iraqi Sunni Al-Zawraa TV now carried on Saudi-based Arabsat," *BBC Monitoring* (Jan. 26, 2007); "Iraqi Sunni Al-Zawraa TV now broadcasting on European satellite," *BBC Monitoring* (Jan. 31, 2007).

[54] "Egypt Takes Militant Iraqi Channel Off Air," *Daily Star* (Feb. 26, 2007), http://www.dailystar.com.lb/article.asp?edition_id=10&categ_id=2&article_id=79858.

[55] Décision n 2007–293 du 3 avril 2007 mettant en demeure la société Eutelsat SA, [Decision No. 2007–293 of Apr. 3, 2007 giving notice to the company Eutelsat SA] *available at* http://www.legifrance.gouv.fr/affichTexte.do?cidTexte=JORFTEXT000000822549&dateTexte=.

Finally, on January 9, 2008, Al Jaburi and Al Zawraa were placed on the U.S. sanctions list, precluded from any financial transactions with U.S. citizens or companies. According to *Intelligence Online*:

> On Jan. 9, the U.S. Treasury published a list of several individuals and entities subject to financial sanctions for backing Iraqi insurgents. Among them was the Iraqi politician Misham Al Jabouri and the satellite television channel he runs out of Damascus, Al Zawraa. Since October, 2006, the station continually ran messages and video clips shot by Sunni Baa'thist militia in their fight against American troops in Iraq. . . .
>
> Starting from last spring, only the Pan-Arab operator Arabsat, which is majority-owned by Saudi Arabia, continued to broadcast Al Zawraa via its *Badr3* and *Arabsat 2B* satellites. The State Department complained in vain to Riyadh before opting for a more aggressive strategy. In March, the frequency on which Al Zawraa broadcasted on Badr 3 (11747 MHz) was constantly jammed, forcing the station to cease its programs before switching to another frequency (11765 MHz).
>
> That manoeuvre won a reprieve for Al Zawraa for several months but the offensive resumed in July. Starting from July 7, reception of the station in Iraq became spotty and the channel remained unavailable for days at a time. On July 30, Al Zawraa finally ended broadcasting in Iraq. The channel sent several messages to its audience to say its signals were jammed. On July 24, the Sunni web forum Hanin.net announced that one of the channel's clandestine stations in Iraq had been bombed and that most of its employees were killed.[56]

The level of official frustration with Al Zawraa, with its inability to locate the production facilities, and the complex efforts to deny the channel access to distribution facilities, had ended with this step. The Al Zawraa case could be seen as a harbinger of the Arab Satellite Broadcast Charter that I discuss in the conclusion.

## D. *Al Manar*

I contrast the preceding examples with the very complex story of Al Manar,[57] the Hezbollah-related broadcasting station based in Lebanon, which was expanded to include a satellite distribution channel targeted at Arabic-speaking populations throughout Europe and beyond.[58] In this case, a much more formal process of

---

[56] "U.S. Pulls Plug on Insurgent TV; Baghdad," *Intelligence Online* (Jan. 17, 2008).
[57] *Al Manar TV*, http://www.almanar.com.lb/NewsSite/News.aspx?language=en.
[58] A statement from the European Union noted:

> In 1991, shortly after Hezbollah actively entered the Lebanese political scene, Al Manar was launched as a small terrestrial station. Although legally registered as the Lebanese Media Group Company in 1997, Al Manar has belonged to Hezbollah culturally and politically since its inception. Today, the terrestrial station can reach Lebanon in its entirety and broadcasts programming eighteen hours daily.
>
> Moreover, Al Manar's satellite station, launched in 2000, transmits twenty-four hours a day, reaching the entire Arab world and the rest of the globe through several major satellite providers. One of the satellite providers which has transmitted Al Manar has been the French satellite Hot Bird 4, owned by the Eutelsat Satellite organization.

regulation began to emerge. The production and distribution of programming was a critical element in Hezbollah's constituency building within Lebanon and provided a link to interested audiences in Europe and elsewhere. To reach audiences in Europe, Al Manar deployed on Eutelsat, but almost immediately faced resistance, including from groups that objected to its statements concerning Jews and Israel.[59] In late 2003, Al Manar was accused, in France, of distributing anti-Semitic programming in violation of French standards.[60] The introduction of the satellite channel into Europe forced the French state into the role of umpire between conflicting interests.

Because Al Manar originated outside of France, and outside of the EU, it presented a jurisdictional and governance crisis. The question arose (and here, it is not necessary to take a position on the nature of the programming) whether the French regulatory agency, the Conseil Supérieur de l'Audiovisuel (CSA), had authority to take action. In February 2004, the CSA and Paris-based Eutelsat entered into an agreement regarding the oversight of satellite broadcasters from outside the EU not licensed by an EU member country.[61]

A Eutelsat press release stated that the organization shared the CSA's "indignation expressed on [the] broadcasting of racist programmes,"[62] but also made it clear that the carrier had no right to censure the programming it carried absent a regulatory requirement that it do so. The problem was a typical one involving satellite channels: There was no national license involved that would govern who had authority over the content of the channel. The CSA, on the other hand, took the position that because the channel was uplinked to Eutelsat, and Eutelsat was a French company,

"EU Rules and Principles on Hate Broadcasts: Frequently Asked Questions," *Europa*, http://europa.eu/rapid/pressReleasesAction.do?reference=MEMO/05/98&format=HTML&aged=0&language=EN&guiLanguage=en.

59  *See* "U.S. Following French Lead in Banning Hezbollah Station," *The America's Intelligence Wire*, Dec. 17, 2004. A week after the French ban, the United States designated Al Manar a terrorist organization, and transmission into the U.S. was banned. The interaction between the informal and the formal in terms of government action is complex but useful to examine. For example, Al-Nour Radio, deemed a Hezbollah-controlled radio station, was named a "specially designated global terrorist entity," a harsher categorization than the Terrorist Exclusion List, along with Al-Manar TV, by the U.S. Department of the Treasury in March 2006. The designation had its intended consequences. It caused the Spanish Hispasat, GlobeCast American, and New Skies Satellite companies to terminate Al-Nour's broadcasting to South America via Hispasat, Asia via AsiaSat, and New Skies Satellite to Europe.

60  *See* U.S. Dep't of State, Report on Global Anti-Semitism (2005), *available at* http://www.state.gov/g/drl/rls/40258.htm. The report discusses Israel's complaints and states that in November 2004, "Al-Manar, the Lebanon-based television network controlled by Hizballah featuring blatantly anti-Semitic material, obtained a limited 1-year satellite broadcast license from the French authorities. This was revoked shortly thereafter due to Al-Manar's continued transmission of anti-Semitic material." France subsequently banned Al Manar.

61  *See* "France: Eutelsat, Regulator Agree to Cooperate on Unlicensed Broadcasters," *BBC Summary of Worldwide Broadcasts*, Feb. 5, 2004.

62  "Cooperation Between Eutelsat and the CSA" (Feb. 3, 2004) (press release), *available at* http://www.eutelsat.com/news/pdf/2004/pr0402.pdf.

the broadcasts (or at least the satellite carrier) were within the CSA's jurisdiction under the EU's Television Without Frontiers directive.

To clarify this authority in anticipation of some concern over power, the CSA already successfully had applied to the public prosecutor, arguing that "[t]he transmission by the Al-Manar channel of thirty episodes of 'Diaspora' may have been seen as anti-Semitic."[63] The CSA president highlighted the difficulties facing the agency when dealing with channels established outside the European Union which still fall under the competence of the French authorities. There were grave jurisdictional issues in engaging in action against satellite operators or their intermediaries through which these external channels were broadcast. The government had to deal with its own strategic concerns: its relationship to domestic communities, its historic relationship to Lebanon, and the convulsive nature of disputes within the Middle East as they found their way to Europe.

The CSA and Eutelsat began a policy of cooperation to check television channels transmitted by Eutelsat for their conformity to European legislation; the National Assembly adopted amendments allowing the CSA authority over operators of satellite networks, power to sanction Eutelsat, and authority to ask the Conseil d'Etat – France's supreme administrative court – to order a carrier to cease transmission of a service where a breach of human dignity, the safeguard of public order, or the protection of minors was involved.[64] Ultimately, by July 2004, the CSA requested the Conseil d'Etat to order Eutelsat to stop transmitting the station. According to the *Agence France-Presse* news agency, this followed the adoption of a new law on July 9 that gave the CSA new powers to ban satellite TV channels not subject to licensing.[65] Even here, the CSA actions were a combination of direct regulation, informal negotiation, and "voluntary" action by Al Manar itself. For example, in November of that same year, the CSA granted Al Manar the right to operate in France as long as it abided by French law and did not incite hate or violence. But just four days later, the station aired a show that prompted new criticism, and on December 13, 2004, the Conseil d'Etat ordered Eutelsat to stop transmitting Al Manar within two days.[66]

---

[63] *See* "France: Broadcast Regulator Explains Anti-Racist Policies," BBC *Monitoring World Media* (Mar. 3, 2004).

[64] *See* French Prime Minister's Office, "Prevailing Against Terrorism: White Paper on Domestic Security Against Terrorism," *available at* http://www.ambafrance-dk.org/IMG/pdf/livre_blanc_english.pdf (French Prime Minister's Office publication discussing its position regarding Al Manar and its subsequent effects to cooperate with European legislation to combat racism).

[65] *See* "Analysis: French Ban on Al-Manar TV Sparks Diplomatic Row," BBC *Monitoring Research*, Aug. 17, 2004.

[66] The text of the July 9 ruling is available at http://legifrance.gouv.fr/affichTexte.do?cidTexte= JORFTEXT000000439399. The text of the December 13 ruling is available at http://www.conseil-etat. fr/cde/node.php?articleid=1096. *See also* Elaine Sciolino, "A New French Headache: When Is Hate on TV Illegal?" *N.Y. Times* (Dec. 9, 2004).

## IV. TOWARD THE FUTURE

Among the models for future treatment of these questions, the EU – in its post Al-Manar consciousness – presents a direction that is formal, regulatory, and bureaucratic. The consistent position on regulating satellite broadcasting within the EU has been that where a broadcast originates within the EU (which was not the case with Al Manar), it is the responsibility of the Member State, the so-called "country of origin," to regulate it. To this end, a series of practical criteria ("establishment" criteria in Article 2 of the Television Without Frontiers directive), for determining which Member State has jurisdiction. These criteria are:

- the location of the head office of the provider of services;
- the place where decisions on programming policy are usually taken;
- the place where the program to be broadcast to the public is finally mixed and processed; and
- the place where a significant proportion of the workforce required for the pursuit of the television broadcasting activity is located.[67]

An additional lens through which this debate can be seen involves a kind of conflict of laws analysis. For instance, in the EU, if a program is lawful in the Member State where it is established, then no other Member State can deny it entry. (There are specific exceptions to this rule, some of which – for example, looking more at the exclusive target audience of an offering – date from the 2007 amendments to the Television Without Frontiers Directive.[68]) It is the standard of the state of origin that determines whether a channel's programming passes muster.[69]

The Al Manar case was an intermediate step in terms of providing transparency in regulation and an effort to shape a systematic approach to satellite carried channels from outside the EU. Indeed, the reaction of the EU to the Al Manar case is the closest we have come to something that anticipates "global governance" or organized consideration of satellite-related delivery issues across many national boundaries. And it is not very close yet. If, as was the case with Al Manar, the satellite channel originates in a third country, outside the EU, different rules apply, according to the

---

[67] *See* Directive 2007/65/EC of the European Parliament and of the Council of 11 December 2007, O.J. (L 332) 37, art. 2, ¶ 3 (amending Council Directive 89/552/EEC on the coordination of certain provisions laid down by law, regulation or administrative action in Member States concerning the pursuit of television broadcasting activities).

[68] *See* "Analysis: French Ban on Al-Manar TV Sparks Diplomatic Row," *supra* note 65, at 31 (graph 34).

[69] For more discussion on the country of origin approach, see Anna Herold, "Country of Origin Principle in the EU Market for Audiovisual Media Services: Consumer's Friend or Foe," 31 J. *Consumer Policy* 5 (2008). The debate over a new Audiovisual and Media Services Directive, which replaced the Television Without Frontiers Directive, partially concerned whether to shift, at least partially, from a country of origin to country of receipt approach.

French precedent. Member States must ensure that such a broadcaster comply with the EU rules if:

- it uses a frequency granted by that Member State,
- it uses a satellite capacity appertaining to that Member State, or
- it uses a satellite up-link situated in that Member State.[70]

Because most TV channels from outside the EU broadcast in Europe using satellite capacities provided either by Eutelsat, which is based in France, or by Astra, which is based in Luxembourg, France and Luxembourg have jurisdiction over a large number of third-country programs received within the EU. During the French proceeding involving Al Manar, the European Commission worked with the French authorities to achieve an EU approach that could be applied to all similar cases.[71] Where signals originating outside of the EU seek EU audiences (using satellites under the jurisdiction of individual Member States), the relevant authorities should block their diffusion (or at least alert the other Member States) if these incoming channels fail to meet EU standards.

In March 2005, after the Al Manar decision, EU officials recognized that difficulties would arise if it were only up to the particular states that had jurisdiction over satellite providers to police hate speech (or what might be generically called hate speech) issues. Better coordination among the states would be essential. The 2007 passage of the Audio Visual Media Services Directive, amending the Television Without Frontiers Directive, makes use of an uplink in a Member State a priority (after use of granted frequency).[72] This distributes jurisdiction over more Member States. What is not yet clear is how many, if any, of the problematic channel providers have shifted uplink sites to take advantage of a different country's jurisdiction, or the extent to which more states will assert authority.

Another problem is presented by third-country broadcasts that can be seen in Europe because of satellite spillover from other countries – that is, where the channel originates outside the EU and the facility used (satellite, frequency, etc.) also is outside the Member State zone. These spillover effects are one reason why the cooperation of regulatory authorities within the EU is insufficient and must be complemented by cooperation with regulators from third countries (for example, the Mediterranean Regulators' Group).

Another perspective – one with the appearance of formality but with great elements of the pragmatic – arises from local efforts to control satellite signals distribution in the

---

[70] *See* Directive 2007/65/EC, *supra* note 67, at 37, art. 2, ¶ 4.

[71] *See* "Conclusions, High-level Group of Regulatory Authorities in the Field of Broadcasting – Incitement to Hatred in Broadcasts Coming From Outside of the European Union," *Europa* Mar. 17, 2005, *available at* http://ec.europa.eu/avpolicy/docs/library/legal/conclusions_regulateurs/concl_reg_fin_en. pdf.

[72] *See also* European Union Committee, "Television Without Frontiers?: Report with Evidence," 3d sess. 2006–07, (Jan. 31, 2007), *available at* http://www.publications.parliament.uk/pa/ld200607/ldselect/ldeucom/27/27.pdf.

Middle East and to use hate speech and similar standards in the process. Most satellite channels viewed in the region are transmitted using transponders of two satellites, Nilesat and Arabsat, both of which are closely tied to regional governments. The management of the two satellites has varied in terms of the stringency of standards or the degree of control involved in determining what channels are transmitted. But as is true in most parts of the world, gaining or keeping a transponder for the distribution of information is primarily a business decision, not one tied to categorization of content.

In February 2008, the Ministers of Information of the Arab League met to develop a regional Satellite Broadcasting Charter (the "Charter") that would impact, even if not decisively, what signals would be carried over satellites controlled by members of the League.[73] They met at a time of great regional frustration occasioned by the extraordinary abundance of satellite signals that were reshaping flows of information in the region.[74] In societies where information, especially via radio and television signals, had been a highly controlled commodity – where an almost universal characteristic of governance was control over the channels of communication – the satellite revolution was providing an irksome new reality.[75] Porousness could lead to new political formations, could undermine stability, and certainly could disturb the state's long-standing control of narrative. Some countries, such as Iraq, barred antennae. With the arrival of Al Jazeera in 1996, there was a sea change, as the channel aggressively covered politics in many Middle Eastern capitals. It was an object of frustration to established autocracies because it seemed to touch an important nerve in the regional audience, which was desirous of receiving more thorough news about their leaders.[76] In addition, there was the persistent concern about western channels bringing western values (or lack of values) and interfering with traditional teachings and ways of life. The state control that had been central to the nature of the state now threatened to dissipate.[77]

---

73  An English translation of the Arab Satellite Broadcasting Charter is available at "Arab Satellite Broadcasting Charter: Principles for Regulating Satellite Broadcasting Transmission in the Arab World," *Arab Media & Soc'y*, Feb. 2008, *available at* http://www.arabmediasociety.com/articles/downloads/20080314081327_AMS_Charter_English.pdf.

74  *See* "Arab TV Broadcasters Face Curbs," BBC News, Feb. 12, 2008, *available at* http://news.bbc.co.uk/2/hi/middle_east/7241723.stm.

75  *See* William A. Rugh, *Arab Mass Media: Newspapers, Radio, and Television in Arab Politics* (Praeger 2004); *see also* Sakr, *supra* note 25.

76  *See* Marc Lynch, *Voices of the New Arab Public: Iraq, Al-Jazeera, and Middle East Politics Today* (Columbia University Press, 2006); *The Al Jazeera Phenomenon: Critical Perspectives on New Arab Media* (Mohamed Zayani ed., Paradigm Publishers 2005); Mohammed el-Nawawy and Adel Iskander, *Al-Jazeera: How the Free Arab News Network Scooped the World and Changed the Middle East* (Westview Press 2002); Hugh Miles, "Al Jazeera," 155 *Foreign Pol'y* 20 (July-Aug. 2006); Naomi Sakr, "Media Development and Democratisation in the Arab Middle East," 6 *Global Dialogue* 98 (Winter/Spring 2004).

77  *See* Rugh, *supra* note 75. *See also* Brookings Doha Center, "Forward or Backward: The 2008 Arab Satellite TV Charter and the Future of Arab Media, Society, and Democracy," at 17 (Mar. 17,

Adopting the Charter was an attempt to control competition among satellite providers and to impose a set of restraints on what the satellite signals would provide. It was drafted to establish regional standards that would be enforced by the signatories, a mode of determining which law applied, and an internal system for complaint by one country to another with a method for ensuring some compliance with regional goals. The Charter provides guidelines as to what should be prohibited or what regulations should govern the behavior of satellite providers. These satellite providers (broadly conceived) should not, according to the Charter, "jeopardize social peace, national unity, public order and general propriety."[78] In addition, the satellite entities should adopt standards requiring them to abstain from inciting hatred or ethnic, color, racial, or religious discrimination, from broadcasting any material that would incite violence or terrorism (interestingly, differentiating between terrorism and "resisting occupation"). Furthermore, the Charter encourages programming that reinforces the religious and ethical values of the Arab society, and prohibits satellites from broadcasting anything that would insult God, revealed religions, prophets, *mazhabs* (religious schools), and religious symbols of each group (with the groups included not fully identified).

There are grace notes that have the flavor of modernization. The satellite broadcasters, according to the Charter, should provide "the largest number possible of programmes and services to maintain the Arab identity and the Islamic culture and values and to highlight the Arab contribution to human civilization." They should promote dialogue and understanding among different cultures. And there is a note of political regional integration to the Charter in the call for satellite agencies to "maintain Arab identity against the negative impact of globalization and reaffirm the specificity of the Arab world." To do this, however, there should be a policy of avoiding the broadcast of "anything that would contradict or jeopardize Arab solidarity." And, of course, the channels should not insult leaders or national and religious symbols.

Al Jazeera, whose frequent criticisms of many Arab governments made it one of the supposed targets of the Charter, organized a panel discussion the day the Charter was issued. In a video report, one commentator pointed out that regulation of Arab satellite channels was motivated by threats to the more mature, state-based channels from "a large number of profit-seeking channels that aim to attract viewers by nudity, charlatanry, and sectarianism."[79] Competition yielded a race to the bottom, he argued, where civility would be sacrificed and sensationalism and lack of objectivity would prevail.

---

2008), *available at* http://www.brookings.edu/~/media/Files/events/2008/0317_arab_media/0317_arab_media.pdf (comments by Saad Eddin Ibrahim).

[78] "Arab Satellite Broadcasting Charter: Principles for Regulating Satellite Broadcasting Transmission in the Arab World," *supra* note 73.

[79] "Al-Jazeera Pundits Discuss Proposed Arab Satellite TV Regulations," *BBC Monitoring World Media*, Feb. 20, 2008.

A second panelist, Abd-al-Bari Atwan, editor-in-chief of *Al-Quds Al-Arabi*, and independent Pan-Arab newspaper based in London, represented a different current of thinking. He argued that the Charter was drafted because "the repressive, dictatorial Arab governments have begun to realize that Arab public opinion is moving strongly," and so Arab information ministers have hastened to "bury this awakening in Arab public opinion" by enacting legislation to "gag and criminalize Arab media." The priority of the ministers of information, he suggested, was to protect the regimes that made those decisions. The objective of the Charter, he argued, was not necessarily to uphold Arab values and ethics, but "to preserve those repressive measures by governments that engage in torture and corruption, squander public funds, and violate human rights."[80]

The Charter gives additional political cover to governments that wish to impose more restrictions, and it seems to augur a new order of pervasive licensing and authorization – or at least to legitimate more extensive supervision.[81] The Charter's existence remains controversial. Some claim that the Charter is so cumbersome as to be ineffective.[82] Others argue that presents no threat because the standards are a "code of honor," a form of self-regulation rather than state enforcement.[83] Yet already there are accounts that the Charter has served to justify additional restrictions by Egypt in contracts for the use of Nilesat;[84] such restrictions might also be imposed on the use of production facilities in media cities in Egypt and elsewhere. Nevertheless, the Charter should be seen in a global context of regulation, alongside a fear of the incompatibility of satellite with domestic control of broadcast signals.

The existence of a pattern of regulation should not be used to justify suppression of dissent or other systematic modes of controlling speech. But comparative insights help in understanding what steps are being taken and in fashioning criteria for judging their appropriateness.[85]

---

[80] *Id.*

[81] "Some satellite television channels based in Egypt are concerned, amid assertions by the government on the need to enforce a document regulating the work of satellite television channels. The Arab information ministers endorsed this document at an emergency meeting in Cairo last month." "Five Private Egyptian Satellite TV Channels Face Prospect of Closure, Ban," *BBC Worldwide Monitoring*, Mar. 7, 2008 (quoting Khalid al-Shami's March 6, 2008 report in *Al-Quds al-Arabi*).

[82] "Al-Jazeera Pundits," *supra* note 79.

[83] *Id.*

[84] *See, e.g.,* "Egypt's Nilesat Halts Transmission of London-Based Al-Hiwar TV," *BBC Monitoring World Media,* Apr. 3, 2008.

[85] *See* "Communication from the Euromed and the Media Taskforce to the Euromed Culture Ministers" Athens (May 29–30, 2008), *available at* http://ec.europa.eu/external_relations/euromed/media/athens_final_communique_0507_en.pdf. For a while, it appeared there might be a "copycat" charter for the so-called Euromed states. Having seen the criticism of the Arab Charter, the Euromed group drafted a Declaration, not a "Charter," seeking to avoid suspicion that they were moving to a binding international legal instrument. Secondly, it would be neutral from a technological point of view, dealing with any kind of audiovisual content (not only that distributed by satellite). Its scope would be any signal received in the Mediterranean area and broadcasted under the jurisdiction of any Mediterranean authority. Personal Communication from Joan Barata Mir, Catalan Regulatory

## V. CONCLUSIONS

This chapter describes a system in which formal law – even formal agreements among countries – may not be descriptive of governmental actions concerning hate-speech-related content on satellites. This chapter discusses the use of explicit transparent modes for regulation and cooperation, such as the coordination effort at the EU level. Further, this chapter describes how informal relationships among states or between states and programming entities are the more relevant determinant of behavior. What emerges is the need to identify or abstract from the preceding examples which points require additional understanding. For example, we see in some aspects of the MED-TV example that control over uplinking is a site for negotiation. We can see in the case of Eutelsat and Al Manar that the act of making available a transponder is a second opportunity for intervention. A more formal act, certainly, is placing a satellite service on a Terrorist Exclusion List and thus criminalizing not only the broadcasting entity but also those who deal with it. We can analyze the passage of a signal from the point of production to the point of reception to determine opportunities that have been used to urge or obtain restriction.

In all of this, the role of "law" – law as a set of properly established criteria to limit governmental intervention – is fugitive and hard to capture. A state's efforts to pressure carriers of satellite signals often will be disguised and hardly subject to any jurisdiction. The state's actions may be speech-repressive and anticompetitive, but still difficult to discern. In many cases, the state will be seeking to secure greater control of the words and images that circulate within its borders. At other times, it will be seeking to prevent the diffusion of disfavored views quite broadly. There are scarce mechanisms or standards to determine what the limits to this kind of conduct should be.

There is no system of global governance with respect to satellite signals, and it is doubtful that such a system will emerge.[86] The EU seeks a more transparent system

---

Commission ("It seeks to identify and to proclaim some common basic principles that we share both European and North-African and Middle East countries. It has been, at least, an interesting exercise of negotiation and a very hard effort in order to find a final version which could satisfy many different kind of authorities belonging to diverse legal and constitutional systems.").

[86] At an early stage – in the mid-1990s – the United States precluded signals from non-U.S. licensed satellites to send them to the United States, except under prescribed circumstances.

Leveraging three years of goodwill and momentum amassed by the WTO negotiations, recent U.S. policy has focused on restructuring the ISOs. In May 1996, the FCC issued a notice of proposed rulemaking known as the Domestic International Satellite Consolidation Order ("DISCO I"), which established criteria to permit foreign-based operators to offer service in the United States.

DISCO I proposed a test in which the granting of a license to a foreign operator to provide services in the United States would be contingent upon a showing that U.S.-based satellites have effective competition opportunities ("ECO-SAT test") in: (i) the home market where the foreign operator is licensed; and (ii) all "route markets" that the foreign satellite intends to service from earth stations in the United States. In light of the recent WTO agreement, however, DISCO I was reconsidered because the WTO agreement allows nondiscriminatory access to markets without consideration of where a foreign operator is licensed.

with respect to certain kinds of content within its borders; conversely, the Arab Charter suggests a somewhat more brutal version of the exercise. In the absence of regulation, informal efforts to persuade, pressure, and even threaten satellite providers are likely to continue. We are beginning to sense patterns emerging, but it is only as the technology itself is becoming slightly overshadowed. Terrorism is the trope that has succeeded in breaking the rules of flows of information where cultural exception, fear of pornography, sweeping concerns about cultural imperialism, and fears for national identity had failed. Terrorism has brought the deacons of free expression to the table of regulation, even of clumsy intervention. What remains to be seen is whether, in this increasingly important area of speech and its distribution, there is a major shift from informal decision making, either as part of leasing or decisions in the shadow of law, toward a model of more transparent jurisdiction, with more traditional regulatory decisions and the invocation of the rule of law.

Henry Wong, Comment, "2001: A Space Legislation Odyssey – A Proposed Model for Reforming the Intergovernmental Satellite Organizations," 48 *Am. U.L. Rev.* 547, 565–6 (1998).

# Index